HEALTH POLITICS
AND POLICY

ISBN 0-8273-4289-6

9 780827 342897

DELMAR SERIES IN HEALTH SERVICES

Stephen J. Williams, Sc.D., Series Editor

HEALTH POLITICS
AND POLICY

Theodor J. Litman, Ph.D.
Professor and Director of Graduate Studies
Division of Hospital and Health Care Administration
University of Minnesota
Minneapolis, Minnesota

Leonard S. Robins, Ph.D.
Associate Professor
Public Administration Program
Roosevelt University
Chicago, Illinois

DELMAR PUBLISHERS INC.®

NOTICE TO THE READER

Publisher and author do not warrant or guarantee any of the products described herein or perform any independent analysis in connection with any of the product information contained herein. Publisher and author do not assume, and expressly disclaim, any obligation to obtain and include information other than that provided to them by the manufacturer.

The reader is expressly warned to consider and adopt all safety precautions that might be indicated by the activities described herein and to avoid all potential hazards. By following the instructions contained herein, the reader willingly assumes all risks in connection with such instructions.

The publisher and author make no representations or warranties of any kind, including but not limited to, the warranties of fitness for particular purpose or merchantability, nor are any such representations implied with respect to the material set forth herein, and the publisher and author take no responsibility with respect to such material. The publisher and author shall not be liable for any special, consequential or exemplary damages resulting, in whole or in part, from the readers' use of, or reliance upon, this material.

Cover design: Wanda Lubelska

For information contact Delmar Publishers Inc.
2 Computer Dr. West
Albany, New York 12212

Printed in the United States of America
Published simultaneously in Canada
By Nelson Canada
A Division of The Thomson Corporation

10 9 8 7 6 5 4 3 2 1

ISBN 0-8273-4289-6

To our families

Contributors

Robert Agranoff, Ph.D.
Professor and Chairperson
Policy and Administration Faculty
School of Public and Environmental Affairs
University of Indiana
Bloomington, Indiana

Odin W. Anderson, Ph.D.
Professor of Sociology
Graduate School of Business and Department of Sociology
University of Chicago
Chicago, Illinois
Department of Sociology
University of Wisconsin
Madison, Wisconsin

Roger M. Battistella, Ph.D.
Sloan Program of Hospital and Health Services Administration
Graduate School of Business and Public Administration
Cornell University
Ithaca, New York

James W. Begun, Ph.D.
Associate Professor
Graduate School of Business and Public Administration
Cornell University
Ithaca, New York

Thomas W. Bice, Ph.D.
Director of the Graduate Program in Health Services Administration
School of Public Health and Community Medicine
University of Washington
Seattle, Washington

Lloyd F. Detwiller, M.A., M.H.A.
Executive Director
Health Sciences Center Hospital
University of British Columbia
Vancouver, British Columbia

David Falcone, Ph.D.
Associate Professor
Health Administration/Political Sciences
Duke University
Durham, North Carolina

Eugene Feingold, Ph.D.
Professor of Medical Care Organization
School of Public Health
Associate Dean
Horace H. Rackham School of Graduate Studies
University of Michigan
Ann Arbor, Michigan

Paul J. Feldstein, Ph.D.
Professor
School of Public Health
Department of Economics
University of Michigan
Ann Arbor, Michigan

William Glaser, Ph.D.
Professor
Department of Health Services Administration
Graduate School of Management and Urban Professions
New School for Social Research
New York, New York

George D. Greenberg, Ph.D.
Senior Program Analyst
Office of the Assistant Secretary for Planning and Evaluation
Department of Health and Human Services
Washington, D.C.

Lynn C. Hartwig
Adjunct Associate Professor
Division of Community and Family Medicine
Duke University
Durham, North Carolina

Peter B. Levine, Ph.D.
Director
Research Department
Minnesota House of Representatives
St. Paul, Minnesota

Theodor J. Litman, Ph.D.
Professor and Director of Graduate Studies
Division of Hospital and Health Care Administration
University of Minnesota
Minneapolis, Minnesota

Theodore R. Marmor, Ph.D.
Professor
Department of Political Science
School of Organization and Management
Yale University
New Haven, Connecticut

James A. Morone, Ph.D.
Assistant Professor
Department of Political Science
Brown University
Providence, Rhode Island

Leonard S. Robins, Ph.D.
Associate Professor
Public Administration Program
Roosevelt University
Chicago, Illinois

Milton I. Roemer, M.D.
Professor of Health Services
School of Public Health
University of California at Los Angeles
Los Angeles, California

Frank J. Thompson, Ph.D.
Chairman and Professor
Department of Political Science
University of Georgia
Athens, Georgia

Foreword

In 1932, Edwin E. Witte, my economics professor at the University of Wisconsin, was sure that 4½ percent of the gross national product (GNP) expended for health and medical services was a reasonable and adequate allocation, if only the total expenditures were distributed rationally! He could not foresee the vast changes in medical technology, utilization, attitudes, and demography that were to take place over the subsequent 50 years and that would have more than doubled the relative share of the GNP allocated to health and medical services.

From 1950 to 1960, when I was deeply involved in the development of the strategy and proposals that eventually led to the enactment of Medicare and Medicaid in 1965, there was not available a book, report, or monograph that conveniently brought together comprehensive information and insight about the interaction of politics, public policy, and the public interest in current medical economic issues. Especially missing were in-depth analyses of diverse options and relevant experiences. The situation was even more barren during the period 1934–1950, when there were attempts to develop feasible proposals amidst the vigorous oppositions of the American Medical Association.

It is true that the Flexner report (1910), the report of the Committee on the Costs of Medical Care (1932), and the pioneering studies undertaken by the committee were important in stimulating proposals for future policy consideration. The pioneering books by I. S. Falk (1936), Louis Reed (1937), and Michael Davis (1955), for example, served as basic resources for provocative analysis during the lean years of program planning in this area.

Today, those of us who teach, think, ponder, question, or debate health policy are overwhelmed by books, reports, monographs, estimates, evaluations, interpretations, and, most of all, proposals, counterproposals, and alternatives related to the subject. The situation today for teachers, students, and practitioners of health policy is different and somewhat confusing compared to that in 1934, 1950, 1960, or 1965, when key decisions affecting the future of health policy were made with a minimum of backup studies and analyses.

Although the detailed outline of any national health insurance plan that is likely to evolve in the future remains a mystery, it is probable that public policy will discard exclusive reliance either on the private, voluntary insurance mechanism or on a public medical-service approach—such as Great Britain, the Soviet Union, and several other countries use.

The provisions of the various health insurance proposals introduced in Congress in recent years also indicate that in the United States some kind of a mixed system will very likely evolve using both the public and private sectors. Although the experience of other countries is of interest, the United States will most likely diverge from the patterns of other countries.

After our struggle with the high unemployment, interest rates, and price level of the 1980s, I believe we will come to a period in which the issue of national health insurance will reappear. The continuing rise in medical and health costs and the continuing increase in the number of the aged will keep the issue alive.

Health policy is open ended, indefinite in duration, universal in interest and concern, controversial and political, and thus a real challenge to those who choose to study and work in this important field. It warrants continuing attention. Litman and Robins have put together a stimulating and broad discussion of these subjects. The present volume is an important effort to throw light on a wide range of key issues, questions, and problems.

Wilbur J. Cohen
Former Secretary of Health, Education and Welfare
Sid W. Richardson Professor of Public Affairs
Lyndon B. Johnson School of Public Affairs
The University of Texas at Austin
Austin, Texas

Preface

A short time before his untimely death from cancer, former Vice President Hubert H. Humphrey noted that the moral test of a government—and we would add a nation—is how it treats those who are in the dawn of life, its children; those who are in the twilight of life, its aged; and those who are in the shadow of life, its sick, needy, and handicapped. For a government (society), he went on to observe, that can neither educate its children, care and sustain its elderly, nor provide hope and meet the needs of its infirmed sick, its poor, and disabled, is a government without compassion and a nation, we would argue, without a soul.

The resolution of such issues, more often than not, tends to be a political one, arrived at in the political arena as part of a political process. It is toward understanding that process and the context within which such decisions are made vis-à-vis health and health care that this book is addressed. It is intended to provide interested students and faculty in the health sciences, government, and public administration with a comprehensive analytical overview of the politics of health. Through an examination of the historical and contemporary involvement of government and politics in the organization, financing, and delivery of health care both here and abroad, it attempts to underscore the important role political factors play in the development of public health policy.

With this in mind, a number of leading academicians and practitioners in the field were invited to prepare original expositions on the politics of health and health care. Since many of the manuscripts were prepared and received before the full thrust of the Reagan presidency had been known or felt, the contributors were given an opportunity to review their pieces in light of the actions and policies of the administration and to add additional comments or observations, if they wished. Response tended to be mixed. Thus, while the results of the 1980 election and its aftermath were regarded by some as the harbinger of a fundamental change in the nature of U.S. social, political, and economic thought, others considered them to be but a brief aberration, a momentary interlude in the nation's long and steady evolution of the role of government in health and human services.

The resulting 16 chapters have been organized around five major topics. Following an overview of the book, Part One provides an incisive review of the major ideological influences that have governed the health policy debate in the United States. The history and development of the U.S. health services enterprise forms the focus of Chapter 3, and we conclude Part One with a discussion of the implications and consequences of government involvement in the organization, financing, and delivery of health care.

In Part Two, our focus shifts to the making of public policy in health. The chapter authors focus on such topics as the importance of executive branch fragmentation in limiting the effectiveness of health policymaking at the federal level; the structure under which health policy decisions are made within the federal executive; the dynamics of health policymaking in the executive branch as it developed with the debate over long-term care policy in the Carter administration; the relative unimportance of congressional structure and process in determining health policy outcomes; and the forces that have a considerable effect on implementation. The whole notion of grants-in-aid and other forms of intergovernmental assistance and their relationship to health is then discussed, and the section concludes with a review of the role of the states in health policymaking and health services delivery.

Part Three explores two facets of the relationship between participatory democracy and the politics of health: the role professional provider groups play in the determination of health policy, and the promises and pitfalls of citizen participation in health. Part Four reviews the history of the politics of public health and the usually sad lack of clout those devoted to public health have had in the political arena, and then examines the politics of regulation and of national health insurance. Part Five explores the relationship of government and health from a cross-national perspective.

Finally, the appendixes contain a set of tables summarizing government health expenditures and a chronology with capsule highlights of U.S. government involvement in health and health care. The appendixes are followed by an extensive research bibliography.

A compilation such as this represents the efforts of a number of people. In addition to our contributors, a special debt of gratitude and appreciation is owed our secretaries: Mary Voight, for her assistance in the early formulation of the project, and Lynne Johnsrud, without whose diligence and forbearance in processing the final manuscript under the most trying of circumstances this book would not have been possible.

Theodor J. Litman
Leonard S. Robins

Contents

HEALTH POLITICS
AND POLICY

PART ONE

*Health Politics
and Policy
in Perspective*

CHAPTER 1

Government and Health: The Political Aspects of Health Care —A Sociopolitical Overview

Theodor J. Litman

When the Eighty-ninth Congress adjourned in 1966, its record of legislative accomplishments made it the most health-minded Congress in U.S. history.[1] Not only had more national health legislation been enacted into law during its first session than had been passed in both sessions of all Congresses in the past decade, but it had appropriated more money for health in the last 2 years of its term than its predecessors had in the previous 168 years. Never before had one session of Congress produced legislation of such far-reaching implications for the health, education, and socioeconomic welfare of the American people than had been enacted in 1965 (Gardner et al., 1967). So extensive was the legislative activity in terms of the number and scope of health actions taken that one observer depicted the period as a turning point in health law (Forgotson, 1967).

As far as health care financing was concerned, the issue was no longer that of public versus private enterprise. According to Anne Somers, that issue had seemingly been settled in favor of the nation's or the United State's unique pluralistic health care economy with its programmatic amalgamation of public and private activities. What had changed was the nature of the mix, which seemed to lean markedly in favor of the public sector

---

[1]A total of 15 pieces of legislation that had direct and far-reaching impact on health services were enacted; the most publicized were Medicare and Medicaid, Titles XVIII and XIX of the 1965 amendments to the Social Security Act. Others included PL 89-239 Heart Disease, Cancer and Stroke amendments of 1965 (Regional Medical Program); PL 89-74 Drug Abuse Control amendments of 1965; PL 89-92 Federal Cigarette and Labeling and Advertising Act; PL 89-105 Mental Retardation Facilities and Community Mental Health Centers Construction Act amendments of 1965; PL 89-109 Community Health Services Extension amendments of 1965; PL 89-115 Health Research Facilities amendments of 1965; PL 89-234 Water Quality Act of 1965; PL 89-272 The Clean Air Act amendments and Solid Waste Disposal Act of 1965; PL 89-290 Health Professions Educational Assistance amendments of 1965; PL 89-291 Medical Library Assistance Act of 1965; PL 89-4 The Appalachian Regional Development Act; PL 89-73 The Older Americans Act; PL 89-333 The Vocational Rehabilitation Act amendments of 1965; PL 89-117 The Housing and Urban Development Act of 1965. A sixteenth bill, PL 89-749, Comprehensive Health Planning, was passed in 1966.

(Somers, 1966). Moreover, with the passage of the National Planning and Resources Development Act (PL 93-641) in 1974 (Rubel, 1975), the question of the federal government's right to interfere in the private practice of medicine appeared to be decided, for all intents and purposes, in favor of government.

The role of the federal government in the organization, financing, and delivery of health care services in the United States at mid-decade seemed assured, and the prospects for adoption of some form of national health insurance seemed imminent, if not a foregone conclusion.

But although the federal initiative of the past 20 years or so had been seen by many as a sociopolitical watershed in which the powers and machinery of government were mobilized to improve access to services, to further distribute justice and equity, and to redress social and economic wrongs (Fein, 1980), times and circumstances change. The heady optimism and faith in the unbridled growth and intervention of the federal establishment of the 1960s and 1970s soon gave way to suspicion, distrust, and disillusionment with government programs. Thus, in spite of a number of notable accomplishments—such as demonstrated gains in access to care and health status among the poor and the elderly (Mooney, 1977), greater rationalization of the health planning process, and increased production of health personnel—skepticism and dissatisfaction with such initiatives began to grow in the face of rising costs, economic stagflation, limited revenues, diminished financial resources, programmatic cutbacks, indifferent if not hostile central administration, and bureaucratic insensitivity to the infringement of federal policies, directives, and regulations on state and local prerogatives, culminating in the Reagan election in 1980.

The response was sudden and pointed. The new chief executive, who had ridden to victory on a promise to get government off the backs of the American people, moved quickly and decisively. Within 6 months of taking office, through the deft and imaginative use of the budgetary process and with the support of a group of conservative Democrats (known as the Boll Weavils) who were ideologically closer to the Republican party than their own, the president succeeded in gaining congressional approval of a package of budget cuts that repealed and modified scores of programs that had become integral parts of the nation's social and economic fabric while reversing the federal expansion of the last half-century and reducing the size and scope of government.

And so, as the United States entered the new decade, it seemed to be embarking on a different course, one reflected in the president's commitment to less social planning and regulation, a smaller public and larger private sector in health as well as other aspects of life, and an abrupt reduction in government, especially in federal funding for social programs. Whether the results of the 1980 election marked a major shift in sociopolitical thought in the United States vis-à-vis the relationship of government to the individual and his or her health care, as many early editorial writers suggested, or was merely an aberrational interlude in the United States' continuing flirtation with the adoption of some form of national health program, remains to be seen. Suffice it to say, however, that the answer is likely to lie in an understanding of the peculiar nature and role of government and politics in American life, with the decision reached, the product of a deliberative political process.

GOVERNMENT AND HEALTH IN THE UNITED STATES

A number of years ago, the noted British social historian T. H. Marshall observed that no modern government could disdain responsibility for the health of its people nor would it wish to do so. Policies, he noted, differ not so much in the aims pursued as in the methods adopted in pursuit of them (Marshall, 1965). But although the notion of a national system of health services has long been a well-established fact in much of the rest of the world, it has been slow to take hold in the United States. Since the first governmental system of health care was established in Germany under Bismarck in 1883, the provision of health and medical care to an entire population on a nationwide basis through some form of national health service or insurance mechanism has been adopted in nearly half of the world's sovereign nations, including most of those in Western Europe. On the whole, this development has generally come about through an evolutionary rather than revolutionary process, a function of the social, cultural, political, and economic fabrics of the various countries involved. In most cases, government programs for the financing of health care services have evolved as part of a broader system of social benefits. To a large extent, each nation's health care system is a reflection of its own particular legacy of traditions, organization, and institutions, and the American experience has been no exception (Litman and Robins, 1971). Thus, to understand where the United States is and may be heading, it is necessary to know something of the past and the nature of the governmental system.

THE UNITED STATES SYSTEM OF GOVERNMENT

As most students of government are aware, ours is a limited system of federalism predicated on the notion of representative government with an emphasis on minority rights, majority rule, and the preservation of individual liberty. Historically, the American conception of freedom has taken the guise of rights to be protected from restraint, rather than duties to be performed, and a suspicion of established authority. Thus, largely in response to government oppression experienced in Europe, the framers of the Constitution provided an extensive system of checks and balances upon the federal establishment. Although Madison and others recognized the need for national supremacy—earlier attempts to rest sovereignty in the state or colonial legislatures as called for under the original Articles of Confederation had proven unsuccessful—they were also aware of the need for protection from the arbitrary use of power by the national government. To pit sovereignty against sovereignty, however, was seen as a formula for disaster.

The solution was outlined in Federalist Paper No. 5:

> In the compound republic of America, the power surrendered by the peoples, is first divided between two distinct governments, and then the portion allotted to each, subdivided among distinct and separate departments. Hence a double security arises to the rights of the people. The different governments will control each other at the same time that each will be controlled by itself.

As set forth under Article I, Section 8 of the Constitution, the relationship between the states and the federal government was fairly well drawn, with the federal government given certain prescribed delegated powers, other powers reserved for the states, and still others left to be exercised jointly.[2]

But the framers were also farsighted and realized that the United States was bound to change over time. As a result, the Constitution was envisioned to be a flexible

---

[2]Significantly, the Constitution did not specify the functions and powers of the states, nor were the lines between national and state powers precisely drawn. Consequently, in order to maintain supremacy of the national

document, confined neither in time nor place. Thus, the role of government in American life has evolved over the past 200 years or so in large part through judicial interpretation and response to executive initiatives and legislative action.

FEDERALISM AND THE CONSTITUTIONAL RELATIONSHIP BETWEEN THE NATIONAL GOVERNMENT AND THE STATES

The question of the proper role of government in general, as well as the relative distribution of powers among the national, state, and local governments in particular, has been the subject of prolonged philosophical debate in the United States, with the line in any given controversy ultimately drawn by the courts. Such deliberations have ranged from Marshall's Doctrine of National Supremacy (*McCulloch v. Maryland*),[3] to the Doctrine of Dual Federalism of the Taney court (*Cooley v. Board of Wardens*)[4] with the states having concurrent powers in those matters considered to be truly local in character, to the Cooperative Federalism of the Cardozo court (Steward Machine Company case)[5] to the concept of Creative Federalism under President Johnson[6] and the New Federalism[7] and new New Federalism of the Nixon and Reagan administrations.

Before the 1930s, both federal and state legislation in the field of social welfare were invalidated by the courts on the basis of the due process clause.[8] In 1937, however, the Supreme Court reversed itself (*West Coast Hotel Company v. Parrish*) and repudiated the old doctrine that the due process could be used to crush social welfare legislation. Nevertheless, it was Marshall's interpretation of the commerce clause and the supremacy of the central government that served as the basis for much of the legislative

---

government over the constituent states in any conflict of authority, the original framers took the following steps: (1) They include a supremacy clause in the Constitution that made the Constitution, federal laws, and treaties of the United States binding on the judges in all states; (2) they required all state officers and judges to take an oath to support the U.S. Constitution including the supremacy clause; (3) they provided for a national guarantee of a republican form of government in each state, which implied the right of the national government to intervene in state governments; and (4) they provided for judicial review of state legislative acts in federal courts. Finally, no state was permitted to nullify or obstruct the acts of the national government (Anderson, 1955).

[3]Chief Justice John Marshall proclaimed that the U.S. government was one of enumerated powers derived from those specifically delegated to it by the Constitution, that is, Article I, Section 8 sets forth 17 enumerated powers, plus those implied from the "necessary and proper clause." Later, in *Gibbons v. Ogden*, Marshall held that Congress's power over commerce was plenary, absolute, and complete, subject to no limitations except that expressly stated by the Constitution. The power to regulate was the power to prescribe rules by which commerce was governed.

[4]This doctrine upheld state action in interstate commerce via the state's police powers. Within the powers reserved by the Tenth Amendment, the states were sovereign, with final determination of the scope of state powers to rest with the national judiciary. Taney allowed for concurrent regulation by the state while acknowledging both state and national government powers. It permitted state action where the federal government failed to act.

[5]This case envisioned cooperation between the two levels of government.

[6]The expression was used by President Johnson in 1964 in a speech given in Ann Arbor, Michigan, and referred to an improved system of federal relations with state and local governments in connection with the transfer of federal funds for a variety of programs and purposes to local governments. It had been used earlier in conjunction with state and federal sharing arrangements such as federal grants-in-aid, interstate compacts, and revenue sharing under the Eisenhower administration.

[7]This term is epitomized in the use of block grants.

[8]For example, *Lochner v. New Nork* (attempted state restrictions on working hours); *Adkins v. Children's Hospital* (minimum wage law); *Hamner v. Dagenhardt* (attempt to restrict child labor in manufacturing).

initiatives of the New Deal (Roosevelt), the Fair Deal (Truman), the New Frontier (Kennedy), and the New Society (Johnson).

State–Federal Regulations

The role of the states in the U.S. political system has changed dramatically over the past 200 years as events and trends have altered the fiscal, functional, and political balance within the federal system and rekindled debate over the proper division of powers and responsibilities among the constituent units (Advisory Commission on Intergovernmental Relations, 1980; Stenberg, 1980).

The expansion of the federal government's role in U.S. life has been neither an historical accident nor an altogether noxious historical legacy, but has come about for good historical reasons (Kennedy, 1981). The Constitutional Convention of 1787, for example, was called largely to cure the crippling chaos of decentralized government under the old Articles of Confederation. In his well-known Federalist Paper No. 10, Madison argued that a federal government, presiding over the large and disparate polity, would be proof against "faction" or the monopoly of political power by a small group. A corollary is that only the central government, by virtue of its aloofness from local passions, is equipped to lift the nation above the petty parochialisms and prejudices of local interests (Kennedy, 1981).

Over the course of the past few years, however, under both the Nixon and Reagan administrations, increasing interest has been expressed in the importance of the relations among the various levels of government. At issue has been how large the federal government's role should be in its relations with its state and local counterparts. The answer has been caught up in philosophical differences that separate not only Democrats and Republicans but also conservatives and liberals within each party (Congressional Quarterly, 1972).

Beginning under Roosevelt's New Deal and continuing under the Democratic administrations of the sixties, a fairly broad agreement was reached in Congress that the federal government should play an active role in areas traditionally within the province of state and local governments, particularly regulation where state laws were either nonexistent or failed to conform to one another. There was also broad agreement that the federal government should have a role in providing financial assistance to states and localities for a variety of purposes, such as fighting poverty, pollution control, local law enforcement, and housing. The issue was no longer legitimacy of whether the federal government should be involved in such areas but rather how it should go about assisting the state and local governments (Congressional Quarterly, 1972).

Traditionally, federal assistance has been in the form of categorical grants-in-aid made to a variety of governmental and other public and private entities for specific purposes. Such grants-in-aid enable state and local governments to preserve their autonomy within a framework of federal assistance; to assure minimum levels of services regardless of income inequities among states and localities; and to help achieve national objectives that states and localities may be unwilling or unable to pursue as well as stimulate, through federal matching, increased investment of state and local funds. Moreover, since federal taxes are generally more progressive than their state and local counterparts, federal grants help reduce interstate inequities both in the level of government services and the tax burden. As a matter of fact, one of the major reasons for the proliferation of categorical grants programs was that not only could the federal government tap far more revenue sources than the states and localities, but the latter officials could not or would not provide funds to deal with certain problems (Congressional Quarterly, 1972).

On the other side of the coin, the expansion of federal power at the expense of state and local government is inherent in such revenue-sharing mechanisms, leading to federal domination or control. It was in reaction to just such concerns, as well as the trend toward centralization of government authority in Washington, D.C., that the concept of block grants was developed. Block grants, which are federal payments to states or local governments for specified purposes such as health, education, or law enforcement, were pushed by Republicans in Congress and the executive branch since the 1960s as a way of returning federal decision making to state and local officials. In contrast to categorical grants, which can only be used for specific programs directed by Congress, with block grants state or local officials may make the decisions on how the money is used within the general program area (Congressional Quarterly, 1981).

The New Federalism

The debate continues with President Reagan's efforts to return many government programs to the states. His proposal, however, although clothed in the mantle of the "New Federalism", represents less a sorting out of functions among the various levels of government than opposition of fiscal conservatives to large-scale public sector spending on particular domestic activities regardless of the level of government (Falkson, 1976).[9] Moreover, although the Reagan proposal to return power and responsibilities to the states has been viewed by some as a watershed in the history of U.S. federalism, critics see the president's New Federalism and Economic Recovery Act as a device to reduce federal expenditures for key domestic activities, and as an abandonment of the national commitments to certain costly social programs, involving the transfer of responsibility to the states and their political subdivisions without adequate funding (Stavisky, 1981).

Such criticisms aside, the president's initiative in this area, like that of his predecessor, Nixon, was directed at a number of real and purported deficiencies associated with the federal government's expanded domestic role in the sixties and seventies. As outlined by Penchansky and Axelson (1974), these include the following:

1. The inefficiency, complexity, and inequity of categorical grants
2. The vesting of policymaking and control in quasiindependent agencies, unaccountable to any constituency, that is, the voters, nor responsive to local needs and priorities, that is, local health service agencies (HSAs)
3. The distortion of state and local priorities through the stifling of local initiative and taxing ability, forcing local governments to structure themselves around categorical programs rather than their own needs
4. The imposition and enforcement of stereotyped, inflexible solutions for local recipients by federal bureaucrats, out of touch and unaccountable to the public

---

[9]The New Federalism proposed by President Reagan should not be confused with that advocated under the Nixon administration a decade or so earlier. The latter embodied a broad spectrum of sociopolitical philosophies advocated by people who shared a common background of experience in state and local government, as well as federal service, and a common belief in the need for reforming the structure of domestic policymaking and program implementation. Although both the new federalists and fiscal conservatives are generally concerned about growth of federal power, only the latter has sought total cessation of public sector spending on social programs (Falkson, 1976).

5. Maldistribution of federal funds to those who master the grants application procedure rather than those who have the greatest need (Penchansky and Axelson, 1974; see also Richardson, 1973)

Moreover, the Reagan proposal seemed to strike a responsive chord with the American public. Although the public was concerned about the impact of such a program on their state and local taxes, and the ability of states and cities to serve the needs of the disadvantaged through block grants, as well as uneasy about the complexity of transferring responsibility from the federal to the state governments, an October 18, 1981 Gallop Poll revealed initial public support, at least in principle, for the President's overture (Gallop, 1981).

As states and local units of government have been forced to struggle with the need to provide more human services in the face of ever diminishing financial resources, proposals to return such functions to their control, without a commensurate transfer of funds, have tended to lose much of their aura and appeal, while the debate over the proper role of government in U.S. life continues.

REPRESENTATIVE GOVERNMENT, INTEREST GROUP POLITICS, AND THE LEGISLATIVE PROCESS

The political process in the United States revolves around two complementary but at times conflicting themes—the notions of participatory democracy and of representative government. To many, the quintessence of the U.S. governmental system is found in Madison's Federalist Paper No. 10:

> Extend the sphere, and you take in a greater variety of parties and interests, you make it less probable that a majority of the whole will have a common motive to invade the rights of other citizens or if such common motive exists, it will be more difficult for all who feel it to discover their own strengths and to act in unison with each other.

From this flows the electoral system of "single-member" districts, a citizen congress composed of members elected on the basis of state and local areas, and a theory of public interest representation. The framers of the Constitution carefully set forth a tripartite structure of government involving an intricate system of checks and balances and a separation of powers among the three branches—the legislative, executive, and judicial.

Legislative Process

The power of Congress to legislate is defined in Article I, Section 1 of the Constitution. In addition to writing federal laws, Congress has the power to conduct investigations; monitor federal agencies; impeach federal officials (including the president); declare war; approve treaties; raise or lower federal taxes; appropriate money; and approve appointments to federal agencies, the judiciary, and the armed forces. It may also override a presidential veto with a two-thirds majority vote in each chamber.

Committee System.   At the heart of the legislative process is the congressional committee system that has existed in the House and Senate since 1789 and allows for a division of work as well as an orderly consideration of legislation. There are about 16 Senate and

22 House standing committees plus a host of special, select, and ad hoc committees and subcommittees. Although the jurisdiction of standing committees is determined by the House and Senate that provide the funding to run them, once running, they are almost independent and can move, stall, or stop legislation under their jurisdiction. Most of the legislative workload is handled by subcommittees where most issues are thrashed out. Generally, only matters of extreme dispute are settled in full committee or on the floor (Grupenhoff, 1982).

Committee assignments are allocated on the basis of seniority and in proportion to the representation of the party's membership in each chamber. Members generally want to be on committees related to their personal interests and backgrounds and the economic interests of their districts or state. Some committees, however, are more powerful than others. Among the latter are the Senate and House Appropriations Committees that control the flow of money to programs authorized by other committees, the Senate Finance and House Ways and Means Committees that consider tax legislation, and the House and Senate Budget Committees that establish national priorities through the preparation of the national budget.

Health and the Committee Structure.[11]   Although the word "health" does not appear in the official title of any congressional committee, at least 14 committees and subcommittees in the House and 24 in the Senate have been identified as having some direct or oversight responsibility in health (Lewis, 1976). Of these, six committees—three in the House and three in the Senate—control much of the legislative activity in Congress. The House committees are as follows:

Ways and Means Committee has the power to tax and was the launching pad for much of the health financing legislation passed in the sixties and early seventies under the chairmanship of Representative Wilbur Mills (Dem., Ark.).

Committee on Energy and Commerce (formerly the Committee on Interstate and Foreign Commerce) and its *Subcommittee on Health and the Environment* have jurisdiction over matters of public health, mental health, health personnel, health maintenance organizations, food and drugs, the Clean Air Act, Consumer Protection Safety Commission, health planning, biomedical research, and health protection.

Committee on Appropriations and its *Subcommittees on Labor, Health and Human Services, and Education* allocate and distribute federal funds for individual health programs.

The Senate committees are:

Committee on Labor and Human Resources has jurisdiction over most health bills referred to it, including health planning, health maintenance organizations, health personnel, mental health legislation, for example, Community Mental Health Centers Act.

---

[11]Whereas 20 years ago, one could be rest assured that any major piece of health legislation would bear the clear imprint of Congressman Wilbur Mills (Dem., Ark.), chairman of the powerful House Ways and Means Committee, and to a lesser degree Senator Russell Long (Dem., La.), then Chairman of the Senate Finace Committee, with the congressional reforms of the seventies, the attendant diffusion of responsibility for health legislation over several committees in both Houses, and the weakening of the committee chairs and party leadership, not only is such determination far less certain today but so too is the prospect of successful passage of legislation on the floor in unaltered form.

This committee formerly included a subcommittee on Health and Scientific Research, which was used by its chairman, Senator Kennedy (Dem., Mass.), as a forum for debate on national health insurance. Under Republican control this subcommittee was abolished, and at the request of the chairman of the full committee, Senator Hatch (Rep., Utah), no subcommittee on health was to be established.

Committee on Finance and Subcommittee on Health, like the Ways and Means Committee in the House, the Senate Finance Committee has jurisdiction over taxes and revenues, including matters related to Social Security, Medicare, Medicaid, national health insurance, and child health and is responsible for many of the Medicare and Medicaid amendments, such as Professional Services Review Organizations (PSROs), prospective reimbursement, and controlling hospital and nursing home costs.

Committee on Appropriations and Subcommittees on Labor, Health and Human Services, and Education, like their counterparts in the House, allocate and distribute federal funds for individual health programs.

It has been estimated that although the tax committees (House Ways and Means and Senate Finance) have jurisdiction over only 15 percent of all health programs' legislation, they control about 70 percent of all federal health dollars expended. The two principal authorizing committees, on the other hand—the House Committee on Energy and Commerce and the Senate Committee on Labor and Human Resources—review approximately 70 percent of all federal health program legislation but directly affect only 15 percent of the total health dollars (Schmidt, 1980).

Once considered stable legislative bodies, with long tenure for members and a committee seniority system that ensured enduring power to multiterm members, especially committee chairs, the House and Senate in recent years have been plagued by high membership and staff turnover, overlapping jurisdictions, and changes in rules that have significantly increased the independence of individual members at the expense of party discipline, diffused institutional accountability, and heightened legislative paralysis.

Of particular concern, as far as it affects the development of congressional policy on health and medicine, has been the high turnover rate among members and their aides who have had a special interest or involvement in these areas. Between 1977 and 1981, for example, while the turnover rate among members in both houses of Congress approximated 40 percent, and for their aides, nearly 90 percent, membership changes in the six key committees and subcommittees that deal with most health legislation were massive, that is, 66 percent, and nearly 90 percent for their staff. Moreover, of the 435 representatives and 100 senators who had voted on the Medicare and Medicaid legislation 16 years earlier, only 68 (13 percent) of the former and 13 (13%) of the latter still remained in office in 1981. Similarly, a survey of the personal aides and professional staffs serving the six legislative committees that organized and funded these programs and continue to have jurisdiction over them revealed not a single staff member remains who had played a significant role during that period (Grupenhoff, 1982).[12] As a result, Congress has been left with a huge vacuum in terms of knowledge and expertise in such

---

[12]A similar concern has been voiced by Levine (Chapter 10 in this volume) at the state level, where continuing budget crises, inadequate compensation, competition from the private sector, the rise of single issue politics, and legislative burnout have eroded the legislative and bureaucratic infrastructure of state government at the very time the federal government has proposed returning more responsibility for the implementation of human service programs to them.

matters at the very time it must grapple with major administration initiatives designed to alter these and related programs greatly.

Role of the Executive Branch.   Despite Congress' predominant role in the legislative process, the executive branch is not without its resources. In addition to proposing, lobbying, and vetoing legislation, it can effectively thwart, if not emasculate, legislative intent by withholding or rescinding funds through the Office of Management and Budget (OMB)[13] and/or weaken enforcement by nominating or not nominating agency heads or appointing persons unsympathetic or antagonistic to direct the program involved.[14]

Interest Group Politics and Health

The efforts of organized interest groups to influence government policy in the United States are an inherent part of the political process and, in large measure, rest on First Amendment guarantees of free speech and the people's right to petition government for a redress of grievances. The increasing complexity of modern life and the attendant increase in the role of government in the everday lives of its citizens has tended to heighten such organizational activity as part of the political process. Thus, as power has moved toward the federal government, there has been a proliferation in interest group activity (in both number and variety) at the national level. Each year hundreds of such organized interest groups attempt to wield considerable influence over government policy, constituting what has been referred to as the Washington Lobby[15] (Congressional Quarterly, 1972; also see Drew, 1967; Felicetti, 1975; Hixson, 1976; Milbrath, 1964; Redman, 1974)

In their efforts to gain results, such organizations, often directed by professionals in the art of government, tend to direct their focus at key points in the decision-making and policy implementation process. If unsuccessful in Congress, for example, a group may continue to pursue its aims in the agency charged with responsibility for its execution. The legislative game, then, does not end with congressional passage of a bill and its subsequent signature; rather, the entire thrust of a piece of legislation may be muted, if not reversed, in the writing of the regulations and/or administration of the act.

In addition to attempting to influence the views of individual representatives and senators or key members of the executive branch on specific issues, many organized interest groups take an active part in the elective process itself, contributing large sums of money to the campaign coffers of individual candidates as well as those of the political

[13]The OMB has been likened to a shadow government (Downey, 1975). Just as Congress has relied on the power of the purse strings to wend its will, so too has the OMB, especially under the directorship of David Stockman in the Reagan administration. Stockman, through his deft use and mastery of the budgetary process, has been far more powerful and has had a much greater impact on public policy, although less publicly accountable, in his role of director of OMB than in his former role as Congressman from Michigan, where he was but one voice among 535.

[14]The latter was epitomized by the controversy in the Reagan administration over the management of the so-called superfund and the Environmental Protection Agency (EPA) under the direction of Anne Gorsuch Burford. Burford, who resigned her position under fire in March 1983, had earned a reputation as a staunch opponent of environment protection laws while she was a member of the Colorado state legislature before appointment to head the EPA.

[15]Especially noteworthy in the area of health has been the role played by Mary Lasker (Drew, 1967; Redman, 1974). An equally if not more important influence on government is that wielded by the large think tanks such as The Brookings Institution, American Enterprise Institute for Public Policy Research, the Urban Institute, and the Rand Corporation (Guttman, 1976; Federation of American Hospitals, 1979).

parties themselves (in many cases hedging their bets by contributing to the candidates on both sides of the political aisle). In the last few years, in fact, considerable concern has been raised over single-issue interest groups and their power to wield a disproportionate influence on the legislative elective process through the creation of lavishly funded political action committees (Congressional Quarterly, 1972).

For the most part, however, interest groups tend to gear their operations to the power structure and procedures of Congress, with much of their efforts directed at the committee system. It has been estimated, for example, that about 90 percent of all legislation passed on the floor of either house was passed in the form previously reported by the committee having jurisdiction over it (Congressional Quarterly, 1972).

The power of committees to draw and prevent legislation as well as determine its nature makes them an inviting target for interest group activity. The Washington Lobby, for example, goes to great lengths to keep abreast of government developments that might have a bearing on the interests of its membership. It makes sure to know and watch the work of committees important to its interests; establish and maintain working relationships with key committee members and their staff; stay informed on potential or actual legislative developments; and provide testing and submit prepared statements setting forth its organization's view before the committee (Congressional Quarterly, 1972).

On the whole, a group's power to influence legislation is as much, if not more than, a function of the financial and personnel resources it can command, the astuteness of its representatives, and its political acumen and skills, as the soundness or righteousness of the ideas or positions it expounds. One observer has noted, "The majority of the American people are not members of special interest groups and hence are much less articulate on particular issues than are the interested minority whose affiliation with some active organization gives them a greater political leverage" (George B. Galloway, as quoted in *Congressional Quarterly*, 1972 p. 4).

Falik (1975) has argued that the power potential of health as a political issue is circumscribed by the equivocal nature of interest group politics. Although the politicalization of health issues helps stimulate public debate, educate the public, and broaden the population base for affirmative legislative action on national health matters, it is equally true that political gamesmanship tends to give disproportionate advantage to those groups that are effectively organized for lobbying. In the health field, this has largely been representative of the medical–educational complex, that is, health professional schools, organized medicine, hospital industry, and third party payors (Falik, 1975; also see Health Policy Advisory Center, 1968). Such vested interest group activity manifests itself in the currying of the support of elected officials in both the legislative and executive branch by representatives of major provider groups in order to gain protection and funding of their favorite programs, for example medical schools for research and training, hospitals for expansion and capital investment, and insurance companies for generous reimbursement formulas (Falik, 1975; also see Feldstein, 1977).

Historically, the most formidable organized interest group in health has been the American Medical Association (AMA), which, year in and year out, is one of the United States' richest and most profligate sources of campaign funding and legislative lobbying.[16] In addition to its long and expensive campaigns against "socialized medicine" and

---

[16]For example, according to an analysis by the public interest group Common Cause, the AMA donated $1.79 million to congressional campaigns in 1976, making it the largest organizational contributor to that year's congressional races (reported in *The Nation's Health*, 1978).

government interference in the practice of medicine (see Carter, 1958; Harris, 1967; Hyde and Wolff, 1954; Means, 1953), the AMA gained a certain degree of notoriety when it successfully blocked the appointment of Dr. John Knowles, director of Massachusetts General Hospital, to the position of assistant secretary, Health, Education and Welfare, for health and scientific affairs in the Nixon administration because of what were considered to be his overly liberal views (Congressional Quarterly, 1972).

Participatory Democracy and Health

Public involvement in the determination of health policy in this country has not been confined to organized interest group activity alone, but has taken other forms as well, e.g., community participation, initiative, and referendum.[17] While community participation represents an extension of our democratic heritage and has been seen as a means to perfect the democratic process (Burke, 1968); initiative and referendum constitute a basic right accorded at the state and local level for the exercise of direct public control over legislation (Roemer, 1965).

Community Participation and Health.   Historically, participation of the public in the making of health policy decisions was subsumed in the involvement of the community power structure in institutional governance—a pluralistic, class-based system. In a series of classic studies, Elling and Lee (1966); Belknap and Steinle (1963), and Holloway et al. (1963) among others have described the relationship between community influentials and voluntary and official health and welfare institutions and its impact on organizational decision making (Elling, 1968; also see Section 8.4 of the bibliography at the end of this book). More recently, Riska and Taylor (1978) have noted that not only are such board members recruited from a very narrow segment of the population, but they share a narrow view on health policy that may be at variance with that of those whom they purport to serve that is, their consumers.

The opportunity for full community or citizen participation in the determination of health policy was institutionalized under the provisions of the model cities (PL 88-164) and health planning legislation (PL 89-749) of the Johnson administration. The movement toward broader participation in human service decision making, including health, has been attributed to diverse factors such as dissatisfaction with professional dominance in the area and a growing recognition of the political nature of decision making regardless of professional input (Silver, 1973). Not surprisingly, the application of the concept has resulted in a collision between what Geiger (1969) has termed "community insistence and professional resistance" and has led in some cases, unfortunately, to a politicalization of the health care delivery system over the issue of who truly represents the community and what "participation" and "community" really mean (Geiger; also see Bellin, 1969, 1970; Brandon, 1977; Gordon, 1969; Moore, 1971; Thompson, 1974; and Feingold, 1973).

Initiative and Referendum.   Finally, a note should be added concerning the use of initiative and referendum in health. Unfortunately, the experience of the scientific communities with such extralegislative devices has been anything but promising. The

---

[17]The initiative is an electoral device that empowers the people to propose legislation; the referendum is an electoral mechanism that accords the people the power to approve or reject legislation enacted by their representatives (Roemer, 1965).

submission of health issues to public referendum, for example, has produced mixed, if not discouraging, results. By far the most extensively studied case has been that related to the fluoridation of water. Of the 600 referenda held on the issue during the 1950s and 1960s, despite widespread endorsement by the health care community, over 60 percent were rejected (Crain, *et al.*, 1968 see also Section 8.5 of the bibliography at the end of this book). Moreover, recent efforts with such campaigns have produced equally dismal results. Of about 19 referenda held on the issue in the United States in the first 6 months of 1980, 17 were defeated (Isman, 1981).

Although a number of reasons have been offered to explain the failure of such proposals at the hands of voters, including ignorance, voter apathy, a growing distrust of government, and the health care establishment (Isman, 1981; Marmor et al., 1960; Gamson, 1961), it is suffice to conclude the following:

The submission of controversial health-related issues for voter approval is risky and should be entered into with great caution.

Reliance on the rationality of the voter, the persuasiveness of scientific evidence, the righteousness of the issues, the prestige of the health professions, and the implausability of the charges of the opposition is presumptuous at best, if not self-defeating.

The successful undertaking of such an endeavor requires considerable political skills, extensive knowledge of the community, and mobilization of broad-based, communitywide support.

THE GROWTH IN THE GOVERNMENT'S ROLE IN HEALTH AND HEALTH CARE IN THE UNITED STATES

EVOLUTION NOT REVOLUTION

It has long been a truism of U.S. political life that government is only permitted to do that which private institutions either cannot or are unwilling to do. The basic economic justification for government intervention, Blumstein and Zubkoff (1973) note, is as a remedy for some market failure. In essence, the traditional basis for government involvement has been a remedial one, that is, when, for whatever reason, the market does not achieve an efficient allocation of resources.

In the area of health and welfare, such a view was perhaps best expressed by a 1965 U.S. Chamber of Commerce Task Force on Economic Growth and Opportunity recommendation on the role of government: "Government programs should be used to help the sick, disabled and aged only if voluntary and private means—truly tried and tested— cannot adequately meet society's needs" (United States Chamber of Commerce, 1965).[18]

A related corollary to the above would add that with the exception of those powers delegated to it by the Constitution, the growth of the federal government's involvement

---

[18]Stevens, (1982), for example, has noted that government hospitals in the United States were established only where community need was self-evident and private efforts were unavailable, for example, to safeguard merchant seamen, protect the general public from infectious and contagious diseases, isolate and treat the mentally ill, and provide care and shelter to the poor (Stevens, 1982).

has generally come about in those areas in which the states have also been found wanting. The Interstate Commerce Act of 1887 was passed only after the states had failed to control the spiraling interstate railroad networks, and enactment of the New Deal came after 4 years of economic collapse that found the states broke, with only 17 having old age pension plans, most which were woefully underfunded (Kennedy, 1981).

The expansion of government or public intervention in health and health care in the United States has essentially been one of evolution rather than revolution, a function of social, economic, and political forces as well as judicial interpretation.

CONSTITUTIONAL BASE

The bases for government involvement in health and health care at the state and federal levels rest on quite different constitutional principles. In the case of the states, this has been through the police powers[19] to "enact and enforce laws to protect the health, safety . . . and general welfare" of the public. The states, for example, have rather broad, comprehensive legal authority to regulate or affect virtually every aspect of the health care system within their boundaries (Grad, 1973; also see Wing, 1976). Such intervention, even by compulsion as in the case of immunization against communicable diseases, has been sustained by the courts [*Jacobson v. Massachusetts*, 197 U.S. 11 (1905)] even in the face of a constitutional challenge to its abridgement of the exercise of First Amendment rights to the free expression of religion (Blumstein and Zubkoff, 1973).[20]

Federal involvement, on the other hand, has rested upon judicial interpretation of the Welfare Clause and, in the case of drugs and medications, the Commerce Clause,[21] which has been honed and expanded over the past 40 years. Historically, for example, the definition of commerce has varied widely and Congress' power in this area has vacilated between restricted regulation and a broad grant of power, subject to judicial interpretation. In periods such as 1880 to 1936, for example, when business has been dominant, the courts have tended to keep government under close reign through a narrow interpretation of the Commerce Clause. On the other hand, in periods in which the government is paramount, such as the past 40 years, the court has given a rather broad interpretation to the word "commerce."

HISTORICAL DEVELOPMENT

Over the course of the past 200 years, the role of government in the organization, financing and delivery of health care services in the United States has evolved from that of a highly constricted provider of services and protector of public health to that of a major financial underwriter of an essentially private enterprise whose policies and procedures have increasingly encroached on the autonomy and prerogatives of the providers of care, as he who pays the piper calls the tune.

---

[19]The police powers of the state are much broader than that of any power of the national government. It is a power that was reserved to the states and never given up by them.

[20]Compulsory fluoridation of water extends the concept of permissible infringement of personal freedom to include protection against a noncommunicable, non-life-threatening condition.

[21]"Congress shall have the power to regulate commerce arising among; foreign nations; the several states and Indians."

Although extensive and, at times, seemingly pervasive, such growth has come about neither capriciously nor because legislators or bureaucrats have had any great desire to interfere in this area of endeavor, but rather because the parties primarily involved—the providers (with the notable exception of organized medicine), consumers, insurance carriers, and politicians—realized and came to recognize the need for assistance and government involvement.

Government's role in health and medical care in the United States has thus evolved over time.[22] In the early days of the republic, for example, there were few organized government health programs at either the state or national level (Lee, 1968). There were no state health departments. Foreign quarantine was the responsibility of each port. Programs for communicable disease control and environmental sanitation were the responsibility of local government. Government intervention in health generally was confined to protecting society from the common risks, such as epidemic disease, and to meeting the essential needs of the poor and the destitute—a heritage from the Elizabethan poor laws. This was coupled with support provided by religious and other charitable agencies, fraternal societies, lodges, and clubs organized by immigrant groups (Falk, 1967b).

For the most part, the federal government's role in matters of health could be characterized as paternalistic, custodial, and, most of all, minimal, consisting essentially of responsibility for the care and treatment of merchant seamen and members of the armed forces—past, present, and future (Falk, 1967b). As a matter of fact, the first major involvement of the national government with illness and the provision of medical care for other than the military services began with the Marine Hospital Service Act in 1798 to provide for sick or disabled seamen.[23] Later this was extended to include American Indians who were held in protective custody on reservations as wards of the state. Out of this developed the Indian Health Service, which in 1976 was the object of a major resolution of the Alaska Medical Society calling for its dissolution as inimicable to the private practice of medicine.

Through much of early U.S. history, health and medical care was considered essentially a private and personal matter—a pattern that continued relatively unchanged for almost 80 years. It remained as such until the 1920s when, with the passage of the Sheppard–Towner Act on Maternity and Infancy in 1921, the federal role in health and medical affairs began to take on its modern form. This act established the first continuing program of federal grants-in-aid to state health agencies for the direct provision of services to individuals, the forerunner of the present-day maternal and child health program. The act, however, largely through the action of the AMA, was allowed to die in 1929 (Schlesinger, 1967; Chapman and Talmadge, 1970, 1971).

The enactment of the Social Security Act in 1935, which marked the beginning of the U.S. system of social welfare, provided the next major development in the growth of the federal involvement in matters of health. From this legislation two concepts of social welfare emerged: (1) social insurance for the working population, that is, unemployment

---

[22]In addition to the specific sources cited, we have also drawn on the following references: Falk, 1967; Foltz and Brown, 1975; Foltz, 1975; Jackson, 1969; Clarke, 1980; Rosen, 1974; Mustard, 1945; Russell and Burke, 1978. For a more detailed capsule outline of the key social, political, and legislative developments that underscored the evolution of the government's role in health and health care in the United States, see Appendix 2.

[23]It is interesting to note that the origin of most of the major national health care systems in the world can be traced to the assumption by government of the responsibility for the medical care of merchant seamen and the maritime trades that were considered crucial to the lifeblood of the nation, dependent as they were on import–export trade (see Straus, 1950, 1965).

insurance, workers compensation, and guaranteed retirement benefits and (2) public assistance, that is, direct financial aid provided by the states for those unable to work.

Although not intended as a medical insurance program for recipients of categorical assistance (considered too costly and neither the time nor the place by President Roosevelt), this precedent-setting law provided for federal grants to the states for public health, maternal and child health, and services for crippled children, as well as for public assistance for the aged, blind, and families with dependent children.

It is interesting to note, however, that while initially invoked and promoted on largely humanitarian grounds, the passage of many pieces of social health legislation, ostensibly those dealing with occupational safety and rehabilitation, rested essentially on utilitarian or pragmatic grounds, that is, returning people to the work force and investing in the future—a reflection of our reliance and belief in the Protestant ethic.

In 1950, the program was extended to include the permanently disabled, and in 1960, a more generous, open-ended federal–state program of medical assistance for the elderly—the Kerr-Mills Act—was enacted. The latter, a conservative response to the more extensive and liberal-backed King-Anderson Medical Care for the Elderly Bill supported by President Kennedy, was a forerunner of the Medicaid law (Filerman, 1962).

The passage of the Hill-Burton Construction Act in 1946, which provided federal assistance to the hospitals whose physical plants had grown increasingly warn and obsolescent following the depression and World War II, served as a prototype for federal involvement in health care. In addition to establishing the principles of local initiative, state review, and federal support sharing, it also called for, via congressional mandate, at least the first vestiges of planning, that is, a state plan. Federal support was further extended to medical education and research in the 1950s and early 1960s, often over the bitter opposition of organized medicine (Anderson, 1966; 1968a; Carter, 1958; Harris, 1967; Hyde and Wolff, 1954; Rayack, 1967).

It remained, however, for the Eighty-ninth Congress under the Johnson administration to bring the federal role in health care to full fruition with the passage in 1965–1966 of legislation providing for the establishment of regional medical programs, comprehensive health planning, extensive aid to medical and other related health profession education, and Titles XVIII and XIX of amendments to the Social Security Act of 1965—Medicare and Medicaid.

Certainly the sleeper here was the Medicaid bill, which was an extension and purported improvement of the earlier Kerr-Mills program and, like its predecessor, relied on the existing welfare system. Quickly and hastily passed as part of a political compromise to appease conservatives, its architects never delineated clear goals nor came to grips with the problems inherent in the entire welfare system—particularly the determination of eligibility, which was left to the states. Moreover, as Medicaid began, policymakers had little if any sense of the potential costs of the program nor the impact of pumping vast sums of federal dollars into the private medical market (Friedman, 1977a,b; also see Davis, 1974, 1975a,b, 1976a,b, 1977; Lewis et al., 1976; Stevens and Stevens, 1970; Stevens and Stevens, 1974; Weikel and Leamond, 1976).

Like the Kerr-Mills program before it, Medicaid tended to epitomize the problems inherent in reliance on the states and a states rights approach to resolving broad social programs. In attempting to retain state autonomy and decision making under the program, for example, the rich states tended to get richer whereas the poor states either took no action or had minimal participation in the program. Moreover, despite the offer of federal assistance, many states, especially in the South, either were unwilling or unable to expend the funds. As a result, there was a considerable lack of uniformity both between and within states, which became even further exacerbated in the face of a decline in the economy. Thus, a number of states encountered excessive costs brought on by an explosion of claimants as a result of the 1970 recession and were forced to cut back severely on their programs or, as was the case of New Mexico, pull out of the program altogether.

In addition, in return for the preservation of local control and the determination of local needs, such programs were subjected to the petty political jealousies and idiosyncratic administrative behavior of local welfare officials and county boards. Moreover, like much of President Johnson's War on Poverty and the welfare system itself, Medicaid proved to be an administrative nightmare. In contrast to Medicare, which had the advantage of being a completely new program administered solely at the federal level by a well-established and accepted entity in the Department of Health, Education and Welfare, using the private sector and the insurance industry as fiscal intermediaries, a major debate soon arose as to whether Medicaid was an income-maintenance or health service program and whether it should be administered by the welfare administration or the Public Health Service—a debate finally resolved in favor of welfare.

Growing concern on the part of the federal and state governments over the administration of the program led to the enactment of several provisions to improve its management. These included the establishment of federal guidelines requiring that the states review on a continuing basis the cost, administration, and quality of the health care services rendered under their programs, including stricter standards to ensure quality care and periodic review of nursing home use.

In 1967, Congress mandated expansion of the program to include early and periodic screening diagnosis and treatment of children and youth under the age of 21 eligible for Medicaid. As a result, not only was the health of low-income children considered a major program priority, but the states were expected to administer and the federal government to oversee a program for the direct provision of health care services (Foltz and Brown, 1975; Foltz, 1975).

Continued disenchantment with the program was reflected in the 1972 amendments to the Social Security Act that called for the withholding of federal funds from states that failed to implement the utilization review and Early and Periodic Screening, Diagnosis, and Treatment (EPSDT) programs mandated by Congress as well as the establishment of PSROs to provide a comprehensive and ongoing review of services rendered under Medicaid and Medicare to determine their medical necessity. This was later followed by repeated efforts under the Nixon, Ford, Carter, and Reagan administrations to constrain costs by reducing services and transferring more of the financial burden back to providers and their patients.

NATURE OF THE GOVERNMENT ROLE IN HEALTH AND HEALTH CARE IN THE UNITED STATES

Both traditionally and historically, responsibility for the medical care of recipients of public assistance, veterans with service-connected disabilities, and other special populations such as Indians and the armed forces and for public health in the United States has rested with government, whereas responsibility for the cost of facility construction and health personnel training has been shared among various levels of government and the private sector. The provision of direct personal health services, on the other hand, is and has been essentially a private endeavor.

For the most part, government intervention in the health care system has tended to embrace the following features:

1. Financial underwriting in order to assure the availability to all in the population through either contributory insurance (e.g., Medicare), general tax revenues (e.g., Medicaid), or both

2. The development and establishment of various standards and procedures to safeguard the quality of services financed through public funds

3. The provision of services wherever possible through nongovernmental practitioners and institutions

4. Extension toward comprehensiveness in publically financed services

5. Direct financial support for the modernization, construction, and equipment of health care facilities and for the education and training of needed personnel (Falk, 1967)

The ownership, financing, and operation of the health services system in the United States, as Anderson (1968a, 1968b) has noted, is diffused with a wide dispersion of sources of funds and decision-making units. It is a pluralistic system in which the public and private sectors find themselves in what he has termed "uneasy equilibrium," with the various sectors negotiating with and accommodating one another.[24] As a matter of fact, the coexistence within the U.S. health care system of a wide variety of providers, organizational forms, and funding sources has been viewed by many as a positive attribute that contributes to the rapid diffusion of new technology, the enhancement of quality of care, and the capacity of the system to innovate and adapt to change (National Center for Health Services Research, 1977).

The flow of government funds to voluntary hospitals has a long and venerable history in the United States. According to Stevens (1982), state funding of voluntary general hospitals prior to the depression was generally on a selective, ad hoc, individualized basis, often in response to specific requests from influencial local groups. Government aid to hospitals at the local level, on the other hand, was determined by a combination of local political conditions, common sense, the strength of local interest groups, and the taxing structures of the respective states. This "distinctive American practice" as Goldwater (1909) termed it, that is, the appropriation of public funds for the support of hospitals managed by private benevolent corporations, is attributed by Stevens (1982) to the lack of distinction that has existed between "public and private" functions in the development of U.S. charitable institutions.

FEDERAL ROLE

As indicated earlier, the federal role in health throughout much of U.S. history has tended to be a constrained one, limited to crisis intervention (Falk, 1967a), the control

---

[24]In contrast to many of its European counterparts, much of the health care delivery system in the United States is in the private sector. As a result, government is forced to bargain because it neither owns the facilities nor hires the personnel (Anderson, 1968b). The request in early 1983 by the Reagan administration for hospitals to reserve beds for use in a possible nuclear attack is a case in point.

and prevention of disease in public health. Typically, as Blumstein and Zubkoff (1973) have noted, federal intervention in the health area has been on an ad hoc basis without an overall plan, formulation of objectives, or theoretical underpining. Moreover, in the absence of any specific formulation, national health policy in the United States has been more or less an amorphous set of health goals, derived by various means within the federal structure (Finch, 1970), with little overall concordance or coordination.

Health Policy at the Federal Level

For the most part, the legislative initiatives in health at the federal level over the course of the past 20 years, as Battistella and Begun remind us in Chapter 2, rested on a set of assumptions and presumptions, many of which were well meaning and seemed to embrace the conventional wisdom of the period but have proven to be overly optimistic, idealistic, or unfounded.

To a large extent, according to Brown (1978) of the Bookings Institution, federal health care policy in the United States has tended to embrace two essentially antithetical models or approaches that today are "nurtured in tension." Thus, while "mainstream" equalizing programs continue to receive strong public support, they are challenged by a set of federal proposals based largely on "revisionist" premises concerning constraints on supply and demand for services. As a result, U.S. health care policy has tended to be discontinuous, inconsistent, and, at times, contradictory. Brown goes on to note that by avoiding hard choices and by reconciling in public policy such seemingly contradictory models, we have tended to institutionalize our ambivalence, while preserving the claims of equality of medical services on one hand and delimiting its scope on the other.

ROLE OF THE STATES

In contrast to their federal counterparts, whose influence over health stems in large measure from its enormous fiscal power, the states have rather broad, comprehensive legal authority for a wide variety of programs. As a result, their role in health has taken a number of forms: (1) financial support for the care and treatment of the poor and chronically disabled, including the primary responsibility for the administration of the federal and state Medicaid program; (2) quality assurance and oversight of health care practitioners and facilities, for example, state licensure and regulation; (3) regulation of health care costs and insurance carriers[25]; (4) health personnel training, that is, states provide the major share of the cost for the training of health care professionals; and (5) authorization of local government health services (Clarke, 1980).[26]

Similarly, although historically the power of the governor has been limited, a throwback to the colonists' distrust of the royal governor in the area of public taxation, the states' chief executive appears to exert considerable influence in determining health policy via the power of appointment. A recent review of the statutory authority governing public health decision making in the 50 states (Gilbert et al., 1983; Gossert and Miller, 1973) found the governor responsible for the appointment of about 91 percent of

---

[25]At the time of this writing, 8 states had adopted programs to regulate hospital costs directly, 7 had enacted some type of comprehensive health insurance legislation, and 18 had sought tighter standards for the sale of Medigap health insurance policies to the elderly (Clarke, 1980; Merritt, 1981b).

[26]Local governments ultimately derive their powers from the states.

the 427 positions on the states boards of health. In 11 states, the members of the board sit at the pleasure of the governor. Moreover, turnover among state health officials has been reported as "brisk" with about 60 percent of them being replaced every 2 years (Association of State and Territorial Health Officials, 1981).

State Expenditures for Health

State spending and responsibility in health have traditionally been directed toward broad public health activities, institutional care of the mentally ill, and the purchase of health care services for the economically disadvantaged. During the past 35 years, state spending in health and other human services has been increasingly shaped by federal prescriptions and initiatives, including a variety of apportionment formulas and project grants. As a matter of fact, a familiar characteristic of the U.S. federal system is that many of the programs that carry out national policies are created and operated by the states under rules established by federal legislation and regulations. Moreover, variable methods of federal funding related to purpose, budgetary limits, formulas, and duration impose similar variability on the states' application of funds to the counties (Kramer, 1972; Davidson, 1978).

Like their federal counterpart, state expenditures for health are provided through direct provision of services and indirect purchase of services and have been the subject of considerable political debate over the scope, cost, level of funding, and appropriateness of such expenditures. For all this costs money, and the funds may not be readily available in times of economic recession. Thus, while many states found themselves with expanding treasuries during the late 1960s and early 1970s, fueled by inflation and aided and abetted by increased federal revenue sharing and a thriving economy, in the face of a serious economic downturn nationally, declining state revenues, reduced federal aid, rising costs, a heightened demand for health and welfare services, threatened taxpayer revolts, and bulging budget deficits,[27] they were forced to cut back greatly on their programs and allow more and more of the burden to fall back on their local counterparts.

The Impact of Federal Initiatives in Health on States and Localities

Finally although the evidence on the extent of the impact of federal initiatives on state and local priorities in health is limited, the key to understanding the ways in which federal aid influences state health goals and programmatic activities appears to lie in the political environment of the state. In a study of six states and four public health programs, for example, Buntz et al. (1978) found that although federal programs facilitate rather than inhibit the attainment of state health goals, federal influence tends to be secondary to that of the state's political environment. A federal program, they note, may elevate an issue to the state's active policy agenda but need not necessarily lead to formulation of a state policy or goals unless interests within the state are receptive. Moreover, the federal influence on state health policy appears to be both state and program specific, reinforcing changes supported at the state level and altering state goals at the margin. Such changes in state goals, however, are likely to occur only when the

---

[27]Unlike the federal government, states are prevented by law from operating with a budget deficit. In the first part of 1983, 40 states reportedly had experienced budget problems as a result of the recession, and, in the case of California, government was forced to issue scripts, that is, IOUs, to creditors until a mutually acceptable budget balancing bill could be worked out between California's governor and the legislature.

political environment of the state is receptive to change. For although the federal government has the power to force states to pay attention to certain national goals, it cannot force them to shift their goals in any fundamental way nor to accept those goals as legitimate.

PUBLIC AND PRIVATE FINANCING OF HEALTH CARE IN THE UNITED STATES

Although initial consideration of the adoption of some form of national health insurance in the United States occurred at about the same time as in Europe—at the turn of the century—and in reaction to similar forces—industrialization, urbanization, the demise of the extended family, and employment practices and policies that heightened the threat of work-related injuries and disease as well as unemployment—unlike Europe, the implementation of social security in the United States came through selected income maintenance programs and the preservation of the voluntary sector (Blanpain, 1978).

Thus, the provision of third-party health insurance coverage in the United States developed primarily on a voluntary basis through Blue Cross–Blue Shield and the commercial insurance industry. The attendant mixture of approaches resulted in a complex pattern of health care financing in which (1) the employed are predominantly covered by voluntary insurance provided through contributions made by their employers and themselves; (2) the aged are insured through a combination of coverages financed out of Social Security tax revenues and voluntary insurance for physician and supplementary coverage; (3) the health care of the poor is covered through Medicaid via federal, state, and local revenues, and (4) special population groups such as veterans, merchant seamen, Indians, members of the armed forces, Congress, and the executive branch have coverage provided directly by the federal government (National Center for Health Services Research, 1977).

According to Kramer (1972), private health insurance primarily has been a collection of payments mechanism that supports and reinforces existing patterns of health services. Government spending for health, on the other hand, has been largely confined to filling the gap in the private sector, that is, environmental protection, preventive services, communicable disease control, care for special groups, institutional care for the mentally and chronically ill, provision of medical care to the poor, and support for research and training. The high cost of public medical care programs, Kramer reminds us, owes its genesis to the markedly unique division of risk taking and responsibility between the public and private sector that has thrust upon government the cost of caring for those segments of the population with the highest incidence of illness and greatest need for care, that is, the aged, poor, mentally ill, retarded, chronically ill, and disabled.

Finally, the use of fiscal stimuli through grants-in-aid, the commitment of major financing programs to retrospective reimbursement of costs on a fee-for-service basis, and reliance on peer review for quality assurance reflect a preference for the achievement of public objectives through strategies that offer inducements, persuasion, and positive rewards to providers for compliance rather than impose penalties or costs for failure to comply (National Center for Health Services, 1977; Anderson, 1968b). Such strategies, however, have been inherently expansive, tending to minimize the need for deliberative allocative choices by increasing the flow of resources into the health care system. Once costs rise and revenues become short, such choices no longer can be put off and questions of constraint and costs are raised.

Government Financing of Personnel Training: The Case of Medical Education

Before the enactment of the Health Professions Educational Assistance Act in 1963, the financing of graduate education in general and health professions in particular was traditionally within the purvue of state government, students, and/or their families. The provision of direct financial aid from the federal government to medical schools in the 1960s and early 1970s to encourage biomedical research and expanded enrollments, bypassing the more traditional intergovernmental transfer approach to funding aid has been depicted by Millman (1980) as "private federalism."

At the state level, medical education tends to be addressed in the context of higher education, rather than as part of health policy, and in response to state and local needs, rather than to those of the nation as a whole, whereas the opposite is true of federal endeavors. As the federal government has assumed an increasing role in the financial support of biomedical research and physician training—to the point where any given medical condition from prickly heat to cancer had its own congressional advocate for federal funding—an unduly large proportion of such support tended to be diverted from a focus on primary care to research and specialty training, distorting the teaching function of the educational institutions and perverting the long-standing reliance of public institutions on the largess of the state legislatures. So entwined had medical school financing become with the federal funding for research and training that the state legislators and policy-makers ended up on the outside looking in (Rogatz et al., 1970; Bloom and Martin, 1976). But if medical school dependence upon federal financial support had become manifest over a 25-year period, there was a point beyond which medical faculties were unwilling to go. This was reached in the late 1970s when, in return for continued federal funding under the Health Professions Educational Assistance Act, 1976 (PL 94-484), Congress mandated that medical schools provide training for United States students studying abroad (US FMS). Following the lead of two private institutions, Yale and Northwestern, and one state, Indiana, U.S. medical schools, citing the abridgement of the right of educational institutions to determine their own admission policy, announced their refusal to go along with such a directive even if it cost them the price of federal support. In the face of such oppositions, Congress "blinked" and the requirement was withdrawn.

The heyday of federal funding of health personnel training, however, appears to have been reached. So active and effective were such efforts that by the end of the last decade, the nation found itself with potentially more physicians and hospital beds than it needed. As a result, beginning in the mid-1970s and escalating rapidly during the Reagan administration, federal goals have moved from a position of fostering a larger supply of health professionals to reducing sharply tax-based support for this purpose, leaving health professional schools and their students caught in the squeeze of rising educational costs, declining federal support, and reduced state revenues (Lewin and Derzon, 1981). Such action, however, may have the salutatory effect of making medical schools and their faculties more responsive to state needs, and, as Lewin and Derzon (1981) note, this may be the case. In contrast to the ebb and flow of federal funding, for example, they found state support for health professions education has grown steadily, that is, at an average annual rate in excess of 10 percent for each profession, from 1974 to 1980, with most such funding directed toward public institutions.

Problem of Cost Versus Services in Government Programs

The amount of money that a nation spends for its health services, Anderson and Newhauser noted in 1969, tends to be a product primarily of a political process arrived at by implicit and explicit public policy decisions within the body politic. An equally appropriate maxim, however, is that whatever government giveth, it can taketh away. In other words, although public programs often initially are enacted on essentially altruistic grounds, for example, increased accessibility to health care services by removing financial barriers to care while defraying costs over a wide segment of the public, once this is done and the costs that originally were borne by patients, their families, and/or the private sector and are now assumed by government rise, there is a strong tendency on the part of the latter to cut back on its commitment by reducing coverage, that is, who and what is covered and increasing the amount paid by those who use the services.

Thus, as costs rise, the tendency is to cut back on the coverage especially if the constituency being served is not a very powerful or influencial one, such as the poor, the socially and economically disadvantaged and, up to the 1960s, the elderly.[28] For as commendable and needy a service may be and as legitimate as government involvement is, the question ultimately gets down to a fundamental economic one: the cost of the service given the limited funds (however defined) available for it.

Therefore, beginning in the latter part of the 1960s early 1970s, the federal government and the states, confronted by escalating costs and depleted resources, began to cut back on the Medicare and Medicaid programs. Thus in contrast to 20 years ago when the dual programs were first enacted and the primary policy concern was increased access to health care services for more U.S. citizens, ostensibly the aged and economically disadvantaged, the programs were so successful that the budget soon became incapable of containing them. As a result, the policy has taken a 180-degree turn toward greater restriction and control, with often devastating consequences on the provision and receipt of services, in many cases proving to be "penny cheap and pound foolish" (e.g., Roemer et al., 1975).

Case of Medicaid.   This conflict between costs and services has been especially true of the Medicaid program, whose expenditures tend to be particularly susceptible to the forces of unemployment and inflation. For not only does the size of its clientele, that is, recipients of public assistance and "the medically indigent," vary with the level of unemployment, but the services it renders are purchased in the general medical marketplace and are susceptible to the impact of inflation. In addition, the negative effect of reduced tax receipts on state and local revenues as a result of a national economic recession tends to place both levels of government in a whipsaw as the demand for services on them rises because of heightened unemployment while their capacity to pay for them diminishes.

Not all states, however, experience the impact of the burden equally. Since the federal contribution to Medicaid expenditures depends on its per capita income relative to the national average 2 years earlier, the federal share is relatively insensitive to the distribution of the burden of the recession among the states as well as the mobility of welfare recipients between and within states (Davis, 1974, 1975, 1976b).

At any rate, in the face of declining economic circumstances and reduced revenues, a substantial growth in the use of inpatient hospital, nursing home, and intermediate care facilities; a loss of general revenue-sharing monies; continued medical care price

---

[28]Historically, considered politically impotent by politicians and political scientists alike, the aged, stimulated by their success in the battle over Medicare, have become an extremely potent electoral force in U.S. political life, heightened by their proclivity to vote. In contrast with their younger counterparts, that is, those under 25 years of age, elderly voters consistently exhibit higher rates of electoral participation (see Donahue and Tibbits, 1962).

inflation; and state and local tax limitations, cutbacks in the program have generally taken a variety of forms, listed below, as our admonition of costs versus services tends to prevail[29]:

1. Reductions in the levels of eligibility, usually by lowering the income ceiling thereby cutting down the number of potential recipients. In the case of the medically indigent, states had wide discretion in their determination of eligibility.

2. Placing limitations on the types and amount of services covered, that is, what and how much. This has generally taken the form of limitations on inpatient hospital services, that is, number of days per spell of illness and/or per year, cutbacks on optional services (other than those specifically mandated under the law), and reduction in services to the medically indigent.

3. Reductions in the amount of reimbursement; placement of ceilings on maximal allowable profit; suspension of payments to providers, that is, physicians, hospitals, and nursing homes, sometimes arbitrarily determined; and, after the services have been rendered, leaving the patient to pay out-of-pocket, if they could, or the provider to absorb the cost—all of which has created considerable bitterness between patients and providers, as well as providers and government. In fact, a major criticism levied at the program by physician and health care institutions was its inadequate reimbursement and excessive red tape. This led many providers to opt out of the program-leaving recipient patients to fend for themselves, avoid care, rely on an increasingly limited number of overworked private practitioners who would see them or on the services of notorious "Medicaid mills," seek care from the hard-pressed public hospitals, or to make up the loss of income by excess visits, overuse of diagnostic lab work, and various forms of creative billing (Fever Chart, 1976).

4. The establishment of requirements for prior authorization or approval before treatment could be rendered as well as restrictions on where services could be obtained.

5. The use of deductibles and copayment provisions in order to force recipients to share in the cost of the services by increasing their out-of-pocket expenses which in turn, it has been argued, not only discourages use but helps offset or reduce the cost to government.[30]

---

[29]In 1981, over half of the states reported significant budget problems with their Medicaid programs. In many cases, Medicaid was the most expensive item in the state's budget, consuming 10 to 15 percent of state general funds. Even more alarming to the states, however, was the fact that the program's costs were rising faster than state revenues. Some 21 states reported either increases in current copayments on some optional services or new copayment requirements on optional services. Almost half the states were considering significant changes in provider reimbursements ranging from decreasing or freezing payment levels for physicians to restructuring nursing home reimbursement formulas. Reduction or elimination of some group from further eligibility was proposed in 14 states (Merritt, 1981).

[30]Such political–economic rhetoric and perhaps, conventional wisdom aside, experience with such cost-sharing measures in the private sector, at least as far as inpatient hospital care is concerned, has proven to be far less cost effective in reducing costs while often denying care for those most in need, delaying the need of more extensive services when such patients are ultimately admitted (Blue Cross Perspectives, 1972). Moreover, such devices focus primarily on the patients rather than the physicians who, through both their gate-keeping and decision-making roles, constitute the primary generators of costs in the institution. The reluctance, on the other hand, of politicians and government officials to impose controls on health care providers is a function of the essentially private character of the U.S. health care system. Thus, drafters of the Medicare and Medicaid legislation were wary of placing onerous restrictions on providers lest they withhold their services or fail to participate in the programs, fearing a possible replication of Canada's experience with a physicians' boycott in Saskatchewan (see Tollefson, 1964). As a result, reliance was placed on the good faith of the medical profession and the provision of financial incentives to hospitals and third-party carriers for cooperation (see Feingold, 1966; Marmor, 1970; Skidmore, 1970).

Case of Medicare.   The situation has been much the same with the federally run Medicare program as the government has sought to recoup or reduce its costs, while reneging on its promises. Thus, beginning with the Nixon and Ford and continuing under the Carter administration, attempts have been made to reduce the costs of the program by placing curbs on provider reimbursement while making the elderly assume more of the costs themselves by increasing the size of the deductible, the amount of copayment required, and the premium for Part B, Supplementary Physician Coverage (e.g. from an initial $3.00 per month in 1966 to $13,50 in 1983), culminating with a proposal by the Reagan administration in early 1983 that called for the imposition of "means test" on program beneficiaries.[31] Such provisions not only are a perversion of the original intent of the Medicare legislation, that is, to relieve the elderly of the fear and heavy financial burden of the high cost of health and medical care while allowing them to retain their sense of dignity through the mechanism of social insurance, but in direct contradistinction to the recommendations of almost every government and nongovernment advisory group and study commission appointed to look at the program since its inception, as well as the 1971 and 1981 White House Conferences on Aging.

Finally, while all such cost-containment measures may well make public officials and their statistics look good,[32] they offer little solace to those who, in many cases through no fault of their own, are in need of care but are ineligible to receive it. Moreover, shifting the cost of such services to those who use them neither solves the problem nor removes the burden, but merely shifts it back on to those least able to bear it.

Thus given the central focus, cost containment has come to assume in government health and social programs, the ultimate question the United States must come to grips with is how much deterrence because of cost is both tolerable and permissible and in what areas. Again, it is the constituency with the least political power—the poor and socially disadvantaged—who are the most likely to feel the brunt of such cuts and to be imposed on.

A CASE FOR A FEDERAL PRESENCE IN HEALTH AND HEALTH CARE

The growth in the federal government's role in health and health care in the United States has not been without its problems and negative consequences, such as escalating costs, bureaucratic inflexibility, excessive regulation, red tape and paper work, arbitrary and, at times, conflicting public directives, inconsistent enforcement of rules and regulations, fraud and abuse, inadequate reimbursement schedules, arbitrary denial of claims, insensitivity to local needs, consumer and provider dissatisfaction, and charges that such efforts tend to promote dependence rather than work. The arguments for decentralizing such programs are all too familiar: The federal government has grown too large, intrusive, and paternalistic; it is too impersonal, distant, and unresponsive; state and local

---

[31]In contrast to the infamous requirement of a pauper's oath to determine eligibility under the old Kerr-Mills program in the early 1960s, which was considered to be particularly demeaning by the elderly, most of whom had lived through the depression and took pride in their independence and unwillingness to accept charity, the Reagan proposal sought to reduce the payment of benefits to the more affluent by placing an upper income limit on eligibility. The eventual result, however, would be the same, that is, the conversion of the program from an earned entitlement available to all to an income-based benefit program limited to just some.

[32]To some, the "cheapest program" of all is the one in which no expenditures are made even though the cost of doing nothing ultimately may be higher.

governments are closer to the people and more familiar with local needs and, therefore, more accessible and accountable to the public and better able to develop responsive programs than are federal agencies (Fein, 1980).

Such problems and criticisms aside, the reason for a national endeavor in this area is not only that more funds are available and collectible at the federal level, but, more important, there is an implied national commitment to action and resolution of the problem.[33] Illness and disease, for example, simply do not recognize jurisdictional boundaries and are nationwide in scope. Chronic disease, alcoholism and drug abuse, hypertension and stroke are as much a threat to the suburban as the inner-city population. Moreover, worldwide transportation and communication systems make a disease anywhere a potential problem everywhere, as exemplified by the various versions of the Asian flu in the 1970s. Thus, although health and human service programs may well be more administratively amenable to state and local control, the latter's track record in this area has been anything but impressive.

While the states, with the prompting of the U.S. Supreme Court in the early 1960s, have tended to improve greatly the administrative and legislative structures that were the object of allegations of incompetence and insensitivity to the needs of the socially and economically disadvantaged just a generation ago, they still possess a number of inherent weaknesses that severely deter their ability to assume a more extensive role in the organization, financing, and delivery of health and human services. In addition to being unequal in financial ability, states differ widely in their needs for services and financial capacity to provide such services. Although innovative and at times ahead of their national counterparts, state action tends to be piecemeal and lacking in uniformity. Moreover, state regulation of nursing homes, health insurance, pollution control, and so on, has often proven to be weak, episodic, and susceptible to industry capture. Finally, states tend to be parochial in their outlook, ready to pursue and preserve their own self-image in competition with other states in regard to population, industry, and the welfare burden leading to serious inequities in the assumption and delivery of services.

A similar situation exists at the local level. Often plagued by antiquated administrative structures, a lack of legal authority, insufficient financial resources, and a dearth of qualified personnel, local efforts frequently have been susceptible to petty conflicts of interests such as rural–urban or urban–suburban differences, racial and economic discrimination, and lack of uniformity in the provision of services or the requirements for eligibility. In some southern and rural counties, county welfare officials in the 1960s and 1970s waged deliberate campaigns to encourage families on relief to go to the more industrialized states or cities of the Northeast and Midwest where welfare payments were higher—even providing one-way tickets so as to reduce their own expenditures for welfare.

Many county officials, moreover, prefer local determination in deciding who should get benefits, regardless of the provisions of the law vis-à-vis eligibility. Some time ago (1968) at a joint meeting on legislative affairs put on by Minnesota's health and welfare departments, a county commissioner from one of the state's southern rural areas was heard to say how he liked to know who was on welfare and determine for himself whether they *really* belonged there and needed what they claimed. "You know, when

---

[33]Nevertheless, as Clarke and others have aptly observed, although federal health policy may constitute a national consensus to do something, the actual implementation of such policy is often dependent on the influence of the "political environment" of the states (Clarke, 1981; see also Buntz, et al., 1978; Altenstetter and Bjorkman, 1978).

you live out there, you kind of get to know who should and shouldn't be on the [welfare] rolls." Federal or state rules and regulations aside, his role, as he perceived it, was that of a self-proclaimed judge and jury.

Similarly, many county boards, in the face of angry taxpayers and disgruntled voters (the taxpayer's revolt), tend to be particularly tight fisted with regard to expenditures for such services, often with self-defeating results. Several years ago, for example, an orthopedic patient at the Kenny Rehabilitation Institute in the Twin Cities would have been able to return home and lead a fairly productive life if the county had agreed to purchase a wheelchair. The county refused to do so, however, on grounds that such an expenditure was a luxury, resulting in a medically unnecessary and prolonged high-cost hospital stay at the county's expense.

Finally, the heavy reliance of local government on the property tax makes the provision of such services extremely difficult. This is especially so in view of the regressive nature of the tax as well as the fact that those who tend to benefit the most from such services or use them disproportionately more are the very ones—the poor and the elderly—who are the hardest hit by the tax and most resistant to increases in it, even to pay for the very services they rely or depend on.

And so, given that many of our problems of health and health care are not restricted to or confined by city, county, township, or state lines and can effectively be resolved only on a broader geographic basis, we have tended to opt for a more global approach. As Anderson (1955) and others have noted, when problems tend to be national in scope, they call for national solutions. And over time, it has been the federal rather than constituent states who have had to act—sometimes alone, sometimes with the aid of the states, and sometimes in the aid of states. It has done so, moreover, consonent with the values and structure of the U.S. social, political, and economic system.

CONCLUSION

The growth in government's involvement in health has been an evolutionary one, a response to changes in times and circumstances. Over the past 40 years, there have been major shifts in the role and posture of the federal government in the organization, financing, and delivery of health care services and its relationship with the states in which the following have occurred:

1. The traditional federal role of sharing the cost of health care gradually has been expanded to include programs of care purchased by the government itself as well as the use of federal funding to initiate and develop new forms of delivery, for example, neighborhood health centers and health maintenance organizations (HMOs) (Penchansky and Axelson, 1974).

2. An increased use of categorical and project grants in health found the federal government involved in the budget funding of local programs and bypassing local governments considered unresponsive to the needs of the poor (Penchansky and Axelson, 1974).

3. The federal focus has shifted from encouraging the expansion of state programs to assuring their integrity and from concern over improving access to services to control over their costs with both patients and providers often caught in the middle.

The progression in such involvement has been a slow and steady one, a function of the nature of the nation's political process and social and economic systems. Incrementalism, rather than fundamental changes in the structure of the health care delivery system, has been the hallmark of federal policies (Falik, 1975). What has evolved then, as Anderson (1968a) has aptly observed, has been a partnership—sometimes rather tenuous and strained—between government (federal and state) and the voluntary system, working together, not as rivals but as partners—not necessarily equally or smoothly, but as partners nevertheless.

Given the experience of the United States over the past half-century with various government entreaties in health, what lessons can be learned? The following are suggested for future consideration:

1. Reform of the health care system in the United States is likely to be incremental, a compromise involving the resolution of a number of interests.

2. National programs require consideration of regional and local problems and needs.

3. Regional variations and the diversity and voluntary–private nature of the health care enterprise makes the imposition of national fee schedules, reimbursement formulas, and facility guidelines difficult if not impossible to achieve.

4. Equality in financing is not sufficient to guarantee equal access to medical care (Davis, 1974).

5. All third-party coverage, whether private or public, such as Medicare and Medicaid, contributes to inflation (Davis, 1974).

6. All modern national health care systems, predicated as they are on sophisticated technology, are inherently costly (Anderson and Newhauser, 1969).

7. Open-ended reimbursement to providers on the basis of cost is inflationary, whereas unrealistic or picayune controls tend to be self-defeating, leading providers to opt out of the system and leaving recipients a limited range of choices of care.

8. Although any government system is likely ultimately to impose restrictions on the autonomy and perogatives of providers, such controls can neither be arbitrary nor capricious but should seek the cooperation of professional interests and the use of financial incentives and rewards.

9. A conflict between cost and services is inherent in government programs.

10. Government efforts to reduce expenditures for health services programs by transferring their costs without appropriate financial safeguards to lesser levels of government or recipients of services does not effectively reduce the overall costs of the services but merely shifts the financial burden to those least able to bear it while depriving those most in need.

11. Utilitarianism, that is, "put people back to work" and "get them off the welfare rolls and onto the tax-paying rolls," rather than humanitarianism and altruism, underscore the ultimate adoption of most government human services programs.

12. Protection against the financial burden of health and medical care is impossible without the placement of a ceiling on the patient's financial responsibility. Unless the family is guaranteed that its share of the cost of care will not exceed some reasonable fraction of income, the goal of preventing or protecting against the financial burden of health care services cannot be achieved (Davis, 1974). While what that level of income or ceiling is or should be is open to debate, it should be noted that artificial financial barriers or income cutoffs tend to be highly susceptible

to the tyranny of inflation, that is, as dollar amounts soar, real value and purchasing power decline.

13. The use of administrative and regulatory controls, such as Medicare's requirement of a three-day hospital stay before a patient may be authorized to be admitted to a nursing home, second opinion requirements, inadequate reimbursement to providers, reduction of the tax deduction for health and medical expenditures, and elimination of deductibility for health insurance premiums, rather than civil or criminal penalties, tend to be misdirected, self-defeating, and ineffective.

14. Programs covering only poor people must be carefully designed so as to avoid adverse incentives and inequities in which some people receive substantial assistance and other equally in need or deserving that is, the near or working poor, receive nothing or practically nothing (Davis, 1974).

15. Assumptions that the elderly are protected against the cost of long-term care by Medicare are ill-founded and wrong. The only government-provided protection the elderly have against the cost of catastrophic illness is Medicaid—a welfare program.

16. Geographic inequities are bound to occur when states have a major role in setting eligibility and benefit levels (Davis, 1974).

17. Government health care programs predicated on the virtues of competition and the free marketplace and a preferred single delivery system ignore the fact that one of the major sources for the high cost of hospital care in the United States has been the virtually unfettered costly competition between health institutions for staff, equipment, and so on, which results in a duplication of services, minimize the value of a diverse pluralistic system of delivery and the variable needs and demands of consumers as well as providers.

18. Whatever the future role of government in health in the United States is to be, it will be the product of a deliberate decision made in the political arena and will likely embrace the unique features of the nation's social, political, economic, and health care system.

HEALTH POLITICS AND POLITICAL SCIENCE[34]

There has been considerable speculation—if not actual sharp intellectual debate—over the years among political scientists specializing in the study of the politics of health as to whether there is something analytically unique *from a political science perspective* about health politics other than its subject matter. We would tend to concur with Falcone (1980–1981) that the politics of health is not *theoretically* different from the politics of other policy areas, for example, defense, welfare, and education. In doing so, however, we wish to stress that insightful political understanding of various policy areas requires not simply general political insight coupled with specialized substantive expertise but also requires that the specific political implications of the substantive issues in various policy areas be carefully analyzed and understood as well. Thus, there are aspects of health politics that, while individually not unique, need to be presented in

---

[34]This section was coauthored by Leonard Robins.

overview form in order to understand developments in the various areas of health politics discussed by the contributors to this volume.

Health politics, for example, is usually conducted in a favorable political climate. The notion of health is a popular one: The public, for good or ill, remains convinced of the efficacy of medicine in promoting and maintaining it and believes that future medical advances guarantee less sickness and longer life. This results in strong popular support for spending money in all fields of health: public health, biomedical research, and especially medical care services. The only important constraint is, obviously, budgetary, that is, people do not want their taxes raised or the budgets unbalanced, which would hurt the economy.

Other fields are not so fortunate when they enter the political arena. Welfare spending, for example, is not merely opposed because of possible adverse tax or spending consequences, but there are important segments of the public that oppose welfare spending in principle. They believe that it is worse than doing nothing, because it encourages laziness and dependency on the part of those receiving welfare.

It would be a mistake, however, to assume that all health policies have the same type of politics. Lowi (1964), for example, describes three major patterns of political conflict that are said to be associated with three different types of public policies—distributive, regulative, and redistributive.[35] Elaborating on Lowi's typology, Marmor (1973) has noted that considerable effort has been expended by political scientists in recent years trying to specify the ways by which different issues are raised, disputed, coped with, and, at times "solved."

It is clear that actual policies are never as distinct as Lowi's typology suggests. All public programs redistribute resources, but most are not primarily attempts to do so. Likewise, all government programs depend on an ultimate capacity to regulate the conduct of citizens, but most do not make such regulation their prime object. And almost all government programs involve the distribution of goods and services among different groups, though the question of which county or which social class should receive them is not always salient.

Given the debate surrounding Lowi's and other's attempts to identify policy arenas and the politics associated with them precisely, no one typology can be presented as being definitive. It is important, however, to recognize that the politics of obtaining funds for biomedical research is not the same as the politics of drug regulation and that neither is the same as the politics of national health insurance.

That different policies may be associated with somewhat different political processes is now relatively commonly accepted by political scientists. Before the work of Lowi, however, this was not generally well recognized, and this failure constituted one of the major reasons for the relative inattention political scientists have given to health. Although the vast majority of political scientists were very concerned with public policy as citizens, they did not feel that public policy was their concern as political scientists. They felt that their proper concerns as political scientists were the political and governmental processes that produce policy—not public policy itself. Political scientists' interest in

---

[35]Distributive policies that parcel out public benefits to interested parties provoke a stable alliance of diverse groups that seek portions of the pork barrel. Regulative policies, which constrain the relationships among competing groups and persons, provide incentives for shifting coalitions, pluralistic competition, and the standard forms of compromise. Redistributive policies, on the other hand, reallocate benefits and burdens among broad socioeconomic population groups and foster polarized and enduring conflict in which large national pressure groups play central roles (Lowi, 1964).

public policy dramatically heightened, however, when, to use research terminology, it came to be increasingly accepted that public policy was, in certain circumstances and for appropriate purposes, an important independent variable in the study of political phenomena as well as the traditional dependent variable to be explained.

What remains unexplained, however, is why health has received relatively little attention in political science as a policy domain in comparison with other fields such as education, law enforcement, and defense. Despite both its practical implications and potential theretical relevance, the politics of health has been a generally neglected area of inquiry among political scientists. In contrast with their counterparts in sociology and economics, the latter—with the notable exceptions of Garceau's (1941) classic pioneering exposition on the political life of the AMA, Eckstein's (1960) landmark analysis of pressure group politics in the British Medical Association, and Glaser's (1960) penetrating look at doctors and politics—have evidenced little interest or involvement in the study of health politics.

The minimal role political science has played in the development of the study of health politics appears to be the result of a variety of factors. Weller (1977), for example, has attributed the discipline's limited contributions to its relatively narrow focus, concentrating on too few groups or too narrow a set of issues, that is, the physician and the medical profession; an overreliance on case studies confined to either a particular group, issue, or piece of legislation; a disciplinary boundary problem over whose purvue health policy belongs, that is, political science, public administration, social welfare, or something else; the complex nature of the health field; and the belief on the part of some political scientists, at least, that the pressure group approach exhausts the possibilities for the political analysis of health.

In addition, the general paucity of available research support for the study of such "politically sensitive" subject matter and the historically "private" character of health care delivery in the United States have come into play. In the case of the latter, although it can persuasively be argued that politics occurs in nearly all endeavors in life, political scientists have traditionally and still primarily do emphasize those political phenomena that essentially relate to government. Thus, whereas the vast bulk of taxing, spending, and employment in the fields of education, law enforcement, and defense have been in the public sector, that for health, at least up to the 1960s, was ostensibly a private endeavor and as such held little fascination or interest for political scientists.

With the passage of Medicare and Medicaid, along with the other legislative initiatives noted earlier, the degree of public involvement in health has changed dramatically. And although the politics of health may never become as important to political science as, for example, medical sociology is to sociology or health economics is to economics, there is reason to believe that it will assume a far greater research significance than it has had within the discipline as political scientists give increasing attention to the politics of public policy in general and that of health in particular.

But if political science has been found wanting as far as its contribution to the politics of health is concerned, the field of health and medical care has been equally remiss in its lack of knowledge and understanding of the political environments within which it operates. Ignorance or neglect of political factors in the organization, financing, and delivery of health care services omits a critical element in the potential resolution of health care problems. For, like it or not, as Kaufman (1966) has succinctly observed, health and health care have become so deeply enmeshed in the body politic that in order to achieve success within it, there is a need for health care administrators and practitioners to learn to understand it, adjust to it, and turn it to their advantage.

Toward this end, the formation of the Committee on Health Politics by a group of interested faculty members in programs in hospital and health services administration in the early 1970s, the introduction of courses and seminars on the politics of health, in programs in health administration, schools of public health and nursing and other health professional schools, and the publication of the *Journal of Health Politics, Policy and Law* are all steps in the right direction and would seem to bode well for the future.

REFERENCES

Advisory Commission on Intergovernmental Relations, *The Federal Role in the Federal System: The Dynamics of Growth*, Washington, D.C.: Advisory Commission on Intergovernmental Relations, 1980.

Altenstetter, Christa and James Bjorkman, *State Health Politics and Impacts: The Politics of Implementation*, Washington, D.C.: University Press of America, 1978.

Anderson, Odin W., "Compulsory Medical Care Insurance, 1910–1950," in Eugene Feingold, ed., *Medicare: Policy and Politics*, San Francisco: Chandler Publishing Co., 1966, pp. 85–156.

Anderson, Odin W., *The Uneasy Equilibrium, Private and Public Financing of Health Services in the U.S., 1875–1965*, New Haven: College and University Press, 1968a.

Anderson, Odin W., "Health Services in a Land of Plenty," in William R. Ewald Jr., ed., *Environment and Policy: The Next Fifty Years*, Bloomington: Indiana University Press, 1968b, pp. 59–102. Also *Health Administration Perspectives No. A7*, Chicago: University of Chicago Center for Health Administration Studies, Graduate School of Business, 1968b.

Anderson, Odin W., "All Health Care Systems Struggle Against Rising Costs," *Hospitals*, Vol. 50, October 1, 1976, pp. 97–102.

Anderson, Odin W. and Duncan Newhauser, "Rising Costs are Inherent in Modern Health Care," *Hospitals*, Vol. 43, February 16, 1969, pp. 50–52.

Anderson, William A., *Nations and States: Rivals or Partners*, Minneapolis: University of Minnesota Press, 1955.

Association of State and Territorial Health Officials, *Internal Newsletter*, Washington, D.C., 1981.

Belknap, Ivan and John G. Steinle, *The Community and Its Hospitals: A Comparative Analysis*, Syracuse: Syracuse University Press, 1963.

Bellin, Lowell E., "Medicaid in New York: Utopianism and Bare Knuckles Public Health . . . ," *American Journal of Public Health*, Vol. 59, May 1969, pp. 820–825.

Bellin, Lowell E., "The New Left and American Public Health—Attempted Radicalization of the American Public Health Association Through Dialectic," *American Journal of Public Health*, Vol. 60, June 1970, pp. 973–981.

Blanpain, Jan with Luc Delesie and Herman Nys, *National Health Insurance and Health Resources. The European Experience*, Cambridge: Harvard University Press, 1978, pp. 2–3.

Bloom, Bernard S. and Samuel P. Martin, "The Role of the Federal Government in Financing Health and Medical Services," *Journal of Medical Education*, Vol. 51, March 1976, pp. 161–169.

Blue Cross Perspectives, Vol. 7, No. 3, 1972, pp. 1–5.

Blumstein, James W. and Michael Zubkoff, "Perspectives on Government Policy in the Health Sector," *Milbank Memorial Fund Quarterly*, Vol. 51, Summer 1973, pp. 395–431.

Brandon, William, "Politics, Administration and Conflict in Neighborhood Health Center," *Journal of Health Politics, Policy and Law*, Vol. 2, Spring 1977, pp. 79–99.

Brown, Lawrence D., "The Scope and Limits of Equality As a Normative Guide to Federal Health Care Policy," *Public Policy*, Vol. 26, Fall 1978, pp. 481–532. Also Brookings Institution General Series Reprint No. 350, Washington, D.C.: The Brookings Institution, 1977.

Buntz, C. Gregory, Theodore F. Macaluso and Jay Allen Azarow, "Federal Influence on State Health Policy," *Journal of Health Politics, Policy and Law*, Vol. 3, Spring 1978, pp. 71–78.

Burke, Edmund, "Citizen Participation Strategies," *Journal of the American Institute of Planners*, Vol. 34, No. 5, September 1968, p. 287.

Carter, Richard, *The Doctor Business*, New York: Doubleday and Co., 1958.

Chapman, Carleton B. and John M. Talmadge, "Historical and Political Background of Federal Health Care Legislation," *Law and Contemporary Problems*, Vol. 35, Spring 1970, pp. 334–347.

Chapman, Carleton B. and John M. Talmadge, "The Evolution of the Right to Health Concept in the United States," *The Pharos*, Vol. 34, January 1971, pp. 30–51.

Clarke, Gary J. "State Government: Where the Action Is," *The Nation's Health*, April 1980, p. 16.

Clarke, Gary J., "The Role of the States in the Delivery of Health Services," *American Journal of Public Health*, Vol. 71, January 1981, Supplement, pp. 59–69.

Congressional Quarterly, "Background," *1971 Congressional Quarterly Almanac*, Washington, D.C.: Congressional Quarterly, Inc., 1971, pp. 698, 2-A.

Congressional Quarterly, "Lobbies: The Washington Lobby: A Continuing Struggle to Influence Government Policy," *Congressional Quarterly Guide. Current American Government*, Washington, D.C.: Congressional Quarterly, Inc., Fall 1972, pp. 1–4.

Congressional Quarterly, "Block Grants: An Old Republican Idea," *Congressional Quarterly*, March 14, 1981, pp. 449.

Crain, Robert L., Elihu Katz and Donald B. Rosenthal, *The Politics of Community Conflict—The Fluoridation Decision*, Indianapolis: Bobbs-Merrill Co., 1968.

Davidson, Stephen M., "Variations in State Medicaid Programs," *Journal of Health Politics, Policy and Law*, Vol. 3, Spring 1978, pp. 54–70.

Davis, Karen, "Medicaid Payments and Utilization of Medical Services by the Poor," *Inquiry*, Vol. 13, June 1976a, pp. 127–135.

Davis, Karen, "Achievements and Problems of Medicaid," *Public Health Reports*, Vol. 91, July–August 1976b, pp. 309–316. Also Brookings Institution General Series Report No. 318, 1977.

Davis, Karen, "Equal Treatment and Unequal Benefits: The Medicare Program," *Milbank Memorial Fund Quarterly/Health and Society*, Vol. 53, Fall 1975a, pp. 449–488. Also Brookings Institution General Series Report No. 317, 1974.

Davis, Karen, "National Health Insurance. Benefits, Costs and Consequences," Washington, D.C.: The Brookings Institution, 1975b.

Davis, Karen, "Lessons of Medicare and Medicaid for National Health Insurance," Brookings Institution General Series Report No. 295, Washington, D.C., The Brookings Institution, 1974.

Donahue, Wilma and Clark Tibbits, eds., *Politics of Age*, Ann Arbor: Division of Gerontology, University of Michigan, 1962, see especially pp. 36–47, 48–59, 63–74.

Downey, Gregg W., "OMB, The Secrets of the Secret Agency," *Modern Health Care*, September 1975, pp. 23–27.

Drew, Elizabeth, "The Health Syndicate—Washington's Noble Conspirators," *Atlantic Monthly*, Vol. 220, December 1967, pp. 75–82.

Eckstein, Harry, *Pressure Group Politics: The Case of the British Medical Association*, Palo Alto: Stanford University Press, 1960.

Elling, Ray H. and Ollie Lee, "Formal Connections of Community Leadership to Health Systems," *Milbank Memorial Fund Quarterly*, Vol. 44, Part I, July 1966, pp. 294–306.

Elling, Ray H., "The Shifting Power Structure in Health," *Milbank Memorial Fund Quarterly*, Vol. 46, January 1968, pp. 119–144.

Falcone, David, "Health Policy Analysis: Some Reflections on the State of the Art," *Policy Studies Journal*, Vol. 9, No. 2, Special No. 1, 1980–1981, pp. 188–197.

Falik, Marilyn, "Health as a Political Issue: The National Foci," *Health Politics, A Quarterly Bulletin*, Vol. 5, Summer 1975, pp. 12–17.

Falk, Isidore S., "Medical Care in a University Teaching Program for Hospital Administration," *Medical Care*, Vol. 5, January–February 1967a, p. 6.

Falk, Isidore S., "Medical Care and Social Policy," *Medical Care in Transition*, PHS Publication No. 1128, Vol. 3, June 1967b, pp. 269–274.

Falk, Isidore S., "National Health Insurance for the United States," *Public Health Reports*, Vol. 92, September–October 1977, pp. 399–406.

Falkson, Joseph, "Minor Skirmish in a Monumental Struggle: HEW's Analysis of Mental Health Services," *Policy Analysis*, Vol. 2, Winter 1976, pp. 93–119.

Federation of American Hospitals, "Brookings and AEI: Testing Grounds for 'Shadow Cabinets' and Policy Ideas," *Review*, Vol. 12, February 1979, pp. 29–33.

Fein, Rashi, "Social and Economic Attitudes Shaping American Health Policy," *Milbank Memorial Fund Quarterly/Health and Society*, Vol. 58, No. 3, 1980, pp. 349–385.

Feingold, Eugene, *Medicare: Policy and Politics*, San Francisco: Chandler Publishing Co., 1966.

Feingold, Eugene, "Citizen Participation: A Review of the Issues," *The Citizenry and the Hospital*, 1973 Duke Forum, Durham: Duke University, 1973, pp. 8–16.

Feldstein, Paul J., *Health Associations and the Demand for Legislation: The Political Economy of Health Care*, Cambridge: Ballinger Publishing Co., 1977.

Felicetti, Daniel A., *Mental Health and Retardation Politics: The Mind Lobbies in Congress*, Lexington, Mass.: Lexington Books, 1975.

"Fever Chart," *American Medical Association News*, March 22, 1976.

Filerman, Gary L., "The Legislative Campaign for the Passage of a Medical Care for the Aged Bill," Unpublished Master's thesis, University of Minnesota, 1962.

Finch, Robert, "Testimony Given Before the United States Congress Senate Committee on Government Operations," *The Federal Role in Health* (The Ribicoff Report), Senate Report No. 809, Ninety-first Congress, 2nd Session, Washington D.C.: U.S. Government Printing Office, 1970, p. 224.

Foltz, Anne-Marie, "The Development of Ambiguous Federal Policy: Early and Periodic Screening Diagnosis and Treatment." (EPSDT), *Milbank Memorial Fund Quarterly/Health and Society*, Vol. 53, November 1975, pp. 35–64.

Foltz, Anne-Marie and Donna Brown, "State Response to Federal Policy: Children, EPSDT and the Medicaid Muddle," *Medical Care*, Vol. 13, August 1975, pp. 630–642.

Forgotson, Edward H., "1965: The Turning Point in Health Law—1966 Reflections," *American Journal of Public Health*, Vol. 57, June 1967, pp. 934–946.

Friedman, Emily, "Medicaid: The Promise Path," *Hospitals*, August 16, 1977a, pp. 51–56.

Friedman, Emily, "The Problems and Promises of Medicaid," *Hospitals*, Vol. 51 (series), April–November 1977b.

Gallop, George, "Gallop Poll: Transfer of Power to States Favored," *Minneapolis Tribune*, October 18, 1981, p. 26A.

Gamson, William A., "Social Science Aspects of Fluoridation. A Summary of Research," *Health Education Journal*, Vol. 19, 1961, pp. 159–169.

Garceau, Oliver, *The Political Life of the American Medical Association*, Cambridge: Harvard University Press, 1941.

Gardner, John W., Wilbur J. Cohen and Ralph K. Huitt, *1965: Year of Legislative Achievements in*

Health, Education and Welfare, Health Education and Welfare Indicators, April 1965–February 1966 (Reprint), Washington, D.C.: U.S. Government Printing Office, 1967, p. iv.

Geiger, H. Jack, "Community Control—or Community Conflict? *NTRDA Bulletin*, November 1969 (Reprint).

Gilbert, Benjamin, Merry-K Moos and C. Arden Miller, "State-Level Decision Making for Public Health: The Status of Boards of Health," *Journal of Public Health Policy*, Vol. 3, March 1983, pp. 51–63.

Ginsburg, Paul B. and Larry M. Manheim, "Insurance, Copayment and Health Services Utilization: A Critical Review," *Journal of Economics of Business*, Vol. 25, Spring–Summer 1973, pp. 142–153.

Glaser, William A., "Doctors and Politics," *American Journal of Sociology*, Vol. 66, November 1960, pp. 230–245.

Goldwater, S. S., "The Appropriations of Public Funds for the Partial Support of Voluntary Hospitals in the United States and Canada," *Transactions of the American Hospital Association*, Vol. 11, 1909, pp. 242–294.

Gordon, Geoffrey, B., "The Politics of Community Medical Projects: A Conflict Analysis," *Medical Care*, Vol. 7, November–December 1969, pp. 973–981.

Gossert, Daniel J. and C. Arden Miller, "State Boards of Health, Their Members and Committments," *American Journal of Public Health*, Vol. 63, June 1973, pp. 486–493.

Grad, Frank, *Public Health Manual*, Washington, D.C.: American Public Health Association, 3rd edition, 1973.

Grupenhoff, John T., "The Congress: Turnover Rates of Members and Staff Who Deal With Medicine/Health/Biomedical Research Issues," *Communications*, No. 1, Fall 1982 (Science and Health Communications Group).

Guttman, Daniel and Barry Wittner, *The Shadow Government: The Government's Multi-Billing Dollar Giveaway of its Decision-Making Powers to Private Management Consultants, Experts and Think Tanks*, New York: Pantheon Books, 1976.

Harris, Richard, *A Sacred Trust*, New York: New American Library, 1967.

Health Policy Adivsory Center, Institute for Policy Studies, "Medical Empires: Who Controls?" *Health-PAC Bulletin*, No. 6, November–December 1968, pp. 1, 3–6.

Hixson, Joseph, *The Patchwork Mouse: Politics and Intrigue in the Campaign to Conquer Cancer*, New York: Anchor-Doubleday, 1976.

Hodgson, Godfrey, "The Politics of American Health Care," *The Atlantic*, Vol. 232, October 1973, pp. 45–61.

Holloway, Robert G., Jay H. Artis and Walter E. Freeman, "The Participation Patterns of 'Economic Influentials' and Their Control of a Hospital Board of Trustees," *Journal Health and Human Behavior*, Vol. 4, Summer 1963, pp. 88–98.

Hyde, David R. and Payson Wolff, "The American Medical Association: Power, Purpose and Politics in Organized Medicine," *Yale Law Journal*, Vol. 63, May 1954, pp. 938–1022.

Isman, Robert, "Fluoridation: Strategies for Success," *American Journal of Public Health*, Vol. 71, July 1981, pp. 717–721.

Jackson, Charles A., "State Laws on Compulsory Immunization in the United States," *Public Health Reports*, Vol. 84, September 1969, pp. 787–794.

Kaufman, Herbert, "The Political Ingredient of Public Health Services: A Neglected Area of Research," *Milbank Memorial Fund Quarterly*, Vol. 44, Part 2, October 1966, pp. 13–34.

Kennedy, David M., "The Federal Role: It's Still Necessary," *Minneapolis Star and Tribune*, editorial page, 1981.

Kramer, C., "Fragmented Financing of Health Care," *Medical Care Review*, Vol. 29, August 1972, pp. 878–943.

Lee, Philip R., "Role of the Federal Government in Health and Medical Affairs," *New England Journal of Medicine*, Vol. 279, November 21, 1968, pp. 1139–1147.

Lewin, Lawrence S. and Robert A. Derzon, "Health Professions Education: State Responsibilities Under the New Federalism," *Health Affairs*, Vol. 1, No. 2, 1981, pp. 69–85.

Lewis, Charles, "Medicare," in Charles Lewis, Rashi Fein and David Mechanic, *A Right to Health. The Problem of Assess to Primary Medical Care*, New York: John Wiley & Sons, 1976a, pp. 144–164.

Lewis, Charles, "Medicaid," in Charles Lewis, Rashi Fein and David Mechanic, *A Right to Health. The Problem of Access to Primary Medical Care*, New York: John Wiley & Sons, 1976b, pp. 165–187.

Lewis, Charles, Rashi Fein and David Mechanic, *A Right to Health. The Problem of Access to Primary Medical Care*, New York: John Wiley & Sons, 1976.

Lewis, Ted, Jr., "The Incredible Machine. How it Grew," *Prism*, January 1974, p. 17.

Litman, Theodor J. and Leonard Robins, "Comparative Analysis of Health Care Systems: A Socio-Political Approach," *Social Science and Medicine*, December 1971, pp. 573–581.

Lowi, Theodore, "American Business, Public Policy, Case Studies, and Political Theory," *World Politics*, Vol. 16, July 1964, pp. 677–715.

Marmor, Judd, Viola W. Bernard and Perry Ottenberg, "Psychodynamics of Group Opposition to Health Programs," *American Journal of Orthopsychiatry*, Vol. 30, April 1960, pp. 330–345.

Marmor, Theodore, *The Politics of Medicare*, London: Routledge Kegan Paul, 1970; Chicago: Aldine Publishing Co., 1973.

Marshall, T. H., *Social Policy in the Twentieth Century*, Hutchinson University Library, 1965.

Means, James Howard, *Doctors, People and Government*, Boston: Little, Brown and Co., 1953.

Merritt, Richard, "State Health Reports," *The Nation's Health*, January 1981a, p. 5.

Merritt, Richard, *1981 IHPP Survey*, Washington, D.C., Intergovernmental Health Policy Project (Suite 505, 1919 Pennsylvania Avenue, N.W., Washington, D.C. 20006), 1981. Reprinted in "State Health Reports," *The Nation's Health*, 1981b (several issues).

Milbrath, Lester W., *The Washington Lobbyists*, Chicago: Rand McNally, 1964.

Millman, Michael L., *Politics and the Expanding Physician Supply*, Montclair, N.J.: Allanheld, Osmun and Co., 1980.

Mooney, Anne, "The Great Society and Health: Policies for Narrowing the Gaps in Health Status between the Poor and the Nonpoor," *Medical Care*, Vol. 15, August 1977, pp. 611–619.

Moore, Mary L., "The Role of Hostility and Militancy in Indigenous Community Health Groups," *American Journal of Public Health*, Vol. 61, May 1971, pp 922–930.

Mustard, Harry S., *Government in Public Health*, Boston: Commonwealth Fund, 1945.

National Center for Health Services Research, *Controlling the Cost of Health Care*, NCHSR Policy Research Report 1970–1977, DHEW Pub. No. (HRA) 77-3182, Hyattsville, Md: National Center for Health Services Research, 1977.

The Nation's Health, "Common Cause: Money Talks on Health Issues," December 1978, p. 5.

Penchansky, Roy and Elizabeth Axelson, "Old Values, New Federalism, and Program Evaluation," *Medical Care*, Vol. 12, November 1974, pp. 893–905.

Rayack, Elton, "The American Medical Association and the Development of Voluntary Insurance," Part I, *Social and Economic Administration*, Vol. 1, April 1967, pp. 3–25; Part 2, ibid., July 1967, pp. 29–55.

Redman, Eric, *The Dance of Legislation*, New York: Simon & Schuster, 1974.

Richardson, Elliot L., "The Maze of Social Programs," *Washington Post and Times Herald*, Vol. 96, January 21, 1973, p. 3C, as reported in *Medical Care Review*, Vol. 30, 1973, p. 147.

Riska, Elaine and James A. Taylor, "Consumer Attitudes Toward Health Policy and Knowledge about Health Legislation," *Journal of Health Politics, Policy and Law*, Vol. 3, Spring 1978, pp. 112–123.

Roemer, Milton I., "Government's Role in Medicine: A Brief Historical Survey," *Bulletin of the History of Medicine*, Vol. 18, July 1945, pp. 145–168.

Roemer, Milton I., Carl E. Hopkins, Lockwood Carr and Foline Gartside, "Copayments for Ambulatory Care: Penny-wise and Pound Foolish," *Medical Care*, Vol. 13, June 1975, pp. 457–466. (See also comments by Chen, pp. 958–63; Dyckman, pp. 968–69, and authors' response pp. 963–64.)

Roemer, Ruth, "Water Fluoridation: Public Health Responsibility and the Democratic Process," *American Journal of Public Health*, Vol. 55, September 1965, pp. 1337–1348.

Rogatz, Peter, Robert Bruner and Donald Meyers, *Health Services Working Conference, Farleigh Dickinson University*, June 15, 1970, unpublished paper, Farleigh Dickinson University, 1970, pp. 19–46.

Rosen, George, *From Medical Police to Social Medicine*, New York: Science History Publications, Neale Watson, 1974.

Rubel, Eugene as reported in "Health Planning Act Seen As Declaration of Federal Role in Health Care System," *American Medical News*, July 7, 1975, p. 14.

Russell, Louise B. and Carol S. Burke, "The Political Economy of Federal Health Programs in the United States: An Historical Review," *International Journal of Health Services*, Vol. 8, No. 1, 1978, pp. 55–77.

Schlesinger, Edward R., "The Sheppard–Towner Era—A Prototype Case Study in Federal–State Relations," *American Journal of Public Health*, Vol. 57, June 1967, pp. 1034–1070.

Schmidt, Terry L., "The Congressional Process. An Overview of How a Bill Becomes a Law," *Group Practice Journal*, Vol. 29, January 1980, pp. 9–29.

Silver, George A., "Participation and Health Resource Allocation," *International Journal of Health Services*, Vol. 3, No. 2, 1973, p. 117.

Skidmore, Max J., *Medicare and the American Rhetoric of Reconciliation*. Tuscaloosa: University of Alabama Press, 1970.

Somers, Anne R., "Some Basic Determinants of Medical Care and Health Policy. An Overview of Trends and Issues," *Health Services Research*, Vol. 1, Fall 1966, pp. 193–208.

Stavisky, Leonard P., "State Legislatures and the New Federalism" (Books Reviews), *Public Administration Review*, Vol. 41, November–December, 1981, p.701.

Stenberg, Carl W., "Federalism in Transition: 1959–79," Advisory Commission on Intergovernmental Relations, *Intergovernmental Perspective*, Winter, 1980, pp. 4–9.

Stevens, Robert and Rosemary Stevens, *Welfare Medicine in America: A Case Study of Medicaid*, New York:Free Press, 1974.

Stevens, Rosemary and Robert Stevens, "Medicaid: Anatomy of a Dilemma," *Law and Contemporary Problems*, Vol. 1970, Spring 1970, pp. 348–425.

Stevens, Rosemary, "A Poor Sort of Memory: Voluntary Hospitals and Government Before the Depression," *Milbank Memorial Fund Quarterly/Health and Society*, Vol. 60, No. 4, 1982, pp. 551–584.

Straus, Robert, *Medical Care for Seaman: The Development of Public Medical Services in the United States*, New Haven: Yale University Press, 1950.

Straus, Robert, "Social Change and the Rehabilitation Concept," in Marvin B. Sussman, ed., *Sociology and Rehabilitation*, Washington, D.C.: American Sociological Association, 1965, pp. 1–34.

Thompson, Theodis, *The Politics of Pacification: The Case of Consumer Participation in Community Health Organizations*, Washington, D.C.: Howard University Institute for Urban Affairs and Research, 1974.

Tollefson, E. A., *Bitter Medicine. The Saskatchewan Medicare Feud*, Saskatoon, Saskatchewan: Modern Press, 1964.

United States Chamber of Commerce, 1965 Task Force on Economic Growth and Opportunity

Report, *Poverty, the Sick, Disabled and Aged*, Washington, D.C.: U.S. Chamber of Commerce, 1965.

Weikel, M. Keith and Nancy A. Leamond, "A Decade of Medicaid," *Public Health Reports*, Vol. 91, July–August, 1976, pp. 303–308.

Weller, G. R., "From Pressure Group Politics to Medical–Industrial Complex. The Development of Approaches to the Politics of Health," *Journal of Health Politics, Policy and Law*, Vol. 1, Winter 1977, pp. 444–470.

Wing, Kenneth R., *The Law and the Public's Health*, St. Louis: C. V. Mosby, 1976.

CHAPTER 2

The Political Economy of Health Services: A Review of Major Ideological Influences

Roger M. Battistella
James W. Begun

The present prominence of health policy in the national political affairs of the United States is not unwarranted. It is a manifestation of the enormously strategic position that health services command in the general economy and in the aspirations of people for the good life. It is also a reflection of the requirements for accountability that have accompanied the increased dependence of consumers and providers on public financing.

Due to developments such as the aging of the population, the growing importance of diseases that require lengthier and costlier forms of treatment, and the rising demands for equity in the distribution and quality of publicly funded services, government is under constant pressure to increase the size of health outlays. These pressures are occurring, however, at a time when the economy is encountering an unprecedented combination of unemployment and inflation.

The many attempts to reconcile demands for health spending with the declining availability of resources have failed. The policies of the past decade characteristically have been piecemeal, inconsistent, and contradictory (Battistella and Rundall, 1978a). At the same time, the climate of urgency and confusion accompanying the succession of measures to control expenditures obscures recognition of some remarkable health policy achievements beginning in the 1960s. These include the virtual elimination of the hospital and physicians' services utilization gap between upper- and low-income people, the modernization and technological upgrading of the nation's hospitals, the return to the community of many physically and mentally disabled persons previously destined to spend their lives in oppressive institutional settings, the correction of aggregate deficiencies in the supply of health personnel, and the protection against the high cost of medical services for the aged and low-income groups. Whether attributable to health services or other causes, U.S. citizens have also benefited from notable increase in life expectancy (Roemer, 1980a). Another largely unrecognized achievement is the transformation of the organizational and managerial profile of health services from turn-of-the-century handcraft to modern industrial–corporate lines (U.S. Department of Health and Human Services, 1981).

It is against this backdrop of mixed and confused events that this political–economic examination of health services in the United States is undertaken. Political–economic inquiry involves the study of changes in economic relationships and the composition of political power within a framework of superordinate values regarding what is fair and just. In the ensuing analysis, health policy is presented largely as the outcome of the interplay of political and economic orientations whose influence has varied over time. For convenience, these orientations have been organized under four principal headings: the normative approach, the rationalist approach, the neoconservative approach, and the neo-Marxist approach. After evaluating these ideological influences, the future prospects for equity in health services in an age of limited economic resources will be established.

As it is presumptuous to claim that it is possible to sum up neatly and accurately the complex events affecting the development of health services over a span of roughly two centuries, the following generalizations are offered as a starting point for more carefully constructed departures.

THE NORMATIVE APPROACH

The predominant approach to health services in the United States until recently has been normative in character. That is to say, individuals and groups have sought to influence the role of government in the health services field mainly on the basis of strong convictions about what is or ought to be highly valued. Disagreement has arisen over the extent to which government programs depart from goals perceived to be important (Donabedian, 1973).

At the core of policy disputes one can usually discern the influence of the enlightenment philosophers (Locke, Hobbes, Montesquieu, and Rousseau in particular), whose perspectives on human nature and the function of government gave justification to American independence and inspired the formulation of human rights guaranteed in the U.S. Constitution. Among the more important concepts associated with this school of thought are individual freedom, equality, compassion, fraternalism, and the malevolence or benevolence of power.

Normative positions on general philosophical issues have been used in the classification of political parties and the actions of government. Individuals and groups believing that human nature, though mixed, is essentially good or perfectable, that human intelligence is superior to natural forces in problem solving, and that government is largely an instrument for the advancement of individual and community welfare are classified as liberal. Individuals and groups taking a less sanguine view of human nature and exhibiting a distrust of power, especially in government, are usually classified as conservative. These normative positions are the source of most controversies over the direction and control of health services.

The normative approach to health services emerges clearly in the uncompleted saga of national health insurance in the United States. Armed with the knowledge of precedents of governmental intervention in Germany and England under conditions of widespread unemployment and medical needs similar to those prevailing in the United

States at the turn of the century, reformers unsuccessfully sought to humanize many of the demeaning aspects of charity and welfare medicine anchored in Elizabethan Poor Law practices. In doing so, they endeavored to establish the principle that health services ought to be provided as a right on the basis of medical need regardless of ability to pay (Davis, 1975).

After nearly 50 years of frustration, these efforts were rewarded partially with the passage of Medicare in 1965, which established a compulsory program of hospital benefits for retired and disabled workers and a voluntary program of physicians' benefits. At the same time, reformers succeeded in vastly enlarging the influence of the federal government in the operation of state and local public assistance programs, in eliminating some of the harsher features of eligibility tests, and in broadening the reach of welfare medical programs beyond the indigent to include the working poor. Most of these gains were incorporated in the Medicaid program.

Marked by intense ideological differences, the battle for national health insurance swirled around the issue of whether access to health care was a privilege or a right. Arrayed on the side of privilege were the professional interest groups, [e.g., American Medical Association (AMA), American Hospital Association (AHA), American Dental Association (ADA)] They feared restrictions on their freedom to pursue unrestricted economic rewards, their autonomy in clinical decision making, and their powers for self-regulation and governance. Their cause was championed by political, commercial, and manufacturing organizations, for example, the National Association of Manufacturers, the Chamber of Commerce, and the Young Americans for Freedom viewing themselves as custodians of competitive market values (Bowler, 1978).

Both sides of the national health insurance issue received considerable support from academic economists who, through a variety of logical deductions and empirical claims, sought to legitimize the objectivity of their adopted parties. Competitive market economists, led by Milton Friedman (1962), argued both then as well as now that medical care is a private good in that the benefits accrue to the individual rather than society. Consequently, the rules of the competitive market should apply in order to maximize individual freedom and economic efficiency.

Because competitive market proponents consider medical care to be much like economic goods and services in general, they, to the consternation of many of their allies in the medical profession, assert that restricting the practice of medicine to licensed doctors of medicine is an abridgement of market efficiency and an enticement to abuse. This is the logical result of their belief that human nature is incorrigibly acquisitive and selfish. Conservative economists are prepared to make only the slightests allowance for negative health care externalities endangering the welfare of others, such as environmental pollution, and lifestyle hazards, such as smoking and alcohol and drug abuse. To the fullest extent practical, they prefer to use market incentives (taxes and fines) rather than publicly administered programs to safeguard community well-being (Fein, 1980).

On the other hand, economists immersed in the sociopolitical history of medicine stress the vulnerability of the sick to exploitation in the marketplace due to the special dimension of anguish in illness and other constraints on consumer rationality. The professional status of medicine is seen as a functional instrument for community integration as well as the enrichment of individual welfare. Economists holding that health care is a right typically argue that spending for maternal and child health services and the working-age population is also a good investment in economic growth. Perhaps the best recognized defense of the special character of health service is that prepared by Kenneth Arrow (1963), who concluded that health services are based largely on nonmarket relationships that substantially curtail the relevance of competitive theory. Sociologists opposed to using the market to ration health services tend to underscore the moral and utilitarian aspects of health services. The late Talcott Parsons (1951), for example, was foremost among his colleagues in the scholarly defense of the idea that health care is a social good (1951).

SHORTCOMINGS OF THE NORMATIVE APPROACH

The normative approach to health policy prevailed up to the mid-1960s. Since then it has fallen into disfavor. Its critics are prone to deride the normative approach for being "value laden," for being overly argumentative and rhetorical, and for using data to buttress policy preferences rather than scientific aims (Battistella, 1972a).

The accusation in brief is that normative analysis tended to simplify the issues and to portray antagonists in hues of good and evil. For example, organized medicine, led by the AMA, often was pictured as a reactionary monolith, whereas groups favoring reforms in the organization and financing of solo fee-for-service medicine were stereotyped as disciples of subversive socialist and communist teachings. Likewise, progress in the implementation of welfare state principles was characterized as well-intentioned but impractical foolishness or as tangible proof of the innately noble affinity of human nature for altruism and justice (Battistella and Wheeler, 1978).

Criticism of the normative approach is not without its own shortcomings, however. It is seldom dispassionate, since it originates from interests advocating a purportedly superior alternative. Also, the handicaps under which the normative approach functioned are rarely acknowledged. One such handicap that invited appeals to emotion rather than reason was the shortage of reliable data to guide decision making. For example, nationwide registration of births did not occur until 1933. Reliable information on the population's need for health services was not available until passage of the National Health Survey Act of 1956, which provided for a continuing survey and special studies of sickness and disability in the United States. Later, related developments caused an explosion in the amount of information on the cost effectiveness of new technologies and the quality and economy of services given by providers. In addition, considerable progress has been made in the coordination of intergovernmental statistical reporting systems and the disaggretation of data for subnational health services planning, monitoring and evaluation (Jonas, 1981).

The fact that proponents of social justice in the availability of health services typically are characterized as misguided idealists or worse, whereas proponents of free enterprise medicine often are viewed more favorably, mirrors a powerful attachment to competitive market values in U.S. culture. The emotional power of this belief system poses a barrier to dispassionate study and discussion, and organized hospital and medical interests have adroitly sought to deflect criticism by ensconcing themselves behind rhetorical bulwarks in defense of free enterprise (Harris, 1966).

Free enterprise values have persevered. Even after Medicare and Medicaid, U.S. health services remain predominantly private. Public outlays for health care, for example, represent only about two-fifths of total spending, in marked contrast to other highly industrialized free market nations in Western Europe where public sources account for the large majority of health financing. The United States, moreover, remains the only major industrial power without a comprehensive national health insurance program (Simanis, 1980). Finally, the situation in the health sector closely approaches that of the economy as a whole, where government spending accounts for only about 30 percent of the gross national product (GNP). In other highly developed capitalist economies, on the other hand, the amount of national wealth commanded by government ranges from a low of 40 percent to a high of 60 percent (Thurow, 1980).

GROWTH OF GOVERNMENT INTERVENTION IN THE HEALTH SECTOR

Although the United States is less a welfare state than other industrial market economies, substantial changes have occurred in the political economy of health services. The enshrinement of free market values in national folklore and in medical politics masks a slow but steady advance of governmental intervention. From the Great Depression to the present, the perception of health services has been transformed from that of a *private good* to that of a *public good*, with the result that the U.S. government is now involved with health services in a big way.

Ironically, some of the greatest pressure for increased public financing and regulation has resulted from decisions taken to buttress and preserve the private features of U.S. health services (Ebenstein, et al., 1970).

The collapse of the national economy in the decade before World War II not only strained the ability of state and local government to continue vital public health services, but it signaled financial ruin for voluntary hospitals deprived of patient revenues and philanthropic funds. In both cases, the federal government intervened to lend the assistance necessary.

The wartime Supreme Court ruling relaxing wage and price controls to allow labor unions to bargain for health insurance and other fringe benefits helped restore the flow of revenues from private-paying patients. However, access to capital remained a problem. At the behest of the American Hospital Association, the government enacted the Hospital Survey and Construction Act of 1946 to discourage destructive competition among hospitals within the same service area and to subsidize the construction of new beds in medically underserved areas (Commission on Hospital Care, 1947). As the economy unexpectedly prospered after the war, the federal program became established as a principal source of money for plant modernization and expansion. In a similar vein, public subsidies for health professional education were increased. From 1965 to 1979, the number of medical schools grew from 84 to 124, and since 1970, when efforts to expand the physician supply began to take hold, the ratio of active physicians to population has increased 25 percent (U.S. Department of Human Services, p. 188,) (*Journal of the American Medical Association*, 1965, 1980). These subsidies were the product of supply-side economic thinking. The presumption was that once deficiencies due to inadequate productive capacity and to the barrier effects of high tuition costs were corrected, market forces would result in a redistribution of physicians from medically overserved to underserved areas and from specialties in which there was an oversupply to those requiring more practitioners.

Whereas the unexpected expansion of the postwar economy made it possible to enrich the package of benefits provided to enrollees by private health insurance, competition between profit-making and nonprofit-making carriers resulted in the erosion of arrangements designed to bring insurance within the financial reach of many low-income and high-risk individuals. Unlike community rating in which everyone paid the same regardless of his or her health status, experience rating methods favored by commercial carriers assigned premiums such that the groups most in need of protection were required to pay the most. As it became more difficult for aged and low-income people to be insured privately, there was a corresponding resurgence of the hospital bad debt problem and political agitation from population groups deprived of access to private care. The enactment of Medicare and Medicaid was an accommodation to these problems pursued in the context of prevailing free-enterprise values (Harris, 1966).

The popular interpretation of Medicare and Medicaid as economic and administrative failures underscores an important lesson from U.S. health policy: The design of publicly funded medical care programs is influenced less by dictates for efficiency than by cultural tradition and political philosophy. Other highly developed countries choosing to finance health services centrally under a unified system of planning and administration have achieved far greater results in raising health standards while spending considerably less of their gross national product (Roemer, 1980b).

The mammoth capital requirement of biomedical research was another important force in drawing the federal government more deeply into the health services field. The perception that scientific medicine had reached the takeoff stage and that the conquest of many dreaded diseases was imminent, fueled a veritable explosion of federal support after World War II. Beginning with the creation of the National Cancer Institute in 1950, the number of federally sponsored national research centers has multiplied to the point where the National Institutes of Health is a conglomerate of specialized research institutes with an annual operating budget of nearly $3 billion (Rushmer, 1980).

Further intervention followed in the wake of the revelation that orthodox supply and demand relationships do not operate in the health field. Experience revealed that subsidies to expand supply and productivity did not function as predicted by economic theory. Increasing the supply of physicians and hospital beds and the introduction of sophisticated technology did not result in lower prices and the desired redistribution of services. To the contrary, they only seemed to compound problems of costs and maldistribution. For reasons largely accepted as peculiar to the health field, it was concluded that supply created its own demand (Fein, 1980).

The passage of the Comprehensive Health Planning Act of 1966 and its further-reaching successor, the National Health Planning and Resources Development Act of 1974, served to limit the unilateral powers of hospitals to expand and modernize and restricted new hospitals in their choice of location. Enactment of the Professional Standards Review Organization Program in 1972 constrained the freedom of physicians with respect to the admission of patients to hospitals and lengths of stay and opened clinical decisions to the compulsory scrutiny of medical peers. Finally, the provision of federal incentives for the spread of prepaid group practice vis-à-vis the Health Maintenance Organization Act of 1973 struck at the heart of free enterprise medicine in challenging the viability of solo fee-for-service practice.

RATIONALIST APPROACH

For whatever reason, the dominant presence of government in the health sector became an established fact before the 1960s ended—if not as a percentage of total spending, certainly in terms of fiscal leverage and the growth of planning and regulatory activities.

Regardless of differences in outlook on the desirability of enlarging the role of public financing in the health sector, it was hard for informed people to disagree that because of inflation it was costing the government a lot of money just to stand still. The pressure to stem inflation was intensified by the conviction that the imperatives for greater public financing were strong and that some form of national health insurance was inevitable (U.S. Department of Health, Education and Welfare, 1976).

For reasons as yet not fully clear, annual price increases for hospital and health services have had a history of being higher than those for consumer goods and services in general. Moreover, the immediate effect of Medicare and Medicaid has been to widen the gap in rates of increase (Council on Wage and Price Stability, 1976).

During periods of recession, standing still has also proven costly. Loss of wages and private health insurance due to unemployment expands the size of the population eligible to receive Medicaid coverage. A less obvious but by no means unimportant effect of recession is the incentive for state and local governments to seek, through creative accounting practices and program restructuring, to transfer more of the cost of public-assistance medical programs to the federal government whenever financing is a shared responsibility (Bulgaro and Webb, 1980).

Additional concerns stemmed from the recognition that spending for other social welfare services had also shot upward and that, together with health spending, they accounted for roughly one-half of the federal budget. Although some observers celebrated this as an irrefutable signal of the triumph of welfare-state principles, others fretted about the demise of conservative economic and political values. Still others became apprehensive about the implications of changes in the composition of the federal budget for productivity and for the ability to generate savings sufficient to finance investments in economic growth necessary to pay for social services (Janowitz, 1976).

The political and economic tensions accumulating during this period from the activism of government and the ascendency of welfare-state principles helped to provoke the reaction against the normative approach to policy decision making. Although conflict among overtly competing values helped to define issues and solutions, there often was a steep price to pay in terms of legislative paralysis. Additionally, the unwillingness to compromise and cooperate obstructed sound administration and program evaluation. These shortcomings prompted interest in alternatives that could depoliticize decision making (Battistella and Smith, 1974).

Moreover, the sheer magnitude of health outlays precipitated curiosity about the returns to society. In combination with mounting concerns over the share of national wealth consumed by government, these tensions stimulated efforts to quantify the costs and benefits of government programs (Battistella and Smith, 1974).

The hiatus resulting from a slowing of economic growth on the one hand and rising demands for more and better services on the other was a provocation to find painless ways to reconcile conflict and diffuse responsibility for unpopular decisions. This led harried officials to look to the introduction of purportedly objective and value-free decision-making techniques derived principally from microeconomic theory. Because of a utilitarian economic or technical means–end orientation in which the calculation of self-interest is considered synonymous with rational behavior, this form of decision making is described in the policy-analysis literature as the rationalist approach[1] (Smith, 1978).

---

[1]Use of the label "rationalist" to identify this school of thought is not meant to imply that the approach is more "rational" than the normative approach (or, for that matter, the neomarxist and neoconservative perspectives introduced later in this chapter.) Both approaches are rational since they make the same use of reason, are subject to the same rules of logic, and are ultimately subject to the same test of how closely they match reality. The distinction is that one approach (the normative) starts with certain overt beliefs about what should be based

Resisted at first by health professionals socialized in the venerable code of medical ethics that rejected the placement of a money value on health and life, the rationalist approach ultimately prevailed, and skepticism concerning the application of quantitative methods became more the exception than the rule (Smith, 1978). Familiarity with cost–benefit analysis, systems analysis, program budgeting, and other quantitative techniques, especially in the areas of accounting and finance, became widely established as indicators of managerial competence.

The significance of the rationalist approach extends beyond the introduction of decision-making techniques. It encompasses a belief in the efficiency of centralized administration, economies of scale, and scientific management and planning principles. These principles comprise the management paradigm of big business. In the search for efficiency and effectiveness in the health sector, the tendency was to look to big business and industry in the hope that their presumably superior management methods could be transferred (Battistella and Chester, 1972).

Notwithstanding the image of clarity and conciseness associated with decision making in the private sector, the term "scientific management" is somewhat vague. To believers in competition, scientific management achieves cost control and efficiency payoffs from market discipline and the application of quantitative methods in cost accounting, finance, marketing, and production. To other observers, however, the purpose of these methods is to escape market discipline through the substitution of corporate power and planning for idealized laws of supply and demand. The confusion is multiplied by the contradiction whereby those actually engaged in planning retain ideological loyalty to the sanctity of economic and political relationships derived from the theory of perfect competition (Battistella and Chester, 1972).

The ascension of the rationalist approach coincided with a period of increased activity in the restructuring of health services. The desirability of a more rational organizational pattern of hospital and physicians' services, with fewer but larger units of production caring for defined populations, was something that cut across political differences in the health politics of the 1970s. The commonly agreed upon goal was to transfer health services from a "cottage industry" to a modern corporate structure (Battistella, 1972a). The language and values of the rationalist approach have a catholic appeal. They capture a rich cultural folklore extolling the innate superiority of market forces over those of government. They also appeal to people believing in the efficacy of scientific management, whether in the planning of health services or in the running of complex corporate enterprises.

The broad-based attractiveness of the rationalist approach facilitated the establishment of a consensus for change strong enough to overcome the status quo in the organization of health services. The merger and consolidation movement among nongovernmental community hospitals is one significant example. Roughly one-third of all hospitals and one-fourth of all hospital beds in the United States now are counted as components of multihospital systems. Between 1975 and 1979 the number of hospitals joining group arrangements rose by 33 percent (Demkovich, 1980). Additionally, near-

---

on philosophical convictions. In purporting to deal solely with what can be measured, the other approach (rationalist) conceals from view the behavioral assumptions underlying quantitative methods. In point of fact, both are value laden, since both are based on beliefs about how people should behave. The term "rationalist" is used because of its prominence in the field of policy analysis and to highlight the political implications of allegedly objective-quantitative methods. Another choice would have been to substitute the word "empirical" for "rationalist." The authors are indebted to Edmund D. Pellegrino for his suggestion to clarify the reasons for choosing the "rationalist" label.

ly one-fourth of the nation's active nonfederal physicians practiced in medical groups in 1975 in contrast with 18 percent in 1969 (U.S. Department of Health, Education and Welfare, 1975).

The ramifications of the rationalist approach for the restructuring of health services are extensive. Rationalist logic and values are imbedded in a number of diverse developments of the 1970s, for example, health planning, health maintenance organizations, professional standards review organizations, and the imposition of quotas on the supply of medical graduates by specialty. It is unlikely that change of such magnitude could have occurred in such a brief period of time if the policy issues had remained as highly politicized as they were during the peak influence of the normative approach.

SHORTCOMINGS OF THE RATIONALIST APPROACH

In retrospect, much of the optimism accompanying the introduction of rationalist methods was misplaced. Far more was promised than could be delivered (Battistella and Smith, 1974), and many weaknesses of the rationalist approach have become evident.

First, the ideas that decisions should be based on facts alone and that facts speak for themselves are illusions. It suggests that irrefutably valid data are readily obtainable and that analytic methods for the accumulation of facts are value free. Policy decisions about Medicaid reimbursement of abortion charges, for example, are predominantly valuative ones. The same applies to national health insurance.

Second, the assumptions contained in rationalist models fail to penetrate adequately the complex environment in which decisions are taken. There is nothing indisputably objective in the assignment of interest rates for establishing the relationship between values at different points in time or the assignment of the opportunity cost of capital diverted from more productive alternative expenditures. These decisions are a matter of judgment. They involve assumptions about the future that are speculative, and they reflect the values of the analyst. The assignment of high interest and discount rates discriminates logically against the taking of long-run actions in preference for the short run. The bias is compounded whenever the economy is beset by a high rate of inflation.

Third, many aspects of good medical care are difficult to quantify. The concept of cure has no application to a vast number of health problems that constitute the reality of health needs today—chronic and mental diseases and disabilities. Given the low likelihood of achieving a cure for disorders of this sort, the total effect of medical intervention is more important to assess, and this too is highly subjective and complex in principle.

Whether people are satisfied with the caliber of medical services they receive and whether they view themselves to be in good or poor health are highly subjective phenomena that have important effects on utilization of services and treatment outcomes. For the most part, quantification in cost–benefit forms of analysis works best when what is being studied bears a relationship to conventional market activities and prices.

Fourth, rationality often is used as a guise for action based on the philosophical precepts of competitive market theory in which selfishness and greed have been elevated to the status of a moral system. The philosophical case of rational analysis does not accept that medical acts are an important aspect of the human relationship of giving and receiving, constituting the moral experience of mutual help (Campbell, 1978).

Fifth, the mounting realization that many health policy issues are highly subjective and qualitative suggests that allegedly objective techniques may be less important in the future. One such issue involves medical technology and ethical rights to treatment and to death. Another centers on entitlements to publicly supported health services. The tradeoff between economic productivity and the quality of the environment is another example of the saliency of issues that cannot be debated without regard to political and social values.

Generally speaking, the application of the rational approach has not succeeded in meeting its economic and efficiency objectives. If anything, there is reason to believe that it may have exacerbated governmental efforts to contain health care expenditures. Indeed, the "rational" models behind the government's cost containment strategy helped create situations in which health care providers were given "perverse" economic incentives to defeat controls. Due to the inability of the rational models to capture the complexities of the health field, for example, government found itself in the bizarre position of reimbursing hospitals for the services of financial experts whose jobs entail devising ways to manipulate or subvert the cost-cutting goals of government regulation (Battistella and Eastaugh, 1980a, 1980b).

Additional unintended consequences may arise in the future from the imposition of the scientific management paradigm in the case of services that are intrinsically labor intensive and highly personalized in nature. The scientific management outlook not only contains a bias for technological expansion capable of undermining priorities for cost containment, but it has a bureaucratic proclivity at variance with the essentially human dimensions of the doctor–patient relationship.

It is shortsighted to assume that most health policy problems can be solved by subjecting the medical profession to management discipline, and control, especially with respect to primary care (Battistella and Rundall, 1978a, 1978b). Such an assumption understates the value to society of the doctor–patient relationship in which the bond of mutual confidence and respect is the key for minimizing disruptions in social and economic activities, many of which are associated with anxieties and symptoms for which no clinical cause can be established. Given the limitations on the life span and the aging of the population, good health increasingly is the result "of physician and patient working together, often in the face of uncertainty and fear" (Fuchs, 1974) rather than simple, one-time interventions ordered by the physician.

NEOCONSERVATIVE APPROACH

Interest groups who have convinced government to assume a larger role in the financing of health services take justifiable pride in technological progress and improvements in social and territorial justice in the distribution and use of health resources. But success has not been without dilemma and paradox. For many reasons, the political climate today is less optimistic, and it has become fasionable to question the practicality of continuing present levels of public spending.

Upwardly spiraling prices for health services cause many people in and outside of government to wonder whether investments have reached the stage of diminishing returns. This has contributed to a spirit of disillusionment manifested in the popularity of the cliché that health problems will not be solved by more government spending. Considerable skepticism has developed about the relationship between health services and health status. Indeed, it is generally accepted that nonhealth services, such as housing, nutrition, lifestyle, and environmental safety, are far more critical. Equally important, it is now generally agreed that the benefits of early diagnosis and treatment have been greatly overstated.

These changing economic circumstances foreshadow an adjustment of the liberal agenda for health services' reform. Although not always explicit in health policy polemics, the liberal platform traditionally rested on a number of well-reasoned assumptions. Most important of all was the belief that economic growth would produce the resources to create a more just society without anyone's suffering on the way. Prosperity would be sustained, moreover, by a sufficiently high birth rate for maintaining demand and a large enough supply of gainfully employed workers to generate the funds to pay for health and social services required by the aged and the disabled (Donnison, 1979). The favorable conditions prevailing at the time of the introduction of Medicare and Medicaid were expected to continue, thereby lessening the chances of a reaction against an expanding role for government. The crowning goal of reform was to be a system of universal health insurance in which comprehensive services would be provided free at the time of use on the basis of medical need. These assumptions have been weakened by the unsatisfactory state of the economy, and the new economic climate poses some major economic and political implications for the future of public intervention.

At the same time, conservative policies are by no means immune to the implications of the decline in the state of the economy. It does not logically follow that the reappearance of scarcity represents a vindication of conservative economic thinking, nor does it follow that competitive market principles will triumph in redefining health care as a private good subject to price and income rationing. There is no reason to assume that the gap between the reality of health care delivery and the theoretical assumptions of free market competition is any less today than in previous years. If anything, the assumptions have become more questionable.

Turn-of-the-century views of the marketplace are discordant with contemporary pressures for rationalization and budgetary planning. Moreover, uncategorical castigations of governmental intervention in the health sector are profoundly indifferent to political reality.

Medicare and Medicaid are not, as contended by promarket polemicists, a folly perpetrated out of ignorance, irrationality, or the machinations of special interest groups, but are an expression of the genuine will of the American people. Government-sponsored health programs are wanted because, as Fuchs (1979) has put it, they meet certain wants better than the alternatives do. Arcane arguments about whether health care services meet the test of a private or public good are largely irrelevant. Health has become established in public opinion as something so meritorious that its provision is regarded more as a right than a privilege.

On the other hand, it may be equally naive for liberals to expect that should the economy recover it will be possible to reapply the axiom that the solution to social problems is greater federal spending. Clearly, there is too much evidence to the contrary for policymakers to be swayed by such arguments. There is no disputing, however, that government now bears the major responsibility for the redistributive function. Although there is no reason government cannot take away what it has given, this is more easily said than done. It is unlikely that the quest for equity and social justice will abate. For many reasons, not the least of which is the absence of viable alternatives, and including rising quality-of-life aspirations and the aging of the population, the long-run political pressure is for more rather than less egalitarianism.

The imposition of absolutes from the dogmas of the left or the right belies the complexities of modern policy. The paramount imperatives for social cohesion point to a search for balance in the pursuit of interdependent goals of equity and efficiency (Fuchs, 1979). Recognition of the necessity for a trade-off between these two goals constitutes the basis for a new political consensus joining pragmatically minded persons from left and right of center of the health policy spectrum.

It is significant that the term "neoconservative" has been used in the policy litera-ture as a designation for politically influential and intellectually stimulating left-of-center individuals who agree on the need for a more eclectic and pragmatic approach to social change. This conclusion results from their reexamination of many liberal precepts be-hind the social and political reforms of the past several decades (Steinfels, 1979).

Neoconservatives may differ on important issues such as defense spending, affirma-tive action, and abortion, but they remain supportive of the basic contours of the welfare state. Neoconservatives also possess a common conviction on the need to redefine the partnership between government and the private sector to better accommodate the changing complexities of a mature economy in which low-productivity service industries constitute the principal source of employment. The dilemma of reconciling political aspirations for equality in an era of economic limits is an overarching preoccupation.

What constitutes ground for a distinct school of thought is an outlook emphasizing the constraints on political power to affect change and the virtues of public restraint in dealing with many social problems. In addition to focusing on the difficulties of estab-lishing and sustaining the necessary consensus for effective action in today's social and political environment, neoconservatives are alert to the lengthening administrative and technical lead times required for the solution of many problems. This perspective prompts them to conclude that far more harm than good results from the sharp and erratic short-term actions typical of many contemporary government policies. Neocon-servatives also share a deep faith in individual opportunity and achievement, rather than parity among social groups, as the best pathway for human progress (Steinfels, 1979).

There is less argument on the meaning of the neoconservative label when applied specifically to health policy. It is used casually to refer to the rising influence of conser-vative economists and the popularity of procompetition health services delivery models. However, the label is more accurately reserved for health liberals who upon reexamina-tion of fundamental assumptions directing health policy during the post-World War II era underwent a conversion comparable to that of their counterparts in the broader sphere of policy. There are reasons to believe that such a process, by no means com-pleted, actually did begin during the 1970s.

The ability of the health sector to enlarge its share of the gross national product from 4.5 percent in 1950 to nearly 10 percent in 1980 was in large part due to the prevalence and depth of trust in some key assumptions, which collectively constituted the prevailing conventional wisdom. Among these were the following beliefs. First, concentrated, large-scale spending for biomedical research and development will signifi-cantly improve the population's life expectancy and health levels. Second, the best place to care for patients is in the hospital, since that is where the best technology and medical services are concentrated. Third, medical specialization is both necessary and desirable. In an era of rapid proliferation of knowledge and rising public expectations for technical competence, general practice and family medicine are outmoded. Fourth, spending for health services is finite because of the eventual satiation of unmet medical needs and the benefits of preventive medicine and health education. And fifth, the role of government in health services should be confined to restoring and buttressing the capital require-ments of high-technology services and the purchasing power of consumers (Battistella, 1972b).

Dissatisfaction among policymakers with the unintended consequences and failures of the above keystone assumptions contributed to many of the uncertainties about the future of public intervention in health care delivery. Contrary to expectations, it became increasingly apparent during the 1970s that (1) spending for health services was limitless; (2) development of high-technological medical services was reaching the stage of diminishing marginal social benefits; (3) neglect of generalist, first-contact medical services was terribly costly in economic and human terms; (4) modern medical diagnosis and treatment inadvertently contributed to a surprisingly large amount of illness and disability; (5) there was an oversupply of hospital beds; (6) increasing the supply of physicians was not the solution to problems of maldistribution by location and type of practice; (7) it was perilous to rely on professional self-regulation alone for the attainment of goals of economy and quality; (8) unrealistically high public confidence in the benefits of medical treatment was resulting in the medicalization of many social problems that could be better dealt with through other means; and (9) the magnitude of health spending was an impediment to economic growth.

Skepticism and disillusionment about the value of health services were fostered by a succession of highly critical publications beginning early in the decade, both in the United States and abroad (Carlson, 1975; Cochrane, 1979; Fuchs, 1974; Illich, 1976; Maxwell, 1974; McKeown, 1976; Pocincki et al., 1973; Powles, 1973; Torrey, 1974; U.S. Congress, 1976a, 1976b; U.S. Department of Health, Education and Welfare, 1976).

The disassociation of many prominent health liberals from the conventional wisdom is possibly best exemplified in the specially prepared 1977 edition of *Daedalus*, "Doing Better and Feeling Worse:Health in the United States," edited by Dr. John H. Knowles (Knowles, 1977). The issues contained a number of far-ranging revisionist interpretations by politically and intellectually influential authors such as David E. Rogers, Donald S. Frederickson, Lewis Thomas, and Renee Fox. The contributions to the publication were linked by a concern that despite the accomplishments of the U.S. health care system, things had recently gone "strangely awry" (p. v) and new solutions were required.

Although they harbor many dissimilar views, health policy neoconservatives have a common outlook regarding some of the fundamental choices affecting the future of health policy. Given the recency of their conversion, however, the neoconservative outlook is less established in experience than in the extrapolation of logical consequences and probabilities.[2]

For the most part, health neoconservatives remain committed to the basic goals of the welfare state and retain a preference for equity over efficiency. On the other hand, they accept the reality of resource scarcity and concede the shortcomings of orthodox liberal doctrine geared to the uncompromised growth of health services and governmental intervention. *Pragmatism* is a distinguishing feature.

Health neoconservatives remain open to the possibility that pricing may be acceptable under carefully specified conditions. In an age of limits, what purpose is served by encumbering public financing with services that are of questionable medical value? Assuming that technology assessment capabilities exist, it is both practical and desirable from a health promotion standpoint to restrict public financing to services determined to meet safety and efficacy standards (U.S. Congress, 1980b). Surely services of unproven safety have no place in the market in a society obligated to protect the health of its

---

[2]The writings of Wildavsky (1979) and Glazer (1971) provide some insights into the application of the neoconservative philosophy to health care, as they are members of the broader neoconservative establishment who have commented specifically on health policy.

citizens, although nonharmful services of questionable efficacy might be left to the market.

The shortcomings of quantitative models and techniques notwithstanding, neoconservatives are not opposed to efforts to better establish the effectiveness and costs of health services in comparison with alternative expenditures. But informed decision making requires that the hidden values of putatively objective methods be made explicit and that the analyses not be skewed in ways that fail to capture the highly subjective contributions of health services (Wildavsky, 1979).

Pricing may also be acceptable to pragmatists looking for ways to supplement revenues for health services, although it is essential that prices do not constitute a deterrent to early diagnosis and treatment in the case of services of proven efficiency.

The experience of the 1970s suggests that even liberals not easily associated with neoconservatism recognize the practical uses of the market. For example, in the case of health maintenance organization policy, liberal legislators and union allies sought to accelerate the growth of prepaid group practice by turning competitive market rhetoric against forces of organized medicine who had successfully used the same tactic in defense of solo fee-for-service practice in the past. Because of this tactic, organized medicine no longer was able to condemn the structural reform of solo fee-for-service practice as socialist-inspired malice (Ehrbar, 1977). Nor did liberals hesitate to support the aggressive antitrust measures used by the Federal Trade Commission (FTC) to weaken the monopoly powers of the health professions—a move dramatically counter to long-standing historical justifications for the insulation of health services from unbridled competition and for the bestowal of professional privilege (Iglehart, 1978).

Neoconservatives are poised to accept the possibility that the principle of universalism at the core of liberal health policy may be politically unattainable in a poorly performing economy and that the interests of the disadvantaged can be protected by the substitution of the principle of selectivity. Increasingly, the concept of compulsory national health insurance no longer is viewed as economically or politically feasible.

The neoconservative approach is rising in appeal despite the fact that it lacks the coherence and consistency of orthodox liberal and conservative dimensions. Interest in restraint and compromise is by no means confined to former liberals. Whether willingly or reluctantly, there are many pragmatic conservatives who eschew the dogma of orthodox conservatism (Lodge, 1970). Many pragmatic conservatives also appreciate the functional significance of health services in a highly developed society. Representatives of big business, in particular, recognize the importance of political stability in an age when the large capital requirements for new technologies are lengthening the necessary lead times before investments can be returned in the form of profits. The practical point is not lost on corporate management and sophisticated investors that the demand for their products depends on consumer purchasing power (Galbraith, 1973). The devastating implications for sales of one-fifth of the population having insufficient disposable income to participate fully in a consumer-oriented economy undoubtedly was a factor in the decision by big business to recommend passage of national health insurance and a guaranteed annual income for the poor in the mid-1970s (Committee for Economic Development, 1973). More recently, the Washington Business Group on Health, which represents 200 national corporations, has indicated its opposition to the Reagan administration's intention to repeal or financially starve the existing health planning system. Employers are said to prefer planning to other alternatives because, imperfections aside, health planning remains "the most effective forum for industry to be responsive participants in health resources allocation" (Demkovich, 1981).

SHORTCOMINGS OF THE NEOCONSERVATIVE APPROACH

The neoconservative position in health policy shares weaknesses associated with the larger neoconservative movement. Perhaps most important, proponents of the approach often are viewed as having abandoned their commitment to fundamental notions of justice and equity in favor of political expediency. The neoconservative approach lacks a clear and simple vision of a "just" society, instead promoting movement toward a workable system that will enjoy broad public support and will incorporate elements from both the left and the right of the political spectrum.

A related potential danger is that many of the more powerful and eloquent ideological voices may be stilled in the name of pragmatism. Ideological exchange serves a valuable function by educating people and alerting them to visions of what is right and just rather than what is workable.

In the field of health services, a particular danger is that the goal of equity in health services delivery may be abandoned or lessened in priority in the face of the exigencies for health care cost containment. With the tide of politics running in a conservative direction, the pressures for containment of costs and curtailment of governmental health benefits are so strong that managerial values may submerge traditionally salient health goals. The pressures to consider health services to be the same as any other economic commodity may be detrimental to the humanitarian and social purposes of health care (Fein, 1980).

Finally, the trade-off between efficiency and equity raises some disturbing questions, particularly with respect to restricting publicly financed services solely to persons in need. If it makes good economic sense not to give services free to persons who can afford to pay for them privately, what are the longer run political and moral consequences of a system of health services segmented by differences in employment status, income, and age? Are programs for the poor destined to provide poor services whenever competition for scarce resources occurs between social groups?

THE NEO-MARXIST APPROACH

During the heyday of the normative era, defenders of the status quo in U.S. medicine displayed a talent for reducing proposals for health services reform to the level of Marxist-inspired subversion and conspiracy. As a tactic for galvanizing public attention and diverting legislative attention from the substantive complexities of health policy, appeals to fears of subversive foreign ideologies were highly successful. From today's perspective, however, the spirit of reform was far less radical than the rhetoric suggested.

Health reformers promulgated the social aims of medicine: community integration, social and economic role performance, and disease prevention and health promotion. Proponents of social medicine stressed that society has an obligation to protect the health of its members and that social and economic conditions have an important effect on health and disease. They also shared a belief in the value of scientific investigation and study for improving the organization and delivery of health services (Rosen, 1958).

Ironically, it was not until the normative approach was in the process of being displaced by rationalism that the Marxist presence was experienced overtly in the U.S. health policy scene. Whether this was due to the political exhaustion of right-wing critics or the complacency of traditional health care reformers after passage of Medicare and Medicaid in the mid-1960s is difficult to establish. Perhaps it represented an outpouring of frustration on the part of the Vietnam War generation whose idealism was shattered by the persistence of poverty and discrimination in an affluent society.

Although still outside the mainstream of health policy, the insights and positions of the Marxist perspective are the subject of curiosity among policymakers as well as scholars and students.

To what extent recent Marxist writing qualifies for the "neo"-designation is difficult to say. Much of it is steeped in classical themes of social class oppression resulting from capitalists' ownership of the modes of production and their resolute pursuit of profits above all else, including environmental protection, the safety and efficacy of foods and drugs, and the health of workers. The apotheosis of the working class as uncorrupted by materialism also persists, as does belief in the remedial effects of nationalization (Elling, 1977; Krause, 1977; McKinlay, 1979; Sidel, 1977).

The chief difference today is in the focus. Rather than proceeding within the framework of entrepreneurial capitalism, contemporary Marxist analysis deals with the effects of new concentrations of power in advanced industrial societies. Hence inquiry is directed at managerial capitalism (the power of national and multinational corporations) and science and technology. Industrialism is regarded as an ideology, independent of private or state ownership, in which health and health services are subordinated to productivity and capital accumulation goals. Power, in this context, accrues to the managers of capital (not the owners) to technocrats possessing the necessary skills and knowledge, and to bureaucracies administering and regulating economic activity. One of the consequences is that traditional class conflict is replaced by tension between those at the top responsible for running industrialized society and those at the bottom—the consumers of goods and services. Thus, social class has largely lost its importance as a category of social analysis. Due to welfare state policies, the working class in developed capitalist societies has been absorbed as part of the larger consumer mass and is subject to the manipulation of a corporate elite (Waitzkin, 1978).

Applied to the health sector, the conflict pits the medical bureaucracy (notably the medical profession) and the health services delivery system against consumers and patients. The result is manifested in an increase in illness attributable to physicians and health care institutions. In order to perpetuate its power, the medical profession finds it advantageous to medically addict the population (Navarro, 1977a).

The neo-Marxist approach has added to the confusion in health policy for the same reason that neoconservatism has. It encompasses a polyglot body of interests ranging at the extremes from stalwart believers in the continuing relevance of Marxist doctrine to anarchistic-leaning proponents of libertarianism. Analyses frequently pivot on subtle but important distinctions between consumption and production in the attribution of re-sponsibility for social problems and whether identifiable interests are the actual per-petrators or agents of oppression (Navarro, 1977b).

Despite its underlying utopianism and romanticism, the neo-Marxist school has made some important contributions, particularly the debunking of a number of myths prevalent in the normative period and the steering of public attention to some new realizations.

First, belief in the power of morality as an engine for social justice has weakened. Neo-Marxist writers have argued with some effect that past reforms are not solely due to the intrinsic altruism of human nature. They contend that change is unlikely without the manipulation of events by powerful, self-serving interests in the private sector, such as insurance companies and hospital supply and pharmaceutical corporations. Medicare and Medicaid have been reinterpreted in this light, as have the Flexner-inspired reforms of medical education (Berliner, 1973; Berliner, 1975; Bodenheimer, 1977).

In a related vein, the self-esteem and public repute of reformers have been assailed by charges that professed humanitarian motives are but a neat (not always conscious) disguise for paternalism. Reformers who are upper class in family background and/or education are less trustworthy than others when examined in this light (Frankenberg, 1977).

As viewed by Navarro (1973), the neo-Marxist emphasis on economic structure and class relations contrasts sharply with the importance given by power-elite theorists to the role of personalities in struggles for reform. Besides romanticizing the contribution of individuals, power-elite writers tend to see change in terms of conflict resolution among different groups and actors in which control of knowledge, technology, money, and the legal right to perform specified services determine the outcome (Alford, 1975; Feldstein, 1977; Marmor, 1973).

Second, belief in the benevolence of the medical profession has diminished, and even moderate observers have become alert to the potential use of professionalism as a cover for group aggrandizement (Begun, 1981). Marxist-spirited critics form part of a circle of skeptics divided in ideology but united in their distrust of the profession. Left-of-center critics typically are moved to curtail professional freedom and to demythologize medicine in order to free patients from medical oppression (Ehrenreich and Ehrenreich, 1974). Bureaucratic discipline in publicly accountable organizations, together with opportunities for citizen participation in the planning, monitoring, and evaluation of services, is the recommended solution. For the sake of individual freedom and economic efficiency, right-of-center critics recommend going still further—the weakening of restrictions on entry to medical practice, on the employment of physicians in bureaucratic organizations, and on competition among organized medical providers (Freidson, 1970).

Illich (1976, 1977) has called for more radical measures: (1) the total debureaucratization of society; (2) the breaking down of professional and other monopolies; (3) the return to classical market competition in which enlightened self-interest prevails; and (4) the maximum restoration of individual self-reliance and autonomy in all matters, including self-responsibility for health. In advanced industrial society, bureaucracy and professionalism, rather than capitalist or class exploitation, are seen as the omnipresent danger to individual freedom and the exercise of free will.

A third contribution of neo-Marxism has been that belief in the monolithic structure of organized medicine has dissolved. Until the mid-1960s, the stereotype of an all-powerful, reactionary American Medical Association entered into most policy deliberations. The medical schools and teaching hospitals, in contrast, seemed to be an exception. This image was an inaccurate one that sidetracked awareness of the implications of a shift in real power to scientific and technological interests.

Neo-Marxist observers were among the first to report that the major teaching hospitals and medical centers had become the chief obstacle to making quality health services more widely available to low-income populations. Few recognized at the time that the enormous capital requirements of high technology, superspecialty medicine were being served without proper consideration for cost-effectiveness or the availability of primary health care to underserved populations (Ehrenreich and Ehrenreich, 1970).

Neo-Marxists not only were among the first to understand the powerful forces in biomedical science and technology causing medical centers to take on many of the features of private corporations, but they also pointed the way for an analysis of the implications of this trend for the provision of medically questionable procedures and the availability of first-contact services attuned to everday health needs (Kotelchuck, 1976).

Finally, belief that medicine possesses little in common with big business has declined. The corporatization of U.S. medicine and the attractiveness of investments in the health economy to major financial and industrial corporations are subjects developed by neo-Marxist analysts and popularized in terms of the medical–industrial complex (Salmon, 1977).

SHORTCOMINGS OF THE NEO-MARXIST APPROACH

To be sure, conceptualization of health services as an instrument in the service of a ruling establishment is not without insight. The drawing of connections between medicine and the structural features of society opens the mind to the realization that reforms are not always conducted purely for humanitarian reasons. The manner in which analysts with a Marxist orientation examine industrialization as a process cutting across national differences in ideology allows the identification of factors more fruitful than those bound to individual personalities or highly localized circumstances. On the other hand, this approach has a number of weaknesses.

First, the presumption of selfish intent is one sided. In taking a pessimistic view of the motives of the powerful, neo-Marxism suffers the same limitation ascribed to conservative believers in the doctrine of market competition, the only difference being that the latter see selfishness as universal to human nature. For example, it is improbable, given the array of interests involved, that health programs introduced during the turbulent sixties (neighborhood health centers, community mental health centers, citizen participation in comprehensive health planning, etc.) were designed principally to repress insurgency by buying off indigenous leaders with good-paying jobs, by using demonstration projects as a way to dodge action, or by educating blacks and Hispanics to middle-class values (Higgins, 1980). This goes too far in discounting the spirit of reform instrumental in the passage of legislation and the administration of new programs.

Second, neo-Marxist analyses are frustrating to follow. They tend to rely heavily on assertion instead of data. The theory often suggests a conspiratal group design to keep and expand controls. The proclivity is to generalize on the basis of a series of policy decisions that may not be representative. For example, although it may indeed be true that some of the health programs launched during the sixties were a means of containing unrest, it is doubtful whether that applies to all of the many developments in health care, housing, education, and social security occurring at the same time. Not all the recipients were in the frame of mind to revolt (Higgins, 1980). Undoubtedly more complex reasons were involved in the cases of Medicare and Medicaid, to cite only two examples.

Finally, there is a distributing disregard for precision in the use of concepts and categories. Neo-Marxist writing is burdened with revolutionary rhetoric and pugnacious tone that impedes serious reflection and thoughtful analysis. It seldom is clear just what is meant by "the ruling class," "the state," or "the system." Vagueness as to who makes policy and who has responsibility for implementation and administration complicates the task of establishing relationships with the ruling class. Similarly, many categories suggest a homogeneity that does not always hold up on close inspection (Higgins, 1980).

FUTURE PROSPECTS FOR EQUITY
IN HEALTH SERVICES

There are many reasons to doubt that progress in equity will continue unabated. A general recognition that the once-affluent economy has entered an age of limits, coupled with mounting political disillusionment with the liberal ideology behind recent health and welfare reforms, suggests that it will be difficult to sustain past gains, let alone move ahead (Russell, 1980). Indeed, the present resurgence of conservative political doctrine and the return from near obscurity of rhetoric extolling the virtues of minimalist government, can be interpreted to bode ill for the future of welfare-state policies.

The vulnerability of publicly financed health services is compounded by the disintegration of confidence in propositions about the relationship between health and medicine and by the waning status and power of the medical profession. Contrary to what was long accepted as true, health spending is now viewed as inimical to economic growth, and the medical profession increasingly is denounced as an obstacle to progress.

Worry about the future of equity in health services is understandable in the present circumstance. Economic stringency and the sheer size and importance of the health sector invite scrutiny and a search for economies (U.S. Congress, 1980a). Progress in the pursuit of equity may have to be deferred until economic conditions improve. What is worse, economic necessity may require cutbacks in the scope of benefits currently provided under government programs, and sacrifices may be unevenly distributed by geography and social class. It is unlikely, however, in the long run that any or all of these events will culminate in the restoration of classical conservative doctrine and the return of health services to the status of a private good in which rationing is conducted by the unhindered play of the competitive market (Ginzberg, 1978).

The doctrine of market competition is no better equipped to withstand empirical testing today than it was in the past. If anything, its premises have been rendered more outmoded by social and economic development. The substitution of one discredited doctrine for another would be an act of folly. The possibility of this occurring belies the limitations on political power and omits the significance of structural factors impacting on health policy in a highly developed society. More than other forms of government, government in the United States speaks with many voices. The independence of the permanent bureaucracy and the role of special interests in national political life add to the constraints imposed by the constitutional separation of powers.

Were equity for the poor the only issue, the reestablishment of health services as a private good would be politically less difficult. The economic significance of the health sector in the modern economy, both as a major employer and as an important consumer of the goods and services produced by suppliers in private industry, further hinders the prospects for radical transformation. The closing of presumably redundant hospital beds is more easily discussed than done, as evidenced by experiences in the 1970s in New York City and in 1982 in Minneapolis–St. Paul (Battistella and Eastaugh, 1980b). The already extensive system of political alliances dependent on the maintenance of high levels of spending for health services will broaden as middle-class fears deepen about the prospects for family income security in the event of serious illness.

People today are living longer and have higher expectations about the quality of life, both of which have led to continuing use of medical care. The prolongation of life often is less important than amelioration of pain, suffering, and restrictions on activities. Public demand for health services is destined to remain high.

No matter what the motives involved, once government has engaged in the financing of health services, it becomes entrapped in a series of internal contradictions. Public financing inevitably leads to issues of accessibility and costs, the solutions to which lead to attempts to get more value for money spent through better management and more productive organization of health services. As discussed earlier, these pressures already have spurred a considerable amount of relationalization in the health sector. It is improbable that the pressures for rationalization will soon end. There are few alternatives open to government, and some are more appealing in the abstract than in practice.

The first is to seek to reeducate people about the limitations of scientific medicine and the need to become less dependent on physicians (Kass, 1975). This alternative misses the sociopsychological point of why people seek organized health services. It glosses over the fact that people often are not emotionally and physically free to reject medicine (Pellegrino, 1979). It also loses sight of the larger social and economic functions of health services. In focusing too much on short-term expediency, this strategy for cost containment may only compound the problem.

In addition to the dangers of improper treatment, self-responsibility begs the question of how illness should be validated to minimize disruptions in day-to-day community functioning. Chaos would ensue if people were allowed to determine on their own that they were too sick to carry out their normally assigned duties. Easily quantifiable effects, in terms of job absenteeism, lost productivity, declining quality of services, and expenditures for sick leave and disability entitlements, would only partially reveal the ramifications.

In putting the blame for illness on the individual, self-responsibility proposals divert policy from more important social and environmental causes of bad health (Guttmacher, 1979). They also tend to overstate the capabilities of behavior modification techniques for dealing with the problem. And they lead to the politically naive conclusion that society should and can withhold free treatment from those whose illness can be presumed to be the result of their own foolishness (Battistella, 1978b).

A second alternative the government can follow centers on the elimination or control of environmental hazards, through regulation and economic incentives for the installation of antipollution devices, and occupational safety and health measures. This, too, founders on the shoals of impracticability since such measures are better received when economic times are good. The costs of introducing such measures during an economic downturn endanger both profits and jobs, with the result that interests standing to gain the most in the long run (workers and local community economies) often are the most vociferous critics of such reforms. At the macro level, the costs involved can be an obstacle to the accumulation of capital for financing investments necessary to economic recovery. Because the economic burdens are much lower when corrective measures are built into the design of new physical plants, it makes more sense to adopt an incremental approach tied to the scheduled obsolescence of buildings and production processes (Battistella, 1978b; Mosher, 1980).

A third alternative involves the restriction of public financing to health services that meet rigorous standards for safety, efficacy, and cost efficiency. This has extraordinary appeal on humanitarian, scientific, as well as economic grounds. However, as described earlier, there are many methodological and ethical pitfalls in the conduct of analyses of this sort, and the findings remain too unreliable to provide unequivocal guidance to policymakers. Despite the substantial shortcomings, this alternative is deeply imbedded in the mindset of the generation of decision makers new to health services policy and administration (Battistella and Rundall, 1978b). Therefore, its influence can be expected to continue. The results could be highly favorable for equity purposes, provided savings were directed at improving the range and quality of services available to populations afflicted with conditions that have remained peripheral to the priorities of modern medicine: the disabled, the mentally ill, the chronically sick, and the frail aged.

Furthermore, the incorporation of cost–benefit logic in the minds of policymakers is bound to spotlight glaring examples of how public funds can be spent to better coordinate health services with economic-growth objectives. Whether historically due to a surplus of workers or to ideological reasons, U.S. policy has been indifferent to investment-in-human-capital health programs. For example, the absence of an organized system of maternal and child health services in the United States ranks as an exception to the rule found in most developed economies. Together with the prospects for productivity from a qualitatively strengthened labor force, maternal and child health services provide a far greater yield in lower future treatment costs than do adult disease prevention and health education investments.

Insofar as health professionals begin to apply cost–benefit logic to compete more successfully for scarce public resources, recognition of the returns from simple and inexpensive industrial medical programs will also improve. Indeed, it can be anticipated that the more astute and aggressive hospitals entering an era of steady-state budgeting will capitalize on the opportunity to develop specialized prevention and treatment programs for employers seeking ways to manage their financial liabilities for occupationally related disorders.

A fourth alternative that government is already pursuing involves managing the supply of health personnel and facilities. The combination of regulations and economic incentives currently found in the health sector is predicated, as mentioned earlier, on the belief that the usual laws of market competition do not prevail (Ginzberg, 1978). Regardless of whether they are pursued in or outside the framework of formal health planning, government measures to control the availability of physicians and hospital beds inevitably are accountable to political demands for equity in their distribution among medically underserved populations. This, too, augurs well for equity in the years ahead.

A fifth alternative is market competition. Although the subject of considerable discussion as the putative course of government in the 1980s, the actual meaning of market competition is unclear. Believers in the superiority of orthodox competitive economic theory interpret it as the long-awaited triumph of reason. On the other hand, groups who have faith in the power of the state to improve the quality of life fear that the political popularity of competitive-market language heralds the disengagement of government from the health sector and the end of equity. This possibility has been commented on earlier in this section. The practical use to which rhetoric is employed by politicians for getting things done in a pluralistic society is conducive to hyperbole. Moreover, political pragmatists generally subscribe to the adage that in human affairs reason is occasionally the compass but emotion is always the steam. As pointed out earlier in discussing the substantial progress made in the rationalization of health services, there are numerous practical advantages to ascribing vaunted cultural folk symbols to conceal controversial change.

When pondered in this context, proposals for increasing the role of competition in health services take on a significance considerably removed from literal translations. Competition has become a metaphor for a major restructuring of traditional practices in the financing, organization, and delivery of personal health services. Some of the more notable aims of this effort include (1) the replacement of retrospective reimbursement with prospective-budgeting systems; (2) the transfer of assumption of financial risks from insurance companies and government to providers; (3) the imposition of restrictions on consumer freedom of choice through the assignment of individuals to organized groups of providers agreeing to provide a specified range of benefits within territorially defined areas; (4) the mandating of private industry and state government to share responsibility for the financing and administration of nationally uniform standards; (5) the introduction of controls on the supply of practitioners by specialty, possibly including their distribution; and (6) the transformation of health services from small-scale to large-scale units of production, conducive to the application of scientific management techniques for production and quality control.[3]

The restructuring of health services is not necessarily harmful to equity in health services. Indeed, many of the changes now underway have multiple implications. If introduced often in the name of cost containment, they also have important positive ramifications for the availability and quality of health services.

On the other hand, there is always the possibility that preoccupation with short-run imperatives for savings may prompt measures that place an unfair burden on the poor. The revival of competitive market values and corollary ideologies attributing poverty to laziness and moral weakness certainly leans in this direction (Beauchamp, 1976).

Inability or refusal to recognize the political importance of quality of life values and the needs of contemporary industry for stable markets carries the risk of grave harm to social cohesion and economic prosperity. What critics from both the right and the left often fail to recognize is that the most important social contributions of health services do not neatly conform to conventional organizational and political principles.

The tensions described in this review of the political economy of health services did not occur overnight, nor can they be attributed mainly to the policies of competing political parties. They were observable in the early 1970s, and the implications were evident in broad outline (Battistella, 1972a). Indeed, even then it could be seen that comprehensive universal health insurance was an idea whose time had passed (Battistella, 1973). The only subsequently major changes involve matters of degree more so than of kind and a broadening awareness within the health community that things would not improve soon regardless of the outcome of national political elections. Evidence from many other highly industrialized nations of widely differing political and economic backgrounds suggests that the causes are structural in nature. They are the likely manifestation of a process of adjustment to the large-scale institutional changes resulting from the transition from industrialization to a higher stage of social and economic development (Battistella, 1978).

The complexities of the changes now occurring in social, political, and economic institutions are a reminder that establishing the right balance between equity and efficiency will not be easy. The enormous challenge of accommodating public policy to an unfamiliar decision-making environment, in which denial rather than gratification is becoming the rule, deserves the attention of all groups committed to the preservation of equity in an era of limits.

---

[3]In many instances the more subtle and politically feasible aims of the 'procompetition movement" actually are antithetical to the classical free market model. This further demonstrates a gap between rhetoric and reality in the movement to increase "competition" in the medical marketplace.

REFERENCES

Alford, Robert R., *Health Care Politics: Ideological and Interest Group Barriers to Reform*, Chicago: University of Chicago Press, 1975.

Arrow, Kenneth J., "Uncertainty and Welfare Economics of Medical Care," *American Economic Review*, Vol. 53, December 1963, pp. 941–969.

Battistella, Roger M., "Rationalization of Health Services: Political and Social Assumptions," *International Journal of Health Services*, Vol. 2, August 1972a, pp. 331–348.

Battistella, Roger M., "Post-Industrial Europe: Implications for Health Services Structure," *International Journal of Health Services*, Vol. 2, November 1972b, pp. 465–476.

Battistella, Roger M., "Towards National Health Insurance in the USA: An Examination of Leading Proposals," *Acta Hospitalia*, Vol. 13, Summer 1973, pp. 3–22.

Battistella, Roger M., "Health Policy Development in Other Highly Industrialized Nations," in Roger M. Battistella and Thomas G. Rundall, eds., *Health Care Policy in a Changing Environment*, San Francisco: McCutchan, 1978a, pp. 23–51.

Battistella, Roger M., "Individual Responsibility for Disease Prevention and Health Maintenance: Potential for Productive Interventions," in Roger M. Battistella and Thomas G. Rundall, eds., *Health Care Policy in a Changing Environment*, San Francisco: McCutchan, Publishing Co., 1978b, pp. 274–293.

Battistella, Roger M. and Theodore E. Chester, "Role of Management in Health Services in Britain and the United States, *The Lancet*, Vol. 1, March 18, 1972, pp. 626–630.

Battistella, Roger M. and Steven R. Eastaugh, "Hospital Cost Containment: The Hidden Perils of Regulation," *Bulletin of the New York Academy of Medicine*, Vol. 56, January–February 1980a, pp. 62–82.

Battistella, Roger M. and Steven R. Eastaugh, "Hospital Cost Containment," in Arthur Levin, ed., "Regulating Health Care: The Struggle for Control," *Proceedings of the Academy of Political Science*, Vol. 33, No. 4, 1980b, pp. 192–205.

Battistella, Roger M. and Thomas G. Rundall, eds., *Health Care Policy in a Changing Environment*, San Francisco: McCutchan Publishing Co., 1978a.

Battistella, Roger M. and Thomas G. Rundall, "The Future of Primary Health Services in the U.S.: Issues and Options," in Roger M. Battistella and Thomas G. Rundall, eds., *Health Care Policy in a Changing Environment*, San Francisco: McCutchan Publishing Co., 1978b, pp. 294–319.

Battistella, Roger M. and David B. Smith, "Towards a Definition of Health Services Management: A Humanist Orientation," *International Journal of Health Services*, Vol. 4, Fall 1974, pp. 701–721.

Battistella, Roger M. and John R. C. Wheeler, "Ideology, Economics, and the Future of National Health Insurance," in Roger M. Battistella and Thomas G. Rundall, eds., *Health Care Policy in a Changing Environment*, San Francisco: McCutchan Publishing Co., 1978, pp. 373–390.

Beauchamp, Dan E., "Public Health as Social Justice," *Inquiry*, Vol. 13, March 1976, pp. 3–14.

Begun, James W., *Professionalism and the Public Interest: Price and Quality in Optometry*, Cambridge: MIT Press, 1981.

Berliner, Howard, "The Origins of Health Insurance for the Aged," *International Journal of Health Services*, Vol. 3, 1973, pp. 465–474.

Berliner, Howard, "A Larger Perspective on the Flexner Report," *International Journal of Health Services*, Vol. 5, No. 4, 1975, pp. 573–592.

Bodenheimer, Thomas, Steven Cummings and Elizabeth Harding, "Capitalizing on Illness: The Health Insurance Industry," in Vicente Navarro, ed., *Health and Medical Care in the U.S.: A Critical Analysis*, Farmingdale, N.Y.: Baywood Publication, 1977, pp. 69–84.

Bowler, Kenneth M., Robert T. Kuderle and Theodore R. Marmor, "The Political Economy of National Health Insurance: Policy Analysis and Political Evaluation," in Kenneth M. Friedman and Stuart H. Rakoff, eds., *Toward a National Health Policy*, Lexington, Mass.: Lexington Books, 1978.

Bulgaro, Patrick J. and Arthur Y. Webb, "Federal–State Conflicts in Cost Control," in Arthur Levin, ed., "Regulating Health Care: The Struggle for Control," New York: *Proceedings of the Academy of Political Science*, Vol. 33, No. 4, 1980, pp. 92–110.

Campbell, Alastair V., *Medicine, Health, and Justice: The Problem of Priorities*, New York: Churchill Livingstone, 1978, pp. 1–5.

Carlson, Rick, *The End of Medicine*, New York: John Wiley & Sons, 1975.

Cochrane, A. L., *Effectiveness and Efficiency: Random Reflections on Health Services*, London: Nuffield Provincial Hospitals Trust, 1979.

Commission on Hospital Care, *Hospital Care in the United States*, New York: The Commonwealth Fund, 1947.

Committee for Economic Development, *Building a National Health Care System*, New York: Committee for Economic Development, 1973.

Council on Wage and Price Stability, *The Problem of Rising Health Care Costs*, Washington D.C.: Executive Office of the President, 1976.

Davis, Michael M., *Medical Care for Tomorrow*, New York: Harper, 1975.

Demkovich, Linda, "Group Management of Hospitals on the Rise," *National Journal*, Vol. 12, August 9, 1980, pp. 1316–1320.

Demkovich, Linda, "Reagan's Ideological Gamble—Eliminating Hospital Cost Review," *National Journal*, Vol. 13, March 14, 1981, pp. 440–443.

Donabedian, Avedis, *Aspects of Medical Care Administration*, Cambridge: Harvard University Press, 1973, pp. 1–30.

Donnison, David, "Social Policy Since Titmuss, *Journal of Social Policy*, Vol. 8, 1979, pp. 145–156.

Ebenstein, William, Herman C. Pritchett, Henry A. Turner and Dean Mann, *American Democracy in World Perspective*, New York: Harper and Row, 1970, 2nd edition, pp. 510–541.

Ehrbar, A. F., "A Radical Prescription for Medical Care," *Fortune*, Vol. 95, February 1977, pp. 164ff.

Ehrenreich, Barbara and John Ehrenreich, eds., *The American Health Empire*, New York: Vintage Books, 1970.

Ehrenreich, Barbara and John Ehrenreich, "Health Care and Social Control," *Social Policy*, Vol. 5, May–June 1974, pp. 26–40.

Elling, Ray H., "Industrialization and Occupational Health in Under-Developed Countries," *International Journal of Health Services*, Vol. 7, No. 2, 1977, pp. 209–235.

Feldstein, Paul J., *Health Associations and the Demand for Legislation: The Political Economy of Health*, Cambridge: Ballinger Publishing Co., 1977.

Fein, Rashi, "Social and Economic Attitudes Shaping American Health Policy, *Milbank Memorial Fund Quarterly. Health and Society*, Vol. 58, Summer 1980, pp. 350–385.

Frankenberg, Ronald, "Functionalism and After? Theory and Developments in Social Science Applied to the Health Field," in Vicente Navarro, ed., *Health and Medical Care in the U.S.: Critical Analysis*, Farmingdale, New York: Baywood Publications, 1977, pp. 21–37.

Freidson, Elliot, *Professional Dominance: The Social Structure of Medical Care*, New York: Atherton, 1970.

Friedman, Milton, *Capitalism and Freedom*, Chicago: Phoenix Books, 1962.

Fuchs, Victor, *Who Shall Live?* New York: Basic Books, 1974.

Fuchs, Victor, "The Economics of Health in a Post-Industrial Society," *The Public Interest*, Vol. 56, Summer 1979, pp. 3–20.

Galbraith, John K., *Economics and the Public Purpose*, Boston: Houghton Mifflin, 1973.

Ginzberg, Eli, "Health Reform: The Outlook for the 1980's," *Inquiry*, Vol. 15, December 1978, pp. 311–326.

Glazer, Nathan, "Paradoxes of Health Care," *The Public Interest*, Vol. 22, Winter 1971, pp. 62–77.

Guttmacher, Sally, "Whole in Body, Mind and Spirit: Holistic Health and the Limits of Medicine," *Hastings Center Report*, Vol. 9, April 1979, pp. 15–21.

Harris, Richard, *A Secret Trust*, New York: New American Library, 1966.

Higgins, Joan, "Social Control Theories of Social Policy," *Journal of Social Policy*, Vol. 9, January 1980, pp. 1–23.

Iglehart, John K., "Adding a Dose of Competition to the Health Care Industry," *National Journal*, Vol. 10, October 7, 1978, pp. 1602–1606.

Illich, Ivan, *Medical Nemesis: The Expropriation of Health*, New York: Pantheon Books, 1976.

Illich, Ivan, *Disabling Professions*, London: Boyars, 1977.

Janowitz, Morris, *Social Control of the Welfare State*, New York: Elsevier, 1976, pp. 41–71.

Jonas, Steven, "Population Data for Health and Health Care," in Steven Jonas, ed., *Health Care Delivery in the United States*, New York: Springer Publishing Co., 1981, 2nd edition, pp. 37–60.

Journal of the American Medical Association, Vol. 194, November 15, 1965, pp. 744–745.

Journal of the American Medical Association, Vol. 243, March 7, 1980, p. 850.

Kass, Leon R., "Regarding the End of Medicine and the Pursuit of Health," *The Public Interest*, Vol. 40, Summer 1975, pp. 11–42.

Knowles, John K., ed., *Doing Better, Feeling Worse: Health in the United States*, New York, W. K. Norton, 1977.

Kotelchuck, David, ed., *Prognosis Negative: Crisis in the Health Care System*, New York: Vintage, 1976.

Krause, Elliot, A., *Power and Illness: The Political Sociology of Health and Medical Care*, New York: Elsevier, 1977.

Lodge, George C., Jr., "Why an Outmoded Ideology Thwarts the New Business Conscience," *Fortune*, Vol. 82, October 1970, p. 106ff.

Marmor, Theodore, R., *The Politics of Medicine*, Chicago: Aldine, 1973.

Maxwell, Robert J., *Health Care: The Growing Dilemma*, New York: McKinsey, 1974.

McKeown, Thomas, *The Role of Medicine: Dream, Mirage or Nemesis?* London: Nuffield Provincial Hospitals Trust, 1976.

McKinlay, John, "A Case of Refocusing Upstream: The Economy of Illness," in E. Gartly Jaco, ed., *Patient, Physicians, and Illness*, New York: The Free Press, 1979, 3rd edition, pp. 9–25.

Mosher, Lawrence, "Industry Takes Aim at the Clear Air Act," *National Journal*, Vol. 12, No. 15, 1980, pp. 1927–1930.

Navarro, Vicente, *Medicine Under Capitalism*, New York: Prodist, 1976, pp. 189–192.

Navarro, Vicente, *Health and Medical Care in the U.S.: A Critical Analysis*, Farmingdale, N.Y.: Baywood Publications, 1977a.

Navarro, Vicente, "The Industrialization of Fetishism or the Fetishism of Industrialization: A Critique of Ivan Illich," in Vicente Navarro, *Health and Medical Care in the U.S.: A Critical Analysis*, Farmingdale, N.Y.: Baywood Publications, 1977b, pp. 38–58.

Parsons, Talcott, *The Social System*, New York: The Free Press, 1951, pp. 428–479.

Pellegrino, Edmund D., "Toward a Reconstruction of Medical Morality: The Primacy of the Act of Profession and the Fact of Illness," *The Journal of Medicine and Philosophy*, Vol. 4, January 1979, pp. 32–56.

Pocincki, Leon S., Stuart J. Dogger and Barbara P. Schwartz, "The Incidence of Iatrogenic

Illness," in *Report of the Secretary's Commission on Medical Malpractice*, Pub. No. (OS) 73-89. Appendix, Washington D.C.: DHEW, 1973, pp. 50–70.

Powles, John, "On the Limitations of Modern Medicine," *Science, Medicine and Man*, Vol. 1, April 1973, pp. 1–28.

Roemer, Milton I., "The Foreign Experience in Health Service Policy," in Arthur Levin, ed., "Regulating Health Care: The Struggle for Control," *Proceedings of the Academy of Political Science*, Vol. 33, No. 4, 1980a, pp. 206–223.

Roemer, Milton I., "Optimism on Attaining Health Care Equity," *Medical Care*, Vol. 18, July 1980b, pp. 775–781.

Rosen, George, *A History of Public Health*, New York: M.D. Publications, 1958, pp. 450–495.

Rushmer, Robert F., *National Priorities for Health: Past, Present, and Projected*, New York:John Wiley & Sons, 1980, pp. 3–40.

Russell, Louise B., "Medical Care," in Joseph A. Pechman, ed., *Setting National Priorities: Agenda for the 1980's*, Washington D.C.: The Brookings Institute, 1980, pp. 169–203.

Salmon, J. W., Monopoly Capital and Its Reorganization of the Health Sector," *Review of Radical Political Economics*, Vol. 8, Spring 1977, pp. 125–133.

Sidel, Victor W. and Ruth Sidel, *A Healthy State*, New York: Patheon Books, 1977.

Simanis, Joseph G. and John R. Coleman, "Health Care Expenditures in Nine Industrialized Countries," *Social Security Bulletin*, Vol. 43, January 1980, pp. 3–8.

Smith, David G., Policy Analysis and Liberal Arts," in William D. Coplin, ed., *Teaching Policy Studies*, Lexington, Mass.: Lexington Books, 1978, pp. 37–44.

Steinfels, Peter, *The Neoconservatives: The Men Who are Changing America's Politics*, New York: Simon & Schuster, 1979.

Thurow, Lester, C., *The Zero-Sum Society*, New York: Basic Books, 1980, p. 7. ╱

Torrey, Fuller E., *The Death of Psychiatry*, Radnor, Penn.: Chilton, 1974.

U.S. Congress, House Sub-Committee on Oversight and Investigations of the Committee on Interstate and Foreign Commerce. *Report on the Cost and Quality of Health Care: Unnecessary Surgery*, 94th Congress, Second Session, 1976a.

U.S. Congress, Office of Technology Assessment. *Development of Medical Technology: Opportunities for Assessment*, Washington, D.C., USGPO, 1976b.

U.S. Congress, The Joint Economic Committee. *Issues in Federal Finance: Special Study on Economic Change*, 96th Congress, First Session, July 1979, Washington, D.C., USGPO, 1980a.

U.S. Congress, Office of Technology Assessment. *The Implications of Cost Effectiveness Analysis of Medical Technology*, USGPO, 1980b.

U.S. Department of Health and Human Services, *Health, United States 1980*, DHHS Pub. No. (PHS) 81-1232, Washington D.C., USGPO, 1981.

U.S. Department of Health, Education and Welfare, *Forward Plan for Health, FY 1977–81*, Pub. No. (OS)76-50024, Washington, D.C., DHEW, 1975.

U.S. Department of Health, Education and Welfare, "Theme: Preparing for National Health Insurance," *Forward Plan for Health, FY 1978–82*, Pub. No. (OS)76-50046, Washington, D.C., DHEW, 1976.

U.S. Department of Health, Education and Welfare, *Health, United States: 1979*, DHEW Pub. No. (PHS)80-1232, Washington D.C., USGPO, 1980.

Waitzkin, Howard, "A Marxist View of Medical Care," *Annals of Internal Medicine*, Vol. 89, August 1978, pp. 264–278.

Wildavsky, Aaron, *Speaking Truth to Power: The Art and Craft of Policy Analysis*, Boston: Little Brown and Co., 1979.

CHAPTER 3

Health Services in the United States: A Growth Enterprise for a Hundred Years

Odin W. Anderson

In the United States, personal health services have been a growth enterprise since 1875—to pick an arbitrary date. They have been embedded in an essentially private sector of the U.S. economy, a mixture of nonprofit and profit enterprises with gradually increasing government support and intervention. The concept of intervention is used deliberately as part of political jargon. It implies that government intrudes in an otherwise normal situation. This mixture has changed over the years primarily as to sources of funding for day-to-day operations and to some degree capital financing. Social and political values in the United States have manifested a great deal of ambiguity as to the responsibilities of citizens as free-standing individuals for their own health care and the extent to which they enter into collective solutions through government. Collective solutions through community fund drives for hospital construction, for example, have had a long history and easy acceptance in the United States. But collective solutions, even through some form of private health insurance, have been adopted cautiously. Early acceptance of life and fire insurance, predictable contingencies, were not regarded as applicable to illnesses and their costs until the 1930s. In general, insurance was considered a normal and prudent means for Americans to protect their own solvency. Medical care for the poor, on the other hand, was regarded as a responsibility of the noblesse oblige of the physician and the charitable tradition of the hospital buttressed in part by local government funding and the compassion of philanthropic organizations.

DEVELOPMENT OF THE UNITED STATES PERSONAL HEALTH SERVICES SYSTEM

For purposes of this discussion, it may be helpful to present briefly the major stages of development of the personal health services system in the United States, including a brief mention of public health and mental hospitals, which preceded and then paralleled the growth of personal health services. The development of personal health services in the United States can be divided into three fairly distinct periods, each with its own characteristics, revealing the evolution of an exceedingly complex and expensive enterprise. These periods are (1) the development of the health services organizational structure, physical facilities, and personnel infrastructure and methods of paying for the services before health insurance—1875 to 1930; (2) the emergence of voluntary health insurance as a means for people to pay for the costs of health services as these became increasingly costly—1930 to 1965; and (3) the application of constraints on the health services in order to manage and direct the pace of rising expenditures and assure greater equality of access and more equitable distribution of facilities and personnel—1965 to the present and likely to continue indefinitely.

THE PERIOD 1875–1930

It took over 50 years for the modern personal health services delivery system to evolve from a general-practice-centered to a specialty- and hospital-centered enterprise. In 1875, physicians and, to some extent, pharmacists were the sole dispensers of professionally recognized health services, two professions with a long and prestigious tradition. On the periphery were recognized and unrecognized midwives who, by the turn of the century, were beginning to be replaced by the medical profession, doctors of osteopathy, chiropractors, and others outside the role of official medicine. A great deal of reliance was placed on home medication. For all practical purposes, the general hospital as it is known today was nonexistent. The poorhouses and almshouses were institutions for taking care of the destitute and the destitute ill who had no families to which to turn. Illnesses were treated mainly in patients' homes and physicians' offices. Physicians and pharmacists were, as they still are, largely private entrepreneurs presumably working within a code of ethics, standards, and services not strictly of a profit-making enterprise but undoubtedly influenced by the laissez-faire atmosphere that characterized the United States in the latter nineteenth-century. There were then as many physicians in relation to the population as there are now. They made a living by treating patients for fees and received very little income from government and philanthropic sources. No other country has been able to support as many physicians from private fee-for-service patients as has the United States. The same was true for pharmacists who eventually established the familiar corner drug store institution because income from prescriptions alone was not sufficient. There were too many pharmacists mainly because physicians frequently did their own dispensing from the relatively simple materia medica of the period. Private practice and fee for service became firmly embedded in the American medical practice tradition.

Two specific medical–technical discoveries sparked the creation of the modern hospital system—antisepsis and anesthesia. Antisepsis made surgery safe from infections, and anesthesia made it relatively painless. Since most surgery had to be performed in a hospital setting, surgery was the medical specialty that initiated growth of the modern hospital. Hospital treatment of medical patients followed in some volume by the turn of the century. (Births in the hospital, however, did not grow to any great volume until the later 1920s.) All this meant, of course, that the health care industry was needing more and more money compared to other goods and services and the gross national product. New money was needed for capital financing of hospitals and for the great increase in surgical procedures. By 1875 surgical procedures had become highly developed in the charity hospitals of the great cities of Europe and on the East Coast of the United States by trial and error on charity patients who were the sole source of "clinical material." But with the advent of anesthesia and antisepsis, the middle and upper classes, who would not have used the historically famous hospitals in Vienna, Paris, Berlin, London, and Edinburgh, began to seek the services of surgeons who, in turn, sought hospital admitting privileges. By 1900 there were 4000 general hospitals in the United States, compared to only a few score in 1875.

The hospitals were established mostly by voluntary community boards and church bodies. The latter had a long history of caring for the sick poor, and this tradition was transformed into the modern general hospital. The capital funds came from the multi-millionaires and the many lesser millionaires who came forth with the tremendous industrial development following the Civil War. These new millionaries were essentially Calvinsts who believed that their material rewards for hard work and prudence should be used in part for the good of the community. A fortuitous and appropriate object of their noblesse oblige was the merging medical–technical infrastructure. Only a small minority of general hospitals were built by the municipalities for the poor. The voluntary hospitals, through their charitable and nonprofit charters, were obliged to provide care for the poor who sought help, but by and large they constituted a minority of the patients. The burgeoning U.S. economy enabled the hospitals to obtain capital funds from philanthropy and daily operating funds from pay patients. The physician, particularly those who expected to be surgeons, made deals with the hospitals to bring in their private patients who paid both the hospital charges and the surgeon's fees. In turn, the surgeons were provided a free workshop in which they provided free care for the poor, an ideal symbiotic arrangement.

The United States has had a long tradition of voluntary self-help on a community level, and the voluntary hospitals have been a prime example of this tradition. The family nurturance functions found expression in the voluntary hospital when the home became unequal to the technical demands and setting of increasingly high technology medicine.

The hospital were thus able to survive and prosper (i.e., with respectable deficits) by serving the large and growing middle class for a fee. Approximately two-thirds of the hospital income came from fees paid by private patients, and one-third came from philanthropy, public funds, and other charities for the poor. It is significant that the general hospitals in the United States were the only hospitals in any country that could survive on income from private patients. Consequently, this country was able to mount a personal health delivery system for private patients, and the poor became a residual of this system. Just the opposite was true in Europe.

By 1909, the self-supporting element of the U.S. population was at times finding it difficult to pay for hospital care. As a spokesman for the American Hospital Association observed, the poor got free care, the rich could afford it, but the cost of hospital care was getting out of the reach of the Third Estate, the broad middle-income class. The political answer surfaced in 16 states between 1916 and 1920 when an attempt was made to pass legislation for some form of compulsory health insurance, a middle-class type of solution. A model bill was formulated by the American Association for Labor Legislation (AALL) made up of social reformers from the ranks of academic economists, social workers, sociologists, and a few sympathetic physicians. Even the American Medical Association (AMA) set up a study commission to investigate the problem of high costs of health services.

But nothing came of it. There was no real grass roots political support. The broad middle-income groups were not sufficiently aroused. The trade unions were indifferent and, in fact, Samuel Gompers, the head of the American Federation of Labor (AFL), was actively hostile.[1] Moreover, labor distrusted government for its persistent injunctions against strikes. Then World War I intervened, and it was discovered that compulsory health insurance was invented in Germany in 1883 under Bismarck. The AMA and the drug and insurance companies went on the offensive with tremendous propagandistic fanfare and won easily because the proponents had no political base. Thus, it was not until the 1930s that the Third Estate, that is, the middle class, found some relief from the high cost of health care through the establishment of voluntary health insurance plans sponsored by the hospitals and medical societies.

Dentists paralleled physicians as private entrepreneurs earning their living from fees from private patients. Since the public perceptions of dental health were then rather primitive, the services of dentists were hardly in great demand. Dentists also benefited greatly from the appearance of anesthesia and antisepsis. In fact, a dentist was the first health professional to use ether for extractions, thus ushering in anesthesiology.

The source of health personnel—physicians, dentists, and nurses—was multifold. During the nineteenth century most of the physicans came from apprenticeship arrangements with practicing physicans and so-called diploma mills established by practicing physicians to train many students at a time in rather primitive arrangements. Later, private and public universities established medical schools related to the basic sciences. Dentists went through a similar proprietary educational period, and eventually dental schools became established in universities. Nurses, on the other hand, were trained by hospitals that, in return, obtained an inexpensive supply of labor. Eventually, as medical science advanced, other types of health personnel, such as laboratory technicians, began to appear.

All this took money, which became available with the growth of the economy as the surplus among other priorities poured into personal health services in increasing volume, as it has to this day. Personal health services were a wanted service and, up to the 1930s, the people of the United States bought it without help of government or private insurance. By the 1930s the personal health services infrastructure was in place as we know it today: voluntary hospitals, privately practicing physicians and dentists, and private pharmacies. But many changes were to take place later external to this structure, chiefly sources of funding, as well as planning and regulation.

Public health services and mental hospitals, have not been a wanted service in the same sense as those of a more personal or individual nature. They have been evolved for a variety of other reasons. Before 1875, cities and counties began to establish health departments when their water supplies apparently became contaminated from the effluents filling up in cities resulting in sporadic cholera epidemics. Later, when communicable diseases in children could be controlled through the aid of immunization and pasteurization, health departments took on an additional function based on bacteriology and epidemiology. Public health nursing for mothers and infants emerged with the addition of public health training to the education of registered nurses. Public health, however, separated itself early from the private practice of medicine. Although public health officers were usually required to be physicians, they did not practice medicine. They were administrators.

---

[1]The AFL at that time was a skilled trade union. There were no industrial unions.

The building of mental hospitals—usually out of the cities and in the country—began before the development of personal health services. They were, and continue to be, more or less separate from personal health services. Mental hospitals are largely publicly owned and operated. Like public health departments, they are not a wanted service, as revealed in the amount of their funding from taxes in relation to the magnitude of the problem. Personal health services through sheer demand and popularity corner the great portion of available funding. This was the state of affairs at the end of the period 1875–1930, and it continues today.

In contrast with the above, the share of the voluntary hospital system was determined by hospital owners, the medical profession, and philanthropy. Government, except by licensure and standards, did nothing to direct the system. The general public presumably approved the structure to date because they used and paid for the system in increasing numbers. The government provided an indirect source of operating subsidy, however, by permitting the hospitals to be tax-exempt enterprises. In addition, capital gifts to hospitals were tax-exempt and interest free. Thus emerged the mixed health services economy, a reflection of the mixed nature of the U.S. economy as a whole.

And so, stimulated by the enormous dynamics of medical science, technology, and money, the acute disease oriented personal health services system in the 1930s was poised for an even more dynamic expansion on top of the one that emerged since 1875. Public health departments and mental hospitals, on the other hand, barely held their own.

THE PERIOD 1930–1965

Whereas the period from 1875 to 1930 witnessed the development of the health service infrastructure, the period from 1930 to 1965 was mainly characterized by the emergence of the third party to pay for the day-to-day operating expenses of this imposing edifice.

In the early 1930s, consumer incomes fell drastically, causing hospital admission rates and payments from private patients to drop as well. Both hospitals and the Third Estate, as well as the poor, became hard pressed. The Great Depression was upon the United States. The 1930s saw the start of the hospital-sponsored prepayment plans, eventually known as Blue Cross. Although such plans would have undoubtedly come about without the Great Depression, their development was likely hastened by it. Hospital stays had become relatively costly and lent themselves to the application of the insurance principle. A relatively predictable number of people would incur hospital expenses. Concurrently and separately, because the hospitals and physician services were two separate interests and enterprises, prepayment plans for physician services in the hospital, mainly surgery, began to appear in the latter 1930s as well. These plans were sponsored by state medical societies and later became known as Blue Shield plans. Again, surgical care, which was relatively costly, lent itself to the insurance principle.

Government continued its health services for the poor through the states, and eventually a shared program between the federal government and the states emerged. During the early formulation of the Social Security Act in 1935, health insurance was considered but not included. The architects of the act who were previously interested in old age pensions and unemployment compensation feared that health insurance would be so controversial as to jeopardize income maintenance of the act itself. Health care reformers pressed for the inclusion of health insurance, but when this became known, the AMA raised such a storm that it was not included in the bill that finally went to the Congress. As was the case from 1916 to 1920, there was no adequate grass roots support for national health insurance, and the AMA once again had an easy victory.

During the 1940s and into World War II, private insurance companies discovered on the basis of the experience of the Blue Cross and Blue Shield plans that hospital care and surgery were insurable and their costs could be predicted. Congress gave the voluntary plans a shot in the arm by decreeing during the wartime control on wages that health insurance—and pensions—were fringe benefits that need not be regarded as increases in wages. This was an example of government encouragement of the private sector, since the portion paid by the employers was tax exempt as a business expense, in other words an indirect public subsidy. Further, signing up for fringe benefits on the part of employees became a condition of employment, an acceptable form of compulsion, whereas direct compulsion in a government program was regarded as a very explosive political issue. Thus, voluntary health insurance received a tremendous stimulus as employees began increasingly to assume a greater share of the premiums and health insurance became part of collective bargaining. In the meantime, bills on national health insurance were moved to the back burner of the congressional kitchen stove from 1937 to 1952, the year Truman (a strong supporter of government health care) ended his presidency; this was a great disappointment to him.

Under the conditions described, the Blue Cross and Blue Shield plans and private insurance companies were spectactularly successful in enrolling employee groups in the major industries, so that by 1952 over one-half of the U.S. population was covered by some form of health insurance, mainly hospital care and physician services in the hospital. With the election of President Eisenhower, the first Republican president since 1932, the venomous controversy over voluntary versus government health insurance subsided only to reemerge a few years later in the form of health services for the aged. For the other 90 percent of the population, voluntary health insurance plans were left with a clear field to demonstrate that they could solve the public's problems.

The salient point in this third-party development was that the existing infrastructure of health services that had emerged since 1875 and had stabilized by 1930 was taken as a given and that the voluntary insurance agencies and the government were concerned mainly with paying its charges. In the case of hospitals, the concept was charges or costs. Physicians were paid by voluntary health insurance by a generously negotiated fee schedule with Blue Shield plans and no negotiations at all with private insurance companies, because there were no contracts with them. In retrospect these reimbursement methods seem administratively irresponsible, but for people who lived through those times, money flowed freely in a rapidly expanding economy. Further, the public was exhorted to "see your doctor early." Visits to physicians and admissions to hospitals increased dramatically from the latter 1930s to the 1960s. For example. hospital admissions increased from 90 per 1000 population per year to 145; the proportion of the population who saw a physician in 1 year increased from 39 to 65 percent. The supply of hospital beds and physicians increased but less in relation to the demand. The physician became increasingly busy and prosperous. The hospital occupancy increased.

To add to the stock of hospitals and beds, particularly in rural areas, Congress in 1946 passed the Hospital Construction Act (Hill–Burton) supported by a cross section of interests such as the American Hospital Association, the American Medical Association, and labor organizations, ordinarily at cross purposes over government health insurance. This act was designed as a one-shot grant to hospitals—public and voluntary—for start-up costs that were to be matched by the hospitals. For the first time, each state took an inventory of its hospital supply, and the grants were made to hospitals within the framework of a loosely knit plan. The act supplied around 25 percent of the expenditures for hospitals that, in turn, generated a considerable sum of money from private and public services, but mainly private.

The main object of the act was to buttress the voluntary hospital, with the public hospital being a relatively minor partner and regarded as spillover from the mainstream of the hospital system. The old sources of capital funds from philanthropy and community fund drives were drying up. Thus, the act came at a very opportune time and provides another example of government support being condoned to assist the private nonprofit sector. The voluntary hospital is obviously an integral part of U.S. local community life mixing the private and public sectors.

By the early 1950s, an era of expansion had been assured with funding for the day-to-day operation of the hospital and physicians' services provided essentially from private sources and that for the supply of hospital beds, physicians, and other personnel from public and private sources. The general economy and the health services economy benefiting from the affluence being created was also in full swing. The existing health services infrastructure continued to be accepted as a given. Within the relatively private and nonprofit nature of the U.S. health services economy, however, there was a development that concerned itself directly with restructuring the delivery of physicians' services and, indirectly, hospital care. This was the emergence of group practice prepayment plans that attempted to replace the solo practice and fee-for-service type of medical delivery by engaging a range of specialists on a salary, providing a full range of physician services from curative to preventive, and serving a known population. The Kaiser Permanente plans were established in the West and the Health Insurance Plan of Greater New York (HIP) in the East. In cities such as Washington, D.C., Seattle, St. Louis, and Minneapolis–St. Paul, similar programs were established more or less on a consumer-cooperative basis. Initially, the opposition on the part of the medical profession to these new arrangements was fierce. Gradually, however, such programs began to take their place in the spectrum of health services delivery types and, in some areas, became regarded as options in labor–management negotiations for health services fringe benefits. Their influence, however, appeared to be out of proportion to their numbers—involving about 4 percent of the population—nevertheless, they soon became reference points for quality health services at a "reasonable" price. It seems that only in the U.S. context, with the organization of private medical group practice giants such as Mayo, Lahey, Crile, and Ochsner plus many lesser ones, was the diversity of delivery types possible. Physicians, in the United States have an entrepreneurial propensity with ability to raise capital unlike any other country. The private group practice concept, which lived on fees, undoubtedly inspired the group practice prepayment concept that lived on premiums divided among physicians for salaries.

The proponents of national health insurance, having failed in their efforts from the 1930s to the early 1950s, began to look for another strategy, and they found it in the aged. Although voluntary health insurance was doing a reasonably adequate job for the mainstream employed segment of the population—at least enough to dampen agitation for universal health insurance—the aged became a burden on the voluntary health insurance and the broad middle-income segment of the population. Again the Third Estate made itself felt.

Toward the end of the period from 1930 to 1965, the private engine of finance was aided and abetted by the public engine of finance with the passage of Medicare for the aged and Medicaid for the poor in 1965. Medicare was a federal program, and Medicaid was a shared federal–state program, as they still are. Medicare took the costs of the care of the aged off the backs of voluntary health insurance and families with aged and ailing relatives. Medicaid assuaged the national conscience regarding the poor and eased the pressure on the shaky revenue structure of the states. The states, however, still had to raise more money to match the federal portion. By then, private and nonprofit insurance agencies were supplying 42 percent of the charges of day-to-day operations of the hospitals and 30 percent of physicians' services, and government was paying for 38 percent of the hospital charges and 6 percent of the physicians services, mainly surgery. The stage was set for a spectacular increase in both price and use. There were no built-in controls on cost. The health services enterprise had become accustomed to being paid what it asked, and the funding sources did not demur because employees, employers, and Congress did not demur either. From 1950 to 1965, expenditures as a percent of gross national product rose from 4.6 to 5.9. Expenditures per capita for all services rose from $78 to $198 without accounting for inflation, which was quite moderate during that period. The private insurance agencies and the government teamed up, as it were, to assure a health service where cost would be of no consequence.

Concurrently, the proportion of people 65 years of age and over was increasing, particularly those 75 years and older. Ineluctably associated with aging is chronic illness and disability and increasing helplessness, overtaxing family financial resources for their elderly. By the 1950s, the expenditure for nursing homes had become a visible portion of the national medical dollar. Only a small portion of this cost, however, could be afforded by direct-pay patients. Public medical assistance for the indigent in nursing homes became a prime source of funding day-to-day operations, which was later buttressed greatly by the Medicaid Act of 1965. True to the U.S. tradition, the market for nursing homes was met largely by the private sector, both profit and nonprofit, with standards set by the states along with the federal Medicaid and Medicare programs. Since the government was incapable or unwilling to supply nursing home beds in sufficient quantity to meet the demand and need, it bought services from the private sector. As with general hospitals, government paid most of what the nursing homes were charging in an affluent economy. Resistance, however, began to appear in the third and last period of development.

THE PERIOD FROM 1965 ONWARD

It was not until the latter 1960s that there began to be general concern by the big buyers of services—government, employers, and labor unions, as well as insurance and prepayment agencies—with the rising expenditure for personal health services, usually referred to as escalating or spiraling costs. Particularly alarming was the pace of the increase, with costs rising faster than that for the economy as a whole as reflected in the consumer price index. The general public was mainly interested in reducing out-of-pocket expenditures, and the buyers of services were interested in keeping reimbursements to providers and insurance premiums low. Hospital expenditures were rising at the dizzying pace of 15 percent annually. Expenditures for physicans' services were close behind. Providers said the increase in expenditures was justified in large part because of improved services and increased use as well as rising labor costs in a labor-intensive enterprise. While no one knew what was an appropriate level of expenditures, there seemed to be general agreement that the contemporary level of expenditures was too high. The theories of costs and expenditures were as primitive as this level of thinking.

It should be noted that the phenomenon of rising costs of health services is not peculiar to the comparatively open and pluralistic U.S. system. The same phenomenon appears in all industrialized countries regardless of funding sources, ownership, and organizational structures. Personal health services are very popular everywhere. In the United States, health services exploded with no obvious potential checks at the time other than what premiums and taxes would bear. Systems abroad also exploded, but they were a part of implicit, if not explicit, political decisions. Budget caps were at least potentially possible given the political will.

This period was thus characterized by an intense concern with how to manage the health service enterprise so that buyers would know what they are buying and providers would know what they are selling. The wide-open era of simply paying what the providers asked was seriously questioned. The payment mechanism was to be used to manage the system rather than act as a mere paying agency. Three methods to do so were to emerge, largely in the following order: monitoring of physician decision making in hospitals, control of hospital beds, and control of hospital reimbursement rates.

Attempts at rationalization—to use an economic term—of personal health services were expressed mainly in the group practice prepayment plans described previously, but they were not simply a means of saving money but one of providing high-quality and comprehensive services efficiently and conveniently. It seemed that saving money was a secondary, although acknowledged consideration. Likewise, the scores of hospital planning councils that were established in the major cities and sponsored by local hospitals and funded in large part by the then Department of Health, Education and Welfare (now the Department of Health and Human Services) were aimed less at saving money as much as at systematizing hospital relationships and cooperation on a local level. Gross duplication of services and equipment, such as cobalt bombs across the street from each other or maternity beds in all hospitals, in the face of a declining birth rate were the objects of attention and interhospital discussions. The council concept was intended to serve as an information clearinghouse on the hospital situation in local areas, the presumption being that the hospitals would recognize their mutual self-interest and survival. These councils may have had other effects, but evidence showed that the reduction in the duplication of services or stablization of the bed supply was not among them.

The seeming lack of success of the hospital council concept led to establishment of the federal Comprehensive Health Planning (CHP) program that incorporated many of the hospital planning councils as agents of the state and was directed at facility planning. A concurrent federal endeavor, also through the states, was the Regional Medical Program (RMP) that aimed at the delivery of services for heart disease, cancer, stroke, and related diseases. It attempted to relate practicing physicians to medical schools and major medical centers whereby they could benefit from the latest knowledge concerning these diseases and refer patients more rapidly. Saving money was not a primary concern; rather, it was hoped that physicians' services might be better integrated. Again, both CHP and RMP failed to accomplish the hardly explicit objectives set for the programs.

In the meantime, expenditures increased apace; the internal and external dynamics of this tremendous growth enterprise was indeed awesome. Two prestigious government commissions, one on so-called hospital effectiveness (1968) followed by one on Medicaid or medical care for the poor (1970) were appointed. The latter expanded its vague charge to consider the entire delivery structure and its problems. The tone in both reports was confusion and frustration, as well there might be. They were ambiguous toward planning and distressed by the prospect of further government intervention, although helpless to suggest anything else. The Medicaid report, however, did begin to refer to competition between delivery options as a means of containing rising expenditures.

More specific attempts at containing expenditures, however, were expressed in the Medicare Act and also applied to Medicaid. In the Medicare Act there was mandated by law the creation of utilization review of physicians' decisions as to length of stay in hospitals; that is, direct monitoring of professional decision making. From the medical profession's viewpoint this was a radical step.

At the state level, legislature after legislature began to pass laws calling for issuance of certificates of need for hospital beds. The building of new hospitals or the expansion or renovation of old hospitals had to be approved by a state planning agency, a control on supply. Also, in state after state, legislation began to be passed to regulate hospital rate setting, a control on price.

In addition, as an outgrowth of the utilization review mandate in 1965, Congress passed a law requiring utilization review of hospital care, that is, physician decision making on an areawide basis by committees (professional standards review organization) made up of physicians. These are now largely in operation. To cap all these developments, Congress passed the Health Planning Act (PL 93-641) in 1974 mandating the creation of over 200 health planning areas administered by health service agencies (HSAs) whose board of governors was to be comprised of a majority of consumers. Consumers were to be appointed by racial, ethnic, income, and area criteria. The health services agencies were to pass on the appropriateness of hospital construction, distribution, and renovation and the purchasing policies of hospitals regarding expensive equipment such as computed tomography (CT) scanners. Further, the health service agencies were to measure health needs in their areas in a master plan according to federal guidelines to be passed up to counterpart state and federal agencies for review and consideration. Congressional intent was to place need determination and control of facility construction at the local level. Needs, as determined by health service agencies, would then be submitted to upper levels of state and federal government. Upper levels of government could then react in terms of their funds and priorities and work out compromises. Congress and perhaps even the bureaucracy were exceedingly chary of imposing a blueprint on the states and local areas, preferring to set up fairly loose guidelines for discussion. It was apparently Congress' intent to put a planning apparatus in place before the enactment of some form of national health insurance so as to have a framework in which to implement such legislation and to have a handle on costs and the direction of the development of the personal health services. Certificate of need and rate control, although state level functions, were in effect turned over to the health service agencies for decision. The state normally respects health service agencies' decisions, and both state and federal governments can withhold payment from hospitals that do not comply. Even so, the current planning apparatus does not seem to have a firm place in national political policy, and the Reagan administration may abolish it altogether. The states, of course, may do as they please to continue supporting the health service agencies using state funds.

The latest approach now being presented—old as a concept but relatively new in terms of government support to contain the cost escalation—is the Health Maintenance Organization (HMO). Health Maintenance Organizations embody several types of prepayment plans that attempt to monitor physican decision making, a fixed premium for comprehensive services, and a known population. These plans have shown that they use hospital services less than the mainstream fee-for-service system and hence tend to cost less. The free enterprise competition concept is thus being carried over to health services delivery by encouraging choice of plans among employed groups with the hope that competition between options will slow the rise in health service costs.

In the meantime, despite Professional Standards Review Organization (PSRO) certificate of need, rate review, and planning, the personal health services economy still grows, expenditures continue to rise, and attempts to manage the system do not seem to have much effect. Between 1965 and 1980, the percent of the gross national product spent for all health services increased from 6.2 to 9.5. The per capita expenditure increased from $217 to $1078. The ultimate weapon, of course, is for the big buyers of services to refuse to provide more money—in short, budget caps—but the pluralistic nature of the funding sources makes this method difficult even though the government is now the source of 40 percent of all expenditures for personal health services. Congress, until recently, has not seen fit to enter into drastic retrenchments, but the time has come.

OBSERVATIONS

In our earlier work, *The Uneasy Equilibrium, Private and Public Financing of Health Service in the United States, 1875–1965* (Anderson 1968), we traced the origin and evolution of government involvement in medical care in the United States up to the passage of Medicare and Medicaid. This chapter is a rethinking and retrospective reformulation of that book. It makes the first and second stages (1875–1930 and 1930–1965) more explicit and adds a third stage beginning about 1965, thus offering a completely new dimension to the analysis of the internal and external dynamics of a modern health services system over 100-year period.

The Medicare and Medicaid programs added to voluntary health insurance increasingly funded by employers opened up vast and virtually uncontrolled resources for increased expenditures. The government still does not own the hospitals, nor does it want to make physicians into salaried employees, nor would Congress ever enact such a plan in the foreseeable future. Thus, the private sector, if it is politically astute in playing the cross currents of the political game in which Congress is so reluctant to set up a highly structured system, will continue to be a counterweight to government "intervention." It seemingly will be encouraged to do so by the Reagan administration. The term "intervention" still implies that government is interfering in a normal situation—because the American people want choices, convenience of access, and the latest technology rather than low cost. Again, the Reagan administration is taking the concept of intervention literally and is trying to reduce its application. The current administration is worrying not so much about the total cost of health services, as to how to have a smaller proportion of this cost in the federal budget.

The equilibrium between the private and public sectors is now as uneasy as it has ever been. It is not clear to either hospitals or physicians to what extent the current government sources of funds for Medicare and Medicaid will be reduced—although it appears to be drastic relative to past funding—or what it means to the current health services whose infrastructure has been built up to the level of the generous funding from all sources. Equity rather than economy was the pervasive sociopolitical objective, and equity is expensive if the badly off are not to reduce the access of the well off. At least to the extent desired during the 1960s, the equity issue is now not as politically prominent nor, apparently, as politically necessary. Cost containment and reducing the government's share of expenditures are now the issues. The evidence is the Reagan administration's clear attempts to weaken the National Health Planning Act and the PSRO activities to monitor physician decision making.

To the extent, however, that the Reagan administration will encourage competition and consumer choice in the hope that this will contain costs, the United States will find that consumers will place a very high priority on personal health services. Although big employers tacitly supported by government may collude with the government to put a cap on expenditures in the private sector as well, in the long run it may be a plausible prediction that employers will throw up their hands and decide to push the whole problem of costs back to government in the form of universal health insurance. For only through government is it possible to put an arbitrary cap on costs for a service that appears to have an insatiable demand as experienced so far. A safe prediction is that the share of the gross national product going to the health services will hit 12 to 15 percent within the next 5 years from all sources, private as well as public, reflecting the people's desires to spend that much on their health care.

BIBLIOGRAPHY

The following is an alphabetical list of the major sources of material for this chapter. Detailed documentation of the actions of interest groups, government commissions, and trends can be found in the three books under Andersen below (1968, 1972, 1976).

American Medical Association, *The Story of America's Medical Schools*, Chicago: The Association, 1960.

Andersen, Ronald, Joanna Lion and Odin W. Anderson, *Two Decades of Health Services: Social Survey Trends in Use and Expenditure*, Cambridge: Ballinger, 1976.

Anderson, Odin W., *The Uneasy Equilibrium; Private and Public Financing of Health Services in the United States, 1875–1965*, New Haven: College and University Press, 1968.

Anderson, Odin W., *Health Care: Can There Be Equity? The United States, Sweden and England*, New York: John Wiley & Sons, 1972.

Anderson, Odin W., *Blue Cross Since 1929; Accountability and the Public Trust*, Boston: Ballinger Publishing Co., 1976.

Anderson, Ronald, Joanna Lion and Odin W. Anderson, *Two Decades of Health Services: Social Survey Trends in Use and Expenditure*, Cambridge: Ballinger Publishing Co., 1976.

Asgis, Alfred J., *Professional Dentistry in American Society: A Historical and Social Approach to Dental Progress*, New York: Clinical Press, 1941.

Boorstin, Daniel J. *The Genius of American Politics*, Chicago: University of Chicago Press, 1953.

Burrow, James, *A.M.A., Voice of American Medicine*, Baltimore: Johns Hopkins Press, 1963.

Carter, Richard, *The Gentle Legions*, Garden City, N.Y.: Doubleday, 1961.

Committee on the Costs of Medical Care, No. 28. *The Final Report of the Committee on the Costs of Medical Care*, adopted October 21, 1932. Chicago: University of Chicago Press, 1933.

Committee on the Grading of Nursing Schools, *Nurses, Patients, and Pocketbooks. Report of a Study of the Economics of Nursing*, New York: The Committee, Fall 1928.

Connery, Robert H. et al., *The Politics of Mental Health: Organizing a Community Mental Health in Metropolitan Areas*, New York: Columbia University Press, 1968.

Corwin, E. A. L., *The American Hospital*, New York: Commonwealth Fund, 1946.

Dahl, Robert A., *Pluralist Democracy in the United States—Conflict and Consent*, Chicago: Rand McNally, 1967.

Davids, Michael M. and Andrew R. Warner, *Dispensaries: Their Management and Development*, New York: Macmillan, 1918.

Davis, Karen and Cathy Schoen, *Health and the War on Poverty; a Ten-year Appraisal*, Washington, D.C.: The Brookings Institution, 1978.

Dietrick, John E. and Robert C. Berson, *Medical Schools in the United States at Mid-Century*, New York: McGraw-Hill, 1953.

Duffy, John, *The Healers, the Rise of the Medical Establishment*, New York: McGraw-Hill, 1976.

Enthoven, Alain C., *Health Plan: The Only Practical Solution to the Soaring Cost of Medical Care*. Reading, Mass.: Addison-Wesley Publishing Co., 1980.

Falk, I. J., Margaret Klem and Nathan Sinai, *The Incidence of Illness and the Receipt and Cost of Medical Care Among Representative Families: Experiences in Twelve Consecutive Months During 1928–31*, Committee on the Costs of Medical Care, No. 26, Chicago: University of Chicago Press, 1933.

Falkson, Joseph L., *HMO's and the Politics of Health System Reform. Chicago:* American Hospital Association, 1980.

Flexner, Abraham, *Medical Education in the United States and Canada; A Report to the Carnegie Foundation for the Advancement of Teaching*, New York: Carnegie Foundation, 1910, Bulletin No. 4.

Gibson, Robert M. and Marjorie Smith Mueller, "National Health Expenditures, Fiscal Year, 1976," *Social Security Bulletin*, Vol. 40, April 1977, pp. 2–22.

Gunn, Selskar M. and Philip S. Platt, *Voluntary Health Agencies: An Interpretative Study*. New York: Ronald Press, 1945.

Jamieson, Elizabeth M. and Mary F. Sewall, *Trends in Nursing History; Their Relationship to World Events*, Philadelphia: W. B. Saunders Co., 1954, 4th edition.

Lowi, Theodore. *The End of Liberalism: Ideology, Policy, and the Crisis of Public Authority*, New York: W. W. Norton & Co., 1969.

Luft, Harold S., *Health Maintenance Organizations; Dimensions and Performance*, New York: John Wiley & Sons, 1981.

Marmor, Theodore R. and Jan S. Marmor, *The Politics of Medicare*, London: Routledge Kegan Paul, 1970.

Means, James Howard, *Doctors, People, and Government*, Boston: Little Brown & Company, 1953.

Mustard, Harry S., *Government in Public Health*, New York: Commonwealth Fund, 1941.

The President's Commission on the Health Needs of the Nation, *Building American Health*, 1952, Vol. 1.

Roberts, Mary M., *American Nursing: History and Interpretation*, New York: Macmillan, 1954.

Rosen, George, *A History of Public Health*, New York: M. D. Publications, 1958.

Shryock, Richard H., *The Development of Modern Medicine*, London: Gollanez,1948.

Shryock, Richard H., *Medicine and Society in America 1660–1860*, New York: New York University Press, 1960.

Sinai, Nathan and Odin W. Anderson, *E.M.I.C., A Study of Administrative Experience*, Ann Arbor: Michigan School of Public Health, University of Michigan, 1948, Bureau of Public Health Economics Research Series No. 3.

Sonnedecker, Glenn, Revision of Kremers and Urdang, *History of Pharmacy*, Philadelphia: J. B. Lippincott Co., 1976, 4th edition.

Stern, Bernhard, *American Medical Practice in the Perspectives of a Century*, New York: Commonwealth Fund, 1945.

"The Truman Memoirs," *Life* Vol. XL, January 13, 1956, p. 104.

Williams, Ralph C., *The United States Public Health Services, 1798–1950*, Bethesda, Md.: Commissioned Officers Association, U.S. Public Health Services, 1951.

Witte, Edwin E., *The Development of the Social Security Act*, Madison: University of Wisconsin Press, 1962.

CHAPTER 4

Implications and Consequences of Government Involvement in Health and Health Care

Lloyd F. Detwiller

The increase in wealth of many nations since World War II has provided the economic means for these nations to solve some of society's moral dilemmas brought about by the uneven distribution of resources among people. Therefore, the idea of Mill and Rousseau that certain basic social benefits should accrue to citizens of a civilized society because of their membership in that society might now be realized.

GOVERNMENT-SPONSORED HEALTH CARE

Since World War II, health care has been chosen by many countries as a basic social benefit, and many governments have embarked on hospital and/or medical care programs. Unfortunately, few of them have thought through a national policy on health. For the most part, policies that at the time of their implementation seemed proper had built-in, long-term problems that were not recognized. The result has been problems with health delivery today.

In North America, universal and comprehensive health care as the citizen's right has been the battle cry of politicians seeking the vote since the early 1930s, especially since World War II. In Europe, the trend began in Germany in the 1860s, with many variations in form and content in other European countries, culminating with the National Health Service in Great Britain in 1948.

Great advances in medical care have been accompanied by comparable increases in cost, which when promised to all, have resulted in fiscal requirements for health services that have paled the strongest of politicians. This is especially the case in the Western democracies, where increasing segments of their economies are changing from the production of goods to the provision of services, with government becoming the major producer of these services.

Bereft of the need to show profit, which is the basis of economic survival in the voluntary free enterprise marketplace, governments have continued to expand their public service programs. This, in turn, has required more taxes in order to provide the social capital necessary to support such programs.

NORTH AMERICAN SOCIETY

North American society is basically individualistic. Government exists to help the individual, not the reverse. Services obtained through governments are intended to be those best provided on a group basis or are for individuals who are not able to look after themselves.

However, great care must be taken in setting out the extent of government participation in order to ensure that the rights of the individual are not usurped by societal action. By the same token, the expectations of the populace must not be raised too high for fear that the government may not be able to provide the services that are expected of it.

There is a fine balance between the two that represents the difference between self-responsibility on the part of the individual in a democratic state and the role of government in a government-directed welfare state.

In many of the Western democracies, health care is one of those services that has changed from an individual responsibility to a governmental one. This is the direct result of political parties promising health care as a right in return for political support. Many governments that have sponsored such health plans are now faced with serious health care cost problems because they were not able to envisage the long-term ramifications of this policy. This was not the result of neglect on their part, rather it occurred mainly because there was not the experience on which to make a considered judgment.

Because of the basic differences between the premise of individualism, hence self-responsibility for health care, and the welfare state in which health is a government responsibility (which the term "right" implies), government-sponsored health systems have had difficulty in fitting into the economic and social fabric of Western democracies. By offering unlimited service to an insatiable public demand, the cost of living up to the political promise has been so great that the health systems have become controversial political issues and, in some instances, liabilities rather than the assets that their proponents thought they would be when they introduced them.

In the short term and especially in times of affluence, they were politically beneficial. Where prosperity declined and tax revenues fell, government-sponsored health systems began to make up an increasing and alarming proportion of the government's budget at the expense of other services.

SYSTEM COST CONTROLS

In programs in which co-insurance, deductibles, and other forms of system self-adjustment were built into the plans in the beginning, the impact of the reduced government revenues was softened. However, if such controls were not part of the original government health program, they were seldom introduced when the plans got into financial trouble, simply because it was not politically expedient to do so.

Instead, governments have attempted to solve their rapidly rising health costs by other methods, hoping to bring their systems under control by regulating the producers of health services rather than the consumers. Even this tactic has failed to bring about the desired reduction in cost escalation. Now, other means are being attempted that involve the consumer. Specifically, governments (e.g., Canada) are attempting to have the populace change its lifestyle, since the majority of illnesses now appear to be directly related to modern-day living. Up to the present, most of these measures have been proposed on a voluntary basis. However, the suggestion is now being made that if individuals are unwilling to change their lifestyles, they may have to be required to do so if they are to be eligible to obtain the full benefit of the government-sponsored health care plan.

Should this happen, there is bound to be a reaction from those individuals who hold dear the concept of total individual freedom. In fact, this rebellion is now occurring in Canada and the United States where government intervention is becoming more evident. Although government intervention may be an acceptable action for many areas such as pollution control and seat belt legislation, it remains to be seen how acceptable it will be if it is applied to overall lifestyle. Articles and editorials on this issue are increasing and are serving to alert the populace of the confrontation and debate that lies ahead (*The Province*, 1978).

Government is oriented to the general welfare of the people, whereas health professionals are oriented to the welfare of the individual at a particular moment. Thus, the government's point of view of spending the tax dollar so as to do the most good for the greatest number of people is, in a way, in opposition to the professional viewpoint of doing everything possible for the individual patient.

Similarly, government must seek the approval of the total community. In other words, the government must evaluate the general desires of a nonprofessional public for political reasons, whereas the health professionals and facilities must satisfy the demands of a select and demanding consumer patient public.

Where government supplies the social capital necessary to run the health system, it may be ultimately necessary for it to dictate the lifestyle. This would seem logical if behavior has the greatest effect on demands for health care and, hence, the cost of meeting the demands. This is especially so if such demands are to be satisfied through a single government health program, with no alternative voluntary plan to share the load.

Examples of such a controlled lifestyle can be found in the USSR and China, where the government controls the economic and social life of the people through regulation of their working conditions, housing, travel, and so on. The belief and adherence to individual freedoms in Western democracies have denied this degree of government lifestyle control, but if the extension of government programs into daily living is continued the same type of centralized control that is seen in these other countries will appear in Western countries.

The term "reasonable manner" has been used in describing how a health system should be used (*Times-Colonist*, 1982). However, the term raises one of the major problems in the design of such a system. Whose criteria are to be followed in the definition of "reasonable manner"? Are the criteria to be those of the individuals seeking treatment, those of the producers of health services, those of the government promising the service, or those of the financiers?

If the money necessary to fund the system come entirely from government, it is going to be the government whose criteria will finally be used! The old adage, He who pays the piper calls the tune, is as applicable to the health system as it is elsewhere in society.

CANADIAN SYSTEMS

In Canada, despite centralized governmental controls, the costs of the Canadian health systems have escalated as elsewhere. There is no doubt that this escalation was the prime reason why the federal authority began to take steps to change its 50 percent cost-sharing formulas as far back as 1971. Not only did the federal government want to level off its degree of financial participation, but it also wanted to shift the problem of systems control to the provinces.

Whereas it was hoped that this change in the financing formula would encourage the provinces to experiment with the delivery system, especially with the primary and custodial levels of care, its most important proposed policy change would be that the provinces would have to bear the full brunt of any extraordinary expenditures that would result if they could not level off the health cost spiral.

The provinces, on the other hand, were resistive to the proposal of the federal government to shift the cost control problem to the provincial level. They pointed out that, in some instances, they had only entered the national plan after manipulation and pressure from the federal government. Why should the provinces, then, look after the unwanted child for the rest of its life, especially when its future demands were bound to increase? The federal authority, as one of the parents, should stay in the marriage unless the separation was mutually acceptable.

In late spring 1976, the federal government proposed a new Equalization Payment Fund to the provinces, which set out a new set of federal and provincial agreements covering hospital and medicare plans, as well as postsecondary education. The government financial aid would be in the form of a per capita cash grant that would be tied to the gross national product along with income tax points. In the case of health, this would replace the 50 percent sharing of provincial health system costs by the federal government.

This formula, with modifications to meet special circumstances for certain provinces, was signed by the federal and provincial governments, which made it more necessary than ever that the provincial governments bring their health care systems under close financial control.

HEALTH CARE AS A RIGHT

As the financing problems of health care systems have increased, the question has been raised as to how and when governments assumed the responsibility for this service. Government's increasing involvement in the field of health stems from the belief that all citizens are entitled to good health care. This humanitarian concept has now been extended to the point where it is being regarded as a right—a right with unlimited availability. There is a fine distinction between a person's health, which is undoubtedly mainly a personal responsibility, and health care, which is a service provided in part by the person but more likely received from health professionals.

A freely exercisable and unlimited right that is universally available cannot help but have important economic consequences. Rights operate much like bank deposits in a reserve system; the system works only as long as all people do not decide to exercise their individual rights simultaneously. Social rights must have social responsibility to limit them; whereas economic resources, unlike rights, are always limited and have a different basis for their allocation.

It is difficult to see how health care can be considered a basic right, comparable to the freedom of speech, the right to worship, and so on, desirable as it may be. Health care is dependent on the service being provided by others and would be impossible to obtain if the health worker refused to provide it. How could government guarantee health care as a right when the service depends on others? In reality, health care is a service that a society may wish to bestow upon itself, but in so doing the society must forego other benefits that might have been provided in its place. This is a rational choice and perhaps a most reasonable one, but it must be recognized for what it is—a political choice. In dealing with a trivial item, the question of right would not be significant; but with health care, society is undertaking a gigantic task.[1]

UNIVERSAL AND COMPREHENSIVE COVERAGE

Another concept in need of assessment is universality. It is attractive, politically, to talk of universality, implying one class of service for all citizens, provided through a single delivery system. On the other hand, the use of a single delivery system denies the person who is prepared to devote a greater portion of resources to health care the opportunity of doing so. The experiences in the United States, Great Britain, Germany, Canada, and elsewhere suggest that neither a completely market-oriented health care system nor an absolute government monopoly, but perhaps a mixture of the two, provides the best way to deliver health care on a national basis.

Universal and comprehensive coverage in the complete sense of the word is not possible in the light of continued advances in health care and the logistics of delivering this service, to say nothing of the cost. When the best health care is promised to everybody, the promise loses its credibility even though it is difficult in today's brokerage politics to offer anything else.

The health care systems of most countries are not self-adjusting and are directed by centralized administrative controls. Usually these controls have failed to keep their costs within acceptable limits, a fact dramatized by the public's outcry but even more so by the governmental rebellion against rising health costs in recent years.

PROBLEMS OF COVERAGE

For the first time in history, the natural law of survival of the fittest is being replaced by man-made legislation that modifies the natural survival process through the application of medical technology or theraputic processes or devices in accordance with the decisions of people. Since demand now exceeds the supply of services, health programs are becoming rationing systems, with the problems of eligibility and entry becoming more important to the individual, perhaps, than new ways of treating disease (Fuchs, 1975). Who is going to get the kidney when only one is available? What are the criteria on which the decision will be based—the highest bidder, good looks, best citizen, parent of

---

[1]For further elaboration on this point, see Detwiller, 1972; Sade, 1971; Chapman and Talmadge, 1970.

a large family, political influence, and so on—assuming that medical acceptance is equal?

The drug interferon, which costs thousands of dollars per treatment, and such diagnostic and treatment devices as computerized axial tomography, positron emission tomography, and nuclear magnetic resonance scanners, which cost $1.5 million each, represent only the beginning of the cost potential that accounts in part for the tremendous increase in health care cost in recent years. A nation may be prepared to support these types of treatment and pieces of equipment as isolated events and/or items connected with research, but to make them available to the total population through a government-sponsored system promising universal and comprehensive health care as a right is quite another matter.

In the past, policymakers have not analyzed their slogans and statements in depth and all too often have been prepared to accept the political and popular misinterpretation of phraseology. This might be acceptable in the short term until the next election but prove to be very troublesome over a longer period of time.

IMPLICATIONS OF THE RIGHT CONCEPT

The promise of government that all people have a right to health care suggests more than a simple interest or preference on the part of the individual. A claim of right suggests an entitlement that a person can demand to have, unless that right is modified by some type of qualification that sets out the conditions under which the principle does not apply. If this is not done, any service considered a right to one person or group must be provided to all regardless of inconvenience, cost, and so on. Moreover, even if the service is provided for all, the next question is whether or not it is of equal quality for all.

If equality is to be the case, it may be necessary to lower the present quality of service to some people in order to have an equal quality of care for everybody, even though there are many people who are prepared to pay for higher quality themselves as a matter of personal preference.

Taken even further, if the amount of social capital going into the health program were totally committed to the delivery system and there was little likelihood of this being increased, people might look unfavorably on research into the development of new health care treatments, simply because there would not be the capital to provide the new treatments to all the population as its right. Carried to the extreme, this would eliminate or seriously reduce research and development of new drugs and procedures that might eradicate a disease or reduce the length of treatment thereby alleviating suffering as well as achieving marked savings in the patient care process.

Denying alternative sources of capital to finance health programs and restricting financial support to the government, prevents those who are willing and able to pay for research, development, and treatment from doing so simply because the same type and level of care has to be available to everybody. Much needed capital is thus denied to the system.

If differences in other sectors of the society, that is, food, clothing, housing, are allowed, why not in health care? Governments do not promise steaks, silk suits, and penthouses to the whole population as a right. Rather, it is willing and receives the support of the population to have differences in the quality and quantity of items that individuals are able to obtain for themselves or are provided to them by government. Why then must there be the same standard of health care for everybody?

Such a notion is part of the Judeo-Christian heritage. But it may no longer be applicable in the pure sense in today's society because of the phenomenal cost of providing all of the benefits of twentieth-century health care to the total population. Perhaps there will soon be a time when people will acknowledge that there needs to be different levels in quality and access in health care delivery simply because of the limited funds made available for this service.

EFFECT OF ECONOMIC RECESSION

In Canada, a welfare state has been created that is similar in many ways to that in Britain and Sweden. Because of the prosperity since World War II, Canada has adopted social programs that are now taxing its population's willingness and perhaps ability to pay for them. Productivity has not kept pace with the charitable social conscience and the country is in trouble because of the current depression.

The social promises of the provincial and federal governments of the 1950s and 1960s are coming back to haunt the people, since the governmental revenues of today are falling far short of the cost of the unemployment insurance plans and welfare programs to say nothing of health care and education. As unemployment increases, an ever-increasing proportion of the population is drawing on its unemployment insurance benefits. As these benefits run out, people are shifting to welfare programs that, in turn, shifts the cost of health care to the government.

The demand for health benefits continues despite the depression so that the cost of the programs becomes increasingly difficult for the government to meet. The monies from income and sales tax, as well as the myriad of other sources of revenue that previously supported the social programs have, in some provinces, dropped so precipitously that the benefits of some programs have not only been reduced but, in fact, canceled (e.g., the decision by the provincial government of British Columbia to cancel its dental program).

The use of social programs for political purposes and the difficulty in administering them equitably is not new. This is especially true when the programs are concerned with the judgment of the individual regarding the demand and/or satisfaction of a personal service such as health.

SOCIAL PROGRAM DILEMMA

When Henry IV of France was crowned King in 1589, he made the following statement, obviously designed to obtain public support for himself at a time when the economy of the country was at a low ebb: "If God grants me the usual length of life I hope to make France so prosperous that every peasant will have a chicken in his pot on Sunday." A shorter version of this, "a chicken in every pot", served as the campaign slogan of the Republican party in the United States during the depression in 1932 (Bartlett, 1955).

While it could be debated what type of chicken should be provided, who would qualify as a peasant, and so on, such determinations are all capable of definition, and hence a calculation could be made of the probable cost of such a political promise. This would not be the case if the king had said that no one would go hungry or everyone would be provided with sufficient food to satisfy his or her appetite. It could not even be questioned whether the intent was to satisfy the appetite barely, moderately, or fully. Since the measure of this is a personal matter, it would be very difficult to discharge such a political commitment, much less develop a mechanism that would evaluate the degree of satisfaction. Add to this the question of whether the process of satisfaction was to be achieved by eating bread and water, peanut butter sandwiches, caviar, roast chicken, baked Alaska, or all of these, and the difficulty of dealing with promises of personal service that have to do with individual values and senses begins to be understood. Demand, under the satisfaction of having an appetite fully satisfied, could be as insatiable and as difficult to meet or control as is the demand for health care today when promised as a right at total government expense.

The constitution of the World Health Organization (WHO) defines health as a state of complete physical, mental, and social well-being, not merely the absence of infirmity. Although this definition, with its terms of "complete physical, mental, and social well-being," is a desirable societal goal, it is difficult to define in concrete terms what is meant by the phrase. Moreover, how is this to be achieved or measured? Whose criteria are to be used? These are very personal and individual first-party judgments, and any attempt to deal with them on a group or third-party basis is difficult.

There is no doubt that the existing affluent society and complex lifestyle have greatly affected the incidence of illness. Unfortunately, it is believed that an individual's health can be abused in any way, and that when bodies are ravaged, people need only go into the health system, have them repaired, and then repeat the process all over again, at no cost or sacrifice to themselves. It is this increasing demand for care that, when reflected in cost, is causing concern to all financing authorities, especially governments. Whether this demand is justified or not is a matter for conjecture, since the true need for care is probably quite different from the demand that is often the result of individual whim or suggestion by third-party individuals.

INFLUENCE OF THIRD-PARTY PREPAYMENT

Since demand is first initiated by the individual in response to a symptom, the volume of demand can vary greatly depending on the priority that the individual assigns to personal health. If there is no need to make any decision as to whether or not something must be sacrificed if treatment is to be obtained, then there is no reason for the individual not to enter the system.

Such a demand process has been fostered through the intervention of third-party prepayment systems between the patient and provider of services. It has usually resulted in increased utilization, especially in the case of government programs. Add to this the urging of television and radio for everyone to see their doctor for any and all ailments, and it is easy to see why patient care demand has sky rocketed.

Prepayment has radically altered the environment of the marketplace in which the demand and supply of the health services have traditionally operated. Instead of asking the public to determine the use of health services through the usual economic considerations, a new approach based on ethical or moral considerations has been introduced. This approach is contrary to the usual practice of allowing the price principle to determine whether or not to purchase an article or service. To expect individuals to base decisions as to whether to seek a service on ethical or moral grounds when their ethics or morals are most likely different from those of their neighbours, suggests that this method of decision making inevitably leads to marked differences in use since there are marked differences in the ethics and morals of individuals.

By removing the necessity of having to forego other desirable items, the public's demand for health care is unleashed because it is believed it can now have health care as well as other desired items. This is the utopia promised to them by the politicians. By contrast, the patient will probably criticize the prepayment authority if it has to increase taxes (if the person is a taxpayer) or increase premiums (if the person is a policy holder) in order to meet the cost of the services that the patient has demanded. Such action could result in withdrawal of vote support or cancellation of the policy.

Third-party prepayment has shifted much of the use decision process from an individual and local level to a group and general welfare level. This change has also had an effect on the contracts among producers of health care, consumers, and financiers of the system. In the days when there was no prepayment insurance and the doctor dealt directly with the patient, there was a direct contractual agreement that the patient would reimburse the doctor in some manner for services rendered. This is not so in the majority of treatments today. Rather, the contract is between the patient and the insuring authority and then the insuring authority and the health service provider. Granted, the patient may be asked to make up a shortage of payment, but in many service policies, this element of the contract may not even be present. Under government prepayment plans, it is only necessary to trace the route of any complaints about services received to find the perceived social contract. Invariably, the complaints are lodged with the local politicians who entered into a political contract with the patient to provide service in return for a vote.

The politicians enter into agreements with the producers of health care to provide their politically promised services for a price, set or negotiated by the government, in line with the funds provided by the legislative branch. It is this regulation of service cost by government that has been the source of argument and confrontation between governments and producers of health services for years.

There is no doubt that government funds will continue to be required in the production of health services, but the proportion of the system costs that will be met from this source will probably vary from time to time in accordance with the wishes of the populace. However, because of increasing health costs, societies throughout the world are searching for ways to solve the health care cost problem. Thus, where there is no overall government plan, the private sector is being threatened with government intervention in order to provide care for everybody and bring costs under control. Conversely, where government plans are in place, private insurance mechanisms are being suggested in order to slow down the escalation of costs and abate consumer demand. In the case of the latter, there is the additional problem of making good the political promise of the best of health care for all, which accentuates the forces that are pushing costs skywards.

It may be that in the long run any government committed to a universal and comprehensive health care program as a political promise would be wise to consider some type of buffer mechanism that would modify the public's demand for the best possible health care in order that it can at least provide a high level of basic health services. If it does not, it may have to adopt other less popular alternatives.

Government should concentrate on health maintenance and prevention rather than only on acute sickness episodes. If this is not done, government may become so hard pressed by the health professions and the public, both directly and indirectly through the media and the ballot box, to continue to extend the system to include the new and expensive treatment programs, and also in such a volume, that it will have difficulty in providing basic essential services.

The long-term answer to insatiable demand may be providing the public with a choice between a private health system and a health care system guaranteed through government. In this way, the government could assure a good level of services, with individuals paying for services over and above the level provided in the government plan. This combination of voluntary and government systems exists in many countries, for example, England, Belgium, Sweden, and Australia.

Although such solutions may be of assistance to those authorities considering the introduction of government-sponsored health plans, the reality facing governments who have assumed full responsibility for the health systems may be that the populace is not yet prepared to take back some degree of self-responsibility.

EFFECT OF LIFESTYLE

From a political point of view, the action just described will probably be taken only after all other avenues have failed. For example, in Canada the proposal to change the lifestyle of the people and hence abate consumer demand has a doubtful future. It began in 1974, when the federal government turned its attention to the consumers of health services in order to do something about the ever-increasing health care costs. The working document, "A New Perspective on the Health of Canadians," published by the Minister of National Health and Welfare, marked a new phase in controls (Minister of National Health Welfare, 1974). Although it pointed out where the health problems lay, it did not contain the phrase "right to health care," suggesting that even then the federal authorities had begun to experience the practical problems of implementing the political policy of health care as a right. Rather, the document emphasized self-responsibility of individuals for their own health and the need for the populace to change its lifestyle.

Canada, of course, is not unique in this regard. Increasingly, health systems are treating diseases of choice or diseases of neglect that are a direct result of the lifestyle. There is an emerging opinion that the way to better health is not to spend more and more on a health care system that is strongly focused on the treatment and cure of illness (Knowles, 1976). In developed countries, it seems health no longer correlates with per capita income and, in fact, higher income seems to do more harm than good. The idea that people can spend their way to better health is vastly overrated. There is little that even modern medical science can do for a lung that has been destroyed by smoking, a skull crushed in an automobile accident, a liver that has ceased to function because of too much alcohol, or a heart attack or ulcer that is the result of too much stress. Yet these are the majority of cases being presented to the system and, in all too many instances, can be classified as provoked illness resulting from high living.

Unfortunately, people believe that the statistical probability for undesired events applies to others and for desired events applies to themselves. There are those, for example, who continue to smoke in the belief that since not every smoker gets lung cancer they will be the exception. Should cancer strike, however, will those people expect the highest quality of care to be immediately available, with little regard for the cost even though they had voted against an increase in health care premiums to improve the system only a short time ago?

Although the public must collectively (government) accept the responsibility for the increases in causes of sickness that are the direct result of a deteriorating environment (pollution), individuals must accept blame for the deleterious effect that their personal lifestyles have had on their health. Smoking, overeating, impaired driving, high living, and so on, all add to self-provoked illness, and hence there must be an acceptance of a greater degree of self-responsibility if these trends are to be changed.

To date, society (government) has not been prepared to implement penalties for those people who voluntarily provoke illness nor rewards for those who try to prevent it. Perhaps it is the right time to introduce incentives to reward health prevention and maintenance, as well as penalties against those who persist in a lifestyle that brings on illness. Although it is very difficult to evaluate the effectiveness of the "lifestyle change" programs to date, they have not been as successful as was hoped. Nevertheless, the growth of jogging and marathon running suggests that the public is perhaps beginning to recognize the problem and support the drive toward a better lifestyle.

CHANGE IN LIFESTYLE

Canada is not the only country concerned over the problem of lifestyle and health. In the USSR, where health care is free, there are articles recommending that the treatment of alcoholics in hospitals and clinics should be made chargeable (*The Province*, 1976). In the United States, health administrators have questioned whether or not Medicaid and Medicare or prepayment plans should pay for the treatment of individuals who self-impose a state of obesity or suffer from self-inflicted illness (Knowles, 1978). In the United Kingdom, recommendations are being made that "free national health assistance should not be given to people suffering from ill health resulting from overeating, drinking, or smoking (*The Province*, 1980).

As a matter of fact, it has been suggested by some (Malleson, 1974) that the day may not be that far off when the physician may only be prepared to treat you if "you cut down on booze, take more exercise and stop smoking." Yet think of the reaction of patients who are told this when their member of Parliament or legislature has guaranteed them all the health care they wish as their right. Now they are told that care is denied or will only be rendered and received if they live up to a set of rules that are being imposed by a party other than the one they entered into a contact with at the ballot box when they voted the member in on the ticket of health care as a right. This is why the original basic principles, on which governmental plans are based, are so important.

An important feature of asking the public to change its lifestyle is that the change makes the consumer/voter a customer/patient. This suggests a return in part to the type of cost-restraint mechanisms that have been so successful in other parts of society. However, when government begins to legislate the public's lifestyle in order to reduce its cost for a health system, care must be taken that such a course of action not be carried very far or it is likely to be resisted in a society that is basically individualistic in nature.

If governments are successful in their appeal to change people's lifestyle and hence lower health costs, this will be admirable. But if people do not respond, what then? The answer is probably to be found in the resolution of the confrontation that is beginning to emerge in Canada between the most influential group determining health costs (physicians) and the authority responsible for paying the health bill (government). This situation has become the subject of public debate, with governments suggesting that patients be given guidelines as "to when and when not to seek medical assistance" and that physicians should consider the cost benefits of annual checkups, and so on.

Organized medicine has responded to these proscriptions by stating that governments, not physicians are responsible for not only the financing of health care but the "mounting prices in health care costs" as well. In Canada, the medical profession has pointed out that the health system is completely open-ended and no checks or balances were built into the system to control an ever-increasing and insatiable demand on the part of the public for service.

The substance of this exchange of opinion is that the government is asking physicians to act as the government's financial watchdog, a role that is in conflict with that of physicians who desire to "do everything possible for the individual patient."

It is the rationing of limited resources to an insatiable demand that is perhaps the greatest challenge of the health care system today. It may be that the final resolution is to abate the consumer demand so that it will equate with the resources available.

The introduction of government into the health process has brought with it a host of new forces that have changed the basic structure on which the demand and supply of health services are based. Although some government health plans were developed on policies that had built in long-range problems, these difficulties were not apparent at the time of their inception. In some instances, they have taken decades to surface, simply because the jurisdiction concerned was prepared to pay the bill incurred until such time as the costs exceeded the political support for the program. When that point is reached (Canada is now well into this stage because of its economic depression), the political process of setting priorities for the services provided through government comes into effect. Funds are apportioned, and if they are not sufficient to support the health services demanded by the population, the rationing process comes into effect in one form or another or new sources of funding are sought after by both the producers of health care (physicians and hospitals) and the financiers (government).

As governments weigh the potential political backlash of increasing taxes for additional revenues or of permitting the producers of health care to raise part of their fees directly from patients, they began to change their perception of their responsibility for management of the health systems.

CHANGE IN PLAN ADMINISTRATION

Up until 1980–1982 senior health plan executives in Canada were usually drawn from the ranks of the health professionals whose jobs were to expand and improve programs. This usually meant higher costs, which was acceptable as long as the economy was buoyant. However, once government budgets became tight, governments began to replace the senior health professionals with individuals who had financial and managerial expertise rather than health experience. It was their jobs to hold down or reduce the health budget in accordance with the realities of reduced government revenues. In many instances, health plan control passed out of the hands of the Health Ministry to the Provincial Treasury Board, a pattern that was not confined to Health but that applied to many other Ministries as well.

At the same time and for obvious reasons, the government has tried to place responsibility for the extravagant costs on the producers of health care, arguing that the systems are inefficient and overadministered.

In desperation in the search for funds, one provincial government actually canceled a benefit program and transferred the subsequent savings ($30 million) to another part of the health system to maintain service. In British Columbia, physicans voluntarily turned back to the government over $30 million to assist the province in meeting its fiscal restraint program because of the depression (*The Province*, 1982a, 1982c).

HEALTH SYSTEM STRIKES

At the same time as these dramatic moves were taking place, hospital employees and physicians elsewhere were threatening to strike for higher wages, even though the awarding of such increases would mean fewer jobs in the system because the total income was fixed. Physicians in several provinces have had short withdrawal-of-service strikes in an attempt to improve the fee structures that they have negotiated with their respective provincial governments. In Ontario, the premier has suggested that doctors should accept a wage cut (*The Province*, 1982b). Although on the surface this activity does cause concern and disruption of services, it is the democratic way of determining the allocation of government revenues and fortunately is recognized as such by those responsible for the administration of the systems.

MAJOR ISSUES

Essentially, the struggle in Canada is between two basic issues: (1) the continued desire on the part of the federal government to impose a series of operating conditions on the provincial governments if the federal authority is going to continue to assist them financially with their health plans and (2) the reaction of the producers of health services to those conditions that place the provincial governments who operate the plans in a very difficult midway position.

CANADA HEALTH ACT

The vehicle to achieve the objectives of the federal authority is the newly proposed (1983) "Canada Health Act," which, at the time of this writing, is under review by the Canadian and provical health associations and the provincial governments (Begin, 1982).

The minister of National Health and Welfare for Canada has warned that because the majority of the provinces allows physicians to extra-bill patients and hospitals to impose user fees, the basic structure of the health plans in Canada is threatened. Exta-billing means that physicans charge patients an additional fee over and above that paid to the physicians by the provincial government in accordance with the regulated fee sched-ule. User fees are charges by hospitals of an amount in addition to the provincial plan per-diem rate paid for services rendered to its citizens (*The Province*, 1982d).

The new Canada Health Act should clarify and define conditions under which the Parliament of Canada can provide transfer payments to the provinces for health insurance programs and provide standards to measure how well the act works. The proposals contained in the act are divided into two parts: First, there are definitions for the four basic conditions of health insurance—universality, accessibility, comprehensiveness, and portability, and, second, there are potential mechanisms to assure Parliament that the standards in practice are being maintained.

REACTION TO THE CANADA HEALTH ACT

Although the Canadian Hospital Association (1982) is generally supportive of the goals of the legislation, it points out that the provincial governments (and the hospitals) will have to be convinced that the changes will improve the overall performance of the health care system with no infringements on their jurisdiction before they will support it (Ontario Hospital Association, 1982). The reaction of the Canadian Medical Association, on the other hand, stands in marked contrast (Canadian Medical Association, 1982; *The Province*, 1982e), claiming that if the minister's new Canada Health Act proposal is accepted, it will do the following:

Convert Canada's high-quality health care insurance program into state medicine.

Make the serious underfunding situation of the hospitals even worse and reduce the ability of hospitals to meet the needs and desires of the communities they serve.

Reduce the financial flexibility of provincial governments and their ability to finance health care.

In addition, it is obvious that the basic issues of private versus state control of medicine is again in the public arena.

Although this public controversy may give the impression that the Canadian health systems are in a state of disarray, such is not the case. They are delivering high-quality service, and although there are points at issue, these are to be expected in an evolving social system.

THE ISSUE

At issue is the degree of socialization, as well as the struggle for control of the system between not only the federal and provincial governments but the producers of service and their financiers. In the final analysis, perhaps, the most important long-term implication of introducing government funds into health systems is that it changes health care into a political service, with the degree of political intervention and control in direct ratio to the proportion of funds provided by government. It is the resolution of this involvement that Canada is working on at the present time.

Will Canada move toward greater government control, which seems to be the direction in which the federal authority is heading with its new Canada Health Act, or will it attempt to reintroduce more patient self-responsibility and local control, which seems to be the theme of the producers of health care, especially the physician? Time alone can tell.

REFERENCES

Bartlett, John, *Familiar Quotations*, Boston and Toronto: Little, Brown and Company, 1955, 13th and Centennial edition.

Begin, Monique, "The Honorable Monique, Opening Statement to the Conference of Federal and Provincial Ministers of Health," Ottawa, Ontario, May 26, 1982.

Canadian Hospital Association, "The New 'Canadian Health Act.' The Preliminary Position," Ottawa, Ontario, Canadian Hospital Association, September 20, 1982.

Canadian Medical Association, "The Canada Health Act," Entre Nous, Ottawa, Canada, Canadian Medical Association, November 15, 1982.

Chapman, Carleton B. and John M. Talmadge, "The Evolution of the Right to Health Concept in the United States," *Law and Contemporary Problems*, Vol. 35, Spring 1970, pp. 334–347.

Detwiller, Lloyd F., *The Consequences of Health Care Through Government*, Office of Health Care Finance, Sydney, Australia, October 1972.

Fuchs, Victor, *Who Shall Live? Health, Economics, and Social Choice*, New York: Basic Books, 1975.

Knowles, John H., *Doing Better and Feeling Worse: Health in the United States*, New York: WW Norton Co., 1976.

Knowles, John H., "Good Health as a Moral Obligation," *The Sun*, Vancouver, B.C., February 23, 1978.

Malleson, Andrew, "Are Doctors as Necessary as We Think?" *The Sun*, Vancouver, B.C., March 21, 1974.

Minister of National Health Welfare, "A New Perspective on the Health of Canadians," Ottawa, Ontario, April 1974.

Ontario Hospital Association," Submission of the Ontario Hospital Association on the Canada Health Act," Don Mills, Ontario, July 16, 1982.

The Province, "Drunk Should Pay Hospitals—Moscow," Vancouver, B.C., June 16, 1976.

The Province, "1984. If the Taxman Doesn't Get You, the Health Police Will," Vancouver, B.C., August 19, 1978.

The Province, "The Cost is Killing for U.K. Patients, London," Vancouver, B.C., March 3, 1980.

The Province, "Denticare Pulled, M.D. Fee Cut Urged," Vancouver, B.C., August 20, 1982a.

The Province, "Ontario Premier Urges Wage Cut for M.D.'s" Vancouver, B.C., September 27, 1982b.

The Province, "Doctors Approve Rebate," Vancouver, B.C., October 24, 1982c.

The Province, "Begin Hits Extra-Billing," Vancouver, B.C., November 8, 1982d.

The Province, "C.M.A. Mounts Lobby," Vancouver, B.C., November 19, 1982e.

Sade, Robert M., Medical Care As a Right: A Refutation," *New England Journal of Medicine*, Vol. 285, December 1971, pp. 1288–1292.

Times-Colonist, "Medical Rationing has Arrived," Victoria, B.C., June 3, 1982.

PART TWO

*Health Decision Making
and the Political Structure*

CHAPTER 5

Health Policy
and the Federal Executive

Eugene Feingold
George D. Greenberg

The federal health policymaking structure in the United States is fragmented, with a large number of health programs in many different agencies, both inside and outside the Department of Health and Human Services. The fragmentation of the policymaking structure of the executive branch reflects the diversity of power and interests that have emerged in the larger health policy system, as well as a fundamental lack of agreement among health interests on health systems goals. There is no consensus on the role of government or its programs vis-à-vis the private sector. The existence of many government programs, and especially the major financial programs of Medicaid and Medicare, creates the impression of an active government role and suggests the potential of an even more active one. The fragmentation and dispersal of those programs, both within and across departments, act in the classic U.S. tradition of checks and balances to restrain government activism. The result is that, on the one hand, government in the United States has less to do with health care delivery and financing than it does in most other Western industrialized countries, and on the other hand, its relatively limited role is large in an absolute sense and has increased rapidly in recent years.

After describing the array of federal agencies and programs, this chapter will review the evolution of the health policymaking structure within the Department of Health and Human Services, the largest federal health agency. Finally, the reasons for continued fragmentation, especially within the Public Health Service, will be assessed and recent administration proposals for block grants and changes in financing programs will be examined to consider their potential impact on the health policymaking structure.

FEDERAL HEALTH PROGRAMS

In 1798, Congress established the United States Marine Hospital Service to provide medical care for sick and disabled seamen. This exercise of the congressional power to regulate interstate and foreign commerce was the first health activity of the federal government and, with minor exceptions, its last for the next one- and one-third centuries—not surprising, in view of the fact that the Constitution did not expressly delegate any powers to the federal government in the area of health.

During the depression of the 1930s, the national government, faced with the collapse of the traditional local public assistance structure, introduced federal public assistance and social insurance programs, which included some financing of medical care. World War II also brought on some limited federal health care financing programs, as well as a major expansion of the military medical care system. However, it was not until after World War II that the federal government directly entered the health arena for the general public on a major scale.

The first postwar activity came in the form of resource building—federal grants for hospital construction and for biomedical research. During the 1950s, public assistance medical care programs were slowly expanded. In the 1960s, the flood began: subsidization of the education of health personnel, Medicaid, Medicare, comprehensive health planning, and a number of programs intended to reorganize the ways in which medical care was delivered—community mental health centers, comprehensive health services for children, neighborhood health centers in low-income areas, maternal and infant care programs, and regional medical programs. In the 1970s, the federal government, faced with a rapid increase in health care costs, tried to restrain the increase with the variety of regulatory measures. The effort at regulation, however, was superficial and ambivalent. Regulatory mechanisms were left largely in private or quasipublic hands, and regulatory tools were unsuccessful in dealing with the problems that faced the health care system.

MANY PROGRAMS IN MANY AGENCIES

The legacy of these activities of the last three and one-half decades is a large number of federal health programs, carried on by many different federal agencies. Many of these federal health programs overlap or affect each other significantly, although the staff of the agency responsible for a particular program often does not know very much about the related activities of other agencies. Efforts to coordinate this melange of activity have had little success. For example, when computed tomographic scanning came upon the scene in the mid-1970s, the congressional Office of Technology Assessment listed eight federal agencies and programs as having a role in assuring the quality of care with respect to computed tomography (CT) (the Bureau of Quality Assurance of the Health Care Financing Administration; the Bureau of Radiological Health, the Bureau of Medical Devices and Diagnostic Products, and the Bureau of Drugs of the Food and Drug Administration; the National Institutes of Health; the Environmental Protection Agency; the National Council on Radiation Protection and Measurements; and the Occupational Health and Safety Administration in the Department of Labor) and six agencies concerned with research on and development of CT scanning (the National Institutes of Health, the National Bureau of Standards in the Department of Commerce, the Energy Research and Development Administration, the National Aeronautical and Space Administration, the National Science Foundation, and the Veterans Administration).

This list of federal agencies concerned with computed tomography deals only with quality of care and research. It does not deal with the operation of hospitals where CT scanning might take place (involving federal agencies such as the Veterans Administration, the Defense Department, and the Public Health Service), nor with federal payment for CT scanning in private institutions (involving the Health Care Financing

Administration), nor with the purchase of CT scanners (involving the Health Systems Agencies and State Health Planning and Development Agencies, regional and state agencies set up under the federal health planning legislation).

Federal health programs are housed in many different agencies. The 1982 Federal Budget, for example, names 16 agencies with health care-related outlays.[1] The largest expenditures, by far, are made by the Department of Defense (DOD) (6 percent of the total expenditure), the Veterans Administration (VA) (8 percent), and the Department of Health and Human Services (DHHS) (77 percent). The expenditures of all the other agencies (excluding health insurance for government employees) add up to less than that of the smallest of the big three. The DOD and VA programs are concerned with the direct provision of care to the military and veterans in government hospitals and clinics, as well as with financing private care for dependents. Overwhelmingly larger than all the others are the expenditures of the Department of Health and Human Services, and it is to that agency that the rest of this chapter will be devoted.

THE DEPARTMENT OF HEALTH AND HUMAN SERVICES

The Department of Health and Human Services spends more money than any other federal agency. Although this is somewhat deceptive as a measure of the department's activities because a substantial part of the DHHS budget consists of the Social Security and Medicare trust funds, the department does carry on a large number of programs. Many of these exist in an atmosphere of contention—public disagreement as to whether the government should be carrying them on at all or, if they are to be carried on, whether they might not be administered differently.

Although three-fourths of all federal health funds are spent by DHHS, health spending is divided within the department among approximately 220 separate health programs or activities, 210 of these in the Public Health Service (PHS) and 10 in the Health Care Financing Administration (HCFA)[2]. These range in size from Medicare payments to hospitals on behalf of aged beneficiaries which constituted a $26 billion activity in fiscal year 1982 (FY 1982), to programs that spend only a few million dollars each. These small programs in the Public Health Service reflect the differentiated structure of health interests, with each subgroup in the health community having its own separately earmarked program and appropriation. The FY 1982 budget for the Health Resources Administration (HRA),[3] one of six bureaus within the Public Health

---

[1]Department of Health and Human Services, Veterans Administration, Department of Defense, Department of Agriculture, Department of Energy, Department of Education, Department of Transportation, Department of Labor, Department of Justice, Department of Commerce, Department of the Interior, National Aeronautical and Space Administration, Department of State, Environmental Protection Agency, National Science Foundation, and Department of Housing and Urban Development.

[2]It is difficult to define the precise number of health programs administered by DHHS because the term "program" is ambiguous and is rarely defined consistently. The figures used here are based on the health activities listed in the Appendix for the Budget of the United States Government, Fiscal Year 1982, for the sake of simplicity and ease of documentation.

[3]In late 1982, the Public Health Service was reorganized and the Health Resources Administration and Health Services Administration (HSA) were merged into a new super agency, the Health Resources and Services Administration. Making up HRSA were four new bureaus: Indian Health Service, Bureau of Health Maintenance Organization and Resource Development, Bureau of Health Professions and Bureau of Health Care Delivery and Assistance.

Service, lists separate activities for institutional assistance, dental assistance, nursing assistance, public health assistance, allied health assistance, and so on. Each PHS program reflects the existence of another interest group with a stake in policy changes.

Although spending by the Health Care Financing Administration is fairly concentrated by comparison (approximately $50 billion spread over 10 programs), the potential effects of this concentration have been diffused because the purchasing power of Medicare and Medicaid is not mobilized behind a consistent set of health system goals. This is symbolized organizationally by the fact that the health care financing function of HCFA is kept organizationally separate within DHHS from the regulatory, delivery, research, and resource development functions of the Public Health Service. To date, Medicare and Medicaid payments have reinforced existing patterns of health care, not challenged them.[4]

The fragmentation of programs within DHHS results from a general lack of agreement on goals and a political process in which "interests favoring particular policies seek the support of others to pass narrowly defined legislation embodying their goals while insulating them from the influence of political superiors who may be responsive to different constituencies" (Greenberg, 1980, p. 63).[5]

Politically, those who support particular goals and policies—whether they be in the department, in Congress, or outside the federal government—work together to pursue the enactment of the policies they favor, the creation and continuation of independent units of the bureaucracy to pursue those policies, and the appropriation of funds for that pursuit. Organizationally, the goals and policies of the department are embodied in many units that pursue specialized goals, working with the congressional subcommittees that oversee them and the clientele that benefit from their programs. These tripartite alliances of specialized agencies, specialized congressional committees, and interest groups, all resisting central control or assignment of priorities, constitute the "iron triangles" identified by political scientists 25 years ago (Jordan, 1981).

As the number of areas in which government policies and regulations impinge upon the society has increased, more groups have had a stake in government action. The groups themselves develop different interests from each other as government policies affect them differently. Thus, there has been a proliferation of categorical programs in government, each apparently responsive to a more narrowly defined and increasingly differentiated set of needs and interests. Major shifts in policy direction become difficult if not impossible, as proposals for change affect established interests and policies in and out of government and each group defends its narrow sphere of control. The secretary of Health and Human Services, in consequence, must devote substantial efforts to establishing and maintaining his or her vision of what the department should be doing.

At the same time, as the number of interests becomes larger and more differentiated, the points at which they impinge upon each other become more numerous. Proposed changes cut across different groups in complex ways producing interdependencies that must be considered and that make rapid change difficult. In addition, the high and increasing costs of the Medicare and Medicaid programs have given the

---

[4]For a discussion of how cost reimbursement formulas were negotiated and how the government compromised on systems reform goals in order to assure participation of sufficient providers to guarantee beneficiaries access to services, see Feder (1977).

[5]Although Greenberg (1980) provides more detailed discussion of the opportunities for and the constraints on management in the Department of Health, Education and Welfare, the organizational predecessor of the Department of Health and Human Services, his argument is equally relevant for DHHS.

secretary and, indeed, the president, an interest in containing costs that is different from the interests of lower-level program administrators and those with whom they deal. This means the higher levels of government will have policy agendas of their own and are less likely simply to ratify the bargains struck by their subordinates and the interest groups and representatives with whom they deal.

ORGANIZATIONAL HISTORY OF THE DEPARTMENT OF HEALTH AND HUMAN SERVICES

A review of the organizational history of the Department of Health and Human Services is helpful in understanding its present functions and problems. Until 1939, there was no single U.S. government agency charged with the broad range of health and social welfare responsibilities that comprise the department's mission. The Public Health Service was a unit of the Treasury Department, reflecting its origin as the agency that, under the direction of the collectors of customs in the various U.S. ports, provided medical care to merchant seamen. The Social Security Board was an independent agency created by Congress in 1935 to administer the new Social Security system. The Office of Education was a unit of the Department of the Interior, largely concerned with data collection.

In 1939, those three agencies and several others were merged into the Federal Security Agency (FSA), newly established to increase efficiency by consolidating government units dealing with social and economic security and health. Gradually other units were created as part of the FSA or transferred to it from other agencies; among them the Food and Drug Administration (FDA) was transferred from the Agriculture Department in 1940. Each of these organizations had its own functions, its own clientele, its own appropriations, its own staff, and its own congressional relationships. Clientele, staff, and members of Congress had reason to be concerned about the loss in independence that might come about if there were to be central control of the agency. Moreover, Paul McNutt, the first FSA administrator, was also chairman of the War Manpower Commission and had little time for FSA oversight. As a result, the FSA acted primarily as a holding company and did not exercise central control over its individual constituents.

Postwar proposals to transform the FSA into a cabinet department were resisted in large part because of fear on the part of organized medicine and other opponents of "socialized medicine" that the designation of FSA as a cabinet department would enhance the status and power of its head, Oscar Ewing, a champion of President Truman's proposal for national health insurance. With the 1952 election of President Eisenhower, who had strongly opposed the idea of national health insurance during his campaign, these fears were mitigated. In 1953, the FSA was transformed into a newly created Department of Health, Education and Welfare (DHEW).

The new department included five major constituent agencies: the Social Security Administration, the Public Health Service, the Office of Education, the Food and Drug Administration, and the Office of Vocational Rehabilitation. There were also several small health, education, and welfare-related organizations such as St. Elizabeth's Hospital in Washington, D.C., and the American Printing House for the Blind.

The new federal department was little more centralized than was the FSA. Each of the constituent agencies maintained a large amount of independence and the secretary of Health, Education and Welfare exercised relatively little control over their activities.

As the number of programs for which the department was responsible increased, there was additional pressure toward fragmentation.

EFFORTS AT COORDINATION

When DHEW was elevated to cabinet status in 1953, staff at the secretarial level was scarce. Congress feared interference with professional health and education functions by a secretary oriented toward welfare, the dominant component of DHEW in 1953, in terms of staff, budget, and program. To prevent such interference, Congress denied requests for increases in staffing for the Office of the Secretary, gave formal legal independence to the secretary's subordinates (the commissioner of education and the surgeon general), prescribed much of DHEW's organizational structure by statute, and assigned specific programs and functions to designated internal organizational units. However, over time, most of these legal restrictions on the secretary's formal powers have been eased. Moreover, a series of reforms specifically designed to improve the "manageability" of the department were undertaken. Steps taken included centralizing supportive services rather than having each constituent agency provide its own, development of an executive secretariat function within the Office of the Secretary to help keep track of policy developments within the department, increasing the amount of policy analysis available to the secretary through development of the Office of the Assistant Secretary for Planning and Evaluation and parallel policy analysis units at the constituent agency level, increasing the secretary's control of the budget through the application of formal management techniques, reorganizing the constituent agencies, and decentralizing the department's grant structure so that the power of Washington-based constituencies might be reduced.

Increases in formal powers, however, may be offset by increases in responsibility, complexity, and the centrifugal forces acting upon the department. Although secretarial ability to manage DHEW has been enhanced by these and other reforms, there are still several factors, some of them inherent in the character of the department and its programmatic responsibilities, that continue to constrain the secretary's ability to give central direction to the department.

Among the factors that constrain the ability to manage DHEW are the following:

1. *Rapid turnover in office.* The average tenure of a DHEW secretary has been slightly over 2 years and the average tenure of assistant secretaries even shorter. Rapid turnover means that new policy directions are difficult to sustain over time, and constituent agencies with independent political support can attempt to wait out the present incumbent.

2. *Narrow congressional definition of program and appropriations.* The DHEW budget takes the form of a large number of fairly narrow appropriations. In the Defense Department, for example, the 1969 authorization of $22 billion for procurement and research programs was a single page in length; by contrast, statutes authorizing $22 billion of Department of Health, Education and Welfare expenditures took up several shelves of a bookcase (Schultze, 1968). Congress has consistently denied the secretary of the DHEW authority to transfer funds from one appropriations account to another. This helps insulate the bureaus and programs and means that there is less flexibility to deal with new problems as they emerge or to deal with social problems that cut across congressional budget categories.

3. *Lack of allocable budget funds.*   There are few discretionary funds in the DHEW budget because increases are eaten up by legally mandated expenditures in programs such as Medicare and Social Security that entitle individuals to services regardless of growth in medical prices or the cost of living. In FY 1976 the "uncontrollable" portion of the DHEW budget (i.e., spending that is mandated by law) surpassed 90% in terms of new budget authority and 95% in terms of outlays or expenditures.

4. *The indirect nature of DHEW grant programs.*   The DHEW was and is dependent on state and local governments and other grant recipients to carry out program objectives. Although grant programs do provide the federal government with some leverage to influence the grantees, there remains a large amount of discretion at the state and local levels. The conduct of the grant programs often reflected the shared professional perspectives of state and federal program officials, but these shared professional perspectives are often not the same as those of the secretary and the political levels of the department.

Given the constraints, the secretary of the DHEW is attracted to legislative and regulatory reform as areas of potential personal influence. Since many of the constraints are legislative in origin, support from Congress is a prerequisite of major change. Moreover, in recent years, the number and volume of departmental regulations has grown considerably, and these regulations often determine whether private businesses and organizations must spend millions of dollars in order to comply with federal requirements and standards. The issurance and revision of regulations is an area of relatively high departmental discretion when compared with the management of grants.

In 1980, the "education" wing of the Department of Health, Education and Welfare was split off to become the core of a newly created Department of Education. The remainder of the DHEW was renamed the Department of Health and Human Services (DHHS). However, both the opportunities for secretarial leadership and the constraints upon the leadership at DHHS were not greatly affected by this change.

HEALTH ACTIVITIES OF THE DEPARTMENT OF HEALTH AND HUMAN SERVICES

The health activities of the DHHS are housed primarily in the Public Health Service and the Health Care Financing Administration. These organizations are subject to the same problem of multiple, vague, and conflicting goals that the department has generally.

The organizational structure of the Public Health Service embodies these multiple conflicting goals. Clientele relationships are built in near the bottom of the organizational hierarchy. Although health activities are primarily overseen by three committees in each house of Congress, several dozen other subcommittees and committees, each with its own narrow focus of interests, have jurisdiction over health and health-related programs. These committees, their members, and their staffs have played an active role in the formation and maintenance of health policy—much more so than in other policy areas in which Congress has been more likely to defer to the president and to agency expertise. The iron triangles are if anything more prominent in PHS than in the rest of the department.

Before World War II, the PHS was primarily concerned with the provision of medical care to federal beneficiaries (e.g., the Coast Guard) and technical assistance to the states in the area of infectious and communicable diseases. It was largely independent of external control and was staffed by a commissioned corps of career public health officers headed by the surgeon-general who reported directly to the administrator of the Federal Security Agency, the predecessor of the Department of Health, Education and Welfare.

After World War II, the activities of the PHS changed substantially: Grants to the states for hospital construction were inaugurated, and support for biomedical research was expanded tremendously—the budget of the National Institutes of Health (NIH) grew from less than $3 million in 1945 to $52 million in 1950 to $1.2 billion in the mid-1960s to almost $4 billion in 1982.[6]

As a legacy from the fight over national health insurance in the Truman administration, PHS officials were very cautious about getting involved in anything that resembled provision or financing of services to people who were not the usual federal beneficiaries. The NIH research programs, in contrast, were particularly appealing: Research support was politically popular and did not raise organized medicine's hackles. The medical profession, particularly academic biomedical researchers, were happy to get federal funds to do what they wanted to do. The process of awarding funds, by making use of external advisory committees and study sections to review applications, brought together a group of able outsiders with common interests, providing them with an organizational base for promoting federal support for biomedical research. The relevant congressional committees were very friendly to research, especially in the wake of the success of the USSR space program in the late 1950s.

This new research support activity, however, created tensions within DHEW. Whereas the PHS had formerly been oriented toward the state health departments, the research activity involved universities, medical schools, and private hospitals. PHS personnel were split between those concerned with the more traditional activities and the NIH staff. NIH was located in Bethesda, Maryland, several miles away from other PHS units, and operated largely independently of the rest of the PHS. The new NIH tail was seen by many as wagging the PHS dog.

In 1965, Congress enacted Medicare and Medicaid. Although these were health financing programs, they were not given to the Public Health Service to administer. Rather, Medicaid, an extension of previously existing public assistance medical care programs, was made the responsibility of the Social and Rehabilitation Service (SRS), the "welfare" arm of DHEW. Medicare became the responsibility of the Social Security Administration (SSA). Both of these were constituent units of the DHEW and PHS had an advisory relationship to them, but little came of that relationship. Public health programs, located in the PHS and overseen primarily by the House Committee on Interstate and Foreign Commerce and the Senate Committee on Labor and Public Welfare, were thus separated from the newly created health care financing programs, located in SSA and SRS and overseen by the House Committee on Ways and Means and the Senate Committee on Finance. The division of health care financing functions from PHS regulatory, research, and resource development functions within the DHEW and the consequent inability to relate health care financing policy to health system reform

---

[6]These changes in the activities and appropriations of the PHS can be traced in its internal documents and annual reports and in congressional appropriations, oversight, and legislative hearings. Much of this information is summarized in (Williams 1951), (United States House of Representatives, 1963), (United States House of Representatives, 1966), (United States Senate 1970), (Greenberg, 1972), (United States Department of Health, Education and Welfare Public Health Service 1980).

goals systematically, reflected the same political forces that produced an identical split in committee jurisdictions over health policy in the Congress.

ORGANIZATIONAL CHANGES IN HEALTH ACTIVITIES

When Secretary John Gardner sought to gain more control over the DHEW in the late 1960s, he and his colleagues concluded, "that it was unrealistic to expect innovative policy leadership in the delivery and financing of medical care and the training of adequate medical and paramedical manpower to evolve among the commissioned officer corps . . . which had been created and designed for a much more limited purpose" (Miles, 1974). Thus, in 1968, the Public Health Service was put under the line authority of the assistant secretary for Health and Scientific Affairs, who had previously performed only a staff function. This took control of the PHS away from the surgeon-general, a career civil servant not fully responsive to the secretary, and gave it to a politically appointed assistant secretary who was subject to the secretary's control.

The assistant secretary was also given formal responsibility for directing overall health policy in the DHEW and coordinating health programs in other parts of the department. This responsibility could have provided the base for more central direction if there were an aggressive assistant secretary and strong support from the secretary, but that is not what happened. Rather, the position of assistant secretary for health, as it was later renamed, was vacant for extended periods at the beginning of the Nixon and Carter administrations, as well as at other times. This meant that working relationships were developed among the top DHEW executives without the participitation of the assistant secretary for health. In addition, the position of assistant secretary for planning and evaluation (ASPE) was created in 1967 to give the secretary a broad analytical overview of all the DHEW's programs and activities, including those in health. The differing organizational perspectives of the assistant secretary for planning and evaluation and the assistant secretary for health can sometimes place them in conflict with each other on health policy issues, with the secretary of the department left the choice of whose advice to accept.

Perhaps more important, the bulk of the DHEW's expenditure for health care was not made by the PHS under the direct jurisdiction of the assistant secretary for health, but rather in the Medicare and Medicaid programs, which continued to be in the SSA and the SRS. Although the assistant secretary for health was given responsibility to coordinate the department's health activities, this general grant of authority was an insufficient foundation for a meaningful role in health care financing programs.

The PHS has remained under the line supervision of an assistant secretary for health since that time. The PHS itself, however, has been reorganized several times. These reorganization efforts have repeatedly displayed several features: the organizational independence of the FDA and the NIH, the influence of the mental health interests, and the uncertain role of the surgeon-general and the commissioned corps.

Throughout the half-dozen reorganizations of the 1960s and 1970s, the FDA has remained largely untouched. It was briefly combined with PHS environmental activities in the 1968 reorganization, but that marriage was unstable and led to divorce in 1970 without any significant changes in FDA operations. It has remained largely independent of the rest of the PHS since then.

Similarly, the major functions and operation of the NIH have not been changed, although manpower training activities have been transferred into and out of NIH, and the National Institute of Mental Health (NIMH) became independent of other institutes in 1966. Control of the NIH, which for many years spent the major fraction of the PHS budget, has largely eluded the assistant secretary for health.

That the NIMH was made independent of NIH in 1966 was a reflection of the existence of a well-organized mental health lobby with strong allies in Congress and the admiration of many for the innovative patient services program support by NIMH. Because NIH was concerned with research, not with patient service, it was felt desirable to make NIMH independent to prevent its service programs from being downgraded. More generally, this is an illustration of the tendency of groups with special concerns to seek higher status and independence for the agencies administering the programs with which they are concerned (see Drew, 1969; Chu and Trotter, 1974; and Connery, 1968).

In the 1968 reorganization, the PHS was broken up into 3 subunits, each reporting to the assistant secretary. The NIMH lost its new independence and became one of the constituents of the subunit charged with provision of services, the Health Services and Mental Health Administration (HSMHA). When the PHS was reorganized again in May 1973, NIMH was returned to NIH, in part because the Nixon administration wanted to reduce or do away with its service delivery functions. However, the mental health interests resisted and, by the end of 1973, NIMH was once more separated from NIH and was renamed the Alcohol, Drug Abuse and Mental Health Administration (ADAMHA).

The replacement of the surgeon-general as head of the PHS by the assistant secretary for Health and Scientific Affairs in 1968 and the simultaneous reorganization of the PHS into three independent subunits left the surgeon-general without a clear role and the commissioned corps demoralized. The surgeon-general was supposedly in day-to-day control of the administration, with the assistant secretary setting policy. In actual fact, however, there was not much for the surgeon-general to do, except in a symbolic fashion, and the office was vacant for several years. The Carter administration solved the problem by appointing the same person assistant secretary and surgeon-general simultaneously. The two positions were again separated under the Reagan administration. However, the role of the surgeon-general remains ambiguous.

Although the PHS continued as a legalism after the 1968 reorganization, it no longer existed as a cohesive entity, as all its functions had been transferred to the three new subunits and the assistant secretary. The size of the type in which the name "Public Health Service" appeared on organization charts dwindled while the subunits' names became more prominent.

In 1973, the PHS was again reorganized, and its name reappeared on the organization charts in all its former glory. In actuality, however, it has not regained that glory. The 1973 reorganization restructured the service from three to five units. The principal change was the dismembering of HSMHA into three new organizations: The Center for Disease Control and the National Institute of Occupational Safety and Health were combined into a new Center for Disease Control, and the remaining activities of HSMHA were divided into two agencies—the Health Resources Administration (HRA) and the Health Services Administration (HSA). In theory, the basis of assigning activities to HSA and HRA was that the former would be concerned with health service delivery and the latter would comprise data-gathering, demonstration programs and manpower training (and, later, health planning). With the later creation of the Alcohol, Drug Abuse and Mental Health Administration (described above), the five units became six: FDA, NIH, HSA, HRA, ADAMHA, and CDC (which now stands for Centers for Disease Control). In 1982, however, the six units once again became five, with the merger of HSA and HRA into a new Health Resources and Services Administration. An effort was also made in 1973 to deemphasize categorical programs and provide the assistant secretary for health with more staff to enable more effective centralized management and coordination. In 1982, however, the Office of Management and Budget proposed elimination of much of that staff and of the line supervision responsibilities for the assistant secretary for health.

Meanwhile, the health care financing programs of the DHEW also underwent reorganization. In 1977, the Medicare and Medicaid programs were taken from the SSA and the SRS and combined into a new agency, the Health Care Financing Administration (HCFA), situated at the same level in the hierarchy as the PHS and SSA.[7]

The PHS units that related to Medicare and Medicaid (primarily performing standard setting and quality assurance functions) were also transferred to HCFA, re-emphasizing the minimal relationship between the PHS (and the assistant secretary for health) and federal programs for financing health care delivery. Inasmuch as President Carter, at that time, was talking about proposing national health insurance (NHI) legislation, this reinforced earlier signals that his proposed NHI program would have little role for the PHS.

The amalgamation of units from three different areas of DHEW, each with its own bureaucratic culture, proved to be difficult. Although there were pressures to combine the operations of the Medicare and Medicaid programs, the difficulties of doing so kept them as separate organizational entities within HCFA for several years, until 1980 when the two programs were forced into a single organizational framework under a functional reorganization ordered by Secretary Califano.

PAST AND FUTURE

The frequent reorganization of federal health activities since World War II reflects the lack of agreement about what those activities should be. Thirty years ago the PHS had a clear mission: technical assistance to states in the area of infectious diseases. Organized medicine tolerated PHS direct delivery of services only to federal wards and others in whom the medical profession was either uninterested or those whom it found unprofitable to serve. Power relationships and boundaries were clear. Biomedical research expanded rapidly after World War II because it did not threaten the private practice of medicine. But research led to pressures to implement research results to improve health outcomes and reform the delivery of health services. This, in turn, led to the proliferation of categorical programs along individual disease and professional lines. Private medicine was not directly challenged; however, programs expanded whenever a particular group could mobilize enough support for a narrowly defined need.

In search of a new mission and role, the PHS has been unable to define one vis-à-vis the many categorical health interests that have entrenched themselves around its individual programs. The search for a stable organization structure is further complicated by the ambiguous relationship between the health services delivery, health regulatory, health research, and health resources development functions of the PHS and the health care financing programs that are kept organizationally distinct within DHHS. Their separation within the department and in Congress mirrors the inability throughout the health care system to enunciate a consistent set of health system goals and to mobilize health financing decisions to pursue them. Financing, once largely a function of the private sector, and regulation, formerly left to the states and the providers, have become

---

[7]As part of this change, the SRS went out of existence and its programs were transferred elsewhere.

federal functions, at least in part. However, because of the lack of agreement on the role of the federal government in restructuring the organization and delivery of health care, agency missions remain ambiguous, agency structure is fragmented around categorical programs, and reorganization remains a constant activity.

Meanwhile, cost control has become the dominant concern of federal as well as state health policymakers. Although other health programs have expanded somewhat, it is the meteoric growth of the Medicare and Medicaid programs that have been the primary source of concern. This concern encouraged federal and state governments to attempt regulation of health care financing, but both have been cautious about putting too many strictures upon medical care providers, especially physicians, and have focused instead on reducing public costs through cutting back on benefits and by increasing consumer cost sharing.

The substantial effect of increased Medicare and Medicaid costs on the federal budget has caused the president and his staff to pay greater attention to health matters, once left largely to the secretary of Health, Education and Welfare and the secretary's associates. Following President Nixon's declaration in the early 1970s that U.S. health care was in a "crisis," the White House Domestic Council and the Office of Management and Budget (OMB) began to take a more active role in health policymaking during his administration. This continued in the Carter administration, where the resulting conflict between the president's staff and the secretary of DHHS resulted in Secretary Califano's dismissal (Califano, 1981). Under President Reagan and his associates, this trend toward greater involvement of the Executive Office of the president in health policymaking has continued.

Within the DHHS, policymaking authority on health matters has also shifted upward, away from the agencies and into the Office of the Secretary that must deal directly with the White House on these matters. Under the Carter administration, the Office of the Assistant Secretary for Planning and Evaluation, not the PHS or the HCFA, was given lead responsibility for developing both the Carter administration's NHI proposal and the bill for hospital cost containment. Under the Reagan administration, the assistant secretary for planning and evaluation has been given the lead to develop the administration's health care competition proposals and to flesh out the initial White House decision to federalize Medicaid.

This centralization of policymaking is true not only of health policy, but of the Reagan administration's social and economic policy more generally, reflecting in part its distrust of the bureaucracy.[8] As policymaking moves to higher levels, interest groups with access to lower-level program officials lose influence and the older politics of "iron triangles" becomes more volatile as the agency corner of the triangle is bypassed.

The Reagan administration's agenda for health attempts to transform the policymaking landscape by replacing the categorical structure of PHS programs with block grants, by transferring federal programs to the states, by reducing federal spending for health programs, and by reducing the direct federal role in health care financing decisions through the strategy of "competition." So far President Reagan has been only partially successful in this ambitious and controversial agenda. In 1981, he proposed that 26 categorical health programs be consolidated into two large block grants. Congress modified his proposals, and several of the categorical programs were retained. The remainder were consolidated into four block grants rather than two: maternal and child health; preventive health; alcohol, drug abuse, and mental health; and primary care. Congress

---

[8]For a discussion of the increased role of the Reagan OMB with regard to health and welfare policy see Demokovich (1982).

did not give the states full discretion in the use of block grant funds but enacted both permanent and transitional limits. Funding was cut substantially, although not quite as severely as the president recommended.

The overwhelming bulk of federal health spending, however, is in the Medicare and Medicaid programs. In 1981, the president proposed to cap Medicaid expenses and strictly limit the future rate of growth of the federal share. Future increases, rather than being shared by both federal and state governments as in the past, would be shifted almost entirely to the states, if they could not live within the sharply limited growth of the federal share. This effort was defeated, although Congress did enact a plan to reduce the federal share somewhat if states exceeded total spending targets.

The administration's legislative proposals in the area of Medicare and in health care competition more broadly had not yet been presented to the Congress when, in his 1982 State of the Union Message, President Reagan proposed in a single, bold stroke to create a "new federalism." This would consist of three phases. First, in fiscal year 1984, the federal government would take full responsibility for the Medicaid program, while the states simultaneously would take full responsibility for food stamps and Aid to Families with Dependent Children (AFDC), the largest public assistance program. Each state would thus conduct—or not conduct—its own food stamp and AFDC program, largely or entirely free from federal requirements.

Second, the proceeds of certain federal excise taxes, totaling $28 billion a year, would be put into a trust fund that would be available for state use. For the next four years (1984–1987), the states could choose whether or not they wished to participate in approximately 40 federal grant programs (including all four of the new health block grants and a number of categorical health grants). If a state participated in those programs, it would have to reimburse the federal government for their cost from the trust fund. If a state chose not to participate, it could use its share of the trust fund for other purposes.

Third, beginning in 1988, federal contributions to the trust fund and the federal excise taxes from which those contributions were drawn would be cut by 25 percent a year. The states could continue the programs if they wished but would increasingly have to pay for them from their own funds, perhaps by instituting state excise taxes to replace the reduced, and eventually eliminated, federal excise taxes. Through this complex series of events, most federal health programs (other than Medicare and Medicaid) would be converted into state programs, to be financed from state funds, and free from federal regulation. Medicaid, a complex state–federal mixture, would become exclusively a federal program.

The State of the Union Message provided only a bare outline of the proposed program. Indeed, the president indicated that the full details of the program had yet to be worked out and that this would be done in consultation with members of Congress and with state and local officials. Among the questions remaining to be answered were whether, and for how long, there would be minimum standards required of the states in the programs that they took over from the federal government. Similarly, it was unclear at what level of services and for what beneficiaries the new all-federal Medicaid program would operate, that is, that of the most generous existing programs, that of the most niggardly, or somewhere in between?

Although the president's proposal was presented as an equal trade in financial terms, some doubted this. Others argued that even if this were true in overall terms, individual states could be affected very differently. It was clear that a great deal of negotiation and specification would be necessary before Congress would approve the proposal.

In July of 1982, the president spoke to the annual meeting of the National Association of Counties, outlining the results of the as yet unfinished negotiations that had been going on with state and local officials. The states would no longer be required to take responsibility for the food stamp program; rather, the first phase of the swap would involve federal assumption of full responsibility for Medicaid in return for state assumption only of full responsibility for Aid to Families with Dependent Children. Second, the number of grant programs to be turned over to the states would be reduced by about 10 percent, and the trust fund would come from general revenues, as well as from excise taxes. (Presumably, this would make it easier for some states to replace the federal funds from state resources after the trust fund was terminated.)

The president promised to send a specific proposal to Congress by the end of the month. When this was not forthcoming, the leaders of the National Governors Association decided to prepare their own plan and offer it to Congress in 1983, preferably with the president's support but, if necessary, without it. The new federalism proposal changed the president's emphasis from his 1981 focus on budget and taxation reduction. The State of the Union Message, however, was followed quickly by the president's budget proposals for fiscal 1983. These included a $6 billion reduction in health program spending, mostly in Medicare and Medicaid. The budget also included a projection of the largest deficit in U.S. history—due to substantially increased denfense spending, previously enacted tax cuts, and the effects of the recession. These budget proposals encountered opposition from several quarters—those who were concerned about the deficit, those who were concerned about the reduced level of nondefense spending, and those who were concerned about the increased level of defense spending.

Block grants and the transfer of federal programs to the states directly challenge the health interests and constituencies entrenched around the individual categorical programs at the federal level. They would eliminate much of the federal responsibility in the health area, whose growth has been described earlier. In the process, the national political movements that helped to enact these programs would be disrupted and forced to focus their attention on 50 state governments. Different patterns of expenditure and control would emerge depending upon the politics of each. National program constituencies would be weakened and would be forced to compete against each other on a state-by-state basis.

The fourth element in the administration's agenda, the competitive strategy, attempted to reduce the government's role in health care decision making by increasing the importance of individual consumer choices. Consumers would be encouraged to obtain health insurance coverage with large cost-sharing amounts by offering them cash rebates if their insurance premiums were less than the employers' contributions to the health plan, or (in the case of Medicare and/or Medicaid) the amount of a government-provided voucher. Increasing the uninsured portion of health care costs would increase consumer awareness of the costs of utilization. Increased consumer cost consciousness would, in turn, it is hoped, encourage insurers to reorganize providers into more efficient delivery systems such as health maintenance organizations (HMOs), which promise to control utilization and reduce future cost increases.

If competition is encouraged among employer-based health plans by reducing or eliminating the nontaxable nature of employment-based health insurance, the administration would gain increased tax revenues at a time when it is under pressure to reduce anticipated budget deficits and is reluctant to do so in other ways. Government health care financing dollars would not be directly used to influence provider behavior. Instead they would be used to create incentives to individual beneficiaries to behave differently since they could substitute cash for Medicare benefits or, alternatively, obtain better coverage for the same voucher if they chose a health plan wisely. The relationship of Medicare and Medicaid to PHS programs and to providers would become increasingly moot as the government simply transferred money to individuals and private insurers began to play the major role in controlling utilization and reorganizing providers into closed panel plans.

Whether or not the president will succeed in this effort depends upon whether he can gain enough support for his goals with regard to the role the federal government ought to play vis-à-vis the private sector in bringing about health systems reforms. In the absence of that support, individual health interests will continue to pursue their own goals at the national level, and those able to mobilize sufficient support will get their programs enacted or retained in the form of categorical programs. If the president is successful, on the other hand, there will indeed be a change in federal health politics of an almost revolutionary nature.

REFERENCES

Califano, Joseph A., Jr., *Governing America*, New York: Simon & Schuster, 1981, pp. 434–435.

Chu, Franklin D. and Sharland Trotter, *The Madness Establishment*, New York: Grossman Publishing Co., 1974.

Connery, Robert H., *The Politics of Mental Health*, New York: Columbia University Press, 1968.

Demokovich, Linda E., "Team Player Schweiker May Be Paying a High Price for His Loyalty to Reagan," *National Journal*, May 15, 1982, pp. 848–853.

Drew, Elizabeth B., "The Health Syndicate," *The Atlantic*, Vol. 224, November 1969, pp. 4ff.

Feder, Jutith M., *Medicare: The Politics of Federal Hospital Insurance*, Lexington, Mass.: Lexington Books, 1977.

Greenberg, George D., "Constraints on Management and Secretarial Behavior at HEW," *Polity*, Vol. 13, Fall 1980, pp. 57–79.

Greenberg, George D., "Reorganization Reconsidered: The U.S. Public Health Service 1960–1973," *Public Policy*, Vol. 23, Fall 1972, pp. 483–522.

Jordan, A. Grant, "Iron Triangles, Wooly Corporatism and Elastic Nets: Images of the Policy Process," *Journal of Public Policy*, Vol. 1, 1981, pp. 95–123.

Miles, Rufes E., Jr., *The Department of Health, Education, and Welfare*, New York: Praeger, 1974.

Schultze, Charles, *The Politics and Economics of Public Spending*, Washington, D.C.: The Brookings Institution, 1968, p. 4.

United States Department of Health, Education, and Welfare Public Health Service, *Inside the Public Health Service*, Washington, D.C.: United States Government Printing Office, 1980.

United States House of Representatives, Committee on Interstate and Foreign Commerce, *Organization of Public Health Service*, Hearings, April, May, June, 1963.

United States House of Representatives, Special Subcommittee on HEW Investigation, *The Department of Health, Education, and Welfare: Background Material Concerning the Mission and Organization of the Health Activities of the Department*, March, 1966.

United States Senate, Committee on Government Operations, Subcommittee on Executive Reorganization and Government Research, *Federal Role in Health*, Report No. 91–809, 1970.

Williams, Ralph C., *The United States Public Health Service 1798–1950*, Washington, D.C.: Commissioned Officers Association of the U.S. Public Health Service, 1951.

CHAPTER 6

Health Policy Debate in the Executive Branch: The Case of Long-Term Care

George D. Greenberg

The evolution of federal health policy in the United States has culminated in a vigorous debate over the role of government vis-à-vis the private sector in achieving health systems goals. The dynamics of health policymaking within the executive branch are exemplified by the debate over long-term care (LTC) policy during the Carter administration. That debate, and, by extension, federal health policy in general, has been characterized by fragmentation, lack of consensus, and incrementalism, which are the results of diffusion of power, uncertain knowledge, and budget constraints.

EBB AND FLOW OF HEALTH POLICY

Public policy since World War II has contributed to major changes in the delivery of health care. An extensive network of health facilities and hospitals has been built, in part through Hill-Burton financing and in part through Veterans Administration (VA) and other direct federal programs. A physician shortage has been converted into a physician surplus. A third-party reimbursement system has been established, in part through the encouragement provided by income tax deductions, and the percentage of health care costs paid out of pocket fell from 55 percent in 1960 to 33 percent in 1978. Medicare and Medicaid have substantially increased health care use among the poor. The availability of third-party reimbursement, especially since the enactment of Medicaid, has helped encourage the rapid growth of the nursing home industry. A large biomedical research effort, budgeted at approximately $3.6 billion in fiscal year (FY) 1982, has been established at the National Institutes for Health (NIH). Thus, government policy has had effects. Even if some of the effects were unintended and some of the results undesirable, the government has succeeded in influencing the development of the health care system over the past 40 years.

Most of these changes were in place by the mid-1970s. Moreover, the previous successes have led to the recognition of new or previously inadequately recognized

114

problems such as escalating costs, problematic quality of care, and continued inequities in the distribution of health resources. Some of the newer problems resulted, in part, from past cures. For example, the expansion of third-party coverage and the creation of more equal access to health care through Medicare and Medicaid are themselves contributing factors to escalating medical inflation. Other problems emerged as previous problems receded from view. For example, as longevity has increased, the problems of the chronically ill have become increasingly important. People who do not die from infectious diseases will live to contract arthritis, heart disease, and cancer.

Several government programs enacted in the 1970s were designed to address this new generation of problems. A system of health planning agencies (Health Service Agencies) and professional standards review organizations (PSROs) was established to help contain health care costs and to help assure quality of care. Health maintenance organizations (HMOs) were encouraged through enactment of a program of loans and subsidies. However, these newer programs have not as yet been institutionalized, and the HSAs and PSROs have been attacked as adding to health systems costs rather than containing them. There has been debate over whether a regulatory or procompetitive approach offers the best hope for a solution. This debate reflects a fundamental lack of agreement over what the role of government vis-à-vis the private health care market should be. Should government use the fiscal power it obtains from purchasing approximately 40 percent of all health care services to contain the escalation of health care costs and to restructure the organization and delivery of health care services? Or should government act instead to restructure its own programs and tax incentives so that people are encouraged to choose health insurance plans with increased cost sharing, thereby creating incentives for private insurers and providers to deliver health care more efficiently?[1]

Similarly, a fundamental question to be resolved in the stalled debate over national health insurance (NHI), which is at the core of the different plans, is the extent to which financing will be used to restructure the health care delivery system. To what extent, for example, will the health insurance markets be left intact or will bealth care financing flow through government.[2] The Reagan administration has supported the procompetitive approach and proposed to dismantle the HSAs and PSROs. It also has sought to reduce the direct subsidies to HMOs while hoping to encourage their growth through the creation of market conditions that will reward the most efficient producers. As noted in Chapter 5, at the time of this writing, the battle over the Reagan administration's agenda of health systems reform had just been joined. To what extent its ambitious policy agenda will be successfully enacted and, if enacted, to what extent it will be able to alter the inertial forces described below, remains to be seen.

POLITICS OF LONG-TERM CARE

Long-term care (LTC) refers to the services required by people who have functional limitations as a result of or in conunction with chronic illnesses or conditions. The

---

[1]For a description of the basic positions, see Sapolsky (1977) and the special issue on "Competition and Regulation in Health Care" in the *Milbank Memorial Fund Quarterly*, Vol. 59, Spring 1981.

[2]For a discussion of the potential relationships between health financing and decisions and health systems reform see McClure (1976).

problems of the chronically ill gain in importance as the aged become an increasingly growing proportion of the population and as medical technology prolongs life. The debate over LTC policy which occurred within the executive branch during the Carter administration is described here in order to illustrate the character of the debate over health policy more generally. The policy area of LTC has been chosen for discussion in part because the problems of the chronically ill remain severe despite advances in acute medical care technology, in part because the characteristics of the policy area of LTC (fragmentation, lack of consensus, and incrementalism) are characteristic of health care more generally, in part because cost escalation in the LTC sector has been more rapid than in the acute care sector, and in part because it is a policy area with which the author is most familiar. The fundamental problems in LTC (escalating costs; overuse of expensive institutional services, e.g., nursing home services; underfinancing of alternatives to institutional care, i.e., ambulatory and preventive services; and problematic quality of care) parallel the problems of the acute care sector, even though LTC policy inevitably concerns the delivery of social services as well as health services and personal care (e.g., bathing, dressing, feeding).

CHARACTERISTICS OF THE POLICY AREA OF LONG-TERM CARE

Fragmentation

There is currently no central focal point for policymaking on LTC issues within the federal government. Major programs are found outside as well as within the Department of Health and Human Services (DHHS). The Veteran's Administration provides for the LTC needs of veterans and in some cases their families. Housing and Urban Development (HUD) finances congregate housing for the elderly and, as the population placed in public housing units 20 years ago grows old, is increasingly confronted by LTC issues. The Department of Transportation finances programs that enable senior citizens to travel more easily to needed medical and social services.

Within the DHHS itself there is no clear policy focus. The Health Care Financing Administration (HCFA) spends the bulk of public dollars for LTC in the form of payments for nursing home services by Medicare and Medicaid. In 1978, for example, out of total public spending of $15.1 billion for nursing home services, Medicaid paid approximately $7.5 billion and Medicare approximately $.4 billion.[3]

Home health expenditures by Medicare and Medicaid, in contrast, totaled only $721 million in FY 1978 and were concentrated on those people who had a medical need for skilled care. Other programs within DHHS (Title XX of the Social Security Act, Title III of the Older American Act) finance nonmedical services in the home setting (respite care, homemaker, nutrition) that are necessary to maintain a frail elderly person at home and delay admission into a nursing home if such an individual does not have a medical need or problem. In FY 1978, Title XX cost approximately $481 million and Title III cost approximately $334 million for these services. The Public Health Service (PHS) also funds a variety of programs related to LTC. Community Health Centers provide primary care to all people, including the elderly, who may have chronic as well as acute health care problems. Chronic disease programs (hypertension, diabetes control) potentially

---

[3]Vladeck (1980) argues that the government should use its oligopolistic power as the principal purchaser of nursing home services to achieve higher quality of care from the industry.

reduce the demand for LTC services. Health manpower programs train geriatric nurse practitioners, nurses aides, and nursing home administrators.

Each of these programs serves different populations, has different eligibility criteria, pays providers differently, uses different service definitions, and has different reporting requirements. This fragmentation at the federal level is mirrored at the state and community levels. It creates difficulties for a social worker or a physician attempting to help a client put together a variety of services from different programs and agencies so that the individual can be maintained in the community outside a nursing home. The easier choice is to place the client in a nursing home in which a full range of services is available. Thus the fragmentation of programs and agencies itself contributes to a set of perverse incentives often leading to inappropriate institutionalization.

During 1980, staff units were established within the Office of the Secretary of the DHHS to provide an overview of the various programs bearing on LTC run by the different DHHS bureaus and agencies. It is unclear whether such staff units can effectively coordinate the diverse programs and policies impinging upon LTC or whether more fundamental organizational change and program consolidation are necessary. Moreover, there is little consensus on the direction such changes should take.

Lack of Consensus on a Policy Approach

The debate over LTC is at least as complex as the debate over national health insurance. Comprehensive reform might take any of several directions, but the price tag on any of them would be large and fundamental decisions must be made on which populations will be covered; what services will be provided; whether financing should flow through the federal treasury or whether a mixed public–private approach is better; and what the relative federal, state, and community roles should be in administration, setting standards, monitoring quality, and reporting. In several important respects, however, the debates are different. Private insurers do not currently cover a significant number of LTC services and therefore have less stake in government financing of LTC benefits than they do in the area of acute care. More importantly, between 60 and 80 percent of LTC services are provided informally by family and friends. There is no agreement on what the continued responsibility of family members should be as a matter of social policy. Should a 40-year-old woman care for her aging mother or should she enter the labor force? Should a middle-aged couple support their aging parents or should they provide for their own retirement or their children's education?

Moreover, there is also concern among policymakers that any expansion of government-supported LTC services will simply displace the current effort of family and friends, leaving recipients with no additional care and driving public costs beyond tolerable limits.[4] Research studies designed to address this "substitution" issue, however, have been relatively rare as well as inconclusive.[5] There are few reliable measures of the amount of time devoted to providing informal care to individuals with different

[4]For a discussion of the LTC policy issues discussed here and below see the following sources: Health Care Financing Administration (1981); *Working Papers on Long-Term Care,* Office of the Assistant Secretary for Planning and Evaluation, 1981, Department of Health and Human Services, October 1981; *Long Term Care: Some Perspectives from Research and Demonstrations,* R. Vogel and H. Palmer, 1981, Health Care Financing Administration, unpublished report, June 15, 1981; and J. Callahan and S. Wallack, 1981, *Reforming the Long Term Care System,* Lexington, Mass.: D.C. Heath, 1981.

[5]See, *In Home Services and the Contribution of Kin,* report prepared for the Office of the Assistant Secretary for Planning and Evaluation, Urban Systems Research and Engineering, Inc., under contract HHS-100-0026.

chronic impairments in different circumstances nor is there agreement on how to price the amount of time given.

The reputed ills of the LTC system have been summarized above. There are a variety of proposals to cure these ills, but each emphasizes a different aspect of the problem. The following brief discussion of some of the major alternatives will illustrate the divergent views, the range of choice, and the difficulty of choosing a proposal:

1. *Finance expanded in-home services.* Proponents argue that greater availability of home health, homemaker, chore, meals-on-wheels, and other in-home services would provide a cost-effective alternative to the provision of care in nursing homes. Opponents claim that available studies that purport to show the benefits of home health services do not adequately control for degree of impairment; that greater availability of in-home services would lead to increased use by less-impaired people, thereby increasing public costs; and that quality of care as well as use will be difficult to monitor in the home setting.

2. *Finance comprehensive assessment and case management services to guide people to appropriate services.* Proponents focus on the fragmentation of the existing system and argue that a case manager can help overcome it by directing people to the most efficient and appropriate mix of services based on a comprehensive assessment of their needs. Proponents hope that inappropriate use of nursing home beds will be reduced if applicants' needs for LTC are comprehensively assessed before an admission is permitted. Opponents argue that assessment and case management are expensive and can have little effect when basic community services to maintain people at home are unavailable. In addition, current assessment techniques may not objectively predict need, and assessment scores may vary according to the training and institutional interests of the person who administers the test.

3. *Replace existing federal categorical programs with flexible block grants to the states.* Proponents argue that LTC presents unique problems in each community and that resources that communities can apply flexibly are needed. In addition, Congress can more effectively determine the appropriate level of funding and the appropriate range of eligible services if LTC were funded through a block grant balancing LTC needs against other national priorities. Communities would, moreover, have financial incentives to use limited LTC resources efficiently. Opponents argue that block grants will not be funded at levels high enough to allow communities to address properly the LTC needs of people.

4. *Enact an LTC insurance program that entitles people to a range of LTC services.* Proponents argue that this is the only mechanism that will ensure that people's needs are met. Opponents argue that individual entitlements lead to inappropriate use and inadequate budgetary controls.

5. *Enact a new categorical federal–state cost-sharing program targeted on LTC populations and services.* Proponents argue such a program would end the fragmentation in existing programs that only serve LTC populations as a by-product and that are not designed to meet LTC needs. For example, Medicare pays for home health, but the home health benefit was designed with the needs of someone recuperating from an acute hospital episode in mind. Under a specific LTC program, service definitions, methods of reimbursement, and so on, could be precisely tailored to the needs of the LTC population. Opponents argue that an additional categorical program will further fragment the abilities of communities to deal with problems comprehensively. Moreover, unless such a program were broadly defined, it is likely to be underfinanced.

6. *Decentralize decisions on LTC benefits to the person and his or her family through the adoption of tax incentives, vouchers, and direct payments to family members.* Proponents argue that such approaches bypass costly governmental regulations and give people incentives to choose the most efficient providers. Opponents argue that tax incentives (e.g., credits similar to the child-care allowance for those who take care of family members) do not help the poor. Moreover, people in need of LTC are often unable to manage vouchers or their own financial affairs.

Incrementalism

Fragmentation and lack of consensus interact to produce deadlock and a pattern of incremental change. The pattern of incrementalism is best illustrated by examining the fate of past LTC proposals in the annual budget and legislative cycles of the DHHS during the Carter administration.

In the spring of 1978 and again in the spring of 1980, planning groups were formed to consider LTC issues from a cross-departmental perspective in order to give the secretary an overview of LTC options in considering the budget proposals and requests of the individual agencies. The planning groups were asked to consider fundamental reforms without regard to costs. Despite this mandate, a series of relatively familiar and inexpensive incremental expansions to existing programs were included in the department's budget when it was submitted to the Office of Management and Budget (OMB) in September. These included proposals such as eliminating the requirement that a recipient be homebound before becoming eligible for Medicare home health benefits, adding occupational therapy to the list of skilled services for which Medicare recipients would be eligible, eliminating the requirement that a recipient be in a hospital for 3 days before becoming eligible for Part A Medicare home health benefits, expanding grants to schools of nursing to improve the training of nurses aides in nursing homes, expanding the level of the nutrition program to the homebound elderly in Title III of the Older Americans Act, expanding the Title XX ceiling and targeting the increase on services for the frail elderly, and expanding LTC-related research and demonstration projects. A selection was made from these and a somewhat broader list of proposals and a new departmental LTC initiative was announced (usually in the neighborhood of $100 million to $150 million in incremental expenditures). The following spring the process would begin again after OMB and Congress failed to approve all but one or two of the proposals. When on occasion one of these limited proposals passed the Congress, a new equally incremental proposal replaced it on the list considered the following spring.

Although the proposals recommended each fall may have had considerable merit, they were clearly incremental reforms that could at best affect the delivery system at the margin if their costs were compared with Medicaid expenditures on nursing homes alone. Large new federal expenditures may not be the best way to reform LTC; on the other hand, the reconsideration of the same series of incremental changes in existing programs during each budget and legislative cycle is simply an indicator of the drift in health policy. Despite the mandate given the planning groups to look across the department, comprehensive solutions were not proposed.

REASONS FOR THE IMPASSE IN HEALTH POLICY

There are three reasons for the impasse in health policy: diffusion of power, uncertain knowledge, and budget constraints.

Diffusion of Power

If the impasse over the passage of government-sponsored health insurance for the elderly in the late 1950s and early 1960s were to be explained, the simple and generally accepted answer would be that the American Medical Association (AMA) possessed the power of a veto group. Today it is clear that the AMA is only one of many health interests and that no one interest has enough power to force (or to block) action.

Twenty-five years ago political scientists explained stability or lack of change in terms of "iron triangles" dominated by executive agencies, congressional committees, and dominant interest groups. Today the system of iron triangles still exists, but its importance has been modified and its influence supplemented by several changes in the political system. First, the number of areas in which government policies and regulations impinge upon the society has increased dramatically so that more and more groups have a stake in government action. Not only does government regulation and spending activate more groups in the private sector, the groups themselves develop different interests from each other as government policies affect them differently. Hugh Heclo (1980, p. 96) has described this phenomenon as follows:

> A key factor in the proliferation of groups is the almost inevitable tendency of successfully enacted policies unwittingly to propagate hybrid interests. The area of health care is rich in examples. Far from solidifying the established medical interests, federal funding and regulation of health care since the mid 1960's have had diverse impacts and therefore have tended to fragment what was once a fairly monolithic system of medical representation. Public Policy has not only uncovered but helped to create diverging interests among hospital associations, insurance companies, medical schools, hospital equipment manufacturers, local health planning groups, preventive medicine advocates, non-teaching research centers, and many others.

Second, as government becomes increasingly involved in programs such as Medicare, it develops independent views and interests from the groups with which it interacts. For example, Medicare gives the government an interest in containing costs, which is different from the interests of physicians, hospitals, and other providers of care. This means the government will have policy agendas of its own and is less likely simply to ratify the bargains struck among interest groups as in some of the simpler models of pluralism.[6]

A third trend, fostered by the complexity of government, the interdependence of policies, and the differential effects of government action, is the growing importance of expertise as a political resource, a phenomenon Heclo has labeled a politics of "issue networks" that is fragmented and kaleidoscopic, built on shifting coalitions of experts who become mobilized as the interconnections of their issues with other issues already on the agenda are activated. Accordingly, Heclo (1980, p. 104) notes,

> There is no single health policy network but various sets of people knowledgeable and concerned about cost-control mechanisms, insurance techniques, nutritional programs, pre-paid plans, and so on. At one time, those experts in designing a nationwide insurance system may seem to be operating in relative isolation, until it becomes clear that previous efforts to control costs have already created precedents that have to be accommodated in any new system or that the issue of federal funding for abortions has laid land mines in the path of any workable plan.

---

[6]Brown describes the attempt by government to solve evident problems of existing government programs as "rationalizing politics." See his analyses of the patterns produced by such politics (Brown, 1978, 1981).

These trends produce somewhat paradoxical results. On the one hand, there appear to be more and more special interests involved with government on the model of the older iron triangles, each autonomous in its own sphere and each controlling its own program relatively free from interference by other interests and groups. On the other hand, if anyone attempts a major reform (apart from enacting a new program to satisfy yet another constituency), a whole host of complexities and interdependencies are engaged, supplementing, but not entirely displacing, the older politics of iron triangles with a less stable and more fluid pattern. Thus there has been a proliferation of categorical interests and programs in government each apparently responsive to a more narrowly defined and increasingly differentiated set of interests. This leads to a politics of "immobilism" and "interest group liberalism"[7] as each group defends its narrow sphere of control. On the other hand, major shifts in policy direction become difficult if not impossible, as proposals for change activate the inevitable interdependencies among interests and policies in unpredictable ways. This leads to a politics of "instability." The joint occurrence of immobilism and instability contributes to the growing perception of an "impasse."

Uncertain Knowledge

Not knowing what to do is an important constraint on action. If the experts agree, the politicians may still not act if there is no popular or social consensus. But if the experts cannot agree, the politicians may not be able to justify their choice and their natural caution will be reinforced. Although there is usually a range of disagreement among the experts in any field, agreement on issues of health policy appears to be minimal; and where there is agreement, the policy issues that need to be resolved appear to be broader than the areas on which there is consensus.

For example, no one knows how to contain health care costs, at least without sacrificing competing goals of quality, access, or freedom of choice. One body of research compares the centralized health financing system of England with that of the United States and suggests that centralization into the public sector of all costs is necessary so someone will pay attention to the total bill (Marmor et al., 1976). Others have examined the relationship of medical cost inflation to the growth of third-party reimbursement and argue that co-insurance is necessary to discipline consumer choices (see Feldstein, 1977). The literature suggests that co-insurance reduces use. Unfortunately there is disagreement over whether the use prevented is necessary or unnecessary. Still another group argues that reorganization of provider and professional incentives is the key to containing costs. They advocate solutions such as the creation of HMOs. In short, the experts and the research are divided not only on technical and methodological issues (e.g., whether controls were adequate, sample sizes large enough, service definitions comparable) but also on the substantive issue of whether the provider, the consumer, or the government is the primary source of the problem.

In addition, research on subjects as complex as the organization and delivery of $200 billion a year in health services is often inconclusive. Key concepts such as costs have been measured in different ways, and replication of studies under similar circumstances is rare. Where threats to internal validity have been adequately controlled (an infrequent occurrence in the quasiexperimental world of health systems research), studies are often based on single communities and may have low external validity. Multisite

---

[7]The phrase is by Lowi (1969).

research conducted according to a planned variation design that can improve external validity is often prohibitively expensive and of relatively high risk. For example, the validity of the randomized experiments designed to test the cost effectiveness of home-maker and day-care services as alternatives to nursing homes was affected by the tendency of case workers to provide additional services to control group members (Weissert et al., 1979). Moreover, policymakers, although hungry for policy-relevant information, are reluctant to make such large investments when budgets are tight, when inevitable limitations of quasiexperimental research designs mean that policy issues will never be finally resolved,[8] and when the lead time on such research is so long that the policy-maker who commissions a study will not be there when the results come in.

Even when the experts agree on a biomedical or epidemiological question, more-over, the policy decision on what to do often involves complex trade-offs among competing values. Even if a procedure is declared to be safe and effective in a consensus development conference, it may be prohibitively expensive or personally obtrusive. If the experts disagree and there are political risks in taking action, another study can always be justified, as demonstrated in the controversy over saccharine. According to H. David Banta and Clyde Behney, "cost-effectiveness analysis has too many methodological and other weaknesses to justify relying solely or primarily on the results of formal studies in making a decision" (Banta and Behney, 1981). Although policy research improves information and choices, it rarely settles complex policy debates.

Constrained Budgets

Spending money is not always the solution to problems. Significant change can often be achieved through budget reallocations and reform of regulations. Nevertheless, constrained budgets severely reduce the choice among alternative policy options to address problems. And even cost-effective reforms require front-end financing.

The costs of even incremental changes are often in the billions. Proposed catastrophic versions of NHI, for example, have been priced from $7 billion to $15 billion in additional federal costs. More comprhensive versions would cost well over $100 billion. Even $7 billion is a very large sum given current budget constraints. Major changes in the benefit structure of existing programs such as adding a drug benefit in Medicare or expanding Medicaid coverage to the "medically needy" in all states may run into billions. Thus, even such comparatively incremental reforms as adding a homemaker benefit to Medicare at a cost of approximately $500 million were priced out of the budget when uncontrollable budget increases largely driven by inflation automatically added over $9 billion to Medicare and Medicaid expenditures between FY 1981 and FY 1982 (Budget of the U.S. Government, 1982).

This dismal budget picture led former Secretary Califano to concentrate on proposals such as hospital cost containment on the theory that medical inflation had to be controlled before the nation could "afford" NHI. Otherwise such a comprehensive plan would soon be priced so high that no one could conceive adding that much to the federal

[8]The interaction between politicians and scientists is a complex one. Although scientific findings rarely resolve policy debates for the reasons cited above, research does feed back upon the political process and influence it. First, information, especially under conditions of uncertainty, is an important political resource in and of itself. Second, the research community may be split, but the politician is constrained to choose one side or the other. Certain positions are simply not viable. Third, and perhaps most important, policy questions may not be fully answered, but often the worst alternatives can be eliminated. More information is usually better than less, unless so little is known that fragmentary results lead in the wrong direction.

budget. The estimated savings from the Carter administration's hospital cost containment bill would have been approximately $2 billion in its first full year of implementation. Whatever the substantive merits of the Carter administration's approach to hospital cost containment, it played a strategic role in creating room for political maneuver in the budget. Although Congress never enacted the hospital cost containment bill, the paper savings of $2 billion theoretically could be allocated to other programs such as the proposal to expand preventive health services to pregnant women and children in Medicaid (CHAP bill). Although Medicare and Medicaid are entitlements and therefore uncontrollable in the absence of legislation modifying the entitlement, the government's estimate of future spending is controllable and is made to conform to proposed legislative changes no matter how unlikely their passage. Even so, the budgetary savings invented in this manner are usually enough to finance only a few incremental program expansions.

CONCLUSIONS

It is popular to describe health care policy as in a crisis that demands a solution. Nevertheless, in a survey conducted in June 1978, 76 percent of the public indicated that they were satisfied or somewhat satisfied with their health insurance coverage, which has led Altman (1981) to observe, "Most patients have faith in their doctor—although they distrust organized medicine—and they look to the medical-care system with an almost mystical view of its powers. Clearly this does not portray a national crisis." The health care crisis, to the extent one exists, is seen by those embedded in the policy elites, not the general population.

The current impasse will end when the public perceives a crisis and general political leadership as well as the health policy elites respond to demands for change. Until such a consensus emerges, there will be little or no popular support for either an expanded federal role in the private health care market or a restructuring of health services delivery along more competitive lines.

When political consensus exists, government takes action even if there is little knowledge of how things work. Thus the election of 74 Democrats to the House of Representatives in the Johnson landslide of 1964 led to the passage of Medicare and Medicaid even though no one could predict accurately their cost or their possible inflationary effect on medical care costs. When political consensus is lacking, the inconclusiveness and methodological weaknesses of research studies and the disagreement among the experts justify inaction. When political consensus exists, one side of the scientific debate is chosen, and even fragmentary evidence may be cited to justify taking action.[9]

Budgetary resources also become available when there is a political demand for action. Not knowing what to do does not preclude spending money on problems that *must* be solved. No one is really sure how to solve the energy crisis, but OPEC is a more visible and understandable enemy than medical cost inflation. Thus President Carter

---

[9]See, for example, Sundquist's (1968) description of the launching of the War on Poverty. Sundquist quotes David Hackett: "I quickly learned from the March meeting that you can't get consensus among professionals, so I had to pick one of the best and rely on his judgment." Foltz (1982) shows how when the scientific community is split, the politicians may choose either side, but are not constrained to side with the majority if one can be identified.

urged passage of a multibillion dollar synfuels program in the very same constrained budget years portrayed above. Although the Reagan administration dropped subsidies for synfuels development from the FY 1982 budget, it recommended unprecedented increases in defense spending.[10]

Finally, if the way in which health care is financed and delivered is to be reformed by any administration, it will need to galvanize the popular support necessary to bypass the fragmented health policy making structure described in Chapter 4 and modify its dynamics as described above.

ACKNOWLEDGMENTS

I wish to thank Larry Brown, John Campbell, George Downs, Judy Feder, Anne-Marie Foltz, Herbert Kaufman, Barbara Manard, Harvey Sapolsky, Deborah Lewis-Idema, and Jack Walker for comments on an earlier draft of this chapter. This chapter was written by George D. Greenberg in his private capacity. No official support or endorsement by the U.S. Department of Health and Human Services is intended or should be inferred.

REFERENCES

Altman, Stuart, "The Design of a National Health Insurance System for the United States," in Stuart Altman and Harvey Sapolsky, eds., *Federal Health Programs: Problems and Prospects*, Lexington, Mass.: D.C. Heath, 1981, p. 206.

Benta, H. David and Clyde J. Behney, "Policy Formation and Technology Assessment," *Milbank Memorial Fund Quarterly/Health and Society*, Vol. 59, Summer 1981, pp. 445–479.

Brown, Lawrence D., "The Formulation of Federal Health Care Policy," *Bulletin of the New York Academy of Medicine*, Vol. 54, No. 1, January 1978, pp. 45–58.

Brown, Lawrence D., "Rationalizing Politics: Notes Toward A Theory," unpublished manuscript, Washington D.C.: The Brookings Institution, 1981.

Budget of the Unites States Government FY 1982, Table 17, p. 596.

Callahan, James, J., Jr. and Stanley S. Wallack eds., *Reforming the Long-Term Care System*, Lexington, Mass.: D.C. Heath, 1981.

Feldstein, Martin, "The High Cost of Hospitals and What to do About it," *The Public Interest*, Vol. 48, Summer 1977, pp. 40–55.

Foltz, Anne Marie, *The Politics of Prevention: Child Health Politics Under Medicaid*, Cambridge: MIT Press, 1982.

Health Care Financing Administration, *Long Term Care: Background and Future Directions*, Health Care Financing Administration, Publication No. HCFA 81-20047, January 1981, p. 15.

Heclo, Hugh, "Issue Networks and the Executive Establishment," in Anthony Kind, ed., *The New American Political System*, Washington D.C.: The American Enterprise Institute, 1980, pp. 96, 104.

Lowi, Theodore, *The End of Liberalism*, New York: WW Norton & Co., 1969.

---

[10]The author is not passing judgment on the substantive merit of any of these proposals.

Marmor, Theodore, Donald Wittman, and Thomas Heagy, "The Politics of Medical Inflation," *The Journal of Health Politics, Policy and Law*, Vol. 1, Spring 1976, pp. 69–85.

McClure, Walter, "The Medical Care System Under National Health Insurance: Four Models," *The Journal of Health Politics, Policy and Law*, Vol. 1, Spring 1976, pp. 22–69.

Office of the Assistant Secretary for Planning and Evaluation, *Working Papers on Long-Term Care*, Hyattsville, Maryland: Department of Health and Human Services, October, 1981.

Sapolsky, Harvey, "A Solution to the Health Care Crisis," *Policy Analysis*, Vol. 3, Winter 1977, pp. 115–123.

Sundquist, James, *Politics and Policy*, Washington, D.C.: The Brookings Institution, 1968, p. 120.

Vogel, Ronald J. and Hans Palmer eds., *Long-Term Care: Some Perspectives for Research and Demonstrations*, unpublished report, Health Care Financing Administration, June 15, 1981.

Vladeck, Bruce C., *Unloving Care*, New York: Basic Books, 1980.

Weissert, William, Thomas Wan, and Barbara Livieratos, *Effects and Costs of Day Care and Homemaker Services for the Chronically Ill: A Randomized Experiment*, Executive Summary, National Center for Health Services Research, January 1979.

CHAPTER 7

Congressional Process and Health Policy: Reform and Retrenchment

David Falcone
Lynn C. Hartwig

Congressional health policy encompasses legislative decisions directly affecting principle actors and institutions in their roles in the health field. Several identifiable legislative and/or centers of power structures affecting the organization, delivery, and financing of health services can be identified. It is our contention that there is little to distinguish the politics of health legislation other than this structural differentiation in Congress, whereby responsibilities are assigned for health issues and the particular "concentration of interests" that characterizes pressure group demands (Falcone, 1980–1981; Falcone, forthcoming).

Since the legislative process with regard to health issues is not immune to the factors affecting all policy areas in recent history (stipulated as post-1960, for purposes of this discussion), trends in congressional behavior are delineated, and an attempt is made to engage in a qualitative multivariate analysis to relate, in a systematic, but ultimately nonscientific, way reform of congressional procedure to changes in health policy.

The general conclusion reached is that it is nearly impossible to ascribe policy developments, or the lack of them, in the health field to variations in the structure and process of congressional decision making. This is not to say that the reforms were insignificant, only that changes in both policy and procedure may also spring, among other sources, from economic and, perhaps consequently, ideological variables; from the substance and style of the presidency; and from "rational" evaluations of the efficacy, efficiency, and effectiveness of past policies.

HEALTH POLICY

Several types of policy directly affect or seek to affect health. Those that come readily to mind are primarily legislative, but they also include judicial and public administrative decisions dealing with the rates of production, geographical and specialty distribution of health personnel, health care financing, assurance of the quality of health personnel, institutions and services, occupational safety and environmental protection, and attempts to limit consumption of presumably destructive substances such as alcohol, tobacco, and synthetic carcinogens. In some instances, the indirect effects on health of housing, income maintenance, or other welfare policies may be even more consequential than the direct effects of policies that patently deal with health. Nevertheless, it is useful to limit the conception of health policy to the conventional notion of public decisions that seek primarily to affect health or principal actors—professional and institutional—in their roles in the health arena. Using this restriction allows statements to be made such as the one above positing that some other policies may ultimately have a more telling impact on health than more strictly health policies or that there is a need for integrating different policy areas (health and welfare are perhaps those most frequently cited).

HEALTH LEGISLATION IN THE 1970s: SURGE AND DECLINE

This section reviews legislative developments from the mid-1960s to the present, focusing on the 1970s, a period of major congressional reform, in an attempt to depict a forward thrust in policy activity followed by a diminution of government intervention.[1] Emphasis is placed on the influence of factors affecting congressional decision making in explaining this policy shift, an emphasis that will be qualified later when legislative reform is assessed alongside other simultaneous influences on health policy.

National health policy before 1972 seemed to show little concern for either actual or future costs as legislation was passed creating program upon program. By 1976 health care costs were described, perhaps hyperbolically, as the "superproblem" in health by Assistant Secretary for Health Theodore Cooper, (Cooper, 1976), and controlling them clearly had become the overriding theme in health policy debate. The reason for this shift is understandable given the rise in federal health outlays over the course of the past 20 years (Table 7-1). However, the magnitude of the federal health bill would not necessarily have produced a cost-containment reaction as long as the "pie" was perceived as ever expanding. The 1974 oil embargo symbolized the end of the "bigger pie" mentality for the United States and the beginning of a surge in high inflation and unemployment.

Health policy, as other policy areas, changed in three ways in the 1960s: (1) the magnitude of government spending at all levels in health rose both in absolute terms from $6.6 billion in 1960 to $104.2 billion in 1980 and as a percent of total health expenditures, that is, from 24.7 to 42.2 percent (Gibson and Waldo, 1982), (2) policy and decision making shifted to the federal level, and (3) the goals of the policy process became implicitly more redistributive and explicitly aimed at improving access to health care. Overall, this policy can be conceived of as having had three broad goals: (1) maintaining quality of care, (2) guaranteeing access to care, and (3) allocating resources in a cost-effective manner (Table 7-2).

Before 1960, health care policy in the United States focused on improving the quality of care through activities of the health professions and state governments. After

---

[1]For a review of major policy developments preceeding this period, see Falcone, (1980–1981).

TABLE 7-1. Federal Health Expenditures (Billions) 1962–1982

Fiscal Year	Total Expenditures	Health Expenditures[a]	Percent
1982 EST	695.3	81.1	11.7
1980	579.6	64.7	11.2
1978	462.2	48.9	10.6
1976	366.5	37.5	10.2
1974	268.4	25.1	9.3
1972	231.9	19.5	8.4
1970	196.6	14.8	7.5
1968	178.9	11.0	6.1
1966	107.0	3.9	3.6
1964	97.7	2.9	3.0
1962	87.8	2.3	2.6

SOURCE: *The U.S. Budget.* Washington, D.C.: Office of Management and Budget, 1962–1982.
[a]Federal health expenditures include health function [651 and 550] and veterans health function [84].

the Flexner report in 1910, for example, a number of medical schools in this country were closed as the educational process for physicians was standardized and the basis for scientific and specialty medicine was created in the basic science departments of educational institutions. At the same time, states passed licensing laws restricting entry into practice to those from accredited schools (Stevens, 1971).

Federal public health activities were limited to hospitals for special people, to communicable disease control, and to some maternal and child health programs. These functions were overshadowed after World War II by the passage of Hill-Burton legislation and the buildup in the 1950s and early 1960s of the research programs of the National Institutes of Health (NIH). The first major federal social policy thrust on the other hand—the Social Security Act (SSA) of 1935—purposefully omitted health proposals from its content. Framers of the act feared medical profession opposition would subvert the entire program. While some of the above policies, such as the reduction in medical school openings, negatively affected access, others, such as Hill-Burton, increased access and improved the quality of the facilities in small communities.

In 1960 a new emphasis upon access as a goal and the shift to greater federal involvement in policy decisions generally resulted in a 15-year period of legislation designed to reduce financial, geographical, organizational, and other barriers to care. The decision makers placed their faith in input process policies, assuming that the outcome would be beneficial; that is, if the resources were provided, people would get the health care they needed and improved health status would result.

Most health legislation between 1968 and 1980 came about either as amendments to the Social Security Act or to the Public Health Service Act (PHSA) of 1944 (Wilson and Newhauser, 1976). (Major exceptions were health programs under the Department of Defense.) Within a very short period, federal health policies laid the foundation for increases in facilities, personnel, and money. Amendments to the Hill-Burton legislation, that is, PL 87-395, PL 88-442, and PL 91-296, provided support for outpatient facilities, nursing homes, and the modernization of hospital and health care facilities in urban areas.

TABLE 7-2. Development of Medical Policy in the United States Over Three Time Periods: 1900–1982

Time period	1900–1960	1961–1972	1973–1980
Goal	Quality	Access	Cost effectiveness
Objectives	Upgrade medical education	Increase number of physicians and other health professionals	Control capital expansion
	Strengthen scientific basis of medicine	Improve geographic distribution	Reduce use of expensive technology
	Strengthen specialty training and practice	Improve specialty distributions	Control number of providers
	Upgrade medical practice	Improve ability to pay	Reduce use of institutions
Policies	Pass state licensing laws	Expand medical schools	PSRO
	Close medical schools	Build new schools	HSA
	Standardize medical education through accreditation	CHP[a]	HMO
	Fund biomedical research	NHSC	Prevention/promotion programs
	Fund hospital construction Hill-Burton	Medicare	Center for health technology
		Medicaid	Primary care programs as cost control mechanism
		Medicaid	
		AHEC	
		Rural health initiatives	
		EPSDT	
		Primary care programs including family medicine	

[a]CHP Comprehensive health planning; NHSC, National Health Services Corps; AHEC, Area Health Education Center; EPSDT, Early and Periodic Screening, Diagnosis, and Treatment; PSRO, professional standards review organizations; HSA, Health Services Administration; HMO, Health Maintenance Organization.

In 1963 health manpower legislation (PL 88-129) authorized support to medical schools for the first time. Later legislation encouraged existing schools to expand enrollment, funded new schools, supported programs to train new health practitioners and primary care physicians, and created Area Health Education Center (AHEC) programs. Federal policies were directed at preventing an impending great physician shortage that was predicted in numerous studies in the 1940s, 1950s, and early 1960s (Sorking, 1977).

Although the legislative debates over Hill-Burton legislation, health manpower, and research funding were hardly mild, several factors tended to limit controversy. For one thing, it was difficult to argue with the need for physicians, hospitals, or research. In addition, the policies were viewed essentially as distributive in nature, benefiting the professional and academic interest group constituencies without outrightly depriving anyone.

Far more controversial was legislation creating national health insurance (NHI) for those 65 years and over and for the poor. Marmor (1973) charts Medicare's progress from impossibility in the 1950s to enactment in 1965 and notes that the House Ways and Means Committee had a central role, first, in preventing passage and, then, after the 1964 election virtually made the legislation inevitable, in greatly expanding the Johnson administration's proposal.

While policymakers from 1961 to 1964 focused public attention on the battles between the American Medical Association (AMA) and labor, the most crucial negotiation took place between then Assistant Secretary Wilbur Cohen and Ways and Means Chairman Wilbur Mills (Dem. Ark). According to Marmor's analysis, Mills had the political sensitivity, power, and technical expertise to block legislation before 1964 and then to steer his own version of Medicare through the Ways and Means Committee and the House. Many of the legislative reforms in the 1970s were aimed directly at breaking Mills' power on Ways and Means, and it is doubtful whether by 1980 any member of Congress could exercise the control Mills did through "persuasion, entreaty, authoritative expertise and control of the agenda" (Marmor, 1973).

Other key elements in President Johnson's health policy were Regional Medical Programs (RMP) designed to help movement of the latest medical knowledge into the communities through a cooperative arrangement between academic institutions and community physicians and Comprehensive Health Planning (CHP). As with many federal programs, CHP began as a permissive program and later became mandatory.

Health legislative activity continued under the Nixon administration, and in 1970 11 major acts of legislation were passed, including such new areas as occupational health and safety, alcohol abuse, and the National Health Service Corps. In 1971 the war on cancer substantially increased support for comprehensive programs targeting this disease.

The major features of legislation passed between 1961 and 1971 were improved access through increased numbers of physicians and other health professionals, construction of facilities, and payment for care. By 1972 the costs of these programs had become visible, whereas their effectiveness measured in terms of improved health status had not. Federal health care costs had increased from $2.3 billion in 1962, to $14.8 billion in 1970, and to $25.1 billion in 1974. The prospect of some form of NHI was seen as imminent, and the consequent effect on inflation was viewed with alarm by federal policymakers (Russell, 1977).

A significant change in the rhetoric of health policy debate was evident in Congress by 1972 during consideration of professional standards review organization (PSRO) legislation and discussion of the National Health Planning and Resources Development Act (NHPRDA) of 1974. Cost control was the prevailing justification for peer review. It was felt that if unnecessary hospitalization and surgery could be averted, Medicare and Medicaid costs could be reduced.

Blumstein (1977) points to the tension posed by legislation that has twin missions of cost control and quality assurance. The act creating PSRO is replete with compromises among the actors in the health policy arena. Two examples are cited: the limitation of such review to hospitals (not physicians' offices) and the delegation of review authority to hospital use review committees where they existed. As the act was implemented, administrative and professional emphasis focused on the quality mission rather than on cost control. Not until 1980 was there any evidence that PSRO was saving government programs more than it cost, and even then, the Congressional Budget Office suggested that costs were simply shifted to the private sector (Congressional Budget Office, 1981).

The national health planning debate began shortly after the 1972 election, with legislative authority for Hill-Burton legislation, Regional Medical Programs, and Comprehensive Health Planning set to expire in June 1973. Again the major problem identified by Congress was cost escalation (Biles, 1975). Congress recognized that government programs had proliferated in an uncoordinated fashion and that inflation in the health system was significantly greater than general inflation. For those in health policy circles desiring to expand health insurance in the United States, regulation was one method of centralizing control of the system. On January 4, 1975, a few days after the National Health Planning and Resources Development Act was signed into law, a staff member of the Subcommittee on Health of the Senate Labor and Public Welfare Committee told an audience of health planners that "you are providing the foundation of an effective, efficient national health insurance program" (Biles, 1975).

Although the new health planning system was given authority to determine the need for health professionals, it had no control over the training or distribution of physicians. After 10 years of federal funding of health professionals' education, congressional action seemed to rest on several assumptions: the medical schools had responded to the federal policy of increasing the output of physicians, nearly doubling the number of spaces by 1974; increased numbers had not altered geographical and specialty maldistributions; each new physician in the system generated considerable sums per annum in expenses (estimates vary from $400,000 to $800,000).

Suggested solutions that would be less costly were to direct physicians into primary care, use nonphysician health personnel, and increase the number of areas receiving members of the National Health Service Corps. For years, differences among various manpower proposals considered by Senator Kennedy's (Dem. Mass.) Senate Subcommittee on Health and Congressman Rogers' (Dem. Fla.) analogous subcommittee in the House prevented final congressional action (LeRoy and Lee, 1977). Rogers' philosophy ultimately was reflected in the Health Professions Assistance Act of 1976. Medical students were not required to enter primary care specialities or practice in underserved areas, but medical schools were required to have 50 percent of their graduates entering primary care residencies by 1980; more coercive policies might be considered if this goal was not met. The critical concept was primary care, and Congress chose the least conflictual but also least meaningful definition—graduates entering internal medicine, family medicine, pediatrics, and obstetrics–gynecology. Finally, Congress approached cost containment from another direction: support for Health Maintenance Organizations (HMO) in the hope of promoting effective preventive medical care.

Price (1975) has described Congressman Rogers' style as consensual and credits him with effectively running his subcommittee based on the traditional norms of comity, reciprocity, and compromise. The effect was to produce legislation that at times pleased no one. Price regards the HMO legislation (PL 95-222) as an example in which the quest for unanimity nearly compromised the bill out of existence. The Nixon administration viewed HMOs as a cost-saving alternative to the fee-for-service system. Kennedy, in an attempt to take the lead, developed a much stronger proposal after extensive hearings. On Rogers' House subcommittee, Dr. William Roy, a freshman Kansas Democrat, submitted an alternative with Rogers' backing and support. Although most proposals before Rogers' committee did not arouse the hostility of the medical profession, HMO legislation was in the class of policies that could substantially alter the delivery of health care. In the House hearings, the AMA argued for a "limited experimental" program. The Kennedy bill was reported out of the Senate on July 21, 1972. Rogers' subcommittee, on the other hand, did not report a bill until late September, giving Commerce Committee Chairman Harley Staggers (Dem. W. Va.), a fiscal conservative, the opportunity to let the bill die as Congress adjourned.

When the measure was reintroduced early in the Ninety-third Congress, the Senate bill was substantially reduced from $5.1 billion to $806 million over 3 years while the Commerce Committee authorized $240 million over 5 years. Many other features of the original proposals were omitted as well, such as special programs for the indigent, for high-risk individuals, and for medically underserved areas. The final conference version favored the House: The authorization was for $325 million over a 5-year period, primarily for feasibility studies and developmental grants. To some extent the outcome was inevitable given the weakened support given to HMOs by the administration during the 1972 campaign, a change that Price (1975) attributes to substantial AMA pressure.

Between 1970 and 1975, Congress created the National Health Service Corps, Professional Standard Review Organizations, and a national health planning system and provided initial support for HMOs. Policymakers waged war on cancer, Cooley's anemia, sickle cell anemia, and sudden infant death syndrome. The prevailing ideology still expected government to provide solutions to the problems identified in the health system. But instead of the open-ended financing of the 1960s, programs needed to be justified in terms of cost effectiveness. New program costs were to be offset by savings to the system. This belief, and the presence of two subcommittee chairmen (Rogers and Kennedy) intent on establishing reputations in the health arena, made the period a particularly productive one.

It is equally true however, that Congress, in the face of major acknowledged cost-control problems, avoided making decisions that would radically change the financing and delivery system (Davis and Schoen, 1978). Equal access to health care had not been assured despite massive government intervention strategies.

By 1977 and the Carter presidency, the Democrats were divided over how to proceed. Senator Kennedy argued that cost could only be controlled by centralizing the insurance system. The President and more fiscally conservative senators and representatives feared that until a mechanism was in place to control at least hospital costs, expansion of the insurance system could strain the federal budget to the breaking point. For whatever reason, the Ninety-fifth and Ninety-sixth Congresses were most notable for the health legislation *not* passed rather than that passed. By the time Carter took office it was evident that one effect of the inflationary economy was public concern over rising taxes. Carter's first thrust then was in cost containment. Two programs were aimed at the rising costs of Medicare and Medicaid. Although the administration was successful in getting a bill passed attacking fraud and abuse in the system, it was unable to get either House to seriously consider a cap on hospital expenditures.

With cost-containment foremost in legislators' minds, why did hospital cost containment fail in both the Ninety-fifth and Ninety-sixth Congresses? One reason may be that it was a bad act that no one believed would work. Or if it worked too well, the availability of services might be sharply reduced. The provider associations certainly argued both points. In the aftermath of its demise, the Carter forces gave the hospital and health lobby credit for defeating the measure. A more likely reason is that the American Hospital Association's voluntary cost-containment program (the so called Voluntary Effort—VE) at least created a sense that hospitals were trying to hold down costs.[2] In addition, the difference between general inflation and that in the hospital sector significantly decreased quelling the desire for reform.

HEALTH POLICY AND THE LEGISLATIVE PROCESS

Ten years ago we would have described the U.S. Congress by noting that it was distinctive among Western democratic legislative assemblies with respect to the power it has retained vis-à-vis the executive, despite the fact that the complexities of policy formation have increasingly placed the responsibility for policy initiation, priority determination, and formulation with the latter branch of government.[3] Whereas most legislatures have had as their principle function the refinement of executive proposals, Congress has remained comparatively capable both of generating policy and of posing the threat of thwarting executive initiatives so that, at least, the calculus of anticipated legislative reaction has been a significant factor in influencing the shape of major policies.

This may still be an accurate distinction, but it is certainly not as definite as before. The reasons why Congress has joined in the often bemoaned decline of legislatures (Loewenberg, 1971) are complex and interrelated: the executive's near monopoly on information needed to make decisions[4]; the fact that perhaps more than ever in twentieth-century legislative history senators and representatives need not adhere to party guidelines in their campaign rhetoric or voting behavior, thus creating a power vacuum in Congress that is exploitable by a vigorous president; the tendency toward plebiscitary democracy that is furthered although, as the Ford and Carter administrations' experiences attest, certainly not determined, by the president's preemptory access to the mass media; and the reliance on variants of neo-Keynesian economics (albeit perhaps implicity) and the resultant blending of fiscal, monetary, and social programs in such a way that a single source ultimately must interdigitate the ingredients of the overall policy mix. In any event, it is clear that a death knell for Congress would be premature, even if the policy initiation capability of this institution has been compromised. This is as true of health legislation as it is for other arenas of congressional concern.

---

[2]In fact, a significant increase in costs occurred after the first year of the voluntary effort owing to deferred capital expansion and unrecovered increases in operating expenses.

[3]This staging of the policy process is borrowed from R. J. Van Loon and Michael Whittington, 1971.

[4]Congress is less caught up in this dilemma than parliaments since it has available, whether or not it is fully used, an autonomous research capability in the general accounting office and in personal and committee staffs that are not duplicated in any other modern democratic legislature.

KEY STRUCTURES IN THE HEALTH POLICY
LEGISLATIVE PROCESS

Congressional decision making is so fluid and complex (e.g., each session of the House and Senate establishes its own procedures although some are emminently predictable), that it is an oversimplication to single out the components of the legislative process responsible for health policy. Nevertheless, it is fairly clear that certain standing committees are central.[5] Their respective turfs are not so readily indentifiable since they are regularly engaged in jurisdictional disputes and because some proponents of legislation use the machine gun approach in advancing their causes; that is, they target as many committees as possible in the hope that one will be a hit.

There traditionally (at least during the period covered by this review of major changes in health policy) has been a Senate Subcommittee on Health within the Committee on Labor and Human Resources (formerly the Committee on Labor and Public Welfare). With the changeover in party control of the Senate in 1981, however, the new chairman of the full committee, Senator Orrin Hatch (Rep. Utah) formerly the ranking minority member of the subcommittee, retained his full measure of discretion over health issues by dissolving the subcommittee, thus leaving health affairs to the full committee.

In addition, there periodically are committees, such as the Senate Special and House Select Committee on Aging, that consider health issues. Moreover, all legislation must undergo the scrutiny of the House Rules Committee and the Senate and House Budget Committees. Finally, the Appropriations Committees are divided into subcommittees with functional responsibilities, one of which is health. Their support is crucial, since many authorizations are beefed up, watered down, or even (although this usually is a breach of collegiality) actually inaugurated at this stage (Redman, 1974). Every prospective grantsman, for example, has keenly felt the meaning of the phrase "authorized but not appropriated." Authorizations usually cover a period of several years, whereas appropriations are voted on yearly.

Other committees occasionally assume prominence in dealing with health issues when their central concerns intersect with this policy area. For example, the Banking and Currency Committees were especially important during the early to mid 1970s because of the impact of the Economic Stabilization Program (wage and price controls), over which they had jurisdiction, on health care institutions.

The potential confusion in the legislative process surrounding the health arena mirrors the difficulty in labeling health policies: Most not only seek to affect quality of care, access, and financing but also, explicitly or implicitly, call for regulation and redistribution of resources. For example, consideration of NHI schemes could require decisions about revenue (House Ways and Means Committee and the Senate Finance Committee), health services delivery (Interstate and Foreign Commerce Committee in the House and the Labor and Human Resources Committee in the Senate), federal–state relations (judiciary in each House), and the organization of government to administer the plan (government operations in the House and Senate).

The effects of fragmentation of responsibilities in the congressional process traditionally have been mitigated by an agile and vigorous leadership, norms of reciprocity

---

[5]In the Senate, there are the Finance, Labor, and Environment and Public Works Committees. And in the House, the Ways and Means, Interstate and Foreign Commerce, and Public Works and Transportation Committees.

and specialization, as well as presidential direction. Recent reforms, however, may have undercut the informal structures and processes that have "greased the skids" of this very frictional mechanism. The irony in this turn of events is that the intention of the reformers was to smooth the way for "liberal" legislation.

REFORM PERIOD

Between 1970 and 1975 Congress, particularly the House of Representatives, passed a series of primarily procedural reforms (Congressional Quarterly, 1976).[6] The focus of the reforms was the committee system and its basis of power—seniority. The major reforms are outlined in Table 7-3 according to how they affected congressional structures, processes, and resources.

From 1911 until the late 1960s a pattern of legislative decision making evolved around powerful committee chairmen who rose to their positions by virtue of their ability to be reelected. Many of these posts, especially the critical positions on Rules and Ways and Means, were held by conservative southern Democrats who were adept at delaying or defeating liberal legislation.

The 1964 election dramatically changed the context of policymaking and the characteristics of Congress. The reforms of the 1970s date to this election and the influx of congressional representatives of the Great Society. From the landslide of 1964 to that of 1974, Congress reflected the proportional change in the number of young voters, the growing demand of minorities and women for influence and power and the rising educational levels and sophistication of the people of the United States. Murphy (1974) has characterized the whole movement as a "new politics," involving three major effects on Congress. The first was a significant decline in the power of the conservative coalition. Southern Democrats in both houses of Congress were being challenged by Republicans in general elections; primary competition was greater; and the constituency in the suburbs, traditionally Republican strongholds, became less conservative. The second and related change was that the composition of the House became more diverse. Black membership increased from five in 1960 to 16 in 1974. Although their numbers did not increase, women began to play a more predominent role. Finally, public interest lobbying forces, such as that of Ralph Nader and the Sierra Club, emerged as a counterbalance to the traditional interest groups.

Reforms were so numerous during the early 1970s and affected so many areas of congressional activity that the particular problems to which they were directed are difficult to discern (Jones, 1977). The problems appear, however, to fall into the following five categories:

1. An unequal and ineffective relationship with the executive
2. The concentration of power in senior committee chairmen
3. Too many barriers in congressional procedure, which allowed a minority of legislators to block programs
4. The inability of junior members, particularly freshmen, to play an active role in the legislative process
5. A weak party structure and inability to effect party platform commitments

---

[6]For an extensive review of these reforms and their background and impact, see Dodd and Oppenheimer (1981).

TABLE 7-3. 1970–1975 Congressional Reforms and Their Impact on Congressional Structures, Processes, and Resources

Congressional Reform	Structure	Process	Resource
Legislative Reorganization Act of 1970		Written committee rules Teller votes on House floor record Role call votes in closed committee made public	
Caucus Rule Changes 1971	Committee on Committees no longer needs to consider seniority in chosing chairman	Ten Democrats can request separate vote on chairman Can hold only one subcommittee chairmanship	
Caucus Rule Change 1973	Steering and Policy Committee created	Caucus must meet regularly even without quorum Open committee meetings Secret vote for chairman can be requested Each Democrat guaranteed one major assignment Majority of caucus can force right to amend on floor	
Subcommittee Bill of Rights 1973	Established subcommittee jurisdictions Set party ratios	Subcommittee chairmen to be elected by full committee caucus Committee chairman must send bill to subcommittee within 2 weeks Guaranteed each member major subcommittee	Provided subcommittee budgets
Hansen Reforms No. 988, October 1974	Required all committees to exercise oversight responsibility through special	House Democrats required to meet to organize in December	

Caucus rule changes December 1974	committee or assign to standing committee	Secret vote for chairman required
	Committee assignments to be made by Steering and Policy Committee	Chairman of Appropriations Subcommittees to be elected
	All committees with over 20 members must have at least four subcommittees	
	Expanded Ways and Means from 25 to 37 members	
	Speaker to nominate Rules Committee members	
Congressional Budget and Impoundment Act of 1974	Created budget committees	Created Congressional Budget Office
	Required budget figures be set then reconciled by end of year	
Caucus rule changes 1975	Conference committee opened	Increased staff of overall subcommittee and minority component

SOURCE: Congressional Quarterly, *Inside Congress*, Washington: Congressional Quarterly, 1976.

The reform movement began with the formation of the Democratic Study Group, an unofficial alliance of liberals concerned about social policy legislation. In 1968 they pushed to revive the Democratic caucus, and in 1973 they were instrumental in creating the Democratic Steering and Policy Committee. Through procedural reforms, power and authority were transferred to these structures and away from the House Ways and Means and Rules Committees, which were viewed as major stumbling blocks for liberal legislation.

Initially, the reforms worked to the benefit of the liberals who proposed them. The rejuvenated caucus and Steering and Policy Committee provided a forum for discussion. The majority of the Democrats were relatively liberal and therefore could control votes taken within the party caucus. The freshman and junior members had been guaranteed seats on major committees and subcommittees hitherto impossible to achieve, and, at the height of the reformists' power, three senior committee chairmen (all southern conservatives) were removed from their posts. The visibility of the legislative process was enhanced when teller votes were recorded, committee sessions were opened to the public, and the budget acts required explicit priority setting in the appropriations process. With this increased visibility, coalition building and compromises became more difficult to negotiate. Members found their interest group constituencies paying close attention to their voting record and uninterested in the necessity to sometimes "make deals."

The intended outcomes of the reforms were to strengthen the party leadership, remove barriers in the legislative process, and democratize (i.e., give more power to more members) the decision-making structure. Observers of the reforms (Reiselback, 1977; Ornstein and Rode, 1977; Oleszek, 1977) maintain that the cumulative effect was to decentralize power so severely that committee chairmen could no longer manage their committees. The sharing of authority and expertise (e.g., staff) with subcommittee chairmen led to the characterization of the 1970s as an era of "subcommittee government" (Davidson, 1977).

The effect of the reforms on the health subcommittees proved less crucial than in other areas. Rogers and Kennedy, though very different in style, were able to get their bills skillfully to conference. Rogers' subcommittee was know as one of the most productive in the House. During the Ninety-second Congress more than one-third of the total bills reported by the Commerce Committee were in the area of health (20 bills) and all cleared the House (Price, 1978).

Health care issues, especially research, personnel training, and hospital building, remained popular. The lower level of AMA opposition[7] and the emergence of interest groups representing numerous other health constituencies meant considerable demand for legislation viewed as distributive or self-regulatory (Feldstein, 1977).

By the late 1970s, when legislation was increasingly viewed as redistributive, the presence of all these groups, their ability to focus almost exclusively on a small number of subcommittee members, and the addition, at least in the House Subcommittee, of more conservative members, prevented Chairman Rogers from mobilizing a moderate, centrist consensus.

---

[7]Although not happy with PSRO or health planning legislation, AMA opposition was mild compared to the fight over Medicare and NHI.

ASSESSING THE POLICY IMPACT OF CONGRESSIONAL REFORM

It appears that the reforms have weakened party and, thereby, congressional leadership. Interest groups that had exploited the hierarchy in the 1960s now proceeded to take advantage of the lack of leadership in the mid- to late-1970s by obstructing those policies they viewed as undesirable.

However, the impact of legislative reforms, when assessed in conjunction with some of the major trends that could have been responsible for the slowdown in health policy developments that followed these procedural changes, seems less plausibly deterministic. A highly controversial body of literature has challenged the traditional political science that places significance on procedural reform (Dye, 1980). Whatever their methodological limitations, the studies making up this literature—referred to, among other labels, as "determinants analyses"—have at least forced people to consider, in qualitative as well as quantitative terms, whether the variations in structures and processes that have been the foci of reform efforts (e.g., the profesionalization and institutionalization of state legislatures) have been merely coincidental with, rather than causes of, policy change. For example, states with professionalized legislatures may also be those wealthy enough to afford policy innovations. It is not necessary to cite further examples of why the relationship between legislative change and policy is difficult to establish, since this will be glaringly obvious in the following attempt to evaluate the meaning for health policy of the 1970s reforms.

FRAMEWORK FOR ASSESSING THE IMPACT OF CONGRESSIONAL REFORM

At the outset of this discussion it should be pointed out that it is assumed that the procedural reforms in the 1970s represented a significant alteration in the power structure of Congress. If this seems to be a banal proposition, consider another view, that is, that the reforms amounted to "dynamics without change" (Alford, 1976), that they were merely cosmetic, simply exchanging subcommittees for full committees as the principal fiefdoms in the feudal domain of congressional decision making. (In this view, what we have regarded as a set of independent *variables* affecting policy change really amounts to a *constant* and, for this reason alone, cannot be expected to have explanatory power.) Of course, this would not be the first time that an amendment of a legislative structure has led to an elaboration of another one to fulfill the function performed by the original. Recall the effects of the Legislative Reorganization Act of 1946, whereby the number of committees was sharply reduced only to result in a proliferation of subcommittees. Congressional history can serve as a mine for testimonials to Anatole France's observation that *"Plus ca change, le plus c'est la meme chose."*

However even eschewing such procedural nihilism, as most observers of congressional behavior have done, and assuming that the legislative reforms were more than chimerical, there are still difficulties in attributing health policy trends to the legislative developments of the 1970s. Other potential causes of policy stagnation have to be considered.

Economic Circumstances

Perhaps the most obvious of the coincidental and interrelated causal factors that compete with legislative reform is the economic downturn that began in the 1970s. This trend illuminates the fact that many health policies are reallocative and that they rest on the presumption that there will be resources to allocate. Theories of public finance that view government expenditures as led by "luxury" categories such as health and welfare and that posit the existence of a ratchet effect that underlies an irreversible incrementalism have to be reconsidered.[8] In short, the law of expanding state activity, which envisions inexorable "progress," should be called into question for reasons quite apart from changes in congressional behavior patterns.

Experience of Government Health Programs

One such factor in the health arena has been the experience of government programs. By way of illustration, Medicare and Medicaid have been far more expensive than predicted and have been accompanied by numerous regulations not unanticipated by watchful observers. Mechanic (1981) has observed that the hesitant and, therefore, perhaps awkward approach to government-sponsored health insurance programs has disaffected both the right and left sides of the ideological spectrum. It has not resulted in easily available and accessible services, but it has been costly both in terms of outright public expenditures and the administrative superstructure it has promoted. Consequently, on pragmatic grounds alone, the efficacy and effectiveness of further government ventures into the financing and regulation of health services delivery could be questioned.

There is also less cynical interpretation of the impact that experience with government health programs has had, that is, that such programs have actually achieved a measure of success and, therefore, have quieted demands for policy change. Most obviously, Medicare has made a wide (if not totally comprehensive) range of services accessible to the heaviest users of health care. Medicaid covers the designated poor, although in a less than ideally humanitarian fashion. And what perhaps most escapes public attention is that government tax expenditures in effect subsidize the private health insurance industry. This has had more than a trivial effect on the numbers of people covered and is somewhat analagous to the more explicit government subsidization of sickness funds in the Federal Republic of Germany and Sweden, for example. The fact that the income tax exemption accorded employees paid health insurance premiums is a form of government expenditure (i.e., in terms of the foregone revenues to the Treasury) did not go unnoticed by the Reagan administration and Republican Senate, which considered the termination of such indirect government support as a means of curtailing government expenditures by putting potential consumers at greater risk and, at the same time, generating revenues. In this policy posture, the government is perhaps further mending the patchwork quilt of programs that has forestalled a more comprehensive health policy.

Another impact of government programs has been the increasing trend toward oligopsony that they have furthered. As Marmor et al. (1976) have pointed out, concentrated interests result in decision makers becoming more cost-conscious purchasers of health services. This historical observation is corroborated by cross-national comparison: Those nations in which a single unit of government (whether national as in Great Britain or provincial as in Canada) is a large subsidizer of health services tend to exhibit more concern about medical care cost inflation than nations in which financial responsibility is divided among levels of government (e.g., the nation and communes in Sweden, the

---

[8]Variants of this theory are carefully reviewed in Bird (1970); see also Dye (1980).

federal government and *landers* in the Federal Republic of Germany) or among governments and other sources of funds (e.g., France with parallel public and private
financing).

The United States still falls in the mixed, pluralistic source of funding classification,
but over time expenditures have become increasingly centralized. Medicare has had a
more profound effect than Medicaid in this regard (Marmor et al., 1976) but the sheer
amounts of money required to underwrite the Medicaid program have also piqued the
fiscal sensitivity of federal, state, and county governments.

Ideological Orientation

In addition to the cynicism and cost consciousness engendered by government health
programs and the resource limitations faced by recent Congresses, there has perhaps
also been an ideological shift to the right. This has not been a distinctively U.S. phenomenon, as it seems that in every nation the basic role of the state is being questioned.
Whether this reemphasis on major ideological issues is a separable phenomenon from
the shrinking of available resources is problematic. Furthermore, it is tempting to read
more fundamental shifts in attitudes into electoral results than is warranted, especially
in view of the unusually low turnout (51 percent) in the 1980 election. On the other
hand, taking the intensity as well as the direction of opinion into consideration, one
could view growth in conservatism as a major development in U.S. political behavior:
Members of the attentive public, whose opinions are most important in policy formulation, have challenged the traditional idea that government should assume responsibility
for potentially private matters. In light of this attitudinal movement in favor of reprivi-
tization (or, at least, a climate of opinion not conducive to intensified government
activity), the policy stasis of the late 1970s is as understandable, if not explainable, by
conventional, civics-text notions about the responsiveness of legislators to their constituents' preferences as it is on the basis of economic, pragmatic, or procedural
considerations.

Again, however, the impact of ideology on policy is questionable. First, ideological
leanings and their policy expression may be regarded as inextricable from economic
circumstances; it is nearly impossible to separate the rhetoric that underlies policy
change from that which merely is convenient to justify it. Second, whatever the causal
mechanism involved, the media seem to have adjudged that there has been an ideological shift and that may amount to a self-fulfilling prophesy in that the assessment is as
important as the phenomenon being analyzed. Third, ideological constraint, even
among the elite (i.e., political leaders) is limited—support for process reform is rarely
divorced from substantial policy implications—e.g., those who favor limitations on debate typically oppose the positions of those who likely will be using the filibuster or
other tactics to obstruct legislation. Finally, to summarize the effects of ideology, this
classification is simply too convenient. The political language is often couched in ideological terms, and post factum analyses of political events tempt people to exchange
ideas in the coin of the realm. Historians and journalists perhaps are especially prone to
succumb to this fallacy, but other social scientists are not immune to such entrapment.

Presidential Character

Another variable set that is analytically troublesome from the standpoint of isolating its
effects from the other influences on policy that have been mentioned is the role assumed

by the president. If one were trying to explain policy primarily on the basis of the types of behavior that constitute what Barber (1972) calls "presidential character," Lyndon Johnson's legislative dexterity could be considered a major factor behind the policy innovations of the mid-1960s; Nixon's Machiavellian pragmatism could be cited as an important influence supporting the drive for NHI during the late 1960s and early 1970s; and the Watergate scandal could be partially credited for the demise of this same policy movement. The weaknesses of the Ford and Carter administrations, for perhaps different reasons, would be adduced to explain the subsequent lack of dynamism in any policy area. But, of course, all these could be questioned in an analytical perspective that included the other effects on policy previously mentioned. For example, except in the most heroic view possible, one cannot discount the impact of economic factors, over which the president clearly has less than total control, on this policy initiation capacity. In addition, some reforms, notably the Anti-Impoundment Act, were specifically designed to undercut the executive's unilateral discretion. Thus, the decline of presidential perogatives on policy during the Nixon, Ford, and Carter administrations were not caused solely by weaknesses in these presidents alone.

CONCLUSION

Legislative events in the 1970s undoubtedly have affected health policy, but their explanatory power is difficult to determine in a systematic research design. It could be argued that health policy, not unlike welfare, education, or other social policies, is now undergoing the retrenchment required by the economic constraints now facing U.S. decision makers as well as leaders of other Western nations. This retrenchment may be linked primarily to legislative reform, government experience with health programs, presidential leadership, a shift in ideological perspective, or, more likely, a combination of these interacting factors. What is important to remember is that health policy is swept in the overall direction of government activity and that, for whatever reason or collection of reasons cited above, it may be that traditional theories of public finance will have to be reformulated to take account of the possibility of a diminution of productivity and, thus, by the logic of the theories themselves, a reduction in the scope of government activity. As changes in legislative structure and procedure occur, one has to be on guard against the temptation to weigh them too heavily in assessing their significance in the determination of health and other social policies. This cautionary note is particularly applicable to the evaluation of the demonstrated incapability of Congress to mount a successful counter initiative to the Reagan administration's budgetary and related social policy proposals. There is little doubt that the dismantling of the leadership structure in the 1970s has been partially accountable for this turn of events, but the other variables considered in this discourse also seem to have come into play in promoting retrenchment and shackling the opposition to the Reagan initiatives.

REFERENCES

Alford, Robert, *Health Politics: Dynamics Without Change*, Chicago: University of Chicago Press, 1976.

Barber, James D., *Presidential Character*, Englewood Cliffs, N.J.: Prentice-Hall, 1972.

Biles, Bryan, Regional Orientation Session Health Resources Planning, Unedited Transcript of Remarks, Atlanta, Georgia, January 13–14, 1975.

Bird, Richard, *The Growth of Government Spending in Canada*, Toronto: Canadian Tax Foundation, 1970.

Blumstein, James F., "Inflation and Quality: The Case of PSRO's," in Michael Zubkoff, ed., *A Victim or Cause of Inflation*, New York: Prodest, 1977, pp. 245–295.

Congressional Budget Office, *The Impact of PSRO's on Health Care Costs: Update of CBO's 1979 Evaluation*, Washington, D.C.: U.S. Congress, 1981.

Congressional Quarterly, *Inside Congress*, Washington: Congressional Quarterly Press, January 1976.

Cooper, Theodore, "Federal Health Policy," *Journal of Health Politics, Policy and Law*, Vol. 1, Spring 1976, pp. 9–12.

Davidson, Roger, "Breaking Up those Cozy Triangles: An Impossible Dream?" in Susan Welch and John G. Peters, eds., *Legislative Reform and Public Policy*, New York: Praeger Publishers, 1977, pp. 30–53.

Davis, Karen and Cathy Schoen, *Health and the War on Poverty: A Ten Year Appraisal*, Washington, D.C.: The Brookings Institution, 1978.

Dodd, Lawrence C. and Bruce Oppenheimer, eds., *Congress Reconsidered*, Washington: Congressional Quarterly Press, 1981, 2nd edition.

Dye, Thomas, *Understanding Public Policy*, Englewood Cliffs, N.J.: Prentice-Hall, 1980, 4th edition.

Falcone, David, "Health Policy Analysis: Some Reflections on the State of the Art," *Policy Studies Journal*, Vol. 9, No. 2, Special Issue No. 1, 1980–1981, pp. 188–197.

Falcone, David, "Health Policy Analysis and Health Policy," in Nagel, Stuart (forthcoming).

Feldstein, Paul, *Health Associations and the Demand for Legislation*, Cambridge: Ballinger Publishing Co., 1977.

Gibson, Robert M. and Daniel R. Waldo, "National Health Expenditures," 1981, *Health Financing Review*, Vol. 4, September 1982, pp. 1–35.

DHEW, *Health 1976–77*, Washington, D.C.: United States Government Printing Office, 1978.

Jones, Charles, "How Reform Changes Congress," in Susan Welch and John G. Peters, eds., *Legislative Reform and Public Policy*, New York: Praeger Publishers, 1977, pp. 11–29.

Leroy, Lauren and Philip Lee, *Deliberations and Compromise*, Cambridge: Ballinger Publishing Co., 1977.

Loewenberg, Gerhard, *Modern Parliaments: Change or Decline*, New York: Aldine Publishing Co., 1971.

Marmor, Theodore, *The Politics of Medicare*, New York: Aldine Publishing Co., 1973.

Marmor, Theodore, Donald Wittmann, and Thomas Heagy, "The Politics of Medical Inflation," *Journal of Health Politics, Policy and Law*, Vol. 4, Spring 1976, pp. 69–84.

Mechanic, David, "Some Dilemmas in Health Policy," *Milbank Memorial Fund Quarterly/Health and Society*, Vol. 59, Winter 1981, pp. 1–15.

Murphy, Thomas P., *The New Politics Congress*, Lexington, Mass.: Lexington Books, 1974.

Oleszek, Walter, J., "A Perspective on Congressional Reform," in Susan Welch and John G. Peters, eds., *Legislative Reform and Public Policy*, New York: Praeger Publishing Co., 1977, pp. 3–10.

Ornstein, Norman and David W. Rohde, "Revolt From Within: Congressional Change, Legislative Policy, and the House Commerce Committee," in Susan Welch and John G. Peters, ed., *Legislative Reform and Public Policy*, New York: Praeger Publishing Co., 1977.

Price, David, *The Commerce Committees*, New York: Grossman, 1975.

Price, David, E., "Policymaking in Congressional Committees: The Impact of 'Environmental' Factors," *American Political Science Review*, Vol. 72, June 1978, pp. 548–574.

Redman, Eric, *The Dance of Legislation*, New York: Simon & Schuster, 1974.

Rieselback, Leroy N., *Congressional Reform in the 70's*, Morristown, N.J.: General Learning Press, 1977.

Russell, Louise, "Inflation and the Federal Role in Health," in Michael Zubkoff, ed., *A Victim or Cause of Inflation*, New York: Prodist, 1977, pp. 225–244.

Sorkin, Alan L., *Health Manpower*, Lexington, Mass.: D.C. Heath, 1977.

Stevens, Rosemary, *American Medicine and the Public Interest*, New Haven: Yale University Press, 1971.

Van Loon, Richard J. and Michael Whittington, *The Canadian Political System*, Toronto: McGraw-Hill, 1971.

Wilson, Florence and Duncan Neuhauser, *Health Services in the United States*, Cambridge: Ballinger Publishing Co., 1976.

CHAPTER 8

Implementation of Health Policy: Politics and Bureaucracy

Frank J. Thompson

The experience of social programs in the United States during the 1960s and 1970s relentlessly reaffirmed a major message: The politics played out after a bill becomes law is as important as that in evidence before passage. Students of implementation have often chosen painful examples to bring this point home. For example, Pressman and Wildavsky (1979) and Bardach (1977) have repeatedly chronicled tales of good policy intentions gone sour through underperformance, delay, soaring costs, and other factors. To be sure, various analyses have occasionally focused on the brighter side. Toward the end of the 1970s, for example, analysts (Rodgers and Bullock 1976; Sabatier and Mazmanian 1979) increasingly turned toward specifying conditions that would contribute to implementation success. On balance, however, the dominant theme of the 1970s seems best expressed by Heclo and Wildavsky (1974), namely, that "the great American weakness . . . lies in implementation."

The emergence of the study of implementation as a growth industry has to some extent found expression among those circles involved in the study of health policy, although their volume of work more readily resembles the Mississippi River at its source than its mouth. Two major types of implementation studies related to health policy stand out. One type focuses on the experience of particular programs such as the complex negotiations and bargaining that transpired between medical providers and the federal bureaucracy after the birth of Medicare (Feder 1977). Also insightful is analysis of the troubles faced in implementing Medicaid's Early and Periodic Screening, Diagnosis and Treatment program (EPSDT). This program, which emphasized medical outreach in order to reduce death and disease among infants and children, met with repeated delays and other woes so that by the late 1970s it had reached only a one-sixth of the some 12 million poor children targeted for attention (Foltz 1975; Congressional Quarterly, 1977). Similarly, work by Thompson (1981, Chapter V with Leonard Robins and Chapter VII with Richard W. Campbell) has attempted to penetrate the dynamics of implementation through a comparative analysis of the evolution of eight health programs.

Aside from these efforts to assess implementation processes, another stream of analysis looks more to the future, attempting to anticipate the implementation problems that various health reforms might face (Marmor, 1980). In 1980, for example, the Urban Institute released a 721-page volume (Feder et al., 1980) that explored many of the issues that would surface in implementing a national health insurance (NHI) program. Matters of physician reimbursement, hospital payment, patient cost sharing, utilization review, and more received judicious scrutiny in this tome.

Although existing works on health policy implementation have fostered understanding, further inquiry is important. Significant gaps in knowledge persist. If additional study cannot assure major breakthroughs, it can still shore up the capacity to describe and explain implementation and to predict the consequences of pursuing certain policy options.

This essay strives to contribute to a foundation for the further exploration of health policy implementation. In this regard, it initially considers some key ingredients of implementation processes. It then examines several forces that leave a considerable imprint on implementation, namely, the policy mandate (or founding statute), qualities of the implementing agencies (especially the limited prestige of public bureaucracies), and the presence or absence of program fixers in the agency's environment. While this essay investigates several themes, it above all stresses that the implementation problem cannot be equated with the bureaucracy problem. Undoubtedly, the limitations of implementing agencies feed the foibles that can arise after a bill becomes law. But the difficulties also have roots in other aspects of the political order.

IMPLEMENTATION INGREDIENTS

Health policy implementation is a deceptively simple phrase. Its meaning seems obvious until matters of formal definition arise; then consensus vanishes. Some, for example, might adopt the common sense notion that health policy implementation involves the carrying out of some formally stated policy. Reasonable as this may seem, other students of the subject would object. Sensitive to the way in which implementation can transform original program goals, one analysis (Farrar et al., 1980) notes that "implementation is not the carrying out of a formulated policy but part of its evolution." The complexities of implementation will no doubt fuel debate concerning appropriate definitions and metaphors well into the future. While foregoing any procrustean effort to resolve this debate once and for all, this essay considers health policy implementation to be the processes of program assembly that occur in response to a health policy mandate; these processes feature strategic, routine, and fortuitous aspects (in the sense of chance rather than good fortune).

Bardach (1977, pp. 57–58) captures the strategic aspect of implementation when he defines it as "the playing out of a number of loosely interrelated games whereby . . . elements are withheld from or delivered to the program assembly process on particular terms." Hence, the implementation of health programs finds various participants (e.g., medical providers, consumers groups, program administrators, unions, key congressional subcommittees) with diverse perceptions and goals mobilizing power resources, forming coalitions, and consciously plotting gambits. Each participant hopes to prevail in the implementation games of special concern to them. Bargaining and compromise often occur. The program assembled as a result of strategic maneuvering in countless games may, of course, differ so greatly from the one envisioned by the founding statute as to undercut any notion of implementation as the "carrying out" of a health policy.

The bureaucratic processes that promulgate health program rules often serve as a particularly important focal point for strategic interaction. Major administrative regulations and guidelines are not simply imposed. Rather civil servants draft them with the intention of giving various interest groups a chance to respond. Formal recognition of this is in the requirement that the bureaucracy publish a "Notice of Proposed Rulemaking" in the *Federal Register* before issuing final rules. The reaction to these initial notices can at times be particularly intense as a case involving the National Health Planning and Resources Development Act (PL 93-641) illustrates. In response to this law, federal administrators in 1977 issued tentative guidelines aimed at reducing excess hospital beds and underused facilities. Among other things, the guidelines suggested that rural hospitals deliver at least 500 babies annually if they were to maintain a maternity ward and delivery room. The guidelines also implied that, regardless of location, inability by a hospital to achieve an average of 80 percent occupancy of its beds would be interpreted as a sign of excess capacity.

The guidelines elicited a massive protest, especially from rural areas. All told, federal civil servants received 55,000 written communications on the guidelines, nearly all of which were negative. Some congressional offices received as many as 10,000 communications. Following this gusher of complaints, the House of Representatives unanimously adopted a resolution demanding that the final guidelines reflect the needs of rural areas to a greater degree (Zwick, 1978). The Department of Health, Education and Welfare (DHEW) subsequently eased the standards somewhat. Final guidelines took pains to mention that Health Systems Agencies (HSA) could, after careful analysis, depart from federal standards in reviewing grant proposals and construction requests. In seven of 11 issue areas, federal civil servants modified standards to take into account the concerns of those in rural areas. For example, the new guidelines made no explicit reference to the number of deliveries an obstetrical unit in a rural hospital should achieve. Instead, the guidelines focused only on hospitals providing care for "complicated obstetrical problems" (*Federal Register*, 1978).

Strategic considerations also shape decisions concerning whether to promulgate any rules at all. The specification of rules need not proceed in some neat, linear fashion once Congress gives civil servants a statute to implement. Consider, for example, the Hill-Burton program that Congress launched in 1946 to spur the construction of hospital facilities. The statute called for equal protection of racial minorities and required hospitals receiving grants to provide some free service to the medically indigent. It was not until October 1978, however, that DHEW promulgated rules governing "free service" that possessed any teeth at all (*Health Resources News*, 1978). During the program's first 30 years, DHEW administrators avoided the conflict with the hospital industry that enforcement of this provision would create. The decision to issue relatively stringent regulations came only after considerable court action and related agitation by representatives of the poor during the 1970s.

Once in place, formal rules help spawn the routines that also comprise a key ingredient of health policy implementation. Standard operating procedures guide much implementation behavior. For example, Medicare employees follow certain routines in determining whether someone is eligible to receive benefits from that program. Standard operating procedures along with other informal decision rules greatly simplify choices for administrators, allowing them to make some decisions almost unthinkingly. Certainly, officials make many choices without the strategic consciousness suggested by the game metaphor.

Ultimately, the strategic and routine combine with the fortuitous, or almost chance events, to create an implementation mosaic. Conveying the importance of the fortuitous has presented difficulties for social scientists who by training tend to emphasize regular or predictable patterns of interaction. Recent work (Cohen et al., 1972), however, represents an intriguing effort to deal with implementation's random qualities. Implementation viewed as a process of organized anarchy could in part be portrayed as the product of four streams: problems, solutions, participants, and choice opportunities. Although none of the streams is completely independent of the others, the model holds that implementation decisions often derive from a somewhat fortuitous confluence of the four.

The strategies, the routine, and the fortuitous thus comprise key ingredients of the implementation of health policy. But what factors shape the particular implementation patterns that emerge and their consequences? Rather than present a laundry list of variables, this chapter will focus on three particularly important ones: the statute, the status of public bureaucracies, and the degree to which fixers are present in the task environment of the implementing agency.

HEALTH STATUTES AS PIVOTAL HYPOTHESES

Observers have often equated implementation difficulties with the "bureaucracy problem." There is undoubtedly something to those definitions of the bureaucracy that refer to it as an organization that cannot learn from its mistakes (Crozier, 1964). The errors of health administrators often push a program toward certain policy pitfalls. But the difficulties faced in implementing health policy stem only in part from a bureaucratic propensity to err. The founding statute and subsequent legislative amendments also do much to rig the implementation game.

A health policy embedded in a statute is in essence a hypothesis. It specifies that if a, b, c, and so on, are done at time one, then x, y, z, and so on, will result at time two. As hypotheses, policies vary enormously in their precision, substance, and plausibility. Precision is a function of the degree to which a policy defines terms, quantifies objectives, specifies timetables for obtaining them, indicates priorities among objectives, and prescribes the administrative structure and procedures to be used in implementing the program (Sabatier and Mazmanian, 1979). With these dimensions in mind, policies can be arranged on a continuum from more precise to less precise. Inextricably intertwined with a policy's precision is its substance. Critical dimensions here include the personnel and fiscal resources allocated to the program, the particular objectives established, and the technological imperatives of the policy (i.e., the kinds of techniques and administrative processes needed to get the program's work done).

Ultimately, the health policy hypothesis achieves some level of plausibility. At times, a formal policy lacks plausibility in that it calls for arrangements that seem destined to foster ineffectiveness, waste, or some other program failure. The Health Maintenance Organization Act of 1973 serves as a useful example in this regard. At other times, the causal notions built into the policy hypothesis ostensibly make sense. For example, the assumption embedded in the Comprehensive Health Manpower Training Act (PL 92-257) that medical schools would increase their enrollments if the federal government used capitation grants to reward them financially for doing so seemed reasonable at the time Congress passed the law in 1971.[1]

---

[1]In retrospect, the assumption seems all the more sound given the substantial increase in medical school enrollments that followed in the wake of capitation legislation (Hadley and Levenson, 1980).

In considering the implications of the statute for implementation processes, an important caveat deserves mention. A health policy may at times perform certain symbolic functions and engender significant sociopolitical outcomes regardless of whether or not officials vigorously move to implement it. The enunciation of legal commitment to certain values with little prospect for follow-up action can be termed "statutory hypocrisy." Such hypocrisy often spawns outcomes that observers view unfavorable. The passage of a health policy could, for example, breed acquiesence as people assume that government has solved some health problems when in fact it has not. But statutory hypocrisy need not automatically possess pejorative connotations. As March (1978) has perceptively noted, there is often "a degree of personal and social wisdom in ordinary hypocrisy." This view holds that if people insist upon consistency between goals and actions, the former will often be more likely to change than the latter. The passage of laws that the bureaucracy does not or cannot implement energetically may at least reinforce commitment to important values in the health arena. In some cases, it buys time for government to pick the moment or to develop the means for delivering on these value commitments.

While recognizing the symbolic functions of health statutes, it remains more pertinent for purposes of this essay to examine potential links between policy characteristics and subsequent implementation problems. Some of the complexities (Bardach, 1980; Greenberg et al., 1977) of understanding these links become evident if one considers the relationship between statutory precision and implementation.

THE PERILS AND POTENTIAL OF PRECISION

Precise laws possess considerable appeal in a democratic society. They seem consistent with ideals about the rule of law and the thwarting of unaccountable bureaucratic power (Finer, 1941; Lowi, 1969). Aside from keeping elected officials in the driver's seat, however, several observers have turned to precise laws as a vehicle for increasing the effectiveness of program implementation. One analysis (Sabatier and Mazmanian, 1979, p. 487) suggests that (given a sound underlying theory) a program's prospects improve when "policy objectives are precise and clearly ranked, both internally [within the statute] and in the overall program of the implementing agencies." Another study (Montjoy and O'Toole, 1979) argues "that the surest way to avoid intra-organizational implementation problems is to establish a specific mandate and provide sufficient resources." Yet, finally, Nakamura and Smallwood (1980) suggest that policy clarity "is a necessary first step toward effective implementation."[2] Observers credit precise mandates with giving an agency a major weapon to turn against those who oppose its mission. Specific statutes also win praise for reducing prospects that an agency's officials will dissipate energy by skirmishing with one another over how to interpret the law. In addition such mandates allegedly expedite evaluation and, thereby, the detection and correction of errors. All this is not to suggest that analysts adhere to a blind and rigid notion that effective implementation requires precision. They certainly recognize that

---

[2]Nakamura and Smallwood (1980, p. 141) subsequently point out that where "implementers are able to amass sufficient power to bend the policy process to their own ends" one is likely to find "one of the most efficient of all the implementation scenarios in terms of producing results and getting things done." But they go on to caution that "this approach can lead to an unchecked accumulation of power that produces a degree of bureaucratic unaccountability that is difficult to reconcile with the tenets of democratic theory."

political processes often make the drafting of precise statutes difficult. But a substantial bias toward precision exists in much of the writing on implementation.

The alleged virtues of precise health statutes cannot be slighted. Indeed, one intriguing analysis (Foltz, 1975) of the difficulties faced in implementing the EPSDT program implies that ambiguous policy had much to do with the problems encountered. Other research (Thompson, 1981) indicates that the vague goals of the National Health Planning and Resources Development Act of 1974 contributed to some of the problems officials faced in implementing this program.

But other evidence from the health arena indicates that precision is no elixer. In its original form, for example, the Health Maintenance Organization Act of 1973 was a precise policy for the near impossible. The law (Falkson, 1980) which provided various grants, loans, and loan guarantees to spur the development of health maintenance organizations (HMOs), was highly detailed. But some of the specific requirements built into the law seriously threatened its plausibility. Among other things, the statute required subsidized HMOs to provide a very rich mix of services and periodically provide open enrollment. These provisos raised serious questions as to whether these HMOs would be able to compete with other plans. As one witness before a House subcommittee hearing remarked, "It's like giving someone $10 to start a Kool-Aid stand which he has to sell at $5 a glass—and then telling him now get out there and compete" (*Congressional Quarterly Almanac*, 1975). In fact, the program did not begin to flourish until Congress approved amendments in 1976. The case of the HMO legislation illustrates how political processes in Congress can at times thwart the application of reasonable theories. It is evident that processes of bargaining, compromise, and coalition formation give birth to ambiguous law. What needs to be stressed is that the same processes directed toward statutory precision can lead to a splicing of incongruous, albeit specific, provisions into a single law.

If precise laws at times undermine effectiveness, vague laws can on occasion spawn creative adaptation, that is, change that helps a program escape policy pitfalls. In 1970, for example, Congress passed an ambiguous, four-page statute that authorized placement of Public Health Service (PHS) physicians in shortage areas as part of what was subsequently called the National Health Service Corps (NHSC). Given this foggy mandate, the program underwent considerable change during the 1970s. At first, agency officials stressed the objective of retaining NHSC physicians in private practice within shortage areas after their departure from the Corps—an effort that met with extremely limited success. By the end of the decade, however, agency officials had turned their backs on this concern. Instead, they stressed the placement of such physicians in federally supported organizations that provided care to the poor (e.g., community health centers). They emphasized reenlistment in the NHSC after a physician's term of duty had expired rather than placement in the private sector. It is at least arguable that this shift permitted the program to achieve a higher level of effectiveness. Retention rates rose along with physician productivity; the program thereby became less of a threat to the credibility of government (Thompson, forthcoming).

The experience of the NHSC as well as that of HMO officials points to the need to reflect more fully on the proposition that "we require the impossible when we expect our bureaucrats to be at the same time literal executors and successful implementers of policy mandates" (Majone and Wildavsky, 1979). At a minimum, students of health policy need to deal with the question of optimal clarity. The appeal of precise health mandates to some extent mirrors conventional notions about rational choice that often assume that good decisions require clear goals. Recently, however, "choice" theorists have begun to distance themselves from this presumption. In this regard, March (1979, pp. 595,603) has argued that when decision makers have confused and contradictory preferences, "precision misrepresents them." In this view, decision making involves guesses not only about the future consequences of various alternatives but about preferences for these consequences. At times, people learn what they want by doing it. Recognition of this phenomenon has driven students of choice to the conclusion that vague tastes or goals may at times be intelligent rather than stupid.

The critical question for health policy implementation thus becomes the following: Under what circumstances will less-precise statutes more readily foster positive program results? In this respect, several conditions, among others, suggest themselves. First, statutory ambiguity more readily fosters creative evolution when Congress cannot turn to a good underlying theory in drafting legislation and problems seem so pressing that something must be done (throwing money at the problem may be the only hope). For example, Congress is probably incapable of drafting a plausible statute that specifies in great detail how best to allocate research funds to reduce the cancer mortality rate.

Second, specific health statutes seem less fruitful when rapidly changing social and economic factors promise to threaten the validity of any precisely worded hypothesis. For example, knowledge of which substances qualify as carcinogens in the workplace and the precise effects of some level of exposure to them remains in a constant state of flux. Therefore, an occupational safety and health law that precisely established maximum exposure levels for some finite set of toxic substances would be destined for rapid obsolescence.

Third, creative program evolution in the face of an ambiguous mandate occurs more readily when a widespread consensus exists within the implementing agency as to its fundamental mission and this mission is not completely at odds with the *general* thrust of the statute. In the case of the National Health Service Corps, for example, top officials responsible for the program shared a strong commitment to delivering care to the disadvantaged through certain kinds of group medical practices. Without internal accord of this kind, vague legislation tends to generate bureaucratic tensions; dysfunctional delay often surfaces as civil servants fight with one another over the proper definition of program goals. Consensus can, of course, dramatically impair implementation if it runs strongly against the whole idea of a legislative initiative. Under this circumstance, sabotage or lethargic implementation tends to crop up. This state of total opposition to a program needs to be kept distinct from the more frequent circumstances whereby civil servants give new legislation, some of whose features they like and others they do not, mixed reviews.

Fourth, foggy health statutes more readily foster creative evolution if the bureaucracy faces an environment relatively free of interest groups intensely opposed to the program's effective and efficient administration. Where such resistance exists, program officials tend to need well-crafted, precise grants of statutory authority or persistent backing from oversight actors. If, for example, Congress wants Medicare officials to stand up to hospitals and physicians on issues involving their payment, it probably needs to strengthen the position of the bureaucracy with clear grants of authority.

No doubt other conditions also boost the correlation between statutory ambiguity and creative program evolution. The central point should be clear, however. Precision hardly qualifies as an unmitigated blessing; the optimal level of clarity varies depending on certain contingencies related to the implementing agency and its environment.

ELUSIVE LINK TO POLICY SUBSTANCE

If complexity marks the relationship between statutory precision and implementation, it also characterizes the interconnection between health policy substance and the behavior that emerges after a bill becomes law. Distillation of a substantive typology that achieves much theoretical fecundity requires additional conceptualization and research. On a general level, however, one can at least note that certain kinds of implementation problems confront more distributive as opposed to more regulatory types of policies in the health arena. A thin line often exists between these general types, with most policies amounting to a mixture of the two. In broad terms, however, a more distributive policy is one that *explicitly* involves government in delivering income, goods, or services to a designated group. Distributive policies, such as Medicaid, often contain a significant regulatory thrust. That is, they frequently attach strings or requirements that must be met as a condition of the subsidy. By contrast, more overt regulatory policies, such as that administered by the Occupational Safety and Health Administration (OSHA), explicitly seek to prescribe and control behavior for a certain group without reference to whether that group has chosen to participate in some government program. Its fundamental technology involves the promulgation of rules or standards, the monitoring of behavior to determine compliance with standards, and the imposition of penalties for failure to comply (Bardach, 1980).

In the health arena, distributive policies have shown susceptibility to three threats in particular. First, pork barrel politics tends to characterize policies that distribute resources explicitly on a geographical basis. Members of Congress, so the argument runs, want to curry favor with constituents and, therefore, prefer to spread program resources over a broad area. Civil servants possess an incentive to cooperate in order to build a large reservoir of support for their program within Congress. Pork barrel politics can undermine the ability of program managers to concentrate resources sufficiently in a given locale to assure effectiveness there. It can lead to a diversion of scarce resources from critical targets. In essence, a substantial amount of money gets transferred from the neediest areas in order to maintain the coalition that provides continued funding and authorization for the program (Bardach, 1977; Arnold, 1979). In the health arena, the placement of Veterans Administration (VA) facilities serves as an example of the pork barrel. The location of these facilities generally has more to do with placating key senators and representatives than with a desire to maximize the access of veterans to care.

A second tendency of distributive health programs is the generation of solutions in search of problems and the subsequent coupling of solutions with inappropriate problems. The major health service programs of the federal government—Medicare, Medicaid, and the VA medical network—have, for example, fallen under considerable criticism for fostering errors of liberality in the delivery of care. In essence, providers with facilities at their disposal and other incentives to provide more rather than less care tend to apply their remedies unnecessarily. This may result in a considerable amount of "flat-of-the-curve medicine" whereby greater medical inputs yield no appreciable improvement in health (Enthoven, 1978a). Moreover, it may well increase the possibility of iatrogenic disease. According to one estimate, as many as a half-million Medicare patients had been hospitalized due to overmedication (U.S. House Committee on Appropriations, 1979).

Inefficient inducement schedules for medical providers comprise a third and related propensity of distributive policies. In sum, government pays physicians and hospitals in a way that gives them minimal incentive to seek out the most cost-effective treatments for different kinds of clients. Under Medicare, for example, hospitals tend to get paid more if they allow certain of their costs to rise. Under the customary prevailing and reasonable charge formula used to pay physicians, those who wish to receive higher payments in the future face ample incentives to boost their fees in a given year (since payment in the current year depends in part on prices charged in the previous one).

Regulatory health policies also reveal propensities to become sidetracked by certain pitfalls. Among other things, they often encounter problems either in avoiding ineffectiveness or in the paradox of credibility. Ineffectiveness derives in part from the capacity of regulatory targets to resist. Groups targeted for regulation may avoid detection, foster delay, or come to dominate the agency. In these and other ways, then, a regulatory agency may become a paper tiger or a defender of its interests against possible competitors. For example, the federally sponsored Health Systems Agencies in many states approved the vast majority of all capital development projects that health care providers submitted to them. To the disappointment of many federal officials interested in holding down increases in health care costs, both the medical providers and consumers represented on the boards of these Health Systems Agencies have often demonstrated little interest in curbing the expansion of health care facilities. Moreover, providers have often proved adroit in evading regulation. Where health planners blocked hospitals from adding certain expensive medical equipment, enterprising physicians have often made end runs around the agency by purchasing the equipment for their own offices and using it there.

By contrast, OSHA's regulatory efforts have tended to flounder on the paradox of credibility. This paradox asserts that the greater the quest for effectiveness by a regulatory agency, the higher the risk of public disapproval. The Occupational Safety and Health Administration avoided domination by business and was often aggressive in promulgating and enforcing its rules. But assertive regulation is hard. Efforts to be effective provoke sharp blasts of criticism and concerted efforts to discredit the agency by the targets of regulation. Furthermore, uncertainty often engulfs the setting of standards and the means for assuring compliance with them. The threat of issuing trivial or erroneous regulations and becoming a nuisance looms large. In sum, aggressive regulation makes it more likely that people will view the agency and its program as unreasonable. Political support for the agency may therefore plummet, and efforts at deregulation may well occur. Such deregulation can involve reducing the number of health and safety rules, completely exempting certain types of employers from regulation, or gutting the agency's will and capacity to enforce the rules that are on the blocks. In the mid-1970s, for example, Congress stripped OSHA of its jurisdiction over agricultural enterprises with fewer than 11 employees, and the Reagan administration moved to weaken enforcement by cutting back inspectors employed by OSHA.

Although the late 1970s and early 1980s saw increased emphasis on the problems of regulatory policy, it deserves emphasis that regulatory and distributive policies carry their own set of implementation risks (Vladeck, 1981). Hence, simple assertions about the general superiority of one type or the other from an implementation perspective are probably not very fruitful. In gauging the plausibility of a policy, one must go beyond these general categories to specific program and contextual variables.

CONGRESSIONAL CAPACITY AND PLAUSIBLE POLICY

Efforts to link the substance and precision of health policy mandates to particular patterns of implementation behavior need to continue. Whatever the specific links uncovered, however, the central point remains: Statutes do much to shape the implementation game. Hence, the capacity of Congress to fashion plausible policy hypotheses ranks as a critical issue for students of implementation.

During the 1960s and 1970s, considerable concern arose that the fragmentation of power within Congress had partially impaired its capacity. This fragmentation springs from a quest by members of Congress for personal clout, which in turn tends to scatter power to subcommittees. Although government by subcommittee enhances a legislator's own prospects for occupying a position with considerable leverage, it tends to weaken Congress as a formulator of policy hypotheses. Groups such as medical providers can turn to an increasing number of decision sites to make sure that their concerns over payment and other issues get taken into account. Legislation thereby increasingly seeks to satisfy a multitude of particular interests and often comes to contain provisions that conflict with one another or otherwise make the policy hypothesis untenable. The statutory sum of all the particular interests often fails to equal a coherent whole. The weakness of political parties[3] (never very strong in U.S. political life) has made it all the more difficult for leaders in Congress or the president to counteract the fragmentation of power (Pressman, 1979; Dodd, 1976). Students of implementation cannot, then, safely stop with a dissection of the bureaucracy's propensities; they also need to pay particuar attention to Congress as an organizational problem.

BUREAUCRACY PROBLEM: A PROPHECY FULFILLED

The statute is, of course, only part of the picture. The capacity of agencies formally charged with implementing a program do much to affect its destiny. Although problems related to equipment, facilities, and supplies can undermine a program, personnel issues often loom as more central to its fortunes. Can those charged with implementing the statute draw on personnel with ample technical, managerial, and political skills? Are these personnel committed to the goals reflected in the statute without being dogmatically inflexible about them? The way in which questions such as these get answered can markedly shape program performance. For example, one reason why OSHA focused so extensively on "safety" rather than "health" violations during much of the 1970s was its inability to recruit enough industrial hygienists. So, too, the personnel needs of the VA medical system prompted the agency to forge tight links with medical schools. Although these links helped the agency obtain a competent staff, it also strongly influenced capital development decisions, that is, where to locate hospitals, and what hardware to purchase, and reinforced an agency bias toward acute hospital-based care (Thompson, 1981).

---

[3]Although during the early 1980s, some signs suggested that the Republican Party in Congress was becoming more homogeneous in outlook and more disciplined, it remains far from clear that this trend will persist and seriously counteract the dynamics that feed fragmentation.

THE INFLUENCE OF BUREAUCRATIC STATUS, OR PRESTIGE

While recognizing the significance of personnel and a host of other factors related to bureaucratic capacity, this section focuses on an agency resource that has received less attention in the implementation literature—bureaucratic status, or prestige. Status ranks among the most important resources an implementing agency can possess. The general reputation of the public bureaucracy for competent and humane action influences its access to other resources and can greatly facilitate or impede implementation. At least to a degree, what the public thinks makes it so.

Government in general and the bureaucracy in particular have long suffered from a poor public image in the United States. Waldo (1980) has gone so far as to suggest that "the ineffectiveness and inefficiency" of the public sector is a belief "so widely and firmly held that one . . . can regard it as a unifying theme of our national creed: something that might be inserted after we hold these truths to be self-evident." In recent times, Vietnam, Watergate, inflation, and economic stagnation have further fueled skepticism and cynicism about the public sector. Survey after survey indicates the sorry state of government's reputation. For example, a Gallup Poll (The Gallup Opinion Index, 1977) conducted in 1977 found that a substantial majority of people in the United States believed that the federal government hires too many people and that these personnel do not have to work as hard as those employed in the private sector. A 1980 survey (Institute for Social Research, 1981) disclosed that over 75 percent of the population believed that the federal government wastes a lot of money. Some 57 percent felt that those running the government did not know what they were doing. Although public confidence in the institutions of U.S. society has generally dwindled, it deserves attention that health care institutions tend to fare better in the public's eyes than does government. Thus, one Harris Poll (Harris, Louis and Associates, 1978) found that over twice as many respondents had "a great deal of confidence in the people running medicine or hospitals" as in those running the federal government. Moreover, although 44 percent of the public believed that hospital administrators represented the public's interest to "a great extent" in hospital matters and 42 percent credited physicians with playing this enlightened role, only 17 percent bestowed this accolade on the federal government vis-á-vis hospitals.

Some view the low status of the federal bureaucracy as a plus, as a vehicle for curtailing bureaucratic arrogance and for keeping civil servants on their toes. But the disadvantage of a sullied reputation often outweigh the benefits. By-products of the federal bureaucracy's reputation include defensiveness, enhanced need for pressure group support, great reliance on private contractors, and dependency on the states.

DEFENSIVENESS

The status problems of public agencies exacerbate the tendency for implementation to become a defensive nonexperimental brand of politics where "a great deal of energy goes into maneuvering to avoid responsibility, scrutiny, and blame" (Bardach, 1977, p. 37). The avoidance of scandal, fraud, and embarrassment rather than performance tends to become the salient administrative concern. Such an orientation corrodes the bureaucracy's willingness to experiment with potentially useful but risky initiatives. It may, for example, help account for the reluctance of Medicare officials to embrace HMOs and other modes of prospective payment more fully. It may also help explain why OSHA administrators have tended to adopt a rigidly legalistic approach to compliance even in the face of evidence that a more flexible posture might better serve safety and health objectives (Bardach and Kagan, 1982).

INCREASED NEED FOR EXTERNAL SUCCOR

The limited prestige of public agencies involved in implementation tends to heighten the agency's need for external political support. Failure to obtain such support greatly increases prospects that a program will flounder on the shoals of ineffectiveness. For example, some of the problems faced by officials charged with implementing the National Health Planning and Resources Development Act (NHPRDA) stemmed from limited public understanding of or sympathy for its regulatory activities and a lack of strong, supportive constituencies. Intense opposition may also create credibility problems for an agency. Some of OSHA's difficulties in sustaining its reputation for competence can be attributed to the warfare that the business community waged against it. Even the vigorous support of organized labor could not counterbalance these attacks.

A successful quest to acquire and sustain a supportive milieu need not, however, invariably bode well for program accomplishments. At times constituencies that back a program push it away from one trap into the grips of another. Thus, the presence of a supportive milieu should prompt the following question: At what price has the support been purchased? The support that health care providers gave Medicare has, for example, partly derived from the program's tolerance of the medical sector's inefficiencies. Given the bureaucracy's limited status as well as the considerable power of the medical lobby, such tolerance may well have been necessary to ensure the effectiveness of the program during its early years. But a case exists that the United States would be better served by the emergence of a more conflictual milieu around the program—one that would feature major governmental forays to encourage greater sensitivity to cost in the delivery of care. Although those responsible for administering Medicare have taken some steps to constrain payments to providers, they have hardly been zealous in this regard. For example, efforts to establish a uniform language of hospital accounting that would help federal officials monitor and evaluate hospital charges have made only modest headway (Thompson, 1981).

The limited status of the bureaucracy, then, fuels the desire of civil servants to avoid conflicts with health care providers over issues of cost effectiveness. With public understanding of issues of medical payment minimal and the bureaucracy viewed as nearly incapable of doing anything right, top administrators negotiate or bargain from weakness. If open conflict erupts, the risk runs high that the public will side with the providers of care rather than with the civil servants. One by-product of this more general circumstance is a regulate and retreat syndrome. Aware of the highly developed entrepreneurial skills of health care providers, yet not indifferent to the goal of more cost-effective implementation, bureaucrats in the health arena often attempt to gain control over the situation by issuing countless pages of regulations. Health care providers see many of these regulations as excessive and niggling; they often manage to apply sufficient pressure to persuade federal civil servants to back off from initial provisions. Given these and related dynamics, regulations constantly seem to be in a state of flux, thereby complicating the administration of the program and conveying inconsistency (Glaser, 1978; Price, 1978). This syndrome reinforces the ineffectual image of the federal bureaucracy.

FLIGHT TO THE MARGINS

The relatively low status of the federal bureaucracy has also been among the forces heightening the tendency to assign programs to "the margins of the state." According to Sharkansky (1979, p. 11), "the margins of the state are those bodies related to the core departments [of government] but with substantial grants of autonomy from them." Core departments tend to appear on official organization charts, to be formally accountable to the head of state, to be staffed by members of the career civil service, and to have their expenditures listed in the official government budget. By contrast, the margins usually lack certain of these attributes. The use of contractors and private nonprofit grantees to accomplish governmental purposes illustrates dependence on the margins.

Numerous examples of this "flight to the margins" dot the health landscape. For example, the bottom tier of the planning structure imposed by the 1974 health planning law consisted primarily of private nonprofit Health Systems Agencies. Similarly, the Medicare program heavily depends on private insurance companies to handle the payment of physicians and hospitals.[4] Support for operations at the margins of the state seems considerable. For example, a Harris Poll (Harris, Louis and Associates, 1978) found that as many people (39 percent in each case) thought that any comprehensive, national health plan should be run by insurance companies as those who thought it should be run by the federal government. A parallel survey of elites (e.g., members of Congress, physicians, hospital trustees) uncovered overwhelming endorsement of insurance company involvement.

The trend toward use of private contractors raises serious issues of accountability. In the case of the medical service programs of the federal government, this question naturally surfaces: Are health insurance companies the masters or servants of government? Under Medicare, these companies have possessed vast discretion and have been far from easy for the federal bureaucracy to harness. Early claims by insurance companies that their close relationships with physicians would allow them to establish effective payment and utilization review practices tended to be long on promise and short on delivery (U.S. Senate, 1970). Federal frustration with the performance of these companies grew to such a point that in 1973 DHEW established the Perkins Committee to examine Medicare's contracts with the insurance industry. Among other things, the committee urged DHEW to develop a more systematic means for measuring carrier performance, spell out methods for rewarding good performance, define ways of terminating those carriers doing poorly, and improve cost reporting and accounting. As the 1970s progressed, DHEW inched toward implementing these recommendations (U.S. House Committee on Appropriations, 1977).

But problems persisted. Consider, for example, the carriers that pay hosptials for serving Medicare patients. Despite soaring program costs, these intermediaries often revealed little commitment to evaluating hospital cost claims critically. This stemmed, first, from an inability of the federal bureaucracy to write specific instructions governing

---

[4]Price refers to arrangements such as these as manifestations of "contract federalism."

reimbursement under the complicated cost-based payment system required by law. Second, it arose from the performance standards applied to these companies. Federal Medicare officials put pressure on the intermediaries to process claims quickly and to hold down administrative costs per claim processed. To spend time examining claims for excess charges could lead to delays in processing and a reputation for being a "bad intermediary." Third, the statutory provision giving hospitals the right to nominate the intermediaries that reimbursed them impeded careful evaluation of hospital claims. An intermediary who tried to get tough with a hospital faced the prospect of being "fired" and seeing the hospital shift to an intermediary with a reputation for being a softer touch. Finally, the private business interests of the intermediaries militated against an aggressive posture toward hospitals. As one DHEW official noted, these companies were "in business outside of Medicare. . . . They have their private business to pursue and one does not gain in business by making enemies. One does make enemies when he begins to tighten the purse strings of the person who he's trying to work with" (U.S. House Committee on Ways and Means, 1979).

The private concerns of companies also militated against efficient administration of the program in another respect. Insurance companies have often attempted to make the government pay a disproportionate share of their overhead costs. By so doing, they have enhanced their competitive position in private markets. Problems such as these have led Feder and Holahan (1980) to conclude that "as long as administrative agents are active in a private market, conflicts of interest remain likely."

Keeping the contractors accountable may be a particular problem in the United States. Sharkansky (1979) suggests that the United States proves less successful in controlling the margins of the state than either Israel or Australia. He points to the entrepreneurial culture of the United States as one source of the problem (as opposed, e.g., to the culture of compliance that is more manifest in Australia). But he also ascribes the accountability problem to the antigovernment sentiments that permeate U.S. political culture. This hostility makes it difficult for government ever to seem "right" in dealing with private sector institutions. Leaders of insurance companies sense this weakness and are not above exploiting it. Ironically, negative attitudes toward the bureaucracy both encourage the rise of the margins and vitiate governmental efforts to guide it.

Antigovernment sentiments also serve as cultural blinders with respect to more direct efforts by public agencies to deliver care. Some evidence (Thompson and Campbell, 1981) suggests that Washington's prime long-term venture into "socialized medicine," the VA medical network, yields results at least as good as, if not better than, programs that rely on private sector providers. Such evidence points to the need for analysts to keep an open mind about the possible advantages of more direct government administration of various health programs. The use of contractors and private nonprofit grantees may at times make considerable sense from an implementation perspective. But no automatic assumptions about the superiority of this strategy seem warranted.

LET THE STATES DO IT

The limited status of the federal bureaucracy has not only helped heighten the appeal of working through the margins of the state, it has also increased the luster of using state and local governments for program implementation. This commitment tends to run higher during Republican administrations but is a persistent current in U.S. political life, as the Medicaid program testifies.[5] Students of implementation have often seen state involvement as problematic—as representing another veto point or decision site at which Washington's policies can flounder. Difficulties presumably rise from a lack of commitment to federal objectives among state officials and from insufficient state capacity.

State Commitment

State officials at times lack commitment to the objectives of federal programs. Some observers have suggested that such commitment may often be particularly limited in the case of programs that seek to help the disadvantaged. In this regard, one analysis (Rosenbaum, 1978) goes so far as to argue that states are counteregalitarian and chiefly serve to limit the redistributive impact of federal policies. Moreover, Vladeck (1979, p. 533) suggests that states have featured "unacceptable variation" in terms of basic health policies "with a total indifference to the poor and minority groups in many of them." Still others (e.g., Sundquist, 1981) have noted how competition among states for business or economic development leads them to be less than enthusiastic enforcers of federal safety and health regulations. Whatever the reason, states at times evince limited commitment to federal programs.

When state officials possess little interest in implementing a federal policy, Washington usually confronts major difficulties in forcing them to do so. A neat hierarchical model does not apply to federal–state relations in the health arena. Rather a kind of bargaining or negotiation at arms length often characterizes these relationships. The central government and the states make bids and counterbids with each trying to get something of what they want (Ingram, 1977). This process as well as other modes of federal–state interaction may yield less than impressive outcomes. Even after federal administrators made concessions to the states with respect to the EPSDT program, for example, many state officials continued to view the program with little enthusiasm. Medicaid posed a number of problems for the states—soaring costs, lack of effective claims systems, abuse by medical providers, and more. In the face of these problems, EPSDT essentially asked the states to drum up additional business. Not surprisingly, many of the states failed to place a high priority on launching vigorous outreach programs for poor children.

The example of EPSDT also points to the reluctance of the central government to penalize the states for noncompliance. The penalties available to federal officials are usually blunt; they often threaten to harm program clients more than the officials responsible for lethargic implementation. In the case of EPSDT, the federal government could withhold 1 percent of the federal share of payments to the Aid to Families with Dependent Children (AFDC) program. Imposition of this penalty would in essence victimize the poor for the failures of state officials. The limited prestige of the federal bureaucracy and the fear of conflict that this generates also reduces the appeal of penalties. The DHEW administrators knew that withholding money from states with poor EPSDT records would provoke opposition from state officials and certain members of Congress; HEW might well lack the resources to prevail in this conflict, and a defeat could further undermine its prestige.

---

[5]Ironically, President Reagan proposed a centralization of the Medicaid program in early 1982. This move, however, hardly reflected a White House conviction that the federal government could do a better job of administering the program than the states. Instead, it was a concession to the states in order to get them to assume responsibility for a vast array of other social programs.

The EPSDT episode should not be read as a sign that the states invariably lack commitment to federal policies, even those that seek to meet the health care needs of the poor. When Congress approved the Medicaid program in 1965, the federal bureaucracy was almost overrun by states eager to obtain federal dollars. An act now, plan later syndrome emerged. States with well-developed staffs passed legislation and requested funds before DHEW had fully clarified and interpreted the provisions of the law. The federal bureaucracy acquiesced. The dominant image was one of a state donkey running wildly after the federal carrot with the driver of the cart (DHEW) holding on for dear life. Even when the costs of Medicaid became more obvious to state officials, many of them moved to cover more services under the program and did not constrain eligibility for care (Thompson, 1981).

If state officials share federal objectives, then, they can often help the federal government achieve a level of effectiveness that might otherwise be beyond its grasp. But where state officials lack sympathy for federal objectives, they can easily impede the implementation of the program. Where federal programs seek to help groups that lack a strong political base at either the state or local levels of government, dependence on an intergovernmental implementation strategy runs a particularly grave risk of implementation breakdown.

State Capacity

Observers (Ingram, 1977) have also questioned whether the states possess the capacity (e.g., skilled personnel, adequate facilities) to implement federal initiatives effectively. The difficulties state officials faced in controlling payment and eligibility errors under Medicaid have often served as ammunition for those who raise this issue. These concerns are far from groundless. Salaries in many state and local governments have remained relatively low. These governments often lack the capacity to compete successfully with the private sector in recruiting and retaining skilled personnel. Recent tax or expenditure limitation initiatives in the states may well exacerbate these problems.

But the evidence does not all point in one direction. Many states have impressive track records in implementing health programs. Administrative reforms during the 1960s and 1970s as well as rising state and local government salaries may well have generated increased implementation capacity at these government levels (Feder and Holahan 1980; Jain, 1981). Moreover, state experience with Medicaid needs to be put in proper perspective. For example, Medicaid administrators experienced more difficulties with eligibility errors than did their Medicare counterparts not because they were necessarily less competent but because eligibility determinations under Medicaid were much stricter. Medicaid determinations involve complex calculations about recipient income with client eligibility fluctuating over relatively short periods of time. By and large, Medicare administrators have not had to contend with these burdens of calculation. One must, then, guard against simplistic judgments about state incapacity as a major source of implementation difficulties and recognize that states vary considerably in this regard. In general, lack of state commitment to federal objectives probably ranks as a more serious implementation problem than inferior capacity.

LEGACY OF LOW STATUS

The tarnished reputation of the federal bureaucracy probably looms as one of the more critical problems (by no means the only one) for the implementation of health programs.

This reputation may, among other things, contribute to excessive caution, dysfunctional weakness in dealing with medical providers, inordinate dependence on as well as difficulties in managing the margins of the state, and (at times, not invariably) excessive deference to intergovernmental implementation strategies. To some extent, the low expectations of the federal bureaucracy undermine prospects for outstanding performance. A self-fulfilling prophecy surfaces.

IN QUEST OF THE FIXER

Implementation problems generated by the statute or the limited prestige and capacity of public bureaucracies hardly need to be insurmountable, especially if the task environment of the implementing agency contains forces conducive to program repair. In this regard, few concepts have a more revered place in discussions of implementation than that of the fixer. A *fixer* is some actor or coalition that carefully monitors a program, accurately diagnoses where it has gone astray, and intervenes to correct a problem (Bardach, 1977, p. 274). A fixer can help compensate for errors that seem destined to afflict a founding statue. Wildavsky (1978) has even cautioned against the stultifying impact of trying too hard to avoid mistakes in the forging of original policies. In his view, "expecting to make errors and pick up after oneself is more satisfactory."

But fixers are often in short supply, especially within the ranks of oversight institutions. Uncertainty and the more general problems of learning comprise part of the problem. It is not always clear what ails a program or how to fix it. Moreover, learning from past experience is far from automatic. In reacting to the past, decision makers frequently "develop myths, fictions, legends, folklore and illusions" (March and Olsen, 1976).

One can, however, easily exaggerate uncertainty and learning disabilities as major factors crippling the efforts of fixers. Members of Congress probably never had so much access to analytically derived information as they did during the 1970s. The General Accounting Office, the evaluation shops of the federal bureaucracy, and others turned out countless studies. The problem was not so much error detection, then, as it was motivating elected officials to undertake the correction of these errors. In this regard, interest group activity and the media often inhibited efforts to deal with program foibles.

INTEREST GROUPS AND THE MEDIA

The forces that appear to debilitate a program are almost always of direct benefit to some group. These groups frequently develop powerful incentives to perpetuate program "weakness." Hospitals and physicians for example, hardly view Medicare's payment practices as flawed just because they fail to provide them with much incentive to control costs. Reforms aimed at making consumers and medical providers more aware of cost factors in the health arena (be they market reforms or those calling for more centralized control by the federal government) can expect to encounter considerable resistance. The barriers to repair may well become even larger. Writing in the *New England Journal of Medicine*, Relman (1980, pp. 963–970) has warned of the rise of a "new medical industrial complex" consisting of "a large and growing network of private corporations engaged in the business of supplying health care services to patients for a profit." In his view the rise of this complex will "probably hinder rather than facilitate rational debate on national health-care policy." The emergence of a limited or no-growth society could also make reform more difficult. Such circumstances heighten the appeal of generating greater outputs per dollar spent. But they also create a zero-sum situation in which a solution often requires some large group to tolerate a reduction in its standard of living (Thurow, 1980). Medical providers can usually defend themselves from these reductions better than clients can. The cuts that do occur may, therefore, foster economy (as with Reagan's efforts to limit Medicaid expenditures) but do little to promote an improved cost-effectiveness ratio.

In addition to interest groups, the media comprise another outside force that can inhibit error correction. Although members of Congress can at times manipulate the media, the ability of television, radio, and the press to set the agenda for politicians ranks as even more impressive. As a rule, implementation problems do not make for interesting news stories. When the media do cover implementation, they tend to examine cases of egregious abuse rather than the more systemic problems that often possess far more relevance for program performance. Media people, for example frequently pay considerable attention to scandals such as outright fraud by medical providers or clients, while giving short shrift to the seemingly dry, technical, but more important issues concerning payment formulas and the day-to-day incentives they establish for medical providers. One cannot count on the media, then, to focus attention on the most critical problems calling for repair.

OVERSIGHT AND FIXING

Interest group pressures and the media, then, often provide little inducement for elected officials to play the role of fixer. Their ability to sidetrack reform becomes even more pronounced in the presence of fragmented power within Congress. Beyond dispersed leverage, members of Congress frequently sense that voters will judge them less in terms of how well the system works than in terms of how well they can explain individual acts.

Rather than engage in the more fundamental issues of fixing programs, legislators often divert their attention to casework or the blame-the-bureaucracy gambit. Members of Congress have grown increasingly interested in cultivating voters through a potpourri of constituent services and frequently intercede on behalf of citizens who must deal with the bureaucracy. Casework yields much political profit for a member of Congress. It creates far fewer enemies than does taking stands on issues that affect programs as a whole. It often does little, however, to strengthen their performance as program fixers (Fiorina, 1977). Aside from this tendency, Congress often plays the blame-the-bureaucracy game. The low status of agencies tempts members of Congress to increase their political popularity by blaming or ridiculing the bureaucracy rather than by helping it diagnose and correct errors. They often prefer the accusatory finger to the helping hand. Members of Congress have, for example, berated federal Medicaid officials for lax administration while simultaneously refusing to provide the staff or funds that might help officials monitor and control developments.

The behavioral propensities of Congress illustrate the importance of drawing a firm distinction between greater oversight and fixing. Until now, the issue with respect to Congress has been framed too much in terms of control. When and how does Congress exert leverage over the bureaucracy? Can it hold federal agencies accountable? These and other questions are important since they go to the heart of critical issues of democratic theory. But a Congress that zealously monitors a program can at times hurt more than it helps.

Overall, then, the obstacles to finding a fixer seem formidable. Vladeck (1980, p. 246) has become so impressed by the barriers of undoing past mistakes as to describe the situation as "the Waist Deep in the Big Muddy Problem: there are many domestic Vietnams, in which the light is always receding from the end of the tunnel."

All this is not, however, to cast a cloud of gloom over prospects for program repair and effectiveness in the health arena. Elected officials do rise to the moment at times. Moreover, sensitivity to the limits of our political institutions (e.g., excessive fragmentation and weak parties) has become so widespread as to become the subject of official government reports (U.S. President's Commission, 1980). Efforts to strengthen these institutions may surface and prove successful.

CONCLUSION

The statute, the limited prestige of public bureaucracies, and the absence of fixers can, then, feed implementation foibles. In considering these problems, this chapter may seem to be yet another exercise in the pessimism that has pervaded the implementation literature. Serious questions persist, however, as to whether the why things do not work tone of much of the writing on implementation is justified, especially in the health arena.

In this regard, it deserves emphasis that the assumptions that undergird judgments of implementation "failure" have often remained fuzzy or even misdirected. Students of implementation have, for example, devoted much ink to the problems generated by delay. In the words of one analysis (Pressman and Wildavsky, 1979) delay "is often difficult to distinguish from program failure." The pathologies of delay have, however, tended to obscure the other side of the coin: The rush to decision often brings problems of its own. Hence, the rapidity with which the Medicaid program took off meant that the states would be on their own in developing procedures needed to assure the effective and efficient administration of the program. Many states were not up to the challenge. By contrast, administrators involved in implementing the HMO legislation of 1973 that sought to encourage the development of prepaid health plans in the private sector moved slowly and cautiously. Their concern with following the letter of the law led them to allocate smaller amounts of grant money than Congress had appropriated. Over the long run, however, the program's slow takeoff may have helped officials avoid legal errors and poor investments.

The implications of delay and other aspects of implementation need, then, to be discussed in terms of more basic and explicit evaluative dimensions. In this regard, certain critical questions suggest themselves. Do civil servants operate within the bounds set by law when they administer a health program? Given some level of program accomplishment do these civil servants hold administrative waste to a minimum? To what extent does the program heighten access to health care among those who need it most, improve the quality of care, constrain medical care costs, or generally foster greater efficiency in the medical sector? Much more fundamentally, does the program enhance the health of the populace? Then, too, does the program seem to engender benign political and economic consequences in a more general sense (e.g., bolster the legitimacy of government by allowing it to appear as a competent and humane problem solver)? These questions, among others, point to important evaluative dimensions.

It would require a Panglossian temperment to expect a health program to perform well on all major dimensions. Short of such a troublefree existence, however, a program can still score impressive achievements. In this regard, considerable evidence suggests that initiatives such as Medicare, Medicaid, the Veterans Administration medical program, and the National Health Service Corps have registered significant accomplishments (Thompson, 1981). Hence, the tale of implementation in the health arena should not be construed as one of woe.

Whatever the validity of this view, it is obviously in some tension with the current national mood. Writing in the late 1970s, Wildavsky (1978, p. 43) asserted that "constellations in the American public policy universe seem to be moving in remarkably similar directions, from concentrating on aggressive design (the war on X, the crusade on Y), through the current quagmire of implementation, and into the strategic retreat on objectives. The age of design is over; the era of implementation is passing; the time to modify objectives has come." The arrival of the Reagan administration seems to bear witness to the sagacity of this view. Within a month after assuming office, the president proposed to cap federal support for Medicaid, eviscerate the HMO program, eliminate new scholarships for the National Health Service Corps, kill the health planning program, and more. Although Congress subsequently revised many of the president's proposals, it did move to reduce federal support for many health programs. Carried far enough, of course, this retreat could do much to solve the implementation problem. Simultaneously, it could raise new problems of inequality, inequity, and inefficiency that some would define as far more serious than those encountered in implementing many health programs. The invisible hand of the market may well be all thumbs when it comes to ensuring the equitable and cost-effective provision of care.

If proclamations of retreat seemed to be the order of the day as the 1980s dawned, it is still too soon for students of implementation to pack up their analytical bags and move on to other subjects. Any retreat may well be limited by the popularity of programs such as Medicare and the VA medical system and the difficulties of rallying political support for procompetition proposals featuring deregulation, cost sharing, and vouchers for medical insurance. On balance, major federal and state involvement in the health policy sphere seems likely to continue. In fact, some surveys of public attitudes toward national health insurance suggest considerable sympathy for an expanded government role in the health sector. For example, one poll (Harris, Louis and Associates, 1978) conducted in the late 1970s found that 29 percent of the public favored the status quo in health insurance, 36 percent supported present arrangements with government requirements for substantial extensions in coverage (e.g., for those confronted with catastrophic illness and for the unemployed), and 32 percent backed comprehensive coverage with a considerable degree of direct government administration and control.[6] Even if this extension of coverage took the form espoused by those who emphasize consumer choice, that is, increasing the play of market forces, and diminishing overt government involvement in providing access to care, implementation issues would require careful attention.[7]

The study of implementation in the health arena can, then, appropriately be kept on the analytical front burner. In this regard, the concepts, approaches, and propositions native to more general discussions of policy implementation can be used to shed light on the specific phenomena found in the health policy sphere. So too, the experi-

---

[6]See also the findings of Goodman and Steiber (1981).

[7]See Feldstein (1977) and Enthoven (1978b) for examples of this kind of strategy. Feder and Holahan (1980) and Rushefsky (1981) also offer critical appraisals.

ence with government programs in the health arena can be used to sharpen and refine broader discussions on implementation. No one should expect this exercise to yield a rigorous theory of implementation analogous to those found in some of the natural sciences. The enormous complexity of implementation can stymie analysis even if researchers possess complete access to pertinent information. And in the political world of implementation, obstacles to such access will often be formidable. If so vaunted a level of understanding cannot be achieved, however, sensitive inquiry can still do much to enhance the ability to describe, explain, and even predict.

Whatever the specific initiatives pursued in studying implementation in the health area, they must consider more than the internal dynamics of the bureaucracy per se. Obviously, these dynamics are important to study. They probably rank among the more malleable components of implementation. But astute analysis requires a broader perspective. Thus, implementation analysis needs to address the problems of Congress as a formulator of policies and of how these policies often rig the implementation game. It needs to assess how certain qualities of political institutions, such as the weakness of political parties, affect Congress. Nor can widespread beliefs about public agencies prevalent in the political culture be ignored given their propensity to become self-fulfilling prophecies. The role of interest groups, the media, and oversight institutions in encouraging or undermining the fixing of programs also commands consideration. The implementation of health programs does not, then, simply revolve around the "bureaucracy problem." Instead it remains deeply intertwined with the more general "health" of the political order. In sum, potent explanations or accurate predictions will not spring from a contextfree theory of implementation. Further specification of the external contingencies that shape implementation looms as critical.

ACKNOWLEDGMENTS

My thanks to Richard W. Campbell, Theodor Litman, Greg Raab, and Leonard Robins for helpful comments on an earlier draft.

REFERENCES

Arnold, R. Douglas, *Congress and the Bureaucracy*, New Haven: Yale University Press, 1979.

Bardach, Eugene, *The Implementation Game*, Cambridge: MIT Press, 1977.

Bardach, Eugene, "Implementation Studies and the Study of Implements," Paper presented at the American Political Science Association Convention, Washington, D.C., 1980.

Bardach, Eugene and Robert A. Kagan, *Going by the Book: The Problem of Regulating Unreasonableness*, Philadelphia: Temple University Press, 1982.

Cohen, Michael D., James G. March and Johan P. Olsen, "A Garbage Can Model of Organizational Choice," *Administrative Science Quarterly*, Vol. 17, March 1972, pp. 1–25.

Congressional Quarterly Almanac, Vol. 33, 1972, p. 494; Vol. 31, 1975, p. 608.

Crozier, Michel, *The Bureaucratic Phenomenon*, Chicago: University of Chicago Press, 1964.

Dodd, Lawrence C., "Congress and the Quest for Power," Paper presented at the American Political Science Association Convention, Chicago, 1976.

Enthoven, Alain C., "Shattuck Lecture–Cutting Cost Without Cutting the Quality of Care," *New England Journal of Medicine*, Vol. 29, June 1, 1978a, p. 1234.

Enthoven, Alain C., "Consumer-Choice Health Plan (Second of Two Parts)," *New England Journal of Medicine*, Vol. 298, March 30, 1978b, pp. 709–720.

Falkson, Joseph L., *HMO's and the Politics of Health System Reform*, Chicago: American Hospital Association, 1980.

Farrar, Eleanor, John E. DeSanctis and David K. Cohen, "The Lawn Party: The Evolution of Federal Programs in Local Settings," *Phi Delta Kappan*, November 1980, p. 167.

Feder, Judith, M., *Medicare: The Politics of Federal Hospital Insurance*, Lexington, Mass.: D.C. Heath, 1977.

Feder, Judith and John Holahan, "Administrative Choices," in Judith Feder, John Holahan and Theodore Marmor, eds., *National Health Insurance: Conflicting Goals and Policy Choices*, Washington, D.C.: Urban Institute, 1980, pp. 35–36.

Feder, Judith, John Holahan and Theodore Marmor, eds., *National Health Insurance: Conflicting Goals and Policy Choices*, Washington, D.C.: Urban Institute, 1980.

Federal Register, Vol. 43, March 28, 1978, pp. 13010–13020.

Feldstein, Martin, "The High Costs of Hospitals and What To Do About It," *The Public Interest*, Vol. 48, Summer 1977, pp. 40–54.

Finer, Herman, "Administrative Responsibility in Democratic Government," *Public Administration Review*, Vol. 1, Summer 1941, pp. 335–350.

Fiorina, Morris P., *Congress—Keystone of the Washington Establishment*, New Haven: Yale University Press, 1977.

Foltz, Anne-Marie, "The Development of Ambiguous Federal Policy: Early and Periodic Screening, Diagnosis and Treatment (EPSDT)," *Milbank Memorial Fund Quarterly Health and Society*, Vol. 53, Winter 1975, pp. 35–64.

The Gallup Opinion Index, Vol. 146, September 1977, pp. 20–24.

Glaser, William A., *Health Insurance Bargaining*, New York: Gardner Press, 1978, pp. 195–196.

Goodman, Louis J. and Steven R. Steiber, "Public Support for National Health Insurance," *American Journal of Public Health*, Vol. 71, October 1981, pp. 1105–1108.

Greenberg, George D., Jeffrey A. Miller, Lawrence B. Mohr, et al., "Developing Public Policy Theory: Perspectives from Empirical Research," *American Political Science Review*, Vol. 71, December 1977, pp. 1532–1543.

Hadley, Jack and Mark Levenson, "Institutional Support for Medical Schools and Teaching Hospitals," in Jack Hadley, ed., *Medical Education Financing*, New York: Prodist, 1980, p. 152.

Harris, Louis and Associates, *Hospital Care in America*, Nashville: Hospital Affiliates International, 1978, pp. 8, 54.

Health Resources News, Vol. 5, November 1978.

Heclo, Hugh and Aaron Wildavsky, *The Private Government of Public Money*, Berkeley: University of Calfornia Press, 1974, p. 12.

Ingram, Helen, "Policy Implementation Through Bargaining: The Case of Federal Grants-in-Aid," *Public Policy*, Vol. 25, Fall 1977, pp. 499–526.

Institute for Social Research, University of Michigan, *1980 Election Survey*, Ann Arbor: University of Michigan Institute for Social Research, 1981.

Jain, Sagar C., ed., "Role of State and Local Governments in Relation to Personal Health Services," *American Journal of Public Health*, Vol. 71, January 1981, supplement.

Lowi, Theodore, *The End of Liberalism*, New York: W.W. Norton & Co., 1969.

Majone, Giandomenico and Aaron Wildavsky, "Implementation as Evolution," in Jeffrey Passman and Aaron Wildavsky, *Implementation*, Berkeley: University of California Press, 1979, 2nd edition, p. 189.

March, James G., "Bounded Rationality; Ambiguity and the Engineering of Choice," *The Bell Journal of Economics*, Vol. 9, Autumn 1978, pp. 599–604.

March, James G. and Johan P. Olsen, *Ambiguity and Choice in Organizations*, Bergen: Universitetsforlaget, 1976, pp. 54–68.

Marmor, Theodore R., *National Health Insurance: Implementation Forecasts and Policy Choice*, New Haven: Unpublished paper, 1980.

Montjoy, Robert S. and Laurence J. O'Toole, Jr., "Toward a Theory of Policy Implementation: An Organizational Perspective," *Public Administration Review*, Vol. 39, September–October 1979, pp. 473.

Nakamura, Robert T. and Frank Smallwood, *The Politics of Policy Implementation*, New York: St. Martin's Press, 1980, p. 33.

Pressman, Jeffrey and Aaron Wildavsky, *Implementation*, Berkeley: University of California Press, 1979, 2nd edition.

Price, Don K., "Planning and Administrative Perspectives on Adequate Personal Health," *Milbank Memorial Fund Quarterly, Health and Society*, Vol. 56, Winter 1978, pp. 22–50.

Relman, Arnold C., "The New Medical-Industrial Complex," *New England Journal of Medicine*, Vol. 303, October 23, 1980, pp. 963–970.

Rodgers, Jr., Harrell R. and Charles S. Bullock III, *Coercion to Compliance*, Lexington, Mass.: D.C. Heath, 1976.

Rosenbaum, Allan, "Federal Programs and State Governments: On Understanding Why 40 Years of Federal Efforts Haven't Fundamentally Altered Economic Inequality in American Society," Paper presented at the American Political Science Association Convention, New York, 1978.

Rushefsky, Mark E., "A Critique of Market Reform in Health Care: The Consumer-Choice Health Plan," *Journal of Health Politics, Policy and Law*, Vol. 5, Winter 1981, pp. 720–741.

Sabatier, Paul and Daniel Mazmanian, "The Conditions of Effective Implementation: A Guide to Accomplishing Policy Objectives," *Policy Analysis*, Vol. 5, Fall 1979, pp. 481–504.

Sharkansky, Ira, *Wither the State?* Chatham, N.J.: Chatham Publishing, 1979, p. 11.

Sundquist, James L., "In Defense of Pragmatism: A Response to 'Is Federalism Compatible With Prefectorial Administration,'" *Publius*, Vol. 11, Spring, 1981, pp. 31–37.

Thompson, Frank J., *Health Policy and the Bureaucracy: Politics and Implementation*, Cambridge: MIT Press, 1981.

Thompson, Frank J., "After the Dance: The Hierarchy Assumption, Implementation, and the National Health Service Corps," *Political Science Quarterly*, forthcoming.

Thompson, Frank J. and Richard W. Campbell, "Implementation and Service Error: VA Health Care and the Commercial Market Option," *Journal of Health Politics, Policy and Law*, Vol. 6, Fall 1981, pp. 419–443.

Thurow, Lester C., *The Zero-Sum Society*, New York: Basic Books, 1980.

U.S. House Committee on Appropriations, *Department of Labor and Health, Education, and Welfare Appropriations for 1978*, Part 6, Washington, D.C.: U.S. Government Printing Office, 1977, pp. 464–465.

U.S. House Committee on Ways and Means, *Intermediary Performance Regarding Fraud and Abuse*, Washington, D.C.: U.S. Government Printing Office, 1979, pp. 5,33,41.

U.S. President's Commission for a National Agenda for the Eighties, *A National Agenda for the Eighties*, Washington, D.C.: U.S. Government Printing Office, 1980.

U.S. Senate, *Medicare and Medicaid, Issues and Alternatives Report 35-719*, Washington D.C.: U.S. Government Printing Office, 1970, pp. 61–66.

Vladeck, Bruce C., "The Design of Failure: Health Policy and the Structure of Federalism," *Journal of Health Politics, Policy and Law*, Vol. 4, Fall 1979, p. 533.

Vladeck, Bruce C., *Unloving Care*, New York: Basic Books, 1980, p. 246.

Vladeck, Bruce C., "The Market vs. Regulation: The Case for Regulation," *Milbank Memorial Fund Quarterly/Health and Society*, Vol. 59, Spring 1981, pp. 209–223.

Waldo, Dwight, *The Enterprise of Public Administration*, Novato, Calif. Chandler and Sharp, 1980, p. 17.

Wildavsky, Aaron, *Speaking Truth to Power*, Boston: Little, Brown and Co., 1978, p. 15.

Zwick, Daniel I., "Initial Development of Guidelines for Health Planning," *Public Health Reports*, Vol. 93, September–October 1978, pp. 407–420.

CHAPTER 9

The Politics and Administration of Intergovernmental Relations in Health

Robert Agranoff
Leonard S. Robins

GROWING CRITICISM OF THE GRANTS-IN-AID SYSTEM[1]

There have been three important waves and ways of thinking about U.S. federalism. The first stressed the competition and divisions between the national and state levels of government. It traced the decline of the constitutional doctrine of *dual federalism:* the concept that some powers were exclusively given to the national level of government, others exclusively to the state level, and the remainder shared concurrently. It traced how the Tenth Amendment to the Constitution became an essentially "dead letter" through various Supreme Court rulings. Finally, it described grants-in-aid as devices by which the national government was able to exert control in fields in which the national government had no clear grant of power. Specifically, grants-in-aid allowed the national government to "bribe" a state to enter a field through an offer of money it could not realistically refuse and then obtain state complaince with national regulations by threatening to cut off the money for the grant-in-aid (Reagan, 1972).

In the 1950s and early 1960s, the major works on federalism and intergovernmental relations of Grodzins (1966) and Elazar (1972) led students of federalism to interpret the U.S. intergovernmental relations system in a considerably different manner. It was realized that the primary source of support and maintenance of the U.S. federal system and an important role for the states in the U.S. federal system is the decentralized U.S. political party system rather than any written legal formulas that are found in the Constitution and expounded by the Supreme Court (Riker, 1964).

In addition, and of more direct relevance, Grodzins and Elazar stressed that the

---

[1]Much of the material in the first two sections is drawn from Robins, (1974).

nation and the states were always primarily partners rather than competitors in the performance of governmental functions. They emphasized and favorably noted upon the fact that when an important problem arose that called for governmental action, both the states and the national government typically attempted to respond with appropriate action. Grodzins and Elazar—though strongly in favor of a major state role in U.S. federalism—generally downplayed efforts at determining which level of government does what best (Elazar, 1972).

Given this perspective on intergovernmental relations, it is not surprising that Grodzins and Elazar did not consider grant-in-aid programs to be usurpation of state power by the national government. Specifically, they emphasized that grants-in-aid typically did not replace state with national power or state with national programs, but rather resulted in an increase in both national and state power. For example, if states do not have the resources to attack a problem and the national government deals with it through a grant-in-aid program in which both the nation and states share responsibility, the national government has increased rather than decreased state power. This example is more than hypothetical; Grodzins and Elazar concluded that vigorous national action typically comes not when the states are acting but rather when the states are not and are not able to act by themselves (Elazar, 1972).

Indirect evidence for this analysis is provided by the attitudes of state officials toward the grant-in-aid system. Several surveys of the attitudes of state officials (the latest in 1978) elicited strong support from them for both the existing grants-in-aid and the grant-in-aid concept of joint national and state control over categorical grant programs (Wright, 1982).

During the Great Society years of President Lyndon Johnson, however, categorical programs multiplied and proliferated in a remarkable, crazy-quilt pattern. Since these were largely conceived, supported, and desired by Washington rather than being joint initiatives, the incentive for the states to cooperate in their implementation was frequently less than with previous categorical programs. Given that the relative lack of interest on the part of the states increased the power of the states in the bargaining over implementation, the conditions attached to these grants were typically qualitatively different from those previously attached to categorical grants—different in ways that tended to increase the degree of national control relative to state control or other recipient control.

First, an increasing number of grant-in-aid programs during this period abandoned the typical 50–50 spending formula that required the states to match federal spending equally. The percentage of matching money required from the states is frequently a good guide to the relative influence of the national government and the states in a grant program. Generally speaking, the higher the percentage of national funds, the greater the degree of national control (Elazar, 1972). In the new grant programs initiated as part of the Great Society, the national contribution was almost always a much higher percentage than that required of the states.

Second, and even more important, project grants rather than formula grants became, during this period, the dominant form of grant-in-aid, and the characteristics of formula grants and project grants have a major impact in determining the relative degree of national and state control over grant programs. "*Formula grants* are grants whose funds are divided among all eligible recipients on the basis of some announced criterion that is applied proportionately across the board and without any discretion in the hands of the grant-giving officials. . . . Formula grants are distributed to all eligible jurisdictions as a matter of "right." The discretion, if there is any, lies in the hands of the recipient governments that decide how much matching money they want to use to obtain a particular federal grant. Federal influence under formula grants lies in the administrative requirements that accompany the grant, rather than in the substance of the grant" (Reagan, 1972, p. 63). States are almost always the recipients of formula grants from the national government.

Project grants are considerably different from formula grants. "Project grants are those made for specific projects only. . . . They are not spread among all potential recipients according to any fixed proportions" (Elazar, 1972, p. 68). Project grants thus typically operate in a manner that enhances national influence in grant programs, for the national government both creates the criteria for projects and does the actual choosing among the applications for support of projects. Project grants, moreover, frequently go to localities, special-purpose governments (e.g., school districts), or even private recipients. Although the states frequently have an important administrative role in grant programs that do not designate them as the recipients (Elazar, 1972), their influence and control over these grants is less than over those grants that designate them as the recipients. In short, the new emphasis on project grants resulted in a major increase in the influence of the national government in grant-in-aid programs.

Describing these and other trends in grants-in-aid more quantitatively and systematically, the number of federal grants increased from less than 100 in the 1950s to nearly 500 by the late 1970s. Nearly 100 of these grants directly or indirectly involved health and medical care.

Indeed, in a major survey of intergovernmental relations, the Advisory Commission on Intergovernmental Relations (ACIR) concluded that the federal government's assumption of progressively greater responsibility for dealing with domestic problems through use of grants-in-aid stands out as a dominant feature of intergovernmental impacts in the decades 1959–1979 (Stenberg, 1980). These grants led to a 72.5 percent increase in the number of state and local government employees and a significant increase in the number and types of regulatory activities (Stenberg, 1980).

This federally stimulated expansion has changed the nature of intergovernmental relationships. Stenberg suggests that the following aspects of the federal assistance phenomenon are particularly noteworthy:

1. *The Dollar Amount.* Aid to state and local governments has increased from $7 billion in fiscal year 1960 to $83 billion in fiscal year 1980. During the same period federal aid has risen from 14.7 to 23.6 percent of state–local expenditures.

2. *Instruments.* The means by which assistance is transmitted has expanded to include a variety of federal–state, federal–local, and federal–private transactions under formula and project categorical grants, block grants, general revenue sharing, procurement contracts, and cooperative agreements.

3. *Participants.* The extent of state and local government involvement has expanded to the point where virtually all general-purpose local units and many special purpose units, as well as newly created special substate or regional units, receive assistance, thus multiplying the number of people affected by intergovernmental actions.

4. *Strings.* The conditions attached to federal programs are often extensive, expensive, and intrusive. In addition to traditional watch dog requirements (e.g., financial reporting and audits), the federal government has increasingly used federal assistance programs as vehicles for achieving national social policy goals, such as affirmative action, environmental quality, historical site preservation, and citizen par-

ticipation. By the late 1970s nearly 60 of these requirements applied to all or most programs, regardless of purpose.

5. *Certainty.*   Although greater federal assistance is available, recipients' capacity to plan for effective use of funds is impaired by uncertainty over amounts, timing, and whether they can be used for recipients' priorities.

6. *Bypassing.*   Federal agencies and congressional committees became increasingly involved in transmitting money directly to local governments, neighborbood groups, private agencies, and community action agencies.

7. *Lobbying.*   Accompanying federal assistance dollar growth, was an increase in the intensity and number of participants in congressional lobbying. The new intergovernmental lobby includes spokespersons for state and local government executive and legislative officials, advocates on behalf of the specialized governmental programs, and units funded by federal assistance and other functional and professional groups that have benefitted from federal largese (Stenberg, 1972, pp. 29–31).

These changes have led Elazar and many other students of intergovernmental relations to become increasingly critical of the grants-in-aid system and to advocate various proposals for diminishing national influence in grant programs. Before turning to their "new" arguments for lessening national control over grant programs, it is important to note that attitudes on this issue are strongly shaped by whose ox is being gored. For reasons that need not be analyzed here, labor and minority groups are, by and large, stronger at the national than at the state level of government (Riker, 1964). Consequently, they have historically tended to be opposed to proposals for weakening the national government's influence in grant programs. The political right, in contrast, has usually been stronger at the state and local governmental levels, and most conservatives tend to be strong advocates of proposals that would weaken national control over grant programs. Second, there are obvious institutional biases in analyzing this question. State and local officials—whether ideologically of the left or right—feel impelled to argue that the discretion of their governments in grant programs should be increased vis-á-vis Washington. National administrators, on the other hand, typically have an opposite viewpoint.

The first of the new arguments is that categorical grants have grown so numerous and confusing that they have themselves become part of the problem rather than the solution. Even some of those who approve of centrally administered categorical grants-in-aid concede that the uncoordinated proliferation of grant programs—project grants in particular—has made the coordinated solving of problems difficult, if not impossible. In the long run, solving problems is the goal and not the delivery of tightly packaged service components. In summary, these critics contend that whatever the merits of any given categorical program in isolation, the "hardening of the categories" has become a serious problem (Sundquist, 1969).

Another criticism of categorical grant-in-aid programs emanating from the Great Society period is that they have harmed general-purpose state and local governments and elected officials (Elazar, 1972). The grants to health departments, school boards, library boards, and so on, have, it is contended, weakened elected state officials and general-purpose local governments, for categorical grants are funded in a manner that tends to remove the professionals and bureaucrats from control by elected officials responsible directly to the public. Specialized local bureaucrats interact with their professional counterparts in Washington rather than being controlled by elected local and state officials (Levin, 1969) (One might also speculate that the same is true at the national level and that professionals and bureaucrats in Washington use the apparent constraints imposed by the states in grant programs to free themselves from the control of their political superiors.)

Those making these criticisms of categorical grants-in-aid importantly differed from the earlier states rights critics of categorical grants, however, for they recognized that national financing and an appropriate national policy role were essential in dealing with many health and social programs. They sought to reform the grant-in-aid system rather than destroy it, and many of them thought the thing to do was to convert categorical into block grants.

THE BLOCK GRANT ALTERNATIVE

There are, on a continuum of greater to lesser control, five types of national programs: nationally run programs, categorical grants, block grants, revenue sharing, and no national programs. These types are outined in Table 9.1, with selected health programs listed under the appropriate categories.

It is important that nationally run programs such as Medicare be placed on a chart that focuses in the relative degree of national influence on various types of grants-in-aid. Otherwise, the clear impression is left that a central position in the degree of national

TABLE 9-1. Relative Degree of National Control from Greater to Lesser Control

Nationally Run Programs	Categorical Grants	Block Grants	Revenue Sharing	No National Programs
Medicare	Medicaid	Public Health Block Grant 314 (d)		
Veterans Administration Hospitals	Family Planning			
	Venereal Disease Control	Preventive Health Services		
Indian Health Service	Immunization	Primary Care		
	Migrant Worker Health	Maternal and Child Health		
	Adolescent Pregnancy	Alcohol, Drug Abuse, and Mental Health		
	Developmental Disabilities			
Hypertension				

control over programs is somewhere between categorical grants and revenue sharing. Within the context of grant-in-aid programs, however, national influence is greatest in categorical grants-in-aid.

"Categorical grants are by and large those for specifically and narrowly defined purposes, leaving very little discretionary room on the part of a recipient government as to how it uses the grant. . ." (Reagan, 1972, p. 59). They are a vehicle for identifying problems, setting priorities, and focusing resources on a national basis. They carry not only restrictions on the use of money but usually also carry planning, accounting, reporting, and personnel requirements. A categorical grant is the kind of program most people think of, in terms of both strengths and weaknesses, when they think of national grant programs. Empirical research on the operation of grant programs, however, indicates that who actually is in control is much less clear-cut than this definition implies (Ingram, 1977; Radin, 1972; Thompson, 1981; Williams, 1980) But a significant degree of national control is almost always intended in categorical programs.

Block grants differ from categoricals in the following five ways: (1) federal aid is authorized for a wide range of activities within a broadly defined functional area, (2) recipients have substantial discretion in identifying problems, allocating resources, and designing programs, (3) administrative, fiscal, reporting, planning, and other federal requirements are kept to the minimum amount necessary to ensure that national goals are being accomplished, (4) federal aid is distributed according to a statutory formula, which has the effects of narrowing federal administrators' discretion and providing a sense of fiscal certainty to recipients, and (5) eligibility requirements are statutorily specified and favor general-purpose governments as recipients and administrative generalists as decision makers (Stenberg and Walker, 1977). In short, block grants are designed to be both theoretically and operationally the opposite of categorical grants.

Revenue sharing is, essentially, money given to the states and localities to assist them in the performance of *their* functions. It is only indirectly relevant to the question of which level of government should perform any given function. For a variety of economic, historical, political, and state constitutional reasons, states and localities have typically relied on property and sales taxes for the bulk of their revenues—taxes that are either very unpopular or hit the poor very hard. The national government, in contrast, has primarily relied on the personal and corporate income tax. A strong case can be made, therefore, that the clearest effect of revenue sharing is to substitute income taxes for sales and property taxes.

The national government may, of course, decide not to become involved in a functional area, that is, to have no national program. This category may also seem unusual in a classification of types of national involvement, but it serves to highlight an essential element in the debate over the desirability of converting categorical into block grants: the danger (or for a conservative perhaps the hope) that the real choice is between a categorical grant or no grant.

BLOCK GRANTS IN HEALTH

In the early 1960s, important objections were raised to the categorical approach to the solution of health problems. In 1961, the ACIR criticized the health categoricals for being overly restrictive. It did not, however, recommend the abolition of categorical grant-in-aid programs for health. Instead, the commission recommended that the states have authority to transfer a certain percentage of funds from one categorical program to another, depending on a state's particular needs and problems (ACIR, 1961).

In 1966, the National Commission on Community Health Services, by contrast, specifically called for a health block grant. The commission felt that "the disadvantage of highly specific grants is the potential distortion of priorities, as viewed from the state or local level." It favorably noted that "the general health grant is available for almost any legitimate purpose, and may be spent by an organization on the basis of its own evaluation of changing needs. A general grant is both flexible and dependable." Its recommendation was that "categorical grants should be reviewed periodically, and phased into the general health grant and the general health grant should be increased both in absolute amount *and as a proportion of total grants*" (emphasis added) (National Commission, 1966).

The group that had been most active over the longest period of time in arguing for a block grant was, however, the Association of State and Territorial Health Officers (AS-THO). In their annual conferences, ASTHO repeatedly argued that the categorical approach incorrectly superimposed national priorities onto states that had vastly different problems and resources.

The advocacy of block grants by groups such as ACIR and ASTHO was hardly surprising, for these are groups that either have an interest in promoting greater state influence in health policy or a known bias in support of increased state influence vis-á-vis Washington in grant-in-aid programs. What needs to be explained, however, is why those, such as the national health bureaucracy, who might have been expected to oppose this shift to block grants did not do so. Although the following might not constitute the total answer, two reasons stand out as being of great importance in the national health bureaucracy's acceptance of the shift to a health block grant.

The first reason for the acceptance of the change to a block grant was the emerging consensus in the health care field that the focus of health care not be on disease categories but should instead be on comprehensive and preventive medical care. Advocates of the comprehensive care approach contended that categorical grants-in-aid reinforced an incorrect approach to health care delivery. A general public health grant would, according to this view, have the virtue of stimulating programs that were more comprehensive and preventive in nature. As former Surgeon General William Steward testified before Congress in support of the 314 (d), Block Grant in the Partnership for Health Act, "it would focus the programs on the multiple problems of individuals and families living in communities throughout the nation, rather than on narrow disease categories" (*House Hearings*, 1966, p. 34). There are generally good feelings between public health professionals at all levels of government. This facilitates smooth administration even when the conditions of a grant are rather rigid. Conversely, professional disagreement will lead to some conflict even when a block grant permits maximum flexibility.

Second, the incentive for the national government to keep control over these programs was minimal because the categorical programs were, from Washington's perspective, relatively insignificant. The categoricals were small in comparison to the overall national expenditures on health and even fairly small as a percentage of the budget spent on health services delivery programs, the relevant unit within the Public Health Service (PHS). Perhaps national health officials preferred to use the lure of a health block grant to obtain support for other proposals they deemed of greater importance.[2]

---

[2]This viewpoint was forcefully expressed in a personal interview with Leonard Robins on February 26, 1970, by George Leonard, Chief, Program Development Branch, Division of Comprehensive Health Planning, Community Health Service, Department of Health, Education, and Welfare.

The public health block grant received smooth sailing in Congress. It was not opposed in Senate and House hearings by a single member of Congress or by any witnesses. The only significant opposition developed over then undersecretary of the Department of Health, Education and Welfare (DHEW) Wilbur Cohen's projection of need and desirable major funding increases (See *Senate Hearings*, 1966). In fact the initial appropriations by Congress fell far short of those requested by DHEW and strongly supported by ASTHO.

The continuation of this pattern led to important changes of opinion by state health officers toward public health block grants. Initially, they had believed the rhetoric that called for a coupling of increased flexibility with increased funding. They slowly recognized that this was not a likely relationship, but many were willing at the margin to trade a slight decrease in funding for a major increase in flexibility, administrative discretion, and lessening of red tape. As funding for the public health block grant continued to decline in real terms, that is, no dollar increase during times of high inflation, however, they gradually grew to strongly oppose extending block grants in any area of health services (Robins and Backstrom, 1976). The ultimate outcome of the public health block grant both contributed to and reinforced this view: Efforts by both the Carter and Reagan administrations resulted in its elimination in 1981.

The reason block grants have always had difficulty obtaining funding is that they are not politically attractive to Congress. Students of congressional spending behavior stress that members of Congress look with favor on concrete programs that seem to meet visible needs directly and are supported by strong clientele groups, on programs over which they can exercise a considerable degree of control, and on programs that offer an opportunity for them to take personal credit for successes (Niskanen, 1971). Categorical programs meet these criteria. They deal with problems such as heart disease and cancer, and by preserving a clear measure of national control, they allow members of Congress to have some influence over them and claim some of the credit for the good they accomplish. In contrast, block grants are frequently amorphous programs over which members of Congress have little control and whose "good works" are seen as coming from state and local governments.

Another long-term problem of block grants is their tendency to become recategorized over time. This can happen in one of two ways. First, new conditions may be attached to the block grant. An example outside of health is the Community Development Block Grant, in which pressures increased, especially during the Carter administration, for more targeting of funds to poor neighborhoods (Kettle, 1980). Second, the block grant may be kept very small and parallel categorical programs established to accomplish objectives that logically should have been assigned to the block grant. This was true in the case of 314 (d), for Congress enacted new programs such as family planning and expanded several ongoing programs such as venereal disease control that should logically have been included in the overall public health block grant.

It is important to emphasize, however, that a similar, albeit reverse, process frequently occurs with categorical programs, that is, over time, state and local recipients frequently increase their authority as they become more knowledgeable about regulations and how they can be manipulated to serve their ends. Thus, it is essential to understand that the grants-in-aid system is not a static one and that federal, state, and local officials are constantly manipulating it to serve their own interests. This understanding is necessary for both enhancing the effectiveness of grants-in-aid and preventing a dramatic decline in intergovernmental programs in favor of a massive sorting out of governmental functions.

THE ALLOCATION OF FUNCTIONS ALTERNATIVE

An important new trend in intergovernmental relations is the growing support for the exclusive allocation of various functional problem areas among states, localities, and the federal government. The reasons given by supporters of "sorting out" functional responsibilities in the federal system, however, differ considerably.

The leading intellectual advocate of this approach is the Advisory Commission on Intergovernmental Relations. In 1981 its executive director called for the following:

> Reexamination of the functional responsibilites of the federal, state and local levels, including assessment of the desirabilities of fully nationalizing some functions while reducing, eliminating, or forestalling federal involvement in others, including consideration of the possible use of instruments other than grants-in-aid to realize national objectives. (Anderson 1981, p. iv)

The primary reason for advocating this position is the belief that the grants-in-aid system has become such a hodgepodge and administrative nightmare that it can be cured only through the dramatic remedy of, to use David Walker's phrase, "decongestion" (Walker, 1981). In short, greater efficiency and accountability are the primary goals to be achieved by sorting out.

Block grants relate to this approach in that the consolidation of categoricals is seen by some as an initial step in sorting out. Devolving the federal government from certain program responsibilities would be a subsequent step. Under this scenario, categoricals are first consolidated, effecting increased flexibility and administrative savings; at some point, total program responsibility would be turned over to the states and perhaps other subnational governments. This approach leaves unclear whether the sorting out would necessarily continue to carry fiscal transfers with it.

The most recent proponents of sorting out—the nation's governors—add to this analysis the important demand that any devolution of functions to the states must be accompanied by the national government's assumption of total responsibility for functions currently jointly performed by national and state governments and that states find difficult to perform. The key to their thinking can be seen through tracing their reactions to the Reagan budget-cutting program of 1981. Before the program's presentation, governors went on record as being willing to accept grant-in-aid cuts of up to 10 percent if they were converted into block grants, thereby allowing them greater flexibility in the use of federal funds. This would enable them to achieve efficiencies and thus be able to absorb the budget cuts. When the cuts, however, were seen to average approximately 25 percent and the grants were discovered to contain unexpected strings, the governors made it clear that they were now in favor of sorting out. The elimination of state revenue sharing and the possibility of eliminating or greatly reducing local revenue sharing has undoubtedly solidified the views of the governors on this point. In other words—words that the governors would not use but that clarify the real issues—the governors are reluctantly but increasingly advocating sorting out over block grants. However, the governors in essence opposed the sorting out proposals of the Reagan administration in 1982, for it bacame clear that the administration had more interest in reducing the federal role than in arriving at a rational plan for rearranging functions between the nation and states (Pierce, 1981). Faced with unacceptable block grant and sorting out proposals, the governors were indeed caught between a rock and a hard place.

Although the motivations of the governors and ACIR differ considerably, the particular programs selected for realignment by those primarily driven by the goal of improved administrative efficiency and those driven by the goal of relief of fiscal stress are remarkably similar. Both favor the federal government taking full responsibility for the provision of welfare and financing personal medical services and the states and localities taking full responsibility for the provision of education, law enforcement, and transportation services.

In fairness, it must be said that whatever one thinks of the sorting out approach, its advocates have gotten the right functions allocated to the right places. The ACIR used the pragmatic measure of "closure," that is, welfare and medical services are now predominantly provided by the federal government, and education, law enforcement, and transportation services are now predominantly provided by state and local governments, hence the swaps should not be too difficult (ACIR, 1977).

More theoretically, the economic logic of "externalities" argues for this division, if a fair division is to be made. States and localities are freer to spend what they think is the correct amount on education, law enforcement, and transportation services than they are on aiding the poor through welfare and personal medical services. The reason is that states and localities often fear that businesses and upper-income residents will move rather than pay for services through higher taxes, thus removing themselves from the consequences of collective decision making. Though the threat is often a bluff and the reality of negative impact is questionable, it is true that the upper-income citizen receives no clear gain from higher welfare expenditures to balance the pain of higher taxes and might even consider them dysfunctional if they are believed to attract more potential welfare applicants to the state or locality.

Conversely, increased spending on education results in a benefit to all citizens as well as in higher taxes, and hence higher taxes might be willingly accepted or even advocated for this function. There is little reason, and may be none, for business and upper-income residents to escape the consequences of collective decision making. Thus, the advocates of sorting out have correctly identified the functions in which economists argue for national funding and those in which they advocate state and local funding.

Two final and more negative points need to be made concerning the sorting out strategy. First, although it is most strenuously advocated by those favoring a reduction of the federal role in the delivery of services and an enhancement of the state and local role, the result might very well be the opposite, particularly if the federal government were to take over financing and administration of welfare and medical services.

Those who advocate dissolving what Elazar described as "the American partnership" should recognize the real possibility that the federal partner will be more able to survive divorce, under almost any terms, than will state and local governments. Despite increased state capacity, there are political and sometimes legal limits on the ability of state governments to tax their citizens to meet a number of the service needs identified in the past few decades. Local governments appear to face even greater problems. Not only do they operate under the supervision of the states, but they are up against both revenue restrictions arising from reliance on property taxes and pressures to provide basic services touching all citizens, such as street maintenance and sanitation. Thus, the prospects for state and local assumption of functions renounced by the national government are not good.

Second, a kind of defacto sorting out process is currently underway, with particularly cruel results for those most in need. The major *nationally run* health and human services programs in the United States—Social Security, Medicare, veterans benefits—have, on the whole, emerged relatively untouched from the major budget cutting endeavors of recent years. Indeed, there have not even really been serious efforts to try and reduce their benefits. In contrast, grants-in-aid for health and human services such as Medicaid, AFDC, and food stamps have been severely slashed. Block grants may have fared worse than categorical grants, but both have come under tremendous budgetary pressures. Another way of categorizing these programs is to note that the main beneficiaries of Social Security, Medicare, and Veterans benefits are the middle class and the aged—groups with relatively high status in U.S. society. In contrast, the poor, minorities, and other stigmatized groups in U.S. society were most hurt by the cuts in grants-in-aid. Proponents of sorting out must face the real possibility that sorting out might empirically mean nationally run programs for the middle class and state run programs—very small state run programs—for the poor. Today's top health policy priority may be cost containment, but most health policy professionals hope to achieve this by containing medical care price increases and by reducing unnecessary medical care use, not by a silent, subtle repeal of the increased access by the poor to medical care achieved over the past 20 years. The states are the administrative jurisdiction directly responsible for slashing Medicaid benefits and eligibility, but they, fortunately, at least are not taking great pride in this form of cost containment.

Instead of such a radical departure from the U.S. grant-in-aid system, a renewed effort to revitalize its performance is proposed. A real effort must be made to improve the effectiveness of grants-in-aid. The first step in such an effort requires a careful examination of the empirical realities of intergovernmental management of programs.

FROM FEDERALISM TO INTERGOVERNMENTAL RELATIONS

The growth in domestic policy areas such as health has created hundreds of new relationships between the federal government and the states, between the federal government and local governments, between the states and local government, between local governments, and between governments and the private sector. These interactions tend to be over the transfer of grant money, priority setting, standards of program design and operation, and rules and regulations. As discussed, these intergovernmental connections have altered formal theories of U.S. federalism, which stressed the *independence and divided functions* of each level, to a new federalism or to intergovernmental relations in which the cutting edge lies in the *actual relationships* among the levels of government as they share in the *performance of expanding functions* (Reagan, 1972). Thus, intergovernmental relations (IGR) has emerged as a result of a complex and interdependent system involving an increase in the number of governmental units, in the number and type of officials involved in such arrangements, in the intensity and regularity of contacts among these officials, in the importance of these officials' attitudes and actions, and in a preoccupation with financial policy issues (Wright, 1982).

Intergovernmental relations (IGR) is commonly perceived to have five distinctive features, which will be illustrated in the context of health policy and politics. First, in contrast to federalism, which tends to emphasize national–state and interstate relationships, IGR also recognizes national–local and interlocal relations, as well as public–private contacts when government programs are involved. In addition to the growing connections between the federal and state governments in the operation of grant programs such as Medicaid, health planning, and numerous public health grants, IGR would also include direct grant programs such as those concerning community health centers, as well as linkages between health organizations involved in governmental programs at the local level. Examples of the latter would include contacts between city and county public health departments or a private agency delivering home health services under contract to the local health department or and a local health inspector's relationship with a nursing home. Of course, IGR involves all contacts between state health officials and local officials. In other words, it encompasses all the permulations and combinations of relations among units of governments and between their operatives.

Second, such arrangements have a human dimension. The individual actions and attitudes of public officials, for example, are at the heart of intergovernmental relations. Thus, IGR is concerned with what the president, members of Congress, governors, state legislators, federal and state bureaucrats, local officials, and key interest group representatives think and do about key health programs. Attitudes and actions about the promotion of Health Maintenance Organizations (HMOs) as a means of cost containment, or regulation–deregulation, or eligibility limits for Medicaid are essential components of IGR. As Anderson once explained, "It is human beings clothed with office who are the real determiners of what the relations between units of government will be" (Anderson, 1960, p. 4).

Third, IGR includes officials' continuous, day-to-day patterns of contact and exchanges of information and views. This means that in addition to health legislation, relationships also include negotiations and discussions over receiving, for example, a state health grant, or an application for an HMO, or the inspection of a hospital. They also encompass the working contacts between governments and the deliverers of health services funded by government programs, such as Medicaid and Medicare vendors, as well as the contractors who process claims and payments. Thus, the participants are primarily concerned with getting things done through relatively informal, practical, goal-oriented arrangements that can be realized within the officials' formal, legal, and institutional context.

Fourth, public officials—legislative, executive, and judicial—at all levels of government participate in reaching intergovernmental solutions. For example, the Hill-Burton hospital construction program primarily involved federal government administration of the legislation through the Division of Medical Facilities within the Bureau of State Services of the U.S. Public Health Service. The division worked through state medical facilities units in public health departments, which themselves operated under state legislative oversight. The states defined medical service areas and allocated construction funding to local communities, which usually involved a variety of local officials. The courts, however, were also called upon to make decisions concerning litigation over equal patient access to Hill-Burton constructed hospitals on the basis of race and income level. Court decisions on these questions affected the regulations written by the Public Health Service, which in turn changed the nature of relationships with state and local officials. When one considers the increasing complexity and interdependence of health programs, it is easy to see that an increasing variety of officials is likely to become involved in IGR.

Fifth, IGR has a policy component generated by the intentions, actions, and inactions of public officials. A program such as Medicaid, for example, is a complex of ideas and issues generated by such actions. In addition to the policy objective of providing payment for the costs of medical services for the poor and medically needy, it was also originally supposed to encourage state expansion of medical services in return for the federal government assuming 50 percent of the costs. Others saw the program as another in-kind benefit for the poor and one that extended benefits to nonwelfare eligible poor. Of course, all of the states did not select the option to extend benefits to this latter group, and not all states met the challenge of expanding services. More important, the program has become so expensive that the emphasis has shifted to reducing costs. How the variety of policy officials involved in a program such as Medicaid regard it and play out their role is an integral part of IGR.

The intergovernmental relations dimension of health programs is particularly important to understand because so many involve the transfer of funds or the imposition of program requirements and regulations among levels and types of governments. For the health official, whether he or she works for government or not, this has meant that complexity has accompanied growth. Numerous categorical grants, block grants, health financing, and regulatory programs have led to federal and state funding and a patchwork of providers in both governmental and nongovernmental sectors (Walker, 1981).

This can be illustrated by examining the units and programs a health official working at the local level would be likely to encounter if he or she mapped out the array. A person might find, within the geographical boundaries of a community, health programs operating under one or more of the following auspices:

1. Several units of local general-purpose governments, for example, cities, counties, towns, townships (particularly hospitals and public health departments)
2. Special-purpose local governments, for example, mental health districts, hospital districts, school districts, sanitary districts, water districts, and in some areas public health districts
3. Direct federal program operations, for example, Social Security Administration Offices (Medicare applications), Veteran's Administration offices, and hospitals
4. Direct state program operations, for example, substate units of state public assistance (Medicaid applications), public health, mental health, rehabilitation, and aging
5. Regional units of state umbrella or consolidated human services departments where substate functions are unified
6. Regional, quasigovernment special-purpose planning agencies, for example, Area Agencies on Aging, Community Action Agencies, and Health Systems Agencies or health planning agencies (where they have been continued under state or local authority after federal support ends)
7. Regional agencies representing general-purpose governments, for example, councils of governments, regional planning agencies, and regional development districts
8. Voluntary and nonprofit health care delivery agencies, for example, hospitals, nursing homes, neighborhood health centers, migrant health centers, visiting nurse associations, mental health centers, and senior centers
9. Proprietary agencies, for example, nursing homes, home health care agencies, hospitals, group and sheltered homes
10. Solo practitioners or group practices, for example, physicians, nurse practitioners, midwives, social workers, and psychologists

SMOOTHING INTERGOVERNMENTAL RELATIONSHIPS
BY ADMINISTRATIVE CHANGES

Growth in the number and types of federal grants, as well as the diversity in recipients and program requirements, brought on attempts to smooth out intergovernmental relationships from the top. Grant recipients, particularly those from general-purpose governments who received many different grants, complained about the fragmentation, resulting lack of coordination, and general lack of accountability in the system. As a result, attempts have been made from as early as 1968 to streamline and consolidate federal requirements as a strategy to facilitate IGR. Many of the actions taken amount to changes in administrative and planning requirements.

The administrative changes ranged far and wide. They included requirements that chief executive officers be notified when grants were awarded; reports and audits be standardized, simplified, and consolidated; and planning and programming efforts be coordinated. Legislative action created programs such as the Integrated Grants Administration, in which state and local recipients were allowed to submit a single application for a set of grants, and the Joint Funding Simplification Act, which permits a single application, audit, and federal agency point of contact for grant applications involving several agencies (Shapek, 1981). Throughout this period, attempts were made to simplify administrative requirements for individual programs, for example, the PHS consolidated requirements for several annual applications for federal funds into a one-page certification. The Public Health Service also instituted joint field audits of selected health services grant programs.

The other thrust involved streamlining of planning requirements, that is, the conditions a recipient must document in an application in order to receive federal funds. When Jimmy Carter became president he ordered a zero-based review of such requirements. As a result some requirements were dropped, and a PHS task force actually proposed a major consolidation of planning efforts. This effort was superceeded by what is perhaps the ultimate in consolidating requirements, the enactment of block grants. Both the older block grants enacted in the late 1960s and mid-1970s, and the nine new ones enacted in 1981 automatically streamline the burden of administrative and planning requirements by reducing the number of programs and the conditions within them. For example, four of the 1981 block grants combine 20 categorical health programs, allowing states to apply for federal funds through an annual submission for each block grant, with no required format or contents; they need only include their own plan describing how the state will follow statutory assurances and intended use of funds.

These changes have made it somewhat easier for states and local governments to work with the federal government. Obviously block grants put less of an administrative burden on the recipient government. However, the fact remains that many programs remain categorical, and the conditions that accompany requirements and divided programs continue to require that officials have to manage their way through the system.

INTERGOVERNMENTAL MANAGEMENT

Altering the framework, such as by enactment of block grants, obviously changes the way intergovernmental actors operate within the federal system. But no matter what the structure of the intergovernmental system happens to be, there will remain a need to manage within that system. All of the restructuring, consolidations, and conversion of grants will not change the basic necessity for officials to administer their way through an essentially mixed intergovernmental system.

Intergovernmental management (IGM) places emphasis on seeking workable solutions to everyday problems. Previously, IGR was described as involving multiple units of government and governmental actors and the actual behavior of actors as they pursue goals and develop and implement policy. Here, IGM, on the other hand, focuses on the goal achievement component of these relationships, inasmuch as management is a *process* by which cooperating officials direct action toward some goal (Massie, 1979). Although the other relationships are also operative on IGM, particularly policy development–policy implementation behavior, the primary emphasis is on the process by which specified objectives are met. In other words, IGM involves the need to develop new and workable means of seeking adjustments in the intergovernmental system when addressing problems that cut across jurisdictional boundaries.

The nature of the grant system in the United States ties governments together within a constitutional and political system that protects and preserves the independence and autonomy of individual governments. As a result, both conflict and cooperation are inherent in IGM. Previously, the cooperative relationships that national and state officials develop while working on grant programs of mutual interest was discussed. But not all interests are mutual. Conflict is inevitable since each level of government wishes to preserve its independence to the greatest degree possible. In IGR, this means that however much a subnational government needs federal dollars, it will strive to maintain as much program independence as possible and will look for ways to redefine national programs to local needs. National officials, on the other hand, are responsible for maintaining standards and requirements based on statutes or other means of national purpose. These differences create the potential for conflict but not necessarily unhealthy conflict, for the resolution of these issues on a daily basis helps define the overall system. Indeed, entire periods of IGR have been characterized by the ebbs and flows of levels of conflict and cooperation between national and other governments (Wright, 1982).

Adjustment and conflict resolution is thus at the heart of IGM because in essence it is a form of coordination. Management between governments means that two or more governments must take action to accomplish a task, which involves a coordinated effort. Any interorganization coordination involves individual or mutual accommodation of the policies and/or procedures of organizations. The literature on coordination between independent organizations suggests that it has been found to be highly problematic because of a series of problems: lack of legal or statutory authority, problems of agency autonomy or turf protection, lack of high-level administrative support or incentives to coordinate, lack of perceived agency interdependence or feeling of resource dependency, lack of general understanding, and difficulties in standardizing procedures (Agranoff and Mahler, 1981). In IGM these barriers must be overcome by focusing on *particular problems.*

Five different IGM strategies, either alone or in combination, have been used by governmental officials to manage their way through and around particular problems of categorical federalism and system fragmentation. These approaches, sometimes appearing under different labels, are (1) administrative changes, (2) program management, (3) policy management, (4) bargaining and negotiation, and (5) problem solving. Each is a variation on the theme of making adjustments while dealing with everyday issues.

ADMINISTRATIVE CHANGES

The first strategy involves the attempt on the part of subnational officials responsible for managing national programs to seek changes in the application of federal regulations or program standards. This approach can involve both long-term strategies—streamlining a body of rules—or short-term strategies—seeking a waiver, exception, or favorable administrative interpretation. For example, states for years pursued a short-term strategy when they sought waivers of the Medicaid and Medicare rules that required stringent hospitalization of recipients, making home-based long-term care nearly impossible. A series of state-by-state waivers made it possible to experiment with partially funded medical services for the home bound. Experimentation is another means of adjusting the rules, such as the case of two ongoing pilot social and health maintenance organizations (SHMO), wherein both individual Medicare and Medicaid benefits are signed over to a SHMO that also administers allocated social services and elderly services funds. Obviously a project such as SHMO requires considerable bending, stretching, and changing of existing rules in order to test if such an approach might work.

Sometimes this strategy merely involves an administrative interpretation. For example, one state Maternal and Child Health (MCH) director sought to have federal officers waive the requirements that massive records, such as annually updated resumes of all program personnel, be included in the annual application. Rather than go through the waiver process, the federal officials verbally informed the MCH director that the requirement could be overlooked, as long as backup documentation was on file in the state health department. Generally, any administrative regulation, standard, or guideline that does not directly derive from the statutes can be changed if the change being sought is for some justifiable program purpose.

Occasionally administrative adjustments are made permanent. State and local governments and public interest groups can press Congress and the federal bureaucracy to make statutory and regulatory changes that promote subnational program interests. For example, for years states opposed provisions in the Medicaid statutes and regulations that resulted in people in need of medical services who were not hospitalized or in nursing homes receiving extremely limited coverage, thereby forcing them into institutional settings. As a result, nearly 40 percent of all Medicaid expenditures went for nursing home care. A change was finally made in 1981, under PL 97-35, allowing states to propose comprehensive waiver programs to finance home care for Medicaid eligible people (*Federal Register*, 1981). Permanent changes, such as the Medicaid waiver program, authorized in law demonstrate the viability of using administrative adjustment as a strategy.

PROGRAM MANAGEMENT

A second strategy is program management, that is, designing and managing individual federal programs so they work from the perspective of the operating jurisdiction. An intergovernmental policy study committee sponsored by the National Science Foundation (NSF) defined *program management* as "the implementation of policy or daily operation of agencies along functional lines" (*Study Committee*, 1975, p. 701). In other words, a jurisdiction with responsibility for implementing a federal program would operate the program from its own perspective. Under such an approach, a state health department with administrative responsibility for the Primary Care block grant would, within the constraints and funding rules imposed by the federal and state governments, use all residual program authority to steer the program and spend dollars according to its needs and priorities. If the state felt that the need for primary services was most acute in rural underserved areas, it would place the highest spending priority in area-based community health centers. Moreover, if no state funds were available for funding primary care in local health departments, they would consider block grant funds as an alternative vehicle. In other words program management is a strategy that asks how within the federal requirements, can we make the program work for our purposes?

POLICY MANAGEMENT

Policy management is a third strategy that often builds on program management. The NSF committee defined *policy management* as "the identification of needs, analysis of options, selection of programs and allocation of resources on a jurisdiction-wide basis" (Study Committee, 1975, p. 701) Accordingly, a state or local health department might assess the array of possible funding sources and programs that operate within the area under analysis and then develop comprehensive policy approaches, incorporating several funding lines. For example, a county health department could take leadership in developing a unified plan for serving the health needs of the poor through efforts combining Primary Care block grant money; Medicaid; local general assistance for those not Medicaid eligible; and dental care money contributed by county revenue sharing, city Community Development Block Grant funds, and private contributions. Such a plan would be carried out by different delivery agents, but it would represent managing intergovernmental programs toward a consistent policy with regard to the health needs of the poor. Obviously, the interest in policy management stems from the need for state and local officials to deal with specific problems through managing their jurisdictions as a whole, by making conceptual and operational sense out of the maze of functional, vertically structured programs, and to assure that the programs are meeting community needs effectively and efficiently (Agranoff and Pattakos, 1978).

BARGAINING AND NEGOTIATION

A fourth strategy is bargaining and negotiation. Following closely the approach used in labor–management relations, it assumes that conflicts between intergovernmental actors are inevitable but that officials can sit down with each other and bargain issues through to a solution (Buntz and Radin, 1983). The most interesting use of bargaining and negotiation was engaged in by three cities—Columbus, Ohio; Gary, Indiana; and St. Paul, Minnesota—through a process called negotiated investment strategy. Under the rubric of general community and economic development, each city initiated a package of intergovernmental program changes that would facilitate development. The changes were negotiated through until a package agreement was agreed upon by federal, state, and local teams that altered specific federal programs (Kunde, 1979). In a similar fashion, under the Department of Health and Human Services' (DHHS) Planning Requirements Reform Demonstration Project, officials from the Illinois Department of Public Health initiated a bargaining process with federal officials to use a state-required public health plan to consolidate plans for 14 U.S. Public Health Service programs into the State Health Plan under 93-641. State officials were most interested in developing federal plans that were consistent with state interests, as well as in reducing planning time and paperwork. Federal health officials were initially unsympathetic to these aims, claiming that statutory intent and program requirements could not be met under the proposal. As a result of the negotiations, the differences were bargained out, and Illinois was able to submit a consolidated plan. Bargaining and negotiation is a particularly useful strategy when a large number of focused changes are being sought, in situations in which substantial conflicts among interested parties have to be worked through.

PROBLEM SOLVING

Problem solving is the fifth and final IGM strategy. Unlike bargaining and negotiation, where conflict is assumed to be inevitable, problem solving involves the interactions of officials—local, state, national—in an atmosphere of perceived common interests, as they jointly reach solutions of importance to a community or state through mutual accommodation. Since it is a very common strategy that virtually any public or non-public health official can engage in, an extensive explanation and case example will be provided.

In a study of successful IGM between all levels and types of governments and the private sector, in six metropolitan areas, Agranoff and Lindsay found that the process involves developing a solution to the problem at hand while recognizing the importance of the legal–jurisdictional, political, and technical issues involved. Each problem that politicians and managers approached involved questions of law or authority, politics, and technical substance that needed resolution as the task was approached. If these issues were confronted, many practical solutions were achieved (Agranoff and Lindsay, in press).

This IGM process can be illustrated by a hypothetical example from a health policy setting. Assume a county public health department administrator wishes to seek a change in the way the federal block grant for Primary Care (community health centers) is operated within the county. The change would allow for a broader definition of care to meet a special need population off site. In this case it is through the use of nurse midwives in rural areas in which physician availability is almost nonexistent. The service is not in the existing state plan.

The official's first concern would be to understand and recognize the legal and jurisdictional issues involved in solving the problem. The local administrator may have to look up federal statutes and state submitted plans and authority. Any use of nurse-midwives would have to be consistent with state statutes and regulations. It may also be necessary for the official to test the legal possibilities for seeking waivers or some other means of changing the way the state plan operates. In other words, the initial task is to see how, legally, a change in the state plan for allocation of services can be made.

A second concern involves achieving political support. The local health administrator would need to ascertain if any county commissioners, state legislators representing the area, mayors, or other officials would be willing to support such a change. Interest groups, particularly medical and nursing associations, either state or locally based, might also have an interest in the issue. If there were both proponents and opponents (and there no doubt would be in this case), their strength would need to be understood and their views brought out in the open. It is important in IGM that all of the politics of the issue be brought out so that accommodations, if necessary, can be reached. The political support of the chief health officer of the state may also be important, since he or she is the person who will ratify the decisions on the state's part. Getting different jurisdictions to ultimately agree on a solution means that elected political and top administrative officials must play out their politics, in order to find out what their interests and stakes are, so that forging a solution to amending the Primary Care Plan can be reached.

A third concern is the technical dimension. The county and state administrators must work together to develop an operating plan that will effect the proposed change. Concerns such as justifying need, standards, licensure and oversight, service delivery plans, contractors, and program evaluation become very real. A plan for use of nurse-midwives and physician back-up will inevitably have to be developed. In other words, the how it is to be done must also be established and agreed upon. All parties to the agreement, in this case county, state, and perhaps federal officials, must be clear as to how the target population will be served. Since this issue is concerned with the delivery of primary health care services, the nuts and bolts of substantive issues are preeminent, adding a technical component ot IGM.

The three previous concerns converge on a fourth—a joint task orientation. Somehow the actors involved must make legal–jurisdictional political, and technical issues work into an agreement that will allow for the use of nurse-midwives under the block grant. This is ordinarily accomplished by bringing all the issues out in the open and seeking adjustments around the goal of attacking the problem at hand.

It is this type of problem–solution process, accounting for and adjusting relevant legal, political, and technical concerns, that represents the type of everyday management that must be sought between jursidictions. Problem solving is a variant of conflict management, which assumes that, unlike bargaining, organizational representatives are brought together in circumstances dominated by issues in which common interests are perceived as more important than conflicting interests. Problem solving involves perceptions of similarities and common concern, relatively open exchange of information, and search and selection of alternatives that benefit more than one party (Brown, 1983). Although problem solving is not a highly visible approach, it is one of the most used and useful strategies to manage intergovernmentally.

In terms of health politics, the five strategies just discussed offer managers opportunities to work with the system as it is. No matter how the system is organized and structured, there will always be a need to fit intergovernmental programs to the immediate setting.

CONCLUSION: MAKING THE SYSTEM WORK

The complexity of the intergovernmental system is such that somehow a means must be devised by which U.S. national program aims in substantive areas such as health are maintained yet sufficient flexibility is provided to make working adjustments on the basis of the process just described. This requires a balanced intergovernmental health system. Vladeck's (1979) study of federal–state relations in three federal program efforts—Medicaid cutbacks, provider licensure, and health planning under PL 93-641–concluded that serious intergovernmental problems arose as a result of a disjunction between administrative or regulatory responsibilities and fiscal accountability. He concludes that as new programs are undertaken, serious attention be given to incorporating an important role for the states, since responsibility for payment must be conjoined with responsibility for administration and regulation. On the other hand, few would dispute that national resources and priorities are a necessary part of financing health programs. Dedicated funding for health programs, through categorical grants, has become a very important device for aggregating support and attention to important health issues. In the words of Tilson (1981, p. 1103), a public health official,

> categories are a convenient shorthand to help a busy Congress understand an essential set of public tasks to which they might otherwise pay little attention. In the process, categories rally a diffuse and often voiceless constituency around key issues and suitable funding when the competitive market fails. Nobody sheds a tear for people suffering from "block grant disease."

Thus, if some sort of symmetry between national aims and state–local responsibility for administration is to be maintained, some sort of balance is needed. The following is a scenario for designing flexible intergovernmental programs, whether they be broad categoricals or block grants.[3]

On a national level, emphasis on maintenance of the program's basic aims and working with state–local delivery agents in achieving results is essential. First, national purpose must be maintained as a legitimate and appropriate part of federal grants. Efforts to reduce what most consider to be excessive conditions in grant regulations should not be confused with maintenance of purpose behind programs. National efforts to target efforts in public health should continue to ensure that programs do, indeed, meet these aims.

Second, these efforts should be based on operationalized national aims. Thompson's (1981) study of eight federal health programs concluded that one essential element of successful implementation was the degree to which Congress and the health bureaucracy could set precise and plausible policy goals in the statutes and regulations. However difficult it may be to be precise in stating aims at the end of a protracted political process, it appears imperative that programs that give subnational agents considerable lattitude in implementing grants must state national aims as a program input.

A third consideration is that states or other units responsible for administering programs should be held accountable for their performance in achieving national aims. If legislation were to be stated in terms of accomplishing national objectives rather than prescribing processes, then fund recipients should be expected to meet minimal standards in working toward national aims. Mogulof (1973, p. 595) has provided the following important clues as to how to do this:

> A goal embraces a particular population at risk, coupled with a specified direction toward which national policy wishes to move that population. If selection of risk populations is a political task and the measurement of movement among these population is a technical one, there remains the problem of specifying appropriate objectives that could help structure the delivery of social services for these population groups.

Accountability, therefore, not based on compliance with detailed program requirements, since means can be left to local choices, but on how well goals are achieved. For example, federal grants for hypertension would concern themselves with the number of

---

[3]Much of the general material in the remainder of this chapter is drawn from Agranoff and Robins (1982).

people screened and cases referred to medical care rather than with the elegance of the documentation. Federal policy would then cease to control inputs so that it can focus on the achievement of national policy (Mogulof, 1973).

Fourth, adequate levels of national funding would appear to be necessary as a trade-off for subnational government administration of national programs. The rationale is based on the assumption that funding must be sufficient to make an impact on those populations at risk deemed important enough to receive national legislative attention. For example, the Women and Infant Children (WIC) program was able to document high levels of success in reducing infant mortality and low birth weight rates as long as funds were appropriated at levels sufficient to meet the needs of most of the target population. When the funds were cut, infant mortality and low birth weights began to increase for the first time since the program started. Although adequacy can only be defined in subjective terms, this formulation suggests that meeting national aims will continue to require sufficient funds to ensure that delivery agents can do the job expected of them.

A fifth and final consideration in this formulation is that federal–state grant relationships must be viewed as an interactive process. Federal health bureaucrats must view their relationship with the states as one of interdependence, whereby officials see each other as important resources of information and technical assistance. Moreover, in a system that encourages diversity in the means of meeting national aims, it is imperative that states not be approached monolithically, but as a group with diverse capabilities, concerns, and commitment (*Planning Requirements Reform*, 1981). What is a successful outcome for one state may be different for another state, and accomplishments vary over time. Achievements must be seen as a slow, evolutionary process in which approaches vary considerably. Indeed, the previously noted planning reform evaluation concluded that "interdependency between state and federal officials will not be sustained if federal officials have a single model of success and rigid commitment to business as usual" (*Planning Requirements Reform*, 1981). Any federal–state process must view both sets of actors as cooperative partners rather than antagonists. Federal constraints on state administrative flexibility may also often not be constraints at all; they often provide the rationale for the enforcement of necessary but locally unpopular components of grant programs.

From a state or local delivery perspective, it is important that agents use the flexibility they have to meet their own priorities within a national framework. First, if health is truly a community affair, then state and local governments must *use* the flexibility they have obtained. Block grants and reduced requirements in federal programs allow jurisdictions to select the array of services they wish to fund. Moreover, resources can be targeted to geographical areas or to special needs constitutents feel are important, as long as broad national purposes are met. Subnational governments under block grants and flexible categoricals have much greater freedom to fit federal grants within the delivery system they choose to design.

A second advantage of this formulation is that increased flexibility allows significant advantages in program design and coordination. For example, the existing federal changes in Medicaid, allowing states to secure waivers for financing health care for people who require home care, coupled with block grants for social services, offer significant opportunities for designing an alternative long-term care program to nursing homes. Although total flexibility will perhaps never be available under a system in which national aims and funding conditions are established, options for program development are increased.

Third, as federal requirements are reduced, the remaining requirements should more easily be met within states' own administrative systems. With fewer requirements and grants, administrative overhead costs should be reduced. For example, the block grants enacted in 1981 allowed states to determine their own application formats, reporting mechanisms, auditing systems, and intended use of funds notifications. Subsequent interpretations by former Secretary Schweiker and his legal staff have stated that "interpretation of statutory provisions is primarily the responsibility of each state" (U.S. Department of Health and Human Services, 1982). Enterprising states will easily be able to adapt their own administrative processes to meet reduced federal reporting expectations.

Fourth, state planning and management systems will have to improve in order to meet the flexibility and performance aims of a balanced grant system. If states and other local delivery agents are to design programs seriously, they will have to develop means of aggregating political preferences, identifying legitimate needs, setting priorities based on preferences and needs, targeting resources, fostering a course of action, and evaluating its impact. Improved administration will also mean efficient reporting and accounting, for states will have to streamline their systems in order to meet federal audit expectations. Most important, jurisdictions will need to develop means of proving to the national government that their programs' performances are consistent with national policy and that they are contributing to national policy aims. All of these issues point to the need for jurisdictional administrative capacity. Under a balanced system, those that have it will be required to use it and those without it will have to develop it.

At both state and national levels, a balanced intergovernmental system requires a broader representational focus. Categorical grants have been popular with Congress because they have specifically rewarded narrow constituencies and groups, for example, cancer, heart disease, hypertension, and hemophilia. As programs become combined into block grants or categoricals become more flexible, they require greater support groups that pursue broader aims. Maintenance and support of more flexible programs would appear to be in the interest of both general health and welfare groups, such as the American Public Health Association and the American Public Welfare Association, and groups of governmental generalists, such as the National Governor's Association and the National Association of County Officials. Health and social service professional groups would appear to be potentially useful in demonstrating to legislatures and executives that increased flexibility in program design can contribute to program aims, convincing Congress that targets are being met and important interests are being represented. Focused representational attention must also be placed in the state capitols inasmuch as an increasing number of decisions are being made there. When federal grants were so specific that resources were nationally targeted and planning and administrative requirements were specified in law and regulations, there was less need to lobby at the state level. Now greater focus has shifted to the states, and general representation seems to be required at both levels.

This chapter has provided the outline of an IGR perspective that would allow the preservation of important national aims, as well as subnational units to tailor programs to their own special configuration of needs and priorities. It is a framework not unlike that of Vladeck's formulation for national health insurance, wherein he proposed that the federal government be responsible for establishing a uniform national entitlement and a uniform method of financing, delegating to the states decisions on how state shares of the total pie are to be allocated. As long as universal entitlements provide a guarantee that states do not dicriminate against one class of citizens in favor of others, he suggests, decisions on the kind of rationing that will be necessary under any finite resources scheme should be left for states or localities to determine so as to best meet special local needs and conditions. Vladeck suggests that under such a formulation, states could become important "laboratories" for social experimentation through means such as offering different packages of "optional services," as direct services providers in areas of need, or for comparing results with the private sector by acting as carriers or intermediaries for all or some parts of the program (Vladeck, 1979). A flexible structure such as this might well be appropriate for many health programs, since it recognizes the need for both national programming and resources and the political and operational realities of operating within a federal system.

REFERENCES

Advisory Commission on Intergovernmental Relations, *Modification of Federal Grants-In-Aid for Public Health Services*, Washington, D.C., 1961.

Advisory Commission on Intergovernmental Relations, *The Federal Role in the Federal System*, Washington, D.C., 1977.

Agranoff, Robert and Valerie A. Lindsay, "Intergovernmental Management: Perspectives from Human Services Problem-Solving at the Local Level," *Public Administration Review*, Vol. 43, No. 3, in press.

Agranoff, Robert and Julianne Mahler, "Mental Health Systems and the Coordination of Services," in Wade Silverman, ed., *Community Mental Health*, New York: Praeger Publishing, 1981.

Agranoff, Robert and Alex Pattakos, "Human Services Policy Management: A Role for University Institutes," *Midwest Review of Public Administration*, Vol. 12, No. 4, December 1978, pp. 257–70.

Agranoff, Robert and Leonard Robins, "How to Make Block Grants Work: An Intergovernmental Management Perspective," *New England Journal of Human Services*, Vol. 2, Winter 1982, pp. 36–46.

Anderson, Wayne, "Introduction," in Raymond Shapek, ed., *Managing Federalism: Evolution and Development of the Grant-in-Aid System*, Charlottesville, VA.: Community Collaborators, 1981.

Anderson, William, *Intergovernmental Relations in Review*, Minneapolis: University of Minnesota Press, 1960.

Brown, L. David, *Managing Conflict at Organizational Interfaces*, Reading, Mass.: Addison-Wesley Publishing Co., 1983.

Buntz, C. Gregory and Beryl Radin, "Managing Intergovernmental Conflict: The Case of Human Services," Unpublished manuscript, 1983.

Elazer, Daniel, *American Federalism: A View From the States*, New York: Thomas Y. Crowell Co., 1972, 2nd edition.

Federal Register, October 1, 1981, pp. 48583–48587.

Grodzins, Morton, *The American System: A New View of Government in the United States*, Chicago: Rand McNally, 1966.

Hearings, Subcommittee on Health of the Committee on Labor and Public Welfare, United State Senate, Eighty-ninth Congress, Second Session, March 16 and 17, 1966, pp. 2–153.

Hearings, Committee on Interstate and Foreign Commerce, House of Representatives, Eighty-ninth Congress, Second Session, October 11, 1966, pp. 1–125.

Ingram, Helen, "Policy Implementation Through Bargaining: The Case of Federal Grants-in-Aid," *Public Policy*, Vol. 25, Fall 1977, pp. 499–526.

Kettle, Donald, "The Management Squeeze: Centralization and Federal Grants," Paper presented at the Annual Meeting of the Midwest Political Science Association, Chicago, Illinois, April 1980.

Kunde, James, "As in the Past, the Cities Propose: Under NIS They Help Dispose," *Nation's Cities Weekly,* November 26, 1979, pp. 4–9.

Levine, E. Lester, "Federal Grants-In-Aid: Administration and Politics," in Daniel Elazar, R. Bruce Carroll, E., Lester Levine, and Douglas St. Angelo, eds., *Cooperation and Conflict: Readings in American Federalism,* Itasca, Ill.: F.E. Peacock Publishers, 1969.

Massie, Joseph, *Essentials of Management,* Englewood Cliffs, N.J.: Prentice-Hall, 1979, 3rd edition.

Mogulof, Melvin, "Elements of a Special Revenue Sharing Proposal for the Social Services: Goal Setting, Decategorization, Planning and Evaluation," *Social Service Review,* Vol. 41, December 1973, pp. 591–602.

National Commission on Community Health Services, *Health is a Community Affair,* Cambridge: Harvard University Press, 1966.

Niskanen, William, *Bureaucracy and Representative Government,* Chicago: Aldine Publishing Co., 1971.

Pierce, Neal, "Reagan Discusses Federalism Initiatives," *Public Administration Times,* December 1981, pp. 2, 4.

Planning Requirements Reform Demonstration Project of the United States Department of Health and Human Services, "An Evaluation Report Prepared for the Office of Assistant Secretary for Planning and Evaluation, 100-79-0190, October 1981."

Radin, Beryl A., *Implementation, Change and the Federal Bureaucracy,* New York: Teachers College Press, Columbia University, 1972.

Reagan, Michael, *The New Federalism,* New York: Oxford University Press, 1972.

Riker, William, *Federalsim: Origin, Operation, Significance,* Boston: Little Brown and Co., 1964.

Robins, Leonard, *The Conversion of Categorical into Block Grants: A Case Study of the 314 (d) Block Grant in the Partnership for Health Act,* Unpublished doctoral dissertaiton, University of Minnesota, 1974.

Robins, Leonard and Charles Backstrom, "The Coming Erosion of Support for Block Grants," *Conference for Federal Studies Notebook,* Vol. 4, Winter 1976, pp. 3–12.

Shapek, Raymond, *Managing Federalism: Evolution and Development of the Grant-in-Aid System,* Charlottesville, Va.: Community Collaborators, 1981.

Stenberg, Carl, "Federalism in Transition: 1959–79," in *The Future of Federalism in the 1980's,* Washington, D.C.: Advisory Commission on Intergovernmental Relations, 1980.

Stenberg, Carl and David Walker, "The Block Grant: Lessons from Two Early Experiences," *Publius, The Journal of Federalism,* Vol. 7, Spring 1977, pp. 31–60.

Study Committee on Policy Management Assistance, "Executive Summary," *Public Administration Review,* Vol. 35, December 1975, special issue.

Sundquist, James, *Making Federalism Work: A Study of Program Coordination at the Community Level,* Washington, D.C.: The Brookings Institution, 1969.

Thompson, Frank, *Health Policy and the Bureaucracy: Politics and Implementation,* Cambridge: MIT Press, 1981.

Tilson, Hugh H., "Intergovernmental Relationships More Different or More Same?" *American Journal of Public Health,* Vol. 71, October 1981, pp. 1103–04.

U.S. Department of Health and Human Services, Memorandum on HHS Policy on Interpretation of Block Grant Statutes, October 15, 1982, Letter from Secretary Schweiker to Governor James Hunt of North Carolina, July 15, 1982.

Vladeck, Bruce, "The Design of Failure: Health Policy and the Structure of Federalism," *Journal of Health Policy, Politics, and Law*, Vol. 4, Fall 1979, pp. 522–535.

Walker, David, *Toward A Functioning Federalism*, Cambridge: Winthrop, 1981.

Williams, Walter, *Government by Agency: Lessons from the Social Program Grants-in-Aid Experience*, New York: Academic Press, 1980.

Wright, Deil, *Understanding Intergovernmental Relations*, Monterey, Calif.: Brooks Cole, 1982, 2nd edition.

CHAPTER 10

An Overview of the State Role in the United States Health Scene

Peter B. Levine

States have participated in virtually every aspect of health care activity in the United States. At times states have been pioneers and leaders by innovating and testing health financing, delivery, or structural schemes. They led the way in establishing health insurance programs, placing health personnel in underserved areas, and requiring certificates of need for large capital outlays. On the other hand, states also have been dragged into health programs, grudgingly changing their statutes to meet federal mandates lest they lose federal dollars. At other times, with little fanfare, states have created or eliminated health statutes or programs to accommodate special interest groups, for example, making changes in licensure at the bequest of health professional groups and changes in health insurance and workers' compensation laws in response to the demands of labor or industry.

STATES' ROLE IN HEALTH CARE

PERSONAL HEALTH CARE ROLE

States have been involved in the direct provision of personal health care, as well as its regulation, for a long time. In recent years, the increased state financing of personal health services has drawn special attention to the state role as a regulator of personal health delivery. In the face of rising costs of health care that have created measureable fiscal stress on their budgets, most states have responded by increasing their regulatory role in personal health care. For example, some states have sought to place a cap on payments to health facilities and/or set minimal rates for government subsidies to individuals. As a principal payor of services for the medically needy, the states' involvement and effect on delivery and financing personal health services has been substantial. With shrinking federal support for health services, both the states' role and the fiscal stress on their budgets are likely to expand.

PUBLIC HEALTH CARE ROLE

The recent attention given to the states' fiscal role in personal health care has overshadowed their traditional public health roles. On the one hand, this is understandable. States spent three times as much of their own money on Medicaid in 1980 as they did for all of the public health programs carried out by state health agencies. On the other hand, states do not have a primary role in financing personal health care. They act as administrative and fiscal agents, adjusting state policies (some states more cleverly or aggressively than others) within the limits of federal mandates.

Conversely, while accepting federal dollars for a variety of public health programs, states retain their principal policy role in public health. This is likely to continue. With local units of government, states monitor water, milk, and food supplies. In addition, they license and regulate health facilities and personnel, watch over their environments, control wastes, and take care of mothers, infants, and school children. In areas such as environmental or occupational health, states follow minimum federal guidelines or standards, but overall they continue to outspend the federal government for public health functions and maintain a hold on policy setting and the administration of public health programs. An informed understanding of the states' role in health care includes a comprehension of these traditional health roles.

FACTORS THAT AFFECT THE STATES' HEALTH ROLE

A state's role in health usually is a reflection of many factors not directly related to health care. Despite their differences, states have some factors in common. They are all affected by rising and shifting costs and federal intervention, and their traditional health functions are similar. However, a state is a product of its particular history, traditions, and culture. Like their people, states are idiosyncratic. The peculiar background of each state is likely to evoke different responses to similar problems. Some states respond to health care needs more vigorously or, at least, differently than others. Special circumstances of demography or climate, political history or wealth create individual needs and elicit various responses. In short, states have more differences than similarities.

This chapter portrays the states' health care roles and functions in the context of these differences and similarities. It describes how and why each state is unique. The chapter begins with a brief description of the rise of health care costs, the shift of health care expenditures to the public sector, and the effects of differences in states' health expenditures. This is followed by an historical and structural perspective on state health roles, including state health care innovations. Finally, states' health roles are summarized in three categories: (1) as administrative and fiscal agents, (2) as direct providers of services, and (3) as regulators of services and personnel.

HEALTH EXPENDITURES AND THE STATES

A traditional distinction between personal and public health services has been the source of funding: personal health services have been paid largely from private funds and public health has been supported by the government. With dramatic increases in government spending for personal health services, this distinction is not quite so clear.

SHIFT FROM PRIVATE TO PUBLIC SPENDING

In 1965, only 25 percent of the total U.S. health bill and 21 percent of all personal health care was paid with government dollars. By 1978, the proportion of personal health care costs paid from government sources had risen to 39 percent. Most of this is attributable to federal programs originally mandated by the Eighty-ninth Congress. In 1965 and 1966 the Eighty-ninth Congress passed an astonishing number (55) of health bills that resulted in sweeping changes in planning, delivery, and financing of health care (Congressional Quarterly Service, 1966). In addition, the War on Poverty programs of the Johnson administration included the seeds of other new government health programs.[1] The fiscal effects of these congressional acts began to be felt a few years later by the United States as a whole and by the states in particular.

In 1965, the federal and the state–local shares of the total U.S. health bill were about equal; both were relatively small. Each spent a little over $5 billion, or 12–13 percent of the total. Interestingly, the state–local share of the personal health care bill was actually slightly larger than the federal share (Advisory Commission on Intergovernmental Relations, 1980a; *Health Care Financing Administration Review*, 1980). This changed considerably following the actions of the Eighty-ninth Congress.

By 1970, the federal government was spending twice as much on personal health care as were state–local governments. In the five years, from 1965 to 1970, the federal portion almost quadrupled, whereas the state–local share doubled. Most of the change was attributable to the 5-year-old Medicaid program that by 1970 was costing taxpayers $5 billion roughly split between federal and state governments (Medicaid/Medicare Management Institute, 1979). In spite of their contributions to Medicaid, the state share of total personal health costs has remained at about 11 percent, relatively unchanged since 1970 (Health Care Financing Administrative Review, 1980). It is at the federal level that the fiscal changes were most noticeable, bolstered by new expenditures for the elderly, mothers, children, migrant workers, and other groups covered by legislation and appropriations of the 1960s. The movement toward greater government fiscal involvement of health care is unmistakable, and the states have shared that enlarged role. For although the latter's share of the U.S. health bill has remained fairly constant, the percent of their own budgets going for health services has increased dramatically.

---

[1]The most notable of these were to be found in the Office of Economic Opportunity (OEO) and Model Cities Legislation that led to the establishment of federally funded Neighborhood Health Centers (NHC). Although not specifically mandated, OEO funds were used to establish the first NHC in the late 1960s. By 1980, NHCs, then mandated by federal law, were budgeted at $350 million.

EFFECT OF STATE SPENDING PATTERNS ON THEIR HEALTH ROLE

During the 1960s and 1970s state government grew noticeably whereas government employment at the federal level declined. In addition to increases in the number of state government employees per 10,000 population, state taxes rose significantly, both as a percent of gross national product (GNP) and as a percent of total government revenues (Health Care Financing Administration Review, 1980).

These state growth patterns, especially when compared to those at the federal level, are interesting and even surprising. However, in the aggregate they can be misleading. The ability of a single state to assume a major fiscal role in health care is usually quite limited. State officials can draw comparisons with other states but do not make program decisions on the basis of aggregate revenue data. Furthermore, the growth of state government employment has often been a result of federal mandates paid for with federal funds, whereas state revenue is frequently a function of factors that states cannot control, such as national economic conditions.

The aggregate spending patterns of states are also interesting, but they characterize states in general and tell little about individual state priorities. In all, states alone spent over $228 billion in 1980, including $85 billion received from the federal government, most of which went to education (U.S. Bureau of the Census, 1980). Payments for health, including hospitals, vendor payments for public welfare beneficiaries, and other health payments comprised the second highest expenditure category. A look at the preferences of individual states, however, is much more informative. For example, in 1980 Idaho's per Capita expenditure for hospitals was $18.12, whereas Rhode Island's was $65.31. For health expenditures other than hospitals and vendor payments, Oklahoma spent $14.09 per capita as compared with Alaska, which spent $86.58, over $30.00 more than the next highest states—Hawaii and Massachusetts (U.S. Bureau of the Census, 1980).

The choices that each state makes are the result of a polyglot of individual and often unique political, historical, and environmental factors. Massachusetts for example, spends comparatively little for education, especially higher education. The patterns of private versus public education in that state may provide some insight into their choice. It is a choice that has little bearing on other states but allows Massachusetts greater fiscal flexibility than most states in making larger health and medical vendor payments. It is clear for many reasons that a state places its own unique value on each government function that affects its health spending. Massachusetts spends proportionately more for health and public welfare than for education; Vermont spends twice as much for health per person than Colorado, Maine, or Nebraska; Wyoming spends a great deal for highways and comparatively little for health (U.S. Bureau of the Census, 1980).

Although most state public health money passes through state health agencies (SHA), for example, about some $3.3 billion in 1978 (Association of State and Territorial Health Officers, 1980), state public health spending patterns are somewhat difficult to discern largely because of the variety of organizational directions states have taken. There are four principal categories of state health expenditures: (1) public health, regulatory, and administrative activities; (2) state hospitals, largely mental health activities; (3) vendor payments to providers of medical care to the needy, and (4) health manpower training.

Not surprisingly, spending by a single agency in one state may be done by three

Table 10-1. Net Per Capita State Aid and Percent of Total to Local Governments[a]

State	Education	% of Total	Public Welfare	% of Total	Health and Hospitals	% of Total	Highways	% of Total	General Support	% of Total
Arizona	$175	64.1	$—	—	$1	0.4	$24	8.8	$68	24.9
California	167	53.0	50	15.9	10	3.2	16	5.1	44	14.0
Colorado	155	72.4	24	11.2	3	1.4	16	7.5	6	2.8
Georgia	119	93.7	—	—	5	3.9	9	7.1	2	1.6
Minnesota	225	63.6	18	5.1	1	0.3	24	6.8	68	19.2
Ohio	121	62.1	16	8.2	6	3.1	24	12.3	20	10.3
Tennessee	82	64.6	—	—	—	—	26	20.5	14	11.0
Wisconsin	180	50.3	26	7.3	13	3.6	26	7.3	107	29.9

SOURCE: Advisory Commission on Intergovernmental Relations, *Recent Trends in Federal and State Aid to Local Governments*, Washington, D.C.: Advisory Commission on Intergovernmental Relations, July 1980, M-118, Table A-33, pp. 94–95. Selected states by function 1976–1977.

[a]Excluding federal government funds passed through to local units.

agencies in another state. Moreover, in almost half the states, state health functions are found in "superagencies" that often include public welfare and/or mental health functions. Finally, although health planning functions are often found in state planning agencies, appropriations for personnel training are usually given directly to colleges and universities.

State–local fiscal relationships also vary from state to state. For example, one reason Rhode Island spends more per capita than any other state for hospitals is the lack of local government spending for health and hospitals in that state. On the other hand, of the $81 million spent by Idaho in 1978 for health and hospitals, only 36 percent was state financed (Advisory Commission on Intergovernmental Relations, 1980). The range of state–local spending for health is reflective of political decisions that are made by state policymakers regarding local government autonomy. A state's decisions on local tax authority, local debt policy, and state appropriations to localities affects how much state and local governments are willing or able to spend for health.

These factors, as well as many others, affect state aid to local units of government. In 1976–1977, for example, 19 states gave no per capita aid to local government for health (Advisory Commission on Intergovernmental Relations, 1980a). General state aids or aids to other program areas may also encourage or make it possible for local authorities to spend their own money on health.

Some of these variations in state aid (excluding Federal pass-through dollars) to local governments are presented in Table 10-1. Note how little state aid goes directly to localities for health and hospitals. The financial ability of a local unit to spend for health, however, is probably more a function of total aid than specific aid programs, although categorical aid may encourage health-specific spending.

EFFECT OF FEDERAL FISCAL ASSISTANCE ON STATES' ROLE IN HEALTH

Most states have come to rely very heavily on federal fiscal assistance. This was not always the case. In fact, the reliance on federal health dollars is a very recent phenomenon.[2] Federal grants-in-aid for public health, for example, had a sputtering start. In 1918, Congress passed the Chamberlain-Kahn Act that lasted only 2 years and provided aid for states to fight venereal disease (Hanlon, 1960a). One year later, in 1921, President Warren Harding signed the Sheppard-Towner Act that provided $1 million to states for infant and maternity programs. Any state could receive a part of the funds by agreeing to follow prescribed federal guidelines. In return, administration of the program was left to the states. The enactment was politically important at the time because it (and subsequent continuous extensions of the law) widened the growing controversy between public and private medicine. Although opposed by organized medicine as an example of state medicine, Harding and most of Congress, perhaps cognizant of the newly enfranchised women voters, supported the measure.

In retrospect, the principal political significance of the act may not have been its effect on the controversy over private versus public medicine, but rather its conception of a new role for state governments in health services. The Sheppard-Towner Act was

---

[2]Early in U.S. history, states provided fiscal assistance to the national government. Limited in its ability to raise funds, the U.S. government needed state grants for military purposes. The first federal aid to states is thought to have begun in 1908 for militia assistance.

the embryo of a process that eventually moved the federal government into traditional state and local activity, that is, human resources planning and financing. The major effects of the act on states, however, were not to come until the 1960s and 1970s. In the meantime, states maintained and enlarged their traditional roles in health services. The states remained as the primary administrative, if not in some cases fiscal, focus for health services in the public sector.

During the period 1965–1978, the federal government assumed greater responsibility in the health field by expanding its use of both transfer payments,[3] the fastest growing and the single largest portion of federal expenditures, and categorical grants-in-aid to the states (Mosher, 1980). Grants to the states, whether for Medicaid, public health, or maternal and child health, have been used to influence states to fulfill the purposes of federal mandates. Once considered gifts and trusts, for many years these grants or payments have been viewed by the courts in a contractual sense (Advisory Commission on Intergovernmental Relations, 1980d). Although states are neither compelled nor obligated to accept a federal grant program (one state, Arizona, refused to participate in the federal–state Medicaid program until 1981), when they do so they also must accept the conditions and standards set by the federal government. Accordingly, acceptance of the money has compounded the federal influence on state and local governments.

Most of the grants or transfer payments for public health and/or medical assistance pass through state governments to individuals, or the funds go directly to local units for the same purposes. A large portion of federal dollars has bypassed the states and gone directly to specific projects, minimizing states' role as provider, administrator, and regulator.

Federal aid to states often requires substantial state contributions. In 1977 about 15 states each contributed more than $100 million to their Medicaid programs, and two—New York and California—spent over $1 billion for Medicaid. These federal programs have changed the revenue needs of many states and explain in part the increase in total state and local taxes as a percent of GNP.

Grants-in-aid in current dollars doubled every five years from 1954 to 1979, rising from $2.9 billion to $83 billion (Mosher, 1980). John Shannon (1980) of the Advisory Commission on Intergovernmental Relations, calls the period from 1954 to 1979 the golden fiscal era for the federal government:

> Why did the federal government move so much farther, faster, and more safely than did the states and the localities into the domestic public sector—an area that historically had been of primary concern to state and local policymakers.
>
> The answer—federal policymakers held several fiscal trump cards which enabled them to expand rapidly in the domestic public sector at little political risk. A fiscal trump can be defined as one that helps policymakers (a) expand programs while cutting taxes, (b) pay for expanded program benefits with tax hikes that meet with little public opposition or (c) co-opt the resources of another level of government. In addition, they could finesse revenue shortfalls with deficit financing.

It is significant to the states that in the last generation the federal government has been doing less and influencing more (Mosher, 1980). In 1978, then Department of

---

[3]Unlike the direct purchase of goods and services traditionally associated with government programs, transfer of payments (both cash and in-kind, such as Social Security, Medicare, and food stamps) go directly to individuals for income support.

Health, Education and Welfare (DHEW) Secretary Joseph Califano estimated that his department indirectly paid the salaries of 980,000 employees to state and local governments, six times more than that employed by the department itself (Mosher, 1980). In the same year there were 78 federal health grant programs, more than any other category (National Journal, 1980). Each program came with its own regulations, guidelines, bureaucratic channels, project directors, and plan requirements. The plans, often duplicative, placed an administrative burden on many states. In many cases, the statements of development and implementation often overlapped, and state employees balanced one plan against another, often using different assumptions regarding similar programs (Remen, 1977).

Grants sometimes overlapped as well and provided money for the same programs. In 1980, for example, there were seven different federal funding sources for community services for the elderly, each of which paid for some or all of 20 different services from medical care to shopping assistance (Hereford, 1980).[4] But although much of the aid went through states, as noted, federal grant programs often bypassed states, going to local governments, quasigovernmental units, and sometimes directly to private and nonprofit organizations willing to carry out federal service mandates. It has been estimated that in 1980 as much as 25 percent of all federal aid bypassed the states (Kailo, 1980). This appears to be changing with federal consolidation, if not elimination, of grant programs and the assumption that states want and should carry the major responsibility for government health programs.

Political scientists in the first half of the twentieth century portrayed the U.S. federal system as a three-layer cake: federal, state, and local governments neatly positioned, related but separate. Since 1950, the federal system has been described as a marble cake. It has been called functional federalism, new federalism, picket fence federalism, and creative federalism. In the health field the states' roles are intertwined with those of the federal and local governments—interdependent and generally indescribable. The complexities of the grants-in-aid system have dramatically altered the federal system and the traditional roles within it.[5]

REDUCTION OF FEDERAL AID TO STATES

In the 1981 federal fiscal year, general revenue sharing (GRS) to states was reduced 33 percent from $7 billion annually to about $4.6 billion. Although little of this state GRS money was spent on health services and the cutbacks should have had little consequences to state health programs, the reduction was a window to future events, coming at a time when states were beginning to feel the general fiscal stress of the worst recession since the Great Depression. Moreover, most states suddenly lost their flexibility to shift state dollars to fill in for lost GRS funds that had been supporting guaranteed services.

Only the energy-rich states, reaping benefits from large severance taxes, were immune from plummeting state revenues. In Minnesota, for example, a state known for its high taxes and concomitant public social programs, an $800 million state surplus

---

[4]Federal funding sources ranged from Titles XVI, XVIII, and XIX of the Social Security Act to the Administration on Aging, the Veterans Administration, and the Housing and Urban Development agencies.

[5]For an extensive examination of recent changes in the grants-in-aid system for funding health and human services, see Chapter 9.

turned into a $750 million deficit in 2 years. State revenues plunged due to changes in the income and property tax and generally declining economy.[6] At the same time, federal health dollars began to diminish as well. For the first time since its enactment, there was a cut in the federal share for Medicaid. In fact, the 15-year golden fiscal era of federal development and control of social programs (1954–1979) had come to a dramatic halt.

The election of Ronald Reagan who had promised a return to greater local control along with a conservative majority in the U.S. Senate in 1980 was, in part, a voter reaction to the increasing federal domination of state and local activity. In the health field, the Reagan administration responded to the electorate by reducing and eliminating federal programs, mandates, and financing and using the block grant mechanism to return health dollars to the states. The latter, however, were considerably smaller than the sum of the categorical grants being replaced, whereas the remaining categorical grants were reduced as well. Moreover, these changes came at a time after federally inspired health programs had raised expectations for their beneficiaries.

Although the states found themselves with fewer federal mandates than before and increasing authority to manage federal dollars, most had less revenue of their own to spend on such programs, were unwilling to raise taxes, and had little hope for borrowing money in highly inflated bond markets. Furthermore, there were competing requirements for state dollars, such as decaying highways and buildings, escalating education costs, and soaring energy prices, and, unlike the federal government, constitutional restrictions on deficit spending.

HISTORICAL AND STRUCTURAL PERSPECTIVES ON STATE HEALTH ROLES

STATES' SOVEREIGN POWERS

The Union and the federal government were born out of an agreement by the states. The Articles of Confederation fashioned a loose arrangement among the states but were abandoned a dozen years after the United States was born. In their place the Constitution was ratified by state legislatures even though they feared a loss in state sovereignty. Under the Articles of Confederation, each state could establish laws on foreign relations and international trade as well as mint its own currency. The confusion this created nearly led to an early demise of the adolescent union. The Constitution's denial of these and other powers to the states, granting them instead to a national government, marks the basic difference between the United States confederation and the constitutional federation that we know today.

Under terms of the Tenth Amendment of the Constitution, powers neither specifically granted to the national government nor denied to the states were reserved for the states or the people. Although these powers are neither listed nor defined by the Constitution, James Madison assured skeptics that the powers were numerous and of concern to the lives, liberties, and properties of the people (Madison, 1787–1788).

---

[6]In response to steadily rising inflation, the state had adopted a system of income tax indexing and lowered property taxes to individuals through higher state property tax credits. The economic downturn nationally left the state's finances reeling as government expenditures soon overtook declining state revenues.

One of the powers the states did not surrender when becoming a member of the Union was police power [*Jacobson v. Massachusetts*, 197 U.S. 11, (1905)]. Under this power, each of the states possesses the authority to constrain private rights when they conflict with the general welfare. It allows states to make laws to provide for public health, morals, and welfare (Grad, 1975). As early as 1877, the U.S. Supreme Court [*Boston Beer Co. v. State of Massachusetts*, 97 U.S. 25, (1877)] described the power as inherent in the sovereignty of the state that could not be contracted away by the legislature. Because of this, state constitutions do not have to provide the legislature with power to enact laws for public health and safety (Fleisher, 1980). Consequently, except for some customary general statements regarding protection of the people, few state constitutions provide specific authority for enacting health laws. The legislature of each state may decide which laws are reasonable and the mode for carrying them out, as long as the law does not contravene other parts of the U.S. Constitution. Legally, a legislature is not even under an obligation to demonstrate that a problem exists before it passes a law. It may, in fact, pass a law to prevent a problem (Grad, 1975). Such action, however, is usually constrained by political or public pressures. Elected bodies are reactive rather than proactive, solving rather than preventing problems, their constitutional authority notwithstanding.

If the states did not surrender their police power when entering the Union, why then has the federal government been so imposing in health matters? According to Article I, Section 8, Clause 1, the U.S. Constitution provides that Congress "shall have the power to lay and collect taxes . . . and provide for the . . . general welfare." Congress regulates states indirectly through the exercise of the taxing and spending power and has the power to spend tax money by giving grants to the states that carry out federally designed programs. The federal government's power to attach strings to federal programs administered by the state was upheld in *King v. Smith*, 392 U.S. 309 (1968). In that case, Alabama's Aid to Families with Dependent Children (AFDC) regulations conflicted with the federal regulations that defined the program. In resolving the conflict, the Supreme Court stated that there is no question that the federal government, unless barred by some constitutional prohibition, may impose the terms and conditions upon which federal money shall be disbursed to the states, and any state law or regulation that conflicts with such federal laws and regulations is to that extent invalid. Alabama's conflicting regulations were declared to be invalid.

In addition Congress regulates states directly through its exercise of the commerce clause. Under Article I, Section 8, Clause 3 of the Constitution, Congress is authorized "to regulate commerce with foreign nations, and among the several states, and with the Indian Tribes." In *Gibbons v. Ogden*, 22 U.S. (9 Wheat.) (1824), the Supreme Court established the rule that still prevails: Local activities that are beyond the reach of Congress under the commerce power are "those which are completely within a particular state, which do not affect other states, and with which it is not necessary to interfere, for the purpose of executing some of the general powers of the governments." Local activities within the reach of Congress are those that affect interstate commerce or the exercise of power over it [*North American Co. v. Securities and Exchange Co.*, 327 U.S. 686, 700, (1946)]. Since food, drugs, cosmetics, and hazardous substances travel in interstate commerce, Congress has power under the commerce clause to regulate these industries. Thus, federal law regulates things such as food, drugs, and cosmetics, the inspection of meat and poultry products, and the labeling of hazardous substances.

The conflict of a state's sovereign powers with those powers reserved for Congress is likely to continue. Historically, it has erupted into states' rights issues in most policy areas including education, control of land and natural resources, commerce, and health care.

The struggle over states' rights began during the writing of the Constitution. The question of a strong central government versus continuing state control was central to the writing of the document. The smaller states were fearful that a strong central government would provide the larger states with control. To allay concerns, each state was allowed equal membership in the Senate, presumably to create equality in at least one legislative body. The trade-oriented states supported a strong federal system to ensure free trade among the states. The agrarian interests supported states' rights because they preferred local control over pricing. The adoption of the Constitution was based on the premise that the Union was a mere league of sovereign states and that the central government was not a separate entity but a sovereign of the states.

The term "states' rights" was probably made popular by its use by the States' Rights Party in the South before the Civil War. The right of a state to secede peaceably and at will was claimed by the sourthern states before and during the Civil War. This controversy was caused by the sectional differences found between the highly agrarian South and the highly industrialized North. Although the claim, for all practical purposes, was negated by the outcome of the Civil War, the effect of these differences on states' values has not been lost.

In the early 1960s, for example, former chairman of the House Ways and Means Committee, Congressman Wilbur Mills, counted on the states' rights fervor of his southern colleagues in Congress to help him pass the Kerr-Mills bill (the forerunner to Medicaid) that called for state administration of federally financed health care for the poor.

The notion of states' rights was again revived in the 1980s by the so-called sagebrush rebellion in which a number of western states sought to lay claim to federal land and the antagonism of the Alaskans to a federally mandated wilderness area. In the field of health and health care, the shift of federal dollars for health and social programs to states using block grants represented an additional response to this development.

STATE POLICY ROLE IN A PLURALISTIC INDUSTRY

There is obviously a great deal of flexibility in determining the focus of government policy setting in the health field. Under the same U.S. Constitution we have had predominantly state control and predominantly federal control. Whether the health care field is better off under a consistent overall national scheme or a variety of state programs is a debate that is likely to continue for many years. Either way, state governments will influence health policy.

In the aggregate, state government exerts influence on the private health care sector, on Congress, and on federal health agencies. The National Governors Association and the National Conference of State Legislatures establish policy positions to influence health policy. State programs developed in one state are often adopted by other states. Individual states, however, rarely develop policy statements for broad-issue areas such as health. Political parties and state executives issue policy goals in the form of party platforms or campaign literature, but these do not guarantee continuity or even acceptance. Snoke and Snoke (1975, p. 620) have argued that in order for a state "to establish an organization whereby it can develop a program, whether for health or for highways, it is important to establish clear definitions, objectives, and priorities."

Although this may apply to specific public programs (e.g., an immunization program), it cannot apply to the broad direction of a state's health program. Statements of objectives and policy often found in the private sector are not analogous to broad public policy statements. State public policy flows from an accumulation of legislative enactments as implemented by an executive. Each enactment evolves from a multitude of pressures, compromises, and quirks of history rather than from clear definitions, objectives, and priorities.

In the context of state policy, health issues compete for attention and resources with the likes of education, welfare, and highways. In the specific context of personal health policy, decisions are being made by an increasing number of players, state elected and appointed officials among them.

Before 1960, the medical profession was largely in control of policy directions for personal health care delivery, financing, and quality. If physicians did not actually make the decisions on supply, location, and type of medical care, their opinions were usually sought and heeded. Burgeoning technology and new methods of financing health care, however, has required special equipment and/or skilled professionals (Feingold, 1977). This led to new costs, changes in organization, and delivery of care, and heightened public expectations for more and better care as well as for greater control. Institutional providers (hospitals, nursing homes, etc.) as well as groups of individual professionals (nurses, social workers, administrators, therapists, etc.) began to participate in the policy process. Unions and insurers increased their influence on health policy in the private and public sectors. With all of these players in an industry that was becoming increasingly complex, policy directions became less clear. Since state government, unlike the private health care sector, has had a commonly accepted and, more importantly, enforceable decision-making process, state officials became participants and ultimate arbiters in an increasing number of health care decisions. Some of the decisions concerning location of facilities, cost of care, numbers and types of professionals, and payment methods are now being made or affected by state government decisions. The schemes to solve health services delivery and financing problems as well as organizational problems will be devised increasingly in the public sector, often by state elected officials.

MISTRUST OF STATES

It was argued strongly during the surge of social legislation in the late 1960s and early 1970s that some states could not be trusted to make choices that would provide services to groups that had little or no political power. Most of the administration of health and other social programs was closely held in Washington, D.C., because of this basic mistrust of some state officials and policies. All states were branded because of the mistrust of a few.

Whereas some states were mistrusted on philosophical grounds, most were not trusted to handle social programs because they were considered administratively unprepared or worse, inept. The legislative and aministrative focal points for deciding on state health issues differed in each state. In the mid-1960s, states had little government focus on personal health care.

On the legislative side, decision-making processes were often haphazard, not continuous, and usually not well understood by the public. Legislative procedures in the states were rarely described, and some were not describable. In a number of states, legislatures met only every other year for brief sessions. Professional legislative policy staff was virtually nonexistent at the state level, and few legislators concerned themselves with health issues unless they happened to be a health professional.

State executive branches were criticized for their lack of purpose, direction, and professionalism. In 1966, one-third of the nation's governors were still elected for 2-year terms. Personnel systems and pay at the state level often lacked the incentives to attract and keep professional staff. Most states were especially criticized for favoring highway improvement, tourism, lower taxes, and so on, over the health of their citizens. In 1964 seven states spent less than $1 million for public health services including some personal services (Council of State Governments, 1966–1967). Since most states had minimal interest in the health field, there was little need to develop or maintain health expertise.

To national policy advocates, the incongruity among the states was unacceptably burdensome. Health policy planners proceeded accordingly, by directing their attentions to building a base at the national level. Consequently, the federal government exercised its prerogatives in health policy, with constitutional superiority as well as an attitude of superiority over the states. Clarke (1981) described the federal view of states as having "long been rife with suspicion, distrust and even out right hostility." During the great surge of federal health activity in the decade 1965–1975, state health officials were rarely consulted about policy or implementation. Professional health care organizations interested in government intervention in personal health care usually sought national policy setting and implementation rather than the state effort. The Medicaid program was one of very few federal endeavors during this period that called for state participation. It was created out of a compromise that the then House Ways and Means chair Wilbur Mills engineered to facilitate the passage of the federally run Medicare program. The Medicaid program, an expansion of the earlier Kerr-Mills program, and state administration of it were a compromise to conservative members of Congress who exclaimed their fear of government medicine by deploring loss of local control.

SEPARATION OF POWERS

State constitutions have generally embraced Montesquieu's concept of separation of powers. That is, like their federal counterpart, they distributed powers among three branches of government: the legislative, the executive, and the judicial. Although states could have chosen other forms of government such as a parliamentary form, they did not. The balance of power among the three branches of government, however, was not what it is today. In practice, if not constitutionally, some of the early state governments were a bit like parliaments in that the governors in most states were elected by the legislatures. Ultimately, the executive gained considerable independence in the various states. This came, first, with longer terms of office; then, with the advent of Jacksonian democracy, governors gained independent election.

By the 1900s it was clear that the state executives had primary and independent responsibility for program implementation. It is this responsibility that is usually recognized in federal legislation and regulations, in the vesting of primary responsibility for the implementation of programs such as certificate of need or health planning directly with the governor, or in the executive branch of state government. Similarly, grants given to states to provide health services to migrant farm workers, children, or other groups usually have been given directly to the state executive branch, whereas evaluation studies, pilot service projects, and planning grants for health activities typically have been awarded to state executive agencies. Clearly, the shortest route to implementation of federal initiatives has often been through the state executive.

Recently, state legislatures have taken vociferous exception to federal grant programs and directives that vest all authority in the states' executives. Legislators argue that their prerogatives are being eroded by federal action. The National Health Planning and Resources Act of 1974, for example, provides that the selection of a state agency to administer federal health planning grants rests with the governor. In the state of New Hampshire, however, after the governor changed his mind twice on the selection, the legislature directed that he designate the state's Department of Health and Welfare as the administering agency. The New Hampshire Supreme Court, responding to the request of the governor for an advisory opinion on the matter, ruled in favor of the legislature. The court found that under the traditional separation of powers doctrine, the legislature had the ultimate responsibility for creating state agencies with prescribed duties (Brown, 1979).

State legislators also have been upset over their partial loss of the states' purse strings. Angered by an apparent loss of power to the executive in managing federal dollars, legislators have sought court intervention. Most courts that have dealt with the issue have invalidated the legislative assertions of power over grant funds (Brown, 1979). However, in the most celebrated case to date [*Shapp v. Sloan*, Pa. A 2d. 595 (1978)] the Pennsylvania Supreme Court ruled in favor of the legislature's broad powers to appropriate federal funds saying, "The framers gave to the General Assembly the exclusive power to pay money out of the State treasury without regard to source of funds." In contrast, nowhere in the federal Constitution is the executive branch given any right or authority to appropriate public monies for any purpose. In most states the problem of determining who has the power to assign the use of federal funds is very important. In South Carolina, for example, federal funds make up 50 percent of total state revenues. According to the National Conference of State Legislatures, every state can recount abuses of bypassing the legislative power of the purse (National Conference of State Legislatures, undated).

Legislative concern over its loss of budgetary control does not end with the executive branch. In a Minnesota case, *Welsch v. Likins*, 373 F. Supp. 487 (1974), a district court found that mentally retarded residents of a state hospital were being denied "adequate" care. The court suspended certain Minnesota laws that prevented the responsible state agency from exceeding its legislatively mandated budget. On appeal, the suspension was vacated, not on the basis of legality or authority, but to allow more time for remedies to take place. By agreement, the executive and legislative branches acceded to the court's findings.

It is clear that the legislature's budget power varies by state. At least 40 state legislatures try to control all state funds, although this is done with varying degrees of success. In short, it is still difficult to identify a single focal point of authority for planning, development, and budget decisions in many states.

DIFFERENCES AMONG THE STATES

Constitutionally, all states are similar in what they may *not* do. They are all subject to constitutional restrictions in that they are denied specific powers. None can unilaterally engage in foreign trade. Constitutional permissiveness, however, opens the doors to the differences in state government structures and procedures. Since each state is a sovereign entity with some powers that are neither listed nor defined, there are local variations in solving similar problems.

The variations are attributable to many local factors, all of which have an effect on health policy decisions. There are many obvious differences: area and population size, demographic mix, topography, and climate. California and New York are not only large states but they have more heterogeneous populations than most states. Surely it is more complicated to make public policy decisions in states such as these then in Utah or in a small New England state. In fact, California enacted 2,700 bills in 1977 and 1978 as compared to 400 in Utah. Whereas the Utah legislature did its work in two short legislative sessions lasting a total of 11 weeks, their California counterparts worked at it for 19 months (Council of State Governments, 1980–1981).

It should come as no surprise that Rhode Island spends much less per capita for highways than does Wyoming. In the same way that Rhode Island's size dictates its level of attention to highways, so does size, demography, topography, and climate affect health care roles in all states. Colorado, for example, was once to tuberculosis patients what Florida is now to the elderly. Florida, with almost 18 percent of its population over 65, has some different health care problems to contend with than does Alaska, which has less than 3 percent of its population over 65. Some states, because of topography, have been forced into a vigorous role in combating air pollution. Ohio, with its many urban centers, handles health planning differently from Kansas.

The urban–rural mix, or more specifically the industrial mix, of a state has had a dramatic, albeit indirect, effect on a state's health role. For example, the general economic downturn and the specific problems encountered by the automobile industry in 1981 created such severe fiscal stress in Michigan that budget cuts almost led to the abandonment of the entire school of nursing at Michigan State University. Such a situation likely would not have happened if Michigan had had more energy producers than energy users in its industrial mix.

To conclude that a state's assumption of a vigorous fiscal role in health is a function of various natural phenomena would not be completely accurate. Government role setting is neither an act of nature nor a result of natural causes. It is the power of each state to make its own decisions in those uncountable areas not denied to them by the Constitution. This can be exercised in a variety of ways. Some states are vigorous in the exercise of their own powers, whereas others resist the use of power to tax or create structures and policies that enhance their roles in health. In short, states are limited or assisted less by natural forces than by a willingness or reluctance to exercise powers to tax or create structures and policies that enhance their roles in health.

STATE INNOVATIONS IN HEALTH

Many states have moved actively to enhance their roles in personal health care. As in many other social programs, the seeds for innovative government health programs have usually been planted at the state level. These new ideas in turn have often been transplanted by federal policymakers into national programs available to or required of all states.

As early as 1911, states individually began to pass workers' compensation bills, and by 1915 workers in 30 states were protected financially from job-related accidents. State interest specifically in health insurance began about the same time. In 1915, a committee of the American Association for Labor Legislation drafted a standard bill to be presented to state legislatures for compulsory health insurance. The standards for the bill included a description of the population to be covered (income group of employed people who earned less than $1,200 per year), a method for meeting the costs of the program (shared by employer, employee, and state), the benefits (cash benefits and medical benefits, usually for 26 weeks), and the organization of services (centralized in each state under a State Social Insurance Commission that included a Medical Advisory Board) (see Williams, 1932). Health insurance bills were introduced in three states in 1916 and in 11 states in 1917. Commissions were set up in eight states in 1917 to investigate and report on health insurance. By 1918 the original standard bill had been revised twice, but none of the states had added the plan to their statutes (Sinai et.al., 1946).

The lack of action was not surprising. The concept received support from organized medicine and some labor leaders. However, Samuel Gompers, the irrepressible leader of the American Federation of Labor, an association he molded from disparate labor units and the principal labor spokesman of his time, opposed it, as did the National Association of Manufacturers (Burrow, 1963). The commissions in the several states produced widely varying results, ranging from strong support to declarations that the concept was unconstitutional. So the standard bill in various forms received wide-ranging discussion in many states, reached the ballot in some, but was never passed. By the late 1930s and early 1940s the idea, having been nurtured in the states for 20 years, finally became a national issue.

However, the concept was far from dead in the states. Although some impatient groups thought that state action was too tedious a process for establishing nationwide social change, others continued to chip away at state policies. In 1935, the newly formed American Association for Social Security developed a model bill for state action on compulsory health insurance. The 1930s depression and later World War II gave new life to these old ideas. From 1939 through 1944, 106 bills were introduced in 15 states (Williams, 1932). Two states—Rhode Island in 1942 and California in 1946—actually enacted short-lived health insurance bills.

Recent state innovations in personal health care are as much a function of fiscal distress as of social change. Renewed interest in health insurance at the state level came again in the 1970s as health costs became as debilitating to individuals as disease itself. Whereas federal officials continued to examine and debate dozens of health insurance proposals each year, several states enacted plans to protect their citizens.

In 1974, 30 years after its first experiment, Rhode Island enacted a catastrophic health insurance plan. The program, tied to private health insurance, offers incentives to the insurance industry for development and to consumers for purchase of health insurance coverage by subsidizing catastrophic health insurance. Six other states, New York, Maine, Alaska, Minnesota, Connecticut, and Hawaii, have also passed health insurance bills that either require minimum benefits in health insurance plans or establish state-supported health insurance. A number of other states have introduced health insurance bills before their legislative bodies. Fiscal difficulties in the early 1980s, however, caused Minnesota and Maine to tighten their health insurance budgets, whereas Alaska, looking for ways to spend its oil money, considered an expansion of its program.

State health insurance programs are a product of a perceived social need for more and better health care. Skyrocketing costs to people exacerbated the need and hurried the establishment of government health programs. In the last decade, it was the cost factor that was the driving force behind most state action. Although some states instituted unpopular cost controls, by the mid 1970s it was clear that health programs were becoming financially out of reach for state government as well.

State governments began to control the construction and purpose of health facilities long before the federal government required states to do so. For example, the requirement for a certificate of need (CoN) for capital expenditures in hospitals was initiated in New York State in 1965, 7 years before an amendment to the federal Social Security Act tied federal reimbursement for Titles V, XIII, XIX to institutional compliance with state review of capital expenditures. At least two dozen states had adopted their own CoN requirements before it became national policy under the National Health Planning and Resources Development Act of 1974.

Many states, moreover, have CoN provisions that are stronger than those required by federal law. Significantly, the Alaska statute includes federal facilities within its scope of coverage, the West Virginia law requires institutions to submit a long-range plan before submitting CoN applications, and the Wisconsin statute encourages decertification of specialized hospital services.

Whether or not physician offices should be covered under CoN has been a key issue at both state and national levels. During 1977 and 1978 many states considered legislation that, to varying degrees, required physicians to obtain a certificate of need when acquiring major office equipment or modifying their office services. Five states, Iowa, Colorado, Wisconsin, North Carolina, and Virginia, adopted such legislation. Hawaii and Minnesota had passed legislation to that effect in 1975, and Michigan and Rhode Island amended their existing CoN statutes in 1978 by extending their applicability to physicians' offices under certain circumstances (Marshall, 1979).

A more direct method of addressing rising health costs initiated at the state level has been state review of hospital rates. Since 1970, more than 18 states enacted legislation requiring disclosure, review, or regulation of hospital rates or budgets.[7] Six states, Connecticut, Maryland, Massachusetts, New Jersey, New York, and Washington have actually been regulating non-Medicare expenses for over 5 years.

Typically, these state rate-setting programs determine prospectively the rates that hospitals may charge. Hospitals know how much they will be receiving for their patient care and establish their budgets accordingly. Proponents of the idea argue that this instills a sense of financial management into hospital administration. Others are skeptical and argue that it retards innovation and quality health care.

The Maryland program was established in 1971. After an initial developmental period, its Health Services Cost Review Commission began setting rates in 1974. In 1977, DHEW's Health Care Financing Administration, on an experimental basis, agreed to permit the Maryland commission to set rates for the Medicare program—an agreement that made Maryland the first state agency in the United States to set rates for all payers. Subsequently, Medicare waivers have been granted for experimental programs in Washington, New Jersey, and western Pennsylvania.

The idea of government rate setting is controversial. Even after decades of experience, disagreement continues as to whether any of the programs actually have slowed the rise of health costs. Although there is considerable pessimism regarding the effects of a national cost-control program, such as the 9 percent cap on hospital expenditures proposed by the Carter administration, a 1980 study demonstrated that the six states

---

[7] The types of hospital rate review or cost-containment programs vary so greatly that the exact number of state programs in existence depends on a definition of the program involved.

with long-standing rate-setting programs showed a slower rate of cost increase than those states without such programs (Biles, 1980).

Although disagreement over the effect of the programs is likely to continue, the management of the programs so far has been left to the states. The programs are closely aligned to other state functions related to health costs: CoN, administration of Medicaid, licensing of providers, and regulation of insurance industry. The state-developed programs have led to a wide variety of experiments tempered by local conditions, problems, and needs.

The rising costs of long-term care, particularly nursing home care, have had a noticeable effect on state expenditures. Largely a private family matter before the passage of Medicare and Medicaid in 1965, financial support for nursing home care has become a troublesome fiscal burden to many states. In 1978, over one-half of the U.S. nursing home care bill was paid by government. State and local governments alone spent $3.6 billion for such care. Nineteen states spent over half of their total Medicaid budgets on nursing homes.

The Medicaid program provides incentives for inpatient long-term care instead of potentially less costly alternatives. States could, of course, provide the alternatives at their own expense, but since these alternatives would have to be offered in addition to nursing home care, most states would likely find this to be financially prohibitive. Some states, however, have received federal waivers to use Medicaid funds for alternatives to institutional long-term care.

One such program—the so-called nursing home without walls—was established in New York in 1977. Born out of fiscal need and designed to meet high medical and social standards, the program established a new category of providers who are responsible for delivering in-home care to eligible Medicaid beneficiaries being considered for nursing home placement. Funding is limited to 75 percent of the average nursing home rate in the patient's county. Each month the state's Medicaid program has saved an average of $550 per patient, so that New York and the federal Medicaid program are both saving money (Clarke and Hereford, 1980). In those states in which federal Medicaid dollars could not be used for such in-home care, it has not proven to be cost effective for states to keep patients out of nursing homes.

Such fiscal disincentives aside, several states have experimented with a variety of noninstitutional long-term care health service programs. Oregon, for example, spends over $2 million of state money annually to provide health services as well as assistance with shopping, housekeeping, and other daily needs for the elderly who cannot manage alone (Hereford, 1980). To hold down nursing home admissions and costs, other states, including Utah, Texas, Virginia, Massachusetts, and Minnesota, have adopted programs to screen prospective nursing home admissions, set nursing home rates, and provide home health services.

Although many state innovations in personal health care such as CoN, rate setting, and home health programs have predated federal initiatives, others have never been nationalized. A surge in medical malpractice suits throughout the United States in the early 1970s spurred changes in state insurance laws to help alleviate the problem. These changes had to be made at the state level where the insurance industry is regulated. Similarly, in the mid-1960s, medical educators began training programs for a new breed of health personnel, such as nurse practitioners, and looked to the states for changes in medical practice laws to accommodate them. Virtually every provider group, for example, chiropractors seeking greater breadth of practice and HMOs seeking a more competitive advantage within a state's insurance laws, has sought statutory changes from its state legislature. Other programs, such as those to allow pharmacists to substitute generic drugs for prescribed brand-name drugs, to fill medical personnel shortages in underserved areas, and to develop family practice programs in medical schools have been tested by states to save money and/or meet social needs.

STATE ROLES IN HEALTH

This chapter has shown how shifting costs and expenses, history and traditions, as well as natural resources and internal political or ideological commitment have altered and varied the direction of state policies in health care. There is no shortage of innovative health programs in the states. Most of the innovations in financing, organization, and delivery of health care have come from the private sector of the health industry. It usually has taken government action, however, to expand these innovations into common practice. Some programs have been adopted by a few states or by the federal government for all states; other programs have been adopted to respond to the peculiarities of only one state. In general, the result has been that state legislators and administrators have taken on an enlarged role in setting the policies, goals, and directions for health care programs. The growth of their policy is likely to continue.

The states' roles in actually implementing health projects, programs, and services can be grouped into three categories. States are (1) administrative and fiscal agents, (2) direct providers of services, and (3) regulators of services and personnel.

THE STATE AS AN ADMINISTRATIVE AND FISCAL AGENT

States plan for health services, choose among alternatives, raise revenues to pay for the services, and establish the institutional frameworks and administrative structures to carry out their plans and decisions. This role is shared with the federal government. State structures and procedures follow federal specifications when states accept federal revenue and states become agents of the national government. In some cases, the federal government has used states as agents to carry out national policy through the administration of grants-in-aid. States have often changed their laws to accommodate national goals.

The responsibility for establishing and financing state administrative structures for health rests with the legislature. Legislative decisions, however, are frequently based on executive recommendations. The first state health structure is thought to have been established in Louisiana in 1855. A board was created to deal specifically with yellow fever and other epidemics. In 1869, at least 40 years before any federal public health activity, Massachusetts set up a State Board of Health to oversee general matters of sanitation, causes of disease, epidemics, and public health (Hanlon, 1960a).

Today, all states have statutes that create structures and procedures to carry out public health functions. These incorporate statewide public health functions as well as those implemented by local governments. The state is ultimately responsible for assuring that public health needs are met by local units of government. If a city or county fails, refuses, or is unable to cope with its health problems, the state may lend assistance. It is not unusual for a state health agency to pass as much as half of its budget on to local health departments. If necessary, a state may assume control or establish structures necessary for delivery of health services in cities and counties. As creatures of the state, local jurisdictions may exercise only those powers expressly granted to them by the state (Winter, 1961). The public health functions of some states are centralized, but most, particularly those with large urban centers, have delegated such responsibility to local authorities. Still, where there is a conflict between the state powers and local powers, even for home-rule municipalities, the courts have generally ruled in favor of the state.[8]

Following Massachusett's lead in creating a state public health agency over 100 years ago, most states vested health functions in a single state agency and a number of local health agencies. Many states also have allowed for the creation of a variety of special health districts (e.g., for sewers, hospitals, or water) used mainly to tax the users of services. Some have given health responsibilities (typically on environmental matters) to state-created metropolitan governments that incorporate a number of contiguous local jurisdictions.

In recent years, the health structures of the states have become considerably more complex. The infusion of federal mandates for health planning, medical assistance, and quality assurance have resulted in more elaborate and often totally new structures in the states. State agencies to respond to environmental problems and to control pollution have been created, sometimes outside of traditional state and local health structures. State welfare departments have taken on medical assistance functions, whereas planning agencies have assumed the health planning mandates. Meanwhile, federal dollars have sometimes been used to create private quality assurance programs separate from state and local government health services agencies.

Curiously, several states have modeled the organization of their health enterprise after the federal government. Arkansas, for example, with its Bureau of Community Health Services and Bureau of Health Resources, went so far as to use titles of federal health agencies. Florida, on the other hand, established a broad functional organization so that federal programs were split into functions across more than one state agency. This was in contradiction to federal regulations that require "single state agencies" to carry out programs such as those for maternal and child health.

One of the most visible health care roles for states in recent years has been that of a fiscal agent. The state role as a fiscal agent is best exemplified by the Medicaid program. Initially thought to be a modest enhancement of the state–federal Kerr-Mills medical assistance program, policymakers and health professionals focused their attention on the Medicare part of the newly passed legislation. Their focus, however, soon changed when the fiscal, administrative, and policy impact of Medicaid began to be felt.

Although half of the $17 billion spent in 1980 for Medicaid was federal dollars, the program had stretched the administrative capacity as well as the imagination and budget of most states. It would be unfair, though, to suggest that states act merely as federal administrative and fiscal field offices for the program. Under provisions of the act, participating states are required to offer a set of optional services that the federal government will share the cost of providing. Within guidelines established by the federal government, states may set income-based eligibility and resource limits. Fur-

---

[8]For example, in *Minnesota Board of Health v. City of Brainerd*, 308 Minn. 24, 241 N.W. 2d 624 (1976), the Minnesota Supreme Court upheld the Minnesota fluoridation law, (Minnesota Statute Section 144.45) that had been challenged on constitutional grounds by the city of Brainerd, Minnesota. The supreme court deferred to both the legislature's factual determination that fluoridated water prevented dental cavities and to the legislative judgment that requiring fluoridation promoted the public welfare.

ther, states establish appropriate fee schedules and reimburse state-approved providers for services. Although the program is based on federal statute and regulation, the states have considerable operational latitude and policy choices in implementing the program. That states have made independent choices can be measured by the differences in program size. For every $1 million of state personal income in 1977, California spent $22.6 thousand, New York, $18.7 thousand, and Wisconsin, $16.0 thousand on Medicaid. At the same time, Wyoming spent $2.7 thousand, Missouri, $5.6 thousand, and Indiana, $6.4 thousand on the program (Hanlon, 1960b). The reason for the differences lies in the basic policy choices made by states regarding eligibility and range of benefits rather than in federal requirements.

To some states the Medicaid program has become a fiscal and administrative nightmare. Setting the "right" policies, creating the administrative structures, and overseeing the management and efficacy of the program have put state executives and legislators into the center of personal health care delivery.

Medicaid is linked to other federal and state programs as well. Administratively, some states have relied on counties to pay bills or determine eligibility. Eligibility is sometimes determined in part on income received from other government-financed programs, including AFDC, Supplemental Security Income (SSI), and food stamps. Medicaid has been used as a carrot to encourage providers to improve services and quality; it has been used as a stick to control the amount and location of health resources. In short, it has placed states in a complicated central health role as administrative and fiscal agents.

Although the Medicaid program imposes a very visible role for states, the states act as administrative and fiscal agents for health in a variety of other programs and services as well. One of these, often overlooked but very costly, is as a buyer of health insurance for state employees. The cost of the coverage that states purchase for their employees is typically as much as state budgets for public health services.

In 1978, there was a total of 3.5 million state employees. At a cost to the states of about $900 per employee, states spent $3.1 billion on employee health insurance.[9] At the same rate, local governments would have spent three times as much. Because of inflation in personal health care costs, total state expenditures for employee health insurance increases almost $500 million each year. Some states have reacted by capping their health insurance benefits and requiring higher deductibles and greater copayments. Even with a direct interest as an employer of large numbers of people and with costs rising, however, few states have used their policymaking powers to hold down health care costs.

States have also acted as administrative and fiscal agents in education and research programs. As in so many areas, it is difficult here to separate the policy power of the state government from its administrative functions. Whereas state legislatures usually control state university budgets, they have little influence over curriculum or research, especially in those institutions that enjoy state consitutional autonomy or have constitutionally established boards.

As with other state health endeavors, education and research vary from state to state and are integrated with federal policy. In those states in which federal dollars dwarf those of the state for health training and research, the state's influence on its own

---

[9]These figures are rough estimates based on discussions with the Minnesota Department of Employee Relations. The estimated $900 per employee figure used here is born out by a 1980 survey of out-of-state salary and fringe benefits. Five reporting states estimated their average percent of payroll for health insurance to be 6.17 percent (State of Washington).

institutions is diminished. It is clear, however, that generally the education of health manpower is a state function, guided by state policymakers usually through the appropriations process. Billions of state tax dollars are spent for institutional support, capital outlays, student aid, and direct support for health manpower training.

The role as fiscal agent has not been an easy one for most states, principally because of the stress that health costs have put on state budgets. Cramped by rising costs of care and declining revenues, some states have been forced into short-term borrowing at high interest rates. Some have reached their constitutional debt limits for raising revenues, thereby limiting their capital budgets for state health facilities. In the face of a budget squeeze, states have often sought to pass the fiscal burden of health costs on to urban health and hospital programs by reducing state benefits, eligibility, and payments for individuals who continue to seek care in local programs. Finally, there is a wide variance in the revenue-raising efforts among the states and local governments. Although there is not a direct correlation between revenues and health services, most states with comprehensive Medicaid programs and other health services have high taxes.

THE STATE AS A PROVIDER OF SERVICES

In addition to financing health care through private vendors, the federal government employs people to provide personal health services to veterans, military personnel, American Indians, and merchant marines. These services represent a small and decreasing share of the federal health budget. States also employ people to provide public as well as personal health services, principally through the provision of hospital services.

Roughly one-third of U.S. hospitals are government operated. Eighty-five percent of these are run by state and local employees (National Center Health for Health Statistics, 1979). Although most of the hospitals are owned by municipalities, the preponderance of beds are state operated. In 1979, states spent over $10 billion ($3 billion more than they spent on Medicaid) to run their hospitals (U.S. Bureau of the Census, 1980).

State health agencies also provide personal health care services directly using their own personnel. These programs cost $2.3 billion in 1978 and accounted for 72 percent of the total budgets. Some of the program areas in which state health agencies provide direct services include maternal and child health, crippled children, communicable diseases, dental health, chronic disease, and mental health.

Another example of the direct provision of health service by state government is in the area of environmental health. As mentioned earlier, growing national concern over environmental threats has caused states to create a variety of structures to cope with these modern problems. The new agencies have been established mainly to handle air and water pollution and solid, radioactive, and other hazardous wastes. Traditionally, states have also directly provided, usually through their state health agencies, environmental services such as food and milk control, sanitation control of health facilities, insect control, housing, hotel, and motel sanitation, and sewage disposal. To be sure, many of the services are provided by local authorities, but states still control and, in fact, often carry out these environmental services.

THE STATE AS A REGULATOR

In the broadest sense, the states' role as regulators includes all of their practices that create or influence change in the health field. This not only includes written rules of the administrative arms of government, but the laws that are the basis of the rules. The threat of law making and other government actions (e.g., legislative committee hearings, executive orders, appropriations) that may influence the success of programs or shape public opinion also serve a regulatory role. It is clear, however, that most people think first of written rules when considering state regulation. These rules, once set, give specific direction and to the general public sometimes seem unalterable.

Federal and state laws, while setting policy directions, often leave much to the imagination of the administrator charged with establishing specific program direction by written rule. In one general statutory statement in the first federal health planning act, Congress established Section 314 (e) of the Public Health Service Act. It was out of this provision, and an equally vague statement in the legislation that created the Office of Economic Opportunity, that federal administrators established the $250 million neighborhood health center program. Federal rules for the program were not established until years after the program was operational.

In general, states have been far more explicit than the federal government in their health statutes. This is probably a function of fewer bills to review, more narrowly defined objectives, fewer interests to satisfy, and lack of legislative staff, which results in bills written by those who will administer the program. The upshot is that state rules frequently follow state legislation rather closely. To be sure, there are many state programs, usually when established directly through appropriations processes rather than a policy process, that are not very explicit.

In some states, the legislative branch has established a rule review and rescinding mechanism to monitor the rule-making process and to ensure that rules meet the intent of legislation. The legislative power to rescind an administrative rule has been questioned but not challenged in court. In fact, most review of administrative rules and procedures occurs in standing legislative committees, and general legislative rule review committees have had comparatively limited success.

The procedures that states have adopted to establish written rules, like almost everything else, vary from state to state. The different procedures alter the influence that an agency may have or the ultimate potential for arbitrariness. For example, Minnesota requires that 25 days before a public hearing on a proposed rule a statement of need and reasonableness be available to the public. Iowa requires similar justification but only if requested to do so by an interested person. In Oregon, and North Dakota, the presiding officer at a public hearing on rules comes from within the agency that is adopting the rules. Minnesota, in contrast, has an independent office for those purposes. Some states require hearings on all contested rules; others require a written petition signed by up to 25 people before a hearing is scheduled. Although half the states have adopted similar legislation for their administrative procedures, most states continue to differ substantially in the specific procedures for rule setting.

Regulating the health industry has been traditionally a state role. In 1894, the New York Constitution was amended to require that private facilities be certified by the State Board of Charities to be eligible for payments from local governments, thus beginning the use of government funds to encourage health standards (Somers, 1969). All states now set quality standards for licensure or certification of health institutions and personnel, either by statute or by written rule. Environmental standards, labor practices, and many other aspects of public life that affect health programs are also guided largely by state, rather than federal, requirements.

In the last 15 years, the traditional state role in setting health personnel and facility standards has come under considerable federal influence. In fact, as early as 1946, the federal Hill-Burton Act that provided construction funds to hospitals throughout the United States, required states to establish minimum standards for hospital operation and maintenance. Model bills establishing such standards were prepared and passed by state legislatures. Unlike licensure of health personnel, fewer than a dozen states had chosen to have health facility licensing laws before the passage of the Hill-Burton Act.

Changes in the Social Security Act in the 1950s increased pressure on the states to broaden their health facility licensing requirements.[10] But it was not until the enactment of the social legislation of 1965–1975, especially Medicare and Medicaid, that the federal regulatory influence became pervasive. In fact, existing state licensing laws (many of which were adopted under earlier federal influence) were considered inadequate by the Congress that passed Medicare and Medicaid. Federal administrators for these programs established their own certification processes and contracted with state health departments to carry out the inspections, at first in units separate from the licensure offices. Before long most states had hospital licensing programs, and licensing of nursing homes and related facilities was begun.

Cost-containment measures such as certificate of need legislation, Medicare, Medicaid, maternal and child health measures, and health planning legislation, greatly expanded the federal influence over state regulatory requirements. Federal appropriations for health programs that bypass state government have carried specific directives often tied to federally mandated regulations. For example, requirements are established for facilities and personnel used by community health centers or HMOs that have received federal dollars. All regulations have budget implications, but some are more direct than others. Federal safety standards for institutions receiving Medicaid funds have cost such institutions (many state owned) millions of dollars in updating. Amendments to the Hill-Burton Act resulted in rules requiring a percentage of "free care" to be delivered by every institution that received financial assistance for capital costs. Failure to comply with CoN or health planning requirements posed the risk of losing Medicare and Medicaid funds. In most states federal requirements are so intermixed with state requirements that it is usually impossible to discern one from the other in written state rules. Together, they include a detailed body of written administrative decisions used by states to regulate the health industry.

The state's regulatory role in health cover much more than facilities and personnel. There are 50 different sanitary codes, 50 separate building codes, 50 sets of rules governing water supplies, and 50 codes regulating sewage treatment and the disposal of waste. Many states, by statute, share the enforcement and even the specific requirements of the codes with local units of governments, with local conditions governing the specifics of the rules and enforcement. In general, however, the regulation of health programs, whether federally mandated or locally shared, remains a state role under its police power.

CONCLUSION

In summary, the role of state government in U.S. health cannot be adequately described outside a context of federalism; health cost trends; the history, structure, and resources

---

[10]The changes required that any state using federal matching funds to pay for care in public or private institutions for welfare recipients must designate an authority to establish and maintain institutional standards.

of state governments; and the variety of ways states make decisions. A state's health role is no longer one of providing public health services as it was 25 years ago, nor is it only a role of innovating delivery or regulatory schemes in response to recent fiscal stress. In this regard, one state's scheme may be another state's anathema. Each state defines its own role according to its own needs in a manner that best fits its peculiar history, politics, and resources. Most states, having accepted federal health funds, agreed to roles and programs set nationally. Yet state health roles still vary dramatically from state to state.

For the most part, from 1965 to 1980 states have been the unseen partner in the public sector of health services. This has begun to change only recently. The states' roles in health, however, are likely to be considerably more visible in the 1980s than ever before. This is true for at least the following reasons:

1. The enlarged government role in personal health in the last 15 years, though mostly at the federal level has affected states. Practically, many people (including the Reagan administration) believe that states have the structures and expertise, not available to them in 1965, to handle health programs.[11] Most states have demonstrated their expertise in developing and handling innovative and traditional health programs. Politically, there is a growing belief among state and federal officials that government-financed health programs are handled best at the state level, according to state-determined needs.

2. Increased fiscal stress in many states due to rising costs and reduced revenues will require difficult expenditure choices, in some cases resulting in severe health program cutbacks. The cutbacks in most states will be in stark contrast to a few energy-rich states that will be able to add services lavishly and public expectations for government-supported health services brought on by trends over the last 15 years. Although the acclaim for increased government support of health services in the last 15 years went to the federal government, state and local governments are likely to be blamed by the public for any forthcoming cutbacks.

3. There is apt to be more government intervention in health services in the 1980s instead of less. A shift to greater state control over heretofore federally supported health programs does not reduce government intervention in health services. Rather, it places the regulation of projects, as well as the policy decisions for the projects, closer to the point of delivery. Furthermore, federal health project funds often went directly to local governments or the private sector, bypassing state governments and thereby minimizing their control. Federal dollars that go directly to state governments for distributions will become a part of the state-controlled budgeting and appropriations processes.

The move of health care issues to the public sector has been heralded by social planners as a move away from pluralistic decision making in health care. It has been seen as an opportunity for restructuring the health care industry through national and state goal setting and government restructuring (Snoke and Snoke, 1975). Such reasoning, however, has failed to recognize that the pluralism of the private health care industry

---

[11]A serious erosion of this professional infrastructure in the face of real and impending budget cutbacks that has seen a major emmigration of highly qualified staff from state government to the private sector greatly endangers such expectations.

was merely being replaced, or added to, by the pluralism of government policymaking. As the health policy role shifts to the states, 50 state executives and legislatures will make decisions for health policy like they do for everything else: inductively rather than deductively, often more politically than substantively, but always incrementally.

REFERENCES

Advisory Commission on Intergovernmental Relations, *Recent Trends in Federal and State Aids to Local Governments*, Washington, D.C.: Advisory Commission on Intergovernmental Relations, M-118, July 1980a, Table A-33, pp. 94–95.

Advisory Commission on Intergovernmental Relations, *The Federal Role in the Federal Systems: The Dynamics of Growth. A Crisis of Confidence and Competence*, Washington, D.C.: Advisory Commission on Intergovernmental Relations, A-77, July 1980b, p. 137.

Advisory Commission on Intergovernmental Relations, *Significant Features of Fiscal Federalism*, Washington, D.C.: Advisory Commission Intergovernmental Relations, M-123, October 1980c, 1979–1980 edition, Table 34, p. 45.

Advisory Commission on Intergovernmental Relations, *Awakening the Slumbering Giant: Intergovernmental Relations and Federal Grant Law*, Washington, D.C.: Advisory Commission on Intergovernmental Relations, M-122, December 1980d, p. 19.

Association of State and Territorial Health Officers, *Comprehensive NPRPRS Report, Services, Expenditures and Programs of State and Territorial Health Agencies*, Washington, D.C.: Association of State and Territorial Health Officers, January 1980, p. 37.

Biles, Brian, Carl Schramm and J. Graham Atkinson, "Hospital Cost Inflation Under State Rate-Setting Programs," *New England Journal of Medicine*, Vol. 303, No. 12, September 18, 1980, p. 664.

Brown, George D., "Federal Funds and National Supremacy: The Role of State Legislatures in Federal Grant Programs," *American University Law Review*, Vol. 28, No. 3, Spring 1979, p. 312.

Burrow, James G., *AMA Voice of American Medicine*, Baltimore: Johns Hopkins Press, 1963, p. 138.

Clarke, Gary J., "The Role of the States in the Delivery of Health Services, *American Journal of Public Health*, Vol. 71, No. 1, January 1981, Supplement, p. 59.

Clarke, Gary and Russ Hereford, eds., "New York's Nursing Home Without Walls Program," *State Health Notes*, No. 12, May 1980.

Congressional Quarterly Service, *Congressional Quarterly Almanacs*, Washington, D.C.: Congressional Quarterly Service, 1965, p. 102; 1966, p. 103.

Council of State Governments, *Book of the States*, Council of State Governments, 1980–1981, pp. 104–105.

Council of State Governments, *Book of the States*, Council of State Governments, 1966–1967, p. 338.

Feingold, Eugene, "Who Controls the Medical Care System?" in Arthur Levin, ed., *Health Services: The Local Perspective*, Proceedings of the Academy of Political Science, New York: Academy of Political Science, 1977, p. 194.

Fleisher, Steve M., "The Law of Basic Public Health Activities: Police Power and Constitutional Limitations," in Ruth Roemer and George McKay, eds., *Legal Aspects of Health Policy: Issues and Trends*, Westport, Conn. Greenwood Press, 1980, p. 9.

Grad, Frank P., *Public Health Law Manual*, Washington, D.C.: American Public Health Association, 1975, p. 5.

Hanlon, John J., *Principles of Public Health Administration*, third edition, St. Louis: C. V. Mosby Co., 1960a, p. 51.

Hanlon, John J., "Data on Medicaid Programs," in John Hanlon, ed., *Principles of Public Health Administration*, St. Louis: C. V. Mosby Co., 1960b, 3rd edition, p. 56.

Health Care Financing Administration Review, Vol. 1, No. 3, Winter 1980, pp. 16–47.

Hereford, Russell N., "Alternatives to Nursing Homes," Unpublished statement of National Conference of State Legislatures, October 3, 1980, pp. 15, 16.

Kailo, Andrea, "Reforming the Federal System: An Agenda for the States," *State Legislatures* National Conference of State Legislatures, Vol. 16, February 1980, p. 8.

Madison, James, "Federal Powers Not Dangerous to the States," *The Federalist Papers*, 1787–1788, No. 45.

Marshall, Mary, Delegate (Virginia) Statement on H. R. 3041 before the Interstate and Foreign Commerce Subcommittee on Health, U.S. House of Representatives, March 29, 1979.

Medicaid/Medicare Management Institute, *Data on the Medicaid Program: Eligibility, Services, Expenditures*, Baltimore, M.: Medicaid/Medicare Management Institute, DHEW, Health Care Financing Administration, 1979, p. 28.

Mosher, Frederick C., "The Changing Responsibilities and Tactics of the Federal Government," *Public Administration Review*, Vol. 40, No. 6, Novermber/December 1980, pp. 541–547.

National Center for Health Statistics, *Health Resources Statistics 1976-77 Edition*, DHEW Pub. (PHS) 79-1509, Washington, D.C.: U.S. Government Printing Office, 1979.

National Conference of State Legislatures, "State Legislative Control of Federal Funds," *State Legislative Report*, Denver: National Conference of State Legislatures, undated, p. 1.

National Journal, Vol. 13, January 3, 1980, p. 7.

Remen, Robert I., Robert N. Wise and John Montgomery, *State Intergovernmental Planning Strategies, Series 7*, Council of State Planning Agencies, 1977, p. 14.

Shannon, John, "A Fiscal Note," *Intergovernmental Perspectice*, Washington, D.C.: Advisory Commission on Intergovernmental Relations, Vol. 6, No. 4, Fall 1980.

Sinai, Nathan, Odin Anderson and Melvin Dollar, *Health Insurance in the United States*, New York: The Commonwealth Fund, 1946, p. 47.

Snoke, P. and A. W. Snoke, "The State Role in the Regulation of the Health Delivery System," *Toledo Law Review*, Vol. 6, Spring 1975, p. 620.

Somers, Anne R., *Hospital Regulation: The Dilemma of Public Policy*, Princeton University: Industrial Relations Section, 1969, pp. 102–107.

State of Washington, 1980 Out-of-State Salary and Fringe Benefit Survey, Department of Personnel and Higher Education Personnel Board.

U.S. Bureau of the Census, *State Government Finances in 1979*, Washington D.C.: U.S. Department of Commerce, Bureau of the Census, 1980, Table 9, p. 38.

Williams, Pierce, *The Purchase of Medical Care Through Periodic Payment*, New York: National Bureau of Economic Research, 1932, pp. 8–9.

Winter, W. O., *The Urban Polity*, New York: Dodd, Mead and Co., 1969, p. 112.

PART THREE

*Health and the Political Process:
The Role of Interest Groups
Politics and Citizen
Participation in Health*

CHAPTER 11

Health Associations and the Legislative Process

Paul J. Feldstein

Several studies have been conducted to evaluate the effectiveness of U.S. federal subsidy programs in the medical care sector.[1] In examination of federal manpower subsidies to increase the number of dentists, it was found that an equivalent number of dental visits could have been produced, at less than one-tenth the cost, if the federal subsidies had been provided in a different manner, namely, if the wages of dental auxiliaries had been subsidized (Feldstein, 1977). Evaluations of the federal Nurse Training Act revealed that an increase in the number of employed registered nurses could have been achieved at between one-fifth and one-tenth the cost had an alternative approach been used, namely, if the wages of registered nurses had been subsidized, thereby increasing their participation rate in the market (Feldstein, 1977). These analyses of the federal manpower subsidy programs have questioned the justification offered for such programs, based, as it was, on the use of health-manpower-to-population ratios to indicate a "need" or "shortage." The method used to distribute the subsidy funds is also open to question. A possible conclusion is that further economic analysis is needed if governmental programs are to be cost effective. The assumption is that with additional information, policymakers would generate better legislation. However, another interpretation of the type of health legislation that results from the legislative process is that the resulting legislation is actually what is intended. Under this hypothesis, the participants in the legislative process are assumed to have rational goals and to be aware of the effects of the legislation that is proposed. If the resulting legislation is not cost effective, it is because it was not meant to be cost effective.

An examination of the beneficiaries of such legislation lends support to this hypothesis. The major beneficiaries of health manpower legislation are the health professional schools, because they are the recipients of the vast majority of funds distributed, and the professional health manpower associations, the American Medical Association (AMA), the American Dental Association (ADA), and the American Nurses' Association (ANA), because government subsidy programs result in relatively small increases in the supply of health professionals.

---

[1]This chapter constitutes a revised and updated version of the author's chapter, "The Political Economy of Health Care," in *Health Care Economics* (Feldstein, 1981), and is based upon his earlier work, *Health Associations and the Demand for Legislation: The Political Economy of Health* (Feldstein, 1977).

If the legislation that results is the outcome intended by a rational and knowledge-able group of participants, then the prospects for improving the cost effectiveness of future health legislation by merely providing additional economic analyses of its intended effects is uncertain. To predict legislative outcomes, it becomes necessary to develop a model, not of the most cost-effective approach to achieving the stated objec-tives of the legislation, but rather of the supply and demand for legislation. In other words, a model of the political economy of health care is required. A theoretical frame-work to explain the outcome of the legislation would include the following participants in the legislative process: legislatures and/or the particular legislative committee with jurisdiction over the proposed legislation; the health interest groups affected by the legislation, such as the American Hospital Association (AHA) and the American Medical Association, the bureaucracy that will administer the legislation, the executive branch of the federal government, and other interest groups such as industry and unions. Those who may be affected by the proposed legislation undoubtedly would like to influence it so that it coincides with their particular interests. For example, legislators favor (or propose) particular legislative actions because they improve their chances of being reelected: If the legislation is viewed favorably by their constituents or other propo-nents, support will be forthcoming to the legislators—in the form of campaign funds, volunteers for helping in the election campaign, or simply votes. The health interest organizations have a demand for legislation because it benefits their members. The demand for legislation by these interest groups, which is an indication of how much a group would be willing to "pay" for those legislative benefits (in terms of campaign funds, etc.), depends upon what benefits the legislation provides beyond the legislative benefits the members of the group already possess. The cost of obtaining these legisla-tive benefits, as determined by the direct monetary and nonmonetary outlays necessary to achieve them, depends, among other things, on the action of other interested parties to that legislation. The greater the adverse affect of the legislation upon other interest groups, the greater will be their willingness to "pay" to forestall or defeat the proposed legislation, which in turn increases the cost of having such legislation passed. The cost of obtaining the legislation may well exceed the positive benefits to members of a group favoring the legislation, in which case they will be unsuccessful in achieving their legislative program.

Another interested participant in the legislative process is the bureaucracy that is to administer the legislation. Bureaucrats wish to see their own bureaucracies survive and grow, thereby justifying their larger salaries as the size of their agencies and respon-sibilities increase. The particular bureaucracy administering the legislation can promise benefits to legislators or particular interest groups if the legislation increases the agen-cy's budget. The executive branch of government, which has overall responsibility for the government budget, may have an interest in the legislation because it would affect total government expenditures. The executive branch of government would like to start new programs so as to increase its own reelection chances. To do so, it may be interested in constraining expenditures on old programs, since new legislation would require additional dollars, which could come either from politically unpopular higher taxes or from underfunding current programs.

These are some of the participants in the legislative process. Other possible partici-pants are industry and labor unions, who would be affected in their costs of production and in number of workers employed or wages, respectively. A complete model to explain the actual outcome of legislation would have to quantify the perceived benefits and the costs of the proposed legislation to all of these participants.

This chapter examines the legislative behavior of one of the participants in the legislative process: the health interest groups. The reason for selecting them is that in the past much of the health legislation at both state and federal levels has been strongly influenced by these groups. In fact, the structure of the U.S. health care system is, in many respects, the result of legislative activity by these health associations. Health interest groups often provide the only testimony on legislation; their positions are well publicized and are presented as being synonymous with that of the public interest. All legislation is complex and requires knowledgeable people to understand it. In the past, the public has been inclined to believe that health legislation is best understood by health professionals and, therefore, has been willing to accept the politics of health as espoused by health professionals.

The potential impact of health interest groups is enormous. From 1965 to 1975 state and federal expenditures on health care more than quintupled, rising from $9 billion to $50 billion. Total expenditures on health care increased during this same period from $39 billion to $120 billion. Had the health legislation that was passed during this period been written in a different fashion—less to the liking of the health interest groups— health expenditures would likely have risen at a slower pace. This massive redistribution of income from patients and taxpayers to health professionals during this same period is an indication of the legislative success of health professionals. Yet few people would maintain that the level of health in the United States has risen as a result of these massive increases in health expenditures.

The belief that legislation can confer large monetary benefits to interest groups is not new. Nearly 200 years ago, in *The Federalist*, James Madison expressed this idea (Madison, 1787). The reason special-interest legislation is enacted is that the economic interests of producers are concentrated whereas the economic interests of consumers are diffused over the many areas of economic activity. The benefits to special-interest groups from legislation are potentially so large as to provide them with ample incentive to secure legislation on their behalf. The cost to each consumer from special-interest group legislation is relatively small, since the costs are spread over a great many consumers. The proponents of such legislation are rarely so bold as to admit that their incomes will be increased by imposing what is the equivalent of a tax on all consumers of their products. Instead, such legislation is presented as being in the public's or country's interests.

Whereas producers often receive their entire incomes from the products they produce, consumers rarely spend more than a small portion of their income on any one product; thus, their economic interests are considered diffuse. Further, for consumers to learn of the special-interest legislation that is being proposed, to ascertain the effects of such legislation on the prices they must pay for the affected products, and to inform other consumers and mobilize them against such legislation is clearly more costly to the consumer than any monetary benefits that would be derived from having the legislation defeated.

The beneficiaries of special-interest group legislation have been documented in a number of studies: Milk producers benefit from milk marketing boards, domestic producers benefit from tariffs on imported goods, maritime workers benefit from maritime subsidies, and northern industrial workers benefit from federal minimum wage legislation. A less obvious but no less important interest group that has benefited from legislation is health associations. The activities of such associations and their success in the legislative marketplace have been virtually unnoticed.

Because expenditures for medical care are a relatively small percentage of consumers' incomes, it is to their advantage to allocate their time and efforts to other activities that have a greater impact on their budgets and incomes. For health professionals, however, health legislation may affect a good share of their income. It is, therefore, in their interests to be involved in the legislative process by contributing money and time to political campaigns, testifying at legislative hearings, and providing information to legislators and the public on their positions.

Most health legislation that is of importance to health associations has been at a state level. This is to the advantage of the health associations, since opponents would have to organize and bear the necessary costs of becoming involved in the legislative process 50 times rather than once. What makes it even more difficult for the consumer to become involved in health legislation at a state level is that such legislation does not outwardly appear to affect the consumers' dollars. State practice acts, which define the tasks to be performed by different health professionals and set the requirements for licensure and state appropriations for medical, dental, and other health professional educational institutions, are policy decisions that appear to be too remote to affect the consumers' pocketbooks.

DEMAND FOR LEGISLATION BY HEALTH ASSOCIATIONS

To gain a better understanding of the type of health legislation that exists in the United States, it is necessary to develop a model of the demand for legislation by health interest groups. Such a framework should indicate the type of legislation different health associations would favor or oppose. If the framework presented is a fairly accurate predictor of the political behavior of different health associations, then it should also be possible to anticipate future legislative changes and the form that such legislation might take. The political behavior of two types of health associations will be examined: first, those health associations that represent the interests of health manpower professions, such as the American Medical Association, the American Dental Association, and the American Nurses' Association and, second, those associations that represent nonprofit providers, namely, the American Hospital Association, the Blue Cross Association (BCA), and the Association of American Medical Colleges (AAMC).

A framework of the demand for legislation will be presented to describe the specific types of health legislation that the various health associations desire. The necessity for having a framework is twofold: (1) It is not possible merely to state that health associations act in their own interests without first defining their interests, and (2) a model is required to indicate how particular legislation works to achieve those interests. Without such a framework, it is not always obvious how legislation promotes the interests of the health associations. The test of the validity of the proposed approach is how accurately the proposed framework predicts the political positions of the health associations. Finally, the implications of such a framework for explaining the political behavior of the health associations with regard to the structure, organization, and financing of medical care will be presented.

SEVERAL CAVEATS

Before discussing the economic model of political behavior, however, it is important to clarify certain situations in which the model would predict that an association would take a certain political position on legislation but it clearly ends up taking a different position. One such situation sometimes occurs when the preferred position of the association is found to be no longer politically possible, and other people and organizations propose positions that are much more to the disadvantage of the association's members. In such situations the current positions taken by the association will be recast to put it in a more favorable light than the alternative being proposed by others. An example of this has been the American Hospital Association's position on cost containment for hospitals. As will be shown, hospitals do not want constraints on what they can charge or on how fast their costs can rise. Although the American Hospital Association's favorable attitude toward prospective reimbursement might be considered a rejection of the proposed framework, when analyzed in terms of both the political climate of the government at the time and the attitudes of others toward hospital cost control, it can be seen that more severe approaches were being suggested and proposed in the form of legislation to place tighter constraints on hospitals. Thus, the American Hospital Association's willingness to accept some minor cost constraints is perfectly consistent with what the model would predict.

Another instance where the model would appear to be inaccurate, when in fact it is not, is when there has been a change in the perceived self-interest of the association's members. Such a change in self-interest would occur when the organization's very survival is threatened. An example of such a situation is Blue Cross's relationship to hospitals. Hospitals started Blue Cross to ensure payment for their services. In many cases, hospitals provided initial capital for Blue Cross, controlled the board of directors, and, until very recently, owned the Blue Cross emblem. One would therefore expect Blue Cross's self-interest to be synonymous with that of hospitals. However, during the last several years Blue Cross has come under attack for not performing its intermediary function adequately, that is, for not monitoring hospital costs or being an innovator in containing the rapid rise in hospital costs. Such behavior is not unexpected because hospitals controlled Blue Cross. But if Blue Cross is to survive as an intermediary under any national health insurance program, then it must demonstrate that it can do more than merely reimburse hospitals. In order to create a new image for itself and survive, Blue Cross has begun, at least in its public statements, to become an adversary of hospitals. Blue Cross's political positions have shifted during the last several years as it has had to redefine its self-interest in order to convince a skeptical group made up of government officials, legislators, unions, and industry that it can perform as an intermediary and should not be replaced in this function by a government agency. A similar situation has occurred with Blue Shield and its relationship to organized medicine.

There are two other minor situations in which it may appear that the political positions of a health association diverge from the self-interest of its members. The first is when an association is fearful that its continually negative position on legislation may be of greater cost to its members than any possible benefits to be derived from opposing it. An example of such a situation is the American Hospital Association's position on applying the minimum wage law to hospital employees. For many years, the AHA was successful in exempting hospitals from such legislation. More recently, however, it did not take a position when such legislation was once again being proposed to include hospital workers. One reason is that hospital workers were now being paid in excess of the minimum wage and so the effect of the AHA would have been small. More importantly, however, the AHA could see that this time such legislation was going to pass and, therefore, it would be a needless loss of political capital to oppose the legislation.

The second example of an association not opposing legislation that is inimical to the interests of its members occurs when it decides to go along with the desires of other health associations in hopes of receiving their support for legislation that is of greater importance to its members' interests. Such trade-offs would not be a refutation of the model's prediction that health associations act in their members' interests regardless of the effect on the "public" interest.

DEFINITION OF HEALTH ASSOCIATION MEMBERS' SELF-INTEREST

Since the predictions made by the economic framework are based on the premise that the health association will demand legislation according to the self-interest of its members, it is necessary to define more precisely the self-interest of the different health associations to be analyzed. Whether legislation has a positive, negative, or neutral effect on the association members' self-interest depends upon what the members perceive their interests to be.

When defining self-interest for a large number of health professionals such as physicians, dentists, and nurses or for organizations that may be quite diverse even though they are considered to be one type of institution such as hospitals, there is a natural tendency to make the definition complex so that it encompasses the diversity. If, however, the self-interest goals are complex or if new goals are specified for each separate piece of legislation, then it is not possible to develop a good predictive model. However satisfying a complex goal statement may be, it is easier to evaluate the effect of legislation using a relatively simply defined goal. Besides, unless the goal that the association is pursuing is easy for its membership to understand, the members may be distressed over the activities on which the association is spending their dues. The true test of whether the specified goal of the association is an accurate measure of the self-interest of its membership is how well the model is able to predict the legislative behavior of the association.

For purposes of this discussion, it is assumed that the legislative goals of the association are *maximization of the incomes of its current members*. Although health professionals have many goals, income in the only goal that all the health professionals in an association have in common. (Increased autonomy and control may be another goal, but it is highly correlated with increased incomes. Income is thus a more general goal.)

The goals or "self-interest" of the associations representing the nonprofit institutions (AHA, BCA, AAMC, and American Association of Dental Schools—AADS) must differ from those of the health professional associations, since such organizations cannot retain any "profits." Hospitals and medical and dental schools are assumed to be interested in *maximizing their prestige*. Prestige for hospitals is seen in terms of their size and the numbers and types of facilities and services. The availability of a full range of facilities and services also makes it easier for a hospital to attract physicians to its staff. Administrators of large prestigious hospitals are held in esteem by their peers and earn high incomes. Prestige for a medical school is usually defined as having students who wish to enter one of the specialties, most probably to become teachers and researchers themselves, having a faculty that is primarily interested in research, and having a low student–faculty ratio. Little prestige accrues to a medical school that trains students to enter general practice or practice in a rural area.

Blue Cross plans have a goal other than that of profit or prestige: It is assumed that Blue Cross seeks to *maximize its growth in enrollment and revenues*. A larger organization provides management with greater responsibility, which justifies greater management incomes. It is further assumed that prestigious hospitals and medical schools and large Blue Cross plans also have some form of satisfying behavior as a goal. For example, a Blue Cross plan with a high percentage of the health insurance market in its area can afford to be less concerned with efficiency. In prestigious hospitals and medical schools, the return to efficiency similarly falls as the organization approximates its prestige goals.

Although there are differences in the objectives of the health associations, the members of these associations all try to make as much money as possible, either to retain it themselves, as in the case of health professionals, or to expend it to achieve either prestige or growth goals. Thus, the model of demand for legislation is the same for all health associations. Basically, each health association attempts to achieve for its members through legislation what cannot be achieved through a competitive market, namely, a monopoly position. Increased monopoly power and the ability to price as would a monopolist seller of services is the best way for associations to achieve their goals.

HEALTH ASSOCIATION LEGISLATION

Specifically, there are five types of legislation a health association will demand. Four of these legislative actions have the effect of increasing the association members' revenues, whereas the fifth should decrease the member's costs of operation. Legislation to increase revenues is legislation that does the following: (1) increases the demand for the members' services, (2) causes an increase in the price of service that substitutes for those services produced by the members, (3) limits entry into the industry, and (4) enables the providers to charge the highest possible price for their services, such as by preventing competition based on prices and by charging different prices according to different purchasers willingness to pay (i.e., price discrimination). Legislative policies that lower the provider's cost of operation are as follows: (1) subsidies to the inputs used in the production of the providers' services and (2) changes in the state practice acts that allow for greater productivity of the inputs used in production. Each of these legislative policies will be discussed in more detail, and illustrative examples of legislative behavior of the various health associations will be given.

DEMAND-INCREASING LEGISLATION

An increase in demand along a given supply curve will result in an increase in price, an increase in total revenue, and, consequently, an increase in income or net revenue. The most obvious way of increasing the demand for the services of an association's members is to have the government subsidize the purchase of insurance for the provider's services. But rather than government coverage for all persons in the population, such as is done in the British National Health Service, the demand for insurance subsidies in the United States is always discussed in relation to specific population groups in society, namely, those persons with low incomes. The reason for selective government subsidies is twofold: First, those persons with higher incomes presumably have private insurance coverage or can afford to purchase the provider's services. The greatest increase in demand would result from extending coverage to those currently unable to pay for the services. Second, extending government subsidies to those currently able to pay for the services would greatly increase the cost of the program to the government. Greater commitment of government expenditures would result in greater government control over the provider's prices and use. Thus, for the purpose of increasing the demand for the provider's services, government subsidies are always requested in relation to specific population groups rather than for the population at large.[2] A related point is that health associations always want an intermediary between the government and the provider of services. The reason is the fear that the government would otherwise interfere in the setting of prices.

An example of such demand-increasing policies is the AMA's program for national health insurance (NHI), which proposed demand subsidies for low-income groups. A Further example of what is preferred by the health professional associations is the AMA's Blue Shield plan. The AMA initially started and controlled Blue Shield. Blue Shield only provided coverage for physician services and covered the patient's entire bill only if the patient's income was below a certain level. The physician was able to charge patients with higher incomes an amount above the Blue Shield fee. In this way, the physician was able to price discriminate, a factor that will be discussed in the following section.

Similarly, the ANA, whose members must work for other providers, has favored demand-increasing proposals that increase the demand for those institutions in which registered nurses work. Increased demand for hospital care will result in increased demand for registered nurses. The ANA has also favored policies that would increase the demand for registered nurses (RNs) directly, such as requiring increases in the use of RNs in hospitals and nursing homes. Another demand proposal favored by nurses in one that would increase their roles, that is increase the number of tasks they would be permitted to perform. If they are successful in this strategy, the demand for nurses will increase because their value will have increased in that they will be able to do more renumerative tasks. Because nurses will be able to be used more flexibly than before, one nurse can then perform the tasks that might have required the hiring of two different types of health professionals. As nurses and other health professionals try to increase their roles, they also wage a struggle in the legislative marketplace to prevent other health professionals from competing with them. One example is the attempt by optometrists to increase their role at the expense of ophtahalmologists. The health professional association that is successful in enabling its members to increase their role while preventing other health professionals from encroaching upon that role will assure an increased demand for its members' services and, consequently, higher incomes.

A major attempt made by the AHA to increase demand has been the establishment and control of the Blue Cross Association. Although the latter originally intended to pay for the costs of hospital care only, thereby lowering the costs of hospital care to consumers and increasing their demand for services, Blue Cross also assured that the hospitals would be paid for their services. Later, the AHA favored government subsidies for the aged under Medicare, which would have increased the demand for hospital care

---

[2]Even when demand subsidies are requested for a particular population group, it is proposed that such demand subsidies be phased in gradually. If the increase in demand is too large, this might create dissatisfaction among the patients because of the limited supply, prices and waiting times would tend to increase rapidly, possibly resulting in pressure on the government to enter the market. If the increase in demand is large, it may result in pressure to cause a greater increase in the number of providers than the association believes is in the best economic interests of its members.

by a high user population with generally low incomes. In doing so, the AHA sought government payment for such services through an intermediary (their own Blue Cross Association) rather than directly from the government, which would have gotten the government more directly involved with the hospitals' charges for Medicare patients.

SECURING THE METHOD OF HIGHEST REIMBURSEMENT

Whether the association members' goal is income, prestige, or growth, the method by which the provider is reimbursed is crucial to the attainment of that goal. High prices, netting larger revenues and increased incomes, facilitate the achievement of institutional objectives through the expenditure of those revenues. There are two basic approaches to being able to secure the highest possible reimbursement for services. The first is to charge different patients or payors different prices according to their ability to pay. This method of pricing, (price discrimination), will result in greater revenues than will a system of charging all patients the same price. The second approach is to preclude price competition among competing providers. Essential to price competition is the provider's ability to advertise differences in prices and any other differences in service, such as availability and competency measures. Price competition is most important for new practitioners or firms entering the area who must let potential patients know they are available and be able to attract them away from established providers. To prevent such competition from occurring, health professional associations have included advertising and other forms of competition in their practice acts as reasons for suspending practitioners' licenses and for assessing penalties for unethical behavior. Since such competitive behavior is not necessarily related to low quality, the inclusion of competitive behavior as part of the unethical practices for which a practitioner can be penalized can only be interpreted as a means of preventing price competition among providers.

Physicians and dentists have a strong preference for "usual, customary and reasonable" (UCR) fees. Such a method of pricing essentially lets the providers charge what the market will bear. Patients with higher incomes (who would be willing to pay more) can thus be charged higher fees than those with lower incomes, as has been the case with the use of Blue Shield income limits. In Kessel's (1958) classic article, "Price Discrimination in Medicine," he describes how county and state medical societies attempted to forestall the development of prepaid group practices, which are a form of massive price cutting since they offer to provide medical services at the same price to all people regardless of income. Similarly, Blue Shield in Spokane, Washington, boycotted physicians if they offered their services through a health maintenance organization (HMO). It ended its boycott only when ordered to do so by the Federal Trade Commission (FTC), acting on its belief that it was an anticompetitive tactic. It is interesting to note that the method that is proposed for payment of providers under proposed legislation is often crucial to its acceptance by the provider association.

The fee-for-service approach, based on UCR fees and used so successfully by the AMA, is being imitated by other health professional associations. Registered nurses are striving to become nurse practitioners who will be able to bill the patient directly under the fee-for-service approach. The ANA has attempted to secure such an amendment to the Medicare law. Other health professionals have also tried to gain the authority to bill under the fee-for-services. Such an approach, using UCR fees, which in most cases are reimbursed by the government or other third-party payor, is the most direct route for a health profession to increase its income.

The methods of reimbursement favored by the AHA for its members are ones that either discourage or do not provide consumers with any incentive to compare prices among different hospitals and methods that enable the hospitals to charge different payors different prices for their services. When hospitals started the Blue Cross Association, Blue Cross plans were required to offer consumers a service benefit plan. A service benefit provides the hospitalized patient with services rather than dollars. In so doing, it actually provides the consumer with an incentive to enter the most expensive hospital, since the services at such a hospital, which are presumably of higher quality, will not cost the consumer anything extra. Thus, under a service benefit policy, hospitals cannot compete for patients on the basis of prices.

If hospitals are to be able to generate sufficient funds to expand their facilities and services, then they must be able to set prices in excess of their costs. The manner in which this is done is to charge different prices to different payors and to set prices for different services according to what the market will bear, that is, according to price elasticity of demand. Hospitals thus prefer multiple sources of payment, rather than one major purchaser of their services, so that they can charge some payors higher prices for the same services. An example of this pricing behavior is to charge commercial insurers and patients responsible for their own bills higher rates than those charged to Blue Cross (which receives a discount) or to Medicare (which pays on the basis of ratio of charges to cost). Another method by which the hospital is able to use price discrimination in its rate setting is to set higher price–cost ratios for those services for which the demand is believed to be more price inelastic, such as ancillary services, than for services that are price elastic, such as obstetrics. That hosptials have used their pricing strategy to their benefit can be seen by the large increase in net revenues after Medicare was instituted. This resulted both from the favorable payments terms and from the inclusion in their reimbursement structure of previously unreimbursable expenses such as unfunded depreciation.

The use of community rating, which was orginally used by Blue Cross as a means of setting premiums, may also be viewed as a method of price discrimination. Under community rating, all groups are charged the same premium regardless of their utilization experience. High-user groups are thus subsidized by low-user groups. High-user groups are also, in many cases, groups of people with low incomes who can not afford to pay the higher premiums. This method of pricing has resulted in the largest enrollment for Blue Cross.

Medical and dental schools, as stated earlier, would rather be reimbursed by the federal and state governments for their costs than charge their students the full costs. The government, for one reason, has a much greater ability to pay than does the individual student. Further, unrestricted operating subsidies allow the school to produce the type of education the faculty prefers without having to respond to the demands of students. That the schools have been relatively successful in charging the government a monopoly price for their services is an observation supported by data that indicate that public medical schools receiving state support have higher per student costs than do private schools. Medical and dental schools are opposed to the government's providing those same subsidies directly to the student. If government subsidies went directly to the student, the student would be able to select the school and the schools would have to compete for students.

Under the current system of providing subsidies, the student can receive a subsidy only by attending a subsidized school. The current system guarantees the survival of the schools and requires the students, not the schools, to compete. Similar to their preference for receiving operating subsidies, the schools prefer to distribute loans and scholarships themselves rather than having the students apply directly to the government for such financial assistance.

LEGISLATION TO REDUCE THE PRICE AND/OR INCREASE THE QUANTITY OF HEALTH MANPOWER COMPLEMENTS

It is difficult in medical care to know when an input, such as a nurse, is a complement or a substitute based just on the task to be performed. A nurse may be as competent as a physician to perform certain tasks; if the nurse works for the physician, however, and the physician receives the fee for the performance of the task, then the nurse is a complement and will increase the physician's productivity. If, however, the nurse performs the same task and is a nurse practitioner operating and billing independently of the physician, then the nurse is a substitute for the physician in providing that service. The essential element in determining whether an input is a complement or a substitute is who controls the use of that input and who receives reimbursement for the services provided by that input.

The legal authority for the different tasks each health profession can perform and the source of stipulations defining under whose direction health professionals must work are the state practice acts. A major legislative activity for each health association is to seek changes in the state practice acts; health associations representing complements attempt to have their members become substitutes, whereas other health associations whose members currently control complements seek to retain the status quo. For the physician, almost all of the health professions and health institutions are complements; nurses and optometrists are examples of professionals who desire to expand their scope of practice and to practice independently of physicians.

With an increase in the demand for health services, providers can increase their incomes if that increased demand is met through greater productivity on their part rather than through an increase in the number of competing providers. The providers' incomes can be increased still further if their productivity increases are subsidized and if they do not have to pay the full cost of increasing their productivity. Examples of legislation that would have the effect of subsidizing increased productivity are educational subsidies, capital subsidies, and changes in the state practice acts to permit greater delegation of tasks. The AHA, for example, has favored the Nurse Training Act (NTA), which in subsidizing the training of RNs resulted in a greater supply of nurses. With a greater number of nurses, nurses' wages would be lower than they might otherwise have been. The AHA has favored both the Hill-Burton program, which provided captial subsidies to modernize hospitals, and educational subsidies to increase the supply of allied health professionals. The AHA has opposed legislative actions that would have increased the hospitals' costs of inputs. It opposed the extension of minimum wage legislation to hospital employees and has called for a moratorium on the separate licensing of each health professional. (Separate licensing of each health professional would limit the hospital's ability to substitute persons and to use such persons in a more flexible manner.)

The AMA has similarly favored both subsidies to hospitals, because hospitals are inputs to physicians, and increases in the supply of RNs under the Nurse Training Act. However, the AMA has opposed the increased educational standards that the ANA wanted to impose on nursing institutions as a condition for receiving funds under the

Nurse Training Act. Higher educational standards for nurses do not necessarily increase the productivity of nurses, but they do limit the supply of nurses and increase the nurse's qualifications as a substitute for the physician.

An interesting example of the AMA's attitude toward a new complement is its position on the physician's assistant (PA). Physician's assistants are potential substitutes for the physician if they practice independently. Thus, the AMA wants to ensure that the fee from services rendered by the PA always goes to the physician. In fact, whether there is direct or indirect supervision of the PA is less important to the AMA in determining its political position toward this new category of health professionals than is who gets the fee. Another important characteristic of the AMA's attitude toward the use of PAs is whether or not the introduction of such personnel in an area will create excess capacity among physicians in the community, resulting in greater competition among them for patients. If the physician did not have sufficient demand to keep as busy as he or she would like, then the introduction of inputs that would increase the physician's productive capacity would be against the interest of those physicians who would like to be busier. However, as 'demand for physician (and dental) services increases, there will be a greater tendency to allow productivity to occur.

Similarly, state practice acts are changed to permit greater delegation of tasks as demand for physicians or dentists increases. One would expect to find those state practice acts with the least delegatory authority in those states in which there is the lowest level of demand per practitioner. The introduction of new types of health professionals and methods to increase productivity is more related to local demand conditions than to the competence of such personnel to perform the tasks for which they were trained.

The AAMC has been relatively successful in its demands for input subsidies. Medical schools have received subsidies for construction, research (which has been used to subsidize teaching programs), teaching hospitals, and the cost of education. It has only been recently that these schools have had to provide something in return for these subsidies. The subsidies received from the states are still unrestricted; however, to continue receiving federal capitation grants the schools had to provide for small enrollment increases. The enrollment increase requirement was later changed and instead the medical schools had to ensure that a certain percentage of their graduating class would practice in underserved areas. The schools have opposed all conditions attached to receiving government subsidies. It is not surprising that the schools have been more successful in their legislative efforts at a state level than at a federal level, where it is relatively easier for opponents to lobby against the schools with Congress.

Blue Cross's main political activity directed toward lowering the price of its inputs has been to favor the development and strengthening of hospital planning agencies. Because Blue Cross reimburses hospitals according to their costs, hospitals have an incentive to add facilities and services and merely pass the costs of these additional services on to Blue Cross and its subscribers, who must then pay higher health insurance premiums. In a number of cases, the addition of facilities and services, and even bed capacity, is duplicative in the community in which they are built. Hospitals compete among themselves for physicians and patients. (And since the hospitals are reimbursed on an individual cost basis and the patient has no incentive under a service benefit policy to select the lowest-cost hospitals, the process of adding duplicate beds and facilities can continue.) Blue Cross's premium consists almost entirely of the costs of hospital care. To remain competitive against commercial insurance companies whose premiums are comprised of a smaller portion of hospital care and whose policies may reimburse patients a fixed dollar amount rather than the complete costs of their hospitalization, it is in Blue Cross's interests to keep the cost of hospital care (both hospital use and the cost per unit) from rising.

Because of the traditional relationship Blue Cross has had with hospitals, it is difficult for Blue Cross to monitor hospital costs directly. An alternative, indirect approach to restraining the cost of the Blue Cross premium and one that would *not* be opposed by the major hospitals in areas in which Blue Cross operates, is to prevent the development of new hospitals and the expansion of beds and facilities in smaller existing hospitals. The existing large hospitals either have the latest facilities and services or would be the likely candidates to receive the approval of the planning agency to add such facilities. As a means of restraining competition; these large hospitals would favor the strengthening of planning agencies. Limiting the increase in hospital beds and the addition of services, whose costs Blue Cross would have to pay even if they were duplicative, would hold down both hospital use and Blue Cross premiums. Although Blue Cross has been a strong advocate of limiting hospital use and duplicative facilities and services, its efforts to date have been less than successful in limiting the rise in hospital costs.

LEGISLATION TO DECREASE THE AVAILABILITY AND/OR INCREASE THE PRICE OF SUBSTITUTES

Any health association will attempt to have the price of a service increased (or its availability decreased) that is considered to be a substitute for the services delivered by its members. If it is successful in doing so, then the demand for services provided by its members will be increased. Three general approaches are used in the legislative arena to accomplish these goals. The first is to have the substitute service declared illegal. If substitute health professionals are not permitted to practice or if substitutes are severely restricted in the tasks they are legally permitted to perform, then there will be a shift in demand away from the substitute service. The second approach, usually used when the first one is unsuccessful, is to exclude the substitute service from coverage for payment by a third party, including any government health programs. This latter policy raises the price of the substitute to a person who is eligible to purchase that service under the third-party coverage. The last approach is to try to raise the costs of the substitute, thereby necessitating a higher price for the services if the substitute is to remain in business. Examples to illustrate the political behavior of health associations in each of these areas will be provided.

For many years, the AMA regarded osteopaths as cultists. It was considered unethical for physicians to teach in schools of osteopathy. Unable to prevent their licensure at a state level, however, the AMA attempted to deny osteopaths hospital privileges. A physician substitute is less than adequate if that substitute cannot provide a complete range of treatment. As osteopaths developed their own hospitals and educational institutions, the medical societies decided that the best approach to controlling this potential increase in the supply of physician substitutes was to merge with the osteopaths, make them physicians, and thereby eliminate any future increases in their supply. An example of this approach, which was used in California until it was overturned by the California Supreme Court, was to allow osteopaths to convert their Doctor of Osteopathy degree to

Doctor of Medicine degree on the basis of 12 Saturday refresher courses. After a merger between the medical and osteopathic societies occurred in California, the Osteopathic Board of Examiners was no longer permitted to license osteopaths.

Optometrists and chiropractors are potential substitutes for ophthalmologists and family practitioners. One approach used by the AMA toward such substitutes has been to attempt to raise their price relative to that of physicians. Medicare, which reduces the price of physician services to the aged under Part B, has been the vehicle for much legislative competition. The AMA has long fought to prevent both the optometrists and chiropractors from qualifying as providers under Part B, thereby effectively raising their price to the aged relative to that of physicians, whose services are reimbursable.

An example of the legislative behavior of dental societies toward substitute providers is illustrated by dentistry's actions toward denturists. Denturism is the term applied to the fitting and dispensing of dentures directly to patients by persons who are not licensed as dentists. Independently practicing denturists are a threat to dentists' incomes, since they offer dentures at lower prices than do dentists. Dentists have, however, been successful in having denturism declared illegal. (Denturists are legal in seven out of Canada's 10 provinces. As a result of their success in Canada, denturists in the United States have become bolder by attempting to have certain state practice acts changed to permit them to practice.) Occasionally, denturists illegally sell dentures to patients. To combat this potential competition, local dental societies, such as those in Texas, have responded in two ways: First, they have offered to provide low-cost dentures to low-income people, and, second, they have pressured state officials to enforce state laws against illegal denturists.

A special ADA commission set up to study the threat of denturists reported that the number of people who are edentulous is much greater in the lower-income levels, and it is among these people that the denturists have met with great success in selling low-cost dentures. An editorial in the *Journal of the American Dental Association* (1976, p. 665) commenting on this special study commission's report proposed the following:

> Organized dentistry should set up some system for supplying low-cost dentures to the indigent or the near indigent all over the [United States], but expecially in those states where the legislatures are considering bills that would allow dental mechanics to construct dentures and deliver them directly to the patient. . . . This is the type of program that would have a favorable impact on the public—not to mention legislators. . . .The supplying of dentures to low income patients by qualified dentists at a modest fee (or even at no fee in special cases) and in quantities meeting the public demands would go a long way toward heading off the movement for legalized denturists.

It is only the threat of competition that results in the dental profession's offer to provide low-cost dentures to the indigent or near indigent. If this competitive threat by denturists is eliminated through dentistry's successful use of the state's legal authority, the net effect will be to cause the public to pay higher prices for dentures.

One of the most important substitutes for registered nurses training in this country is the foreign-trained RN. Because nursing salaries are considerably higher in the United States than in many other countries, there is a financial incentive for foreign nurses to come to the United States. The manner in which the ANA has tried to decrease the availability of a low-cost substitute for nurses trained in the United States has been to make it more difficult for foreign nurses to enter the United States. The ANA has attempted to have the Department of Labor remove the preferential status of foreign nurses from the immigration regulations. The ANA has also proposed that foreign nurses who wish to enter the United States be screened by examination in their home country before being allowed to enter. The ANA's advocacy of screening before admittance to the United States, where the nurses would again be screened by having to pass state board examinations, is consistent with a policy of reducing the inflow of foreign nurses. If the screening examination were administered in the United States, then foreign nurses could still work in some nursing capacity even if they did not pass the examination, and they could then retake it in the future. Establishing an additional screening mechanism before nurses emigrate erects another barrier to nurses' entering the United States; if they do not pass the examination, they are unlikely to emigrate.

Another legislative tactic used by the ANA is to prevent other personnel from undertaking nursing tasks performed by RNs. The ANA has opposed policies that would have permitted physicians to have greater delegatory authority over which personnel can perform nursing tasks; the ANA has opposed permitting licensed practical nurses to be in charge of skilled nursing homes, since this would cause substitutions for RNs who currently perform such functions; the California Nurses' Association opposed a bill that would have authorized fire fighters with paramedic training to give medical and nursing care in hospital emergency departments; and the ANA, as a means of preventing PAs from moving into a role that the ANA would like to see reserved for RNs, has favored a licensing moratorium. Such a moratorium would prevent any new health personnel from being licensed to undertake tasks that RNs perform or would like to be permitted to perform.

Examples of the approach used by the AHA to raise the price of substitutes has been to oppose free-standing surgicenters and to attempt to raise the relative price of for-profit hospitals to patients. *Surgicenters* are outpatient surgical facilities and, therefore, low-cost substitutes for hospitals. Any increase in the use of surgicenters will decrease the demand for inpatient care. In order to limit the availability of such low-cost substitutes, hospitals have argued that surgicenters should be permitted only when they are developed *in association* with hospitals. In this manner, hospitals would be able to control the growth of a competitive source of care, and they would be able to benefit (since presumably they would operate the substitute service) as such surgicenters develop. Hospitals have also favored including surgicenters under certificate-of-need legislation. If such substitutes were subject to the approval of planning agencies, which are heavily influenced by the hospitals in the community, then it is unlikely that a low-cost substitute would be permitted to develop. The existing hospitals would claim that the growth of these institutions would leave them with excess inpatient surgical facilities, which, under cost-based reimbursement, the community (through Blue Cross) would have to pay for anyway.

Methods used by nonprofit hospitals to raise the cost of a substitute are to oppose the granting of tax-exempt status to for-profit hospitals, thereby raising their costs, and to oppose granting Blue Cross eligibility to for-profit hospitals or even to new nonprofit hospitals when the existing nonprofit hospitals claim that there are sufficient beds in an area. Denying third-party reimbursement to potential or actual competitors in effect precludes the use of the facilities by patients whose costs of hospitalization would be reimbursed if they entered a hospital that was eligible for Blue Cross reimbursement.

The political position of Blue Cross with respect to substitutes is similar. Blue Cross would favor having the Social Security Administration (SSA) excluded, by law, from being able to compete with Blue Cross and Blue Shield as intermediaries under any government payment program. Further, Blue Cross opposes granting to commercial insurers the same tax-exempt status that Blue Cross plans enjoy, which causes their competitors' costs to be increased.

LEGISLATION TO LIMIT INCREASES IN SUPPLY

Essential to the establishment of a monopoly position are limits on the number of providers of a service. The justification given by health associations for supply–control policies is that they ensure high-quality care to patients. At the same time, however, these health associations oppose quality measures that would have an adverse effect upon existing providers. This apparent anomaly—stringent entry requirements and then virtually no quality-assurance programs directed at existing providers—can be consistent only with a policy that seeks to establish a monopoly position for existing providers. If the health associations were consistent in their desire to improve and maintain high-quality standards, they should favor all policies that ensure quality. Quality control measures directed at existing providers, such as reexamination, relicensure, and monitoring of the care actually provided, would adversely affect the incomes of some providers; more importantly, such "outcome" measures of quality assurance would make the entry or process measures unnecessary, and thereby permit larger numbers of providers into the industry.

The following examples illustrate measures to assure quality that are in the interests of the members of a health association and those that are not and are, therefore, opposed by the association. The health professions are always in favor of licensing. The profession ends up controlling the licensure process by setting the necessary requirements for licensure and having members of the profession itself comprise the licensing board. Once licensing requirements have been legislated at a state level, the profession, through its representatives on the licensing board, imposes additional requirements. The major requirement is that before any person can take a licensing examination, he or she must have had a specified education, usually of a minimum number of years (which keeps increasing), and this education must have taken place in an educational institution approved by the profession or its representatives. The number of educational institutions is always limited so that, as in medicine and dentistry, there is continually an excess demand by applicants for admission. Limiting the number of educational spaces and specifying an educational curriculum that imposes training requirements in excess of the skills required to practice in the profession reduces the number of people who can take the licensing examination. If the licensure requirement just specified passing an examination, then potential practitioners could secure the necessary knowledge in a number of different ways, in different lengths of time, and in different institutions. In such a situation, the number of people who could potentially take the examination and pass it would be much greater than if the number of those applying to take the examination were limited by the number of approved educational spaces.

The foregoing policies have been successfully developed in medicine and dentistry. Nursing is also moving in this direction through attempts to require that nursing education take place only in colleges that offer a baccalaureate degree. Previously, the predominant place of education for a nursing degree was in a diploma school, generally operated in conjunction with a hospital. By proposing that the educational requirement for nursing be increased, the ANA must be well aware that fewer nurses will be trained since the costs of training have increased (and people trained for a baccalaureate degree might decide to receive training for a profession other than nursing). The ANA also must be aware that with the additional training it would presumably be easier to justify having nurses perform additional tasks, thereby increasing nurses' incomes.

At times the professions impose requirements on new entrants into the profession that are blatant barriers to entry. Examples of such requirements are U.S. citizenship for foreign medical and dental graduates in order to practice in some states and a 1-year residency requirement if a duly trained and licensed professional, such as a dentist, wishes to practice in another state, such as Hawaii. Such requirements cannot be remotely related to a concern for quality. The current method of quality assurance for health professionals is aimed solely at entry into the profession rather than at monitoring the quality of care practiced by the professionals. The inadequate performance of state licensing boards in disciplining their members is evidence of this practice. The public is less protected against unethical and incompetent practitioners than it has been led to believe.

Hospitals, medical and dental schools, and Blue Cross plans are also advocates of supply-control policies, since they provide these institutions with a monopoly position in their market. Since such institutions cannot achieve a monopoly position through the normal competition of the marketplace, they seek to achieve it through legislation. Large hospitals favor certificate-of-need (CON) legislation. The CON agencies, which are likely to be controlled by the administration of the large existing hospitals, will use legislative authority to limit the growth of potential competitors in their areas. With fewer providers in a community, patients will have less choice among providers and the existing providers will more easily be able to increase their costs and prices. The survival of existing hospitals will also be assured, since competing hospitals will have been excluded. Larger hospitals are likely to be favored over smaller hosptials in their re-quests for the addition of specialized facilities. Because many specialized facilities are useful to a limited number of patients in the community, it is likely that a larger hospital will be able to justify having the facility more easily than will a smaller one; also, larger hospitals are more likely to have complementary facilities that may be required for new specialized services. The CON legislation does not control the increase in hospital costs; it merely restricts expansion and additions to capacity and facilities. If another mecha-nism to control the large annual increases in hospital costs must be found, why not use this mechansim to determine which hospital is most efficient and which has the demand that would warrant adding beds and new facilities?

CONCLUDING COMMENTS

Because the separate members of each of the health associations cannot achieve a monopoly position through the normal competitive process, they seek to achieve it through legislation. They then attempt to improve their monopoly position by further demanding legislation that will increase the demand for their services, permit them to price as would a price-discriminating monopolist, lower their costs of doing business, and disadvantage their competitors either by causing them to become illegal providers or by raising their prices. Health associations have been relatively successful in the legislative arena, as is indicated by the large sums of money being spent on their services and by their members' positions in society's income distribution. What are the costs or implications to the rest of society of the success of these interest groups in the legislative marketplace?

THE OUTLOOK FOR LEGISLATIVE CHANGE IN MEDICAL CARE

The incentive and reason for the legislative success of health associations is that the benefits to their members are greater than the costs imposed on individual consumers. Proposed legislative changes that would remove the monopoly protection that members of health associations currently enjoy would be difficult to achieve. Because the members of the health associations have more to lose than the individual has to gain from such legislative changes, they will be more involved in trying to prevent such legislative changes.

Are there alternative approaches to structural change in the delivery system that will achieve the twin goals of quality assurance and minimum cost? One proposal that has been suggested is to place consumers on health institutions and licensing boards. I believe this to be a false panacea. Even assuming that consumer representatives would know the most efficient manner of structuring the delivery system (which is unlikely), it is improbable that they would be effective. Consumers are currently represented on all the boards mentioned. To date, the consumers have not been able to make Blue Cross plans more aggressive in their monitoring of hospital costs, they have not been able to deter their hospitals from establishing duplicative facilities and services, nor have they moved licensing boards to become more active in disciplining their errant members. Consumers are usually nominated by the professions or administrators of the institutions themselves, and it is far easier to remove a particular board member than for a particular board member to change the performance of the profession. Consumers also do not have all the necessary information; they must rely on the professionals and administrators themselves for the appropriate information. Thus it is difficult to conclude that improved performance of an institution or a profession will be in proportion to the number of consumers on their boards.

Another approach that has been suggested to improve the performance of the delivery system is to have greater government intervention and regulation of the industry or profession. When one examines the performance of regulatory agencies in other fields, it can be observed that these agencies rarely perform in the consumer's interests. Such agencies are either captured by the industries they are meant to regulate or respond in a manner that seeks to mimimize outside conflict. There is no reason to believe that health care regulatory agencies would perform any differently. A growing body of evidence with regard to certificate-of-need agencies and state agencies responsible for regulating nursing homes has not produced the hoped for accomplishments. It is unlikely that additional government regulation would succeed any better.

Certain other developments may have some beneficial effects in the legislative marketplace. The first of these is the involvement of a greater number of interest groups in the legislative process. The success of the AMA and the ADA has not gone unnoticed by other health professional associations. Greater competition among health associations in the legislative process is occurring. As more health associations attempt to increase the benefits to their members through changes in the various state practices acts, the cost to the AMA and ADA of preventing such changes increases. The possible gains to these other health associations from becoming substitutes for, rather than complements to, the physician and dentist are very large. They are becoming more willing to assess their members the necessary costs to compete for legislative changes.

Other interest groups that are becoming more active are industry, unions, and the states themselves. As the costs of health care continue to rise at a rapid rate, such costs, when embodied in wage agreements as fringe benefits, are passed on to the worker in terms of lower wages (since the cost of the fringe benefits have increased) and to the consumer in terms of higher prices for manufactured goods (since the wage costs of producing these goods and services have increased). Unions, to receive higher wages for their members, and industry, so as not to have to raise the prices of its products, have become more concerned with the rise in costs of medical services. In the past, certain large unions have attempted to resolve this problem by proposing to shift the costs of medical care to the federal government through national health insurance. It is increasingly being recognized, however, that the costs of health care cannot be completely shifted to other taxpayers and that a significant part of that cost will be borne by industry and labor (ultimately, by consumers) through various payroll taxes. Because both industry and labor are affected by the rise in medical costs and because the costs to each of them of gathering the necessary information and participating in the legislative process are much less than the possible benefits if they are successful in reducing the rise in medical costs, it would be expected that they would become even more active participants in the legislative process.

Several large states have been greatly affected by their share of the cost of administering the Medicaid program. The annual cost to certain states for Medicaid is in excess of $1 billion. These funds are no longer available to meet the demands of other interest groups within a state, and to continue paying such large amounts of money each year may necessitate increases in the state income tax. If these states cannot shift this burden to the federal government, they will become very interested in making legislative changes that will ease their burden.

It is possible that because of the rise of new health interest groups—industry, unions, and the states themselves—there will be greatly increased competition in the legislative process. As a result of this competition, more information will be provided by the different interest groups regarding the cost, quality, and efficiency of different systems of delivery for medical services. It is thus more likely that changes in the state practice acts and in the delivery system will be possible in the future.

A second development related to the foregoing is the role of the government in quality assurance. As more information has become available on the poor performance of health associations in monitoring (through their licensing boards) the quality of care practiced by their members, the government has become more involved. An example of this involvement is professional standards review organization (PSRO) legislation. At a state level it is likely that there will be changes in the state's role in assurance of quality of care. As different health associations seek to become licensed and establish their own licensing boards, there is an awakening interest in preventing this proliferation, which would create an inflexible system to decide which people can perform specific tasks. Some states are moving in the direction of *combining* licensing boards, with a number of different provider groups having representation on those boards. It is possible that such licensing boards would allow greater delegation of tasks and would become more flexible in the prerequisites for licensure. It is hoped that such boards would begin to monitor the quality of care practiced.

In the past, the states have delegated their responsibility for protecting the public from unqualified practitioners to the separate health professions. The states should not be allowed to abrogate their responsibilities in this manner. The state agency responsible for this function should be required to develop performance measures to determine how well it performs its monitoring function. Further, the legislature should hold annual oversight hearings on the performance of the responsible state agency. If this were to occur, interested people, as well as organized interest groups, would be able to participate (at a low cost) in the process of structuring the delivery system and in quality assurance. To further ensure that the responsible state agencies perform their tasks of quality assurance, patients and consumers should have recourse to the courts. Greater publicity and accountability in the area of quality assurance should permit changes and innovations in the delivery system that have in the past been inhibited by health associations whose members' monopoly position would have been adversely affected.

REFERENCES

Feldstein, Paul J., *Health Care Economics*, New York: John Wiley & Sons, 1981.

Feldstein, Paul J., "A Preliminary Evaluation of Federal Dental Manpower Subsidy Programs," *Inquiry*, Vol. 11, No. 3, September 1974, pp. 196–206.

Feldstein, Paul J., *Health Associations and the Demand for Legislation: The Political Economy of Health*, Lexington, Mass.: Ballinger Publishing Co., 1977.

Journal of the American Dental Association, "Action Urgently Needed on Denturist Movement," (editorial), *Journal of the American Dental Association*, Vol. 92, 1976, p. 665.

Kessel, Reuben, "Price Discrimination in Medicine," *Journal of Law and Economics*, October 1958.

Madison, James, *Federalist No. 10*, 1787.

CHAPTER 12

The Citizen Role in Health Politics: Democratic Wishes and Sensible Reforms

James A. Morone

Citizen participation seems a simple idea: If the public is to have a genuine say about societal institutions, it must have that say directly. In the United States, it is a notion with intellectual roots that range from Rousseau to the Students for a Democratic Society (SDS) (Rousseau, 1968; Hayden, 1962), a political heritage that stretches back to the Progressive Era at the start of the twentieth century. Yet neither clear philosophical exposition nor repeated historical experience has resulted in contemporary clarity about broad-based citizen action.

Citizens involvement in government received widespread attention—and notoriety—when the Johnson administration established the Community Action Agencies to carry the War on Poverty into U.S. communities. The agencies were required to provide "maximum feasible participation" by community members. Despite the pyrotechnic community politics that followed, the notion of citizen involvement spread swiftly.[1] Government officials were supplemented by open meetings, special public task forces, boards of citizens, and all manner of required hearings. Programs in every policy area and on every level of government were directed to include the citizenry in their deliberations.[2] By 1975 over half the states had offices coordinating citizen participation programs. President Carter endorsed the trend with an executive order that required "broad opportunities for public participation" (Langton, 1978, p. 5).

In health politics, citizen action progressed more slowly. Hospitals constructed with federal funds were ostensibly required to tap community sentiment as early as 1946.[3] But this vague intimation of participation went largely ignored. In 1966, the

---

[1]For descriptions of the Community Action Program and its politics see Moynihan, 1969; Greenstone and Peterson, 1973.

[2]There are, of course, many different ways that government can institutionalize citizen involvement. For efforts to sort out some differences see Morone and Marmor (1981) and Checkoway (1981a).

[3]The Hospital Survey and Construction Act of 1946 (better known as Hill-Burton). See discussion in Rosenblatt (1978).

Comprehensive Health Planning Act encouraged local agencies to rationalize local health systems with citizen—termed consumer—involvement. However, local health providers quickly dominated the agencies (as they had long dominated local health politics). Citizens were placed on the boards of community mental health centers, neighborhood health centers, and a series of other small programs.[4]

In 1974 consumers were given a larger role. Infused with a Watergate-inspired enthusiasm for reform and alarmed by soaring health care costs, Congress passed the National Health Planning and Resources Development Act of 1974 (PL 93-641). The law mandated considerable public involvement in local health care policy. It appeared to sweep citizens from the peripheries to the center of local health care politics.

That new place did not last long. The National Health Planning Act, and more generally, the entire wave of citizen action reform ended with the ascent of the Reagan administration. However, Republican hostility is hardly the major pitfall confronting reformers.

If citizen action is easy—and occasionally fashionable—to mandate, it is extremely difficult to implement. Similar problems repeatedly snare citizen action efforts. This chapter is about those problems, about what citizen action has been and could become. First, the problems that have bedeviled reform are presented: confused goals, naiveté about power and politics, and a lack of respect for the crushing implications of modern organization; then, how these difficulties affected the National Health Planning Act are considered. The purpose is to describe both the pitfalls into which reformers repeatedly stumble and the promises that their efforts could hold. In an increasingly bureaucratized society there are important uses for citizen action. Past efforts may delineate the course of successful future reforms. But this can be achieved only after some old difficulties have been fully resolved.

HISTORICAL ROOTS OF REFORM

Recent reforms introduce precisely the same "goo-goo" illusions that characterized the Progressive Era. Goo-goo reformers—the term is a derogatory abbreviation of good government—were also plagued by ill-defined goals. political naiveté, and the organizational forms that their innovations took.

The Progressives' dilemma lay in the paradox at the center of their major reform proposal. They sought to overcome the private domination of public institutions by bringing government closer to the people (through referenda, recall mechanisms, etc.) and at the same time they attempted to shift policy from politically charged arenas to neutral nonpolitical ones. Public choices would be made in organizations structured beyond politics in which the techniques of scientific management could be applied. There was no cognizance of the tension between the two reform principles—choices were simultaneosuly turned over to broad publics and apolitical professionals (McConnell, 1966).

Fifty years later, the same reforms were prescribed. The designers of the National Health Planning Act explicitly sought to wed scientific planning techniques to community participation. The problems of the health system—inflation, inadequate access—

---

[4]For example, the 1966 Regional Medical Program, the 1971 Experimental Health Services Delivery Program, and the Emergency Medical Services Program all incorporated citizen volunteers, though seldom in a manner that was central to the agencies operation. For a discussion see Altman et al. (1981).

could be solved with a mixture of techincal methods and town meetings. To be sure, participation is now far more ambitiously conceived; entire populations are to get an opportunity to construct, or at least comment on, public policy. And the intellectual heirs of scientific management wield cost–benefit analyses and planning methodologies. Yet the conceptions remain unchanged: public participation, bolstered by technical expertise, organized beyond politics, smashing selfish private power in search of public good(s).

The problems remain as well. Without a positive vision of the public good, the major policy guide is the policymaking process itself. When concentrated producers— robber barons for the Progressives, hospital associations for contemporary health system reformers—dominate the process, policy will be biased. But how precisely are the reformers' alternatives to operate in practice? How and why are citizens to be empowered?

WHY PARTICIPATION? THE UNCERTAIN PURPOSES OF REFORM

Direct participatory governance is often criticized. It is unprofessional by definition. Where it is successful it is contentious (for more issues are raised, more interests injected). Like many amateur enterprises, it is slow, inefficient, marked by ignorance and often apathy (at times, even achieving a quorum can be a milestone). It bypasses and threatens established (powerful) institutions. And though returning governance to the governed sounds fine, the consequent politics are often less democratic than the institutions that are being supplemented. There are reasons to suspect that the "public" speaking at a hearing is less representative than a public opinion poll. Thus, beneath the sweeping rhetoric of broad representation or maximum participation lies a throng of difficulties.

What is the defense for citizen participation? There are many, often jumbled together, not because citizen participation is a poor idea, but because it is several ideas, some good, others not.

DEMOCRATIC PARTICIPATION

The most radical and sweeping theory contends that people are fully citizens only when they govern themselves directly. The process of participation itself enhances the public, engendering a sense of civic virtue. More important, the common good is freed from the mire of narrow self-interests. When the public governs, the public will dominates. If citizen masses are initially clumsy in their rule, the actual exercise of authority is expected to steady them (Rousseau, 1968; Pateman, 1970; Cole, 1920).

The conceptual key is direct participation. Representation is rejected. "No man's will can be treated as a substitute for, or representative of the will of others" (Pateman, 1970). Government for the people must literally be governance by them.[5]

The democratic argument is often eloquent. But the quest remains illusory. The

---

[5]These theories of direct participation are often cast as contrasts to orthodox democratic theory. The prevailing view, articulated by Joseph Schumpeter (1942) and Robert Dahl (1964) contends that public preferences are most likely to be articulated by officials competing for public approval.

contemporary citizenry will not, cannot, play out this vision of Athenian democracy. It is subverted by stubborn political realities. Issues are complex, fragmented, and persistent. Those who have more invested will, over time, care most—invest most—in the relevant politics. Over time, producer interests tend to win. Hospitals seeking to expand or pharmaceutical firms marketing new drugs will attend public meetings, regardless of inconvenient hours, with lawyers and experts and charts. The public will not do so regularly. They have their own livelihoods to which to attend.

Proponents of participatory democracy retort that the incremental changes implicit in contemporary reform are not appropriate tests for broad theories of societal behavior. Yet, in a vague, often unarticulated fashion, it is precisely their theories that drive the reform. The vision of sweeping citizen action has repeatedly proved seductive to advocates tinkering with policymaking institutions.

The fundamental lesson of public participation is repeatedly taught, repeatedly forgotten. New programs, incorporating new types of policy forums designed to harness civic energy, are launched with great expectations. A short time thereafter, "the hidden price tag of public participation" is ruefully admitted (Cooper, 1979). It is one of the oldest lessons in U.S. political thought: Those with more at stake care more, commit more resources to policy debates. Many successful policy reforms have emerged in the past decade; few of them are rooted in the Rousseauian ideal of mass citizen participation.

COMPETETIVE INTERESTS

A second notion is less eloquent but more practicable. The premise remains the same Progressive critique: Institutions ostensibly making public choices spurn the public interest. Hospitals are motivated more by the imperatives of organizational maintenance than community needs. Political actors, mindful or powerful medical constituencies, too readily champion local providers. Public health bureaucracies are hierarcical and aloof; their concerns are typically bureaucratic—maximizing budgets, adding bodies, avoiding blunders.

The reformers response is to place members of the public directly into public institutions. Citizens sit on governing boards, advisory panels, and ad hoc committees throughout the institutional apparatus of contemporary society. The more power they achieve, the better. Citizens are represented (there is no effort to achieve complete participation) by other citizens who are avowed amateurs. It is precisely their amateur quality that, as when serving on a jury, is expected to lift them beyond narrow self-interested politics. The public interest is best sought by individuals representing (and in some variations of the theory, representative of) the public.

There are practical difficulties: The jury analogy obscures the need for political skills, for these are political positions. The amateurs are immediately confronted by experts, ostentatiously displaying their expertise. They feel pressure from entrenched interests without countervailing support from the public they represent. Their legitimacy is assailed by threatened administrators. Each of these challenges is significant. When legitimacy is questioned, for example, what conception of democracy is to bolster a citizen's claim to represent the public more effectively than established public institutions (like a department of health)? Against all expectations, recent experience suggests that none of these problems is irresistable. Structured properly, consumer representation can survive, even thrive, despite hostility from professionals.

However, a more fundamental, more perplexing problem remains. How are citizen representatives to pursue the public interest? How will they know when they have found it? Not sharing the narrow interests of producers proves no decision rule when the public good is in dispute—and in politics, it rarely is not. In short, for what are consumer representatives to fight? The planning law is tellingly elliptical, even in its definition of consumers, that is, a consumer is one who is not a provider and is not married to one. Surely this is no help to representatives seeking a guide for action.

One facile and unsatisfying solution is the simple call for more. Consumer representatives stand for consumer representation. Hospitals can be judged by the number of consumers who sit on their boards; agencies can be judged by the advisory committees they amass. Representatives call for still more. In some places, the National Health Planning Act experience could be written in precisely these terms. Agencies were evaluated, sued, funded, almost defunded, and occasionally praised for how they filled their boards with members of the public.

A more substantive pursuit of the public interest is obstructed by the varied perspectives that citizens are likely to have. Although they may avoid the narrowness that is likely to characterize a pharmaceutical firm making judgements about its own drugs, the public itself contains many competing perspectives. Where, after all, is the common ground between the wealthy and the poor, the fit and the chronically sick, children and the aged, reckless motorcyclists and those who pay insurance premiums? Even the most straightforward advisory panel is apt to see disagreement between homemakers and business people when clinic hours are discussed.

One solution is to abandon the rhetoric received from earlier reform movements. Citizen activists are not likely to discern overriding public interests. They are not even well equipped to try. Volunteers are unlikely spokesmen for the consumer or citizen perspective, for these are vague categories that do not touch people's lives. They would do better articulating the interests that most concern them or their more immediate constituencies, for example, the problems of the poor, the aged, or the terminally ill.

Naturally, every health interest in a community cannot be represented on one board; but that is not necessary. More traditional governing mechanisms remain, supplemented rather than supplanted by citizens action. Ultimately, the promise of citizen action is in the introduction of voices that are not likely to be heard in traditional policy institutions. The dialog between hospital administrators and city officials, for example, could be significantly broadened by representatives of the poor or the aged.

Political history appears to support this contention. The Community Action Agencies established during the War on Poverty have often been judged as failures. Nonetheless, they appear to have had a profound and beneficial effect on local political processes—the legitimation and political socialization of minority representatives (Greenstone, 1973). Another quasicorporatist experiment that failed—The National Recovery Administration of the New Deal—also left an enduring political legacy (Schlesinger, 1960), the legitimation of labor as a political actor.

Citizen activists and their policy forums fit neatly into the U.S. pluralism of clashing and coordinating interests. Well-structured consumer representation enhances that process by extending the number of interests likely to be heard, by adjusting the number of local interests within the political process. Properly understood, citizen activities are the heirs not of Rousseau or La Follette, but of the James Madison of *Federalist* Number 10.[6]

---

[6]Madison argued that to avoid tyranny, it was more important that a wide range of strongly felt interests be well represented then that many citizens participate in making policy. Thus a crucial ingredient of liberal democracy is an arena in which representatives of a population's major interests can come together and hash out policy. Robert La Follette was an important Progressive senator from Wisconsin.

3

SCIENTIFIC REFORM

The scientific reform tradition also has roots in the Progressive movement, but the emphasis is on science and management rather than public participation. Indeed, this tradition is skeptical of narrow interest representation, amateur activists, and broad notions of democratic participation. Instead, scientific reformers argue that the public interest is best pursued by skilled experts. They stress impartial universalistic policy designed by professionals. Trained public servants (planners, policy analysts) replace politicians and citizen activists; professional computation supplants political competition.

The participatory movements described in the preceding sections are self-conscious revolts against the scientific reform tradition. They follow from the belief that bureaucracies staffed by experts result in aloof institutions concerned primarily with internal rules and self-preservation. The reform tradition unabashedly participates in what is refered to in the next section as the fundamental goo-goo error: the belief that public choices can somehow be lifted above the grime of politics.

PURPOSE OF CITIZEN ACTION: A SUMMARY

Three entirely different notions were tangled together in the reforms of the 1960s and 1970s: mass public participation, the infusion of public choices with scientific wisdom, and the representation of specific interests on policy-making bodies. Any of these, taken alone, is ambitious; seeking to accomplish them all is almost certainly impossible.

In the simple conceptual terms of this section, neither broad participation nor scientific politics is a likely recipe for successful political reform. However, organizing the representation of (often overlooked) political interests may prove a useful innovation. An analysis of the politics and organization of citizen action will help explain why.

POLITICS OF CITIZEN ACTION

Representational systems are political instruments rather than neutral attributes. They structure the political process—some groups and interests are advantaged, others enfeebled. Political outcomes are biased by the parties that are injected into or insulated from political frays. United States theorists have encouraged reformers, suggesting that policy forums that promote the representation of a wide range of interests are less likely to be dominated by single powerful factions. Public-spirited Davids may slay an occasional Goliath if they can find enough allies to join in.

The critical point is that representational schemes may alter politics, but they do not abolish them. Nor do they annul power. Redesigning representational systems will not yield an uncontroversial path to the public interest. There is the shocked realization that reform has not ended political controversy. The rules may be adjusted, political markets balanced a bit, the democratic dice—as Klein (1979, to be published) puts it— loaded a little; however, the political game rolls on.[7] Perhaps the best that can be

---

[7]Rudolf Klein remains one of the wisest observers of social welfare politics in Great Britain and the United States.

accomplished is to add some new faces and inject some new interests to those already crowded around the political table.

Furthermore, an entirely different type of political challenge often confronts reform. New programs are frequently designed without regard to institutional landscapes. They are thrust in the midst of existing organizations. Goals and boundaries overlap; authority relationships are ambiguous. Rather than sift through old policy debates, as their designers intended, the policy forum is apt to be the subject of new ones. Competing boards, agencies, and departments alternatively challenge and ignore the upstart. Substantive policy questions (difficult enough in programs that stimulate citizen action) are interrupted by skirmishing with agency rivals.

For example, when local health planning agencies were established, municipal, county, and state bodies immediately (and somewhat successfully) sought to subordinate the newcomers to existing health agencies. The battle was waged partially in Washington, D.C., (for the new program was designed by Congress) and partially in the communities (in which bureaucratic peace treaties—Memoranda of Mutual Understanding (MOUS)—were hammered out and signed). The role of citizen action—extensive only in the new agencies—was diminished as a consequence of bureaucratic politics that had little to do with the reforms themselves. This odd sort of politics may be a consequence of the patchwork of U.S. federalism.[8]

In sum, citizen action reform in the United States must confront politics on two levels. First, representational schemes simply pour new parties into old battles. Powerful institutions remain powerful. The logic of collective action often favors their domination of policy arenas, regardless of changes in participation and representation. The empire—as Checkoway (1981b) has noted in this context—is always apt to strike back. Second, the politics relevant to a new agency's functions is matched by the politics of bureaucratic competition. Naturally, the two may run together. A medical association, fearful of participatory politics, may challenge the legitimacy of new programs in the name of the local department of health. Reformers in the past two decades—like their goo-goo predecessors—expected the politics of participation to climax with legislative victory. To their surprise, program enactment simply marked the beginning of another round of political action.

ORGANIZATION OF CITIZEN ACTION

The openness and fluidity of direct citizen action contrasts seductively with the bureaucratic rigidities of many U.S. institutions. However, the contrast can be illusory and undermined as reforms are set into operation. Whatever the problem of philosophy or politics, the greatest barriers to direct citizen action are the mundane exigencies of institutional action.

The reform literature exhorts the citizenry and its representatives to an active role. Trappings of participation—giving testimony—are spurned for more substantial power—setting agendas, making choices (see Arnstein, 1969) The mystifying question remains how, in simple procedural terms, are they to do so? Repeated efforts at citizen

---

[8]The British equivalents (Community Health Councils) are also designed with an ambiguous role, but their integration into the National Health Service is plain and relatively unchallenged.

action yield a repetition of the same lesson: the more participants, the more powerful the parliamentarian.

The point is easily illustrated: New England town meetings, a fable of citizen action, were dominated, almost choreographed, by a small Puritan elite (Katznelson and Kesselman, 1975). The stockholders revolt, a tool of reform that briefly terrified corporate management, proved impossible to wield effectively (Vogel, 1978). Citizen health planners, exhorted to control their agency's agenda, spent their meetings resolving their role vis-à-vis their staff instead.

Citizen activists are amateurs. They are not guided by the professional norms that often leave professional public servants aloof from the public; nor are they as intensely interested as producer groups, acting on narrow calculations of profit. These are precisely what qualify citizens for public action. Yet, somehow the unexpert, disinterested citizen must make public choices that rule the experts and the intensely interested. How are they to do so? What follows is as simple as it seems insurmountable.

If decisions must be made, information must be gathered and analyzed, professional staff hired, and a decision-making process set into motion. Paper flows, deadlines proliferate, rules emerge, an ethos develops. Those most imbued in the organizational details and processes become vital, then dominant, sometimes subtly, often not. The power of information, of simply tending the processes and routines, becomes irresistable. The oligarchy of interests that Michels (1962) posited of all organizations is widely understood (if still debated). But in simpler terms all significant actors become captives of the organization itself, co-opted by its processes.

The citizen activists can, of course, play a major role. They can devote time and thus develop expertise. But in doing so, they lose what is distinctive qua citizen actors. They either become specialists or are left in the organization's bureaucratic wake. Either is far from the sanguine vision of town meetings and direct citizen action.

The process of seizing and wielding decision-making authority transforms citizen activists. On this level, power to the people is more a conundrum than a call to action. The people that can take power are no longer representative of the people. Amateur bureaucrats are bound to and by their organization as surely as the professional that the activists originally critiqued.

Organization is crucial. It helps determine the relevant actors, their conflicts, and outcomes. The proparticipatory critique of many public and private institutions is their sheer impermeability; professionalism, bureaucracy, and expertise keep the public distant. Ironically, the institutions that are developed as a reaction must contend with a strong pull toward the same sorts of rigidities.

The major analytical task for citizen activists is synthesizing participation and bureaucracy. Theorists such as John Stuart Mill (1969) and Herbert Simon (1947) suggest an answer in the distinction between ends and means—juries of citizens could choose the goals, staff experts could implement them. In practice, however, overriding value choices and the means by which they are achieved constantly melt into one another. Indeed, the cognizance of that overlap has grown into a widely cited tenet of organizational and policy analysis.[9] Amidst voluminous commentary about recent citizen participation in health policy, the dilemma of organizational form has passed almost un-

---

[9]This is a reference to *incrementalism*, one of the best know theories of U.S. politics and public policy. Incrementalists suggest that U.S. policy is made by small (incremental steps) without much conception of grand design or ultimate purpose (in contrast to the central planning model of Eastern European policy). See Lindblom (1959, 1965).

noticed. The key to both past behavior and future reform may well lie in the organization of reform organizations.

NADER AND THE GRASS ROOTS: A STRATEGY FOR CITIZEN ACTION

The same phenomena that stifle some reformers, assist others. A recent type of reform-er—termed "civic balancers"—define precise goals, then unabashedly embrace contemporary organizational techniques to pursue them.[10] They seek to achieve tasks such as saving endangered whales or impoverished hospitals. But although broad citizen involvement and the rhetoric of public interest may be useful means, when democratic participation clashes with achieving policy goals, it is the former that is likely to be jettisoned.

Civic balancers share the premise of most citizen action reformers: Policy arenas are fragmented, dominated by narrow producer elites, such as hospital and medical associations. Poitical markets must be balanced by groups speaking for broad publics. The difference lies in how these reformers try to do so.

Civic balancers seek to influence policy choices rather than make them directly. They are suspicious of both private and public power; they are acutely aware that political games proceed regardless of organizational design or decision-making methodology. Redesigning governmental bodies is less important than applying steady (balancing) pressure on them. To do so, they use the techniques of the interests they challenge. Reformers build organizations that can coordinate action, sustain interest over time, and wield relevant expertise. This type of reform avoids ill-defined goals and political naiveté. Given the nature of their mission—achieving defineable goals rather than somehow enhancing democratic governance—the strictures of organizing for direct action are less onerous. Their goals are far more modest than those of many citizen activists, and their political influence is often overstated. Nevertheless, they suggest a strategy for citizen activists uncertain about how to proceed.

The same conclusion emerges from each section of this chapter. In conceptual, political, or organizational terms, the major achievement of citizen action is empowering groups organized around specific interests, that is, loading the democratic dice. Where interests have been dormant, for example blacks, handicapped, and the aged, citizen action programs have stimulated entre and political socialization.

The more ambitious aspirations of citizen action have repeatedly failed: Broad participation in the tradition of Rousseau, various assays at some overriding public interest, organizations somehow aloof from the roar of partisan politics, even the substitution of citizens by experts have disappointed advocate and will continue to do so. However, citizen action, where it is organized around a clear objective, can add a voice that is otherwise likely to go unheard.

The classic group model of politics suggests that groups approach government with their demands. For citizen action in health politics, the reverse has been the case. Without prompting, Congress designed policy forums in which individuals and groups might represent the citizenry. An enormous array of quiescent groups was drawn into

---

[10]The term "civic balancers" is taken from Andrew McFarland (1976).

politics. Five years later each congressional twitch drew voluminous (organized) response.

Government institutions can be designed to draw a range of interests—broad and narrow—into policy-making. Institutions can be structured on quasicorporatist principles to stimulate representation of interests that are overlooked, either generally (poor, aged) or in specific policy areas (health care payors).

No promises are made about the public interest or the essence of citizenship. Yet the public choices that emerge are likely to be more equitable for the additional actors. It is a particularly appealing prospect for health politics. The long search for a national policy seems endlessly bogged down in the politics of national health insurance (NHI). The original purpose of the latter reform has turned from insuring the bulk of the population to providing protection for that small increment that remains uninsured while protecting everyone else from the inflation that comes partially from widespread insurance. In the current system of piecemeal, incremental reform, each increment has direct and indirect consequences on many interests. Policy bodies that seek to bring together spokespeople for a wide range of interests may be particulary well suited to the problems of the time.

CITIZEN ACTION IN THE 1970s: THE CASE OF THE NATIONAL HEALTH PLANNING AND RESOURCES DEVELOPMENT ACT

The preceding themes are well illustrated by the National Health Planning and Resources Development Act, the largest citizen action effort in U.S. health politics. The National Health Planning Act established a national network of over 200 community health agencies (Health Systems Agencies—HSAs). After organizing themselves—a task that required juggling broad participation, narrow interest groups, individual citizens, and professional staff—the agencies were set to shape the evolution of local health care systems. Massive planning documents were written and annually amended. These were to be the blueprints of agency action. If communities lacked a needed service, the agency was to stimulate its introduction; if special programs were desired (e.g., rat abatement in Chicago, auto safety in Detroit) the HSA would seek out and organize the necessary actors. Most important, the agencies were asked to determine which hospital and nursing home services were needed. On the theory that unneeded facilities stimulated unnecessary costs, all capital expenditures over $150,000 were to be judged as necessary or redundant (a certificate of need—CON—was issued to the former). Later an inventory of all local services was to be undertaken to determine the appropriateness of each.

The agencies themselves were constructed out of an undifferentiated amalgamation of reform notions. Broad democratic participation, several variants of interest group representation, and the aspirations of scientific reform were liberally written into the law and its regulation.

Democratic participation was mandated in scrupulous detail. Any citizen could comment on, criticize, or commend any aspect of agency life. Documents were to be available at local libraries, meetings were to be advertised in at least two newspapers, and even secretarial salaries were open to review and comment by the populace (Federal Register).

Variations of the interest groups model appeared in the agency structure. The HSA governing boards and committees were to have consumer majorities (51–60%) "broadly representative of the social, economic, linguistic, racial and geographic characteristics" (93-641) of the community. (The rest of the board members were to be providers.) The wording appealed to citizens seeking to do good and to an array of interest groups, some with specific health agendas, others that vaguely qualified as representative of a community's social characteristics. Two tumultuous years of sorting through competing claims for governing board seats followed.

The scientific reform tradition was also included. When distinguishing this planning act from its politically anemic predecessors, Senate committee reports emphasized the professional staff who were to be fluent in "the scientific techniques of health planning" (U.S. Senate Committee, 1974). The law itself was publicized as the marriage of community action and scientific planning. And true to the reformer's distrust of local (biased, captured) health authorities, these agencies almost completely bypassed municipal and county governments. Senator Kennedy and his staff in particular were convinced that local politics would not mix well with either community participation or scientific planning (Altman, 1979; Iglehart, 1975).

Once again U.S. reform had concocted a combination of only partially compatible notions. Several sorts of community action would be mixed with value-free techniques and placed beyond the jurisdiction of local political institutions. From there they would turn policy choices from producer concerns to public interests.

Predictably, the act delighted reformers and appalled the health industry, which was particularly critical of the intrusive, untrained amateur boards. Most analysts drew a similar conclusion. Broadening the range of voices would not alter the outcomes. Board members had neither the will nor the skill to deflect health institutions or health politics from their traditional courses. How, it was asked, can citizens challenge the professionals in an area as technical as medicine? And perhaps more pertinent, why should they seek to do so? In a system dominated by third-party payors, surely citizens would not seek to reduce their health services for some doubtful experiment in cost control. The predictions were clear: Citizens (consumers) would simply legitimate what producers (health providers) were already doing, that is, requesting larger, more sophisticated health care facilities regardless of cost.

Once established, many local boards were challenged. The HSAs were peppered with litigation from providers charging antitrust violations. Sophisticated planning methodologies languished as the agencies battled the local industry for data. Reviews of hospital expansion requests repeatedly pitted a barrage of choreographed citizen groups and witnesses against the local board of consumer representatives. But the most intense battling was often with the local governmental units that the law's designers had sought to bypass. The states won a major place in the planning structure—all decisions about hospital needs were to be reviewed on the state level. Municipalities and counties were generally less successful. Some won a place in the process (10 gained district control of an HSA); other squabbled with, sued, or ignored the local agencies. Only a small number developed working relationships. The progress of the various HSAs could be measured in large part by the political astuteness of their managers, as well as the political muscle of their rivals. Like many reform programs, this one was not organized to deal effectively with the exigencies of political life.

Problems were compounded when many agencies made almost bizzare organizational choices. In the name of community participation, boards of 50, 60, and more people were established. Rather than enhance the citizen's role, this diminished it;

authority necessarily devolved into smaller, often ill-defined, subgroups within the agency. Instead of selecting one representative of the interests of the poor, some agencies sought a half-dozen—too few for the Rousseauian ideal that in a confused fashion underlay the choice and too many for either representative competition or effective agency action.

Once fully constituted, HSAs behaved contrary to most expectations: They became cost-control agencies. Though their cost savings were predictably paultry—they were never given serious cost-control tools—the outcome was remarkable. Why should citizen volunteers across the United States battle long hours to keep local hospitals and nursing homes from expanding? Why should citizens—most of whom do not directly pay their health bills, many of whom represent medically underserved constituencies—eschew a whole range of health system goals in order to become regulators of capital expenditure?

One response fits reassuringly into classic political theories of regulation. After an industry fails to defeat regulation, it embraces it (see Wilson, 1974). A strong CON program can provide a franchise monopoly to existing providers; potential competitors can be shut out in the name of cost control and health system rationality. In this view, citizen boards denying the CON were dominated by hospital administrators protecting their markets; the skeptics had been right about provider control of citizen boards. It is true that in many places health institutions came to appreciate the benefits that the CON could confer. But the program was often thrust upon them, sometimes despite vociferous opposition. And in many cases, providers continued to stand united against it, virulently opposed to what they perceived as governmental usurpation of the industry's role. Providers may have profited from the HSA concern with cost control and they may at times have participated in developing it. However, their behavior is not an adequate account of why it occurred.

Political analysts originally fixed on consumer–provider relationships. The staff was overlooked. (They were there only to inject a scientific perspective into political debate.) In fact, the staff played a major role in HSA politics. Like providers the staff was health professionals with a large stake in HSA outcomes. Unlike providers, the staff tended to have the ideology normally associated with planners—they viewed health in systematic terms, they would spurn CON proposals that did not conform to existing plans and guidelines. When providers and consumers clashed, the HSA staff generally sided with consumers. However, the enthusiasm that has greeted this alliance sometimes obscures the clashing visions that underlie consumer and staff prespectives. After all, the call for citizen action is in part an assault on the professional, bureaucratic, rationalistic spirit that planners embody. Indeed, it is often suggested that the unexpected HSA outcomes are a product of the staff dominating consumers and providers. Certainly the full-time staff played a key role in the life of these agencies. They constituted a serious dilemma for citizen action. Although full-time staff are necessary to keep a professional organization running, how are part-time volunteers to keep up with the professional staff? A partial answer can be found in HSA bylaws: Only the board members vote. Staff may have pressed the HSAs toward cost control, but the choice ultimately was made by the consumers and providers on the governing board.

The process by which HSA choices were made also affected the choices themselves. All the attributes of bureaucratic organization noted above were quickly evident. Rules proliferated, processes grew immutable, vast quantities of paper began to flow; in short, the agenda was set. The bias of the organizational process (tended by the staff) emphasized Certificate of Need regulation. It became difficult to change the subject. Citizen volunteers were either transformed into amateur bureaucrats, volunteering 20 hours a week to pursue capital regulation, or they grew irrelevant.

A final explanation places all these elements in a political and organizational rubric. The HSAs existed in a fragile political equilibrium. Established by an act that terminated earlier planning agencies, challenged by a hostile industry, threatened by jealous municipal and health competitors, the legitimacy of their enterprise was always suspect. The HSA's funding agency—Department of Health, Education and Welfare (DHEW)—found them useful for one purpose: controlling health care costs. With President Carter's health cost-control legislation languishing in a rebellious Congress, it had few levers with which to try to constrain costs. One of the few, weak and indirect as it may have been, was the HSA review of capital expenditures. The DHEW pressed that lever, insisting that individual agencies and the program in its entirety was at stake and that funding and even survival meant cost control. The agencies were mediating an unambiguously articulated DHEW interest when they made cost control, one of the tasks that Congress had assigned them, their overriding and almost exclusive preoccupation and mission.

Other explanations—consumer ideology before board membership, provider self-interest, staff concerns (over jobs or ideology)—all work within this context. But the primal force driving the HSAs was agency survival.

Survival motivated not just the professional staff members but the consumer, sometimes even provider, volunteers. From the perspective of organizational theory it may not be an extraordinary outcome—actors co-opted by their organization; indeed, Selznick populatized the term in precisely such a context. However, it runs counter to everything that was anticipated of citizen action. If citizens were overwhelmed, it was not by providers or special interests but by the processes and norms of their agencies. Ultimately, the fundamental fact moving the volunteers and their HSAs was the exigency—the survival—of the organizations to which they volunteered their time.

CONCLUSION

Future reformers will have to articulate their reform visions more carefully. Seeking achievable goals is nothing like wishing democratic wishes. The areas susceptible to reform, although important, are limited. Limits are imposed not merely by political interests and competing institutions. Rather the imperatives of organizing for political action—hiring staff, setting an organizational process into motion—are inimical to many Progressive notions and are a constraint on the level of direct democratization that can be attained in a society such as that of the United States. Those proposing change will either harness the dynamics of contemporary organization or will have its consequences thrust upon them. This is not to eschew all citizen action reform but to pick among the possibilities more cautiously and wisely. For example, if health politics are dominated by health providers, public institutions would do well to integrate representatives of the poor, or minorities, or the aged. This may expand the number of interests that are heard while policy is made—no small accomplishment.

However, reformers are not likely to pick their way into a democratic idyl, routinely detecting the public interest of the popular will. They will find, rather, the less pleasant world of contemporary bureaucracy: long meetings, complicated forms, silly rules, trying deadlines, and the adjudication of apparently trivial political disputes.

Even so, the implications—for the shape of the administrative institutions and the policies they make—can be significant, perhaps extraordinary.

In a system dominated by large hierarcical actors, the energy underlying the Progressive critique is not likely to be dormant long. We will hear another round of calls for direct citizen action, spurred on again by the perceived impermiability of health institutions—from the Department of Health and Human Services to the local hospitals. That future wave of reformers will have at their disposal a considerable historical record. The experience of the 1970s, should they care to examine it, quite clearly illuminates both the problems of broad citizen action and the possibilities for its success.

REFERENCES

Altman, Drew, "The Politics of Health Care Regulation: The Case of the National Health Planning and Resources Development Act," *Journal of Health Politics Policy and Law*, Vol. 2, No. 4, Winter 1979, pp. 560–580.

Altman, Drew, Richard Greene and Harvey Sapolsky, *Planning and Regulation*, Ann Arbor, Mich.: AUPHA Press, 1981.

Arnstein, Sherry, "A Ladder of Citizen Participation," *Journal of the American Institute of Planners*, Vol. 35, July 1969, pp. 216–224.

Checkoway, Barry, ed., *Citizens and Health Care*, New York: Pergamon Press, 1981a.

Checkoway, Barry, "The Empire Strikes Back: More Lessons for Health Consumers," *Journal of Health Politics Policy and Law*, Vol. 7, No. 1, Spring 1981b, pp. 111–124.

Cole, G. D. H., *Social Theory*, London: Menthuen, 1920.

Cooper, Terry L., "The Hidden Price Tag: Participation Costs and Health Planning," *American Journal of Public Health*, Vol. 69, No. 4, April 1979, pp. 368–374.

Dahl, Robert, *Who Governs?*, New Haven: Yale University Press, 1964. *Federal Register*, Vol. 12812, March 26, 1976, pp. 114–122.

Greenstone, David J. and Paul Peterson, *Race and Authority in Urban Politics: Community Participation and the War on Poverty*, Chicago: The University of Chicago Press, 1973.

Hayden, Tom, et al., *The Port Huron Statement*, Port Huron, Mich.: Students for a Democratic Society, 1962.

Iglehart, John, "State and County Governments Win Key Role in New Program," *National Journal*, Vol. 7, November 1975, pp. 1533–39.

Karznelson, Ira and Mark Kesselman, *The Politics of Power*, Chicago: Hartcourt, Brace and Jovanovich, 1975, chap. 2.

Kelin, Rudolf, "Control. Participation and the British National Health Service," *Milbank Memorial Fund Quarterly: Health and Society*, Vol. 57, Winter 1979, pp. 70–94.

Klein, Rudolf, "Reflections on Health Planning in America," *Journal of Health Politics Policy and Law*, to be published.

Langton, Stuart, *Citizen Participation in America*, Lexington, Mass: Lexington Book, 1978, p. 5.

Lindblom, Charles, "The Science of Muddling Through," *Public Administration Review*, Vol. 19, Spring 1959, pp. 79–88.

Lindblom, Charles, *The Intelligence of Democracy*, New York: The Free Press, 1965.

Madison, James, *The Federalist*, No. 10.

Morone, James and T. R. Marmor, "Representing Consumer Interests: The Case of American Health Planning," *Ethics*, Vol. 91, April 1981, pp. 431–450.

McConnell, Grant, *Private Power and American Democracy*, New York: Knopf, 1966.

McFarland, Andrew, *Public Interest Lobbies*, Washington, D.C.: American Enterprise Institute, 1976.

Michels, Robert, *Political Parties*, New York: The Free Press, 1962.

Mill, John Stuart, "On Representative Government," in Hannah F. Pitkin, ed., *Representation*, New York: Atherton Press, 1969.

Moynihan, *Maximum Feasible Misunderstanding: Community Action and The War on Poverty*, New York: The Free Press, 1969.

Pateman, *Participation and Democratic Theory*, New York: Cambridge University Press, 1970.

Rosenblatt, Rand, "Health Care Reform and Administrative Law: A Structural Approach," *The Yale Law Journal*, Vol. 88, No. 2, December 1978, pp. 243–336.

Rousseau, Jean-Jacques, *The Social Contract*, Baltimore: Penguin Books, 1968.

Schlesinger, Arthur, *The Politics of Upheaval*, Boston: Houghton Mifflin, 1960.

Schumpeter, Joseph, *Captialism, Socialism and Democracy*, Evanton, Ill: Harper and Row, 1942.

Simon, Herbert, *Administrative Behavior*, New York: Macmillan, 1947, Chap. 3.

Vogel, David, *Lobbying the Corporation*, New York: Basic Books, 1978. U.S. Senate Committee on Interstate Commerce and Foreign Commerce, *The National Health Policy, Planning and Resources Development Act of 1974*, Report No. 93–1382, Washington, D.C.: Government Printing Office, 1974.

Wilson, James Q., "The Politics of Regulation," in James McKie, ed. *Social Responsibility and the Business Predicament*, Washington D.C.: The Brookings Institution, 1974.

PART FOUR

The Politics of Health and Health Care: Some Selected Examples

CHAPTER 13

The Politics of Public Health in the United States

Milton I. Roemer

The position of public health agencies in the overall health sector of the United States has been determined by two major influences. One has been the capabilities within the field of public health—a field that may be defined as a population-based approach to promoting health, in contrast to the orientation of clinical medicine to treatment of individual patients. The second influence has been the external circumstances surrounding public health agencies in society, particularly the distribution of authority and responsibility in the health sector as a whole.

Both of these influences have changed over the years, resulting in differing positions for public health organization in various historical periods. The role of public health agencies can be best understood, therefore, by examining the health scene in the United States in the following periods of time:

Beginnings	1800–1870
Maturation in government	1870–1910
Focus on prevention	1910–1935
Expansion and development	1935–1960
Health care progress elsewhere	1960–1980

BEGINNINGS, 1800–1870

Public health activity arose in the United States in the first years of the nineteenth century. As in Europe, it first occurred in the largest cities in which concentrations of population led to the spread of communicable diseases. Typically, in response to epidemics, a board or commission would be appointed to make regulations for the maintenance of a sanitary environment. Even before microorganisms were recognized as causative agents of disease, the hazards of a dirty environment and contaminated water were recognized. John Snow in London had attibuted a cholera epidemic to drinking polluted water drawn from the Thames River in 1849, long before the bacteria causing this disease had been described.

In New York City an epidemic of yellow fever occurred in 1798. A Board of Health, composed of leading citizens, had been established some years before to recommend measures for elimination of filth from the streets, for drainage of swamps, and other objectives of environmental sanitation. In 1804, a full-time city inspector of health was appointed. He and his staff were lodged in the New York Police Department, since the *enforcement* of sanitary regulations was seen as the central task. These personnel were not transferred to a separate agency under a permanent board of health until 1838. Similar developments occurred in Boston, Philadelphia, and a few other cities in this period.

The boards of health were concerned principally with the maintenance of a sanitary environment. Quarantine and isolation of patients with communicable disease were also practiced, since contagiousness was realized (also before the indentification of bacteria). Until the Civil War, boards of health were limited to large cities. In 1849, however, a Sanitary Commission was appointed in Massachusetts to survey health and sanitation problems in the whole state. The report of this commission, chaired by Lemuel Shattuck, appeared in 1850 and made recommendations on vital statistics (including the notification of communicable diseases), smallpox vaccination, many aspects of environmental sanitation, and health education of the general population on hygiene. To implement these ideas, the commission proposed a board of health with permanent staffing at the state level, along with similar boards in the government of every town. Not until after the Civil War—1869—however, was the first *state* board of health set up in Massachusetts.

PUBLIC HEALTH MATURATION IN GOVERNMENT, 1870–1910

As the United States settled down after the Civil War, a more firm structure of government gradually took shape in the main cities and in state capitals. With heavy immigration from Europe and the development of industry, cities grew rapidly as did problems of environmental sanitation. By the end of the nineteenth century, boards of health had been established within the governments of most large cities as well as at the state level.

In 1878 a National Quarantine Act was passed by Congress for the purpose of preventing the entry, by ships from Europe, of persons with communicable disease. The surgeon general of the Marine Hospital Service (which had originated in 1798) was put in charge of quarantine procedures at the principal ports of the United States. In the next year, 1879, a National Board of Health was established by law for "foreign and interstate quarantine." By then, however, the sovereignty of the states on public health matters and other domestic affairs was well established; a National Board of Health was ahead of its time, and in 1883 Congress let it die through withholding appropriations.

Although boards of health and permanently staffed health departments under them were a widespread features of state and local governments by 1900, their functions remained limited to the enforcement of sanitary regulations and of certain measures for the control of acute communicable disease. It was about 1860–1870 that the work of Louis Pasteur and others in Europe had demonstrated the bacterial basis of various infectious diseases. In the 1890s, the principle of immunization (beyond that from smallpox) was formulated, first for diphtheria. This greatly strengthened the capabilities of public health agencies in the control of communicable diseases.

The scope of health department functions did not broaden until the turn of the century, and the initiative was taken first by voluntary groups of citizens. Thus, in 1893 private philanthropy set up milk stations in New York City for poor mothers (who could not nurse their babies). The work of these stations gradually increased to include counseling of mothers on the general care of infants. Then in 1908, the New York City Health Department organized a Bureau of Child Hygiene staffed by full-time nurses. These nurses visited the mothers of newborn babies in tenements, supervised midwives, inspected school children for detection of infectious disease, and conducted child health clinics. A National Association for Study and Prevention of Infant Mortality was formed in 1909 to promote such preventive child health programs throughout the United States.

Parallel developments led to the extension of health department activities to include the detection and follow up of cases of tuberculosis. In 1892 the Pennsylvania Society for the Study and Prevention of Tuberculosis was founded, and by 1904 there were 23 such state and local associations. Among other things, special tuberculosis clinics were organized. In 1905 the Society for Social and Moral Prophylaxis was founded to encourage the prevention of venereal disease (VD), and VD clinics were set up. After the feasibility of these special clinics was demonstrated, public health agencies started similar programs. This greater scope of work strengthened the general image of health departments in the community.

In small towns when health departments were established, it was customary to designate some local physician as health officer. This physicians would have the legal authority to enforce the regulations on sanitation and communicable diseases, although the day-to-day inspections and services were carried out by full-time sanitarians and nurses. In 1908 Jefferson County, Kentucky, appointed the first such full-time public health personnel to work throughout a county and outside city limits.

Thus, by 1910, public health agencies had become well established in state and local governments, although they had not yet acquired a major role in the overall health sector. The influence of voluntary agencies led to incremental expansion of public health functions beyond sanitary hygiene, but still within the sphere of prevention. Even the voluntary agencies were careful to emphasize their preventive objectives in order to avoid controversy with private physicians who were expected to provide all medical treatment.

FOCUS ON PREVENTION, 1910–1935

The focus of public health agencies on preventive work was taken for granted; it was not a point of contention. Thus, when actions were taken to broaden the role of government on nonpreventive aspects of health, there was little reason to assign responsibilities to health departments. In 1910 the first law on worker's compensation for industrial accidents was enacted in New York State, and soon followed by similar legislation in other states. Medical care was among the benefits of injured workers, but health departments were not involved; special new state agencies were established. Even when factory inspection programs were launched to assure safe working conditions, their implementation was assigned to state department of labor or the like. Medical care of the poor was also sometimes a responsibility of local governments, but administration was done by departments of welfare concerned with other aspects of public assistance.

After 1910, various types of health service became increasingly organized, but the preventive focus of Health Departments ruled out any involvement by them. General hospitals were growing rapidly in number and overall bed capacity, so that a rising proportion of personal health care was given within their walls. Most hospitals were voluntary, but even public hospitals were seldom connected with health departments. Physicians were also increasing rapidly in the United States and were suspicious of competition from public agencies. Through their societies, they were always concerned about any governmental encroachment on their domain. Since local and even some state health officers were typically part-time private practitioners, they tended to share this attitude. This was reflected in various ways.

In the American Public Health Association (APHA) (founded in 1872), for example, a sociological section was organized in 1910. It was composed mainly of social workers concerned with the "social and economic aspects of health problems." Medical social work was taking shape in those years in order to help low-income patients coming to hospital outpatient departments and dispensaries. At this time the dominant group in the APHA were local health officers. (When a Committee on Municipal Public Health Practice was formed in 1920, it focused its attention solely on sanitation and quarantine—not even including maternal and child health services.) The American Medical Association (AMA), to which part-time local health officers typically belonged, was attacking all proposals to extend the health role of government. In this atmosphere, it is not surprising that by 1922 the APHA sociological section died a quiet death.

Conservatism in public health was particularly strong at the local government level. At the state level, there was greater likelihood for health departments to be directed by full-time professionals dedicated to a public health movement. Thus in 1916 the Conference of State and Territorial Health Officers discussed a number of proposals then in state legislatures to establish social insurance programs covering workers for medical care costs. (Great Britain had enacted general health insurance for workers in 1911, and the idea was discussed soon after in the United States—as an extension of the worker's compensation acts.) The state health officers gave support to these health insurance proposals and urged "close cooperation of the health insurance system with state, municipal and local health departments and boards." Local health officers, on the other hand, were reluctant to become concerned even with preventively oriented child health clinics.

In 1921, as a result of pressure from the labor movement and children's advocates, the Sheppard-Towner Act was passed by Congress; it established the first federal grants-in-aid for local child health clinics. The program was administered by the Children's Bureau, which had been established in 1912 in the federal Department of Labor (because of concern with banning child labor). Many local health departments, however, declined to accept these grants for fear of alienating private practitioners. The AMA and local medical societies opposed the program vigorously, and in 1928 Congress allowed it to terminate.

In some places, health officers were especially courageous and attempted to broaden the scope of public health work to include general medical services for the poor. In 1919 the Dawson committee in the British Ministry of Health advocated a network of health centers for both preventive and therapeutic ambulatory services. In 1920 a similar proposal was made by Herman Biggs, the health officer of New York State. The private medical profession, however, effectively killed this idea, as it killed a similar proposal by Dr. John Pomeroy, health officer of Los Angeles, a few years later.

By 1932, when the United States was into a deep economic depression and Franklin D. Roosevelt was elected president, the purely preventive focus of public health agencies was no longer challenged. In 1934 the Federal Emergency Relief Administration (FERA) gave the first federal grants to local government for public assistance to the poor, including financial support for medical care. The FERA funds were administered by welfare departments, and local health departments played no part. During this period the construction of public works was federally subsidized to provide jobs, and among other things many health center were constructed. These facilities were used for housing health departments and their preventive clinics but never for the provision of medical care to the poor or other segments of the population.

The depression also caused a decline in the earnings of private physicians. As a result, many of them were glad to accept appointments as local health officers, often regarding this as a form of retirement. Dependence of local public health agencies almost entirely on meagre local government revenues inevitably meant very weak programs, even in the sphere of prevention. The quarters of most departments were typically in antiquated public buildings, with no links to hospitals or other medical facilities. Work in such settings naturally held little attraction for young physicians whose professional lives were ahead of them.

Thus, in the quarter-century between 1910 and 1935 public health agencies became widely established, but their scope was limited to environmental sanitation and preventive control of communicable diseases; the latter function had sometimes become extended to chronic disorders such as tuberculosis and venereal infection (their diagnosis but not treatment). In the overall arena of government, moreover, Health Departments were weak agencies, in comparison, for example, with boards of education or police departments.

The weakness of health departments was manifestly due to both internal and external causes. With untrained private physicians often in charge, there was little initiative to expand public health functions beyond traditional prevention. Even within government, health departments held little attraction as units for handling new or enlarged public tasks such as medical care of the poor; they commanded little respect. Yet without experience, how could they develop new capabilities? It was a vicious cycle.

EXPANSION AND DEVELOPMENT, 1935–1960

Enactment of the Social Security Act (SSA) in 1935 ushered in a very different period in U.S. public health. Early planning of this important legislation had considered the inclusion of a social insurance program for medical care—along with old-age pensions, unemployment compensation, and other benefits. But President Roosevelt did not want to jeopardize enactment of the entire law due to opposition from the medical profession. In place of health insurance, therefore, the act included two titles designed to strengthen public health services by federal grants-in-aid to the states.

Title V on the support of maternal and child health services (MCH) was essentially a resurrection and expansion of the old Sheppard-Towner act of 1921–1928. This title also authorized grants for the diagnosis and treatment of crippled children—clearly a nonpreventive task. Federal MCH activities came under the Children's Bureau in the

Department of Labor, so that this program was handled separately from those for the rest of public health work. Title VI for general public health purposes came under the administration of the U.S. Public Health Service (USPHS), which had evolved in 1912 from the Marine Hospital Service. Because its historical origins had included tax collection from shipowners, the USPHS was, strangely enough, a part of the Treasury Department. In 1939, the USPHS, along with the Food and Drug Administration (FDA) (in the Department of Agriculture), the Social Security Board, and other related programs were brought together under the Federal Security Agency. These activities were not endowed with cabinet status until 1953, when the Department of Health, Education and Welfare (DHEW) was formed.

Federal grants to the states greatly strengthened public health agencies. State health departments everywhere acquired additional trained personnel, and local health departments were expanded. In fact, funds were earmarked to support formal training at university schools of public health. (These schools were also strengthened by the grants, and new schools were established.) Under Surgeon-General Thomas Parran, great emphasis was given to VD control, and hundreds of VD clinics were organized by local public health agencies. Since prevention of the spread of syphilis and gonorrhea required aggressive treatment of cases, this meant that health departments became engaged in personal medical care—if only for this disease category.

As health departments grew stronger, the perception of their proper responsibilities changed. State health departments, for example, developed services in industrial hygiene to study working conditions in industry in order to prevent occupational diseases. Local health departments undertook examinations of school children, often through agreements with boards of education. When World War II started in 1939, special attention was given to building up public health services in the vicinity of military training camps or in rapidly expanding war production areas. In order to promote community support for all sorts of public health activities, the field of health education took shape as a new professional discipline. Dental clinics were organized in health departments to do reparative work on the teeth of children and mothers seen in the MCH program (and in schools).

With the robust expansion of the entire field, there was much discussion about the proper scope of public health activities. The APHA was growing in membership and functions; one outcome was an important study directed by Haven Emerson (Dean of the Columbia University School of Public Health) and published in 1941, titled "Local Health Units for the Nation." Among other things, this report emphasized that health departments should be concerned only with disease prevention. They should provide six basic services: environmental sanitation, communicable disease control, maternal and child health promotion (not treatment), laboratory services (in connection with disease prevention), vital statistics, and health education. This advocacy of the basic six tended to draw the lines in the public health movement between those who favored keeping the field confined to prevention and those who wanted to see it expanded to all aspects of the health of populations, including the planning and organization of medical care (Rosen, 1958).

In the previous period, an important national study had been conducted by a prestigious Committee on the Costs of Medical Care (CCMC). The CCMC staff worked from 1928 to 1932, producing 27 volumes on all aspects of U.S. medical care, private and public. As a follow-up study in 1935–1936, the USPHS with the aid of the Works Progress Administration (WPA) conducted a National Health Survey that revealed a vast burden of untreated disease in the population, particularly in the lower-income groups.

Stimulated by these findings, Senator Robert Wagner (sponsor of the Social Security Act) introduced an amendment to this act in Congress, which would have supported federal grants to the states for the organization of health insurance plans covering workers and their dependents. This was in July 1939; the onset of World War II in September postponed any serious consideration of such an idea.

After the heavy involvement of the United States in Europe and the Pacific during World War II, work began on postwar planning. In 1943, new legislation was introduced in Congress for launching a federally administered national health insurance (NHI) program. This bill went through several versions, one of which assigned administrative responsibility to the USPHS. In support of the concept of public health agency participation in NHI administration, in 1944 the APHA governing council issued a now classic policy statement on Medical Care in a National Health Program. This action marked a turning point in the entire U.S. public health movement. The ideology of the old guard favoring prevention only was defeated and, at least among the most active leaders in the field, was replaced by the view that public health agencies should become concerned with all aspects of health service administration, including the delivery of medical care. In 1948, the APHA established a Medical Care Section, which soon became the largest group in the association.

In 1943, state health departments throughout the United States had been assigned a major new responsibility involving medical care administration. The Emergency Maternity and Infant Care (EMIC) program provided for governmental financing of maternity care (including childbirth) for the dependents of military personnel along with pediatric care of the infant during its first year of life. The EMIC program required the establishment of minimum standards for medical and hospital care, payment for these services, and related matter. Suddenly the state public health agencies found themselves heavily involved with responsibilities clearly beyond the boundaries of prevention.

After the war, another new and significant responsibility was delegated to state health departments. Although no NHI legislation was enacted, in 1946 the National Hospital Survey and Construction Act (Hill-Burton) became law. This federal program to subsidize the construction of hospitals in areas of bed shortage (mainly rural counties) had, in fact, been one section of a comprehensive NHI bill, which was separated and passed. Responsibility for surveying the hospital bed supply in each state and developing a master plan for new hospital construction where needed gave state public health agencies a wholly new type of experience. These agencies were also usually assigned the task of inspecting and licensing all hospitals and related facilities. (The nongovernmental Joint Commission of Accreditation of Hospitals was not established until 1952.)

In the postwar years, the scope and authority of public health agencies were also broadened in other ways. The National Mental Health Act (NMHA) became law in 1946 and provided grants to the states for research, prevention, diagnosis, and treatment of mental disorders. It was administered by a new branch of the USPHS and in most states mental health programs were developed in state health departments. At the local level, various types of mental health clinics were organized within health departments or other public and voluntary agencies.

These years also saw the entry of state and local health departments into the difficult field of chronic (noncommunicable) disease control. Heart disease and cancer had long been the major causes of death in the United States, and demands arose for some public health action. Accordingly, the early detection of chronic diseases became an objective of many public health agencies; mass population surveys with laboratory tests (e.g., blood glucose levels for identification of subclinical diabetes) were conducted. Eventually several such tests were performed on people at one time—a technique that became known as multiphasic screening. Public health agencies also began to promote rehabilitation services in hospitals and nursing homes. Some years later health education on lifestyle (diet, exercise, smoking, etc.) became a customary public health activity for the purpose of preventing heart disease and cancer.

During the 1950s there was further expansion of public health activities at the federal level. The National Institutes of Health (NIH) within the USPHS were greatly expanded for the support of biomedical research both intramurally and through grants to universities and other places. In 1954, the operation of a comprehensive health service for American Indians was transferred from the Department of Interior to the USPHS. In 1956 Congress authorized the USPHS to conduct a continuing national health survey for the identification of every kind of illness in the population and the types and amounts of medical care received by families.

By the end of this period (1960), the scope and importance of federal, state and local public health agencies had clearly become far greater than they were in 1935. Although organized health activities had also expanded under other types of sponsorship—welfare departments, public and private hospitals, voluntary health insurance organizations—health departments were participating actively in the extension of social responsibilities for health. Furthermore, under innovative leadership, health departments assumed unusually broad responsibilities, such as administration of the medical care program for the poor (public assistance recipients) in Maryland or the combined responsibility for public health and public hospitals in Denver, Colorado.

HEALTH CARE PROGRESS ELSEWHERE, 1960–1980

In the 1960s, governmental responsibilities for various aspects of health continued to expand, although principally in organizations other than departments of health. The 1963 Health Professions Educational Assistance Act was administered federally by the USPHS, but the grant went entirely to universities and colleges, without any involvement of state or local health departments. In response to a sort of rediscovery of poverty, the federal Economic Opportunity Act (EOA) was passed in 1964. President Johnson spoke of declaring a war on poverty, and the EOA established a new U.S. Office of Economic Opportunity (OEO) outside the DHEW and reporting directly to the president. In 1965 the OEO launched a program of federal support for neighborhood health centers in impoverished sections of cities and rural areas. These facilities offered poor people a comprehensive range of ambulatory medical services, both therapeutic and preventive.

A special feature of OEO health centers was maximum community participation, meaning the participation of poor people themselves in the determination of policies and administrative practices. Between 1965 and 1971 about 100 neighborhood health centers were established. Although local health departments played a role in the origins of a few of these centers, by 1971 not a single center had any connection with a public health agency.

In 1973, under President Nixon, the OEO was terminated and its neighborhood health centers were transferred to the supervision of the USPHS. In the meantime, several other types of community health centers (as these facilities came to be called) were launched under various new federal grant programs—aggregating to nearly 1,000 such facilities by 1979. In spite of their USPHS federal supervision, very few of these units involved any health department management. The vast majority were operated by newly formed local nongovernmental community organizations. Many facilities were related in some way to hospitals or medical schools, but not to departments of health.

This explosive development of community health centers for the poor did, however, have an influence on local health departments, especially those in large cities. The popularity of comprehensive health services offered in free-standing facilities convinced some public health agencies to broaden the scope of their traditional categorical clinics. Instead of limiting their functions to preventive MCH services or to treating VD, health department clinics began to offer general primary medical care.

A turning point came in 1965, when SSA amendments launched the major health programs soon labeled as Medicare and Medicaid. The problem of financing medical care for the aged had been evident for some years; a greater burden of sickness had to be faced in the later years of life just when most people lost their voluntary insurance coverage because of retirement from work (such insurance being linked so often to employment). The Medicare program gave health insurance protection to people eligible for old-age pensions under SSA. Although some personal cost-sharing was required, most medical and hospitalization costs were met by the government.

The other population group with little protection by voluntary health insurance was the poor. The Medicaid program, depending on both federal and state general revenues, financed a broad range of services for public assistance recipients and certain other medically indigent people. Both Medicare and Medicaid were essentially payment mechanisms for services in the medical mainstream, that is, services from private physicians, community hospitals, and other health care providers serving the population as a whole.

Medicare and Medicaid rapidly became the largest programs for health purposes in the federal government. Their costs soon dwarfed expenditures for all other governmental health-related programs combined. In the administration of these major programs, however, public health agencies at federal, state, and local levels played almost no part. Under Medicare, payments were handled by fiscal intermediaries drawn from Blue Cross and Blue Shield plans and commercial insurance companies. Medicaid was most often managed by state welfare agencies or new bodies established in state governments. Occasionally the state health department was administratively involved, but the local health departments never were. About 1975 a new agency was set up under the federal DHEW solely for Medicare and Medicaid management—the Health Care Financing Administration.

In late 1965 another important federal health program was started; it was to promote improvement in the quality of medical care through various regionalized educational and consultative activities. To make the law politically attractive, it was linked to the three greatest causes of death in the United States (mainly in old people) and designated as the Regional Medical Program for Heart Disease, Cancer, and Stroke (RMP). At the federal level RMP was administered by the USPHS, but no role was played by public health agencies at state or local levels. By 1972 federal RMP grants went to 56 organizations that blanketed the United States; of these 33 were sponsored by universities, four by medical societies, and 19 by other new or existent corporate bodies. Not a single RMP program came under a state or local health department.

In 1966 the first U.S. law on Comprehensive Health Planning (CHP) was enacted. The CHP agencies were to be organized in every state and local area "to support the marshalling of all health resources—national, state, and local—to assure comprehensive health services of high quality for every person." At the state level the governor was to appoint a State Health Planning Council, and in about half the cases this was in the state health department. At the local level, 198 areawide CHP agencies had been established by 1972; of these 150 were new private nonprofit organizations, 45 were special quasigovernmental district councils, and only three had any relationship to local health departments. The principal work of CHP agencies was hospital planning, but their scope theoretically encompasses all organized health activities. One can hardly think of a role more suitable for local public health agencies to perform, but this was almost never the case.

The last straw in the legislative bypassing of public health agencies was the enactment of the National Health Planning and Resources Development Act of 1974. This legislation replaced both the RMP and CHP laws with a nationwide planning program of very broad scope. Once again federal administration was assigned to the USPHS, but at the state level only about half the governors designated the state health department as the administrative agency. More important, by 1979 at the local level, 203 Health Systems Agencies (HSA) were established, of which 178 were private nonprofit entities. Only 25 HSAs were established in any branch of local government, not necessarily involving the local health department. The language of the federal law, in fact, made it difficult for local health departments to play this crucial planning role.

Other types of health care organization developed in the United States during 1960–1980. The Health Maintenance Organization (HMO) Act of 1973 provided for federal promotion of these special forms of medical practice, which organized both the financing and delivery of comprehensive health services in a manner that yielded economies. In 1975, further amendments of the SSA established a nationwide network of Professional Standards Review Organizations (PSRO) to monitor the services provided under Medicare and Medicaid. Both HMOs and PSROs functioned essentially at the community level, but the local health department was almost never involved. Still other important movements for the increased organization of services, such as voluntary health insurance and private group medical practice, were entirely outside the domain of government.

Another health feature of the 1970s was a reopened legislative debate on a national health insurance program. In part because of Medicare and Medicaid, which pumped more money into the health sector without changing patterns of health care delivery, medical care costs rose very rapidly, becoming increasingly burdensome to the average family. Numerous proposals were introduced in Congress, therefore, to extend economic support of medical costs from the aged and the poor to the total population. The various bills differed in their scope and degree of impact on patterns of health care, but (as in the 1940s) legislative agreement could not be reached on any of them. In the late 1970s, in part due to the stalemate on health insurance and in part due to research findings on the role of personal lifestyle in the development of chronic disease, the federal government shifted it priorities. There was a kind of rediscovery of the importance of prevention and health promotion. Thus the health education component of public health programs got a major boost, but this was in the traditional sphere of prevention.

Thus in the period 1960–1980, the long-term trend toward greater organization of health services continued and even accelerated. In terms of dollars spent in an organized framework, including voluntary health insurance and as government at all levels, by 1977 nearly 70 percent of health services involved third parties. In terms of the services delivered to people, a rising proportion was being provided in hospitals—inherently very organized settings compared with physicians' offices. Even ambulatory health care was becoming increasingly organized through diverse types of clinics under both governmental and private sponsorship. Very few of these developments, however, involved public health agencies.

GENERAL INTERPRETATION

We have now considered five periods in the evolution of public health activities in the United States. In the first period (1800–1870), community responsibility began to be taken for the health of populations, mainly in cities in which concentrations of people created greater health hazards. Boards of health were appointed to formulate rules and regulations on environmental sanitation to reduce those hazards. In the second period (1870–1910), public health agencies with full-time civil servants became established as a normal part of state and local governments; then, largely through the influence of voluntary organizations, the scope of these governmental agencies gradually broadened beyond sanitation and the control of the acute communicable diseases.

In the third period (1910–1935), many other forms of organization of the health sector took place. At the same time, private medical practitioners became more important in the average community: they implemented the advancing medical science and commanded great respect. As small businesses selling services for patient fees, however, physicians were much concerned about the encroachment of governmental health programs on their domain. To avoid controversy and opposition from the medical profession, therefore, state and local health departments were careful to confine their activities to disease prevention. Medical diagnosis and treatment were regarded as the exclusive prerogative of private physicians.

The fourth period (1935–1960) was marked by a deep economic depression, a destructive world war, and expansion of the role of government in many spheres. In these circumstances, public health agencies at all levels—federal, state, and local—increased greatly in strength and scope. Although their principal role remained the prevention of disease, health departments (especially at state and federal levels) acquired new responsibilities in medical care administration. The definition of the term "prevention" was also broadened to include the early detection of patients with chronic disease, rehabilitation of the physically handicapped, and ambulatory care of patients with mental disorders.

The fifth period (1960–1980) brought further expansion of organized programs in the health sector. Most of the action took place, however, outside the sphere of government or, if in government, under agencies other than health departments. Large new social programs—Medicare, Medicaid, RMP, CHP, HMO promotion, and so on—greatly enlarged the share of total health expenditures coming under some type of organized arrangements. Public health agencies did not actually decline in their resources and services, but the major social developments in the health sector occurred in other places. Compared to the blossoming of health departments in the previous period, there seemed to be a *relative* decline in their stature in 1960–1980.

What can be identified to account for these changing trends? It is evident that U.S. health care has become increasingly subject to regulation, planning, and social controls over at least the last century. This has been generally opposed by the private sector of

U.S. health services, including not only most physicians and dentists but voluntary hospitals, pharmaceutical companies, and even professional schools as well. All these groups tended to view with alarm the expanding power of government and the diminishing independence of the private health sector.

If these trends could not be stopped, at least their impact could be weakened. Conservatism in the health care system was inevitably mirrored in the halls of the U.S. Congress. The strategy may not have been so crude and deliberate as the military policy of divide and conquer, but its effects were the same. No single public agency would be permitted to become very powerful. Insofar as authority was to be delegated below the national level, it should be dispersed. Medical schools, as well as hospitals, insurance carriers, welfare departments, or wholly new nongovernmental bodies, should play a part. The long history and the established legal status of public health agencies should not be permitted to endow them with a central role in the health sector. Broad authorities in any single type of state or local agency would constitute a continuing threat to the independence of the private sector.

There have also been weaknesses in the caliber of public health personnel. The decade of 1935–1945 was a time of great social change in the United States; it attracted into government many idealists and fighters for improvement in society. By the 1950s, with conservative national governments and the cold war atmosphere in the world, things were different. Physicians and others entering public health tried, in the main, to avoid controversy and to keep the agency on an even keel, not to tackle unmet social needs. The crusaders of the New Deal period were replaced by a cohort of office holders and managers.

The 1960s and 1970s in the United States then brought a new generation of young activists eager for social change, but few of them entered public health work. Health departments, like other parts of government, were seen as representing the status quo; the most spirited young people wanted to work in the community without burearcratic restraint. Public health agencies did not enjoy the swelling flow of financial support they had in the previous period; the principal innovations were occurring in other parts of the health care system. Assignment of health planning responsibilities to wholly new agencies (mainly nongovernmental, in spite of their federal public support) was a particular blow to the public health movement.

Thus, circumstances in the national environment, as well as in the internal staffing of health departments, contributed to the modest role these agencies played in the U.S. health sector of the 1960s and 1970s. Relatively few voices from the public health movement were heard in reaction to the great fragmentation of organized health programs. Aggressive leadership demanding social reforms in the U.S. health sector was replaced by the posture of the low profile.

With the election of the conservative Republican administration in 1981, there has been increasing pressure for termination, if not reversal, of past trends—less social planning and regulation, a smaller public sector and a larger private sector in health as in other aspects of life, and an abrupt reduction in governmental financing for social programs, particularly at the federal level. In the case of public regulations, a major effort has been made to reduce their impact on the health services, if not eliminate them entirely. The central thrust has been to maximize private health services and minimize regulatory controls, transferring responsibilities whenever possible from the federal to the state and local levels.

At this point, one can, of course, only speculate about the future. Will the whole structure of organized health services in the United States continue to go downhill? Or will a reaction set in to reestablish public responsibility for health services in general and public health activities in particular? If a reconstruction period should occur in the later 1980s, one might even expect that health departments—with their long tradition in local, state, and federal governments—may regain a central position in the structure of government, with major responsibilities for the planning and delivery of health services in the United States.

REFERENCES

Jain, Sager C., ed., *"Role of State and Local Governments in Relation to Personal Health Services,"* *American Journal of Public Health*, Vol. 71, January 1981, Supplement.

Jonas, Steven, et al., *Health Care Delivery in the United States*, New York: Springer Publishing Co., 1977.

Last, John M., ed., *Maxcy-Rosenau: Public Health and Preventive Medicine* New York: Appleton-Century-Crofts, 1980, 11th edition.

Mustard, Harry S., *Government in Public Health*, New York: Commonwealth Fund, 1945.

Rosen, George, *A History of Public Health*, New York: MD Publications, 1958.

Silver, George A., *A Spy in the House of Medicine*, Germantown, Md.: Aspen Systems Corp., 1976.

CHAPTER 14

The Politics of Health Care Regulation

Thomas W. Bice

During the 1970s, mounting expenditures for health services in the United States prompted both the federal and state governments to impose a variety of regulatory controls on the health services industry. Their principal targets were hospital services, the most costly and rapidly increasing component of health care spending. Regulation was extended over hospitals' investment decisions, their use by patients, and their revenues. Still, health care costs continued to rise, albeit at somewhat lower rates in the more stringently regulated states. By the close of the decade, policymakers had lost enthusiasm for regulatory solutions, and the 1980 election brought to power a presidential administration firmly committed to deregulation and the invigoration of market forces in the health services industry.

This chapter chronicles the rise and apparent decline of health care regulation during the 1970s. It focuses on the forces that gave impetus to the regulatory movement and shaped the structure and performance of particular regulatory efforts. The chapter begins with overviews of the structure of the health services industry and of earlier attempts to modify the industry's organization and functioning. This is followed by a discussion of the origins and nature of the principal regulatory approaches devised during the 1970s and of the market-oriented strategies that were developing alongside them. The chapter concludes with an analysis of poltical forces that are likely to shape health care regulation in the near future.

The regulatory programs enacted during the 1970s were directed at changing institutional behaviors that were rooted in fundamental structural features of the health services industry. These included the traditional patterns of relationship between physicians and hospitals and the means by which their services were reimbursed (Fuchs, 1973). Organizational and financial arrangements among health care providers had developed largely without direction from public policy (Anderson, 1968). However, many of the public policies and programs instituted after World War II reinforced traditional institutional arrangements, thereby contributing to the health care cost crisis of the 1970s. The structural features of the industry and the earlier public policies that have fueled expansion and rising costs are reviewed below.

THE HEALTH SERVICES INDUSTRY

The health services industry in the United States has traditionally been organized on the foundations of independence among providers of services and fee-for-service payment. Bolstered by ethical proscriptions against the corporate practice of medicine, physicians have preferred to practice as independent entreprenuers or in small partnerships. They have eschewed joining group practices and working as employees of hospitals and other institutions and have opposed the growth of ambulatory care services attached to inpatient facilities (Roemer, 1981). In consequence, health services in the United States have been divided rather distinctly between ambulatory care provided in physicians' offices and acute inpatient care rendered in hospital settings.

Despite the largely independent development of ambulatory and inpatient care, physicians' preferences have greatly influenced the nature and operation of hospitals and therefore their costs. Serving on the staffs of hospitals, physicians exert pressures on institutions to acquire and make available to them the equipment and personnel they regard as necessary for the treatment of their patients. As the medical profession has undergone specialization, hospitals' offerings of facilities and services have grown and diversified accordingly. Physicians are free to employ these increasingly expensive facilities in the treatment of their patients, but they have no direct stake in the financial solvency of the hospitals (Redisch, 1978). Such arrangements encourage physicians to be insensitive to the costs of inpatient care.

The independence that characterizes relationships among physicians is mirrored in the relationships among a community's hospitals. Health care planners and expert panels and commissions have pleaded for regionalized or coordinated hospital care since the 1920s (Pearson, 1976). Until recently, however, hospitals have remained largely autonomous institutions, each striving to offer a full range of services. Several forces combine to encourage and preserve autonomy. Lay boards of trustees take pride in directing institutions that provide for all their communities' health care needs, as do community groups that use particular hospitals, administrators who manage them, and physicians who staff them. Attempts to regionalize or merge facilities formally, therefore, typically encounter resistance among groups who would lose access to or control over fully equipped facilities (Starkweather, 1981).

The autonomous growth of hospitals has resulted in excess capacity and oversupplies of expensive inpatient equipment and services. Lacking knowledge of their communities' overall needs for services, hospitals have added beds, equipment, and services to the point of superfluity. The Institute of Medicine estimated that in the 1970s the United States had 100,000 excess hospital beds (Institute of Medicine, 1976). Other studies have indicated that the availability of complex equipment and services could be reduced without jeopardizing the quality of health care (McClure, 1976).

The fee-for-service mode of paying for health services and the widespread reliance on insurance join organizational features of the industry to promote growth in the availability and use of services. Paid on the basis of the numbers of services they provide, physicians face economic incentives to deliver more care (Monsma, 1970). Similarly, hospitals benefit financially from high censuses and from providing high-cost services. The practice of paying hospitals for the costs incurred in caring for patients has encouraged them to acquire and use expensive technologies and has blunted their sensitivity to costs of services (Abernethy and Pearson, 1979).

The growth of health insurance has facilitated the expansion and use of expensive services in two ways. First, as health care costs have risen, employees have demanded and received increasingly broad insurance coverage from employers in the form of fringe benefits. Protected against the economic consequences of high-cost services, they are relatively insensitive to the costs of care at the point of its delivery. Second, the assurance that third parties will cover the costs of services affords hospitals favorable status in credit markets, which, in turn, promotes further expansion and the acquisition of expensive technologies (Kelling and Williams, 1978).

HEALTH CARE POLICY

The federal government and the states have never articulated an overarching, internally consistent health care policy. Rather, they have promoted several relatively distinct programs, each intended to deal with particular problems. From the close of World War II through the 1960s, however, the general direction and effect of government's involvements in health care were to encourage the growth of the health services industry, to improve its services, and to promote citizens' access to them. The major exception to this pattern of growth was the inauguration of publicly supported comprehensive health planning in the mid-1960s, which laid the organizational foundation for subsequent efforts to regulate the investment decisions of health care institutions.

GROWTH-ORIENTED POLICIES

Three general types of policy initiatives have been used, primarily at the national level, to promote the development and use of health services: subsidies to the industry, tax policy, and health care financing schemes. All provided infusions of public funds into the health care sector, with limited incentives to alter fundamental organizational features of the industry. Indeed, they tended to reinforce prevailing relationships among providers and their preferred reimbursement mechanisms.

Subsidies for the development of health care resources began with the 1946 Hill-Burton program (Lave and Lave, 1974). This initiative made available federal formula grant funds to assist in the construction of nonprofit hospitals, primarily in low-income rural areas. A popular program, it was frequently amended to broaden the types of projects eligible to receive federal assistance through cash grants, loans, and loan guarantees. In the mid-1950s, the federal government established the National Institutes of Health (NIH) to provide grant funds for the support of biomedical research and development. In the 1960s federal programs to train physicians, dentists, nurses, nurse practitioners, and other health personnel were instituted.

Changes in tax policy also supported growth. Important in this respect were initiatives that prompted people to purchase health insurance. During World War II, exemption of employer contributions to group health insurance plans from the federal corporate income tax and the treatment of portions of individual outlays for health insurance and health care as deductible expenses from personal income taxes (Congressional Budget Office, 1980) had the effect of lowering the out-of-pocket price of health services and encouraging employees to take income in the form of health insurance coverage. In turn, the lower net price of health services due to insurance increased demand for health care.

The most significant policies in terms of their direct effects on public spending for health care are the Medicare and Medicaid programs. Enacted in the mid-1960s, they were the culmination of nearly a half-century of public debate surrounding national health insurance (NHI) proposals (Marmor, 1973). The financing arrangements and administrative procedures adopted for Medicare and Medicaid programs were strongly influenced by health care providers (Feder and Spitz, 1979). In effect, the federal and state governments initially agreed to purchase services without disturbing prevailing modes of organization and financing. Beneficiaries were guaranteed their freedom to choose health care providers. Physicians were permitted to charge reasonable and customary fees, and hospitals were paid for services on the basis of retroactively determined costs. Controls imposed on providers were relatively few and weak. Certification for hospitals' participation in Medicare was placed in the hands of the Joint Commission for the Accreditation of Hospitals, and organization created by the American College of Surgeons (ACS), the American Medical Association (AMA), and the American Hospital Association (AHA). Review of the use of hospital services was left largely to the hospitals themselves.

HEALTH CARE PLANNING

The first attempts to rationalize the organization of health care at the national level were initiated during the Johnson administration. Two programs were enacted in rapid succession, each charged with planning health care services. Both, however, were prevented by statutory constraints from exerting authority over health care providers.

The Regional Medical Program (RMP) was created to improve the delivery of services for the treatment of heart disease, cancer, and strokes. Based on a report produced by a prestigious national commission, Congress initially set out to establish federally funded regional centers that would link major teaching and research centers with community practitioners. This intention was deleted from the final legislation, however, largely as a result of opposition by the AMA. The AMA viewed the proposed centers as government intrusions into the practice of medicine that would divert patients from private practitioners. Hence the act that emerged from Congress explicitly forbade the centers to interfere with prevailing patterns of medical practice. The RMPs thus became largely channels for directing federal grants to educational and other programs throughout the United States until their authorization was allowed to elapse in 1974 (Bodenheimer, 1969; Glaser, 1973).

The second planning effort enacted during the Johnson administration—the Comprehensive Health Planning (CHP) Act—eventually became the organizational framework through which regulatory programs were administered (Hyman, 1975). At its outset, however, it also lacked authority to alter the organization of health services and institutions. The authorizing legislation created a national network of regional and statewide planning agencies comprising representatives of health care consumers and providers. In the spirit of the consumer movement of the 1960s and the War on Poverty's support of maximum feasible citizen participation in public sponsored reforms, the boards of CHP agencies were to include a majority of consumers.

The CHP agencies were to develop comprehensive plans that specified the numbers and types of services needed by populations in their jurisdictions. Regional CHP(b) agencies were to plan for regions within states, and statewide CHP(a) agencies were to do so for entire states. However, neither type of agency was empowered to compel either practitioners or institutions to abide by their plans. Like the RMP program, legislation creating CHP agencies directed them not to interfere in the organization and practice of medicine. Planning was to effect improvements, not through command and control, but by developing consensus among interest groups in communities.

RISE OF REFORM

By the late 1960s, the various threads of existing health policy were coming to be viewed as being internally inconsistent and intolerably costly. Moreover, mounting health care expenditures were attributed to systemic features of the health services industry. Liberal and conservative policymakers alike urged reforms. Proponents of extensive national health insurance schemes favored the imposition of strict controls over the industry as a precondition for expanding public financing for health care. Opponents of national health insurance stood against regulatory strategies, favoring instead reforms that would marshal market forces to effect efficiencies in the delivery of health care. Organized medicine opposed both strategies, for each would infringe upon cherished autonomy and threaten the continuation of fee-for-service medicine.

While Congress debated alternatives at the national level, several states initiated cost-containment programs. A short time thereafter, the federal government enacted other programs and, at the same time, launched efforts to encourage competitive solutions to the health care cost crisis. Inevitably, these courses were to lead to contradictory ends and to define the substance of health care policy debate in the 1980s.

REGULATORY REFORMS

The early 1970s witnessed the birth of three major regulatory strategies: capital expenditures and services controls, utilization review, and rate controls. Each was fashioned to deal with a particular aspect of the health care cost problem, and each was established largely independently of the others.

Certificate-of-Need Controls

Certificate-of-need (CON) regulation attempted to control growth of expenditures for inpatient services by limiting health care institutions' investments and offering of new services to those services certified as needed by regulatory agencies (Salkever and Bice, 1979). It aims to prevent institutions from investing in unnecessary expansion of capacity and in duplicating expensive equipment and services.

The first CON program was adopted by New York State in 1965, and by 1972 about half the states had imposed similar controls (Salkever and Bice, 1979). In that year Congress passed the section 1122 amendment to the Social Security Act (SSA), which provided participating states with federal funds to conduct capital expenditures reviews. This incentive led additional states to engage in this form of regulation. Finally, the National Health Planning and Resources Development Act of 1974 (PL 93-641), which revamped the U.S. health planning program, provided strong inducements for all states to adopt CON programs. Provisions of the law threatened to withhold various federal grants from states that failed to enact conforming programs.

Certificate-of-need programs were initally administered by the health planning agencies created by the CHP program. With the enactment of PL 93-641, those agencies were abolished and replaced by regional Health Systems Agencies (HSAs) and State Health Planning and Development Agencies (SHPDAs). The former were responsible for preparing plans for their regions and for conducting initial CON reviews of institutions' capital investment proposals. The SHPDAs, as state governmental agencies, were set up to devise statewide plans and render final decisions on CON applications. Like their predecessor CHP(b) agencies, HSAs are participatory bodies that are required to include a majority of consumer representatives on their governing boards (Atkisson and Grimes, 1976).

The introduction of CON controls evoked a storm of controversy. Drawing upon experience from other industries in which similar controls had been in effect, critics argued that CON regulation would inevitably encourage the growth of monopolies and provider cartels (Havighurst, 1973). Protected against competition from new entrants, they contended, existing institutions would be free to raise prices and to engage in other cost-increasing activities. Opponents of CON controls were especially critical of the potentially distorting effects of the complex, multitiered political structure that was devised to administer the regulation. Indeed, as the various versions of the health planning bill moved through Congress and after the enactment of the law, debate over who should control CON decision making became a major issue.

The National Health Planning and Resources Development Act and its CON provisions were at their outset testimony to the federal government's strong interests in controlling the expansion of the health services industry. Unlike the CHP program that had preceded it, the new planning legislation assigned broad authority to the secretary of the Department of Health and Human Services (DHHS) to formulate national planning goals and guidelines and to oversee the formation and functioning of state and regional planning agencies. Furthermore, the legislation directed state governments to enact and administer regulations that conformed to federal prescriptions. Despite these extensive federal prerogatives, the act placed most of the day-to-day administrative responsibilities in the hands of state and regional planning bodies.

Several governors regarded the federal government's extensive responsibilities as unwarranted intrusions into states' rights and entered into lawsuits to enjoin the secretary from implementing the law (Glantz, 1977). North Carolina, Missouri, and other states opposed the federal government's attempts to impose CON regulation. Governors of several states resisted the secretary's attempts to influence the designations of planning regions and the compositions of planning agencies' boards. However, the courts consistently upheld the constitutionality of the act and supported the secretary's exercise of authorities granted under the law. The planning program and its CON provisions nevertheless remained an irritant to many governors and state legislatures.

A measure of the continued opposition to federal control over health planning was the barrage of dissenting comments evoked by the secretary's publication of national health planning guidelines in 1978 (U.S. Department of Health, Education and Welfare, 1978). These guidelines set forth quantitative standards for optimal numbers of hospital beds and specific types of services. It was unclear, however, whether the guidelines were intended as binding national standards or merely as benchmarks for planning agencies. Under pressure from industry representatives and state governments, Congress yielded to the latter interpretation, thereby weakening the federal government's authority to enforce stringent planning targets.

Similar types of conflict surfaced within states between state and regional planning agencies. In some cases SHPDAs pursued rigorous constraint-oriented goals, whereas the regional HSAs emphasized planning objectives and were relatively permissive in their application of CON regulation (Cohodes, 1981). In other states, these priorities were reversed among state and regional agencies.

Perhaps the weakest link in the planning and regulatory network is the local HSA. Several observers have noted that the participatory structure mandated by PL 93-641 is based on erroneous political theory, namely, one that conceives of consumers as unswerving advocates of strong regulation (Vladeck, 1977). In fact, studies of the planning process reveal that consumer board members frequently join providers in supporting the growth of facilities and new services (Brown, 1981; Morone, 1981). Furthermore, attempts to meet the participatory requirements of PL 93-641 by representing minority members and other disadvantaged groups are likely to dampen agencies' attempts to control expansion of services. When agency decisions regarding CON applications reach the public at large, still more pressures toward weak enforcement materialize (Altman et al., 1981).

By the close of the 1970s, support for CON regulation had dwindled among federal policymakers. Research on the program had failed to substantiate planners' claims that it was containing either the growth of the hospital industry or the costs of hospital care (Sloan and Steinwald, 1980). Amendments to PL 93-641 in 1979 broadened governors' authorities over health planning at the expense of the secretary of DHHS and exempted various providers from CON coverage (Budetti, 1981; Havighurst, 1981). The election of the Reagan administration posed further threats to the continuation of health planning and regulation. Dedicated to eliminating the federal government's regulatory role, it slashed the program's budget as the first step in its strategy of returning planning and CON functions to the states (Davis, 1980).

Utilization Review

To win the support of health care providers for the Medicare and Medicaid programs, Congress initially placed few restrictions on physicians' and hospitals' freedom. The original legislation directed hospitals to establish utilization review committees to certify that hospital care rendered to beneficiaries was appropriate. However, it did not provide for rigorous enforcement or oversight of such activities. By the late 1960s mounting costs of the Medicaid program had prompted several states to impose utilization review to eliminate unnecessary hospital use. In 1972, Congress enacted the Professional Standards Review Organization (PSRO) amendment to the Social Security Act, which mandated such reviews nationally for beneficiaries of Medicare and Medicaid (Blumstein, 1978).

The legislation established a national network of PSROs that was to set and enforce standards of care for patients with particular health problems. These standards were to specify normal ranges of lengths of hospital stays as well as the uses of ancillary services. With these standards, PSROs were to compare an individual physician's practices to norms and call upon practitioners to justify practices that deviated from them. In situations in which physicians refuse to comply with PSRO standards, the secretary DHHS may withhold payment to the offending practitioners.

The legislation that created the PSRO program was ambiguous regarding its intent, and it evoked strong opposition from several quarters. As a result, implementation was slow and beset by controversy. A fundamental problem of the program since its inception has revolved around whether it was intended primarily to improve the quality of health care or to reduce use of hospital services and thereby contain costs (Havighurst and Blumstein, 1975). The principal author of the legislation, Senator Wallace Bennett (Rep., Utah), reasoned that both objectives could be met simultaneously. Holding that hospitalization and many medical procedures involved risks to patients, he argued that reducing unnecessary admissions and procedures would result in both improved quality and lower costs. As the DHHS moved to implement the program, however, varying interpretations of its quality versus cost-containment objectives materialized and persisted over the ensuing decade.

However one defines the program's intent, it provoked ferocious opposition from organized medicine. The AMA mounted an unsuccessful campaign to block passage of the law and has subsequently given it only mild and divided endorsement. It viewed the effort as an unwarranted intrusion of the federal government into the physician-patient relationship and as an attempt to impose "cookbook" medicine on the nation's physicians. It argued vehemently that the program would raise the cost of care and lower its quality by replacing physicians' clinical judgment with rigid bureaucratic standards of practice.

Other health care providers voiced opposition to the program as well. Nurses, psychologists, and others opposed the creation of agencies composed entirely of physicians who would be empowered to regulate their practices. Likewise, hospitals and health maintenance organizations (HMOs) expressed displeasure at the imposition of external reviews over their institutions.

Amidst protracted controversy, the PSRO program was slowly and, in many cases, begrudgingly implemented. Individual PSROs were to pass through two preliminary stages before becoming fully operational. By 1979, agencies had been created in 189 of the 195 designated PSRO areas, almost all of which had attained the second level of development. None, however, had achieved the status of a fully operational agency (Health Care Financing Administration, 1979).

Despite the long-standing dispute over the objectives of the PSRO program, its support among federal policymakers came to rest primarily on its ability to contain hospital costs. Thus, when a 1977 program evaluation failed to show that it had substantially reduced hospitalizations among Medicare beneficiaries, the Carter administration attempted to eliminate the program's funding. Fiscal support was restored, however, only to suffer the same judgment in 1981 at the hands of the Reagan administration. A victim of the Reagan administration's domestic budget cutting and animus toward federal regulation, its future as a federally supported program is in peril (Davis, 1980).

Hospital Rate Setting

The third prong in the regulatory strategy that developed during the 1970s focused on controlling hospitals' revenues. Such efforts were initiated during the 1960s under private auspices and by state governments, and hospital rates were controlled nationally under the Nixon administration's Economic Stabilization Program. Subsequently, however, Congress rejected attempts by the Carter administration to impose a national hospital revenue control program (Abernethy and Pearson, 1979). Rate setting has therefore developed primarily at the state level, with relatively little direction from the federal government.

The principal objective of all rate-setting programs is to encourage greater efficiency by subjecting institutions to the rigors of fixed rates or budgets (Bauer, 1978). In practice, however, the organizational frameworks within which rates are set and the means used to establish and enforce them vary widely (Coelen and Sullivan, 1981). By the late 1970s, some form of revenue review or control was in place in about half the states. Most of these were sponsored by hospital associations and Blue Cross plans; others were mandated by state governments. Generally speaking, the latter invoked more stringent controls.

The impetus for the early rate-setting programs came from state insurance commissioners and Medicaid agencies acting in response to rapidly increasing health insurance premiums and Medicaid expenditures. In several states, hospitals were also receptive to experimentation with reimbursement methods due to increasingly stringent definitions of allowable costs being used by their Medicaid agencies. Since Medicaid programs paid hospitals retroactively, denials of payment for services resulted in financial losses to hospitals. To avoid such shortfalls, hospitals pressed their state associations to join with local Blue Cross plans and state governments in fashioning prospective payment schemes. The federal government, in turn, encouraged the development of experimental prospective payment programs by authorizing waivers of Medicare's retroactive reimbursement procedures.

Although the federal government has not directly imposed rate setting nationally, it has indirectly stimulated the development of state programs. The Economic Stabilization Program of the early 1970s placed wage and price controls on the economy generally and retained special controls on hospitals after they had been removed from other sectors of business (Ginsburg, 1978). This experience alerted the hospital industry to the difficulties it would face in a nationally uniform rate-setting program and reinforced its resolve to combat federal rate-setting initiatives. The industry thus greeted the 1977 Carter administration's hospital cost-containment proposal with strong and effective opposition (Abernethy and Pearson 1979). Provisions of that proposal would have exempted from federal controls states that had implemented rate controls. Hence, hospital associations in several states reluctantly agreed to accept state regulations to avoid being placed under the control of more remote, and possibly more stringent, federal agencies.

Unlike the other major regulatory efforts of the 1970s, rate controls appear to have had at least some success in limiting the growth of expenditures for hospital services (Coelen and Sullivan, 1981). In consequence, they are likely to remain as cornerstones of the regulatory apparatus of states in which they have become institutionalized. Where they were enacted to avert federal controls, however, they may experience the fate of Colorado's program (Rice, 1981). In that case, once it appeared that the threat of federal intervention had disappeared, Colorado's hospital industry led a successful campaign to repeal the state's program. On the other hand, as will be discussed later in the chapter, states that have not had strong programs are beginning to take more direct steps to control Medicaid costs that may obviate the need for industry-wide rate controls.

MARKET-ORIENTED REFORMS

While the states and the federal government were fashioning regulatory efforts to deal with rising health care costs, other reforms were being initiated that sought to invigorate market forces to attain these ends. Specifically, three channels of policy developed during the 1970s: encouragement of the growth of health maintenance organizations, enforcement of federal antitrust laws, and market-oriented national health insurance plans. Eventually, these strategies came into conflict with regulatory approaches and gave rise to a national debate that posed them as competing policy paradigms.

Health Maintenance Organizations

Among its visionary proposals for the organization and financing of health care, the Committee on the Costs of Health Care, in the 1930s, recommended prepaid group practices. Under such arrangements, defined populations receive a full range of ambulatory and inpatient services from an organization in return for a fixed annual premium. The notion thus envisions placing physicians and hospitals under a single budget constraint that, in turn, may promote the efficient use of services and resources.

Despite these presumed advantages, prepaid group practices have been strongly resisted by organized medicine. By placing physicians under the employment of hospitals or other organizations, they run counter to ethical proscriptions against the corporate practice of medicine. Furthermore, their prepayment provisions are antagonistic to physicians' preferences for fee-for-service payment. Early attempts to establish prepaid group practices thus met strong resistance from the medical profession (Roemer, 1981). State and local medical societies in several states succeeded in persuading legislatures to enact prohibitions against their development, and, where these efforts failed, physicians boycotted colleagues and institutions that participated in prepaid plans.

In the face of such opposition, prepaid group practices took root in only a few communities. Nevertheless, experience over the years has indicated their ability to provide relatively more efficient medical care than the dominant fee-for-service practice mode. Studies have repeatedly shown that populations enrolled in large, well-established prepayment plans used fewer hospital days per capita, resulting in substantially lower overall costs (Luft, 1981). Furthermore, the integration of services effected by these plans came to be seen by critics of the health care industry as an exemplary model for improving the continuity and quality of health care. As the health care cost problem grew in the early 1970s, the prepaid group practice arrangement thus gained increasing visibility as a potential solution to systemic problems of the industry.

Embraced by liberals and conservatives alike, the prepaid group practice—renamed the health maintenance organization (HMO)—became the cornerstone of market-oriented reform. Despite strong opposition from the AMA, Congress enacted legislation in 1973 that provided federal subsidies to encourage the development of HMOs. The measure received broad support. Fiscal conservatives saw HMOs as the solution to rising health care costs, and proponents of national health insurance viewed them as a means of expanding the scope of covered benefits without substantially increasing costs (Falkson, 1980; Brown, 1983). Together, these perspectives led Congress to require federally certified HMOs to offer rich benefit packages at low prices, a formula that virtually assured slow growth (Starr, 1976).

The HMO strategy also ran counter to federal regulatory policy as expressed in the CON provisions of PL 93-641 of 1974. One arm of federal policy channeled subsidies to stimulate growth, whereas another erected barriers to new development. Proponents of the market-oriented HMO argued that the participatory nature of planning and regulatory bodies made them especially likely to be hostile to HMO development (Havighurst, 1973). Seeing planning agencies as being dominated by groups supporting existing health care institutions, HMO advocates contended that HMOs should be exempted from CON regulation.

These arguments were heeded by Congress in its reauthorization of the health planning act in 1979 (Budetti, 1981; Havighurst, 1981). Having lost much of its enthusiasm for regulatory controls and beginning tentatively to move toward competitive solutions, Congress directed the U.S. planning agencies to use CON controls to promote competition. In so doing, HMOs were to be exempted from CON regulation.

Antitrust Enforcement

The federal antitrust laws are the purest testimony to the commitment to free enterprise in the United States. They speak clearly and forcefully to the illegality of combinations and conspiracies aimed at thwarting competition. Like other legal doctrines, however, special circumstances are recognized that exempt particular practices from prosecution that might otherwise be adjudged as culpable (Gellhorn, 1976). Historically, health care providers enjoyed several such immunities, which shielded them from the antitrust laws. Beginning in the mid-1970s, however, a series of landmark judicial decisions removed several of these protections and opened the medical profession and hospitals to prosecution for anticompetitive practices (Havighurst, 1980; Miller, 1980). Applauded by proponents of market-oriented reforms in health care, these decisions greatly restricted organized medicine's control over its own members and removed many of its means of controlling health care institutions and competing health care practitioners.

The specific legal issues, decisions, and implications are too numerous and complex to consider here. The general effects of antitrust enforcement are clear, however. Namely, they opened a channel of influence over the organization and functioning of the health services industry that permitted greater competition, and they challenged several of the premises upon which regulatory strategies had been founded. Earlier it had been assumed, for example, that consumers of health care were insufficiently informed to choose among alternative providers. From the antitrust perspective, such presumed ignorance was seen as a possible consequence of the prohibitions by professional organizations against advertising. Likewise, the medical profession's traditional opposition to the corporate practice of medicine came to be viewed as a conspiratorial means of preventing insurance companies from exercising legitimate controls on behalf of their subscribers.

By defining the practice of medicine as a business, the antitrust perspective saw market failures as being the consequences of conscious anticompetitive practices. Proponents of regulation, on the other hand, had conceived of them as by-products of the unique features of medical markets. Advocates of market-oriented reforms thus adopted the antitrust instrument as a means of alerting policymakers to fundamental structural causes of the health services industry's inefficiencies. In turn, they criticized regulatory strategies for at best merely dealing with symptoms of problems and at worst reinforcing them. The antitrust movement thus added elements of skepticism in the late 1970s to the already growing disenchanchment with regulatory strategies.

Market-Oriented National Health Insurance

The early 1970s brought a resurgence of public debate on the issue of national health insurance that led to controversy about the relative strengths of regulatory versus market-oriented reforms. Debate initially centered on differences among specific provisions and estimated costs of the countless proposals tendered by the Nixon administration, members of Congress, and interest groups (Davis, 1975). Seemingly, consensus had been achieved regarding whether there would be a national health insurance scheme; the legislative task at hand was to select an approach from the array of alternatives.

Initially, the lines of debate were drawn between plans proffered by liberal Democrats led by Senator Edward Kennedy and those proposed by the Nixon administration and the AMA. The former called for virtual universal coverage of the nation's population under a federally administered health insurance plan, accompanied by extensive regulation of the health services industry. The latter proposed relatively minor modifications of existing financing schemes and considerably less active government involvement. The more ambitious proposals eventually foundered on the immensity of their implied costs to the public treasury and on the specter of the vastly extended regulatory apparatus they envisioned. This specter, in turn, prompted proponents of market-oriented reforms to lay out their competing scenarios in equal detail.

The most thoroughgoing exposition of the market-oriented approach was embodied in the "Consumer Choice Health Plan" (Enthoven, 1978). It envisioned promoting price competition among HMO-like organizations that would offer various benefit packages to consumers. Cost consciousness among providers would be instilled by an organizational framework and financing schemes that subjected hospitals and physicians alike to the rigors of fixed budgets. Such arrangements, in turn, would obviate the need for external investment and rate controls. Competing health care organizations' investment decisions and rate structures would be disciplined by market forces.

To promote awareness of costs among consumers, market-oriented schemes would limit subsidies. Under national health insurance, government would provide fixed contributions to groups of consumers, and tax subsidies for the purchase of private insurance would be eliminated. In principle, consumers would thereby be encouraged to purchase insurance plans that promised to return the greatest benefit for the prices paid.

By the close of the 1970s, as the sputtering national economy moved public attention to other domestic issues, the prospects for national health insurance had evaporated. However, continuing increases in health care costs sustained debate on the relative merits of regulatory and market-oriented cost-containment strategies. With the election of the Reagan administration, the balance in the dispute shifted dramatically to the side of market-oriented strategies for containing costs. Moreover, the competitive approach provided a positive legislative agenda that reinforced the administration's antiregulatory stance.

THE FUTURE OF HEALTH CARE REGULATION

By the early 1980s, it appeared that the regulatory era had ended. Federal programs enacted during the previous decade had failed to stem the growth of health care costs and were slated by the Reagan administration for extinction. Should this occur, the federal government will cease to be a major force in the direct regulation of health care institutions' investment decisions and of the use of hospital services.

The wane of regulation sponsored by the federal government does not mark the end of controls over the health services industry, however. Indeed, more draconian measures may be afoot. Both the federal and state governments, as well as the private sector, are increasingly turning to reform of reimbursement mechanisms to control health care costs. Price controls are likely, therefore, to become a significant regulatory device.

The emerging movement to impose price controls differs from earlier attempts. The hospital cost control bills sponsored by the Carter administration and the prospective rate-setting programs established by several states sought to control directly all or most hospital revenues. Newer forms of price control are more decentralized and selective. They rely on payers' market power to encourage providers to compete for exclusive contracts. Those providers that offer the lowest bids are selected to be preferred providers for the beneficiaries of particular insurance programs. Under such arrangements, insurers will not pay for care rendered to beneficiaries in hospitals that are not designated preferred providers. The state of California adopted this approach in 1983 for its Medicaid program, and the idea is gathering support among private insurers and business coalitions in other parts of the United States as well.

Meanwhile, the Reagan administration had advanced two related reimbursement schemes that would indirectly control providers' revenues. One envisions setting prices that hospitals charge Medicare on the basis of patients' diagnoses and the mixes of services they use. The other proposes paying providers prospectively for care rendered to Medicare beneficiaries. The latter scheme would presumably encourage Medicare enrollees to seek out the least costly plans.

Were the preferred provider approach and other forms of prospective payment to be widely adopted, the need for direct regulation of providers' business decisions would presumably become superfluous. Providers would have incentives to use their resources in the most efficient manner in order to compete favorably for preferred provider contracts and for enrollees. Hence, the locus of regulatory activity would shift from planning and rate-setting agencies to the agencies and organizations that pay for health care—Medicare, Medicaid, and private insurers. Undoubtedly, these agencies and organizations would ultimately take on responsibility for ensuring that services they purchase are appropriate and of high quality by imposing utilization and quality controls.

Thus, as of the early 1980s, it would appear that payment-oriented regulation will become the principal instrument for controlling the costs of health care. However, this approach is based on several assumptions that have yet to be tested. First, it assumes that governments have no particular interest in the fates of health care institutions that do not provide services to beneficiaries of public reimbursement programs. Second, it assumes that the people of the United States will accept infringements upon their privilege to seek care from providers that they themselves choose. Finally, it rests on the yet to be demonstrated belief that health care providers will develop integrated systems of services and will compete among themselves on the basis of price. These assumptions will likely set the health care policy debate of the 1980s and beyond.

REFERENCES

Abernethy, David S. and David A. Pearson, *Regulating Hospital Costs: The Development of Public Policy*, Ann Arbor, Mich.: AUPHA Press, 1979.

Altman, Drew, Richard Greene and Harvey M. Sapolsky, *Health Planning and Regulation: The Decision-Making Process*, Ann Arbor, Mich.: AUPHA Press, 1981.

Anderson, Odin W., *The Uneasy Equilibrium*, New Haven; College and University Press, 1968.

Atkisson, Arthur and Richard Grimes, "Health Planning in the United States: An Old Idea with a New Significance," *Journal of Health Politics, Policy and Law*, Vol. 1, Fall 1976, pp. 295–318.

Bauer, Katherine, "Hospital Rate Setting—This Way to Salvation?" in Michael Zubkoff, Ira E. Raskin and Ruth Hanft, eds., *Hospital Cost Containment*, New York: Prodist, 1978, pp. 324–369.

Blumstein, James F., *"The Role of PSRO's in Hospital Cost Containment,"* in Michael Zubkoff, Ira E. Raskin and Ruth Hanft, eds., *Hospital Cost Containment*, New York: Prodist, 1978, pp. 461–485.

Bodenheimer, Thomas S., "Regional Medical Programs: No Road to Regionalizarion, " *Medical Care Review*, Vol. 26, December 1969, pp. 1125–1166.

Brown, Lawrence D, "Some Structural Issues in the Health Planning Program," in Institute of Medicine, *Health Planning in the United States: Selected Policy Issues*, Washington, D.C.: National Academy Press, 1981, pp. 1–46.

Brown, Lawrence D., *Politics and Health Care Organization: HMO's as Federal Policy*, Washington, D.C.: The Brookings Institution, 1983.

Budetti, P. P., "Congressional Perspectives on Health Planning and Cost Containment: Lessons from the 1979 Debate and Amendments," *Journal of Health and Human Resources Administration*, Vo. 4, No. 1, 1981, pp. 10–19.

Coelen C. and D. Sullivan, "An Analysis of the Effects of Prospective Reinbursement Programs on Hospital Expenditures," *Health Care Financing Review*, Vo. 2, No. 1, 1981, pp. 1–40.

Cohodes, D. R., "Interstate Variation in Certificate of Need Programs," in Institute of Medicine, *Health Planning in the United States: Selected Policy Issues*, Washington, D.C.: National Academy Press, 1981, pp. 47–80.

Congressional Budget Office, *Tax Subsidies for Medical Care: Current Policies and Possible Alternatives*, Washington, D.C.: U.S. Government Printing Office, January 1980.

Davis, Karen, *National Health Insurance: Benefits, Costs and Consequences*, Washington, D.C.: The Brookings Institution, 1975.

Davis, Karen, "Reagan Administration Health Policy," *Journal of Public Health Policy*, Vol. 2, December 1980, pp. 312–322.

Enthoven, Alain C., "Consumer-Choice Health Plan," *New England Journal of Medicine*, Part I, Vol. 298, March 23, 1978, pp. 650–658; Part II, Vol. 298, March 30, 1978, pp. 709–720.

Falkson, Joseph L., *HMO's and the Politics of Health System Reform*, Bowie, Md.: Robert J. Brady Co., 1980.

Feder, Judith and Bruce Spitz, "The Politics of Hospital Payment," *Journal of Health Politics, Policy and Law*, Vol. 4, Fall 1979, pp. 435–463.

Fuchs, Vistor R, "Health Care and the United States Economic System—An Essay in Abnormal Physiology," in John B. McKinlay, ed., *Economic Aspects of Health Care*, New York: Prodist, 1973, pp. 57–94.

Gellhorn, D., *Antitrust Law and Economics in a Nutshell*, St. Paul, Minn.: West Publishing Co., 1976.

Ginsburg, Paul B., "Impact of the Economic Stabilization Program on Hospitals: An Analysis with Aggregate Data." in Michael Zubkoff, Ira E. Raskin and Ruth S. Hanft, eds., *Hospital Cost Containment*, New York: Prodist, 1978, pp. 293–323.

Glantz, L. H., "Legal Aspects of Health Facilities Regulation," in H. H. Hyman, ed., *Health Regulation: Certificate of Need and Section 1122*, Germantown, Md.: Aspen System Corp., 1977, pp. 75–104.

Glaser, William A., "Experiences in Health Planning in the United States," Paper presented at the Conference on Health Planning in the United States: Past Experiences and Future Imperatives," New York: Columbia University, June 1973.

Havighurst, Clark C., "Regulation of Health Facilities and Services by 'Certificate of Need'," *Virginia Law Review*, Vol. 59, 1973, pp. 1143–1232.

Havighurst, Clark C., "Antitrust Enforcement in the Medical Services Industry: What Does it All Mean?" *Milbank Memorial Fund Quarterly/Health and Society*, Vol. 58, Winter 1980, pp. 89–123.

Havighurst, Clark C., "Health Planning for Deregulation: Implementing the 1979 Amendments," *Law and Contemporary Problems*, Vol. 44, No. 1, 1981, pp. 33–76.

Havighurst, Clark C. and J. M. Blumstein, "Coping with Quality/Cost Tradeoffs in Medical Care: The Role of PSRO's," *Northwestern Law Review*, Vol. 70, 1975, pp. 66–68.

Health Care Financing Administration, *Professional Standards Review Organization 1979 Program Evaluation*, Washington, D.C.: U.S. Department of Health and Human Services, 1979.

Hyman, Herbert H., *Health Planning: A Systematic Approach*, Germantown, Md.: Aspen Systems Corp., 1975.

Institute of Medicine, *Controlling the Supply of Hospital Beds*, Washington, D.C.: National Academy of Sciences, 1976.

Kelling R. S., Jr. and P. C. Williams, "The Projected Response of the Capital Markets to Health Care Facilities Expenditures," in G. K. McLeod and M. Perlman, eds., *Health Care Capital: Competition and Control*, Cambridge: Ballinger Publishing Co., 1978, pp. 275–304.

Lave, Judith R. and Lester B. Lave, *The Hospital Construction Act: An Evaluation of the Hill-Burton Program, 1948–1973*, Washington, D.C.: The American Enterprise Institute for Public Policy Research, 1974.

Luft, Harold S., *Health Maintenance Organizations: Dimensions of Performance*, New York: John Wiley & Sons, 1981.

Marmor, Theodore R., *The Politics of Medicare*, Chicago: Aldine Publishing Co., 1973.

McClure, Walter, *Reducing Excess Hospital Capacity*, Final report of Contract No. HRA-230-76-0086, Bureau of Health Planning and Resources Development, U.S. Department of Health, Education and Welfare, 1976.

Miller, F. H., "Antiturst and Certificate of Need: Health Systems Agencies, The Planning Act, and Regulatory Capture," *Georgetown Law Journal*, Vol. 68, 1980, pp. 873–918.

Monsma, G. N. Jr., "Marginal Revenue and the Demand for Physicians' Services," in Herbert E. Klarman, ed., *Empirical Studies in Health Economics*, Baltimore: Johns Hopkins Press, 1970, pp. 145–160.

Morone, James A., "The Real World of Representation: Consumers and the HSA's," in Institute of Medicine, *Health Planning in the United States: Selected Policy Issues*, Washington, D.C.: National Academy Press, 1981, pp. 237–265.

Pearson, David A., "The Concept of Regionalized Personal Health Services in the United States, 1920–1975," in Edward W. Saward, ed., *The Regionalization of Personal Health Services*, New York: Prodist, 1976, pp. 10–14.

Redisch, M. A., "Physician Involvement in Hospital Decision-Making," in Michael Zubkoff, Ira E. Raskin and Ruth Hanft, eds., *Hospital Cost Containment*, New York: Prodist, 1978, pp. 217–243.

Rice, Donald, "Government Regulation of the Hospital Industry in Colorado," *Journal of Public Health Policy*, Vol. 2, March 1981, pp. 58–69.

Roemer, Milton I., *Ambulatory Health Services in American: Past, Present, and Future*, Rockville, Md.: Aspen Systems Corp. 1981.

Salkever, David S. and Thomas W. Bice, *Hospital Certificate-of-Need Controls*, Washington, D.C.: The American Enterprise Institute for Public Policy Research, 1979.

Sloan, Frank A. and Bruce Steinwald, "Effects of Regulation on Hospital Costs and Input Use," *Journal of Law and Economics*, Vol. 23, No. 1, 1980, pp. 81–109.

Starkweather, David B., *Hospital Mergers in the Making*, Ann Arbor, Mich.: Health Administration Press, 1981.

Starr, Paul, "The Undelivered Health System,"*The Public Interest*, Vol. 42, No. 1, 1976, pp. 66–85.

U.S. Department of Health, Education and Welfare, Health Resources Administration, "National Guidelines for Health Planning," *Federal Register*, Vol. 3, March 28, 1978, pp. 13040–13050.

Vladeck, Bruce C., "Interest-group Representation and the HSA's: Health Planning and Political Theory," *American Journal of Public Health*, Vol. 67, January 1977, pp. 23–29.

CHAPTER 15

National Health Insurance and the Next Half-Step

Theodore R. Marmor

The debate about compulsory national health insurance (NHI) has extended over fully one-third of the life of the United States. Teddy Roosevelt first made national health insurance an issue in the Bull Moose campaign in 1912. Since then, and with varying degrees of intensity, the issue has held a place on the national political agenda. In the 1960s, NHI returned squarely to center stage; enactment of Medicare and Medicaid represented the culmination of a decade-long struggle to provide health care to the aged. But Medicaid and Medicare did not resolve the essential political controversy surrounding NHI. The basic question of how the government should create a universal health insurance program remained despite national programs for the poor and the elderly.

Over the years, national health insurance has come to mean different things to different people. Conceptions of what NHI *should be* affect both the likelihood of a program's enactment and the impact a program would have on the health care system. This chapter first characterizes the prevailing views of NHI and their use in the continuing national health insurance debate.[1]

One of the consequences of the ideological intensity generated by the NHI debate in the United States is that very little time and attention has been devoted to the nuts-and-bolts issues of implementation. When the issue of policy direction is uncertain, political incentives press actors to mobilize supporters not to design operational measures to ensure policy compliance. And when the policy choice is deeply controversial— as with NHI—implementation estimates are part of the arsenal of policy warfare not aids to policy design. Thus we cannot expect that the NHI debate will focus on issues of implementation despite their substantial practical significance.

---

[1]For further discussion of these issues, as well as extensive discussion of the institutional and regulatory components of NHI program, see Feder et al. (1980).

COMPETING NATIONAL HEALTH INSURANCE PROPOSALS

A typology of NHI proposals can be developed on several different criteria. One is administrative: In what people and institutions is administrative control vested? A second focuses on the definition and scope of benefits provided: Who is eligible to receive what medical services? A third is fiscal: Who pays and how—through premiums, payroll taxes, or user charges?[2]

The differing political perspectives on NHI are best understood when proposals are characterized by their source of financing and scope of benefits. No descriptive category can be exclusive, and it is necessary to refer to administrative and other considerations when discussing both financing and benefit criteria.

The use of financing and benefit provisions as base criteria gives a spectrum of proposals broken into the following distinctive bands:

1. *Narrow coverage, minimal federal financial role.*   Proposals in this class address an exlicitly defined problem or population segment. Catastrophic medical expense is the problem most frequently addressed. Some proposals define catastrophic expense as set out-of-pocket expenditures; other proposals define it as a percentage of income rather than fixed amount. Proposals that emphasize catastrophic protection may provide other coverage as well. Typically, this coverage concentrates on discrete populations—the old, the poor, or the very young.

2. *Wide coverage, limited federal financial role.*   The NHI proposals that fall within this second category would provide wider benefit and population coverage than proposals in category 1 above but would still call for a limited federal financing role. The limitation would be achieved through distribution of premium costs among employers, employees, and government and through reliance on private insurance companies to underwrite benefits. Plans of this kind could be voluntary, with participation at the discretion of employers and individuals, or mandatory, with all employers and individuals required to obtain coverage. Most plans in the second category combine employment-based coverage with public plans for the poor and the elderly to constitute a universal health insurance plan or plans for the entire population by aggregation.

   Plans along this line are national in scope, extending their reach to specified beneficiaries wherever they are in the United States. They propose government health insurance in the sense of coercing participation, although the compulsory financing is formally off the budget. They also constitute schemes of universal insurance in the sense that for practical purposes, all people in the United States fall into one or another of the subplans. These are proposals for universalizing health insurance by aggregating different plans, not be creating one plan for all.

3. *Wide coverage, large federal financing role.*   The most far reaching of the proposals within this third category, the Kennedy-Corman bill[3] prominent through most of the 1970s, proposed a federal monopoly of the medical insurance business. Rather than

---

[2]For a somewhat dated but still relevant discussion, see Davis (1975).

[3]Introduced in the Ninety-fourth Congress.

relying on the private insurance market, this plan proposed to establish a single NHI program for all U.S. residents—employed or unemployed, old or young, rich or poor. Benefits would have been extremely broad and patients would not have shared the costs at time of service use. The plan would have been financed jointly by payroll taxes and general revenues and administered by the federal government. Administration in this plan would have gone beyond payment of claims to allocation of a predetermined national health budget, by type of medical service, to regions and localities.

This plan's universal scope, comprehensive benefits, and public financing were similar to NHI plans in other Western industrial nations. This similarity, however, should not obscure considerable diversity in financing and administration. In Great Britain, for example, the national government not only pays for all services, it also owns the health facilities and employs the providers. In Canada, the national government pays only a portion of total expenses; the rest is paid by the provincial governments, which, within certain nationally uniform conditions, administer their own plans.

It should be noted that an accurate description of financing provisions is not as easy as it might appear to be. Three distinct cost figures are involved. The first is the total cost of any NHI program, that is, the sum of the costs to individuals, employers, subfederal units of government, and the federal government. The second cost figure includes costs incurred by government at all levels, and the third is the federal cost alone. (In public discussion, cost figures are sometimes used in misleading ways as, for example, when the federal cost is used to mean total program cost. Total program cost figures would, if complete, incorporate private contributions and private payments.)

POLITICS OF NATIONAL HEALTH INSURANCE

The foregoing classification of various legislative proposals highlights the primary source of controversy in political debates on national health insurance—the legitimacy and desirability of government intervention in health care. Government intervention involves fundamentals such as the redistribution of income, status, and influence and the legitimacy of highly valued political beliefs. Because the stakes are so high, NHI generates ideologically intense debate matched by few other issues in U.S. politics.

The antagonists in the debate are well defined and well known, and they have remained relatively stable over time.[4] One camp wishes to shift medical care financing from the private to the public sector in the belief that private financing of medical care has produced intolerable inequities in the distribution of services. The members of this coalition are united in their belief that universal, government-financed health insurance is the crucial missing element in the panoply of social welfare programs enacted in the 1930s.

Historically, large industrial labor unions, the Congress of Industrial Organizations (CIO), and later the United Auto Workers (UAW), have spearheaded the recurrent demands for NHI in the United States. More recently, their special aim has been to eliminate health insurance costs, generally the most expensive fringe benefit, from

---

[4]For a more extensive discussion of this topic refer to Bowler et al. (1977) and Marmor (1973).

contract negotiations with management. They are convinced that a compulsory, tax-financed health program would provide their membership with comprehensive coverage at lower cost to union families. The leadership of the NHI movement also includes a number of prominent individuals, most of whom were central figures in the formulation and enactment of the original Social Security Act (SSA) and every social welfare program since then. For 40 years they have been involved in administering federal social insurance and welfare programs, advising the president and members of Congress on health and welfare matters, and advocating government-financed health insurance.[5] The industrial unions and social insurance reform leaders have been regularly bolstered by a loose coalition of liberal church, professional, service, and consumer organizations intermittently united in their support of NHI.

An equally broad coalition, ranging in membership from medical and hospital groups to the U.S. Chamber of Commerce and the Young Americans for Freedom, has traditionally opposed comprehensive government health insurance. This coalition views government financing as synonymous with government control, and government control as synonymous with impersonal and inadequate medical care. Medical professionals particulary have feared NHI as a threat to their professional status and discretion. These groups have favored, at most, limited federal involvement in a NHI program.

The arguments and the alignments in the NHI debate have remained much the same over time. The nature of the battlefield has changed, but the antagonists and the underlying principles at stake have hardly changed at all.[6] Unions and other pro-NHI forces have consistently found support among the national leaders of the Democratic party, and the position of the health industry has been generally supported by Republicans.

The historically vitriolic debate over NHI has helped to maintain the bipolar coalitions. The emergence of voluntary private insurance programs in the 1930s momentarily dampened but did not eliminate the demand for government intervention. For two decades after World War II government health insurance proposals—for all, the elderly, or the poor-were salient. The enactment of Medicare in 1965 brought a temporary halt to the long-standing cleavage between the coalitions, and for nearly 5 years the public discussion of medicine centered on the problems of implementing Medicare and Medicaid and dealing with the unprecedented level of inflation that followed their enactment.

Although heralded as major innovations, both programs had been preceded by smaller steps taken to expand the government role in the financing of medical care. Some veterans, for example, have for years enjoyed free government health care. This building-block approach to national health insurance, which establishes government intervention by increments of discrete population groups, might have been expected to have moved beyond dispute the basic principle of a major government role in medical care. But this has not been the case. As the disagreements narrow, the antagonists nonetheless contend sharply. The stakes are still seen to be very high.

The 1968 presidential election was the first since World War II in which the

[5]These include Wilbur Cohen (secretary of the Department Health, Education and Welfare—DHEW, 1968–1969); I. S. Falk (Social Security Administration, 1936–1954); Robert Ball (Commissioner of the Social Security Administration, 1962–1973); and Nelson Cruikshank (Advisory Council Social Security Financing, 1957–1958 / Health Insurance Benefits Council, 1965–1972).

[6]An excellent narrative account of the struggle for a compulsory health insurance program in the United States is provided by Daniel Hirschfield (1970). Although focusing on the period from 1932–1943, he provides a useful account of the work undertaken on behalf of compulsory health insurance in the early decades of the twentieth century. For the relationship of Medicare and Medicaid to this earlier history see Marmor (1973).

candidates felt no compunction about ignoring the issue of NHI. But that hiatus was temporary, and when the debate reemerged it was to be importantly shaped first by the vocabulary of "crisis" and then by the inflationary experience of the late 1960s and 1970s.

The leading advocates of NHI in the early 1970s comprised the so-called Committee of 100, chaired initially by Walter Reuther of the UAW union. These advocates renewed the practice of treating NHI as the answer to the "crisis" in U.S. medicine. Not only were some of the proponents and proposals familiar, but so were the ingredients of the debate. Medical care problems were cited as if no dispute about their existence and magnitude was possible. Public choice, the nation was told, consisted of selecting the proper response to the crisis in cost, distribution, access, and quality of U.S. medical care. The debate was structured as if the solutions were reasonable responses to worsening conditions when, in fact, the solutions were framed out of long-standing political and ideological conviction.

The crisis rhetoric, moreover, has been bipartisan, even if the proposed solutions to the crisis are not. President Nixon, referring to the U.S. medical care system in 1969, warned that "unless action is taken, both administratively and legislatively . . . within the next two to three years, we will have a breakdown in our medical care system with consequences affecting millions of people throughout this country" (Nixon, 1969). Senator Edward Kennedy's 1972 book, *In Critical Condition*, captured the views of many politicians about the problems of U.S. patients in the 1970s (Kennedy, 1972), where as a series of articles on "Our Ailing Medical System," in *Fortune* magazine alleged that "American medicine, the pride of the nation for many years, stands . . . on the brink of chaos" (Fortune, 1970). Labor leaders maintained almost ritualistically that "there is little [they] can add in the way of new facts and figures to further prove what is generally accepted: that there is a medical care crisis in America" (Meany, 1971).

Because of the central role expenditure levels played in political debate, they deserve discussion here. In 1950, the United States spent $12 billion on medical care; by 1977 the national medical care bill exceeded $160 billion. Per capita expenditures grew from $78 to $730 in the same period. Within a quarter-century, the percentage of the gross national product committed to medical care has more than doubled reaching around 10 percent in the early 1980s amounted to over 9.1 percent (U.S. Department of Health, Education and Welfare, 1980).

Increases in medical expenses predate enactment of Medicare and Medicaid and are generally attributed to the expansion of insurance coverage. Public insurance programs, after all, are intended to reduce financial barriers to care and can therefore be expected to increase the volume of services provided. But experience with insurance in general and public insurance in particular reveals that the price as well as the volume of services rise with insurance coverage. Part of the price increase undoubtedly reflects the rising cost of necessary resources and changes in the quality of the service provided. Some proportion, however, represents a transfer of income to providers, the social value of which has been called into question.

Historically, medical prices have risen faster than prices for consumer goods and, as overall prices have risen, medical prices have increased even more rapidly. Before 1966, consumer prices exclusive of medical services rose at 2 percent per year, medical prices at 3.2 percent per year. Between 1966, when Medicare and Medicaid went into effect, and 1971, when price controls were introduced, general prices increased at 5.8 percent per year and medical prices at 7.9 percent per year (U.S. Executive Office of the President, 1975). The rise in hospital prices has been particularly rapid, with increases in expenses per day often exceeding 14 percent annually since the removal of price controls in 1973. The appropriateness of this increase has been subject to particular challenge because hospital occupancy rates have been declining (U.S. Executive Office of the President, 1976).[7]

Because of the government's sizable commitment to health care, these expenditure increases take their toll on the federal budget. In 1965, before Medicare and Medicaid, the federal government spent 4.8 percent of its budget ($5.2 billion) on health care. By 1969, the share of the budget allocated to health care had doubled. Rising continually, federal health expenditures represented 12.4 percent of the federal budget in 1977 (U.S. Executive Office of the President, 1979).

To return to the political arena, these expenditure increases have significantly affected the debate on NHI. Until recently, the issue of cost took a particular and limited form. How to reduce or eliminate the financial barriers between individuals and adequate medical care. Within the space of a few years, cost has become a fundamental political constraint. The cost question is properly framed not by asking how the U.S. citizen can secure medical care, but rather, how the U.S. government can afford a national health insurance program. Concern about the organization, quality, and distribution of medical care has somewhat receded in importance. But the question of overall program costs in a NHI plan now casts a pervasive and distinctive shadow over all other issues in a way that it never did before. Paul Starr (1982) has observed the following:

> It hardly needs pointing out that the concern with cost control reflects the condition of the economy and particularly the uneasiness over inflation. As one of the four most inflationary sectors of the economy (the others have been energy, food and housing), medical care is an inevitable target of anti-inflation policies. But even if fiscal and inflationary pressures were to subside, the search for cost restraints in medical care would persist. For medical costs cause concern not only because of their magnitude, but also because of increasing skepticism about their legitimacy. The studies, frequently reported in the press, of unnecessary surgery, excess hospital capacity, duplication of technology and so on reflect a crisis of confidence in the value of medical services and methods of resource allocation. Similar doubts now surround education, welfare program, and many other areas of social policy. Rising costs and diminished confidence set the debate about health insurance today in a new context: the old reformers, as well as the physicians, took the value of medical care for granted. They just wanted more of it for everybody. Now reformers want less of some services, more of others, but most of all, control of what it all adds up to.

Specifically, the cost issue dominates the debate on the desirability of greater government intervention in the health sector. Based on expertise to date, many NHI opponents argue that expansion of insurance coverage will serve primarily to exacerbate the recent growth in medical care expenditures. Although some segments of the population would benefit from greater insurance protection, the bulk of the population, it is argued, would suffer from higher taxes, premiums, or rising costs for whatever medical bills NHI did not cover. Even the benefits associated with expanded protection have been questioned. Although third parties pay 94 percent of the expenses for hospital care, they only pay 61 percent of the expenses of physicians' services. Expansion of

---

[7]Expenditure and utilization data are presented in Gibson and Fisher (1978).

coverage, therefore, is directed primarily at physicians' services. As insurance lowers prices to consumers, there is reason to believe that physicians will provide and patients will receive services for which costs exceed health benefits derived. Finally, beyond these effects on the health sector, there is opposition of the expansion of the federal budget that NHI would entail. Many believe a larger federal budget would divert resources from more productive activities, to the detriment of the nation's economic health.

These considerations have been used to justify the assertion that the United States cannot afford NHI. This argument is espoused by a new breed of conservative Democrats who have joined with Republicans in opposition to NHI. The counterargument, made by liberal Democrats and their constituencies, is that NHI is required to bring the current medical inflation under control, in other words, that the United States cannot afford not to have NHI, specifically of the third variety.

The latter position has been taken by Senator Kennedy who maintains that comprehensive coverage and expenditure control can be compatible. Fiscal concerns, however, have led Kennedy and his organized labor supporters to abandon their insistence on a single, government-run NHI plan. Instead, they are willing to approach NHI by aggregating public and private plans. But the benefits their 1979 plan would offer and the controls it would establish on all health spending remained very much the same as those in earlier bills.

Carter, on the other hand, was reluctant to offer such comprehensive coverage or to undertake such extensive government control. Caught between the concerns of his economic advisers that a major increase in government spending would be inflationary and the pressure of his social policy and political advisers to improve insurance coverage available to U.S. citizens, Carter's compromise position was to offer comprehensive coverage in phases: first, catastrophic coverage, then, coverage of the very young, and, finally, Medicaid and Medicare reform. This provided for more extensive population coverage (and therefore more public spending) than his economic advisers recommend but for less coverage than Kennedy had proposed.

The 1980s promise to see another change in the battlefield of NHI, though again the underlying principles at stake remain largely unchanged. Before turning to specific NHI proposals, a number of potentially significant trends in progress should be noted. Accurately predicting the changing structures of institutions and political arrangements is a hopeless task. A given set of variables, such as the ones to be discussed, can be identified as significant, however, even as we acknowledge that, other factors and events outside our field of vision will come into play.

One trend to note is the proportion of the elderly in the United States. They now represent 11 percent of U.S. residents, and this percentage is expected to increase to about 12.5 percent in the year 2000 (Crystal). The most rapidly increasing group among the aged in the next 15 years will be those over 85. The second trend in progress is a dramatically rising supply of physicians. In 1960, there were 148 physicians for every 100,000 people in the United States; by 1975, this figure had risen to 175 per 100,000. By 1995, it is estimated that there will be well over 200 physicians per 100,000 population (Starr, 1977; Hadley, 1980). And although the number of physicians had been rising, the number of hospital beds had been relatively stable. Hence, the ratio of hospital beds to physicians had been falling (from about 3.15 general beds per active physician in 1968 to about 2.83 in 1976 (National Center for Health Statistics, 1979).

Although changes in demography and the physician supply will by no means determine the course of future events in the private and public world of health care, the course of those events will play out in an environment conditioned by those variables.[8]

The increasing proportion of elderly in the U.S. population will not only cause an absolute increase in the volume and intensity of health care services provided nationwide, along with attendent cost increases that will generate greater pressure for cost-containment measures, but it will also strengthen an already powerful interest group determined to protect its perogatives in present publicly funded health care programs. The issue of Medicare and Medicaid integration into any NHI system will elicit increasing attention from interest groups speaking on behalf of the elderly.

The increasing physician supply could also lead to higher expenditures for health care, since contrary to economic logic, physicians practicing fee-for-service medicine (as the majority do) do not typically engage in price competition. On the other hand, the physician surplus may also lend impetus to the growth of alternative delivery systems, such as health maintenance organizations (HMOs). More physicians means an increase in the supply available to HMOs, which are likely to be able to recruit young physicians at lower salaries. Because the growth of HMOs is believed by some to be an essential ingredient in creating much-needed competition in the health care sector, this development could tie in with a change in the political climate surrounding the NHI debate. Finally, the decreasing ratio between hospital beds and physicians may place hospitals in an unprecedentedly strong position to demand compliance with more economical rules of practice should hospitals be fiscally constrained by reimbursement methods.

In the coming decade, the NHI debate may emerge as one part of the new contest between the reinvigorated champions of competition and the supporters of the dispersed regulatory bodies that try to cope with the health care industry. Rising governmental budgets, coupled with increasingly frequent charges of waste and inefficiency in governmental bureaucracies, have led some to propose that social service delivery systems be structured to accommodate market incentives. In medical care, these procompetitive proponents promise that a return to the market will lead to cost containment, more equitable allocation of scarce medical resources, the creation of more rational delivery systems, and the delivery of more appropriate and perhaps better medical care. In a sense, this creates a new position between that of the older positions of advocacy for or against NHI; it allows government involvement in the competitive transformation of a private industry—the best of both worlds!

The appeal of procompetitive arguments is so broad that the President's Commission for a National Agenda for the 1980s argued confidently that "an expansion of the role of competition, consumer choice, and market incentives rather than government control is more likely to create the much needed stimulus toward greater efficiency, cost consciousness, and responsiveness to consumer preferences so visibly lacking in our present arrangements for providing medical care." (President's Commission for a National Agenda, 1980). Similar claims have received a widespread coverage in trade journals, the popular press, and on Capital Hill.

SOME ALTERNATIVE APPROACHES

Although each of the alternatives is labeled procompetitive, the positions advanced under this banner are in fact diverse and distinguishable. They vary in degree of change

---

[8]For a more extensive discussion, see Starr (1981) and Marmor (1973).

proposed for U.S. medicine, the rationale for such change, and their mechanisms, implementability, and effects. Although some constitute components of competition-based NHI programs, others propose to introduce competition in some part of the present mix of private and public insurance programs.[9]

The first approach would enhance consumer sovereignty. Advocates of this approach hold that the market for medical care is no different from other markets; if consumers face incentives that encourage sensible decisions about the amount of care and level of insurance needed, they will change their consumption patterns and consequently alter the medical care system. Second, there is the view that medical competition exists within fee-for-service medicine not between fee-for-service and other delivery and financing models, as would be preferable. In this view, sensible reforms would encourage the development of groups of physicians, primarily in prepaid practice arrangements, as alternatives to fee-for-service medicine. Finally, the proponents of antitrust initiatives hope to reduce the market power of medical care providers. The corollary, though often unspoken, to these proposals is that most if not all of the present health care regulatory apparatus should be dismantled as procompetitive reforms are implemented.

Until President Reagan's election, the liberals' response to competition proponents was scattered; a spate of countervailing articles has been published discussing the difficulties that would be encountered in attempting to implement procompetitive reforms and/or the undesirability of the impact of those reforms assuming that implementation was possible.[10] The liberal critique is only now evolving, but some rudimentary features can be summarized as follows.

First, procompetitive proposals share questionable analyses of the effects of current command and control regulation; they typically compare present circumstances of regulatory disarray with future circumstances of uncorrupted competition. They draw analogies between regulation in health care and regulation in other industries when projecting the impacts of their proposed changes. These analogies, however, ignore or downplay the differences between the market for medical care and the markets for other economic goods, as well as the many different forms of regulation that pervade the medical care sector. In fact, although procompetitive proposals all reject present and proposed command and control regulations, all require market correcting regulation to improve the workings of the market so admired.

Second, the course of implementation of numerous procompetitive strategies has not been sketched. Often proponents disdain the messy politics or organizational behavior that must be accounted for in various scenarios. The propensity for organizations to satisfice, that is, to achieve an attainable and satisfactory rather than optimal level of profitability, the capacity of medicine to engage in perverse competition that lets costs float up rather than be driven down, the relative ignorance of precisely how HMOs will

---

[9]The principal procompetition bills introduced in the Ninety-sixth Congress were (1) The National Health Care Reform Act (HR7527), introduced by Representatives Gephardt and Stockman; (2) The Consumer Health Expense Act (HR7258), introduced by Representative Janes; (3) The Health Cost Restraint Act (HR5740), introduced by Representative Ullman; (4) The Medical Expense Protection Act (HR6405), introduced by Representative Martine; (5) The Health Incentives Reform Act (S1968), introduced by Senator Durenberger; (6) The Comprehensive Health Reform Act (S1590), introduced by Senator Schweiker. There are in fact three separable threads of procompetitive logic, though all have interrelated elements.

[10]For elaborations and variations see Marmor et al. (to be published) and Rosenblatt (to be published) both dealing with competition in health care as well as Sigelman (to be published), Brown (1981), Vladeck (1981), and Weiner (1981).

achieve savings, and the unlikelihood that competitive strategies could be adopted in a pristine, doctrinaire form without the addition of distorting amendments and modifications foisted on them by interest groups are only a few of the factors that engender skepticism of the claim that competitive reforms would perform as predicted.

Third, assuming that procompetitive reforms were desirable and would resemble the vision of their proponents when implemented, changes that would enhance the market structure in the long run do not provide solutions to immediate problems. The encouragement of alternative delivery mechanisms would not solve present problems with geographical maldistribution of medical resources. The possible attainment of a long-run market equilibrium would not solve current cost problems. Even if equilibrium were possible, it would be slow to evolve, and until it did, there might be significant underinvestment in health be relatively uninformed consumers.

Fourth, regardless of the arguments of procompetitive proponents that the structure of the health care system should be encouraged to develop in a manner that encourages efficiency while equity considerations can best be dealt with separately in explicit political decisions to provide assistance to the disadvantaged members of the society, considerations of structure and equity are not so easily divorced. The powerful interest groups created or abetted through structural reforms militate against the creation of political forums in which the disadvantaged or consumers in general will be represented or, if represented, successful in pressing for the vouchers, subsides, or other forms of monetary or informational assistance they will require to receive needed treatment.

The procompetitive reform proposals that directly affect the industry rather than consumers could only be enacted if a powerful political personality acted as an entrepreneur, creating the political pressure to counterbalance concentrated interests and to create a public policy seen to generate public goods. After all, if market mechanisms accomplish all that their proponents promise, consumers will benefit and most providers will suffer. Even if they do not succeed in reducing the medical care inflation rate and ultimately the proportion of the U.S. resources devoted to medical care, they would redirect resources. For example, in the first approach, the insurance industry might suffer; in the second and third approaches, fee-for-service practice would be on the defensive. Additionally, one must remember that parts of the health care industry have adapted to regulation and thereby benefited from it. For example, some hospitals have increased their market share through regulatory interference with a competitor's expansion, and others have learned to manipulate their charges to maximize regulated reimbursement rates. These actors will not welcome all forms of procompetitive reform.

When President Reagan submitted his budget proposals in winter 1981, no procompetitive programs could be found among the various reductions in funding for Medicaid, Professional Standards Review Organization (PSRO), HMOs, health planning, aid to health professions, veteran's medical care, and the various programs netted in block grants.

In contrast to other areas of the budget, the administration was not really very successful in its proposals concerning health care. Powerful interests supporting current arrangements were able to beat back a cut in Medicaid spending, maintain some categorical health programs, retain some subsidy for HMOs, continue health planning, retain some manpower training programs, and maintain funding for veteran's medical care. In the face of increased pressure for more budget retrenchment, however, the administration is likely to find procompetitive proposals increasingly attractive.

The banner of procompetitive reform could be used to cloak a variety of changes in financing or regulatory programs that make at best nominal improvements in the competitive positions of alternatives to fee-for-service practice and, at worst, simply reduce government expenditures by forcing consumers to bear greater proportions of the cost of their medical care.

The experience of the Carter administration, when the political power of a Democratic president and Congress was shown insufficient to force enactment of NHI, or even hospital cost containment, and the prospects of a Reagan administration, in which the dismantling of health care regulation rather than the construction of even market-based health programs will probably take precedence, may be disheartening to NHI advocates. But with a history of decades of altercation on NHI and a complex and rapidly transforming medical industrial complex confronting the United States, no realistic prognosis can be any more promising.

REFERENCES

Bowler, M. Kenneth, Robert T. Kudrle and Theodore R. Marmor, "The Political Economy of National Health Insurance: Policy Analysis and Political Evaluation," *Journal of Health Politics, Policy and Law*, Vol. 2, Spring 1977, pp. 100–130.

Brown, Lawrence D., "Competition and Health Cost Containment: Cautions and Conjectures," *Milbank Memorial Fund Quarterly*, Vol. 59, Spring 1981, pp. 145–189.

Crystal, Stephen, "Health Resources for All the Aged by the Year 2000: A Prospectus for New Strategies," On file at the Committee on U.S. Health Goals for the Year 2000, Washington D.C., Institute of Medicine National Academy of Sciences, as cited in Paul Starr and Theodore Marmor, "The Future of American Medicine: A Social Forecast Through 1995," unpublished paper prepared for the Conference on Health Care in Industrialized Society in 1995, May 1980, p. 4, on file, Yale University Center for Health Studies.

Davis, Karen, *National Health Insurance: Benefit, Costs, and Consequences*, Washington D.C.: The Brookings Institutions, 1975.

Feder, Judith, John Holahan and Theodore R. Marmor, eds., *National Health Insurance: Conflicting Goals and Policy Choices*, Washington D.C.: The Urban Institute, 1980.

Fortune, "Our Ailing Medical System," *Fortune*, vol. 81, January 1970.

Gibson, Robert M. and Charles R. Fisher, "National Health Expenditures, Fiscal Year 1977," *Social Security Bulletin*, Vol. 41, July 1978, p. 16, Table 6.

Hadley, Jack, "Physician Supply and Distribution," in Judith Feder, John Holahan and Theodore R. Marmor, eds., *National Health Insurance: Conflicting Goals and Policy Choices*, Washington D.C.: The Urban Institute, 1980, pp. 235–240.

Hirschfield, Daniel S., *The Lost Reform*, Cambridge: Harvard University Press, 1970.

Marmor, Theodore R., *The Politics of Medicare*, Chicago: Aldine Publishing Co., 1973.

Marmor, Theodore R., Richard Boyer, and Julie Greenberg, "Medical Care and Procompetitive Reform," *Vanderbilt Law Review*, to be published.

Meany, George, Statement of the AFL-CIO, *Hearing on National Health Insurance*, Committee on Ways and Means, Vol. 11, October–November 1971, p. 239.

National Center for Health Statistics, Health Resources Statistics 1976–1977, Washington D.C.: U.S. Government Printing Office, 1979, pp. 141, 305.

Nixon, Richard, "The Nation's Health Care System," *Weekly Compilation of Presidential Documents*, Vol. 5, July 10, 1969, p. 963.

President's Commission for a National Agenda, *A National Agenda for the Eighties*, Washington D.C.: President's Commission for a National Agenda for the Eighties, 1980, pp. 78–79.

Rosenblatt, Rand, "Health Care, Market, and Efficiency: A Dissenting View," *Vanderbilt Law Review*, to be published.

Sigelman, Daniel W., "The 'Competitive' Prescription for Health Care: Survival of the Fittest?" *Journal of Health Politics, Policy, and Law*, to be published.

Starr, Paul, "A Coming Doctor Surplus?" *Working Papers for a New Society*, Vol. 4, Winter 1977, p. 18.

Starr, Paul, "Transformation in Defeat: The Changing Objectives of National Health Insurance, 1915–1980," *American Journal of Public Health*, Vol. 72, January 1982, pp. 78–88.

Starr, Paul, *The Social Transformation of American Medicine*, New York: Basic Books, 1981.

U.S. Department of Health, Education and Welfare, *Health: United States, 1979*, PHS Publication No. 80–1232, Washington D.C.: U.S. Government Printing Office, 1980.

U.S. Executive Office of the President, Office of Management and Budget, *Special Analyses, Budget of the United States Government, Fiscal Year 1975*, Special Analysis J., "Federal Health Programs," 1976, p. 136.

U.S. Executive Office of the President, Council on Wage and Price Stability, "The Problem of Rising Health Care Costs," Staff Report, Spring 1976, p. 7.

U.S. Executive Office of the President, Office of Management and Budget, *Special Analyses, Budget of the United States Government, Fiscal Year 1979*, p. 242.

Vladeck, Bruce, "The Market vs. Regulation: The Case of Regulation," *Milbank Memorial Fund Quarterly*, Vol. 59, Spring 1981, pp. 209–224.

Weiner, Stephen M., "Reflections on Cost Containment Strategies," *Milbank Memorial Fund Quarterly*, Vol. 59, Spring 1981, pp. 269–296.

PART FIVE

Health Politics:
A Cross-National Perspective

CHAPTER 16

Health Politics: Lessons From Abroad

William Glaser

THE NATURE OF MODERN GOVERNMENTS

GOVERNMENT AS A COMMITTEE

Every government can be conceived as a committee. Each committee member is a high official based in a ministry or in a major government organization. The committee consists of those leading officials who share in decisions about the government as a whole, as well as the major decisions about their own substantive sectors. Every government has a cabinet on paper, but the decision-making committee usually is not identical with it. The committee includes leaders not in the cabinet list. Some cabinet members are functional specialists not included in major government-wide decisions. Each committee member has private sector constituency groups in addition to the agency he or she runs in the government. Some people have larger political empires than others.

Governments in the world differ in the size, configuration, and membership of their committees. Certain roles, however, recur in all, such as the members who lead in budgeting, revenue collection, defense, and foreign relations. The comparable committee members vary among countries in their own political resources (the size and influence of their agencies and private sector constituents), the demands upon them by agency subordinates and private constituents, their careers (how they were recruited), and their independent authority (who appointed and can remove them). In addition, certain roles—for example, heads of police, economic planners, and mobilizers of the population (such as heads of political parties), are in the committee in some countries but not in others. Committees vary in homogeneity: In some countries, the members are from the same social background and political factions; in others, they are mixed and must constantly negotiate agreements.

Countries vary in the power of the chair, or head of the government. A dictatorship is a committee in which the chair has greater power to remove members and to substitute his or her own ideas for theirs. In no country, however, tyrannical, does the leader ever rule alone, as historical research always shows. In fact, dictators usually specialize so narrowly in a few topics—often foreign affairs—that the rest of the committee has considerable authority in domestic affairs.

305

Specific policies are not originated by the full committee. They originate in individual agencies—and often earlier in the demands of the private-sector constituents. In practice in all modern governments, the detailed review and design of each policy is done by a subcommittee of the full committee, that is, a few of the members specially affected by that policy, with staff assistance and perhaps substantial participation by the chair's office. The full committee meets periodically to screen, usually adopt, and sometimes reject the recommendations of its several subcommittees.

Federalism is a peculiar arrangement in that it is multilevel. The national committee must interact with regional committees to get things done. In unitary systems, the committee at the top can make decisions for the entire population, without dealing with independent clusters of power.

International relations is an interaction among coequal committees. Many modern governments have assemblies representing the private sector. Some are picked in periodic national elections (i.e., legislatures). At present, most assemblies in the world have very limited importance and uncertain roles; the election for an assembly in effect is the election deciding the groups from which the governing committee will be selected, and the committee thereafter runs the assembly. However, if the election results are so fragmented that a simple majority or simple coalition does not result, members of the assembly bargain among themselves to pick or terminate the committee and, therefore, have much power over it.

Most elected assemblies consist of political brokers (politicians) who act as the speaker for regions and interest groups. A few countries now extensively use advisory assemblies consisting of representatives of the principal special interest associations.

GOVERNMENT AS A COMMITTEE IN THE UNITED STATES

The United States is an unusual government in the weakness of its committee members, the disorderly method of running the committee, the great power of the political assembly (the national Congress), and the extensive power of the agency supposedly specializing in settling disputes (the national judiciary). Moreover, the same picture of committee weakness, lack of system, and diffusion of power is common in many (not all) state governments, as well as in their national counterpart.

In the United States, committee members have not risen through the governmental system and rarely have prestige and a political following at the time of their appointment. They are often complete newcomers to government, to their agencies, and to their functional specialities. They are picked because of the personal tastes of the chair, and they are easily removable by the chair with no repercussions.

The committee in the United States does not work as systematically as in other countries. The president or governor rarely meets regularly with the leading policymakers. He or she confers with different ones at different time and often dispenses with meeting, enumerating new policies without collective discussion and advice. When an identifiable full committee meets periodically, there may not be any specialized subcommittees to polish the proposals, thereby overburdening the full group or presenting it with poor documents. The absence of a systematic collective committee procedure makes presidents and governors vulnerable. They do much more of the work and get far more of the political heat than their counterparts in other countries. The U.S. government is hampered by constant internal intrigues about who joins in and who is left out of decisions.

The United States differs from other countries in how its political culture determines public attitudes toward politicians and civil servants. In Europe, government was long tied to a class structure characterized by great inequality and obedience; the public deferred to leaders, even if it disliked them. The public and rulers were drawn from the same nationality. The public could complain about oppression by their own priviledged classes but not about foreign conquests. The United States, on the other hand, rebelled, at least in historical terms, relatively recently against foreigners. The only European counterparts with such late eighteenth- and nineteenth-century historical experiences are Belgium, Eastern European countries, and in a sense, Italy. In such countries, government is "foreign" and never to be trusted. Politicians and civil servants are installed from the general public, without a special aristocratic and respectful mandate and without secure tenure. The public demands services from these politicians and civil servants constantly and removes them or reshuffles them easily. Politicians and civil servants in the United States lack the respect and mandate for action that is common in Europe and Canada. Denounced frequently as tyrants when they are not doing anything, American politicians and civil servants shrink from regulatory action against substantial numbers of citizens. The diffused structure of power in the United States enables politicians and civil servants to curry favor with interest groups by blocking regulatory action by others.

In Europe and Canada, the problem of political revolution has been to democratize government, not to handcuff and fragment it. The aristocratic oppressors of the past are now elected. If a mandate has been given in an election or a law has been passed, the politicians and civil servants form a common front in implementing it.

SOCIAL FORCES

The foregoing describes the machinery of government in the making and implementing of decisions. Some actions are initiated by the politicians and civil servants themselves. However, most actions originate with groups in the population whose proposals may be extensively or only slightly revised by the politicians and civil servants. Interest groups also press the government to oppose other groups' policies. The same government official must cope with conflicting demands; or different officials sympathetic to rival interest groups may confront each other.

Every country has pressure groups representing physicians, hospitals, and other health care providers. Countries differ, however, in the characteristics of these groups: in the completeness of their membership, number (some countries have several medical and hospital associations whereas others have only one), homogeneity, political militance, resources, and so forth. Several countries have increasingly important pressure groups with members who are not clinical providers in their own right but who live off health, such as unions representing hospital workers.

Most developed countries use insurance mechanisms, or sick funds, as they are usually called for financing health services. They differ, however, in the number, status (governmental or private), political orientation, resources, and influence of their respective sick funds. In some developed countries, sick funds are an active force upon government; in others, health financing is channeled through government budgets and sick funds are small and impotent.

Several pressure groups performing other principal functions also have an interest in health, either because their members are consumers, as with trade unions and farmers' associations, or because they are heavy payers of health care costs, as with associations. Because of their multiple functions, these groups often take inconsistent stands. For example, trade unions are usually critical of health care expenditure on physicians' fees but oppose strict cost control on hospitals, which employ their members.

INITIATING AMBITIOUS PROGRAMS

It is easy to enact new programs. Interest groups want things for themselves; if private action disappoints, they expect government to help. Politicians are in the business of acting, doing good, meeting the society's needs, doing for the people what the people cannot do for themselves. Politicians are gratified by visible achievement in legislation and in new programs, gratified by getting credit. They are reelected if they win the gratitude of voters—both previous supporters and past adversaries—and they lose if their opponents can accuse them of ineptitude and do-nothingism.

Similarly, civil servants like new programs, provided their lives are not strained by confusion and by expansion in the agency. Life becomes more interesting if the agency adds something new, provided that the civil servants' ability to run existing programs is not impaired. Civil servants looking for promotions welcome new programs and help initiate them.

When new administrations come to power, they are supposed to fulfill several pledges in their electoral platform. At times, a health program is included. Until the 1960s, most countries had shortages in health care facilities or deficiencies in financing, and occasionally a political party that took office pledged to remedy them. Usually they were the parties of the left, since the richer citizens were more able to find and buy medical care. However, if the country's medical services were poor, government remedies were likely to be endorsed even by the conservative political parties although more ambiguously than the left. Therefore, adding health services through government has until recently enjoyed a political consensus, with varying enthusiasm by interest groups and parties.

Until the cost consciousness of the 1970s enforced priorities planning, governments were motivated to enact a great deal of legislation. In governments effectively controlled by committees, a limited number of new programs was enacted. If the committee was dominated by an elected assembly or if the assembly was independent and the capital city was full or political entrepreneurs, many programs were enacted.

GREAT BRITAIN'S NATIONAL HEALTH SERVICE

A large and sweeping reorganization of familiar institutions is possible only under the most unusual political conditions. Enactment of the British National Health Service (NHS) is the best example. A citadel of capitalism adopted government ownership of all essential health care facilities and government employment of nearly all physicians and other health care workers. Nearly all health spending passes through the budget of the national government. No other developed country has anything exactly like this. Instead, they have national health insurance (NHI), with varying degrees of governmental regulation and government subsidization.[1]

New health programs are not enacted because of good ideas but because of felt deficits in private action. A domestic revolution such as the NHS can occur only when private medical services are in disaster. And so they were in Great Britain. National health insurance had already existed since 1911 but seemed to have failed. Hospitals were bankrupt, lacking in facilities, unable to pay adequate wages to enough people, and unequally located. Many patients could not pay physicians, who had to give priority to private patients. Physicians had to concentrate where they could find business, not where all the people lived. Physicians' offices were primitively equipped.

The problems were so serious and the normal solution, that is, national health insurance, so inadequate that all political parties and leading politicians agreed on the need for a governmental program of some sort. Along with pensions and programs for full employment, a national health service was recommended by the all-party coalition government during World War II (Beveridge, 1942; Willink, 1944).[2]

By historical accident, the Labour party happened to be in office just after the war when legislation was enacted. Many details would have differed if the Conservatives had been responsible, since they were more responsive to private owners (such as the voluntary associations who owned hospitals) and since they were closer to the medical associations. But the decision-making procedure would have been much the same, since it was the British government in action.

Under the British system, a new government of the day assigns to several ministers the lead responsibility in designing programs (with the aid of the incumbent civil servants in their new agencies and with the aid of any outside advisors they choose). The new government gives the lead minister the responsibility of discussing needs and plans with private interest groups, publicizing the program in the country, steering the law through the assembly, writing budgets, and managing the program during its early years. During the euphoric early years of a new government, each committee member is so busy that he or she lets the others alone to design their programs. Subcommittees keep other members informed of plans that affect them by each lead minister, but the code prescribes deference and log rolling. If the minister of finance complains that resources are insufficient, the solution in every government has been to avoid a showdown: The new program begins modestly, but it is not turned down; the day of reckoning is put off, but the day of political credit is not.

The National Health Service was designed and enacted in this fashion. The Labour party won the national election of July 1945 and assigned its principal leaders to the enactment of the several parts of its long agenda for transforming a society in ruins. The new minister of health, Aneurin Bevan, was given full responsibility for designing and selling the NHS. He began with strong assets: He was leader of the left. Unexpectedly, he proved a political genius in program creation, namely, in meetings with all interest groups to learn their positions, constructing institutional arrangements that would be acceptable and workable in the short run, anticipating the long-term consequences of proposals and devising long-term solutions, dividing and conquering by identifying and

---

[1]Two exceptions to the insurance model are Sweden, which has slowly evolved toward a decentralized version of Great Britain's NHS, and Canada, which runs all payments to providers through the budgets of provincial governments.

[2]The disappointing experience under national health insurance is reported by Harris (1946).

winning allies in the potential opposition, inspiring the public, selling his concessions to his own constituency, and so on. In the writing of both the original bill and the implementing regulations defining the institutional details, Bevan worked with a subcommittee of the leaders, the Social Services Committee of Cabinet.[3] Relations were easy in this stage of euphoric program creation. The treasury had as yet no fears, its chancellor was encouraging, and the other ministers did not think the new NHS would impinge on their jurisdictions and budgets.[4]

Certain constitutional and political features of British government make it possible for the entire committee (cabinet) and each individual minister to be very decisive. The monarch is in theory supreme and nearly totalitarian. Acting for the sovereign (i.e., providing all the monarch's advice) is an assembly, Parliament, elected in a fashion that nearly always guarantees a large majority for one party. Unlike other democracies, Britain almost never has a peacetime coalition government, and therefore its leadership is politically homogeneous, albeit sometimes faction-ridden. Britain's cabinets rarely have small majorities and can govern without the distraction of snap votes. In control of Parliament, the cabinet is effectively supreme over the government and society; each minister is supreme over his or her agency and civil servants. The code of Whitehall requires complete fidelity by the civil servants. During its 5-year mandate, a cabinet can enact and implement whatever policies it chooses, no matter how unpopular and politically suicidal—as the ministries of Ramsey McDonald and Neville Chamberlain illustrate. As long as Bevan kept his ministers informed and sympathetic, he was fully empowered to create and launch the NHS.

To make the system work requires strong nerves and ability. Some prime ministers and ministers have backed down, despite their mandates, when faced by domestic uproars.[5] A minister can dither away the opportunity if he or she is baffled by the ever-present complications and controversies. But Bevan developed expert understanding of the health system and could also formulate main themes. As a result, his actions were consistent as well as intelligent.

Bevan experienced one of the fundamental and inescapable problems of health politics, namely, the struggle for supremacy with the medical profession. This recurs in every attempt to pay or to organize medical services through government. The issue is not merely levels of pay and procedures; every other statute bearing on an occupation or industry arouses such arguments. But physicians are peculiarly passionate and apparently unreasonable, because they are being converted from charismatics to conventional mortals. Before government's regulators and auditors entered, they were complete monopolists, applying specialized knowledge to solving acutely anxiety-provoking problems with an air of total certainty, demanding and often getting unlimited resources, enjoying the public's reverence and complete dependence. Even when the rest of society favors a health program, such as like the NHS in 1946–1948, the physicians may become militantly opposed because their special status is changed and they are being made accountable. Usually they can arouse enough sympathy from the electorate and enough discomfort from the politicians to obtain major concessions in the design of the new program. Since the politicians are trying to launch a popular program and reap

---

[3]The model for modern cabinet government everywhere, Britain was perhaps the first with standing subcommittees to review and polish bills and regulations bearing upon several ministries.

[4]The writing of the NHS is recounted in Willcocks (1907), Eckstein (1958), Foot (1973), and Abel-Smith (1964).

[5]An example was the government of Prime Minister Edward Heath from 1970 to 1974. It made much-ridiculed U-turns on many domestic policies, including income, support for failing industries, and industrial relations.

credit, they will do anything to persuade the physicians to stop rocking the boat. The physicians may be put in control, although the incorporation of rules, prospective reimbursement, and audits means they have lost the total discretion of a charismatic elite. They are often bought off with high pay and expensive facilities. Great Britain experienced one of the first grave political battles with the medical profession; one of Bevan's achievements was navigating this baffling course, so different from the negotiations with a mundane noncharismatic interest group (Foot, 1973; Eckstein, 1960).[6]

MEDICARE AND MEDICAID IN THE UNITED STATES

In the United States major new programs to deliver health care are often discussed but rarely enacted. Enough is done in the private sector to deprive the issue of the necessary urgency. Instead, national and state legislatures have enacted many subsidies for special purposes in health.

Two of the few major laws dealing with basic health delivery for a large segment of the population was the Medicare and Medicaid acts of 1965. Their political history was typical of a new, big spending program. President Lyndon Johnson's new administration had come to power with some decision-making characteristics peculiar to the United States and quite different from those of other countries. The impetus within the executive branch came largely from one man, the new president, rather than from a collective group of leaders who had been in a shadow cabinet together before taking over the government. Another uniquely American feature was the large role played by legislators who are only legislators, and not ministers and heads of agencies too.

Several health problems manifestly existed after World War II, namely, the need to help the aged and the poor pay the increasingly expensive hospital and ambulatory bills and the need to alleviate the financial strain for states, which traditionally paid medical costs of welfare recipients. The problems were difficult for some, annoying to many, but not catastrophic on a national scale. Therefore, a strong national demand for action did not exist, comparable to the circumstances leading to profound reforms such as enactment of the New Deal in the United States or of the National Health Service in Great Britain. Without such urgency, foreign governments put health (or any other problem) low on their relatively short legislative agendas; in the United States, less-than-catastrophic problems invite minor tinkering that subsidizes rather than restricts private interests.

In other democracies, the creation and enactment of an important new program follows a definite sequence. The target is always whether the lead committee member in that field (usually a minister) shall draft and push a statute and regulations. Such programs are in preparation for years, and information and advice is directed at that minister's office. The interest groups and specialized publications in that field diagnose the social problem and recommend action. Special committees of the political parties—consisting of the activists on rival sides in the private sector—hold meetings, write reports, and press to add their issues to electoral platforms. As the issue becomes more serious and more widely discussed, the ministry commissions and publishes special reports (called variously white papers, green papers, and papers of other colors) from

---

[6]My first research about health politics dealt with the political orientations of U.S. physicians, and I was struck then by their detachment from conventional politics, their peculiar superiority to it all, so unique to a charismatic elite (see Glaser, 1960).

private consultants or from standing or ad hoc commissions of interest group leaders. If the winning side in an election has compaigned on the issue, the new committee member specializing in the subject is authorized to prepare the new law and program. The proposal is screened by the special interagency subcommittee, approved by the full committee, and rapidly enacted by the Parliament. Great Britain's NHS and most country's national health insurance laws were prepared and enacted in this way.

The government of the United States, on the other hand, has always been somewhat less structured than other governments in the sense that creation of a new program had not followed a standard sequence. Focal decision points do not exist. Anyone can speak up in any forum, and the loser in one forum finds another forum. Recently, U.S. politics has become less structured than ever, as interest groups proliferate and become more resourceful, as positions of authority are weakened (such as chairmen of congressional committees), and as elected politicians become less secure electorally.

As in other countries, issues are debated for many years in the United States. Because private sector solutions (or half-solutions) are often devised for underservicing and underfinancing in health, tremendous deficits are avoided and fundamental reorganizations of health by government are unusual. For example, where as every other country started to debate national health insurance at the same time as the United States (about 1910), the United States alone has never enacted it, despite repeated renewals of the discussion. The United States lacks a standard decision-making sequence that will either cut the Gordian knot or permanently suppress a losing proposal. The United States' political pot is always full of proposals that are constantly reworked.

In other democracies nowadays, the assembly gives perfunctory debate and automatic approval to the governing committee's proposals. In the United States, the Congress is an important site for the entire policy debate. Every member is an independent entrepreneur, and every legislative committee chair has his or her own resources. If a problem is diagnosed in the country or if a new scheme is proposed and it strikes a chair's fancy, hearings may be called and a staff report commissioned. The chair can introduce bills proposed by interest groups or ask the legislative staff to prepare them. None of these activities need to be serious preludes to legislation; most are not coordinated with the executive branch but are mechanisms of education for the legislators or mechanisms of publicity for the interest groups. In every other developed country, the executive branch controls the schedule of the legislature; but in Washington, the executive branch can merely ask to testify at a committee hearing. Proposals percolate in Washington for years, dying with each Congress and reappearing with modifications in the next. A coalition of many leaders in both the House and Senate is needed to move a proposal toward enactment, and it must mobilize enough votes. Collaboration with the executive branch is very helpful, since the president and cabinet secretaries can excite the mass media, their constituency of interest groups, and some votes in the Congress. But a well-led and determined coalition in Congress can enact a scheme regardless of the apathy or even the opposition of the executive branch.

After World War II, several Democratic presidents campaigned on platforms endorsing universal national health insurance or specific insurance programs for the aged and poor. In other countries, action would have followed. At first, the administration proposals were discussed and shelved by Congress; alternatives were circulated but also shelved. Limited stopgaps such as the Kerr-Mills bill in the 1960s were passed. The landslide victory of Lyndon Johnson in 1964, however, strengthened advocates, and the landslide defeat of Barry Goldwater broke the alliance between the Republicans and the American Medical Association (AMA).

In parliamentary countries, the political opposition opposes, but government of the day control majorities capable of legislating. In the diffuse power structure of the United States, the opposition must either split or be willing to go along with a bill in order to legislate.

The administration had produced proposals for insuring the aged and paying for the poor, drafted in the Department of Health, Education and Welfare (DHEW) under a veteran civil servant turned assistant secretary (Wilbur Cohen). The president was enthusiastic throughout the preparation, ensuring the cooperation of the White House staff, the budget office, and the treasury. Other agencies deferred to the head of DHEW. In parliamentary countries, the administration's bills would have been the only agenda item before the legislature. But in the United States, they were only some of the proposals before Congress.

The creative leadership for Medicare and Medicaid was preformed by a leader of Congress, the chairman of the House Ways and Means Committee, Wilbur Mills. He performed most of the Aneurin Bevan role in Great Britain, with Wilbur Cohen, Secretary of DHEW, playing a contributing part. Mills conducted committee hearings open to all witnesses (private and governmental), conferred informally with politicians, civil servants, interest group leaders, and fellow house members; studied all the competing proposals; guided his staff in drafting; and ultimately stitched them together. By combining several bills—a familiar and sometimes confusing technique on Capitol Hill— Mills produced a plan with much greater benefits than that proposed by DHEW. Mills steered his bill through his full committee and through the House; monitored its progress through the Senate; and led the conference committee that reconciled differences. Then he and his staff kept in touch with the DHEW officials who wrote the implementing regulations.[7]

As usual, the drafters had to cope with the passionate fears of the medical profession. For years, the AMA had campaigned in elections and in the mass media against any legislation, preferring private insurance and professional control. To appease the AMA, Congress emasculated Medicare by making it the world's only national health insurance program without any form of prospective reimbursement or fee schedules. Every physician was guaranteed "customary" charges and full coverage of his or her costs. As in the enactment of all big health programs, the passage had to be made politically painless, with the financial consequences deferred to the future.

Because the committee controls the assembly in other democratic countries, and since the two trust each other, the statutes usually are short, clearly written, simple, and as readable as any prose. Details are added in regulations. Britain's National Health Service Act of 1946 was a typical statement of principles, passed before the institutional details were settled. The minister and the cabinet were allowed to settle the structure and procedures with a minimum of new amending legislation thereafter.

However, the United States experiences a constant struggle for supremacy between executive and legislative branches. The Congress does not trust the executive branch to implement its intent—this was especially true during the 1970s—and therefore passes detailed laws spelling out behavior that in other countries is left to administrative regulations and administrative discretion. The intricate American legislation is actually much less explicit than appears on first reading. This is particularly true when a law had been quickly pasted together from many bills without laborious feasibility and

---

[7]For a description of the creation of Medicare and Medicaid see Marmor (1973) and Stevens and Stevens (1974).

costly research in the policy planning staff of a ministry. Both Medicare and Medicaid proved very ambiguous and controversial in their implementation. Both seemed to commit government to pay providers with few direct cost and quality controls. Both were unclear about patient cost sharing. Moreover, the roles of the national and state governments in Medicaid were ambiguous and therefore trouble prone. In later years, both Medicare and Medicaid spent far beyond expectations, and Medicaid generated constant tension between national and state governments. In other countries, a program is allowed to stabilize in practice; the ministry has discretion to implement it. In the United States, on the other hand, Congress quickly investigates when it hears of trouble and tinkers with a law every few years. So, Medicare and particularly Medicaid have undergone repeated embarrassing reviews by congressional committees, and the laws have been frequently amended.[8]

ENACTING CONSTRAINTS

Major health programs follow a common cycle. At first, for years deficits in care exist and remedies are proposed. But physicians and other private providers successfully resist the intrusion of government. Limited private programs and public subsidies patch things up for a while. When deficits in facilities or financing so exhaust private money that services collapse, a law is passed. To appease the physicians, they and the hospital are guaranteed more generous payment than ever before with minimum controls. Utilization, medical fees, and hospital charges prove higher than expected, and the treasury complains.

The politicians in charge of the budget (called variously the minister of finance, minister of budget, president of the treasury board, etc.) perceives the problem when he or she must allocate next year's available money among spending ministries and must cut requests. But the civil servants in treasury have been at the job longer, are skeptical of all spending ministries, and have anticipated the problem much earlier. Economists work with statistical projections of trouble. They view health as a chronic financial problem, always exceeding its predicted costs, always drawing more from the government's appropriations than expected. The treasury is also the watchdog of the official health insurance funds and must keep going back to the assembly for higher payroll taxes (i.e., the official insurance premiums) on employers and subscribers. If the politicians limit the increases in taxes, the treasury must subsidize the sick funds from the general budget. So the ministry of health (or whatever ministry oversees the sick funds) inevitably faces a serious showdown with treasury involving the entire committee. Previously we have described how governments make easy big decisions, namely, the decisions to offer benefits and spend money. The struggle to control the costs of these programs shows how they make their difficult big decisions.

GREAT BRITAIN

The first unlimited service benefits program in a developed country, the British NHS was the first to experience problem of constraining costs. Heated at the time, the issues seem tame from the perspective of the spendthrift 1970s.

---

[8]Certain aspects of the subsequent evolution of Medicare and Medicaid may be found in Stevens and Stevens (1974) and in Feder (1977).

At the start, cost overruns occurred in dentistry. The planners had underestimated demand and productivity. Dentistry was the only part of the NHS using fee for service. Dentists took full advantage of the method, worked quickly, lengthened their hours, earned far higher incomes than predicted, and caused great overruns in the total budget for dentistry. Within the government, no disagreements existed over the need to cut spending back to the budgetary predictions. A ministry headed by the leader of the left did not want to enrich a profession.

The minister of health had plenary authority under British constitutional practice and could act. At first Bevan placed ceilings on the earnings of individual dentists and impounded the excess; then he cut the rates in the fee schedule. The ministry listened to the protests of the British Dental Association but ultimately went ahead, since it was backed up by the cabinet, Parliament, and mass media (Lindsey, 1962).

The next efforts to control costs, however, split the cabinet and contributed to its electoral defeat. The NHS each year cost more than expected. The situation was discussed annually in the financial subcommittee of the cabinet. The full committee then agreed to the supplementary estimate, and the additional money was approved by Parliament. Treasury would have preferred that NHS stay within its budget, but price controls on services were possible only in dentistry. Cutting expenditure in medicine was possible only by reducing utilization, and the Labour party in general and the NHS in particular were pledged to all services anyone needed. Therefore, the only remedy was to find money beyond general treasury revenue.

At first, all NHS benefits were completely free and were an article of faith with the left. Treatment was supposed to be governed only by need and not be related to any payment at point of service. The only new revenue that treasury could think of, arising from within NHS, was charges for services. It recommended charges for three items most likely to be ordered and wasted: drugs, spectacles, and dentures. Such charges would have the added advantage of deterring unnecessary utilization; if the patient paid part, he or she was more likely to order only what would be used.

To these proposals, Bevan reacted with the outrage he himself had to face when the physicians felt he was destroying *their* basic principle of professional control. He opposed treasury on the principle of free services for the poor. He opposed the entire cabinet over the priorities of the government: The cabinet had carefully decided to restrain all domestic expenditure so that more money could be spent on national defense. In every country, cost control of health involves defeat over priorities as well as defeat over the propensity to run inflationary deficits.

When creating the NHS, Bevan was the lead minister, carrying along the rest of his committee and assembly. Now he had to be a negotiator within a committee with competing priorities, a team player. At first he made a deal with treasury to buy time: The National Health Service Amendments Act of 1949 authorized the levying of a charge on prescriptions, but that year's national budget did not impose it. But subsequent events precipitated a showdown. The Korean War led to rearmament. The new budget required a shift in NHS financing, and it was prepared by a new chancellor of the exchequer (Hugh Gaitskell) who was less willing to make political concessions to the left. The prime minister's health deteriorated, and he was less effective in mediation. When the Labour party declined in the 1950 election, Bevan thought that the only long-term political remedy was an adamant appeal to the electorate by a pure left position. An impasse resulted of the sort that committees desperately avoid: Both Bevan and the chancellor of the exchequer threatened to resign if their rival positions were not adopted. No compromise was negotiated, the cabinet came down for charges, the new budget included charges for spectacles and dentures, and the NHS Amendments Act of

1950 authorized them. Bevan resigned with a spectacular attack on the charges, rearmament, and British foreign policy (Foot, 1973; White, 1981).

As often happens in health policy, the controversial change later becomes routine. The Labour party lost the election of 1951, in large part because of its factional disarray. The new conservative government repeated the principle of charges for drugs, spectacles, and dentures in the NHS Amendments Act of 1951. Charges have been normal ever since, going up and down in each budget according to the cycle of social generosity and fiscal responsibility projected that year by the government of the day. No other developed country (except Japan) has offered completely free drugs, spectacles, and dentures under national health insurance.

FRANCE

Through its vertical budget system—aggregate spending on health is a line in the government's budget—Britain has controlled spending more firmly than any developed country. In a field with potentially unlimited demand on resources to save lives, the result in Britain has been chronic complaint by clinical researchers and by hospital consultants about underfunding of facilities. Some specialists find more jobs and much better pay abroad, and they emigrate.

Countries that expanded their health benefits later than Great Britain, that used insurance mechanisms, and that were richer, experienced spending booms and ultimately had to make great efforts to control costs. At first, the issue was remuneration of the physicians. Later, during the 1970s, the problem was control over the largest and fastest growing item, namely, the hospitals.

France had to cope with the payment of physicians when its governments were impotent and it was unable to control costs. A remedy was found only when the governmental system changed. The events that followed demonstrate the conditions and consequences of impotence as well as show how institutional changes in government can make a big turnabout.[9]

The French Third and Fourth Republics were ruled by weak governments. No party controlled the assembly, and all cabinets were coalitions selected from rival voting blocs in the assembly. Particularly in the Fourth Republic, members of the assembly were often eager to overthrow cabinets, to embarrass other parties and politicians, and to gain ministries themselves. Any difficult issue strained every committee, since it aroused the members' diverse ideological reactions and electoral strategies. To preserve the committee, leaders played safe by avoiding the difficult issues that would divide the assembly and break up the committee. A powerful national interest group such as the medical association could exercise great leverage upon the system.

France was one of the last developed countries to enact national health insurance. The physicians' protests, indicating that they were apprehensive about falling under the control of lay people in government and the sick funds, delayed its passage until 1928 and implementation until 1930. The program went into effect by the unique devise of indirect payment, a method practiced on a large scale elsewhere only in the Blue Shield program in the United States. The patient recovered money from the sick funds, and the physician never directly contacted the public authorities. In theory, the sick fund reim-

---

[9]The events are described in Glaser (1970) and Hartzfield (1963).

bursed the patient almost 80 percent of the fee he or she paid the physician, and fees were set by an agreement between each local sick fund and local medical society. In practice, this was not enforced: Many medical societies refused to sign meaningful fee schedules; where some did, many individual physicians refused to adhere.

As prices, incomes, and costs rose throughout the French economy during the 1950s, physicians' charges rose faster than the sick funds' reimbursements to the patients. The government and sick funds had promised the public extensive coverage of benefits by including them under a compulsory law and by taxing them, but it could not deliver. Patients had to pay a steadily greater proportion of their costs, and the cabinet and Parliament could do little. The situation was a principal reason for the discrediting of parliamentary government in France.

Only a strong and clever government can cope with a defiant medical profession. The Fourth Republic collapsed over Algeria and, by chance, was superseded by a very powerful committee. The once omnipotent assembly recalled General de Gaulle, gave him emergency powers to solve the Algerian crisis, and abdicated. Another style of French government was now resurrected, namely, a dictator depending on popular acceptance, working with a small committee specializing in sectors of domestic policy, certain of faithful implementation of their decrees by the civil service.

A small subcommittee of specialists in health screened long-standing proposals for reform originating both within and outside of the ministries. They consisted of senior civil servants and the ministers in health and labor, leading professors of medicine (including the father of de Gaulle's prime minister), and other reformers among interest groups (such as the sick funds). They listened to but no longer negotiated with the medical association, whose once formidable political leverage had disappeared overnight.

The leaders' confidence about facing down the physicians was built up by a series of decrees in late 1958 and 1959 that reorganized the hospitals and medical education. The teaching hospitals were reshaped with full-time medical staffs and modern facilities. The administration of the public hospitals was reorganized, including a structure of consolidation and regionalization that remains only a mirage elsewhere.[10] Gradually, the subcommittee worked up the plan that was certain to produce an explosive showdown with the physicians.

The decision was approved by the full committee and was issued in May 1960 as an ordinance with the full force of law, signed by President de Gaulle. It was therefore the personal order of the twice saviour of France, equipped with even more charisma than all the physicians together. According to the ordinance, fee schedules would bind nearly all physicians and would cover nearly all patients. A government commission could set ceilings on the negotiated fee schedules and could prescribe fees in districts where no collective agreements existed. If the local medical society did not sign a collective agreement with the social security fund, any individual physician could do so. If a physician was not covered by a collective or individual agreement, his or her patients would be reimbursed by the fund at much less than the usual rate. If the local medical society did not sign a collective agreement, the social security fund retained the right to establish a polyclinic in the area.

The French national federation of medical associations (CSMF) had never encountered a political decision it had not controlled in advance. Not clearly knowing what to

---

[10]The contents and creation of the hospital decrees are reported in Jamous et al. (1967) and Comet (1960).

do, it gambled by calling its first strike against national health insurance. Patients continued to be treated and continued to pay as before, but many (not all) physicians refused to fill out the receipts that patients customarily sent to the funds for reimbursement. Success in a big political fight requires good judgment and luck, and the federation lacked both. The strike could hardly have come at a worse time. The country was worried over Algeria—during mid-1960 de Gaulle seemed to be failing—and few could sympathize with a well-paid profession's self-centered maneuvers to charge the public without limit. The federation's action was widely denounced.

The strike was actually meaningless. The federation had unwisely declared war without weapons as well as without allies. Since the office practitioners did not have direct relationships with any public agencies, there were no services or information they could withhold; since the physicians did not wish to cut off their own incomes, they had to continue treating and charging patients as before. Refusing to fill out official forms was no weapon: Physicians had to give some kind of receipts to their patients, and the funds accepted them for reimbursement. The federation could have won only if every physician followed it. But only some of the Paris and Lyons doctors were so militant and prosperous as to practice outside social security. Most others were content to accept the official fee schedules and would have signed individual agreements had not the federation surrendered and allowed the local societies to sign collective agreements. Thus, most French physicians now practice according to the ground rules of social security and under price ceilings, a situation unthinkable to the secretive independent practitioner of the past. But this decisive—even if belated—victory by the social security system was possible only because an authoritarian regime had replaced a democracy.

During subsequent years, the medical association negotiated the details of the system they were compelled to accept. It negotiated conditions of service, the fee schedule (i.e., a relative values scale), and the monetary level of fees with the sick funds. In case of deadlocks, the government can always intervene and impose a settlement. The government agencies are always united in their commitment to limit the fees of physicians; increasingly they became dominated by the ministry of Finance and ministry of Budget, which have parachuted their elite corps of economists (the *inspectorat des finances*) into key jobs, including those in the ministry of Health. Every decree has been drafted by a lead agency (such as health) and then polished and approved in a cohesive interagency subcommittee of civil servants, usually representing health, labor, agriculture, finance, and budget.[11] Therefore, the medical association has been at an increasing disadvantage. But the sick funds and government have not dictated punitively: The physicians might still appeal to the public that lives are threatened by the bureaucrats' stinginess; the authorities prefer to buy peace and buy the cooperation of the physicians rather than suffer political wounds from fights.

Gradually, government has tightened its rules and price controls over more physicians, so that nearly all are now covered. One reason for the growth of government's power is that the tables are turned. Until 1958, the medical association was united and government was disunited. By the late 1970s, the French government had become highly united in health finance policy and the medical association had split. The rival medical federations fought each other more adamantly than they fought the government. Each is willing to sign contracts with the government and sick funds at the other's

---

[11]Many examples of such preparation of regulations are described in Glaser (1980a).

expense, and the contracts give the public authorities more power over the work and payment of all physicians.[12]

CANADA

By the 1970s, nearly every country had severe problems of health care costs, particularly the tendency for hospital costs to rise faster than revenue and gross national product (GNP). Various methods were used to cope with the problem, depending on the system of government and the methods of financing already in place. These were intricate problems of budgeting and of setting rates for organizations (especially for hospitals) rather than price controls over physicians. Therefore, these did not involve highly personalized struggles between a few glamorous leaders of government (such as Bevan, Johnson, and de Gaulle) and the leaders of the medical association. The struggles became bureaucratic exchanges among civil servants, finance officers, and auditors, with policies approved by political leaders. Within every government, policy was set and implemented by constant interagency communication.

Federal countries such as the United States have had a particularly complicated task in creating and implementing policies to control costs. In every federal system, regional, or local government is traditionally and constitutionally the level to regulate and to subsidize hospitals and other health care providers. But regional and local resources have been limited; when the demand for better facilities and wider coverage of the public spread after World War II, the national government became involved. Once the faucet was turned on, the question became how to turn it down. During the 1970s the big problem in federal countries has been how to define responsibilities and powers, who should have the principal authority over grants and over providers.

Canada was the first federal country to open Pandora's box in health and the first to close it. After World War II, private insurance was unable to cover inpatient and ambulatory care widely. The provincial governments could not expand coverage and benefits sufficiently and could not build up facilities, since they lacked the taxes with flexible yields. The remedy was successful appeal to the national government for federal–provincial shared-cost programs in hospital construction, hospital benefits for the population, ambulatory medical care (called Medicare in Canada) for the population, and other areas. Several programs had fixed ceilings and eventually expired. Hospital and medical care benefits had unlimited commitments; hospitals and physicians treated all patients as they chose, the provincial governments paid the providers in full, and the provincial governments collected half their costs from the national government.[13]

The provincial premiers and politicians were happy to deliver on their promises to improve social services; they could take credit without getting the blame of heavy taxation, since half the money was a "free gift" from Ottawa. The provincial treasuries were happy to get cash without having to levy equivalent taxes, although they would have preferred complete discretion about spending. The hospitals and physicians welcomed the money. At first the provincial ministries of health were satisfied, since they

---

[12]The recent negotiating system is summarized in Glaser (1978).

[13]Creation of these programs by the provinces and by the national government is presented in Taylor (1978). The operations of the federal–provincial shared-cost programs in hospitalization, Medicare, and other fields are summarized in Smiley (1963) and Carter (1971).

could build up hospital and ambulatory services. Eventually, however, they chafed that they could not use the earmarked money for other providers that were most cost effective or that were higher in their ministries priorities, such as nursing homes, community health centers, day care, and home care. Politicians and civil servants in health resented the audits and investigations by the national government; they wrangled frequently in federal–provincial meetings over the costs that could be shared by Ottawa.

Politicians and civil servants in the national government became disenchanted. They felt that they received no political credit for expanding health services—since the money was distributed by the provinces—but they got the blame for heavy national taxes and for inflationary deficits in the national budget. The ministers and civil servants in finance and in the treasury board complained that a large part of the national budget was uncontrollable and unpredictable, that the provinces were wasteful because they spent "50-cent dollars." On the other hand, many civil servants in the national Department of Health were proud of a program that had produced such good modern care and wished to preserve it, lest the provinces make cuts and jeopardize patients.

Each level of government had to develop a policy, since the federal–provincial arrangement was not permanent. The grants were seed monies so the provinces could implant hospital services and ambulatory care, that is, Medicare. Eventually the provinces were supposed to take them over. Every 5 years, the provinces and national government negotiated a division of tax money, and Ottawa began to propose that the provinces take over hospitalization and Medicare completely, along with the responsibility (and political blame) for levying the taxes.

Canadian national and provincial governments are much like Britain's, with cabinet subcommittees to work out common positions. The lead agency at each level of government in designing and negotiating the periodic Fiscal Arrangements Acts was the ministry of finance. The financial subcommittees in each provincial and national government—called Treasury Boards or another less formal name—became the sites for working out the fate of the hospitalization and ambulatory programs. Health was represented, but meetings were chaired either by the minister of finance or by the government's minister for the budget. The economists did the staff work.

When each Fiscal Arrangements Act was approaching renewal, the federal ministers and the finance officers suggested proposals about tax sharing and grants with the provinces, the interagency subcommittees reacted and approved, and cabinet approved. The federal minister of finance then announced the offer in the standing federal–provincial conference of finance ministers. Each provincial government then worked out its position in its own subcommittee and cabinet meetings. Federal–provincial meetings of civil servants and ministers in finance settled details. The finishing touches to a new agreement often were made in a federal–provincial Conference of First Ministers (i.e., the prime minister of Canada and the premiers of the provinces). The agreement was then written up in a new Fiscal Arrangement bill, introduced into the Parliament of Canada by the national minister of finance or by the prime minister. Upon passage it was a law of Canada, since it involved the national government's taxes and cash transfers from the national to the provincial governments.[14]

During the 1970s, Canada experienced the same escalation in health care costs as did other countries, and the senior civil servants in the national ministry of finance became convinced that the shared financing system was a cause. The open-ended obliga-

---

[14]Such negotiations are described in Simeon.

tion to pay hospital and ambulatory costs must be removed from the national budget, they said, making it more predictable. If the provinces had full responsibility for both spending and taxing, they would be more vigilant about waste and overuse and would look for less expensive substitutes for hospital care.

Several civil servants in the Department of National Health and Welfare criticized reversion of the hospitalization and medical programs back to the provinces, particularly if the transfers were unconditional. They feared that the provinces might reduce health services and use the new tax money for other things. Health and Welfare Canada, for a long time the biggest agency in Ottawa, would have nothing left to do and careers would end. But the civil servants in health were bypassed. In accordance with the original theory that the federal grants were only seed money, the cabinet and prime minister had decided for reversion to the provinces as early as the late 1960s. The only remaining issue was the financial terms of the transfer. Responsibility for the negotiations was given to the national and provincial financial ministers and financial civil servants who favored reversion. The national minister and deputy minister of health had to endorse reversion and cooperate. The lower civil servants in health continued their regular federal–provincial meetings to implement the final years of the shared-cost programs and to lay the groundworks for the future. Several specialists in health finance in Health and Welfare Canada—along with a few others from finance—prepared the detailed financial analyses of the hospitalization and ambulatory care programs needed by the negotiators from finance. The different levels of government faced each other with united teams.

The issue was formally precipitated in 1975, when the minister of finance introduced the national budget into Parliament. Solidly backed by his own cabinet and ministries, he gave formal notice for terminating the federal–provincial shared-cost program in hospitalization, and he announced a fixed limit on the federal contribution to Medicare, the ambulatory medical care program. Ottawa had the great advantage of initiative and ultimate power, since the programs were tax and spending laws of the national government. Several years of intricate bargaining then ensued between the national government and all the provinces, with much exchange of statistical projections about program costs and tax yields. It was a struggle between bright young econometricians, without a place for spell-binding political orators. So much of Canadian governmental decision making has come to revolve around fiscal federalism, that the principal politicians in Ottawa and most provinces have become transformed into intelligent advocates of economic briefs. The provincial governments not only interacted collectively with the national government at the federal–provincial meetings, but they had to meet separately by themselves and work out common positions. All these interactions and the constant need for decisive responses to new offers required each government to keep its own elements unified. Although the premiers and ministers of finance were given full negotiating authority, they had to keep their ministries of health informed and cooperative.[15]

Under the Fiscal Arrangements Act of 1977, Ottawa continues to collect personal and corporate income taxes for itself and for all provinces except Quebec, which has its own tax collection system. The provinces assume the financing and mangement of hospitalization insurance, Medicare, and postsecondary education. In return, the national government gives the provinces larger shares of the personal and corporate in-

---

[15]Details of the negotiations are described in Glaser (1979).

come taxes. Cash grants are offered for several provincial extended health care programs. National equalization payments to the poorer provinces continue, with some changes in the formulas. If a province's revenues decline because of a downturn in economic activity, the national government makes fiscal stabilization payments or transition payments. If the new changes in personal income tax arrangements cause a province to lose money, the national government makes revenue guarantee payments. The transition and revenue guarantee payments insure every province against losses and are designed to get the agreement of all.[16] The national government controls its costs better than before; unlimited commitments to pay provincial health costs are no longer in the national budget. The provincial governments now try to conserve funds by imposing tighter bids on hospital budgets,[17] by fostering less expensive extramural care, and by driving harder bargains with the physicians over fees.

WEST GERMANY

Canada and the United States make federal–provincial decisions by extraconstitutional methods. In Canada, the provinces remain powerful and a system of federal–provincial negotiating committees exists in health and all other fields. In the United States, state governments have become emasculated, they come to Washington like any other interest group, and much is decided in Congress, as if the United States were a unitary country.

West Germany differs. The national and provincial governments make decisions together under a structure defined by the constitution. The provinces hold the seats in the upper house of the *Bundestrat*, the national legislature. Besides running their own internal affairs, the West German provincial governments shape a great deal of the legislation for the nation because of their leverage in Parliament.

Within each government, the committee members must work out proposals for action by their own assembly for negotiation with the other level of government, and they must work out their reactions to the other level's proposals. As in every government, each committee member has a functional responsibility. In both the national and provincial governments, West German political custom gives great responsibility to each agency head and to each bureau chief within each agency. When any proposal is planned and drafted, one agency head is designated the leader (the *federfuhrend*, or the one who signs). It is then that leader's responsibility to coordinate the work with other agencies bearing on the issues, as well as to decide whom to consult and how to do it. To avoid trouble, the officials of the federfuhrend agency make many contacts. Ad hoc interagency committees exist for individual projects, chaired by the lead agency. An important understanding is that each agency defers to the leadership of whoever is federfuhrend, avoiding recriminations and invasion of the other's turf, because one is then protected in one's own work. Within an agency the work of each official is conducted with comparable autonomy.[18]

Between 1969 and 1972, the office of Chancellor Willy Brandt tried to expand and

---

[16]The new fiscal arrangements are summarized in Lewis (1977), Carter (1977), and Courchene (1979).

[17]Described in Glaser (1980b).

[18]The autonomous power of each minister, interministerial coordination at higher levels of government and interbureau coordination at lower levels within each ministry in national and provincial governments are analyzed in Mayntz and Scharpt (1975).

become coordinator among all portfolio ministries, such as the developments in most other democracies. The West German portfolio ministries refused to cooperate, insisted that the chancellor reduce the staff, and later cemented their victory by installing as new Chancellor the minister of finance, Helmut Schmidt, who had led the fight against the expansion of the chancellor's office.[19] So, the federfuhrend practice remains. If a chancellor intervenes to coordinate several ministries in a common subject, the role is personal rather than institutional. The chancellor confers with them in a nonthreatening way and must demonstrate deep knowledge of the subject. The ministry coordinates with its opposite number in the other level of government (e.g., the national and provincial ministries of health) without routing the communication through the intergovernmental relations staffs of the federal chancellor and of the provincial minister–president.

In West Germany, essential glue is supplied by the political party. Leaders from the same party are remarkably solidary in helping each other, in supporting each other's policies, and in opposing the adversaries. Many policies are developed in the national and provincial party commissions and are carried out when the party has power. Members of a cabinet work together if they are from the same party, even if formally independent. National and provincial politicians from the same party cooperate, a provincial government helps national leaders of the same party. Struggles over changes in leaders and policies occur without damaging party solidarity. In few countries are political parties such an important force in organizing opinion, mobilizing the electorate, and coordinating the leaders as they are in West Germany.

Political parties, however, can be very divisive and weaken government if they are constantly maneuvering against each other and if they embarrass and handcuff officials from other parties. Coalition governments usually are very weak, unable to make big decisions, full of feuds, and often at the mercy of the divided assembly elected by the population; but not in West Germany. The rules of the game prescribe that coalition partners work together and that their party blocs in the legislature support them faithfully. The national government has been governed by coalitions for the last dozen years, as occasionally have been some provinces. Each party is given certain cabinet posts, and each minister runs his or her own show completely. The leaders of the two or three coalition partners—usually holding the three ranking ministries in the cabinet—are expected to communicate constantly.

The power of political parties has had one unexpected effect in West German government: The upper house of Parliament can be mobilized against the lower. Throughout the 1970s, the national government has been led by the Social Democrats (SPD), usually in coalition with the Free Democrats (FDP). The Christian Democrats (CDU and CSU) are more widely organized across the country and have always won a majority of provincial governments. Therefore, the CDU has had a majority of the votes in the upper house (the *Bundesrat*) of the Parliament where the delegations are sent by provincial governments, whereas the SPD and FDP have had majorities in the popularly elected lower house (the *Bundestag*). Recent cabinets have been SPD–FDP coalitions, since they were constructed according to the party composition of the Bundestag.

Involved governmental systems often founder over difficult, big decisions such as the containment of health costs. The West German government has had a mixed record, able to expand benefits more easily than to restrain them. The country has had a long-

---

[19]The unsuccessful attempts during the early 1970s to increase the power of the chancellor's office and coordinate the portfolio ministers are described in Von Beyme et al. (1976).

standing fear of inflation. During the 1950s, an interministerial committee was appointed to propose an improved health insurance system, including restraints on costs. The issue was so important that the chair of the interagency committee was given to Chancellor Konrad Adenauer, not merely to the lead ministry—the minister of labor. Although the national government produced its bill without internal divisions, the parliamentary and political system gave interest groups chances to object. A common conservative belief that cost sharing by the patient deters wasteful use was ingenuously included by the government in the bill. But a change from a paid-in-full to a cost-sharing policy invariably produces explosions on the left. As a matter of fact, with the exception of small charges for supplies, such as the British reforms of 1949–1951, no entire country has ever made this change for clinical care itself. The uproar over cost sharing and other changes caused the West German government to back away and shelve its bill in 1961, without putting it to a final vote in Parliament.[20]

The episode demonstrates the great difficulty in enacting restrictions upon health finance and health services. The strongest possible democratic government proposed them, led by the most successful leader of any West German democratic government (Adenauer), who was personally involved in writing the bill and selling it to interest groups. His collaborators, such as the minister of labor, were important figures themselves. The CDU had a majority in both the Bundestag and Bundesrat. Nevertheless, proposing so many restrictions in one package—on physicians as well as on patients—aroused a coalition of protesters. Trouble demoralizes voters, and the CDU lost some of its strength in the national election of 1961. Adenauer and his associates then decided to start over with a reform that required fewer deprivations, could win support of the trade unions (the traditional constituency for health insurance), and could be enacted without protest. A new minister of labor was appointed for that task.

The result was expansion of coverage, expansion of benefits, guarantees of higher fees to physicians, and a continuation of paid-in-full services without cost sharing by patients. Popular health laws are expensive. By the 1970s, West Germany, like other countries with national health insurance but without British control by vertical government budgeting, was experiencing a rapid cost escalation. Restraining utilization or raising additional revenue by patient cost sharing was taboo. No West German politician would have dared endorse it, and the Social Democrats (then in office) opposed it ideologically. In theory, costs should be controlled by vigorous bargaining by the sick funds with health care providers, such as the physicians, whom they face directly. In theory, the provincial governments should control costs of hospitals by regulating their rates strictly. But the sick funds and the provincial governments had to grant rates that at least covered the providers' costs, which supposedly were rising (particularly the wages of employees) out of the control of physicians and the hospitals themselves. The sick funds bargained over charge per service and the provincial governments regulated daily rates of hospitals, but the providers could increase revenue and costs through greater volume. Provincial governments were not adamant regulators because they were also owners of some hospitals and thus were interested in higher charges from the sick funds. Therefore, the problems for the national government were to place a ceiling on the total health expenditure and, since outright nationalization of all service was impossible, to strengthen the resolve of the bargainers and regulators.

But the political barriers to a strong law were greater than in 1959. Instead of a

---

[20]For details, see Safran (1967).

strong one-party majority in the assembly and committee, West Germany was ruled during the 1970s by a coalition (SPD and FDP), which controlled only the Bundestag. The CDU controlled a majority of the provincial governments and therefore a majority of the seats in the Bundesrat. The SPD–FDP coalition did not have two-thirds of the seats in the Bundestag and lacked the margin to override negative votes in the Bundesrat. Therefore, the coalition had to write bills that the Bundesrat would pass. A careful scenario was worked out for the health bill to make sure nothing went awry.

Within the executive branch, the lead agency was the ministry of labor, since it oversaw the social security laws. A new minister was installed for the job, and he brought with him several new senior civil servants and staff planners. They set to work collecting ideas, particularly those that the key interest groups would be willing to implement. For example, the national leadership of the medical association and sick funds had been trying to negotiate guidelines about fair increases in fees. Every provincial medical association and every provincial sick fund were encouraged to adopt the guidelines voluntarily. The staff in the ministry of labor visited interest groups and political party caucuses in the Bundestag to gain political support and avoid trouble. Many trips were taken to provincial capitals, in accordance with the national government's rules of procedure, requiring the sharing of legislative drafts with the provinces and consideration of their reactions.

The civil servants met among themselves to provide advice to the ministry of labor draughtsmen. This was very delicate, since the SPD and FDP had opposing views on state intervention and the free market. The draughtsmen had to be particularly alert to any signals coming from the civil servants of the ministry of interior, not because interior was involved in health, but because the minister was the leader of the FDP. Presumably any objections or questions posed by the civil servant from the interior reflected the views of the leader of the FDP. It was thus essential to persuade the civil servant from the interior, who would then persuade his boss. At the same time, discussions were held at higher ranks of the coalition involving the chancellor (leader of the SPD) and the leader of the FDP.

Because the Bundestag was so closely divided and the Christian Democrats had a majority in the Bundesrat, the civil servants had to consult with the CDU caucus in the Bundestag repeatedly. To get a bill through both houses, there would have to be either a grand coalition among all the parties or enough votes within the CDU would have to be split away. But who spoke for the CDU and could deliver votes? The national party leadership could speak for the CDU in the Bundestag. But each CDU provincial government made up its own mind, and ultimately the Bundesrat would decide. So, the minister of labor and the civil servants began negotiations with the CDU leaderships in the provinces that would have swing votes in the Bundesrat, such as Lower Saxony. In such cases, the ideologies and ambitions of the CDU ministers–president had to be taken into account.

During the communication with the groups, it became an art to assign the right emissary to the appropriate interest group and to the appropriate party caucus. The negotiations with the employers association were crucial. Concerned with the cost explosion and burdened with mounting social security taxes, the employers supported the final bill. This made it possible for parts of the CDU to support it. For the first time in 40 years, a law about health was passed over the opposition of the medical profession. In a pattern that might become common in other countries, the historical alliance between physicians and business was broken.

As the draughtsmen collected ideas, it became evident that the political parties had diametrically opposed policies. Much of the Social Democratic party and the draughts-men in the ministry of labor wanted strict price controls and quantity controls so that the annual increase in West German health care costs would match the annual increase in the GNP. A fixed amount of money might be budgeted for each sector, such as physi-cians' services; if use was higher than predicted, unit prices would be reduced. The average income of each class of health employee therefore could be planned in advance.

Such global budgeting was anathema to the CDU and to the medical profession. Something like it had existed in West German national health insurance before 1965 but had been abandoned. The CDU feared the SPD—in power for one of the few times in West German history—would use the cost control remedies as a first step toward outright national government ownership of sick funds and of health services and a first step toward national government employment of the physicians. The left wing of the SPD had long favored such a national health service.

Instead, the CDU insisted on safeguarding the autonomy of the sick funds, the associations of providers, and the owners of services. Beyond this principle, the CDU was divided. The conservative wing (based in Bavaria but scattered throughout central West Germany) opposed any national legislation. The liberal wing, which controlled national party headquarters and the leadership in the Bundestag, contended that some-thing had to be done. If not, the CDU would later be blamed for obstruction, inflation; and bankrupting the social security accounts, and the SPD could pass a stronger law. The internal debate became linked with the maneuvers by the leader of the conserva-tives (Franz Joseph Strauss of Bavaria) to overthrow the leader of the national party (Helmut Kohl) and become the next chancellor. To deal with costs, the CDU national leadership favored a voluntary assembly among the leading interest groups in health to set guidelines for prices and spending during the next year. It would include the participants in the annual guidelines conferences that were already being conducted, that is, the national headquarters of the physicians and sick funds, as well as involve representatives of trade unions, employers, and other health professions. Such a stand-ing assembly (called a *Konzertierte Aktion*, or KA) had maintained harmonious relations between industrial management and labor for several years. Although the medical professions wanted no cost control law at all, the creation of a KA was the least evil; in these sessions the physicians might find conservative allies against the sick funds and the trade unions.

Because the national government feared that hospital owners were spending grants from Bonn for construction and equipment too wastefully, the bill converted the grants into shared costs. Ten percent of such expenditures would be paid by the hospital owners for new capital development, five percent for renovations. The bill included several other provisions that would improve cost control and that had been recom-mended by ministries, parties,or interest groups in the past. The pension system and the payment of health care for the retired were improved. This part of social security had long fallen primarily on the employers, who feared it would eventually bankrupt them. A new fee schedule would be designed for all sick funds, including those for the middle classes. The general sick funds had long pressed for standardization as a step toward controlling the more generous (and more expensive) middle-class funds.

The draughtsmen combined ideas and modified wording so (they hoped) the bill would survive first passage in the Bundesrat without an excessively hostile report. The views of the CDU, employers, and physicians were incorporated. The traditional bilat-eral negotiations between sick funds and physicians at the provincial level were pre-served but were to be preceded by several guideline-producing stages at the national level. The connection between rises in health care costs and rises in the GNP was reduced to an idea to be taken into account by the negotiators. Other criteria for the negotiators were added in order to please the physicians: Increases in spending for their services were justified by increases in demand and by the improved technical quality of care. But the SPD-led ministry of labor was not willing to hand leadership over cost control to the providers, who it believed had created the problem; therefore, it did not add a KA to the draft.

The government drew the line against appeasing the physicians. One clause was designed to increase competition in the ambulatory care by allowing hospital physicians to treat any insured outpatient. This proposal enraged the office-based physicians throughout the country. In Lower Saxony they suspended practice briefly in protest, one of the few strikes by physicians in postwar Europe.

During the informal consultations, the provinces had objected to the ten percent and the five percent sharing of the costs of investments, since they would have to pay much of this. But the ministry of labor and the cabinet thought this essential to discourage the excessive building and expansion of hospitals. Ten percent provincial cost sharing struck them as ridiculously low and they thought that the provinces should be grateful.

Preoccupied with writing language about ambulatory care that would mollify the CDU, the employers, and the politically formidable medical profession, the government quickly devised a method of hospital cost control that nearly wrecked the bill. All private hospitals, public hospitals, urban governments, and provincial governments would have to contribute some of their own money or lose some of the *Bund* financial help upon which they had come to depend. A solid opposition coalition of provinces arose, combing the SPD and CDU provinces, a rarity in the now divided and causus-ridden Bundesrat. The national government gambled further that its case was justified and would eventually win over critics. It insisted on retaining the hospital cost controls. In response, the CDU provinces in the Bundesrat sent the bill on to the Bundestag after an exceptionally long and critical floor debate, with a long and critical report. The attacks continued in the Bundestag and were not appeased by modified and additional wording in existing clauses by the committees.

The bill then went back to the Bundesrat for second passage. Its fate demonstrates the control over legislation gained by the federal–provincial voting system in the Bundesrat. The national government had ignored the principal objections of the CDU provinces and of the Bundesrat in general: The bill still included cost sharing for hospital investment and still omitted a KA. It was rejected by the Bundesrat in a barrage of criticisms and was submitted to the joint conference committee of the two houses, the *Vermittlungsauschuss*.

The national government needed the vote of the two CDU provinces in the Bundesrat. Soundings had already been taken. Important influences in rounding up provinces would be the national leaderships of the CDU and of the FDP. The CDU needed to pass a bill and avoid the stigma of obstructionism, provided that a KA was the keystone. The FDP had supported development of the bill in the national cabinet and could influence CDU ministers–president in those provinces ruled by CDU–FDP coalitions. The most likely defectors from the opposition were two provinces with CDU–FDP coalitions.[21] Saarland was won over most easily: It was the poorest province,

---

[21]In fact, the FDP had helped the CDU pluralities in these provinces form provincial cabinets in order to help its national coalition partner, the SPD, run the blockade in the Bundesrat.

it suffered budgetary strain from the cost explosion, and it was interested in improving health care services (as evidenced by its customary role as permanent chair of the Bundesrat's committee on health). The other possibility was Lower Saxony, ruled by the liberal wing of the CDU and led by a minister–president eager for national attention. The price was high: Both provincial governments (especially Saarland) insisted on removal of the cost sharing for hospital investment; both governments (especially Lower Saxony) insisted on adoption of a KA in health; and Lower Saxony's volatile office-based physicians insisted that they be allowed to retain their clinical freedom and monopoly over ambulatory care.

To obtain a law, the national government surrendered to the two CDU-led provinces. The KA was inserted. All cost controls over hospitals were removed. The right of hospital physicians to treat ambulatory patients was limited, and the national minister of labor gave a speech in the Bundesrat assuring the physicians (and the CDU of Lower Saxony) of their professional autonomy. The ministers–president of Lower Saxony and of Saarland announced their support of the bill. The remaining CDU provinces in the Bundesrat condemned the law, but Lower Saxony's votes gave it a bare majority. Officially, it is the *Krankenversicherungs-Kostendampfungsgesetz* of 1977.[22]

The national government had succeeded in getting one of the most politically difficult of all laws—the control over health care costs—through the obstacle course of West German intergovernmental decision making. It had been a triumph of intergovernmental and intergroup negotiation by the minister of labor and his civil servants. But had anything survived? The KA was now the keystone. The voluntary effort conducted by the national headquarters of the physicians and sick funds was now official. Since failure would give the SPD an excuse to call for a new law with direct controls, the medical association made sure that its stage in the negotiations would be productive. With the national leaderships of the sick funds and with its own provincial offices, it carefully rehearsed the forthcoming public performance. The KA held its first meeting in March 1978; it agreed to increase physicians' payments for both fees and services by 5.5 percent. Although the provincial units of the insurance physicians signed contracts with the sick funds for no more, the dentists refused to agree on any guidelines and the KA deadlocked over them.

To accomplish anything seemed a triumph, but the biggest problem had been bypassed, namely, the hospitals. The staff of the ministry of labor resumed negotiations with the interest groups, party caucuses, and provinces to produce a law focusing on the containment of hospital costs. The starting point was the article in the 1977 bill that had been struck out by the Mediation Committee. The guarantees of defeat, that is, the ten percent cost sharing of capital expenditures by the owners and the five percent for renovations, were dropped. Hospital planning would be strengthened. The role of the sick funds as watchdogs over money would be strengthened: Somewhat like their bargaining with the associations of physicians over money, they would bargain with associations of hospitals over rates. But by now the subject had become so sensitive, the provinces had become so suspicious of tampering with hospital finance, and the text was such an obscure patchwork that the bill got nowhere. Since the weakly regulated hospital spending was far more important in total costs than the fees monitored in the KA, costs continued to rise, exceeding 9 percent of the GNP by the late 1970s, one of the world's highest proportions at that time.

---

[22]English-language summaries of the bill may be found in Stone (1979), Geissler (1978), and Landsberger (1980).

Although disappointing, the results show the difficulty in restraining costs when government does not own the facilities (as in Britain) and does not control all spending for services through the government budget (as in Britain and Canada). Under national health insurance, the law can only set guidelines for providers, sick funds, and regulators. But a government with great political will (such as in France at times) can impose strict rules and can create the machinery to enforce them.

THE UNITED STATES

If the problem is distribution of the government's own money, government can make difficult decisions because it must. Imposing regulation on the private sector is more sensitive, and government must be organized to formulate a proposal and to carry it through. If the executive is weak and the legislature strong—particularly a supreme legislature characterized by internal political rivalries—the prospective losers from regulations and from spending cutbacks can block action. A political system that has centers of leverage for both the advocates and opponents of hard decisions can enact some changes but not the most difficult ones.

The United States is usually a government with a very powerful legislature and a weak and often disorganized executive. As the Medicare experience showed, it can produce spending laws that yield political credit but shelves controls and cutbacks that arouse protest. By the 1970s, the succession of grants and entitlement programs in health had run their course, and the problems were to set priorities and restraints. But the decision-making system could not cope with them. American political culture presumes against government regulation and for private enterprise, even when regulation is being enacted and implemented. This presumption is particularly strong in fields in which private action is thought very successful, such as health.

The stillborn Hospital Cost Containment Act of 1977 was prepared within DHEW at a time when the Carter administration gave maximum responsibility to each operating department to develop its program. The authors did not have to coordinate either the content or politics of their proposals with other agencies. The administration was easily sold on the need for the bill.

The DHEW was not under legal obligation to consult systematically with interest groups and state governments, as in some other countries. Nor did it consult informally and circulate drafts, lest critics be ready with attacks. The secretary announced his general intentions in February 1977, but the details were not shared until the bill was ready.

Announced in April 1977, the bill controlled all inpatient revenues for nearly all short-time acute care and specialty hospitals in the United States. Controlling Medicare and Medicaid payments alone was considered a mistake, since hospitals might then overcharge private insurance accounts to make up the difference. Besides, the problems were thought to be protection of all purchasers of hospital services and stabilization of the entire medical economy. The only solution was across-the-board spending control of an entire industry, an extraordinary action in peacetime. This was presented as an emergency step, to be replaced by a more permanent but still undefined method of cost control a few years later.

The bill prescribed global budgeting tied to changes in general inflation and the GNP. Each hospital could increase its revenues per admission no more than the formula—calculated from data about general price movements and the GNP—allowed.

The target was control over revenues, that is, the combination of prices and services, and not over prices alone. The authors were convinced that if prices were limited, health care providers would increase work per case in order to increase income. The method gave hospitals the choice of varying charges and service intensity, provided ceilings were not exceeded.

Another part of the bill authorized DHEW to limit hospital capital expenditures and the supply of hospital beds. If occupancy fell below a certain level, no new beds would be allowed and existing ones would be shut. Hospital capital expenditures and beds would be distributed across the country according to population.[23]

Still in its first months in office, the Carter administration believed that such a direct method of controlling a manifestly serious problem could not fail to win quick enactment.[24] Instead, it could not fail to lose, since such an approach to controlling cost had no large and politically militant constituency. It principal enthusiasts were government budget officers. In other countries, the natural constituency is the sick funds and their allies, the trade unions. Here, however, Blue Cross, Blue Shield, and the private insurance companies were apprehensive at such a massive entry of government regulation, particularly by Washington, when the government agencies they normally confronted were state insurance commissions and state rate regulation agencies. In contrast with West Germany, where the ministry of labor had acquired a constituency for its control bill by framing it in collaboration with the sick funds, trade unions, and the Social Democratic Party, DHEW had written its cost control bill in secrecy, uncontaminated by the self-interest of the special groups. Trade unions in the United States interpreted the strict global budgeting not as ensuring better value for their members but as a check on wage increases for hospital employees, and therefore they too had the orientation of providers. Finally, although provincial governments in federal systems should be supporters of cost controls in health because they administer payments or are the responsible overseers, not only did the proposed U.S. bill bypass the states, so did most of the health spending. Medicare, for example, was a national program, where as increasing proportions of the Medicaid money were from Washington and most of the rest was private. Worthy schemes without committed political friends do not progress far in democracies.

In effective modern governments, the lead minister never stands alone behind his or her proposal. It is shaped with the senior civil servants in the agency. The latter often become leading authorities on the subject matter, respected by both providers and consumers in the private sector. They have become impartial, serving successive committees of different political complexion. The elite civil servants in an agency can obtain united support throughout the government by the automatic backing from their counterparts in other agencies. But the United States lack such an elite permanent civil service. The cost-containment bill discussed here, for example, was written by the secretary and young experts whose tenure began and ended with the Carter administra-

---

[23]A good summary of the cost problem, the terms of the original bill, and the possible consequences in practice is *The Hospital Cost Containment Act of 1977: An Analysis of the Administration's Proposal* (Washington, D.C.: Congressional Budget Office, 1977). Earlier and later bills to control hospital costs are described in Congressional Research Service of the Library of Congress, *Hospital Cost Containment*, prepared for the Subcommittee on Health, Committee on Ways and Means, and Subcommittee on Health and the Environment, Committee on Interstate and Foreign Commerce, U.S. House of Representatives (Washington, D.C.: U.S. Government Printing Office, 1979).

[24]For details about the history of the Carter administration's bill and its rivals, see Glaser (1979) and Abernathy and Pearson (1979).

tion. Therefore, their scheme did not appear sound and impartial to the private sector and other government agencies.

When writing bills and negotiating legislative decisions in the United States, it is difficult to find responsible people who can speak for the executive and legislative branches. If DHEW began as the lead agency in hospital cost containment, eventually the treasury and the White House became active, and their views diverged. For something as important as health, two committees in each House processed bills. Every member made up his or her own mind. Since Congress did not negotiate a final bill with the executive branch, it did not miss a fully empowered executive spokes person. Congress has become accustomed to the absence of leadership; members want to be autonomous and have eliminated the special powers of their own nominal leadership. Therefore, legislation oozes along, amended and supplemented in successive discussions and votes.

The drafters of the cost-containment bill did not use their stage to learn the views and future political intentions of all the prospective key actors. The drafting was an armchair exercise based on bright thoughts. Not only does secrecy deprive a bill of better ideas, but is antagonizes potential supporters and legitimizes support of rival schemes. Chronic secrecy by a democratic government eventually discredits it.

The drafters and political leaders in the initiating ministry developed no scenario about future contingencies. They failed to discover that substantial political support was absent for what they considered important. Pressing Congress for difficult laws that no one really wants is a serious waste of political capital and damages an administration's capacity to accomplish anything.

Within the context of the American system of government, the executive branch is merely another lobby on Capitol Hill, asking members and committees to consider its proposals. It is often at a disadvantage, since its small lobbying staff is spread over many issues, whereas the interest groups aggrieved by each proposal can focus their efforts.

Although the executive branch's proposal attracts special attention, it does not monopolize the debate. Every critic and rival can draft their own bill and get it introduced. The result is a potpourri. As the issue is discussed and members of Congress get signals from their constituents, attention shifts to new bills, rarely remaining with the first ones, such as the administration's. A common upshot in a congressional committee is to combine several bills hastily. Such was the case with hospital cost containment during 1978. The patchwork is done by the members and their staffs, usually without the agreement of the executive branch. If the result is enacted, it is very complex and confusing.

Political party organizations cannot unify and mobilize members of Congress on legislation in a disciplined fashion. However, party identity influences action because it affects whom the members and their staff associate with, who sends them advice and requests. Often a consensus builds within clusters of legislators who regularly associate. On hospital cost containment, some Republicans first pushed for state rather than national regulation, then they shifted from state regulation to private voluntary self-regulation. Gradually Congress swung their way.

Members of Congress react most strongly to the people who hire and fire them, namely, the interest groups and individuals from their districts, regardless of party. Because of their extensive grass roots organization and popularity, interest groups in health (such as state hospital associations) can be quite formidable. Drafters of bills in the executive branch must foresee what will motivate them to lobby. To the surprise of the Carter administration, the state hospital associations became the most effective lobbyists on Capitol Hill, influencing members throughout.

The United States has a peculiar federal system. A program can be administered by the national government alone, by all the state governments, or by a mosaic in different places. The United States does not have a consistent policy on structure, presuming that the states alone should administer a program and forbidding them to evade the responsibility. Trying to regulate health as an exclusively national effort invites anger if not defeat, because state governments resent invasion of their turf and because existing state regulatory efforts might be superseded or handcuffed. Much confusion during the legislative history of hospital cost containment from 1977 through 1979 revolved around the role of the state governments in this traditional area of state power.

When American legislators adopt the common practice of combining bills, the absence of a standard structure for running a program can produce troublesome results. For example, early hospital cost-containment bills proposed price controls by the national government, regulation by state governments, and direct negotiations between the private carriers and the hospitals (called voluntary effort). A widely supported bill in 1979 proposed a series of fallbacks: If private negotiations failed to achieve a targeted limit on growth, state regulation would automatically be triggered; and if state regulation were absent or ineffective, national regulation would be triggered. Despite its plausibility, this arrangement exploded in tremendous fights: The participants in private negotiation opposed being superseded by government regulators and presented their own data showing that the trigger misfired; similarly, no state commission quietly accepted national intervention.

Government displacement of negotiators occurs outside the United States only as arbitration, that is, imposing an agreement if the parties failed. But government never deposes a bargaining arrangement that is merely too expensive. Superseding negotiators for making the wrong decision requires a permanent change in the law and in the system.

Enactment of health cost containment is difficult at best, but hopeless without strong union support. Therefore, the Carter administration quickly appeased the unions by exempting wages from controls. Any wage increase for hospital workers would automatically pass through and be fully covered in the revenues earned by hospitals. The controls would apply to everything else in the hospitals' budgets. This concession appeased the unions and motivated them to lobby for the Carter proposal. It, however, discredited the bills, since the biggest item of cost was exempt. Any other supplier could make a case for exemption. The hospital association, for example, could argue that only an intelligent method of examining and deciding every cost individually makes good public policy and that arbitrary ceilings are not legitimate if they are arbitrarily selective. The power of trade unions and the failure to tie wage determination into the method of controlling hospital spending are the biggest difficulties in hospital cost containment in every country.

LESSONS FOR THE UNITED STATES

THE NEED TO IMPROVE DECISION MAKING

In every country today, one hears about problems of public management and decision-making overload. Too many interest groups, citizens and officials want to participate in each decision. Many programs are enacted, large amounts of money are spent, and some programs commit government to spend more money every year. Everyone finds it difficult to keep track of so many activities; many programs work out differently than expected; considerable waste and conflict occur.

Several important books have described the overload affecting Western governments.[25] In many countries, traditional methods of overseeing the administration have been changing, either because of modernizing trends in public management or because of breakdowns due to the overload.

Nowhere are these problems as evident and troublesome as in the United States, where one often hears of a "crisis of competence in government" (Sundquist, 1980). Americans traditionally favor flexibility and competition instead of permanent structure. Often their government appears chaotic during social change, and the antipathy toward macroorganization produces few standing mechanisms to oversee and improve the system itself. Instead, Americans produce a constant stream of commissions and reports about government, whose sheer number and ephemeral character contribute to, rather than solve, the situation.[26]

The confused history and ultimate breakdown of hospital cost-containment legislation in the United States are typical outcomes. The national government can vote to spend but cannot terminate obsolete programs (unless they contain an automatic expiration date) or prioritize them. The system has great difficulty in enunciating the problem for which legislation is being proposed, since everyone is too busy and no one is in charge of an issue. Alternative actions are not clearly debated nor are their full consequences, such as the alternative national, state, and private sector methods of hospital cost containment, thoroughly explored. Combining them all in one bill begs the questions. Legislating without forethought and hoping that institutional details will be worked out later aggravates the management problems. Since both the executive and legislative branches leave so many matters unclear, private parties invite judges to settle them, adding to the conflicts and confusion.

Certain constitutional features of the United States differentiate its government from others, notably the separation of powers. Its size makes it difficult to manage. Its serious internal social divisions, particularly its intermittent civil war among the races, create greater tensions then those of others countries. Some Americans conclude that the United States is so different, that the high-level decision-making experiences of other countries are irrelevant. But that is fatalism, a rationalization that the current chaos is irremediable. Others look for remedies and are eager for ideas from any source. Once, despite its special features, American government operated with greater structure and identifiable centers of responsibility and power, more like other countries. The following are lessons about macro-decision-making derived from other countries and addressed to the deficiencies in the United States.

HEALTH ISSUES

Since health is a fundamental source of anxiety, a health program offering benefits can easily be passed. The public wants it and politicians compete to reap the credit. All too

---

[25]See, for example, Crozier (1975) and Rose and Peters (1978).

[26]One of the few standing specialists in U.S. government organization, the Advisory Commission on Intergovernmental Relations, during recent years has conducted major projects and a conference to assess the situation. (See Advisory Commission on Intergovernmental Relations, 1980.) The plenary meeting of the National Governors' Association in August 1980 called for a National Commission on Federalism to sort out the chaos and redesign the system.

often they are too easy to pass. Premature and wasteful programs might be enacted unless the government has a very careful system of screening and prioritizing its commitments. Unless they are enacted with termination dates and expenditure ceilings, health programs commonly experience cost overruns.

Since physicians and health care providers are accustomed to demanding and getting all the resources they need to save lives, they fight any meaningful cost-control mechanisms and fight any monitoring structures that give people management supremacy. Legislators should beware of bargaining away cost-control and monitoring clauses in order to enact a spending program. Their best chance of getting controls is during enactment of the package the providers and the public want. Separate enactment later is very difficult, as the German experience in 1978 showed.

Taxpayers complain over excessive taxes and spending for other programs but much less frequently over health finance. Most other spending programs are transfers to other people, but health spending is viewed as a potential benefit to one's self when it is urgently needed.

The appeal of any charismatic group (such as physicians) to the public is formidable politically. If a government wishes to enact a program fought by the medical profession, it must make sure it is internally unified, that supporters are lined up among interest groups, and that it sends into battle an attractive national leader of its own. Since the medical profession has great grass-root support throughout the country, its rivals must organize equivalent support everywhere. If legislators are independent and subject to great influence by the local medical associations, the physicians' rivals must reward and protect them politically.

To enact a major change in health institutions or health financing, tremendous problems must be overcome. The reformers must be led by a political virtuoso, and substantial factions of the physicians and hospital leaders must cooperate.

If clinical services have been free, one cannot reimpose cost sharing by patients. Either the protests cause the executives and legislators to back away, or the electorate is mobilized for revenge.[27] On the other hand, small charges for supplies (drugs, spectacles, dentures, prostheses, etc.) are normal.

A negative policy such as health cost containment cannot easily be imposed by external order. The most effective path is voluntary, a habitual orientation by a new generation of lay mangers and physicians trained in modern canons of cost effectiveness.

LEADERSHIP

A lead agency must be designated to prepare a plan, prepare the scenario of political maneuvers and pitfalls, and discuss the drafts with key actors (interest groups, legislators, provincial governments in federal systems). Someone must be in charge and remain in charge throughout the political difficulties encountered by every major health proposal.

The minister must have the personal skills and political strengths necessary to hold

---

[27]The most prominent victim of this lesson is the Liberal party of Saskatchewan. Faithful to conservation truisms, it enacted charges on visits to physicians a short time after winning the 1967 election, which led to its defeat by the new Democratic party (NDP) in 1971. The latter repealed the copayment. In every subsequent election, the NDP has warned the voters that a liberal victory will bring back copayments. The issue has helped the NDP win every election in the province by a landslide since.

productive discussions with the medical association, the hospital association, the trade unions, and businesses. In the United States, the secretary must be skillful with Congress. He or she must have a cadre of civil servants on the assignment, with similar skills. The minister must be committed to spend most of his or her time on the effort: No important health plan can be passed otherwise; defeat is politically expensive. If the minister is not up to the task, the proposal will lose and the regime will be wounded.

Selection of the right person for the ministry of health is more difficult than is generally assumed. Such a person must have the vigor, glamor, independent political power, and skills to dramatize a new proposal, persuade the public and legislature, and impress the interest groups. But since ambitious spending commitments such as one's pet schemes often get out of hand, there must be a willingness to compromise with one's colleagues. Leaders outstandingly successful in the first role are often unfitted for the second, as the erratic career of Aneurin Bevan demonstrates. The American "solution" is to avoid the first type of leader: Most cabinet officers are not independently powerful but are pedestrian team players, subordinate to the president. This is a reason why pressure groups and members of Congress dominate the creation and reshaping of proposals and the U.S. executive branch is lost in the shuffle.

Leadership is not only a person but an institution. Effective modern governments are led by teams of ministers and senior permanent civil servants in each agency. The minister expresses the views of the government of the day and its social constituency, negotiates with other members of the committee, and sells the proposal to its assembly and public. The senior servants draft in detail a project that is feasible and fits other government programs; they convey impartiality and expertise to the providers and the public and mobilize the support of other agencies. The United States does not yet have this kind of civil service, but it needs it. Effective programs cannot be drafted, sold, implemented, and corrected by political agency heads aided by young personnel deputies, both with limited experience in the subject field and short tenure in government. The result in the United States is to lose control over program formation to the interest groups that possess the expertise and permanent involvement.

Once a decision is made it needs to be implemented with political will. Dithering leaders, such as former President Carter and Prime Minister Edward Heath, have short and ineffective tenures. But since a leader is stuck with a big commitment, its merit and political consequences should be thought through carefully in advance.[28] Scuttling an unproductive proposal means a loss of political capital—as in Chancellor Konrad Adenauer's cost-sharing proposal—but a resourceful leader can get off the plunging vehicle in time and can survive to try something else.

COORDINATION

Health proposals invariably affect several agencies, and therefore coordination is necessary from the start. Unless the government has a very definite code of behavior (as in West Germany), the lead ministry cannot reliably coordinate with everyone nor compromise when appropriate. The lead ministry's officials are too busy dealing with outside groups, too committed to their drafts.

---

[28]The British political system can give a brave prime minister plenary authority to act but not the wisdom and luck to adopt a successful policy.

Although once a common practice, the ministry of finance cannot be a dispassionate coordinator either. It is too committed to its own position on spending. In the United States, moreover, many finance officers have thinly concealed philosophies about the substance of health care that should enter into policy but should not dominate it.

The usual pattern is coordination by the office of the head of government. Health issues are difficult enough at times to require much work by the head himself. President Carter's noninvolvement in his hospital cost-containment bill was a reason for its political weakness. Clement Attlee's diffidence while healthy and absence while ill let the interagency conflict over NHS charges get out of hand in 1951. The head's staff should coordinate, not originate, new policies that are substituted for those of the ministries. Excessive meddling by the White House instead of coordination, for example has contributed to Washington's confusion in recent years.

One effective method of coordination is to spread through the higher civil service people trained in the same way. For example, members of the *inspectorat des finances* rule not only the French ministries of finance and budget but now also occupy top posts in the spending ministries, such as health. They move their respective ministries in the same direction voluntarily by common conviction, instead of playing cat-and-mouse games with interagency coordinators. The United States has still to develop such esprit de corps and professionalization among its higher civil servants.

Powerful political parties can ensure unity among ministers and can ensure the cooperation of legislators. But they can create serious problems if the opposition is adversarial in style and equal in discipline. Every issue becomes raised to a partisan struggle, even health issues that otherwise might divide the population less intensely or on other principles. If the assembly is closely divided, the government cannot enact its proposals, or the cabinet itself lives under the constant shadow of overthrow. In an environment of disciplined rival parties, one cannot often pick up support for meritorious proposals from members of the opposition.

INTERGOVERNMENTAL RELATIONS

If the United States ever develops a true federal system, that is, one in which state governments would have principal responsibilities and powers in health and in other, classic police-power fields, it must develop a national–provincial and interprovincial negotiating system.

Major intergovernmental negotiations that produce a result require common fronts. Each level of government requires thorough and constant internal coordination. This is the opposite of the undisciplined picket-fence federalism of the United States. If a ministry has extensive discretion to deal with its counterpart on the other level of government (such as in West Germany), coordination within its own government by some method (personal contacts, legal rules, political party discipline, participation by the office of head of government) is especially important.

SUMMARY AND CONCLUSION

The people speak, but their voices are many. Most governments have been organized diffusely, with individual officials responding to diverse constituencies and regions. History is a cycle between governments organized centrifugally and others that try to get control of situations, either in order to respond to social pressures coherently or in order to mobilize the society to fulfill the leaders' own ambitions.

Every government is a committee of leaders and an assembly of representatives of the population. The committee writes programs and pushes for their enactment, but in some centrifugally organized governments much initiative comes from the assembly. All governments can be persuaded to enact popular programs. A cohesive committee capable of setting priorities and controlling its assembly has a range of choices: It can reject some popular demands but can also adopt innovations making great changes in traditional practices and in group interest. Restricting popular programs requires cohesive committees that have resourceful members, that control their assemblies, and that are led by chief executives willing to risk their political capital.

It is easy to be fatalistic about one's own government. Faced by the highly diffuse operations of the present government of the United States, one is tempted merely to explain and not to reform, to say that the situation—whether called freedom or chaos—is inevitable and unchangeable. However, a government with the unique record of continuous operation for two centuries that the United States has, must have the capacity to change, to adapt, to act upon each new generation's unique social agenda and external threats. American methods of making and implementing decisions have been reformed many times. Just as the founders at the first Constitutional Convention leaned heavily on lessons from other countries during the creation of a new system, so today, one can think of the rest of the world as a demonstration laboratory of organizational forms, inspiring the people of the United States to think of new ways to organize in the face of modern complexity and modern hyperactivity, new ways to strike the balance between order and liberty.

REFERENCES

Abel-Smith, Brian, *The Hospitals 1800–1948*, London: Heinemann, 1964, Chaps. 27–29.

Abernathy, David S. and David A. Pearson, *Regulating Hospital Costs*, Ann Arbor, Mich.: AUPHA Press, 1979

Advisory Commission Intergovernmental Relations, *The Federal Role is the Federal System: The Dynamics of Growth—A Crisis of Confidence and Competence*, Washington, D.C.: Advisory Commission Intergovernmental Relations [ACIR], July 1980, summary report.

Beveridge, William, *Social Insurance and Allied Services*, London: H.M. Stationery Office, CMD. 6404, 1942, Para. 106, 437.

Carter, George E., *Canadian Conditional Grants Since World War II*, Toronto: Canadian Tax Foundation, 1971.

Carter, George E., "Financing Health and Post-Secondary Education: A New and Complex Fiscal Arrangement," *Canadian Tax Journal*, Vol. 25, September–October 1977, pp. 534–550.

Congressional Budget Office, *The Hospital Cost Containment Act of 1977: An Analysis of the Administration's Proposal*, Washington, D.C.: Congressional Budget Office, 1977.

Congressional Research Service of the Library of Congress, *Hospital Cost Containment*, Washington, D.C.: U.S. Government Printing Office, 1979.

Comet, Paul, *L - Hopital Public*, Paris: Berger-Levrault, 1960, 1st edition.

Courchene, Thomas J., *Refinancing the Canadian Federation: A Survey of the 1977 Fiscal Arrangements*, Montreal: Canadian Economic Policy Committee, C.D. Howe Research Institute, 1979.

Crozier, Michael J. et al., *The Crisis of Democracy*, New York: The Trilateral Commission and New York University Press, 1975.

Eckstein, Harry, *The English Health Service*, Cambridge: Harvard University Press, 1958.

Eckstein, Harry, *Pressure Group Politics: The Case of the British Medical Association*, London: Allen & Unwin, 1960.

Feder, Judith M., Medicare: *The Politics of Federal Health Insurance*, Lexington, Mass.: Lexington Books, 1977.

Foot, Michael, *Aneurin Bevan: A Biography*, London: Davis-Poynter, 1973, Vol. 2, Chaps. 3–4.

Geissler, Ulrich, *Health Care Cost Containment in the Federal Republic of Germany*, Bonn-Bad Godesburg: Wissenschaftliches Institute der Ortskrankenkassen, 1978, pp. 11-21.

Glaser, William, "Doctors and Politics," *American Journal of Sociology*, Vol. 66, November 1960, pp. 230–245.

Glaser, William, *Paying the Doctor*, Baltimore: Johns Hopkins Press, 1970, pp. 124–134.

Glaser, William, *Health Insurance Bargaining*, New York: Gardner Press and John Wiley & Sons, 1978, chap. 3.

Glaser, William, *Federalism in Canada and West Germany: Lessons for the United States*, New York: Center for the Social Sciences, Columbia University, 1979. (Distributed by the National Technical Information Service.)

Glaser, William, *Paying the Hospital in France*, New York: Center for the Social Sciences, Columbia University, 1980[a].

Glaser, William, *Paying the Hospital in Canada*, New York: Center for the Social Sciences, Columbia University, 1980[b].

Harris, R. W., *National Health Insurance in Great Britain 1911–1946*, London: Allen & Unwin, 1946.

Hatzfeld, Henri, *Le grand tournant de la medecine liberale*, Paris: Les Editions Ouvrieres, 1963

Jamous, Haroun, Jacques Commaille and Bernard Pons-Vignon, *Contribution a ure Decision Politique*, Paris: Centre d'Etudes Sociologiques, Centre National de la Recherche Scientifique, 1967.

Landsberger, Henry, *West Germany's Health Cost Control Law 1977*, Washington, D.C.: National Health Planning Information Center, 1980.

Lewis, Perrin, "The New Federal-Provincial Fiscal Arrangements," *Monthly Review of the Bank of Nova Scotia*, March–April, 1977.

Lindsey, Almont, *Socialized Medicine in England and Wales*, Chapel Hill: University of North Carolina Press, 1962, pp. 411–414.

Marmor, Theodore R., *The Politics of Medicare*, Chicago: Aldine Publishing Co., 1973.

Mayntz, Renate and Fritz W. Scharpf, *Policy-Making in the German Federal Bureaucracy*, Amsterdam: Elsevier Scientific Publishing Co., 1975.

Rose, Richard and Guy Peters, *Can Government Go Bankrupt?* New York: Basic Books, 1978.

Safran, William, *Veto Group Politics*, San Francisco: Chandler Publishing Co., 1967.

Simeon, Richard, *Federal-Provincial Diplomacy: The Making of Recent Policy in Canada*, Toronto: University of Toronto Press, 1972, chap. 4.

Smiley, Donald V., *Conditional Grants and Canadian Federalism*, Toronto: Canadian Tax Foundation, 1963.

Stevens, Robert and Rosemary Stevens, *Welfare Medicine in America*, New York: The Free Press, 1974, Part I.

Stone, Deborah A., "Health Care Cost Containment in West Germany," *Journal of Health Politics, Policy, and Law*, Vol. 4, Summer 1979, pp. 176–199.

Sundquist, James, "Crisis of Competence in Government," in Joseph A. Pechman, ed., *Setting*

National Priorities: Agenda for the 1980's. Washington, D.C.: The Brookings Institution, 1980.

Taylor, Malcolm, *Health Insurance and Canadian Public Policy: The Seven Decisions that Created the Canadian Health Insurance System.* Montreal: McGill-Queen's University Press, 1978.

Von Beyme, Klaus, et al., *German Political Systems*, Beverly Hills: Sage Publications, 1976, pp. 53–63.

White, Michael, "Have We Been Here Before?" *Health and Social Service Journal*, Vol. 9, January 1981, p. 9.

Willcocks, Arthur J., *The Creation of a National Health Service*, London: Routledge, Kegan, and Paul, 1967.

Willink, Henry, *A National Health Service*, H.M. Stationery Office, Cmd. 6502, 1944.

APPENDIX 1

Government Expenditures
for Health
in the United States
for Selected Years

TABLE 1. Federal, State, and Local Government Expenditures for Health and Medical Care

	Amount (in Billions)			Total[a] Per Capita	Total as Percent of All National Health Care Expenditures (Public and Private) (%)[a]
Year	Federal	State and Local	Total		
1950	$ 1.6	$ 1.8	$ 3.4	$ 22.24	26.8
1955	2.0	2.6	4.6	27.05	26.0
1960	3.0	3.6	6.6	36.10	24.5
1965	5.5	5.2	10.8	54.57	25.9
1966	7.4	6.1	13.6	67.82	29.5
1967	11.9	7.0	19.0	93.75	37.0
1968	14.1	8.0	22.1	108.15	38.0
1969	16.1	8.8	24.9	120.72	37.9
1970	17.7	10.1	27.8	133.22	37.2
1971	20.3	11.3	31.7	149.87	38.1
1972	22.9	12.5	35.4	165.88	37.9
1973	25.2	14.1	39.3	182.15	38.1
1974	30.4	16.6	47.1	216.44	40.5
1975	37.1	19.1	56.2	255.49	42.4
1976	42.6	20.3	62.9	283.51	42.0
1977	47.4	22.7	70.1	312.67	41.4
1978	53.7	25.7	79.4	350.27	41.9
1979	60.8	29.3	90.1	393.31	42.0
1980	70.9	33.3	104.2	449.96	42.2

SOURCE: Health Care Financing Administration, *Health Care Financing Review*, September 1981.

[a]Detail may not add to totals due to rounding.

TABLE 2. Federal Government Health Budget Outlays[a]

Fiscal Year	Medicaid and it's Predecessors	Medicare	Dept. of Defense	Veterans Services	Indian Health Services	Federal Civilian Employees Health Insurance	Research	Medical Facilities Construction[b] and Other	Total	Percent of Total Federal Budget
1960	$ 200	N.A.	$ 880	$ 879	N.A.	—	$ 448	$1,093	$ 3,500	3.8
1965	555	N.A.	937	1,115	$ 71	$ 149c	1,040	1,293	5,160	4.4
1966	766	$ 65d	1,107	1,161	75	165c	1,315	1,274	5,928	4.4
1967	1,205	3,395	1,432	1,252	83	202c	1,364	1,868	10,801	6.8
1968	1,834	5,347	1,648	1,343	94	223	1,547	2,096	14,132	7.9
1969	2,298	6,598	1,750	1,431	107	230	1,528	2,614	16,556	8.9
1970	2,607	7,149	1,760	1,651	120	233	1,577	2,969	18,066	9.2
1971	3,374	7,875	1,957	1,874	143	350	1,565	3,040	20,178	9.5
1972	4,166	8,819	2,341	2,256	170	502	1,776	4,501	24,531	10.6
1973	4,997	9,479	2,468	2,587	198	561	2,002	3,738	26,030	10.6
1974	5,833	11,348	2,741	2,787	216	729	2,078	3,457	29,189	10.9
1975	7,056	14,781	3,085	3,287	283	1,029	2,453	4,816	36,790	11.3
1976	8,381	17,777	3,232	3,793	332	1,397	2,818	5,883	43,613	11.9
1977	9,714	21,391	3,815	4,708	395	1,654	3,147	4,812	49,636	12.4
1978	10,960	25,551	3,354	5,174	467	1,837	3,715	4,277	55,335	12.2
1979	12,407	29,148	4,332	5,509	555	1,991	3,929	4,875	62,746	12.7
1980e	13,957	35,034	4,696	6,424	635	2,195	4,599	6,734	74,274	12.8
1981e	16,452	40,006	5,608	6,822	688	2,660	4,829	7,064	84,129	12.7
1982e	17,334	44,877	6,034	7,661	718	2,962	5,186	10,089	94,861	12.8

SOURCES: U.S. Office of Management & Budget, *Special Analysis. Budget of the United States Government*, various years: Social Security Administration, "*Social Welfare Expenditures*", *Social Security Bulletin*, various years: U.S. Department of Health and Human Services, Indian Health Service: U.S. Office of Personnel Management.

[a] Data include administrative expenses. 000,000 omitted.

[b] Except Veterans Administration, Department of Defense, and Indian Health Services facilities construction.

[c] Fiscal year estimates based on calendar year data provided by U.S. Office of Personnel Management.

[d] July to December.

[e] Estimated.

N.A., not available.

TABLE 3. Amount and Percentage Distribution of Personal Health Care Expenditures by Type of Expenditure and Source of Funds, 1981

	Type of Expenditure							
	Personal Health Care		Hospital Care		Physician Services		Other	
Source of Funds	Amount[a]	Percent	Amount[a]	Percent	Amount[a]	Percent	Amount[a]	Percent
Private	$146.7	60.3	$51.9	46.3	$38.3	73.5	$56.5	71.4
Public	96.7	39.7	60.3	53.7	13.8	26.51	22.6	28.6
Federal	70.8	29.1	46.5	41.4	10.8	20.6	13.6	17.2
State/Local	25.9	10.6	13.8	12.3	3.1	5.9	9.0	11.4
Totals	$243.4	100 %	$112.2	100 %	$52.2	100 %	$79.0	100 %

SOURCE: Health Care Financing Administration, Bureau of Date Management and Strategy, *Health Care Financing Trends*, Vol. 3, June 1982, pp. 3, 5.

[a]Amount in billions.

APPENDIX 2

Chronology and Capsule Highlights of the Major Historical and Political Milestones in the Evolutionary Involvement of Government in Health and Health Care in the United States

1730	American seamen (then British subjects) taxed to pay for hospital care.
1760	New York City adopts licensure requirement for physicians to practice medicine.
1772	New Jersey legislature adopts an act to regulate medical practice requiring that all persons wishing to practice medicine be examined and approved by any two judges of the Supreme Court. This act serves as a colonial prototype of later state boards of medical examiners.
1780	Virginia taxes seamen for hospital care.
1798	The Fifth Congress passes act to tax seamen for health care and establishes the U.S. Marine Hospital Service to provide medical care for sick and disabled seamen—in essence, the first prepaid medical care program in the United States.
1809	The Commonwealth of Massachusetts adopts the nation's first compulsory vaccination (small pox) law.
1846	In response to a call from the New York State Medical Society, a preliminary meeting of delegates from medical societies and colleges from throughout the United States is held at New York University to explore the establishment of a national physicians' organization (a forerunner of the American Medical Association—AMA).
1847	The American Medical Association is established. Under its charter, representation is to be comprised of delegates from state, county, and local medical societies, institutions, and medical colleges in a fixed numerical ratio.
1869	The first state board of health is set up in Massachusetts.
1872	The American Public Health Association (APHA) is founded.
1878	National Quarantine Act is passed.
1891	The National Confederation of State Medical Examining and Licensing Boards is founded.
1899	The classic legal recognition for the practice of state aid to church-related welfare

institutions such as hospitals is given by the U.S. Supreme Court in the Case of *Bradfield v. Roberts* 175 US 299 (1899).

1904   A uniform curriculum, recommended to all faculties, is adopted by the National Confederation of State Medical Examining and Licensing Boards.

1905   The U.S. Supreme Court upholds the constitutionality of Massachusetts Compulsory Vaccination Law [*Jacobson v. Commonwealth of Massachusetts* 197 US 11 (1905)].

1906   The first bill to establish a national children's bureau is introduced.

1906   The first food and drug act is passed.

1909   President Theodore Roosevelt calls together a conference (later to be known as the first White House Conference on Children) of some 200 professional and lay leaders interested in the care of dependent children.

1910   The Flexner Report, commissioned by the Carnegie Foundation, condemns the current state of medical education in the United States and proposes major reforms that are to transform medical education from a guild apprenticeship model to a university–hospital-based enterprise modeled after that of the Johns Hopkins University.

1912   On a vote of 54 to 20 with 17 not voting in the Senate and 177 to 17 with 190 not voting in the House, a bill calling for the establishment of a children's bureau is passed and approved by President Taft.

1912   Social insurance, including health insurance, is endorsed in the platform of the Progressive party and espoused by its candidate, Theodore Roosevelt.

1913   The American College of Surgeons (ACS) is formed to further a more structured examination of surgical practice in the United States.

1916–1920   Several state commissions study a standard bill for health insurance and conclude that it is neither needed nor wanted. State interest then wanes.

1916   Samuel Gompers, one of organized labor's early patriarchs, reaffirms his opposition to any form of government-sponsored compulsory health insurance as infringing upon labor's right to bargain.

1917   Congress passes amendment to War Risk Insurance Act to provide medical benefits to veterans with service-connected disabilities.

1917   The AMA's house of delegates passes resolution stating principles to be followed in government health insurance plans.

1918   First federal grants to states for public health services.

1920   The AMA's house of delegates reverses its position, declaring its unequivocal opposition to compulsory health insurance.

1920   Congress passes the first Vocational Rehabilitation Act. Passage rests less on humanitarian than utilitarian terms, that is, it would put people on the productive tax rolls.

1921   Congress enacts the first Maternity and Infancy Act (Sheppard-Towner) which provided grants to states to develop health services for mothers and children. The act is a prototype for federal grants-in-aid to the states.

1924   Congress passes World War Veteran's Act providing more liberal hospital benefits to all war veterans.

1924   A bill to remove a prohibition against contraceptives and information on contraception fails to win congressional approval.

1929   The first Blue Cross plan in the United States is established at Baylor University in Dallas, Texas.

1929   Assailed and opposed in Congress as "drawn chiefly from the radical, socialistic, behavioristic philosophy of Germany and Russia" and denounced by the AMA as an "imported socialistic scheme," the Sheppard-Towner Act is allowed to lapse.

1930   The National Institute of Health (NIH) is created as the administrative home for the medical research of the Public Health Service (PHS).

1932   The report of the Committee on the Cost of Medical Care (CCMC) is published calling for the organization of the U.S. medical services on a group practice, pre-payment basis. Despite the preeminence of its compilers and extensive documentation, the report is rejected out of hand by the AMA as socialistic and inimical to the best interests of the people of the United States.

1933   Enactment of the Federal Emergency Relief Act affords the first federal financing of medical care for the aged as funds are made available to states through the Federal Emergency Relief Administration (FERA) to pay medical expenses for people receiving relief. However, in most states, only emergency medical and dental care are provided for.

1935   On January 17 President Franklin D. Roosevelt sends to Congress the report of the President's Committee on Economic Security, which is to form the basis of the Social Security Act (SSA) passed later that year. The report endorses the principle of compulsory national health insurance (NHI) but makes no specific program recommendations. In his accompanying message, the president states that he is not planning to recommend adoption of "so-called health insurance at this time," His decision not to recommend national health insurance reportedly is based, in part, on the fear that opposition to it would endanger passage of the entire Social Security Act, and, in part, on the belief that the nation's medical facilities were inadequate to sustain such a program and needed to be beefed up first through public health facility grants and other similar efforts.

1935   July 15 the first government health insurance bill is introduced in the Congress—the Epstein Bill sponsored by Senator Capper.

1935   Congress passes and the president signs (August 14) the Social Security Act (PL 74-241), which includes provisions for grants-in-aid to states for maternal and child care, aid to crippled children, aid to the blind, the aged, and other health-impaired people.

1935   The first National Health Survey is conducted.

1936   Congress authorizes federal regulation of industrial safety in companies doing business with the government through passage of the Walsh-Healy Act (PL 74-846).

1937   The first categorical institute, the National Cancer Institute, is established under the National Cancer Institute Act (PL 75-244).

1938   The National Health Conference calls for expansion of public health services, provision of medical services to people at the lowest income levels at public expense, and medical insurance at the state level for the rest of the population.

1938   The LaFollette-Bulwinkle Act (venereal disease—VD control) (PL 75-540) provides grants-in-aid to states and other authorities to investigate and control VD.

1938   The federal Food, Drug and Cosmetic Act (PL 75-717) extends federal authority to act against adulterated and misbranded food, drugs, and cosmetic products, banning new drugs until approved by the federal Food and Drug Administration (FDA).

1939   Senator Robert Wagner (Dem., N.Y.) introduces a bill based on recommendations of the 1938 National Health Conference calling for federally subsidized state medical care compensation. No action is taken, however.

1939   The Public Health Service is transferred from the Treasury Department to the new Federal Security Agency by the Reorganization Act of 1939 (PL 76-19).

1939   The AMA, the District of Columbia Medical Society, and the Harris, Texas, Medical Society are indicted for violation of the Sherman Antitrust Case over their efforts to restrict physicians in prepaid group practice from practicing medicine.

1940   After a lengthy trial, the AMA and the District of Columbia Medical Society are found guilty of restraint of trade in their battle against prepaid medicine. Despite their legal reversal, organized medicine is successful in getting legislation passed at the state level prohibiting the corporate practice of medicine. Many such restrictions remain in existence today and limit the growth and development of health maintenance organizations (HMOs).

1941   The Nurse Training Act (PL 77-146) gives schools of nursing support to increase their enrollments and help strengthen their facilities.

1941   The Physicians Forum, a liberal-based physician's organization, is formed by dissident members of the New York County Medical Society to work for the adoption of compulsory health insurance.

1942   Rhode Island becomes the first state to pass a health insurance law.

1942   A *Fortune* magazine poll reports that 75 percent of the public favors national health insurance.

1943   The first Wagner (Sen. Robert, Dem., N.Y.), Murray (Sen. James E., Dem., Montana), Dingell (Rep. John D., Sr., Dem., Mich.) Bill (S1161, HR2861) calling for sweeping revisions and broadening of the Social Security Act including a compulsory national health system for people of all ages, financed through a payroll tax, is introduced in the Senate and the House. No action is taken on the measure, however, by the seventy-eighth Congress. Opponents call the bill "the most virulent scheme ever to be conjured out of the mind of man" and depict a revised version to mean "the end of freedom for all classes of Americans."

1944   President Roosevelt, in his January 11 State of the Union Message, outlines an Economic Bill of Rights, which includes "the right to adequate care and the opportunity to achieve and enjoy good health." Although interpreted by many to imply that the president favored a national health insurance system, no subsequent recommendations of any such enabling legislation to Congress is forthcoming.

1944   The APHA adopts a set of principles on comprehensive health care for all people in the United States financed through social insurance supported by general taxation or by general taxation alone.

1944   All public health service authorities are consolidated into a single statute (42 U.S. Code) under the Public Health Service Act (PL 78-410).

1945   Wagner, Murray, and Dingell reintroduce the same broad bill that they had sponsored in 1943.

1945   November 19, President Harry S. Truman sends a message on health legislation to Congress calling for comprehensive, prepaid, medical insurance for all people of all ages, to be financed through a 4 percent rise in the Social Security Old Age and Survivors Insurance Tax. His proposal is quickly introduced in the Senate and House by Senators Wagner and Murray and Representative Dingell. The bill, however, languishes in Congress and no action is taken.

1946   The National Mental Health Act (PL 79-487) authorizes major federal support for mental health research, diagnosis, prevention and treatment, establishes state grants-in-aid for mental health, and changes the PHS Division of Mental Health to the National Institute of Mental Health.

1946   Recognizing a shortage in health care services and the antiquated status of the nation's hospital facilities, Congress enacts the Hospital Survey and Construction Act (PL 79-725) (Hill-Burton) providing for national direct support for the development of community hospitals, ostensibly rural facilities, and for the first time attempts to mandate, at least rudimentary standards for construction and the insistence on regional planning. At the same time, however, the act carries a hidden time bomb that only comes to light 30 some years later, that is, a requirement that recipients provide a "reasonable volume of services to those unable to pay"—a free care obligation—and make their facilities "available to all persons residing in their service areas"—a community service obligation.

1946   California passes a compulsory health insurance act.

1948   National Health Act (PL 80-655) establishes the National Heart Institute, pluralizing NIH.

1949   Flushed with success after upset victories in the 1948 presidential and congressional elections that found the Democratic party in control of both houses of Congress plus the White House, President Truman again calls for compulsory national health insurance in his January 5 State of the Union Message.

1949	Hearings on bills embodying the proposals sponsored by Senators Murray and Wagner (S1679) and Representative Dingell and others (HR43121) produces bitter controversy and heavy lobbying on both sides of the issue.
1949	The AMA sets up $3.5 million war chest and mobilizes a massive campaign to defeat what they consider to be socialized medicine and a threat to the free practice of medicine in the United States, using the talents of the California public relations firm of Whitaker and Baxter for a fee of $100,000 and assessing each physician $25 to support their efforts. No congressional action in either house is taken.
1950	The president repeats his earlier request for compulsory national health insurance, but again no congressional action is forthcoming. Instead, Congress moves to help the states provide medical care for welfare recipients supported by the four federal–state public assistance programs for the indigent, that is, Old Age Assistance (OAA), Aid to Dependent Children (ADC), Aid to the Blind (AB), and Aid to the Permanently and Totally Disabled (APTD). Amendments to the Social Security Act provide for federal sharing with the states in vendor payments, that is, paymets to providers as well as the direct payments of living expenses to recipients.
1950	PL 81-507 establishes the National Science Foundation as an autonomous entity and strengthens the concept of federal support for university-based research in physical, medical, and social sciences.
1951	Durham-Humphrey amendments (PL 8-2-215) establishes category of prescription drugs requiring labeling and medical supervision.
1952	The Joint Commission on Accreditation of Hospitals (JCAH) is established.
1952	A bill (S3001, HR 7484-85) is introduced in Congress by Senator Murray and Representatives Dingell and Celler (Emanuel D., Dem., N.Y.) calling for the payment of hospitalization costs for retired people and their dependents or survivors under the Social Security Old-Age and Survivors Insurance (OASI) System. No action is taken, however.
1953	The Federal Security Agency (FSA) is transformed into the Department of Health Education and Welfare (DHEW) and elevated to cabinet status.
1954	The Hill-Burton Act amended (PL 83-482, Medical Facilities Survey and Construction Act) to expand the scope of the program to include nursing homes, rehabilitation facilities, chronic disease hospitals, and diagnostic or treatment centers.
1954	Responsibility for maintenance and operation of Indian Health facilities is placed in PHS rather than Bureau of Indian Affairs (PL 83-568).
1955	The U.S. major trade unions—the American Federation of Labor (AFL) and Congress of Industrial Organization (CIO)—merge (AFL-CIO) and set health insurance for the aged as a top priority.
1955	The American Hospital Association's Board of Trustees passes a resolution recommending federal subsidies to the states to begin voluntary health insurance programs for older people, and the concept is approved by the association's house of delegates.
1955	PL 84-377 Polio Vaccination Assistance Act provides assistance to state vaccination programs.
1956	The Social Security Act is further amended to permit separate federal matching funds for medical care payments on an individual basis in addition to cash assistance.
1956	The Dependents Medical Care Act (PL 84-569) sets up CHAMPUS program of primarily inpatient medical care for military dependents.
1956	The National Health Survey Act (PL 84-652) provides for a continuing survey and special sickness and disability studies of the U.S. population.
1956	PL 84-941 transfers responsibility for the Library of Medicine to the Public Health Service.
1957	The Forand (Rep. Aime J., Dem., R.I.) Bill (HR9467) calling for an increase in the Social Security OASI payroll tax to provide for up to 120 days of combined hospital and nursing home care as well as necessary surgery for aged OASI beneficiaries is

introduced. Although no action is taken by the Congress, the Forand bill begins to draw increasing public interest and debate. Both the American Hospital Association (AHA) and American Nurses Association (ANA) endorse the bill.

1958   The AMA sets up the joint council to improve the health care of the aged comprised of the AMA, AHA, the American Dental Association (ADA), and the American Nursing Home Association, which concludes that the health care of the aged does not need improvement. Not represented in the council is the ANA, which in 1957 had supported in principle the Forand bill.

1958   PL 85-929, the Food Additive Amendment to the Food, Drug and Cosmetics Act, requires premarketing clearance for new food additives, establishes a generally recognized as safe (GRAS) category, and prohibits under the so-called Delaney clause, the approval of any additive "found to induce cancer in man or animal."

1959   The House Ways and Means Committee holds hearings on Forand's reintroduced bill, but no action is taken.

1959   Blue Cross negotiates contract with Civil Service Commission to provide health insurance coverage for federal employees. Contract serves as a foot in the door and a prototype for Blue Cross' later involvement in Medicare and Medicaid.

1960   The Forand bill becomes a major political issue, supported on one hand by organized labor and liberal Democrats and opposed on the other by the AMA, most Republicans including President Eisenhower, most business and insurance groups, and political conservatives.

1960   March 31, the House Ways and Means Committee on a 17 (Dem. 7, Rep. 10) to 8 (Dem. 8, Rep. 0) vote to table the Forand bill. Voting in favor of killing the bill are Committee Chairman Wilber D. Mills (Dem., Arks.) and six other southern representatives.

1960   May 4, in testimony before the Ways and Means Committee, the Eisenhower administration unveils its own "Medicare" program, which it proposes will help the needy aged meet the costs of catastrophic illness without using the compulsory national health insurance feature proposed under the Forand bill. Under the administration's plan, federal matching grants would be offered to the states to help them pay for a varied list of specified medical, hospital, and nursing costs for elderly persons with incomes of $2,500 a year or less ($3,800 for a couple). Individuals would have the option of receiving cash payments to help them purchase private commercial health insurance.

1960   August, Congress passes the Kerr (Sen. Robert S., Dem., Okla.)–Mills (Rep. Wilbur D.) Bill (PL 86-778—Title XVI of the Social Security Act) providing additional federal matching funds to the states for vendor payments under the Old Age Assistance Act as well as federal matching funds for the medically needy aged, creating a new public assistance category—Medical Assistance for the Aged (MAA). The significance of the MAA program (Bernard and Feingold, 1970) lay in (1) its recognition of medical indigence, (2) its introduction of open funding by the federal government, and (3) the introduction of some minimal standard to the substance and administration of public assistance medical care.

1961   The King-Anderson bill, embodying President Kennedy's proposal to provide health insurance for the elderly through the social security system is introduced in both houses of Congress by Senator Anderson (Clinton, Dem., N. Mex.) and Representative King (Cecil, Dem., Calif.) [Note: As a senator, the president had earlier sponsored a Senate version of the Forand bill (S 2915)]. Although normally an administration's legislative initiatives are sponsored by the highest ranking member of the president's party on the committee with jurisdiction over it, since both Senate Finance Committee chairman Harry F. Byrd (Dem., Va.) and Ways and Means chairman Mills were opposed to the president's proposal, the bill carried the sponsorship of Congressman King and Senator Anderson. The latter had earlier proposed a revised version of the Forand-Kennedy bill in the Senate

	Finance Committee in 1960 but it was rejected. Hearings on the proposed legislation are held by the Ways and Means Committee but no action is taken.
1962	The AMA sets up AMPAC, a political action committee analogous to the AFL-CIO's COPE to fight the Kennedy proposal for medical care for the aged.
1962	PL 87-692, the Migratory Workers Assistance Act, authorizes federal aid to clinics serving migratory agricultural workers and their families.
1962	PL 87-781, Kefauver-Harris drug amendments require improved manufacturing practices, better reporting, assurances of efficacy, as well as safety and strengthened regulation of the drug industry.
1962	January 3, the AHA drops its opposition to federal funding averring that the source of funding is of secondary importance and federal assistance a necessity.
1962	Continued inaction by the House Ways and Means Committee leads Senator Anderson to offer a revised version of the administration's medical care for the aged proposal as an amendment on the floor of the Senate, to the Public Welfare Amendment (HR10606) that already had been passed by the House. The Anderson amendment, cosponsored by five Republicans, headed by Senator Jacob K. Javits (Rep., N.Y.), proposes a one-quarter of one percent increase on the OASDI payroll tax on each employer and employee and three-eighths of one percent on the self-employed, as well as a rise to $5,200 in the wage base for the tax, with additional revenues to be earmarked to pay for all or most of the costs of a long list of hospital (90 days inpatient care), nursing home (180 days, skilled care), and diagnostic services for people 65 years of age and older eligible for OASDI old age benefits, as well as certain other people not otherwise eligible for OASDI benefits.
1962	July 17, In a dramatic roll call vote, Senate Republicans and Southern Democrats unite to kill the Anderson amendment on a 52 (Dem. 21, Rep. 31) to 48 (Dem. 43, Rep. 5) vote.
1963	Health Professions Educational Assistance Act (PL 88-129) provides construction money for health professions schools, funds tied to increased enrollment requirements to assist with the school's operating expenses, plus loans and scholarship programs. It authorizes support to medical schools for the first time and establishes the presence of the federal government in health-related educational institutions.
1963	The Blue Cross Association of America under the leadership of its president, Walter McNerney, issues report in support of government financing of medical care for the aged, noting the problem the high cost of health care poses for the elderly, the hospitals, and the third-party carriers as well.
1963	PL 88-156, Maternal and Child Health and Mental Retardation Planning Amendments initiate program of comprehensive maternity, infant care and mental retardation prevention.
1963	PL88-164, Community Mental Health Centers Construction Act seeks to bring comprehensive mental health services to patients in their own communities and further deinstitutionalization.
1963	PL 88-206, Clean Air Act, authorizes direct grants to state and local governments for air pollution control. Establishes federal enforcement in interstate air pollution.
1963	The AMA raises several million dollars to fight Medicare.
1964	PL 88-525 authorizes the food stamp program for low–income people to purchase nutritious foods for a balanced diet.
1964	PL 88-581, Nurse Training Act, provides special federal effort for training professional nursing personnel.
1964	The Hill-Burton act amended to set aside monies for the modernization and replacement of health care facilities.
1965	Congress amends the Social Security Act (PL 89-97) providing for medical care for the elderly (Medicare—Title 18) and grants to the states for medical assistance to the poor (Medicaid—Title 19), on a vote of 307 to 116 in the House and 70 to 24 in the Senate, and President Lyndon B. Johnson signs it into law on July 30. The act also extends social security coverage to physicians.

1965   The conservative Association of American Physicians and Surgeons urges its 16,500 members not to cooperate with the program. The AMA, on the other hand, cautions against a physician's boycott. The legislative defeat leads to the forced retirement of Dr. Morris Fishbein, former editor of the *Journal of the American Medical Association* (1924–1949) and the long-time, erstwhile spokesman of organized medicine as executive secretary of the AMA. He is replaced by Dr. Frank Blasingame who later is summarily dismissed in 1968.

1965   PL 89-239 amends the Public Health Service Act and establishes a nationwide network of Regional Medical Programs (RMPs) for heart disease, cancer, and stroke. The legislation is an outgrowth of the President's Commission on Heart Disease, Cancer and Stroke headed by Dr. Michael DeBakey.

1965   PL 89-272, Clean Air Act Amendments provide for federal regulation of Motor Vehicle Exhaust (Title I) and establishes program of federal research and grants-in aid in solid waste disposal (Title II).

1965   PL 89-290, Health Professions Educational Assistance Amendments, provide scholarships, loans, and construction aid to schools of medicine, osteopathy, and dentistry. Introduces provision of 50 percent forgiveness of loans for service in personnel shortage areas.

1965   Congress authorizes a program of Special Project Grants for health of school and preschool children under Title V of the Social Security Act Amendments (PL 89-97), including the delivery of compulsory health services to low-income children. Out of this legislation comes the Children and Youth (C and Y) projects and clinics administered through the Maternal and Child Health Service (see Lewis et al., 1976).

1965   PL 89-73, The Older Americans Act, establishes an Administration on Aging within DHEW headed by a commissioner of aging appointed by the president. It declares 10 objectives for older people, which are the joint responsibility of federal, state, and local governments.

1965   PL 89-92, The Federal Cigarette Labeling and Advertising Act, requires that all cigarette packages or containers offered for sale in the United States must bear the warning statement: "Caution: Cigarette Smoking May be Hazardous to your Health." The new law preempts the field of cigarette labeling, precluding any federal, state, or local authority in the area.

1966   An amendment (PL 89-749) to the Office of Economic Opportunity (OED) legislation formalizes the Comprehensive Health Services Program, including the provision for the establishment of neighborhood health centers.

1966   PL 89-749, The Comprehensive Health Planning Act, is passed to promote comprehensive planning for health services, personnel, and facilities in federal– state– local partnership.

1966   PL 89-614 broadens eligibility to CHAMPUS and extends benefits beyond inpatient care.

1966   PL 89-642, Child Nutrition Act, establishes federal program of research and support for child nutrition, including authorization for school breakfast program.

1966   PL 89-751, Allied Health Professions Personnel Act, provides initial effort to support the training of allied health workers.

1967   Amendment to the Social Security Act seeks to raise the quality of care provided in nursing homes, establishing a number of conditions of nursing home participation under Medicare and Medicaid. Creats a new class of facility—the intermediate care facility. Establishes educational requirements for long-term care facility administrators (Kennedy amendment). The latter constitutes the first time that educational requirements for licensure are mandated by legislative fiat at the federal level.

1968   PL 90-407, amends the National Science Foundation to include major support of applied research in the sciences.

1968   PL 90-490, Health Manpower Act, authorizes formula institutional grants for training all health professionals and adds pharmacy and veterinary medicine to the professions covered.

1969   PL 91-173, Federal Coal Mine Health and Safety Act, provides for protection of the health and safety of coal miners.

1969   PL 91-190, National Environmental Policy Act, creats the Council on Environmental Quality to advise the president on environmental matters; requires preparation of environmental impact statements before major federal actions.

1969   In an effort to slow the rise in Medicaid costs, the secretary of DHEW issues regulations setting an upper limit (75th percentile of customary charges) on fees to be paid to individual practitioners.

1970   PL 91-222, Public Health Cigarette Smoking Act, bans cigarette advertising from radio and television.

1970   PL 91-596, Occupational Safety and Health Act (OSHA), provides federal program of standard setting and enforcement to assure safe and healthful conditions in the workplace.

1970   PL 91-616 establishes National Institute of Alcohol Abuse and Alcoholism and provides comprehensive aid program to states and localities.

1970   PL 91-623, Emergency Health Personnel Act, provides for assistance to health manpower shortage areas through the establishment of the National Health Service Corps.

1971   In his February health message to Congress, President Nixon introduces the notion of health maintenance organizations (HMOs) as the cornerstone of his administration's national health insurance proposal.

1971   The health industry is singled out for special stringent controls under the Economic Stabilization Act (and are the last segment of the economy to be relieved of such controls 3 years later).

1971   PL 92-157, Comprehensive Health Manpower Training Act, covering programs for students in medicine, osteopathy, dentistry, veterinary medicine, optometry, pharmacy, and podiatry replaces institutional formula grants with capitation grants. Provides for schools to receive a fixed sum of money for each student in return for agreeing to increase its enrollment by a specified percentage. Adds interest subsidies and loan guarantees to outright grants for construction (the sole previous financing mechanism under earlier programs) as the federal government assumes an active role in the funding of primary care. The act is the most comprehensive piece of health manpower legislation to date. A shift from support to control is evident (Losteller and Chapman, 1979).

1972   PL 92-303 amends the Federal Coal Mine Health and Safety Act, providing benefits and other assistance for coals miners suffering from black lung disease.

1972   PL 92-426 establishes a Uniformed Services University of the Health Sciences and an Armed Forces Health Professions Scholarship Program.

1972   PL 92-433, The National School Lunch and Child Nutrition Amendments, add funds to support nutritious diets for pregnant and lactating women and for infants and children (the WIC program).

1972   PL92 -541 authorizes the Veterans Administration (VA) to help establish eight state medical schools and provides grant support to existing medical schools.

1972   PL 92-573, Consumer Product Safety Act, creates Consumer Product Safety Commission and transfers enforcement of hazardous substances, flammable fabrics, poison prevention packaging acts to the commissions.

1972   PL 92-585, Emergency Health Personnel Act Amendments of 1972, establishes Public Health and National Health Services Corps scholarships.

1972   PL 92-603, amendments of the Social Security Act. Establishes, over the bittter opposition of organized medicine, Professional Standards Review Organizations (PSROs) to monitor the need and quality of care rendered to recipients of federal health programs. Extends health insurance benefits to the disabled and end-stage renal disease patients.

1972   PL 93-154, Emergency Medical Services Systems Act, provides aid to states and localities to establish coordinated cost-effective Emergency Medical Service (EMS) Systems.

1972   Blue Cross at McNerney's urging and in response to public pressure concerning conflict of interest, severs formal ties with AHA.

1973   PL 93-272, Health Maintenance Organization Act, provides assistance for the establishment and expansion of HMOs. Authorizes $375 million over a 5-year period for grants, loans, and loan guarantees for feasibility studies, development studies, and initial operations for new and exising HMOs.

1973   Supreme Court declares laws outlawing abortion unconstitutional.

1974   PL 93-247, Child Abuse Prevention and Treatment Act, creates a National Center on Child Abuse and Neglect, authorizes research and demonstration grants to states and other private and public agencies.

1974   PL 93-296, Research in Aging Act, establishes National Institute on Aging within the National Institutes of Health (NIH).

1974   PL 93-523, Safe Drinking Water Act, requires the Environmental Protection Agency to set national drinking water standards and aid states and localities in their enforcement.

1974   Moss (Sen. Frank, Dem., Utah) Senate Subcommittee on Nursing Homes issues extensive report detailing abuses in the nursing home industry.

1975   PL 93-641, The National Health Planning and Resources Development Act, sets up national designation of local health systems areas and authorizes major federal reorganization of health planning programs. Establish a national certificate of need (CON) program.

1975   Rhode Island enacts first state comprehensive health insurance program.

1976   PL 94-484, Health Professions Educational Assistance Act, requires medical schools to have 50 percent of their graduates nationally entering primary residencies by 1980. Continues capitation payments but no longer requires enrollment increases as a condition for funding. Mandates that recipient schools reserve positions in their classes for U.S. students studying at foreign medical schools as a condition for receiving federal financial support. The latter provision is heatedly opposed by the U.S. medical schools as an unwarranted infringement on their right to determine admissions. Northwestern, Indiana, and Yale universities announce that they will not comply even if it should mean loss of federal funding.

1976   Medicare and Medicaid are transferred from the Social Security Administration and Social and Rehabilitation Service (SRS) and combined into a new agency, the Health Care Financing Administration (HCFA).

1976   Over the strenuous opposition of the hospital industry, Congress tightens up the immigration rules amending the Immigration and Nationality Act (Sections 101 and 212) to restrict the entry of alien physicians into the United States and imposes stringent constraints on the licensure of foreign medical graduates including the requirement of passage of the VISA and/or FLEX exam, declaring that "there is no longer an insufficient number of physicians and surgeons in the United States" and that "there is no further need for affording preference to alien physicians and surgeons in admission to the United States."

1977   PL 95-210, Rural Health Clinics Act, extends Medicare and Medicaid coverage to new health practitioners in rural clinics.

1977   The Carter administration proposes placing a cap (9 percent) on increases in hospital revenues to be reimbursed by federal programs by limiting what they can spend. The industry counters by proposing its own voluntary program deemed Voluntary Effort (VE).

1977   PL 95-215, Health Professions Education Amendments. Bowing to medical school pressure, Congress repeals the requirement that medical schools, as a condition of receiving capitation funds, must reserve an adequate number of positions in their classes for United States citizen foreign medical students (USFMS).

1978   The DHEW secretary, Joseph Califano, issues controversial bed supply guidelines to control excess hospital bed capacity in the United States. Rural and western sections of the country take strong exception seeing the proposal as a further intrusion of the federal government on what they consider to be a local or state matter.

1980   The Department of Education is split off as a separate department from DHEW and the remainder is renamed the Department of Health and Human Services (DHHS).

1980   Medicare and Medicaid amendments of the Omnibus Reconciliation Act of 1980 (PL 96-499) results in significant changes in both programs, including simplification of methods for state reimbursement of nursing homes, increased funding for state Medicaid fraud-control units, changes in utilization review requirements, coverage of nurse–midwife services, reimbursement under both programs for hospital swing beds, and a measure for state enrollment in Medicare part B.

1981   President Reagan proposes the consolidation of 26 categorical health programs into two large block grants. Instead, Congress responds by creating four health block grants: preventive health (combining eight programs: home health, rodent control, water fluoridation, health education, risk reduction, health incentive grants, emergency medical services, rape crisis centers, and hypertension), health services, primary care, and maternal and child health care, authorizing all for 3 years or until the end of fiscal year (FY) 1984. (The Omnibus Budget Reconciliation Act. of 1981, HR 3982.) Several other programs originally targeted for block grants, that is, family planning, childhood immunization, VD research and treatment, migrant health center, tuberculosis, primary care research and demonstrations, retain their categorical status, and a new adolescent family life program is authorized.

1981   Capitation grants to schools of medicine, osteopathy, dentistry, veterinary medicine, optometry, podiatry, pharmacy, and nursing are eliminated.

1981   The provision for free medical care for merchant seamen is eliminated as of October 1, 1981, with existing public health hospitals slated for closure by end of fiscal year 1982.

1982   President Reagan proposes in a single bold stroke to create a "new federalism" transferring responsibility of many human services to the states.

1982   Office of Management and Budget considers proposals to trim the cost of Medicare by requiring the elderly to demonstrate need as a condition of receiving benefits. The introduction of a means test is acknowledged to constitute a significant change in the program, making Medicare less of an insurance program and more of an income assistance one.

1982   Congress passes the Tax Equity and Fiscal Responsibility Act (TEFRA) authorizing Medicare reimbursement for hospice services.

1983   Congress establishes a new Medicare hospital prospective payment (reimbursement) system based on the use of diagnostic related groups (DRGs) as part of the 1983 Amendments to the Social Security Act (PL98-21), signed into law June 1983.

1983   On September 1, the Health Care Finance Administration ushers in a new era of Medicare hospital reimbursement with the publication of regulations implementing the DRG-based prospective payment system.

REFERENCES

Becker, Dorothy D. and Ruth R. Johnson, *Chronology Health Professions Legislation, 1956–1979*, DHHS Publication No. HRA 80–69, Bureau of Health Professions, Washington, D.C.: U.S. Government Printing Office, 1980.

Berliner, Howard S., "The Origins of Health Insurance for the Aged," *International Journal of Health Services*, Vol. 3, No. 3, 1973, pp. 465–474.

Bernard, Sydney E. and Eugene Feingold, "The Impact of Medicaid," *Wisconsin Law Review*, Vol. 1970, No. 2, 1970, pp. 726–755.

Blendon, Robert et al., eds., *Baselines for Setting Health Goals and Standards*, Papers on the National Health Guidelines, DHEW Publication No. HRA 76–640, Washington, D.C.: United States Government Printing Office, 1976, pp. 19–28.

Chapman, Carleton B. and John M. Talmadge, "Historical and Political Background of Federal Health Care Legislation, Health Care: Part I," *Law and Contemporary Problems*, Vol. 35, Spring 1970, pp. 334–347.

Chapman, Carleton B. and John M. Talmadge, "The Evolution of the Right to Health Concept in the United States, *The Pharos*, Vol. 34, January 1971, pp. 30–51.

Congressional Quarterly, "Medical Care for the Aged," *Congressional Quarterly Special Report*, Washington, D.C.: Congressional Quarterly Service, Inc., August 1963, pp. 15–17.

Corning, Peter A., *The Evolution of Medicare . . . From Idea to Law*, Office of Research and Statistics, Social Security Adminstration, Department of Health, Education and Welfare, Research Report No. 29, Washington, D.C.: U.S. Government Printing Office, 1969.

Feingold, Eugene, *Medicare: Policy and Politics*, San Francisco, Calif.: Chandler Publishing Co., 1966.

Fishbein, Morris, A *History of the American Medical Association*, Philadelphia: W.B. Saunders Co., 1947.

Gardner, John W., Wilbur J. Cohen and Ralph K. Huitt, *1965: Year of Legislative Achievements in Health Education and Welfare*, Office of the Secretary, DHEW, Washington, D.C.: United States Government Printing Office, 1965.

Lewis, Charles E., Rashi Fein and David Mechanic, A *Right to Health*, New York: John Wiley & Sons, 1976.

Losteller, John O. and John E. Chapman, "The Participation of the United States Government in Providing Financial Support for Medical Education," *Health Policy and Education*, Vol. 1, No. 1, 1979, pp. 27–65.

Bibliography

GENERAL REFERENCE GUIDES TO CONGRESS, LEGISLATION, AND GOVERNMENTAL AFFAIRS

Current Government Documents

Bills and Resolutions. One free copy of all legislation is printed daily after it is introduced and is available from one's member of Congress. One free copy of a bill, committee report, conference report, or public law may be obtained by sending a request along with a self-addressed mailing label to either Senate Document Room S-325 or House Document Room H-226, U.S. Capitol, Washington, D.C., 20510.

Congressional Directory. Issued annually. Contains brief biographical sketches of each member of Congress, complete rosters of standing and special committees assignments by members, as well as maps of all congressional districts. Also lists major executives of all government agencies and members of the diplomatic corps. Available from the Superintendent of Documents, Government Printing Office (GPO).

The Congressional Record. Published in its present form since 1973. A verbatim transcript, subject to revision by members of Congress, of the proceedings and floor debates of the U.S. Senate and House of Representatives, including extension of remarks and materials inserted at the request of members of Congress. Bound sets consist of 15–20 parts per year, including separate index and, since 1947, *Daily Digest* volumes. A *Daily Digest* is included at the back of each issue. Single copies may be obtained by sending 75¢ to the Congressional Record Office, H-112, U.S. Capitol, Washington, D.C., 20515.

Committee Reports. When each piece of legislation goes to the floor, it is accompanied by a report that generally analyzes the bill, describes its purposes, and states the view of the committee's members as to the desirability of its enactment. Available from the publications clerk of the appropriate committee.

Digest of Public General Bills. Cumulative compilation providing a brief description of each public bill introduced during the session. Published approximately five times per year. Indexed by subject matter. Available from the Government Printing Office.

Federal Register. Published 5 days each week. Contains notices of proposed rule making as well as proposed regulations and changes and all legal documents of the executive branch. Available from the Government Printing Office (GPO).

Forum. Bimonthly publication. Official magazine of the Health Care Financing Administration (HCFA). Covers all aspects of health care financing as well as HCFA programs and activities. Available from the Government Printing Office.

General Accounting Office Reports. Issued on an irregular basis by the General Accounting Office (GAO), the investigative and program auditing arm of Congress, pursuant to a special request by a congressional committee. Single copies may be obtained free of charge by writing the U.S. General Accounting Office, Document Handling and Information Services Facility, P.O. Box 6015, Gaithersburg, MD, 20760. A free monthly listing of reports with summaries may be obtained by writing the General Accounting Office, 441 G Street N.W., Washington, D.C., 20548.

Health Care Financing Review. Quarterly publication of the Health Care Financing Administration's Office of Research, Demonstrations and Statistics. Presents statistics on Medicare, Medicaid, national health expenditures, and related subjects, as well as reports on agency-supplied research, demonstration, and evaluation projects. Available from ORDS, HCFA, Room 1-E-9 Meadows Bldg., 6340 Security Blvd., Baltimore, MD 21235.

Index to U.S. Government Periodicals. Published quarterly. Index to articles appearing in periodicals produced by over 100 federal departments and agencies.

Monthly Catalog of U.S. Government Publications. Monthly publication with annual cumulative index. Lists every document published by the federal government that is made available to the public, including House and Senate documents, hearings, and reports, as well as those of federal departments and agencies. Available from the Government Printing Office.

Perspective. Published three to five times a year. HCFA's how to publication for Medicaid and Medicare carriers, Medicare carriers and intermediaries, state, and local agencies. Articles address program techniques, procedures, and operations' management. Available from Health Care Financing Administration (HCFA).

Rules of the House and Senate. Published separately for the House and Senate at least once each Congress. Provides a useful reference on jurisdiction of committees, procedures in handling of legislation, precedents, etc.

Social Security Bulletin. Official monthly publication of the Social Security Administration. Offers feature articles, regular reports, notes, statistics, and analyses of public and private expenditures for hospital care and physicians services. Provides review of private health insurance and Medicare and Medicaid experience. Available from the Government Printing Office.

U.S. Code. There are 14 volumes and supplements. Published every 6 years, with annual supplements until the next publication. Compiled by subject under 50 titles. Includes all the general and permanent laws of the United States. Available from the Government Printing Office.

U.S. Government Manual. Issued annually. Official handbook of the federal government. Describes purposes and programs of most government agencies, including listings of top personnel. Contains brief references to the statuatory authority for federal programs by department or agency as well as organization charts and statements of purpose of various administrative units in the executive branch and the names and titles of principal administrative officers.

U.S. Statutes at Large. Official edition of federal laws arranged numerically in order of enactment. Includes subject and name index, list of bills enacted into law, guide to legislative history of bills enacted, and tables of laws affected. Usually consists of one or more volumes for each legislative session.

Commercial Publications

Almanac of American Politics. Contains biographies, group ratings, committee assignments, voting records, and lobby interests of members of Congress as well as political, demographic, and economic make-up of each member's state or district. Published by E. P. Dutton, 2 Park Avenue, New York, New York, 10016.

Commerce Clearing House Congressional Index. Weekly looseleaf publication. Lists, indexes, summarizes, and reports progress of bills and resolutions in Congress. Pending measures are indexed by number, subject, author, and headline term. Voting records of members of Congress on each bill and status tables of action taken on each bill in the House and Senate are given. Published by Commerce Clearing House, 4025 W. Peterson Avenue, Chicago, Illinois, 60646.

Congressional Information Service/Index to Publications of the U.S. Congress (CIS). Private commercial reference work. Abstracts and indexes all congressional committee hearings and all House and Senate reports, documents, and special publications. Available from Congressional Information Service, 4520 East-West Highway, Washington, D.C., 20014.

Congressional Quarterly's Guide to the Congress of the United States. A 1,000-page volume documenting the origins, development, and operations of the U.S. Congress. Explains how Congress works, including its powers, pressures on it, and prospects for change.

Congressional Quarterly Weekly Report (CQ). Weekly report, published since 1945, of major congressional actions in the House and Senate. Contains all roll call votes taken in each chamber plus weekly political roundups. Includes rosters, updated committee and subcommittee assignments, presidential texts, and so on.

Congress and the Nation. Volume I (1945–1964), Volume II (1965–1968), *Congressional Quarterly*. A 3,100-page two-volume set. Documents all major legislative actions and national political campaigns from 1945 to 1968. Published by Congressional Quarterly, Inc.

Congressional Quarterly Almanac. Published each spring since 1945. Presents a thorough review of the legislative and political activity of each session of Congress, as well as summary of the terms of the U.S. Supreme Court.

Congressional Staff Directory. Published annually. Contains biographical sketches of many members of Congress and staffs, lists of employees of members and committees. Available from Congressional Staff Directory, 300 New Jersey Ave. S.E., Washington, D.C.

National Health Council's Relations Handbooks: 1740 Broadway, New York, New York, 10019.

Congress and Health: An Introduction to the Legislative Process and its Key Participants. Provides description of how a bill becomes a law. Gives practical information on how to determine the current status of a bill. Lists committees and subcommittees having significant impact on health legislation, including a brief description of their jurisdictions as well as names, photographs, and phone numbers of the six most important health subcommittees and the names of their staff members who handle health issues.

Congressional Staff Aides for Health Legislation. Directory of the names, addresses, and phone numbers of senators and representatives and their staff aides assigned responsibility for health matters.

Private Health Organizations' Government Relations Directory. Lists major private health organizations and groups with major interest in health policy as well as names and phone numbers of their staffs assigned to lobby in Washington, D.C.

National Health Directory. Published annually. Directory of more than 6,000 key health and medical officials within Congress, including health legislative aides, federal agencies, state governments, federal regional offices, and congressional districts. Complete list of members of the six major congressional committees on health; current titles, addresses and phone numbers of health decision makers in offices of the governor, state agencies, and state legislators. Available from Science and Health Communications Group, Inc., 1740 N. Street, N.W., Washington, D.C., 20036.

National Journal Report. Weekly periodical reviews congressional activities, lobbying, campaign and policy issues. Includes chart of roll call votes. Spotlights federal officials and election campaign reports and analyzes executive action. Especially informative is the discussion on health policy issues by John Iglehart.

Washington Report on Medicine and Health, Jerome Brazda, ed. A four page newsletter published weekly by McGraw-Hill (50 issues a year). Provides brief coverage on current status as well as speculation on probable fate of health bills on Capitol Hill. Also notes publication of regulations, agency plans, and proposals. McGraw-Hill, 1221 Avenue of the Americas, New York, New York, 10020.

Washington Report on Health Legislation. A lengthier companion to the *Washington Report on Medicine and Health*. Published 50 weeks a year by McGraw-Hill. Summarizes provisions of major legislation. Lists recently introduced bills along with their sponsors and the congressional committees to which they have been referred. Includes charts of roll call votes on some key amendments. McGraw-Hill, 1221 Avenue of the Americas, New York, New York, 10020.

Other Sources

American Medical News. Weekly tabloid-size newspaper published by the AMA. Distributed free to association members as part of their dues and offered on subscription basis to others. Covers policy positions and activities of organized medicine at both the national and state level as well as governmental actions of interest to the medical profession.

Drug Research Reports (The Blue Sheet). A weekly newsletter published by a commercial firm, providing special coverage of government activities in the drug, medical, and allied research fields. Reports on congressional committee hearings and health bills and reviews congressional and executive branch actions in the area of health and health care.

Hospitals. Semimonthly journal of the American Hospital Association. Particular attention is directed to two sections: "News at Deadline" and "Washington Briefs," located at the beginning and end of each issue, which focus on policy developments and government actions affecting the hospital industry.

The Nation's Health. Tabloid-size newspaper of the American Public Health Association. Contains reports of current status of state and federal actions in the field of health and health care and comments on government activities as they relate to the public's health.

Medical Care Review. Quarterly. Originally published by the School of Public Health at the University of Michigan and now published under the auspices of the Health Administration Press. Includes items from several of the nation's leading newspapers, for example, the *New York Times*, the *Washington Post*, the *Wall Street Journal*, and the *Christian Science Monitor*, as well as abstracts of new releases from the Department of Health and Human Services, the *Congressional Record*, and the major health care journals.

POLITICS OF HEALTH AND HEALTH CARE

General

Begun, James W. and Ronald C. Lippincott, "A Case Study in the Politics of Free-Market Health Care," *Journal of Health Politics, Policy and Law*, Vol. 7, Fall, 1982, pp. 667–687.

Bellin, Lowell E., "The Intellectual Decline of the Health Care Left," *Medical Care*, Vol. 18, September 1980, pp. 960–968.

Brown, J. H. U. and Southwest Research Consortium, *The Politics of Health Care*, Cambridge: Ballinger Publishing Co., 1978.

Cater, Douglass and Philip R. Lee, eds., *Politics of Health*, New York: Medcom Press, 1972.

Edelman, Murray, "The Political Language of the Helping Professions," *Politics and Society*, Vol. 4, No. 3, 1974, pp. 295–310.

Facchinetti, Neil J. and W. Michael Dickson, "Access to Generic Drugs in the 1950's: The Politics of a Social Problem," *American Journal of Public Health*, Vol. 72, May 1982, pp. 468–475.

Falcone, David, "The Challenge of Comparative Health Policy for Political Science," *Journal of Health Politics, Policy and Law*, Vol. 1, Summer 1976, pp. 196–213.

Fox, Daniel M. and Robert Crawford, "Health Politics in the United States," in Howard E. Freeman, Sol Levine and Leo G. Reeder, eds., *Handbook of Medical Sociology*, New York: The Free Press, 1979, 3rd edition, pp. 392–411.

Goldsmith, Seth B., "Political Party Platform Planks: A Mechanism for Participation and Prediction?," *American Journal of Public Health*, Vol. 63, July 1973, pp. 594–601.

Hodgson, Godfrey, "The Politics of Health Care: What is it Costing You?" The Atlantic, Vol. 232, October 1973, pp. 95–61.

Hodgson, Godfrey, "The Politics of Health Care: What is it Costing You?" in David Kotelchuck, ed., *Prognosis Negative, Crisis in the Health System*, New York: Vintage Books, 1976, pp. 304–316.

Kaufman, Herbert, "The Political Ingredient of Public Health Services: A Neglected Area of Research," *Milbank Memorial Fund Quarterly*, Vol. 44, October 1966, Part 2, pp. 13–34.

Krause, Elliott, "Health and the Politics of Technology," *Inquiry*, Vol. 8, September 1971, pp. 51–59.

Lepawsky, Albert, "Medical Science and Political Science, *Journal of Medical Education*, Vol. 42, October 1967, pp. 905–917.

Lewis, Irving J., "Science and Health Care—The Political Problem," *New England Journal of Medicine*, Vol. 281, October 16, 1969, pp. 888–896.

Lewis, Oscar, "Medicine and Politics in a Mexican Village," in Benjamin D. Paul, ed., *Health, Culture, and Community*, New York: Russell Sage Foundation, 1955, pp. 403–434.

Margolis, Richard J., "Where Does it Hurt: America's Medical Crisis and the Politics of Health Reform," *The New Leader*, Vol. 57, April 15, 1974, pp. 3–35.

Marmor, Theodore R., Amy Bridges and Wayne L. Hoffman, "Comparative Politics and Health Policies: Notes on Benefits, Costs, Limits," in Douglas E. Ashford, ed., *Comparing Public Policies: New Concepts and Methods*, Vol. 4, Beverly Hills: Sage Publications, 1978, pp. 59–80.

Marmor, Theodore R., Donald A. Withman and Thomas C. Heagy, "Politics, Public Policy and Medical Inflation," in Michael Zubkoff, ed., *Health: A Victim or Cause of Inflation*, New York: Prodist, 1976, pp. 299–316.

McKinlay, John B., ed., *Politics and Law in Health Care Policy, A Selection of Articles from the Milbank Memorial Fund Quarterly*, New York: Prodist, 1973.

McKinlay, John B., ed., *Politics and Health Care. A Milbank Reader*, No. 6, Cambridge: MIT Press, 1981.

Mechanic, David, *Politics, Medicine and Social Science*, New York: John Wiley & Sons, 1974.

Middleton, William J., "Politics of Liberating the Health System," *The Black Scholar*, Vol. 5, May 1974, pp. 16–25.

Millman, Michael L., "Politics and the Expanding Physician Supply," unpublished doctoral dissertation, Columbia University, 1977, Microfilm No. 77-24, 110.

National League for Nursing, *People, Power, Politics for Health Care*, New York: National League for Nursing, 1976.

Navarro, Vicente, "Social Class, Political Power and the State: Their Implications in Medicine—Parts 1 and 2," *Journal of Health Politics, Policy and Law*, Vol. 1, Fall 1976, pp. 256–284.

Powell, John E., *Medicine and Politics: 1975 and After*, Turnbridge Wells, England: Pitman Medical, 1976.

Record, Jane Cassels, "Medical Politics and Medical Prices: The Relation Between Who Decides and How Much it Costs," in Kenneth M. Friedman and Stuart H. Rakoff, eds., *Toward a National Health Policy: Public Policy and the Control of Health Care Costs*, Cambridge: Lexington Books, 1977.

Riska, Elainne and James A. Taylor, "Consumer Attitudes Toward Health Policy and Knowledge About Health Legislation," *Journal of Health Politics, Policy and Law*, Vol. 3, Spring 1978, pp. 112–123.

Silver, George A., "Medical Politics, Health Policy, Party Health Platforms, Promise and Performance," *International Journal of Health Services*, Vol. 6, No. 2, 1976, pp. 331–343.

Swanson, Bert E., "The Politics of Health," in Howard E. Freeman, Sol Levine and Leo G. Reeder, eds., *Handbook of Medical Sociology*, Englewood Cliffs, N.J.: Prentice-Hall, 1972, 2nd edition, pp. 435–455.

Weaver, Jerry L., "Health Care Costs as a Political Issue: Comparative Responses of Chicanos and Anglos," *Social Science Quarterly*, Vol. 53, March 1973, pp. 846–854.

Weller, G. R., "From 'Pressure Group Politics' to 'Medical-Industrial Complex': The Development of Approaches to the Politics of Health," *Journal of Health Politics, Policy and Law*, Vol. 1, Winter 1977, pp. 444–470.

Wildavsky, Aaron, "Doing Better and Feeling Worse: The Political Pathology of Health Policy," *Daedalus*, Vol. 106, Winter, 1977, pp. 105–123.

Zola, Irving K., "In the Name of Health and Illness: On Some Socio-Political Consequences of Medical Influence," *Social Science and Medicine*, Vol. 9, February 1975, pp. 83–87.

Abortion

Roemer, Ruth, "Abortion Law Reform and Repeal: Legislative and Judicial Developments," *American Journal of Public Health*, Vol. 61, March 1971, pp. 500–509.

Schneider, Carl E. and Maris A. Vinovskis, *The Law and Politics of Abortion*, Lexington, Mass.: Lexington Books, 1980.

Steinhoff, Patricia G. and Milton Diamond, *Abortion Politics: The Hawaii Experience*, Honolulu: University of Hawaii Press, 1977.

Cancer

Eisenberg, Lucy, "The Politics of Cancer," *Harpers*, Vol. 243, November 1971, pp. 100–105.

Epstein, Samuel S., *Politics of Cancer*, San Francisco: Sierra Club Books, 1978.

Hixson, Joseph, *The Patchwork Mouse, Politics and Intrigue in the Campaign to Conquer Cancer*, Garden City, N.Y.: Anchor Press/Doubleday and Co., 1976.

Lally, John J., "Social Determinents of Differential Allocation of Resources to Disease Research: A Comparative Analysis of Crib Death and Cancer Research," *Journal of Health and Social Behavior*, Vol. 18, June 1977, pp. 125–138.

Levine, Adeline G., *Love Canal, Politics and People*, Lexington, Mass.: Lexington Books, 1982.

Markle, Gerald E. and James C. Peterson, eds., *Politics, Science and Cancer: The Laetrile Phenomenon*, Boulder, Colo: Westview Press, 1980.

Rettig, Richard A., *Cancer Crusade: The Story of the National Cancer Act of 1971*, Princeton, N.J.: Princeton University Press, 1977.

Strickland, Stephen P., *Politics, Science and Dread Disease: A Short History of United States Medical Research Policy*, Cambridge: Harvard University Press, 1972.

Whelan, Ellen Haas, "Government: Hindrance or Help in the Cancer War?," in Bernard H. Siegan, ed., *Government, Regulation and the Economy*, Lexington, Mass.: Lexington Books, 1980.

Chronic Disease, Disability, and Rehabilitation

Berkowitz, Edward D., "Rehabilitation: The Federal Government's Response to Disability, 1935–1954," unpublished doctoral dissertation, Northwestern University, 1976. Also, New York: Arno Press, 1980.

Brandt, Allan M., "Polio, Politics, Publicity and Duplicity: Ethical Aspects in the Development of the Salk Vaccine," *International Journal of Health Services*, Vol. 8, No. 2, 1978, pp. 257–270.

Gary, Lawrence, E. and Betty J. Penn, *The Socio-Political Impact of Sickle Cell Disease*, Washington, D.C.: Howard University Institute for Urban Affairs and Research, March 1977.

Howards, Irving, Henry P. Brehm and Saad Z. Nagi, *Disability: From Social Problem to Federal Program*, New York: Praeger Publishers, 1980.

Krause, Elliott A., "The Political Sociology of Rehabilitation," in Gary L. Albrecht, ed., *The Sociology of Physical Disability and Rehabilitation*, Pittsburgh, Pa.: University of Pittsburgh Press, 1976, pp. 201–222.

Morris, Robert, ed., *Allocating Health Resources for the Aged and Disabled. Technology versus Politics*, Lexington, Mass.: Lexington Books, 1981.

Spingarn, Natalie Davis, *Heartbeat: The Politics of Health Research*, Washington, D.C.: Robert B. Luce, 1976.

Wilkenson, Doris Y., "For Whose Benefit? Politics and Sickle Cell," *The Black Scholar*, Vol. 5, May 1974, pp. 26–31.

Drugs

Blank, Charles H., "Delaney Clause: Technical Naivete and Scientific Advocacy in the Formulation of Public Health Policies," *California Law Review*, Vol. 62, July–September 1974, pp. 1084–1120.

Campbell, Rita Ricardo, *Drug Lag; Federal Government Decision Making*, Hoover Institution Studies No. 55, Stanford, Ca.: Hoover Institution Press, 1976.

Greenberg, Daniel S., "Report of the President's Biomedical Panel and the Old Days at the FDA," *New England Journal of Medicine*, Vol. 294, May 27, 1976, pp. 1245–1246.

Landau, Richard L., ed., *Regulating New Drugs*, Chicago, Ill.: University of Chicago, Center for Policy Study, 1973.

Peltzman, Sam, *Regulation of Pharmaceutical Innovation: The 1962 Amendments*, Research Evaluative Studies No. 15, Washington, D.C.: American Enterprise Institute for Public Policy Research, 1974.

Rock, Paul E., ed., *Drugs and Politics*, New Brunswick, N.J.: Transaction Books, 1977.

Schroeder, Richard C., *The Politics of Drugs: Marijuana to Mainlining*, Washington, D.C.: Congressional Quarterly, 1975.

Silverman, Milton and Philip R. Lee, *Pills, Profits and Politics*, Berkeley, Calif.: University of California Press, 1974.

Steslicke, William E., *Doctors in Politics: The Political Life of the Japan Medical Association*, New York: Praeger Publishers, 1973.

Wardell, William M. and Louis Lasagna, *Regulation and Drug Development*, Washington, D.C.: The American Enterprise Institute for Public Policy Research, 1975.

Health Maintenance Organizations

Bauman, Patricia, "The Formulation and Evolution of the Health Maintenance Organization Policy, 1970–1973," *Social Science and Medicine*, Vol. 10, March–April 1976, pp. 129–142.

Falkson, Joseph L., *HMO's and the Politics of Health System Reform*, Chicago: American Hospital Association and Robert J. Brady Co., 1980.

Moran, Donald W., "HMO's, Competition and the Politics of Minimum Benefits," *Milbank Memorial Fund Quarterly/Health and Society*, Vol. 59, No. 2, Spring 1981, pp. 190–208.

Health Planning (also see Regulation)

Altman, Drew, "The Politics of Health Care Regulation: The Case of the National Health Planning and Resources Development Act," *Journal of Health Politics, Policy, and Law*, Vol. 2, Winter 1978, pp. 560–580.

Altman, Drew and Harvey M. Sapolsky, "Writing the Regulations for Health, *Policy Sciences*, Vol. 7, December 1976, pp. 417–438.

Binstock, Robert H., "Effective Planning Through Political Influence," *American Journal of Public Health*, Vol. 59, May 1969, pp. 808–813.

Brown, Lawrence D., *The Political Structure of the Federal Planning Program*, Washington, D.C.: The Brookings Institution, 1982.

Conant, Ralph W., "The Politics of Health Planning," *Hospital Progress*, Vol. 50, January 1969, pp. 51–56.

Desario, Jack, "Demise of Health Planning in the United States: The Politics of Incremental Health Policy Formation," *Journal of Health Politics, Policy and Law*, Vol. 3, June 1982, pp. 164–177.

Feingold, Eugene, "The Changing Political Character of Health Planning," *American Journal of Public Health*, Vol. 59, May 1969, pp. 803–807.

Hyman, Herbert H., ed., *The Politics of Health Care: Nine Case Studies of Innovative Planning in New York City*, New York: Praeger Publishers, 1973.

Ingman, Stanley R., "Politics of Health Planning," unpublished doctoral dissertation, University of Pittsburgh, 1971, Microfilm No. 71-23, 656.

Kaufman, Herbert et al., "The Politics of Health Planning," *American Journal of Public Health*, Vol. 59, May 1969, pp. 795–813. [(1) Herbert Kaufman: Introduction, pp. 795–796; (2) Basil J. F. Mott: The Myth of Planning Without Politics, pp. 797–803; (3) Eugene Feingold: The Changing Character of Health Planning, pp. 803–807; (4) Robert H. Binstock: Effective Planning Political Influence, pp. 808–813.

Klarman, Herbert E., "National Policies and Local Planning for Health Services," *Milbank Memorial Fund Quarterly/Health and Society*, Vol. 54, Winter 1976, pp. 1–28.

Levin, A. L., "Health Planning and the U.S. Government," *International Journal of Health Services*, Vol. 2, No. 3, 1972, pp. 367–376.

Mott, Basil J. F., "The Myth of Planning Without Politics," *American Journal of Public Health*, Vol. 59, May 1969, pp. 797–803.

Mott, Basil J. F., "Politics and International Planning," *Social Science and Medicine*, Vol. 8, May 1974, pp. 271–274.

Rothstein, P., *The Closing of St. Francis Hospital: A Case Study in the Politics of Health Planning*, New York: Health Policy Advisory Center of the Institute for Policy Studies, 1968.

Seder, Richard H., "Planning and Politics in the Allocation of Health Resources," *American Journal of Public Health*, Vol. 63, September 1973, pp. 774–777.

Warde, James J., "The Role of Local Government in Health Planning," *Journal of Health Politics, Policy and Law*, Vol. 1, Winter, 1977, pp. 387–390.

Health Policy

Bauman, Patricia, "The Formulation and Evolution of the Health Maintenance Organization Policy, 1970–1973," *Social Science and Medicine*, Vol. 10, March–April 1976, pp. 129–142.

Blumstein, James F. and Michael Zubkoff, "Public Choice and Health: Problems, Politics and Perspectives on Formulating National Health Policy," *Journal of Health Politics, Policy and Law*, Vol. 4, Fall 1979, pp. 382–413.

Brown, Lawrence, *The Scope and Limits of Equality as a Normative Guide to Federal Health Care Policy*, Washington, D.C.: The Brookings Institution, 1979, General Series Reprint, No. 350.

Brown, Lawrence, "The Formulation of Federal Health Care Policy," *Bulletin of the New York Academy of Medicine*, Vol. 54, January 1978, pp. 45–58.

Davis, Karen, "Reagan Administration Health Policy," *Journal of Public Health Policy*, Vol. 2, December 1981, pp. 312–332.

Dunham, Andrew B. and Theodore Marmor, "Federal Policy in Health: Recent Trends and Different Perspectives," in Theodore J. Lowi and Alan Stone, eds., *Nationalizing Government: Public Policies in America*, Beverly Hills, Calif.: Sage Publications 1978.

Falcone, David, "The Challenge of Comparative Health Policy for Political Science," *The Journal of Health Politics, Policy and Law,* Vol. 1, Summer 1976, pp. 196–213.

Fein, Rashi, "Social and Economic Attitudes Shaping American Health Policy," *Milbank Memorial Fund Quarterly/Health and Society,* Vol. 58, Summer 1980, pp. 349–385. Also in John B. McKinlay, ed., *Issues in Health Care Policy,* Cambridge: MIT Press, 1981, pp. 29–65.

Ingraham, Norman R., "Formulation of Public Policy in Medical Care: Dynamics of Community Action at Local Level," *American Journal of Public Health,* Vol. 51, August 1961, pp. 1144–1151.

Klein, Rudolf, "Economic versus Political Models in Health Care Policy," in John B. McKinlay, ed., *Issues in Health Care Policy,* Cambridge: MIT Press, 1981, pp. 66–79. Also in "Models of Man and Models of Policy: Reflections on *Exit, Voice* and *Loyalty* Ten Years Later," *Milbank Memorial Fund Quarterly/Health and Society,* Vol. 58, Summer 1980, pp. 416–429.

Marmor, Theodore R. and John B. Christianson, *Health Care Policy. A Political Economy Approach,* Beverly Hills, Calif.: Sage Publications, 1982.

Marmor, Theodore R., Amy Bridges and Wayne L. Hoffman, "Comparative Politics and Health Policies: Notes on Benefits, Costs and Limits," in Douglas E. Ashford, ed., *Comparing Public Policies: New Concepts and Methods,* Beverly Hills, Calif.: Sage Publications, 1978, Vol. 4, pp. 59–80.

Marmor, Theodore R., Donald A. Withman and Thomas C. Heagy, "Politics, Public Policy and Medical Inflation," in Michael Zubkoff, ed., *Health: A Victim or Cause of Inflation,* New York: Prodist, 1976, pp. 299–316.

McKinlay, John B., ed., *Issues in Health Care Policy. A Milbank Reader,* Cambridge: MIT Press, 1981.

Mechanic, David, "Some Dilemmas in Health Care Policy," *Milbank Memorial Fund Quarterly/Health and Society,* Vol. 59, Winter 1981. Also in John B. McKinlay, ed., *Issues in Health Care Policy,* Cambridge: MIT Press, Winter 1981, pp. 80–94.

Rhoads, Steven E., ed., *Valuing Life: Public Policy Dilemmas,* Boulder, Colo.: Westview Press, 1980.

Riska, Elainne and James A. Taylor, "Consumer Attitudes Toward Health Policy and Knowledge About Health Legislation," *Journal of Health Politics, Policy and Law,* Vol. 6, No. 2, 1976, pp. 331–343.

Silver, George A., "Ordering Social Objectives: National Health Service and National Health Insurance as Policy Options in Organizing the Medical Care System," *Yale Journal of Biology and Medicine,* Vol. 5, 1978, pp. 177–184.

Straetz, Ralph A. and Marvin Lieberman, "Health Policy Studies by Political Scientists," *Policy Studies Journal,* Vol. 3, Winter 1974, pp. 195–200.

Straetz, Ralph A., Marvin Lieberman and Alice Sardell, *Critical Issues and Health Policy,* Lexington, Mass.: Lexington Books, 1981.

Hospitals

Derzon, Robert A., "The Politics of Municipal Hospitals," in Douglass Cater and Philip R. Lee, eds., *Politics of Health,* New York: Medcom Press, 1972.

Feder, Judith and Bruce Spitz, "The Politics of Hospital Payment," *Journal of Health Politics, Policy and Law,* Vol. 4, Fall 1979, pp. 435–463.

Jaeger, Boi Jon, "Government and Hospitals: A Perspective on Health Politics," *Hospital Administration,* Vol. 17, Winter 1972, pp. 39–50.

Joskow, Paul L., *Controlling Hospital Costs. The Role of Government Regulation,* Cambridge: MIT Press, 1981.

Lindsay, Cotton M., *Veterans Administration Hospitals: An Economic Analysis of Government*

Enterprise, Washington, D.C.: American Enterprise Institute for Public Policy Research, 1975.

Lumpton, David M., *The Politics of Medicine in China: The Policy Process 1947–1977*, Boulder, Colo.: Westview Press, 1977.

Raphaelson, Arnold H. and Charles P. Hall, Jr., "Politics and Economics of Hospital Cost Containment," *Journal of Health Politics, Policy and Law*, Vol. 3, Spring 1978, pp. 87–111.

Rosner, David, "Gaining Control: Reform Reimbursement and Politics in New York's Community Hospitals, 1890–1915," *American Journal of Public Health*, Vol. 70, May 1980, pp. 533–542.

Influenza

Berliner, Howard S. and Warren J. Salmon, "Swine Flue, the Phantom Threat," *Nation*, Vol. 223, September 25, 1976, pp. 269–272.

Neustadt, Richard E. and Harvey V. Fineberg, *The Swine Flue Affair: Decision-Making on a Slippery Disease*, Washington, D.C.: U.S. Government Printing Office, 1978.

Osborn, June, *Influenza in America, 1918–1976: History, Science and Politics*, New York: Prodist, Neale Watson Academic Publishers, 1977.

Silverstein, Arthur M., *Pure Politics and Impure Science. The Swine Flue Affair*, Baltimore, Md.: The Johns Hopkins University Press, 1981.

Viseltear, Arthur J., "Immunization and Public Policy: A Short Political History of the 1976 Swine Influenza Legislation," in June E. Osborn, ed., *Influenza in America, 1918–1976: History, Science and Politics*, New York: Prodist, Neal Watson Academic Publishers, 1977.

Medicine and the Medical Profession (Doctors and Politics)

Anderson, Odin W., "PSROs, The Medical Profession and the Public Interest," *Milbank Memorial Fund Quarterly/Health and Society*, Vol. 54, Summer 1976, pp. 379–388.

Bonner, T. N., "Social and Political Attitudes of Midwestern Physicians," *Journal Hist. Med. and Allied Sciences*, Vol. 8, April 1953, pp. 133–164.

Cain, Leonard D., Jr., "The AMA and the Gerontologists: Uses and Abuses of 'A Profile of the Aging: USA'," in Gideon Sjoberg, ed., *Ethics, Politics, and Social Research*, Cambridge: Schenkman Publishing Co., 1967, pp. 78–114.

Carter, Richard, *The Doctor Business*, New York: Doubleday & Co., 1958.

Chase, Edward T., "The Politics of Medicine," in Marion Sanders, ed., *The Crisis in American Medicine*, New York: Harpers, 1961, pp. 1–19.

Colombotos, John, "Physicians and Medicare: A Before-After Study of the Effects of Legislation on Attitudes," *American Sociological Review*, Vol. 34, June 1969, pp. 318–334.

Dodds, Richard W., "A Framework for Political Mapping of Conflict in Organized Medicine—Especially Pediatrics," *Medical Care Review*, Vol. 27, November 1970, pp. 1035–1062.

Eckstein, Harry, *Pressure Groups Politics: The Case of the British Medical Association*, Palo Alto, Calif.: Stanford University Press, 1960.

Garceau, Oliver, *The Political Life of the American Medical Association*, Cambridge: Harvard University Press, 1941.

Glaser, William A., "Doctors and Politics," *American Journal of Sociology*, ol. 66, November 1960, pp. 230–245.

Gordon, Gerald and Selwyn Becker, "Changes in Medical Practice Bring Shifts in the Patterns of Power," *Modern Hospital*, Vol. 102, February 1964, pp. 89–91.

Lewis, R., "New Power at the Polls: The Doctors," in H. Turner, ed., *Politics in the United States: Readings in Political Parties and Pressure Groups*, New York: McGraw-Hill, 1955, pp. 180–185.

Means, James Howard, *Doctors, People, and Government*, Boston: Little, Brown & Co., 1953.

Melicke, Carl A., "The Saskatchewan Medical Care Dispute of 1962: An Analytic Social History," unpublished doctoral dissertation, Microfilm No. 68-7435, University of Minnesota, 1967.

Millman, Michael L., *Politics and the Expanding Physician Supply*, Montclair, N.J.: Allanheld, Osmun and Co., 1980.

Stauffer, Robert B., *The Development of an Interest Group: the Phillippine Medical Association*, Quezon City: University of the Phillippines Press, 1966.

Tollefson, E. A., *Bitter Medicine*, Toronto: University of Toronto Press, 1964.

Medicare and Medicaid: Government Health Insurance

Anderson, Odin W., "Compulsory Medical Care Insurance, 1910–1950," in Eugene Feingold, ed., *Medicare: Policy and Politics*, San Francisco, Calif.: Chandler Publishing Co., 1966, pp. 85–156.

Anderson, Odin W., "The Medicare Act: The Public Policy Breakthrough, or Wheeling, Dealing and Healing," in Irving L. Webber, ed., *Medical Care Under Social Security—Potentials and Problems*, Institute of Gerontology Series, Gainsville, Fla.: University of Florida Press, 1966, Vol. 15, pp. 9–26.

Anderson, Odin W., *The Uneasy Equilibrium: Private and Public Financing of Health Services in the U.S., 1865–1975*, New Haven, Conn.: College and University Press, 1968.

Bernard, Sydney E. and Eugene Feingold, "The Impact of Medicaid," *Wisconsin Law Review*, Vol. 1970, No. 3, 1970, pp. 726–755.

Bernstein, Betty J., "The Politics of the New York State Medicaid Law of 1966: An Analysis," unpublished doctoral dissertation, Microfilm No. 69-21,237, New York University, 1969.

Bernstein, Betty J., "Public Health—Inside or Outside the Mainstream of the Political Process? Lessons from the Passage of Medicaid," *American Journal of Public Health*, Vol. 60, September 1970, pp. 1690–1700.

Brewster, Agness W., *Health Insurance and Related Proposals for Financing Personal Health Services . . . A Digest of Major Legislation and Proposals for Federal Action, 1935–1957*, Division of Program Research, Social Security Administration, Washington, D.C.: U.S. Government Printing Office, 1958.

Corning, Peter A., *The Evolution of Medicare . . . From Idea to Law*, Office of Research and Statistics, Research Report No. 29, Social Security Administration, Washington, D.C.: U.S. Government Printing Office, 1969.

Feder, Judith M., Medicare: *The Politics of Federal Medical Insurance*, Lexington, Mass.: D. C. Heath and Lexington Books, 1977.

Feingold, Eugene, *Medicare: Policy and Politics*, San Francisco, Calif.: Chandler Publishing Co., 1966.

Filerman, Gary L., "The Legislative Campaign for the Passage of a Medical Care for the Aged Bill," unpublished masters thesis, University of Minnesota, 1962.

Foltz, Anne-Marie, *An Ounce of Prevention. Child Health Politics Under Medicaid*, Cambridge: MIT Press, 1982.

Gentry, John T. and Morris Schaefer, "The Impact of State and Federal Policy Planning Decisions on the Implementation and Functional Adequacy of Title XIX Health Care Programs," *Medical Care*, Vol. 7, January 1969, pp. 92–104.

Harris, Richard, "Annals of Legislation: Medicare—All Very Hegelian," *New Yorker*, Vol. 42, July 2, 1966, pp. 29–62.

Harris, Richard, "Annals of Legislation: Medicare—We Do Not Compromise," *New Yorker*, Vol. 42, July 16, 1966, pp. 35–91.

Harris, Richard, "Annals of Legislation: Medicare—A Sacred Trust," *New Yorker*, Vol. 42, July 23, 1966, pp. 35–63.

Harris, Richard, *A Sacred Trust*, New York: New American Library, 1967.

Hirshfield, Daniel S., *The Lost Reform: The Campaign for Compulsory Health Insurance in the United States from 1932–1943*, Cambridge: Harvard University Press, 1970.

Marmor, Theodore R., *The Politics of Medicare*, Chicago, Ill.: Aldine Publishing Co., 1973, revised American edition.

Rose, Arnold M., "The Passage of Legislation: The Politics of Financing Medical Care for the Aging," in Arnold M. Rose, ed., *The Power Structure*, New York: Oxford University Press, 1967, pp. 400–455.

Skidmore, Max J., *Medicare and the American Rhetoric of Reconciliation*, Tuscaloosa, Ala.: University of Alabama Press, 1970.

Stevens, Rosemary and Robert Stevens, "Medicaid: Anatomy of a Dilemma," *Law and Contemporary Problems*, Vol. 1970, Spring 1970, pp. 348–425.

Stevens, Robert and Rosemary Stevens, *Welfare Medicine in America: A Case Study of Medicaid*, New York: The Free Press, 1974.

Vuori, Hannu, "Ideology Versus Interest: The Case of Medicare," *Social Science & Medicine*, Vol. 2, September 1968, pp. 355–363.

Weikel, M. K. *A Decade of Medicaid. Some State and Federal Perspectives on Medicaid*, Special Report of Medicaid–Medicare Management Institute, Washington, D.C.: Health Care Financing Administration, 1979.

Mental Health

Bardach, Eugene, *The Skill Factor in Politics: Repealing the Mental Commitment Laws in California*, Berkeley, Calif.: University of California Press, 1972.

Connery, Robert H., *The Politics of Mental Health*, New York: Columbia University Press, 1968.

Chu, Franklin D. and Sharland Trotter, *The Madness Establishment: Ralph Nader's Study Group Report on the National Institute of Mental Health*, New York: Grossman Publishers, 1974.

Falkson, Joseph L., "Minor Skirmish in a Monumental Struggle: HEW's Analysis of Mental Health Services," *Policy Analysis*, Vol. 2, Winter 1976, pp. 93–119.

Felicetti, Daniel A., *Mental Health and Retardation Politics: The Mind Lobbies in Congress*, New York: Praeger Publishers, 1975.

Foley, Henry A., *Community Mental Health Legislation: The Formative Process*, Lexington, Mass.: Lexington Books, 1975.

Foley, Henry A., *Madness and Government*, Washington, D.C.: American Psychiatric Press, 1983.

Rumer, Richard, "Community Mental Health Centers: Politics and Therapy," *Journal of Health Politics, Policy and Law*, Vol. 2, Winter 1978, pp. 531–559.

National Health Insurance

Anderson, Odin W., "Compulsory Medical Care Insurance, 1910–1950," in Eugene Feingold, ed., *Medicare: Policy and Politics*, San Francisco: Chandler Publishing Co., 1966, pp. 85–156.

Anderson, Odin W., "The Politics of Universal Health Insurance in the United States: An Interpretation," *International Journal of Health Services*, Vol. 2, No. 4, 1972, pp. 577–582.

Cairl, Richard E. and Allen W. Imershein, "National Health Insurance Policy in the United States—A Case of Non-Decision Making," *International Journal of Health Services*, Vol. 7, No. 2, 1977, pp. 167–178.

Evang, Karl, "The Politics of Developing a National Health Policy," *International Journal of Health Services*, Vol. 3, No. 3, 1973, pp. 331–340.

Falk, I. S., "Proposals for National Health Insurance in the USA: Origins and Evolution, and Some

Perceptions for the Future," *Milbank Memorial Fund Quarterly/Health and Society*, Vol. 55, Spring 1977, pp. 161–192.

Goodman, Louis J. and Steven R. Steiber, "Public Support for National Health Insurance," *American Journal of Public Health*, Vol. 71, October 1981, pp. 1105–1108.

Gordon, Jeoffry B., "The Politics of Community Medicine Projects: A Conflict Analysis," *Medical Care*, Vol. 7, November–December 1969, pp. 419–428.

Hirshfield, Daniel S., *The Lost Reform: The Campaign for Compulsory Health Insurance in the United States, 1932 to 1943*, Cambridge: Harvard University Press, 1970.

Lubove, Roy, "The New Deal and National Health," *Current History*, Vol. 72, May–June 1977, pp. 198–199, 224–227.

Marmor, Theodore R., "Politics of National Health Insurance: Analysis and Prescription," *Policy Analysis*, Vol. 3, Winter 1977, pp. 25–48.

Marmor, Theodore, R., NHI in Crisis: Politics, Predictions, Proposals," *Hospital Progress*, Vol. 59, January 1978, pp. 68–72.

Numbers, Ronald L., *Almost Persuaded: American Physicians and Compulsory Health Insurance, 1912–1920*, Baltimore, Md.: The Johns Hopkins University Press, 1978.

Numbers, Ronald L., *Compulsory Health Insurance, The Continuing Debate*, Westport, Conn.: Greenwood Press, 1982.

Prussin, Jeffrey A., "National Health Insurance: Anatomy of a Political Issue," *Medical Group Management*, Vol. 23, March–April 1976, pp. 22–25.

The Poor

Coute, Richard A., *Poverty, Politics and Health Care: An Appalachian Experience*, New York: Praeger Publishers, 1975.

Dans, Peter E. and Samuel Johnson, "Politics in the Development of a Migrant Health Center," *New England Journal of Medicine*, Vol. 292, April 24, 1975, pp. 890–895.

Davis, Karen, "A Decade of Policy Developments in Providing Health Care for Low-Income Families," in Robert H. Haveman, ed., *A Decade of Federal Antipoverty Programs: Achievements, Failures and Lessons*, New York: Academic Press, 1977, pp. 197–231.

Rose, Marilyn G., "Federal Regulation of Services to the Poor Under the Hill-Burton Act: Realities and Pitfalls," *Northwestern University Law Review*, Vol. 70, March–April 1975, pp. 168–201.

Shenkin, Budd N., *Health Care for Migrant Workers: Policies and Politics*, Cambridge: Ballinger Publishing Co., 1974.

Stevens, Robert and Rosemary Stevens, *Welfare Medicine in America: A Case Study of Medicaid*, New York: The Free Press, 1974.

Stone, Deborah A., "Diagnosis and the Dole: The Function of Illness in American Distributive Politics," *Journal of Health Politics, Policy and Law*, Vol. 4, Fall 1979, pp. 507–521.

Public Health

Bellin, Lowell E., "Medicaid in New York: Utopianism and Bare Knuckles in Public Health, 3. Realpolitik in the Health Care Arena: Standard Setting of Professional Services," *American Journal of Public Health*, Vol. 59, May 1969, pp. 820–825.

Bellin, Lowell E., "The New Left and American Public Health—Attempted Radicalization of the A.P.H.A. Through Dialectic," *American Journal of Public Health*, Vol. 60, June 1970, pp. 973–981.

Bernstein, Betty J., "Public Health—Inside or Outside the Mainstream of the Political Process? Lessons from the Passage of Medicaid," *American Journal of Public Health*, Vol. 60, September 1970, pp. 1690–1700.

Conant, Ralph W., *The Politics of Community Health*, Washington, D.C.: Public Affairs Press, 1968.

Courtwright, David T., "Public Health and Public Wealth: Social Cost as a Basis for Restrictive Policies," *Milbank Memorial Fund Quarterly/Health and Society*, Vol. 58, Spring 1980, pp. 268–282.

Gilbert, Benjamin, Merry K. Moos, and C. Arden Miller, "State-Level Decision Making for Public Health: The Status of Boards of Health," *Journal of Public Health Policy*, Vol. 3, March 1982, pp. 51–63.

Gordon, Jeoffry B., "The Politics of Community Medicine Projects: A Conflict Analysis," *Medical Care*, Vol. 7, November–December 1969, pp. 419–428.

Greenberg, George D., "Reorganization Reconsidered: The U.S. Public Health Service, 1960–1973, *Public Policy*, Vol. 23, Fall 1975, pp. 483–522.

Kaufman, Herbert, "The Political Ingredient of Public Health Services: A Neglected Area of Research," *Milbank Memorial Fund Quarterly/Health and Society*, Vol. 44, October 1966, Part 2, pp. 13–34.

Levine, Adeline G., *Love Canal. Science, Politics and People*, Lexington, Mass.: Lexington Books, 1982.

Snoke, Albert W., "What Good is Legislation—or Planning—If We Can't Make it Work? Need for Comprehensive Approach to Health and Welfare," *American Journal of Public Health*, Vol. 72, September 1982, pp. 1028–1033.

Regulation

Altman, Drew, "The Politics of Health Care Regulation: The Case of the National Health Planning and Resources Development Act," *Journal of Health Politics, Policy and Law*, Vol. 2, Winter 1978, pp. 560–580.

Avellone, Joseph C. and Francis D. Moore, "The Federal Trade Commission Enters a New Arena: Health Services," *New England Journal of Medicine*, Vol. 299, August 31, 1978, pp. 478–483.

Chesney, James D., "The Politics of Regulation: An Assessment of Winners and Losers," *Inquiry*, Vol. 19, Fall 1982, pp. 235–245.

Cohen, Harris S., "Regulating Politics and American Medicine," *American Behavioral Scientist*, Vol. 19, No. 1, 1975, pp. 122–136.

Curran, William, Richard Steele and Ellen Ober, "Government Intervention on Increase," *Hospitals*, Vol. 49, May 16, 1975, pp. 57–61.

Grabowski, Henry G., *Drug Regulation and Innovation*, Evaluative Studies No. 28, Washington, D.C.: American Enterprise Institute for Public Policy Research, 1976.

Joskow, Paul L., *Controlling Hospital Costs—The Role of Government Regulation*, Cambridge: MIT Press, 1981.

Kavaler, Florence, Howard R. Kelman, and Alan P. Brownstein, "Regulating Health Care. Prospects for the Future," *Journal of Public Health Policy*, Vol. 1, September 1980, pp. 230–240.

Krause, Elliott A., "The Political Context of Health Service Regulation," *International Journal of Health Services*, Vol. 5, No. 4, 1975, pp. 593–608.

Levin, Arthur, *Regulating Health Care. The Struggle for Control*, New York: Academy of Political Science, 1981.

Levine, Adeline G., Love Canal: Science, Politics, and People, Lexington, Mass.: Lexington Books, 1982.

McCaffrey, David P., *OSHA and the Politics of Health Regulation*, New York: Plenum Publishing Corp., 1982.

Mendeloff, John, *Regulation Safety. An Economic and Political Analysis of Occupational Safety and Health Policy*, Cambridge: MIT Press, 1979.

Mosher, James F. and Lawrence M. Wallack, "Government Regulation of Alcohol Advertising: Protecting Industry Profits Versus Promoting the Public Health," *Journal of Public Health Policy,* Vol. 2, December 1981, pp. 333–353.

Rice, Donald, "Government Regulation of the Hospital Industry in Colorado," *Journal of Public Health Policy,* Vol. 2, March 1981, pp. 58–69.

Schwartz, Teresa M., "Protecting Consumer Health and Safety: The Need for Coordinated Regulation Among Federal Agencies," *George Washington Law Review,* Vol. 43, May 1975, pp. 1031–1076.

Miscellaneous

Brumback, Clarence L., "The Politics of Smoking Prevention: A Report from the Field," *Journal of Public Health Policy,* Vol. 2, March 1980, pp. 36–41.

Gordon, Linda, "The Politics of Birth Control, 1920–1940: The Impact of Professionals," *International Journal of Health Services,* Vol. 5, No. 2, 1975, pp. 253–278.

Kalisch, Beatrice J. and Philip A. Kalisch, "Discourse on the Politics of Nursing," *Journal of Nursing Administration,* Vol. 6, March–April 1976, pp. 29–34.

Koplin, Allen N., "Anti-Smoking Legislation. The New Jersey Experience," *Journal of Public Health Policy,* Vol. 2, September 1981, pp. 247–255.

Law, Sylvia and Stephen Polan, *Pain and Profit: The Politics of Malpractice,* New York: Harper and Row, 1978.

Littlewood, T. B., *The Politics of Population Control,* South Bend, Ind.: University of Notre Dame Press, 1979.

Raphaelson, Arnold H. and Charles P. Hall, "Politics and Economics of Hospital Cost Containment," *Journal of Health Politics, Policy and Law,* Vol. 3, Spring 1978, pp. 87–111.

Roth, William, *The Politics of Daycare: The Comprehensive Child Development Act of 1971,* Discussion Paper No. 369–76, Madison, Wis.: University of Wisconsin, Institute for Research on Poverty, December 1976.

Steslicke, William E., *Politicization of Medical Malpractice in Michigan,* Ann Arbor, Mich.: University of Michigan, Department of Medical Care Organization, April 18, 1977.

THE POLITICAL ECONOMY OF HEALTH

Alford, Robert R., "The Political Economy of Health Care Dynamics Without Change," *Politics and Society,* Vol. 2, Winter, 1972, pp. 126–164.

Bowler, M. Kenneth, Robert T. Kudrle and Theodore R. Marmor, "The Political Economy of National Health Insurance: Policy Analysis and Political Evaluation," in Kenneth M. Friedman and Stuart H. Rakoff, eds., *Toward a National Health Policy: Public Policy and the Control of Health Care Costs,* Lexington, Mass.: Lexington Books, 1977.

Bowler, M. Kenneth, Robert T. Kudrle, Theodore R. Marmor and Amy Bridges, "Political Economy of National Health Insurance—Policy Analysis and Political Evaluation," *Journal of Health Politics, Policy and Law,* Vol. 2, Spring 1977, pp. 100–133.

Brenner, M. Harvey, "Health Costs and Benefits of Economic Policy," *International Journal of Health Services,* Vol. 7, No. 4, 1977, pp. 581–623.

Eyer, Joseph, "Does Unemployment Cause the Death Rate Peak in Each Business Cycle? A Multifactor Model of Death Rate Change," *International Journal of Health Services,* Vol. 7, No. 4, 1977, pp. 625–662.

Feldstein, Paul J., *Health Associations and the Demand for Legislation, The Political Economy of Health*, Cambridge: Ballinger Publishing Co., 1977.

Ginzberg, Eli, "The Political Economy of Health," *Bulletin New York Academy of Medicine*, Vol. 41, October 1965, pp. 1015–1036.

Helt, Eric H., "Economic Determinism: A Model of the Political Economy of Medical Care," *International Journal of Health Services*, Vol. 3, No. 3, 1973, pp. 475–485.

Kelman, Sander, "Toward the Political Economy of Medical Care," *Inquiry*, Vol. 8, September 1971, pp. 30–38.

Kelman, Sander, "Special Section on Political Economy of Health," *International Journal of Health Services*, Vol. 5, No. 4, 1975, pp. 535–693.

Kelman, Sander, "Introduction to the Theme: The Political Economy of Health," *International Journal of Health Services*, Vol. 5, No. 4, 1975, pp. 535–538.

Kelman, Sander, "Toward the Political Economy of Medical Care," in Lewis E. Weeks and Howard J. Berman, eds., *Economics in Health Care*, Germantown, Md.: Aspen Systems Corp., 1977, pp. 39–48.

Klein, Rudolf, "The Political Economy of National Health: Report from London," *The Public Interest*, Vol. 26, Winter 1972, pp. 112–125.

Krause, Elliott A., "Health and the Politics of Technology," *Inquiry*, Vol. 8, September 1971, pp. 51–59.

Krause, Elliot A., *Power and Illness, The Political Sociology of Health and Medical Care*, New York: Elsevier North-Holland, 1977.

Lichtman, R., "The Political Economy of Medical Care," in Hans Peter Dreitzel (ed.), *The Social Organization of Health*, New York: Macmillan, 1971, pp. 265–290.

Marmor, Theodore R. and Jon B. Christianson, *Health Care Policy. A Political Economy Approach*, Beverly Hills, Calif.: Sage Publications, 1982.

Marmor, Theodore R., Amy Bridges and Wayne L. Hoffman, "Comparative Politics and Health Policies: Notes on Benefits, Costs and Limits," in Douglas E. Ashford, ed., *Company Public Policies: New Concepts and Methods*, Vol. 4, Beverly Hills, Calif.: Sage Publications, 1978, pp. 59–80.

McKinlay, John B., *A Case for Refocussing Upstream: The Political Economy of Illness, Applying Behavioral Science to Cardiovascular Risk*, proceedings from the American Heart Association Conference, Seattle, Washington, June 17–19, 1974, pp. 7–17.

McKinlay, John B., "A Case for Refocussing Upstream: The Political Economy of Illness," in E. Gartly Jaco, ed., *Patients, Physicians, and Illness*, New York: The Free Press, 1979, 3rd edition, pp. 9–26.

Mendelson, Mary A. and David Hapgood, "Political Economy of Nursing Homes," *Annals of the American Academy of Political and Social Science*, Vol. 415, September 1974, pp. 95–105.

Navarro, Vicente, "Political Economy of Medical Care, An Explanation of the Composition, Nature and Functions of the Present Health Sector of the United States," *International Journal of Health Services*, Vol. 5, No. 1, 1975, pp. 65–94.

Navarro, Vicente, "The Political and Economic Determinants of Health and Health Care in Rural America," *Inquiry*, Vol. 13, June 1976, pp. 111–121.

Navarro, Vicente, "Social Class, Political Power, and the State and Their Implications in Medicine," *International Journal of Health Services*, Vol. 7, No. 2, 1977, pp. 255–292.

Navarro, Vicente, "The Crisis of the Western System of Medicine in Contemporary Capitalism," *International Journal of Health Services*, Vol. 8, No. 2, 1978, pp. 179–211.

Renaud, Marc, "The Political Economy of the Quebec State Interventions in Health: Reform or Revolution?" unpublished doctoral dissertation, University of Wisconsin, 1976, Microfilm No. 77-3421.

Rice, Dorothy P. and Douglas Wilson, "The American Medical Economy: Problems and Perspectives," *Journal of Health Politics, Policy and Law*, Vol. 1, Summer 1976, pp. 150–172.

Russell, Louise B. and Carol S. Burke, "The Political Economy of Federal Health Programs in the United States: An Historical Review," *International Journal of Health Services*, Vol. 8, No. 1, 1978, pp. 55–77.

Schatzkin, Arthur, "Health and Labor-Power: A Theoretical Investigation," *International Journal of Health Services*, Vol. 8, No. 2, 1978, pp. 213–234.

Somers, Herman M., "Observations on Policy and Politics in the Health Care Economy," in Blue Cross Association, eds., *Health Care in the American Economy: Issues and Forecasts*, Chicago, Ill.: Health Services Foundation, 1977.

Stevenson, Gelvin, "Profits in Medicine: A Context and an Accounting," *International Journal of Health Services*, Vol. 8, No. 1, 1978, pp. 41–54.

Waitzkin, Howard B., "How Capitalism Cares for our Coronaries: A Preliminary Exercise in Political Economy," in Eugene B. Gallagher, ed., *The Doctor-Patient Relationship in the Changing Health Scene*, DHEW Pub. No. (NIH) 78-183, Washington, D.C.: U.S. Government Printing Office, 1978, pp. 317–332.

Windham, Susan R., "National Health Insurance as an Issue in Political Economy—The Implications of the Kennedy Health Security Act for Developing a Strategy to Effect Major Reorganization of Health Care Delivery in America," Unpublished Doctoral Dissertation, Brandeis University, 1977, Microfilm No. 77-15, 274.

GOVERNMENT AND HEALTH

Anderson, Odin W., *The Uneasy Equilibrium: Private and Public Financing of Health Services in the U.S., 1865–1975*, New Haven, Conn.: College & University Press, 1968.

American Nursing Home Association, Government Relations Department, *An Analysis and Partial Legislative History of Title II of Public Law 92-603 (H.R.I.), The Social Security Amendments of 1972*, Washington, D.C.: American Nursing Home Association, February 1, 1973.

Becker, Dorothy D. and Ruth R. Johnson, *Chronology of Health Professions Legislation 1956–1979*, DHHS Publication No. (HRA) 80-69, Washington, D.C.: U.S. Government Printing Office, 1980.

Blumstein, James F. and Michael Zubkoff, "Perspectives on Government Policy in the Health Sector," *Milbank Memorial Fund Quarterly/Health and Society*, Vol. 51, Summer 1973, pp. 395–431.

Brian, Earl W., "Government Control of Hospital Utilization, A California Experience," *New England Journal of Medicine*, Vol. 286, June 22, 1972, pp. 1340–1344.

Burger, Edward J., Jr., *Protecting the Nation's Health: The Problems of Regulation*, Lexington, Mass.: Lexington Books, 1976.

Carey, Sarah C., "A Constitutional Right to Health Care: An Unlikely Development," *Catholic University of America Law Review*, Vol. 23, Spring 1974, pp. 492–514.

Carleton, William G., "Government and Health Before the New Deal," *Current History*, Vol. 72, May–June 1977, pp. 196–197, 223–226.

Carnegie Council on Policy Studies in Higher Education, *Progress and Problems in Medical and Dental Education: Federal Support Versus Federal Control*, San Francisco: Jossey-Bass, 1976.

Chapman, Carleton B. and John M. Talmadge, "Historical and Political Background of Federal Health Care Legislation," *Law and Contemporary Problems*, Vol. 35, Spring 1970, pp. 334–347.

Chapman, Carleton B. and John M. Talmadge, "The Evolution of the Right to Health Concept in the United States," *Pharos*, Vol. 34, January 1971, pp. 30–51.

Clark, Duncan W., "Politics and Health Services Research: A Cameo Study of Policy in the Health Services in the 1930's," E. Evelyn Flook and Paul J. Sanazaro, eds., *Health Services Research and R & D in Perspective*, Ann Arbor, Mich.: Health Administration Press, 1973, pp. 109–125.

Cohen, Elias S., "Integration of Health and Social Services in Federally Funded Programs," *Bulletin of the New York Academy of Medicine*, Vol. 49, December 1973, pp. 1038–1050.

Cooper, Barbara S. and Nancy L. Worthington, *Comparison of Cost and Benefit Incidence of Government Medical Care Programs, Fiscal Years 1966 and 1969*, Office of Research and Statistics Staff Paper No. 18, DHEW Pub. No. (SSA) 75-11852, Washington, D.C.: U.S. Government Printing Office, September 1974.

Densen, Paul M., "Public Accountability and Reporting Systems in Medicare and Other Health Programs," *New England Journal of Medicine*, Vol. 289, August 23, 1973, pp. 401–406.

Detwiller, Lloyd F., "The Right to Health," *Hospitals*, Vol. 45, February 16, 1971, pp. 63–66.

Detwiller, Lloyd F., *The Consequences of Health Care Through Government*, Research Publication No. 6, Sydney, Australia: The Office of Health Care Finance, October 1972.

Fenninger, Leonard D., "Health Manpower and the Education of Health Personnel," *Inquiry*, Vol. 10, March 1973, Supplement, pp. 56–60. Comment: Malcolm C. Todd pp. 61–65; Myron E. Wegman pp. 66–68. Discussion, pp. 69–73.

Feshbach, Dan, "What's Inside the Black Box: A Case Study of Allocative Politics in the Hill-Burton Program," *International Journal of Health Services*, Vol. 9, No. 2, 1979, pp. 313–339.

Foley, Henry A., *Community Mental Health Legislation: The Formative Process*, Lexington, Mass.: Lexington Books, 1975.

Fox, Peter D., "Access to Medical for the Poor: The Federal Perspective," *Medical Care*, Vol. 10, May–June 1972, pp. 272–277.

Frank, Kenneth D. "Government Support of Nursing Home Care," *New England Journal of Medicine*, Vol. 287, September 14, 1972, pp. 538–545.

Friedman, Kenneth M. and Stuart H. Rakoff, *Toward a National Health Policy: Public Policy and the Control of Health Care Costs*, Lexington, Mass.: D.C. Heath, 1977.

Ginzberg, Eli, "The Political Economy of Health," *Bulletin of the New York Academy of Medicine*, Vol. 41, October 1965, pp. 1015–1036.

Havighurst, Clark C., "Controlling Health Care Costs: Strengthening the Private Sector," *Journal of Health Politics, Policy and Law*, Vol. 1, Winter 1977, pp. 471–498.

Health Resources Administration, *Health Resources Studies: Government Controls on the Health Care System: The Canadian Experience*, DHEW Pub. No. (HRA) 77-246, Washington, D.C.: U.S. Government Printing Office, 1977.

Iglehart, John K., "The Carter Administration's Health Budget: Charting New Priorities with Limited Dollars," *Milbank Memorial Fund Quarterly/Health and Society*, Vol. 56, Winter 1978, pp. 53–77.

Jaeger, Boi Jon, "Government and Hospitals: A Perspective on Health Politics," *Hospital Administration*, Vol. 17, Winter 1972, pp. 39–50.

Jonas, Steven, David Banta and Michael Enright, "Government in the Health Care Delivery System," in Steven Jonas, ed., *Health Care Delivery in the United States*, New York: Springer Publishing Co., 1977, pp. 289–328.

Katz, Daniel, et al., *Bureaucratic Encounters: A Pilot Study in the Evaluation of Government Services*, Ann Arbor, Mich.: University of Michigan, Institute for Social Research, 1975.

Kennedy, Edward M., "The Congress and National Health Policy," *American Journal of Public Health*, Vol. 68, March 1978, pp. 241–244.

Kennedy, Virginia C., "Interpreting Legislative Voting Patterns on Health Issues: A Method and Rationale," *Journal of Community Health*, Vol. 1, Spring 1976, pp. 188–195.

Kessel, Reuben A., *Ethical and Economic Aspects of Governmental Intervention in the Medical Care Market*, Washington, D.C.: American Enterprise Institute, Center for Health Policy Research, 1977.

Klarman, Herbert E., "Major Public Initiatives in Health Care," *The Public Interest*, Vol. 34, Winter 1974, pp. 106–123.

Lally, John J., "Social Determinants of Differential Allocation of Resources to Disease Research: A Comparative Analysis of Crib Death and Cancer Research," *Journal of Health and Social Behavior*, Vol. 18, June 1977, pp. 125–138.

Lashof, Joyce C. and Mark H. Lepper, "Federal–State Local Partnership in Health," in USPHS, Health Resources Administration, eds., *Health in America: 1877–1976*, Washington, D.C.: U.S. Government Printing Office, 1976, pp. 122–137.

Lave, Judith and Lester Lave, *The Hospital Construction Act: An Evaluation of the Hill-Burton Program, 1948–1973*, Washington, D.C.: American Enterprise Institute for Public Policy Research, 1974.

Leroy, Lauren and Philip R. Lee, eds., *Deliberations and Compromise, The Health Professions Educational Assistance Act of 1976*, Cambridge: Ballinger Publishing Co., 1977.

Lostetter, John O. and John E. Chapman, "The Participation of the United States Government in Providing Financial Support for Medical Education," *Health Policy and Education*, Vol. 1, No. 1, 1979, pp. 27–65.

Marmor, Theodore R., "Origins of the Government Health Insurance Issue," in David Kotelchuck, ed., *Prognosis Negative: Crisis in the Health Care System*, New York: Vintage Books, 1975, pp. 293–303.

Marmor, T. and D. Thomas, "The Politics of Paying Physicians: The Determinants of Government Payment Methods in England, Sweden and the United States," *International Journal of Health Services*, Vol. 1, No. 1, 1971, pp. 71–78.

McEwan, E. D., "A Case for Government Sponsored Health Care Research and Development in the Formulation of Health Policy and an Account of Early Experience of Government-Sponsored Health Care Research in One Jurisdiction," *International Journal of Health Services*, Vol. 3, No. 1, 1973, pp. 45–58.

McNeil, Richard Jr. and Robert E. Schlenker, "HMO's, Competition and Government," *Milbank Memorial Fund Quarterly/Health and Society*, Vol. 53, Spring 1975, pp. 195–224.

Meilicke, Carl A., "The Saskatchewan Medical Care Dispute of 1962: An Analytic Social History," unpublished doctoral dissertation, University of Minnesota, 1967, Microfilm No. 68-7435.

Mooney, Anne, "The Great Society and Health: Policies for Narrowing the Gaps in Health Status Between the Poor and the Nonpoor," *Medical Care*, Vol. 15, August 1977, pp. 611–619.

Naimark, Arnold, "Ethical Questions Posed by Community and Government Pressures on Medical Education in Canada," *Bulletin of the New York Academy of Medicine*, Vol. 54, July–August 1978, pp. 687–696.

Neustadt, Richard E. and Harvey V. Fineberg, *The Swine Flu Affair: Decision-Making on a Slippery Disease*, Washington, D.C.: U.S. Government Printing Office, 1978.

Palley, Howard A., "Policy Formulation in Health, Some Considerations of Governmental Constraints on Pricing in the Health Delivery System," *American Behavioral Scientist*, Vol. 7, March–April 1974, pp. 572–584.

Phelps, Charles E., "Public Sector Medicine: History and Analysis," in Institute for Contemporary Studies, eds., *New Directions in Public Health Care: An Evaluation of Proposals for National Health Insurance*, San Francisco: The Institute for Contemporary Studies, 1976.

Rakoff, Stuart H. and Kenneth M. Friedman, eds., "Health, Health Costs and the Role of Government," in Kenneth M. Friedman and Stuart H. Rakoff, eds., *Toward a National Health Policy: Public Policy and the Control of Health Care Costs*, Lexington, Mass.: Lexington Books, 1977.

Rhein, Reginald W. and Larry Marion, *The Saccharin Controversy, A Guide for Consumers*, New York: Monarch Press, 1977.

Roemer, Milton I. and Mary H. McClanahan, "Impact of Government Programs on Voluntary Hospitals," *Public Health Reports*, Vol. 75, June 1960, pp. 537–544.

Rudolf, Ronald J., "Physician Care and Government Programs: Analysis of the Distribution of Health and Health Services in New York City and the Nation," unpublished doctoral dissertation, Rutgers University, 1976, Microfilm No. 77-7277.

Russell, Louise R., "Inflation and the Federal Role in Health," in Michael Zubkoff, ed., *Health: Victim or Cause of Inflation?* New York: Prodist, Neale Watson Academic Publishers, 1976, pp. 225–244.

Sade, Robert M., "Medical Care as a Right: A Refutation, *New England Journal of Medicine*, Vol. 285, December 2, 1971, pp. 1288–1292.

Schelling, Thomas C., "Government and Health," in Institute for Contemporary Studies, eds., *New Directions for Public Health Care: An Evaluation of Proposals for National Health Insurance*, San Francisco: The Institute for Contemporary Studies, 1976.

Schlesinger, Edward R., "The Impact of Federal Legislation on Maternal and Child Health Services in the United States," *Milbank Memorial Fund Quarterly/Health and Society*, Vol. 52, Winter 1974, pp. 1–13.

Schlesinger, Edward R., Martha M. Skoner, Estelle D. Trooskin, Janet R. Markel and A. Frederick North, "The Effects of Anticipated Funding Changes on Maternal and Child Health Projects: A Case Study of Uncertainty," *American Journal of Public Health*, Vol. 66, April 1976, pp. 385–388.

Schwartz, Joshua I., *Public Health: Case Studies on the Origins of Government Responsibility for Health Services in the United States*, New York: Cornell University Program in Urban and Regional Studies, 1977.

Snoke, Albert W., "What Good is Legislation—or Planning—If We Can't Make It Work? The Need for a Comprehensive Approach to Health and Welfare," *American Journal of Public Health*, Vol. 72, September 1982, pp. 1028–1033.

Sobel, Lester A., *Health Care: An American Crisis*, New York: Facts on File, 1976.

Somers, Herman M., "Health and Public Policy," *Inquiry*, Vol. 12, June 1975, pp. 87–96.

Steiner, Gilbert Y., *The Children's Cause*, Washington, D.C.: The Brookings Institution, 1976.

Stevens, Robert and Rosemary Stevens, *Welfare Medicine in America, A Case Study of Medicaid*, New York: The Free Press, 1974.

Strickland, Stephen P., "Medical Research: Public Policy and Power Politics," in Douglass Cater and Philip R. Lee, eds., *Politics of Health*, New York: Medcom Press, 1972.

Strickland, Stephen P., *Research and the Health of Americans: Improving the Policy Process*, Lexington, Mass.: Lexington Books, 1978.

Stuart, Bruce C., "Who Gains from Public Health Programs," *Annals of American Academy of Political and Social Science*, Vol. 399, January 1972, pp. 145–150.

Walsh, Margaret E., *The Health Profession Educational Organization and the Governmental Process*, New York: National League for Nursing, 1974.

Wikler, Daniel I., "Persuasion and Coercion for Health: Ethical Issues in Government Efforts to Change Life-Styles," *Milbank Memorial Fund Quarterly/Health and Society*, Vol. 56, Summer, 1978, pp. 303–338.

Williams, A. P. Jr., et al., *Policy Analysis for Federal Biomedical Research*, Santa Monica, Calif.: Rand Corp., March 1976, Rand Report No. R-1945-PBRP/RC.

Wilson, Walter A., "The Future Role of Government in Dental Practice and Education," *Journal of the American College of Dentists*, Vol. 40, April 1973, pp. 111–116.

Wing, Kenneth R., *The Law and the Public's Health*, St. Louis, Mo.: C. V. Mosby Co., 1976.

Zubkoff, Michael and James Blumstein, *Framework for Government Intervention in the Health Sector*, Lexington, Mass.: D.C. Health, 1976.

FEDERALISM, THE FEDERAL GOVERNMENT, AND HEALTH AND HEALTH CARE

Altenstetter, Christa and James W. Bjorkman, "The Rediscovery of Federalism: The Impact of Federal Child Health Programs in Connecticut State Health Policy Formation and Service Delivery," in R. Thomas and C. O. Jones, eds., *Public Policy-Making in a Federal System*, Beverly-Hills, Calif.: Sage Publications, 1976, pp. 217–237.

Altenstetter, Christa and James W. Bjorkman, "Policy, Politics and Child Health, Four Decades of Federal Initiative and State Response," *Journal of Health Politics, Policy and Law*, Vol. 3, Summer 1978, pp. 196–234.

Altman, Stuart H. and Harvey M. Sapolsky, eds., *Federal Health Programs. Problems and Prospects*, Cambridge: Lexington Books, 1981.

Banta, David, "The Federal Legislative Process and Health Care," in Steven Jonas, ed., *Health Care Delivery in the United States*, New York: Springer Publishing Co., 1977, pp. 329–345.

Baydin, Lynda D., "The End-Stage Renal Disease Networks: An Attempt Through Federal Regulation to Regionalize Health Care Delivery," *Medical Care*, Vol. 15, July 1977, pp. 586–598.

Berkowitz, Edward D., "Rehabilitation: The Federal Government's Response to Disability, 1935–1954," unpublished doctoral dissertation, Northwestern University, 1976. Also, New York: Arno Press, 1980.

Bloom, Bernard S. and Samuel P. Martin, "The Role of the Federal Government in Financing Health and Medical Services," *Journal of Medical Education*, Vol. 51, March 1976, pp. 161–169.

Blumstein, James F., "Foundations of Federal Fertility Policy," *Milbank Memorial Fund Quarterly/Health and Society*, Vol. 52, Spring 1974, pp. 131–168.

Brown, Lawrence D., "The Formulation of Federal Health Care Policy," *Bulletin of the New York Academy of Medicine*, Vol. 54, January 1978, pp. 45–58.

Bryant, John H., Myron E. Wegman, Reuel A. Stallones, Lester Breslow and Cecil G. Sheps, "The Impact of the New Federalism on Schools of Public Health," *Milbank Memorial Fund Quarterly/Health and Society*, Vol. 51, Fall 1973, pp. 435–472.

Budetti, Peter P., John Butler and Peggy McManus, "Federal Health Program Reform: Implications for Child Health," *Milbank Memorial Fund Quarterly/Health and Society*, Vol. 60, No. 1, Winter 1982, pp. 155–181.

Buntz, C. Gregory, Theodore F. Macaluso and Jay A. Azarow, "Federal Influence on State Health Policy," *Journal of Health Politics, Policy and Law*, Vol. 3, Spring 1978, pp. 71–86.

Carter, G. M., D. Schu, J. E. Koehler, R. L. Slighton and A. P. Williams, Jr., *Federal Manpower Legislation and the Academic Health Centers: An Interim Report*, Santa Monica, Calif.: Rand Corp., April 1974, Rand Report No. 4-1464-HEW.

Chapman, Carleton B. and John M. Talmadge, "Historical and Political Background of Federal Health Care Legislation," *Law and Contemporary Problems*, Vol. 35, Spring, 1970, pp. 334–347.

Decker, Barry, "Federal Strategies and the Quality of Local Health Care," in Arthur Levin, ed., *Health Services: The Local Perspective*, Proceedings of the Academy of Political Science, Vol. 32, No. 3, New York: The Academy of Political Science, 1977, pp. 200–214.

Derzon, Robert A., *A Legitimate Role of Government in the Private Health Services System, 1979*,

Michael M. Davis Lecture, Chicago: University of Chicago Center for Health Administration Studies, Graduate School of Business, 1979.

Drew, David E., John G. Wirt, F. W. Finnegan, M. C. Fujisaki and A. L. Laniear, *The Effects of Federal Funds Upon Selected Health-Related Disciplines*, Santa Monica, Calif.: Rand Corp., March 1976, Rand Report No. R-1944-PBRP.

Dunham, Andrew B. and Theodore Marmor, "Federal Policy and Health: Recent Trends and Different Perspectives," in Theodore J. Lowi and Alan Stone, eds., *Nationalizing Government: Public Policies in America*, Beverly Hills, Calif.: Sage Publications, 1978.

Edwards, Charles C., "The Federal Involvement in Health, A Personal View of Current Problems and Future Needs," *New England Journal of Medicine*, Vol. 292, March 13, 1975, pp. 559–562.

Foltz, Anne-Marie, "The Development of Ambiguous Federal Policy: Early and Periodic Screening, Diagnosis and Treatment (EPSDT)," *Milbank Memorial Fund Quarterly/Health and Society*, Vol. 53, Winter 1975, pp. 35–64.

Foltz, Anne-Marie, *Uncertainties of Federal Child Health Politics: Impact in Two States*, DHEW Pub. No. (PHS) 78-3190, Hyattsville, Md.: National Center for Health Services Research, 1978.

Fox, Peter D., "Access to Medical Care for the Poor: The Federal Perspective," *Medical Care*, Vol. 10, May–June 1972, pp. 272–277.

Fritschler, A. Lee, *Smoking and Politics: Policymaking and the Federal Bureaucracy*, Englewood Cliffs, N.J.: Prentice-Hall, 1975.

Glaser, William A., *Federalism in Canadian Health Services—Lessons for the United States*, Preprint Series, New York: Center for the Social Sciences, Columbia University, December 1977.

Gold, Byron D., "Role of the Federal Government in the Provision of Social Services to Older Persons," *Annals of the American Academy of Political and Social Science*, Vol. 415, September 1974, pp. 55–69.

Hageboeck, Helen E., "An Analysis of the Impact of Federal Legislation on Community Based Health Services to Functionally Dependent Adults," unpublished doctoral dissertation, University of Iowa, 1978, Microfilm No. 79-02, 907.

Jaeger, Boi Jon, "Hospitals and the Federal Government: A Study of the Development and Outcomes of Public Policy," unpublished doctoral dissertation, Duke University, 1971, Microfilm No. 72-10, 887.

Jones, E. Terrence, "The Impact of Federal Aid on the Quality of Life: The Case of Infant Health," *Social Indicators Research*, Vol. 1, September 1974, pp. 209–216.

Judd, Leda R., "Federal Involvement in Health Care After 1945," *Current History*, Vol. 12, May–June 1977, pp. 201–206, 227–228.

Koleda, Michael, Carol Burke and Jane S. Willems, *The Federal Health Dollar: 1969–1976, A Chartbook Analysis of Activities Supported and Strategies Pursued in Federal Expenditures for Health*, Washington, D.C.: Center for Health Policy Studies, National Planning Association, February 1977.

Komaroff, Anthony L. and Paul J. Duffell, "An Evaluation of Selected Federal Categorical Health Programs for the Poor," *American Journal of Public Health*, Vol. 66, March 1976, pp. 255–261.

Lostetter, John O. and John E. Chapman, "The Participation of the United States Government in Providing Financial Support for Medical Education," *Health Policy and Education*, Vol. 1, No. 1, 1979, pp. 27–65.

Martin, Edward D., "Federal Initiative in Rural Health," *Public Health Reports*, Vol. 90, July–August 1975, pp. 291–297.

Mooney, Anne, "The Great Society and Health: Policies for Narrowing the Gaps in Health Status Between the Poor and the Nonpoor." *Medical Care*, Vol. 15, August 1977, pp. 611–619.

National Planning Association, *Chartbook of Federal Health Spending, 1969–1974*, Washington, D.C.: National Planning Association, Center for Health Policy Studies, August 1974.

National Planning Association, *The Federal Health Dollar: 1969–1974*, Washington, D.C.: National Planning Association, Center for Health Policy Studies, 1977.

Penchansky, Roy and Elizabeth Axelson, "Old Values, New Federalism and Program Evaluation," *Medical Care*, Vol. 12, November 1974, pp. 893–905.

Perkoff, Gerald, "The Impact of Federal Programs, Long-Term Dialysis Programs: New Selection Criteria, New Problems," *The Hastings Center Report*, Vol. 6, June 1976, pp. 8–13.

Prussin, Jeffrey A., "The Nursing Home Administrator as an Effective Political Advocate: An Overview of the Federal Arena," *Journal of Long Term Care Administration*, Vol. 4, No. 4, 1976, pp. 1–13.

Raskin, Ira E., "Conceptual Framework for Research on the Cost–Effective Allocation of Federal Resources," *Socio-Economic Planning Sciences*, Vol. 9, February 1975, pp. 1–10.

Rich, Robert F., "Selective Utilization of Social Sciences Related Information by Federal Policy-Makers," *Inquiry*, Vol. 12, September 1975, pp. 239–245.

Roemer, Milton I. and Mary H. McClanahan, "Impact of Government Programs on Voluntary Hospitals," *Public Health Reports*, Vol. 75, June 1960, pp. 537–544.

Russell, Louise B., "Effects of Inflation on Federal Health Spending," *Medical Care*, Vol. 13, September 1975, pp. 713–721.

Russell, Louise B., "Inflation and the Federal Role in Health," in Michael Zubkoff, ed., *Health: A Victim or Cause of Inflation?*, New York: Prodist, Neale Watson Academic Publishers, 1976, pp. 225–244.

Russell, Louise B. and Carol S. Burke, "The Political Economy of Federal Health Programs in the United States: An Historical Review," *International Journal of Health Services*, Vol. 8, No. 1, 1978, pp. 55–77.

Russell, Louise B., Blair Bourque, Daniel Bourque and Carol Burke, *Federal Health Spending, 1969–1974*, Washington, D.C.: Center for Health Policy Studies, National Planning Association, August 1974.

Schlesinger, Edward R., "The Impact of Federal Legislation on Maternal and Child Health Services in the United States," *Milbank Memorial Fund Quarterly/Health and Society*, Vol. 52, Winter 1974, pp. 1–14.

Shannon, James A., "Federal Support of Biomedical Sciences, Development and Academic Impact," *Journal of Medical Education*, Vol. 51, July 1976, Supplement, pp. 1–98.

Smith, David G., "Emerging Patterns of Federalism: The Case of Public Health," in Mary F. Arnold, L. Vaughn Blankenship and John M. Hess, eds., *Administering Health Systems, Issues and Perspectives*, Chicago, Ill: Aldine Publishing Co., 1971, pp. 131–142.

Stone, Deborah, "The Problem of Monopoly Power in Federal Health Policy," *Milbank Memorial Fund Quarterly/Health and Society*, Vol. 58, Winter 1980, pp. 50–53.

Vladeck, Bruce C., "The Design of Failure. Health Policy and the Structure of Federalism," *Journal of Health Politics, Policy and Law*, Vol. 4, Fall 1979, pp. 522–535.

Warner, Judith S., "Trends in the Federal Regulation of Physicians' Fees," *Inquiry*, Vol. 13, December 1976, pp. 364–370.

Warren, B. S., "Coordination and Expansion of Federal Health Activities," *Public Health Reports*, Vol. 9, May–June 1975, pp. 270–277.

White, Ben B., *Falling Arches: The Case Against Federal Intervention in the Practice of Medicine*, Hicksville, N.Y.: Exposition Press, 1977.

Williams, A. P., et al., "The Effect of Federal Biomedical Research *Programs on Academic Medical Centers*, Santa Monica, Calif.: Rand Corp., March 1976, Rand Report No. R-1943-PBRP.

Zwick, Daniel I. and Clyde J. Behney, "Federal Health Services Grants, 1965–1975," *Public Health Reports*, Vol. 91, November–December 1976, pp. 493–495.

Federal Bureaucracy

Chu, Franklin D. and Sharland Trotter, *The Madness Establishment*, Ralph Nader's Study Group Report on the National Institute of Mental Health, New York: Grossman Publishers, 1974.

Falkson, Joseph L., "Minor Skirmish in a Monumental Struggle: HEW's Analysis of Mental Health Services," *Policy Analysis*, Vol. 2, Winter 1976, pp. 93–119.

Feder, Judith M., "The Social Security Administration and Medicare: A Strategy of Implementation," in Kenneth M. Friedman and Stuart H. Rakoff, eds., *Toward a National Policy Health Policy: Public Policy and the Control of Health Care Cost*, Lexington, Mass.: Lexington Books, 1976.

Fredrickson, Donald S., "The National Institute of Health: Yesterday, Today and Tomorrow," *Public Health Reports*, Vol. 93, November–December 1978, pp. 642–647.

Greenberg, George D., "Reorganization Reconsidered: The U.S. Public Health Service 1960–1973," *Public Policy*, Vol. 23, Fall 1975, pp. 483–522.

Greenberg, George D., "Constraints on Management and Secretarial Behavior at HEW," *Polity*, Vol. 13, Fall 1980, pp. 57–79.

Miles, Rufus E. Jr., *The Department of Health, Education and Welfare*, New York: Praeger Publishers, 1974, pp. 168–243.

Sherman, John F., "The Organization and Structure of the National Institutes of Health," *New England Journal of Medicine*, Vol. 297, July 1977, pp. 18–26.

Thompson, Frank J., *Health Policy and the Bureaucracy Politics and Implementation*, Cambridge: MIT Press, 1981.

Federal–State Relations in Health and Health Care

Altenstetter, Christa and James Bjorkman, "Federal Impacts on State Health Policy: Lessons from Connecticut and Vermont," New Haven, Conn.: Yale Health Policy Project, 1975.

Altenstetter, Christa and James W. Bjorkman, "The Impact of Federal Child Health Programs in Connecticut State Health Policy Formation and Service Delivery: The Rediscovery of Federalism," in R. Thomas and C. O. Jones, ed., *Public Policy Making in a Federal System*, Sage Yearbooks in Politics and Public Policy, Beverly-Hills, Calif.: Sage Publications, 1976, Vol. 111, pp. 217–237.

Altenstetter, Christa and James W. Bjorkman, *Federal–State Health Policies and Impacts: The Politics of Implementation*, Washington, D.C.: University Press of America, 1978.

Buntz, C. Gregory, Theodore F. Macaluso and Jay A. Azarow, "Federal Influence on State Health Policy," *Journal of Health Politics, Policy and Law*, Vol. 3, Spring 1978, pp. 71–86.

Foltz, Anne-Marie, *Uncertainties of Federal Child Health Politics: Impact in Two States*, DHEW Pub. No. (PHS) 78-3190, Washington, D.C.: National Center for Health Services Research, April 1978.

Foltz, Anne-Marie and Donna Brown, "State Response to Federal Policy: Children, EPSDT and the Medicaid Muddle," *Medical Care*, Vol. 13, August 1975, pp. 630–642.

Lashof, Joyce C. and Mark H. Lepper, "Federal–State–Local Partnership in Health," in United States Public Health Service, Health Resources Administration, eds., *Health in America: 1776–1976*, DHEW Pub. No. (HRA) 76-616, Washington, D.C.: U.S. Government Printing Office, 1976, pp. 122–137.

Passel Peter and Leonard Ross, *State Policies and Federal Programs: Priorities and Constraints*, New York: Praeger Publishers, 1978.

Price, Isabel, "What's Happening to Federally Aided Health Programs Under State Departments of Human Resources," *Public Health Reports*, Vol. 93, May–June 1978, pp. 221–231.

Robins, Leonard, "The Impact of Decategorizing Federal Programs: Before and After 314 (d)," *American Journal of Public Health*, Vol. 62, January 1972, pp. 24–29.

Robins, Leonard, "The Impact of Converting Categorical into Block Grants: The Lessons from the 314 (d) Block Grant in the Partnership for Health Act," *Publius*, Vol. 6, Winter 1975, pp. 49–70.

Scherr, Lawrence, "Coping with Intrusions by State and Federal Government Agencies," *Federal Bulletin*, Vol. 65, No. 3, 1978, pp. 69–80.

Snoke, Albert W. and Parnie S. Snoke, "Linking Private, Public Energies in Health and Welfare Planning," *Hospitals*, Vol. 50, August 16, 1976, pp. 53–58.

Webb, Bruce J., "Impact of Revenue Sharing on Local Health Centers," *The Black Scholar*, Vol. 5, May 1974, pp. 10–15.

ROLE OF THE STATES IN HEALTH AND HEALTH CARE

Altenstetter, Christa and James W. Bjorkman, *Federal-State Health Policies and Impacts: The Politics of Implementation*, Washington, D.C.: University Press of America, 1978.

Bentak, J. M., ed., *A Digest of State Laws Affecting Prepayment of Medical Care, Group Practice and HMO's*, Rockville, Md.: Health Law Center, Germantown, Md.: Aspen Systems Corporation, 1973.

Blendon, Robert J., "The Prospects for State and Local Governments Playing a Broader Role in Health Care in the 1980's," *American Journal of Public Health*, Vol. 71, January 1981, Supplement, pp. 9–14.

Brown, Ray E., "Health Facilities and Health Services," *Inquiry*, Vol. 10, March 1973, Supplement, pp. 17–22. Comment: Melvin A. Glasser, pp. 23–25; J. D. Wallace pp. 26–28. Discussion pp. 29–39.

Chirikos, Thomas N., "State Health Manpower Policy: An Appraisal," *Journal of Community Health*, Vol. 2, Spring 1977, pp. 163–177.

Clarke, Gary J., *Health Programs in the States, A Survey*, New Brunswick, N.J.: Rutgers–The State University, Eagleton Institute of Politics, 1975.

Clarke, Gary J. *Health Expenditures by State Governments*, Washington, D.C.: Georgetown University Health Policy Center, 1976.

Clarke, Gary J., "The Role of the State in the Delivery of Health Services," *American Journal of Public Health*, Vol. 71, January 1981, Supplement, pp. 59–61.

Colner, Alan N., "The Impact of State Government Rate Setting on Hospital Management," *Health Care Management Review*, Vol. 2, Winter 1977, pp. 37–49.

Connor, Gerald R., "State Government Financing of Health Planning," *American Journal of Health Planning*, Vol. 1, October 1976, pp. 48–51.

Davidson, Stephen M., "Variations in State Medicaid Programs," *Journal of Health Politics, Policy and Law*, Vol. 3, Spring 1978, pp. 54–70.

Ellet, T. Van, *State Comprehensive and Catastrophic Health Insurance Plans: An Overview*. Washington, D.C.: George Washington University, Intergovernmental Health Project, 1980.

Ellet, T. van, *Medigap: State Responses to Problems with the Sale of Health Insurance to the Elderly*, Washington, D.C.: George Washington University, Intergovernmental Health Policy Project, 1980.

Freedman, Ben, "Cost of Fragmentation of State Government Operated Health Services," *Inquiry*, Vol. 12, September 1975, pp. 216–227.

Gilbert, Benjamin, Merry-K Moos and C. Arden Miller, "State Level Decision Making for Public Health: The Status of Boards of Health," *Journal of Public Health Policy*, Vol. 3, March 1982, pp. 51–63.

Jain, Sager, ed., "Role of State and Local Governments in Relation to Personal Health Services," *American Journal of Public Health*, Vol. 71, January 1981, Supplement.

Jain, Sager, ed., *Role of State and Local Governments in Relation to Personal Health Services*, Washington, D.C.: American Public Health Association, 1981.

Kovner, Anthony R. and Edward J. Lusk, "State Regulation of Health Care Costs," *Medical Care*, Vol. 13, August 1975, pp. 619–629.

Laird, Maureen, "State Roles in Financing Medical Education," *Journal of Medical Education*, Vol. 51, March 1976, pp. 206–209.

Lavin, John H., "How Would You Fare Under States Health Insurance?," *Medical Economics*, Vol. 53, September 6, 1976, pp. 77–81.

Merritt, Richard and Susan Mertes, *State Innovations in Health*, Washington, D.C.: George Washington University, Intergovernmental Health Policy Project, 1980.

Miller and Byrne, Inc., *Annotated Bibliography: The Impact of Public Health Service Programs and State Government*, Rockville, Md.: Miller and Byrne, April 1977.

Renaud, Marc, "On the Structural Constraints to State Intervention in Health," *International Journal of Health Services*, Vol. 5, No. 4, 1975, pp. 559–572.

Rosenkrantz, Barbara G., *Public Health and the State: Changing Views in Massachusetts, 1842–1936*, Cambridge: Harvard University Press, 1972.

Schramm, Carl J., "Regulatory Hospital Labor Costs: A Case Study in the Politics of State Rate Commissions," *Journal of Health Politics, Policy and Law*, Vol. 3, Fall 1978, pp. 364–374.

Schwartz, Jerome L., "Strategies for Monitoring the Effects of Proposition 13 on Health Services," *Journal of Health Politics, Policy and Law*, Vol. 4, Summer 1979, pp. 142–154.

Snoke, Parnie S. and Albert W. Snoke, "State Role in the Regulation of the Health Delivery System," *University of Toledo Law Review*, Vol. 6, Spring 1975, pp. 617–646.

STATE–LOCAL RELATIONSHIPS

Berger, Stephen, "The Interplay of State and Local Government in Health Care," in Arthur Levin, ed., *Health Services: The Local Perspective*, Proceedings of the Academy of Political Science, Vol. 32, No. 3, New York: The Academy of Political Science, 1977, pp. 63–67.

Fowinkle, Eugene, "The State Role in the Delivery of Local Health Services," in Arthur Levin, ed., *Health Services: The Local Perspective*, Proceedings of the Academy of Political Science, Vol. 32, No. 3, New York: The Academy of Political Science, 1977, pp. 53–62.

Gayer, David, "The Effects of Medicaid on State and Local Government Finances," *National Tax Journal*, Vol. 25, December 1972, pp. 511–519.

LOCAL GOVERNMENT

Bellin, Lowell E. "Local Health Departments: A Prescription Against Obsolescence," in Arthur Levin, ed., *Health Services: The Local Perspective*, Proceedings of the Academy of Political Science, Vol. 32, No. 3, New York: The Academy of Political Science, 1977, pp. 42–52.

Koppel, J. and J. Clark, *The Role of County Government in Medicaid*, Washington, D.C.: National Association of Countries, July 1976.

Ingraham, Norman R., "Formulation of Public Policy in Medical Care: Dynamics of Community Action at Local Level," *American Journal of Public Health*, Vol. 51, August 1961, pp. 1144–1151.

Levin, Arthur, ed., *Health Services: The Local Perspective*, Proceedings of the Academy of Political Science, Vol. 32, No. 3, New York: The Academy of Political Science, 1977.

Miller, C. Arden, "Issues of Health Policy: Local Government and the Public's Health," *American Journal of Public Health*, Vol. 65, December 1975, pp. 1330–1334.

Millman, Michael, "The Role of City Government in Personal Health Services," *American Journal of Public Health*, Vol. 71, January 1981, Supplement, pp. 47–57.

Mytinger, Robert E., "Barriers to Adoption of New Programs as Perceived by Local Health Officers," *Public Health Reports*, Vol. 82, February 1967, pp. 108–114.

Piore, Nora, Purlaine Lieberman ani James Linnane, "Financing Local Health Services," in Arthur Levin, ed., *Health Services: The Local Perspective*, Proceedings of the Academy of Political Science, Vol. 32, No. 3, New York: The Academy of Political Science, 1977, pp. 15–28.

Piore, Nora, Purlaine Lieberman and James Linnane, "Public Expenditures and Private Control? Health Care Dilemma in New York City," *Milbank Memorial Fund Quarterly/Health and Society*, Vol. 55, Winter 1977, pp. 79–116.

Robins, Leonard, "Controlling Health Care Costs," in Arthur Levin, ed., *Health Services: The Local Perspective*, Proceedings of the Academy of Political Science, Vol. 32, No. 3, New York: The Academy of Political Science, 1977, pp. 215–226.

Schwartz, Jerome L., "Strategies for Monitoring the Effects of Proposition 13 on Health Services," *Journal of Health Politics, Policy and Law*, Vol. 4, Summer 1979, pp. 142–154.

Shonick, William and Walter Price, "Reorganizations of Health Agencies by Local Government in American Urban Centers: What Do They Portend for 'Public Health'," *Milbank Memorial Fund Quarterly/Health and Society*, Vol. 55, Spring 1977, pp. 233–271.

Shonick, William and Walter Price, "Organizational Milieus of Local Public Health Units: Analysis of Response to Questionnaire," *Public Health Reports*, Vol. 93, November–December 1978, pp. 648–665.

PARTICIPATORY DEMOCRACY

Political Parties and Health

Goldsmith, Seth B., "Political Party Platform Planks: A Mechanism for Participation and Prediction?" *American Journal of Public Health*, Vol. 63, July 1973, pp. 594–601.

Silver, George A., "Medical Politics, Health Policy, Party Health Platforms, Promise and Performance," *International Journal of Health Services*, Vol. 6, No. 2, 1976, pp. 331–343.

Interest Group Politics and Health

Alford, Robert R., *Health Care Politics: Ideological and Interest Group Barriers to Reform*, Chicago, Ill.: University of Chicago Press, 1975.

Binstock, Robert H., "Interest-Group Liberalism and the Politics of Aging," *Gerontologist*, Vol. 12, Autumn 1972, Part 1, pp. 265–280.

Congressional Quarterly, *Legislators and Lobbyists: Medicare Over the Years*, Washington, D.C.: Congressional Quarterly, May 1968, 2nd edition.

Drew, Elizabeth, "The Health Syndicate—Washington's Noble Conspirators," *Atlantic Monthly*, Vol. 220, December 1967, pp. 75–82.

Feldstein, Paul J., *Health Associations and the Demand for Legislation, The Political Economy of Health*, Cambridge: Ballinger Publishing Co., 1977.

Feldstein, Paul J., "Health Associations and the Legislative Process," University of Michigan, 1982.

Felicetti, Daniel A., *Mental Health and Retardation Politics: The Mind Lobbies in Congress*, New York: Praeger Publishers, 1975.

Flash, William, Milton Roemer and Sander Kelman, "Stalking the Politics of Health Care Reform: Three Critical Perspectives on Robert Alford's 'Health Care Politics Ideological and Interest Group Barriers to Reform'," *Journal of Health Politics, Policy and Law*, Vol. 1, Spring 1976, pp. 112–129.

Marmor, Theodore and D. Thomas, "Doctors, Politics and Pay Disputes: Pressure Group Politics Revisited," *British Journal of Political Science*, Vol. 2, October 1972, pp. 421–442.

Novello, Dorothy J., "People, Power and Politics for Health Care," in National League for Nursing, eds., *People, Power, Politics for Health Care*, New York: National League for Nursing, 1976, pp. 1–8.

Poen, Monte M., *Harry S. Truman Versus the Medical Lobby: The Genesis of Medicare*, Columbia, Mo.: University of Missouri Press, 1979.

Pond, M. Allen, "Politics of Social Change: Abortion Reform, The Role of Health Professionals in the Legislative Process," *American Journal of Public Health*, Vol. 61, May 1971, pp. 904–909.

Rosen, George, "The Committee of One Hundred on National Health and the Campaign for a National Health Department, 1906–1912," *American Journal of Public Health*, Vol. 62, February, 1972, pp. 261–263.

Ward, Paul D., "Health Lobbies: Vested Interests and Pressure Politic," in Douglass Cater and Philip R. Lee, eds., *Politics of Health*, New York: Medcom Press, 1972.

Weller, G. R., "From 'Pressure Group Politics' to 'Medical–Industrial Complex': The Development of Approaches to the Politics of Health," *Journal of Health Politics, Policy, and Law*, Vol. 1, Winter 1977, pp. 444–470.

Wier, Richard A., "Patterns of Interaction Between Interest Groups and the Canadian Political System: The Case of the Canadian Medical Association," unpblished doctoral dissertation, Georgetown University, 1970, Microfilm No. 70-23, 874.

Community Power Structure and Health

Arnold, Mary F. and Isabel M. Welsh, "Community Politics and Health Planning," in Mary F. Arnold, L. Vaughn Blankenship and John M. Hess, eds., *Administering Health Systems: Issues and Perspectives*, Chicago: Aldine–Atherton, 1971, pp. 154–175.

Belknap, Ivan and John G. Steinle, *The Community and Its Hospitals: A Comparative Analysis*, Syracuse, N.Y.: Syracuse University Press, 1963.

Berg, Robert L., "Movers' and 'Statics' Refine Political Strategies in HSA's," *Hospital Progress*, Vol. 58, September 1977, pp. 64–69.

Blankenship, L. Vaughn and Ray H. Elling, "Effects of Community Power on Hospital Organization," in Mary F. Arnold, L. Vaughn Blankenship and John M. Hess, eds., *Administering Health Systems: Issues and Perspectives*, Chicago: Aldine Publishing Co., 1971, pp. 176–196.

Blankenship, L. Vaughn, "Organizational Support and Community Leadership in Two New York State Communities," unpublished doctoral dissertation, Cornell University, 1962.

Blankenship, L. Vaughn and Ray H. Elling, "Organizational Support and Community Power Structure: The Hospital," *Journal of Health and Human Behavior*, Vol. 3, Winter 1962, pp. 257–269.

Elling, Ray H., "The Hospital Support Game in Urban Center," in Eliot Freidson, ed., *The Hospital in Modern Society*, New York: The Free Press, 1963, pp. 73–111.

Elling, Ray H., "The Shifting Power Structure in Health," *Milbank Memorial Fund Quarterly*, Vol. 46, January 1968, Part 2, pp. 119–144.

Elling, Ray H. and Sandor Halebsky, "Organizational Differentiation and Support: A Conceptual Framework," *Adm. Science Quarterly*, Vol. 6, September 1961, pp. 185–209. Also in W. Richard Scott and Edmund Volkart, eds., *Readings in the Sociology of Medical Institutions*, New York: John Wiley & Sons, 1966, pp. 543–557.

Elling, Ray H. and Ollie J. Lee, "Formal Connections of Community Leadership to the Health System," *Milbank Memorial Fund Quarterly*, Vol. 44, July 1966, Part I, pp. 294–306.

Elling, Ray H. and Milton I. Roemer, "Determinants of Community Support," *Hospital Administration*, Vol. 6, Summer 1961, pp. 17–34.

Freeborn, Donald K. and Benjamin J. Darsky, "A Study of the Power Structure of the Medical Community," *Medical Care*, Vol. 12, January 1974, pp. 1–12.

Gossert, Daniel J. and C. Arden Miller, "State Boards of Health, Their Members and Commitments," *American Journal of Public Health*, Vol. 63, June 1973, pp. 486–493.

Hanson, Robert C., "The Systemic Linkage Hypothesis and Role Consensus Patterns in Hospital-Community Relations," *American Sociological Review*, Vol. 27, June 1962, pp. 304–313.

Holloway, Robert G., Jay H. Artis, and Walter E. Freeman, "The Participation Patterns of 'Economic Influentials' and Their Control of a Hospital Board of Trustees," *Journal of Health and Human Behavior*, Vol. 4, Summer 1963, pp. 88–98.

Hunter, Floyd, Ruth C. Schaffer, and Cecil G. Sheps, *Community Organization: Action and Inaction*, Chapel Hill: University of North Carolina Press, 1956.

Kupst, Mary Jo, Phil Reidda and Thomas F. McGee, "Community Mental Health Boards: A Comparison of Their Development, Functions, and Powers by Board Members and Mental Health Center Staff," *Community Mental Health Journal*, Vol. 11, Fall 1975, pp. 249–256.

Laur, Robert J., "A Study of the Extramural Sector of Governing Board Responsibility in Non-Profit General Hospitals: Trustee Interest in Interorganizational Relations," Unpublished Doctoral Dissertation, University of Minnesota, 1969, Microfilm No. 69-20, 032.

Miller, Paul A., "The Process of Decision-Making Within the Context of Community Organization," *Rural Sociology*, Vol. 17, June 1952, pp. 153–161.

Perrow, Charles, "Organizational Prestige: Some Functions and Dysfunctions, *American Journal of Sociology*, Vol. 66, January 1961, pp. 335–341.

Saunders, J. V. D. and J. H. Bruehing, "Hospital–Community Relations in Mississippi," *Rural Sociology*, Vol. 24, March 1959, pp. 48–51.

Smith, David B. and Carl G. Homer, "The Hospital Support Group Revisited," *Journal of Health Politics, Policy and Law*, Vol. 2, Summer 1977, pp. 257–265.

Smith, Richard A., "Community Power and Decision Making: A Replication and Extension of Hawley," *American Sociological Review*, Vol. 41, August 1976, pp. 691–705.

Thacker, Stephen B., Carolee Osborne and Eva J. Salber, "Health Care Decision Making in a Southern County," *Journal of Community Health*, Vol. 3, Summer 1978, pp. 347–356.

Warnecke, Richard B., Saxon Graham, William Mosher and Erwin B. Montgomery, "Health Guides as Influentials in Central Buffalo," *Journal of Health and Social Behavior*, Vol. 17, March 1976, pp. 22–34.

White, Marjorie A., "Attitudes of Influentials Toward Health and Illness Care Delivery," unpublished doctoral dissertation, Case Western Review University, 1976, Microfilm No. 76-28, 428.

Community Participation

Anderson, Donna M. and Markay Kerr, "Citizen Influence in Health Service Programs," *American Journal of Public Health*, Vol. 61, August 1971, pp. 1518–1523.

Anderson, John B., "Associations Between Participation in Community Mental Health Planning and Adherence to Community Mental Health Ideology: A Study of Citizen Participation in Two Community Mental Health Center Planning Projects," unpublished doctoral dissertation, Ohio State University, 1973, Microfilm No. 73-26, 760.

Andrejewski, Norman S., Carl G. Homer and Richard H. Schlesinger, "Consumer Participation in Health Planning," *Health Education Monographs*, No. 32, 1972, pp. 23–36.

Arnold, Mary F. and Isabel M. Welsh, "Community Politics and Health Planning," in Mary F. Arnold, L. Vaughn Blankenship and John M. Hess, eds., *Administrating Health Systems: Issues and Perspectives*, Chicago: Aldine Publishing Co., 1971, pp. 154–175.

Bazell, R. J., "Health Radicals: Crusade to Shift Medical Power to the People," *Science*, Vol. 173, August 6, 1971, pp. 506–509.

Bellin, Lowell E., Florence Kavaler, and Al Schwarz, "Phase One of Consumer Participation in Policies of 22 Voluntary Hospitals in New York City," *American Journal of Public Health*, Vol. 62, October 1972, pp. 1370–1378.

Brandon, William, "Politics, Administration and Conflict in Neighborhood Health Centers," *Journal of Health Politics, Policy and Law*, Vol. 2, Spring 1977, pp. 79–99.

Burlage, Robb K., "Confrontation: Consumer Forces will Liberate Systems," *Modern Hospital*, Vol. 3, December 1968, pp. 81+.

Cornely, Paul B., "Community Participation and Control: A Possible Answer to Racism in Health," *Milbank Memorial Fund Quarterly/Health and Society*, Vol. 48, April 1970, Part 2, pp. 347–362.

Dana, Bess, "Consumer Health Education," in Arthur Levin, ed., *Health Services: The Local Perspective*, Proceedings of the Academy of Political Science, Vol. 32, No. 3, New York: The Academy of Political Science, 1977, pp. 182–191.

Danaceau, Paul, *Consumer Participation in Health Care: How it's Working*, Arlington, Va.: Human Services Institute for Children and Families, 1975. Also available from Springfield, Va.: National Technical Information Service, 1975.

Doong, Jean, Consumer Participation in Health Planning: An Annotated *Bibliography*, Health Planning Bibliography Series No. 2, DHEW Pub. No. (HRA) 77-14551, Rockville, Md.: National Health Planning Information Center, 1976.

Douglass, Chester W., "Effect of Provider Attitudes in Community Health Decision-Making," *Medical Care*, Vol. 11, March–April 1973, pp. 135–144.

Douglass, Chester W., "Representation Patterns in Community Health Decision-Making," *Journal of Health and Social Behavior*, Vol. 14, March 1973, pp. 80–86.

Douglass, Chester W., "Consumer Influence in Health Planning in the Urban Ghetto," *Inquiry*, Vol. 12, June 1975, pp. 157–163.

Duvall, Wallace, L., "Consumer Participation in Health Planning," *Hospital Administration*, Vol. 16, Fall 1971, pp. 35–49.

Falkson, Joseph L., "Review Article: An Evaluation of Policy-Related Research on Citizen Participation in Municipal Health Service Systems," *Medical Care Review*, Vol. 33, February 1976, pp. 156–221.

Feingold, Eugene, *Citizen Participation: A Review of the Issues, The Citizenry and the Hospital*, 1973 National Forum on the Citizenry and the Hospital, Durham, N.C.: Duke University, Program in Hospital Administration, 1973.

Fox, Daniel M. and Jean W. Wofford, "Citizen Participation: A Substitute for Action," *Health Education Monographs*, No. 32, 1972, pp. 37–40.

Glogow, Eli, "Community Participation and Sharing in Control of Public Health Services," *Health Service Reports*, Vol. 88, May 1973, pp. 442–448.

Gordon, Jeffrey B., "The Politics of Community Medicine Projects: A Conflict Analysis," *Medical Care*, Vol. 7, November–December 1969, pp. 419–428.

Gosfield, Alice, *PSRO's: The Law and the Health Consumer*, Cambridge: Ballinger Publishing Co., 1975.

Gosfield, Alice, "Consumer Accountability in PSRO's," *University of Toledo Review*, Vol. 6, Spring 1975, pp. 764–803.

Gosfield, Alice, "Approaches of Nine Federal Health Agencies to Patients' Rights and Consumer Participation: An Overview of Responses of Agency Representatives to an Interview Survey," *Public Health Reports*, Vol. 91, September–October 1976, pp. 403–405.

Greer, Ann L., "Training Board Members for Health Planning Agencies: A Review of the Literature," *Public Health Reports*, Vol. 91, January–February 1976, pp. 56–61.

Grossman, Randolph M., "Voting Behavior of HSA Interest Groups: A Case Study," *American Journal of Public Health*, Vol. 68, December 1978, pp. 1191–1194.

Hersch, Charles, "Social History, Mental Health and Community Control," *American Psychologist*, Vol. 27, August 1972, pp. 749–754.

Hessler, Richard M., "Consumer Participation, Social Organization and Culture: a Neighborhood Health Center for Chicanos," *Human Organization*, Vol. 36, Summer 1977, pp. 124–134.

Hollister, Robert M., "From Consumer Participation to Community Control of Neighborhood Health Centers," unpublished doctoral dissertation, Massachusetts Institute of Technology, 1971.

Holton, Wilfred E., Peter K. New, and Richard M. Hessler, "Citizen Participation and Conflict," *Administration in Mental Health*, Vol. 1, Fall 1973, pp. 96–103.

Jonas, Steven, "A Theoretical Approach to the Question of 'Community Control' of Health Services Facilities," *American Journal of Public Health*, Vol. 61, May 1971, pp. 916–921.

Jonas, Steven, "Limitations of Community Control of Health Facilities and Services," *American Journal of Public Health*, Vol. 68, June 1978, pp. 541–543.

Kane, Daniel, "Community Participation in the Health Services System," *Hospital Administration*, Vol. 16, Winter 1971, pp. 36–43.

Kane, Thomas J., "Citizen Participation in Decision-Making: Myth or Strategy," *Administration on Mental Health*, Vol. 3, Spring 1975, pp. 29–45.

Kelman, Howard R., "Evaluation of Health Care Quality by Consumers," *International Journal of Health Services*, Vol. 6, No. 3, 1976, pp. 431–441.

Klein, Rudolf and Janet Lewis, *The Politics of Consumer Representstion: A Study of Community Health Councils*, London: Center for Studies in Social Policy, 1976.

Koseki, L. K. and J. Hayakawa, "Consumer Participation and Community Organization Practice—Implications of National Health Legislation," *Medical Care*, Vol. 17, No. 3, March 1979, pp. 244–254.

Kramer, Marlene, "Consumer's Influence on Health Care," *Nursing Outlook*, Vol. 20, September 1972, pp. 574–578.

Lavery, Thomas J., "Consumer Participation at a Neighborhood Health Center," unpublished doctoral dissertation, University of Iowa, 1978, Microfilm No. 70-01, 899.

Lipsky, Michael and Morris Lounds, "Citizen Participation and Health Care: Problems of Government Induced Participation," *Journal of Health Politics, Policy and Law*, Vol. 1, Spring 1976, pp. 85–111.

Marmor, Theodore R. and James A. Morone, "Representing Consumer Interests: Imbalanced Markets, Health Planning and the HSA's," *Milbank Memorial Fund Quarterly/Health and Society*, Vol. 58, Winter 1980, pp. 125–165.

McNamara, John J., "Communities and Control of Health Services," *Inquiry*, Vol. 9, September 1972, pp. 64–69.

MacStravic, Robin E., "Community Participation and Influences in Health Care Delivery: Expectations, Performance and Satisfaction," unpublished doctoral dissertation, University of Minnesota, 1973, Microfilm No. 74-10, 539.

MacStravic, Robin E., "Scalability of Community Participation in Health Program Decisions," *Health Services Research*, Vol. 10, Spring 1975, pp. 76–81.

Metsch, Jonathan M. and James E. Veney, "Measuring the Outcome of Consumer Participation," *Journal of Health and Social Behavior*, Vol. 14, December 1973, pp. 368–374.

Metsch, Jonathan M. and James E. Veney, "A Model of the Adaptive Behavior of Hospital Administrators to the Mandate to Implement Consumer Participation," *Medical Care*, Vol. 12, April
1974, pp. 338–350.

Metsch, Jonathan M. and James E. Veney, "Consumer Participation and Social Accountability,"
Medical Care, Vol. 14, April 1976, pp. 283–293.

Metsch, Jonathan, Martin Weitzner and Ann Berson, "Impact of Training on Consumer Participation in the Delivery of Health Services," *Health Education Monographs*, Vol. 3, Fall 1975, pp.
251–261.

Milio, Nancy, "Dimensions of Consumer Participation and National Health Legislation," *American
Journal of Public Health*, Vol. 64, April 1974, pp, 357–363.

Millis, John S., "The Future of Medicine: The Role of the Consumer," *Journal of the American
Medical Association*, Vol. 210, October 20, 1969, pp. 498–501.

Moore, Mary L., "The Role of Hostility and Militancy in Indigenous Community Health Advisory
Groups," *American Journal of Public Health*, Vol. 61, May 1971, pp. 922–930.

Mushkin, Selma J., ed., *Consumer Incentives for Health Care*, New York: Prodist, 1974.

New, Peter Kong-Ming, Richard M. Hessler and Phyllis B. Carter, "Consumer Control and Public
Accountability," *Anthropological Quarterly*, Vol. 46, July 1973, pp. 196–213.

Newman, Ian Mount, ed., *Consumer Behavior in the Health Marketplace, A Symposium Proceedings, 1976*, Lincoln, Neb.: University of Nebraska, Nebraska Center for Health Education,
1976.

Nutt, Paul C., "Merits of Using Experts or Consumers as Members of Planning Groups: A Field
Experiment in Health Planning," *Academy of Management Journal*, Vol. 19, September 1976,
pp. 378–394.

Oakes, Charles G., *The Walking Patient and the Health Crisis*, Columbia: University of South
Carolina Press, 1973.

Office of Consumer Education and Information, Health Maintenance Organization Service, *Selected Papers on Consumerism in the HMO Movement*, DHEW Pub. No. (HSM) 73-13012,
Washington, D.C.: U.S. Government Printing Office, 1973.

Padgett, Edward R., "The Political Effects of Consumer Participation—A Political Scientist's
View," *Health Education Monographs*, No. 32, 1972, pp. 67–78.

Padilla, Elena, "Community Participation in Health Affairs," in Arthur Levin, ed., *Health Services:
The Local Perspective*, Proceedings of the Academy of Political Science, Vol. 32, No. 3, New
York: The Academy of Political Science, 1977, pp. 227–237.

Palmer, Boyd Z., Roger L. Sisson, Lorrinne Kyle and Adele Hebb, "Community Participation in
the Planning Process," *Health Education Monographs*, No. 32, 1972, pp. 5–22.

Papp, Warren, R., "Consumer-Based Boards of Health Centers: Structural Problems in Achieving
Effective Control," *American Journal of Public Health*, Vol. 68, June 1978, pp. 578–582.

Partridge, Kay B., "Community and Professional Participation in Decision-Making at a Health
Center," *Health Services Reports*, Vol. 88, June–July 1973, pp. 527–534.

Partridge, Kay B. and Paul E. White, "Community and Professional Participation in Decision-
Making at a Health Center: A Methodology for Analysis," *Health Services Reports*, Vol. 87,
April 1972, pp. 336–342.

Pecarchik, Robert, Edmund Ricci and Bardin Nelson Jr., "Potential Contribution of Consumers to
an Integrated Health Care System," *Public Health Reports*, Vol. 91, January–February 1976,
pp. 72–76.

Ready, William E., "The Consumer's Role in the Politics of Health Planning," *Health Education
Monographs*, No. 32, 1972, pp. 51–58.

Riska, Elianne and James A. Taylor, "Consumer and Provider Views on Health Policy and Health
Legislation," in E. Gartly Jaco, ed., *Patients, Physicians and Illness*, New York: The Free
Press, 1979, pp. 356–359, 3rd edition.

Rivkin, M. O. and P. J. Bush, "The Satisfaction Continuum in Health Care: Consumer and Provider Preferences," in Selma J. Mushkin, ed., *Consumer Incentives for Health Care*, New York: Prodist, 1974.

Rogatz, Peter and Marge Rogatz, "Role for the Consumer," *Social Policy*, Vol. 2, January–February 1971, pp. 52–56.

Rosen, Harry, Jonathan Metsch and Samuel Levey, eds., *The Consumer and the Health Care System: Social and Managerial Perspectives*, Health Systems Management Series No. 9, New York: Halsted Press (Spectrum Publishers), 1977.

Salber, Eva J., *Caring and Curing, Community Participation in Health Services*, New York: Prodist, 1975.

Sanders, Irwin T. and Ann Brownlee, "Health in the Community," in Howard E. Freeman, Sol Levine and Leo G. Reeder, eds., *Handbook of Medical Sociology*, Englewood Cliffs, N.J.: Prentice-Hall, 1979, 3rd edition, pp. 412–436.

Sheps, Cecil G., "The Influence of Consumer Sponsorship on Medical Services," *Milbank Memorial Fund Quarterly/Health and Society*, Vol. 50, October 1972, Part II, pp. 41–72.

Silver, George A., "Community Participation in Health Resource Allocation," *International Journal of Health Services*," Vol. 3, No. 2, 1973, pp. 117–131.

Smith, Richard A., "Community-Power and Decision Making: A Replication and Extension of Hawley," *American Sociological Review*, Vol. 41, August 1976, pp. 691–705.

Stamps, Paula L., Thomas E. Duston, Edward J. Rising, Donald Allen and Marcia Bondy-Levy, "How Consumers Exercise Control Through Their Bill-Paying Patterns," *Inquiry*, Vol. 15, June 1978, pp. 151–159.

Steinberg, Marcia K., "Consumer Participation in a Health Care Organization—The Case of the Health Insurance Plan of Greater New York," unpublished doctoral dissertation, City University of New York, 1977, Microfilm No. 77-14,590.

Stokes, Ann, David Banta and Samuel Putnam, "The Columbia Point Health Association: Evaluation of a Community Health Board," *American Journal of Public Health*, Vol. 62, September 1972, pp. 1229–1234.

Stoller, Eleanor Palo, "New Roles for Health Care Consumers—A Study of Role Transformation," *Journal of Community Health*, Vol. 3, Winter 1977, pp. 171–177.

Strauss, Marvin D., "Bibliography on Consumer Participation," *Health Education Monographs*, No. 32, 1972, pp. 79–86.

Strauss, Marvin D., "Consumer Participation in Health Planning," *Health Education Monographs*, No. 32, 1972, (entire issue). Also Thorofare, N.J.: Charles B. Slack, 1972.

Taylor, Rex, "The Local Health System: An Ethnography of Interest Groups and Decision-Making," *Social Science and Medicine*, Vol. 11, September 1977, pp. 583–592.

Thompson, Theodis, "Consumer Involvement in Health: A Conceptual Approach to Evaluating the Consumer Participation Process in Neighborhood Health Centers," unpublished doctoral dissertation, University of Michigan, 1973, Microfilm No. 74-15,907.

Thompson, Theodis, *The Politics of Pacification: The Case of Consumer Participation in Community Health Organizations*, Washington, D.C.: Institute for Urban Affairs and Research, Howard University, 1974.

Thomson, Ruth, "The Whys and Why Nots of Consumer Participation," *Community Mental Health Journal*, Vol. 9, Summer 1973, pp. 143–150.

Tichy, Noel M. and June Irmiger Taylor, "Community Control of Health Services," *Health Education Monographs*, Vol. 4, Summer 1976, pp. 108–131.

Tranquada, Robert E., "Participation of the Poverty Community in Health Care Planning," *Social Science and Medicine*, Vol. 7, September 1973, pp. 719–728.

Vladeck, Bruce C., "Interest Group Representation and the HSA's: Health Planning and Political Theory," *American Journal of Public Health*, Vol. 67, January 1977, pp. 23–29.

Young, T. Kue, "Lay-Professional Conflict in a Canadian Community Health Center: A Case Report," *Medical Care*, Vol. 13, November 1975, pp. 897–904.

Westermeyer, Joseph, "Absentee Health Workers and Community Participation," *American Journal of Public Health*, Vol. 62, October 1972, pp. 1364–1369.

Politics of Public Referenda on Health: Fluoridation Controversy

Abelson, Robert P., and Alex Bernstein, "A Computer Simulation Model of Community Referendum Controversies," *Public Opinion Quarterly*, Vol. 27, Spring 1963, pp. 93–122.

Burns, James MacGregor, "The Crazy Politics of Fluorine," *New Republic*, Vol. 128, July 13, 1953, pp. 14–15.

Burt, B. A., P. D. Bristow and T. B. Dowell, "Influencing Community Decisions on Fluoridation," *British Dental Journal*, Vol. 135, July 1973, pp. 75–77.

Conant, Ralph W., "Bibliography of Social-Scientific Studies in the Fluoridation Controversy," *Journal of Oral Therapeutics & Pharmacology*, Vol. 3, November 1966, pp. 203–211.

Crain, Robert L., "Fluoridation: The Diffusion of an Innovation Among Cities," *Social Forces*, Vol. 44, June 1966, pp. 467–476.

Crain, Robert L., Elihu Katz and Donald B. Rosenthal, *The Politics of Community Conflict: The Fluoridation Decisio*, Indianapolis: Bobbs-Merrill Co., 1969.

Dalzell-Ward, A. J., "Fluoridation and Public Opinion," *Health Education Journal*, Vol. 17, November 1959, pp. 247–258.

Davis, Morris, "Community Attitudes Toward Fluoridation," *Public Opinion Quarterly*, Vol. 23, Winter 1960, pp. 474–482.

Dickson, S., "Class Attitudes to Fluoridation," *Health Education Journal*, Vol. 28, September 1969, pp. 139–149.

Douglass, Chester W. and Dennis C. Stacey, "Demographical Characteristics and Social Factors Related to Public Opinion on Fluoridation," *Journal of Public Health Dentistry*, Vol. 32, Spring 1972, pp. 128–134.

Dwore, Richard B., "A Case Study of the 1976 Referendum in Utah on Fluoridation," *Public Health Reports*, Vol. 93, January–February 1978, pp. 73–78.

Evans, Caswell A., Jr. and Tomm Pickles, "Statewide Antifluoridation Initiatives: A New Challenge to Health Workers," *American Journal of Public Health*, Vol. 68, January 1978, pp. 59–62.

Eveland, Charles L., "The Political Significance of Dental Health Orientations in the Fluoridation Controversy: A Post-Referendum Assessment," unpublished doctoral dissertation, University of Michigan, 1969, Microfilm No. 70-4076.

Fish, D. G., E. S. Hirabayashi and G. K. Hirabayashi, "Voting Turnout on a Fluoridation Plebiscite," *Journal of the Canadian Medical Association*, Vol. 31, February 1965, pp. 88–93.

Flanders, Raymond A., "The Denturism Initiative," *Public Health Reports*, Vol. 96, September–Pctober 1981, pp. 410–418.

Frankel, John M. and Myron Allukian, "Sixteen Referenda on Fluoridation in Massachusetts: An Analysis," *Journal of Public Health Dentistry*, Vol. 33, Spring 1973, pp. 96–103.

Gamson, William A., "Public Information in a Fluoridation Referendum: A Summary of Research, *Health Education Journal*, Vol. 19, March 1961, pp. 47–54.

Gamson, William A., "Social Science Aspects of Fluoridation: A Summary of Research," *Health Education Journal*, Vol. 19, September 1961, pp. 159–169.

Gamson, William A., "The Fluoridation Dialogue: Is It An Ideological Conflict?" *Public Opinion Quarterly*, Vol. 25, Winter 1961, pp. 526–537.

Gamson, William, A. and Peter H. Orons, "Community Characteristics and Fluoridation Outcome," *Journal of Social Issues*, Vol. 17, No. 4, 1961, pp. 66–74.

Gamson, William A. and Carolyn G. Lindberg, "An Annotated Bibliography of Social Science Aspects of Fluoridation," *Health Education Journal*, Vol. 19, November 1961, pp. 209–230.

Gamson, William A., "Social Science Aspects of Fluoridation: A Supplement," *Health Education Journal*, Vol. 24, September 1965, pp. 135–43.

Green, Arnold L., "The Ideology of Anti-Fluoridiation Leaders," *Journal of Social Issues*, Vol. 17, No. 4, 1961, pp. 13–25.

Grossman, J., "Problems in the Translation of Social Science Theory to Field Action: An Example in the Case of Fluoridation," *Journal of Dental Research*, Vol. 45, November–December 1966, Supplement, pp. 1595–1601.

Hahn, Harlan, "Voting Behavior on Fluoridation Referendums: A Reevaluation," *Journal of American Dental Association*, Vol. 71, November 1965, pp. 1138–1144.

Hahn, Harlan, "Health Concerns and Attitudes Regarding Fluoridation," *Public Health Reports*, Vol. 84, July 1969, pp. 655–659.

Hutchison, John A., "A Small-Town Fluoridation Fight," *Scientific Monthly*, Vol. 77, No. 5, 1953, pp. 240–243.

Isman, Robert, "Fluoridation: Strategies for Success," *American Journal of Public Health*, Vol. 71, July 1981, pp. 717–721.

Jackson, D., "Attitudes to Fluoridation: A Survey of British Housewives," *British Dental Journal*, Vol. 132, March 21, 1972, pp. 219–222.

Kegeles, S. Stephen, "Some Unanswered Questions and Action Implications of Social Research in Fluoridation," *Journal of Social Issues*, Vol. 17, No. 4, 1961, pp. 75–81.

Kegeles, S. Stephen and Gloria Latter, "Population Characteristics and Fluoridation Referendums," U.S. Public Health Service, Division of Dental Health, unpublished paper, 1962.

Kimball, Solon T. and Marion Pearsall, "The Health Inventory at Work: The Fluoridation Project," in Solon T. Kimball and Marion Pearsall, eds., *The Talladega Story: A Study in Community Process*, Tuscaloosa: University of Alabama Press, 1954, pp. 100–115.

Kirscht, John P, "Attitude Research on the Fluoridation Controversy," *Health Education Monographs*, No. 10, 1961, pp. 16–28.

Kirscht, John P. and Andie L. Knutson, "Science and Fluoridation: An Attitude Study," *Journal of Social Issues*, Vol. 17, No. 4, 1961, pp. 37–44.

Kirscht, John P. and Andie L. Knutson, "Fluoridation and the 'Threat' of Science," *Journal of Health and Human Behavior*, Vol. 4, Summer 1963, pp. 129–135.

Lantos, Joseph, Lois A. Marsh and Ronald P. Schultz, "Small Communities and Fluoridation; Three Case-Studies," *Journal of Public Health Dentistry*, Vol. 33, Summer 1973, pp. 149–159.

Linn, E. L., "Effect of Community Leaders and Organizations on Public Attitudes Toward Fluoridation," *Journal of Public Health Dentistry*, Vol. 29, Spring 1969, pp. 108–117.

Linn, E. L., "An Appraisal of Sociological Research on the Public's Attitudes Toward Fluoridation," *Journal of Public Health Dentistry*, Vol. 29, Winter 1969, pp. 36–45.

MacRae, P.; C. R. Castaldi and W. Zacherl, "Dental Health, Socioeconomic Level, Interest Response to Polio Vaccination Program, and Voting in a Fluoridation Plebiscite," *Journal of Dental Research*, Vol. 43, October 1964, Supplement, pp. 898–899.

Markle, Gerald E., James C. Petersen and Morton O. Wagenfeld, "Notes from the Cancer Underground: Participation in the Laetrile Movement," *Social Science and Medicine*, Vol. 12, No. 1, 1978, pp. 31–37.

Marmor, Judd; Viola W. Bernard and Perry Ottenberg, "Psychodynamics of Group Opposition to Health Programs," *American Journal of Orthopsychiatry*, Vol. 30, April 1960, pp. 330–345.

Masterton, G., "A Study of Responses to a Questionnaire on Fluoridation," *American Journal of Public Health*, Vol. 53, August 1963, pp. 1243–1251.

Mausner, Bernard, "The Fluoridation Controversy: A Study in the Acceptance of Scientific Authority," *Journal of American College of Dentists*, Vol. 24, September 1957, pp. 202–205.

Mausner, Bernard and J. Mausner, " A Study of the Anti-Scientific Attitude," *Scientific American*, Vol. 192, February 1955, pp. 35–39.

Mazur, Allan, *The Dynamics of Technical Controversy*, Washington, D.C.: Communication Press, 1981.

McNeil, Donald R., *The Fight For Fluoridation*, New York: Oxford University Press, 1957.

McNeil, Donald R., "Political Aspects of Fluoridation," *Journal of the American Dental Association*, Vol. 65, November 1962, pp. 659–662.

Metz, A. Stafford, "Research Directions in Fluoridation," in *Social Science Research Opportunities in Dental Health*, U.S. Public Health Service, Division of Dental Health, Washington, D.C.: U.S. Government Printing Office, 1965, pp. 31–35.

Metzner, Charles A., "Referenda for Fluoridation," *Health Education Journal*, Vol. 15, September 1957, pp. 168–177.

Metzner, Charles A., "Planning a Survey to Secure an Objective Understanding of the Public's Reactions to Fluoridation," in *Proceedings of the Fourth Workshop on Dental Public Health*, Continued Education Papers No. 69, Ann Arbor, Mich.: University of Michigan, 1965, pp. 134–142.

Mitchell, Austin, "Fluoridation in Dunedin: A Study of Pressure Groups and Public Opinion," *Political Science (New Zealand)*, Vol. 12, March 1960, pp. 71–93.

Mueller, John E., "The Politics of Fluoridation in Seven California Cities," *Western Political Quarterly*, Vol. 19, March 1966, pp. 54–67.

Mueller, John E., "Fluoridation Attitude Change," *American Journal of Public Health*, Vol. 58, October 1968, pp. 1876–1882.

Murray, J. J., "Water Fluoridation: A Choice for the Community," *Community Health (England)*, Vol. 6, September–October 1974, pp. 75–83.

O'Meara, B. J., "Observations on a Fluoridation Plebiscite," *Canadian Journal of Public Health*, Vol. 51, May 1960, pp. 207–209.

O'Shea, Robert M. and Lois K. Cohen, "Social Science and Dentistry: Public Opinions on Fluoridation, 1968," *Journal of Public Health Dentistry*, Vol. 29, Winter 1969, pp. 57–58.

O'Shea, Robert J. and S. Stephen Kegeles, "An Analysis of AntiFluoridation Letters," *Journal of Health and Human Behavior*, Vol. 4, Summer 1963, pp. 135–140.

Paul, Benjamin D., "Synopsis of Report on Fluoridation," *Massachusetts Dental Society Journal*, Vol. 8, January 1959, pp. 19–21.

Paul, Benjamin D., "Fluoridation and the Social Scientists: A Review," *Journal of Social Issues*, Vol. 17, No. 4, 1961, pp. 1–12.

Paul, Benjamin D.; William A. Gamson; S. Stephen Kegeles, et al., "Trigger for Community Conflict: The Case of Fluoridation," *Journal of Social Issues*, Vol. 17, No. 4, 1961, entire issue. Benjamin D. Paul, "Fluoridation and the Social Scientists—A Review," pp. 1–12; Arnold Green, "The Ideology of Anti-Fluoridation Leaders," pp. 13–25; Arnold Simmel, "A Signpost for Research on Fluoridation Conflicts: The Concept of Relative Deprivation," pp. 26–36; John P. Kirscht and Andie L. Knutson, "Science and Fluoridation: An Attitude Study," pp. 37–44; Harry M. Raulet, "The Health Professional and the Fluoridation Issue: A Case Study of Role Conflict,' pp. 45–54; Irwin T. Sanders, "The Stages of a Community Controversy: The Case of Fluoridation," pp. 55–65; William A. Gamson and Peter Irons, "Community Characteristics and Fluoridation Outcome," pp. 66–74; S. Stephen Kegeles: "Some Unanswered Questions and Implications of Social Research in Fluoridation," pp. 75–81.

Petersen, James C. and Gerald E. Markle, "The Laetrile Controversy," in Dorothy Nelkin, ed., *Controversy: Politics of Technical Decisions*, Beverly Hills, Calif.: Sage Publications, 1979, pp. 159–179.

Petterson, Elof O., "Abolition of the Right of Local Swedish Authorities to Fluoridate Drinking Water," *Journal of Public Health Dentistry*, Vol. 32, Fall 1972, pp. 243–247.

Pinard, Maurice, "Structural Attachments and Political Support in Urban Politics: The Case of Fluoridation Referendums," *American Journal of Sociology*, Vol. 68, March 1963, pp. 513–526.

Plaut, Thomas F. A., "Analysis of Voting Behavior on a Fluoridation Referendum," *Public Opinion Quarterly*, Vol. 23, Summer 1958, pp. 213–222.

Ramirez, A., R. B. Connor, R. M. Gibbs, H. G. Griggs, J. O. Neilsen and O. W. Reeder, *Anomie and Political Powerlessness: Their Relationship to Attitudes and Knowledge Concerning Fluoridation*, Birmingham, Ala.: University of Alabama, School of Dentistry, 1969.

Raulet, Harry M., "The Health Professional and the Fluoridation Issue: A Case of Role Conflict," *Journal of Social Issues*, Vol. 17, No. 4, 1961, pp. 45–53.

Roemer, Ruth, "Water Fluoridation: Public Health Responsibility and Democratic Process," *American Journal of Public Health*, Vol. 55, September 1965, pp. 1337–1348.

Rosenstein, David I., Robert Isman, Tomm Pickles and Craig Benben, "Fighting the Latest Challenge to Fluoridation in Oregon," *Public Health Reports*, Vol. 93, January–February 1978, pp. 69–72.

Rosenthal, Donald B. and Robert L. Crain, "Executive Leadership and Community Innovation: The Fluoridation Experience," *Urban Affairs Quarterly*, Vol. 1, March 1966, pp. 39–57.

Sanders, Irwin T., *The Physician and Fluoridation: A Summary of Research Findings*, Cambridge: Harvard University School of Public Health, August 1960, Document No. 16-S, Social Science Program.

Sanders, Irwin T., The Stages of a Community Controversy: The Case of Fluoridation," *Journal of Social Issues*, Vol. 17, No. 4, 1961, pp. 55–65.

Sanders, Irwin T., "The Involvement of Health Professionals and Local Officials in Fluoridation Controversies," *American Journal of Public Health*, Vol. 52, August 1962, pp. 1274–1287.

Sapolsky, Harvey M., "Science, Voters, and the Fluoridation Controversy, *Science*, Vol. 62, October 1968, pp. 427–433.

Sapolsky, Harvey M., "The Fluoridation Controversy: An Alternative Explanation," *Public Opinion Quarterly*, Vol. 33, Summer 1969, pp. 240–248.

Scism, Thomas E., "Fluoridation in Local Politics: Study of the Failure of a Proposed Ordinance in One American City," *American Journal of Public Health*, Vol. 62, October 1972, pp. 1340–1345.

Shaw, C. T., "Characteristics of Supporters and Rejecters of a Fluoridation Referendum and a Guide for Other Community Programs," *Journal of the American Dental Association*, Vol. 78, February 1969, pp. 339–341.

Simmel, Arnold G., "A Signpost on Fluoridation Conflicts: The Concept of Relative Deprivation," *Journal of Social Issues*, Vol. 17, No. 4, 1961, pp. 23–36.

Simmel, Arnold G., "The Structuring of Opinion on a Controversial Topic: Studies and Explanations of Fluoridation Conflicts," unpublished doctoral dissertation, Columbia University, 1969, Microfilm No. 70-17,047.

Smith, Richard A., "Community Power and Decision Making: A Replication and Extension of Hawley," *American Sociological Review*, Vol. 41, August 1976, pp. 691–705.

Stephens, Douglas W., "Why Fluoridation Was Defeated in Long Beach, California, *Oral Hygiene*, Vol. 48, May 1958, pp. 30–34.

Sturgeon, L. W. C., "A Plebiscite on Continuing Fluoridation in Thorold, Ontario," *Canadian Journal of Public Health*, Vol. 49, October 1958, pp. 425–429.

Thomas, C. R., "The Press and Fluoridation Referenda in Selected Wisconsin Cities," unpublished master's thesis, University of Wisconsin, 1966.

Turk, Herman, *Organizations in Modern Life: Cities and Other Large Networks*, San Francisco, Calif.: Jossey-Bass, 1977.

Walsh, Diana C., "Fluoridation: Slow Diffusion of a Proven Preventive Measure," *New England Journal of Medicine*, Vol. 296, May 12, 1977, pp. 1118–1120.

Warner, Morton, "Communication Overkill in a Fluoridation Campaign," *Canadian Journal of Public Health*, Vol. 63, May–June 1972, pp. 219–227.

Wilson, Robert N., *Community Structure and Health Action*, Washington, D.C.: Public Affairs Press, 1968.

REFERENCES

Litman, Theodor J., *The Sociology of Medicine and Health Care: A Research Bibliography*, San Francisco, Calif.: Boyd & Fraser Publication Co., Vol. I, 1976; Vol. II, 1983 (tentative).

Congressional Quarterly, Inc., *Congressional Quarterly's Guide to Congress* Washington, D.C.: Congressional Quarterly, Inc., 1976, 2nd edition.

Cirn, John T., *A Guide to Doing Library Research in American Health, Policy and Politics*, University of Iowa, Graduate Program in Hospital and Health Administration, 1979 (mimeo).

Vose, Clement, *A Guide to Library Sources in Political Science: American Government*, Washington, D.C.: American Political Science Association, 1975.

Index